Natural Language Processing: Emerging Neural Approaches and Applications

Natural Language Processing: Emerging Neural Approaches and Applications

Editors

Massimo Esposito
Giovanni Luca Masala
Aniello Minutolo
Marco Pota

MDPI • Basel • Beijing • Wuhan • Barcelona • Belgrade • Manchester • Tokyo • Cluj • Tianjin

Editors
Massimo Esposito
Institute for High Performance
Computing and Networking
National Research Council
of Italy
Naples
Italy

Giovanni Luca Masala
School of Computing
University of Kent
Canterbury
United Kingdom

Aniello Minutolo
Institute for High Performance
Computing and Networking
National Research Council
of Italy
Naples
Italy

Marco Pota
Institute for High Performance
Computing and Networking
National Research Council
of Italy
Naples
Italy

Editorial Office
MDPI
St. Alban-Anlage 66
4052 Basel, Switzerland

This is a reprint of articles from the Special Issue published online in the open access journal *Applied Sciences* (ISSN 2076-3417) (available at: www.mdpi.com/journal/applsci/special_issues/NLP).

For citation purposes, cite each article independently as indicated on the article page online and as indicated below:

LastName, A.A.; LastName, B.B.; LastName, C.C. Article Title. *Journal Name* **Year**, *Volume Number*, Page Range.

ISBN 978-3-0365-2271-5 (Hbk)
ISBN 978-3-0365-2272-2 (PDF)

© 2022 by the authors. Articles in this book are Open Access and distributed under the Creative Commons Attribution (CC BY) license, which allows users to download, copy and build upon published articles, as long as the author and publisher are properly credited, which ensures maximum dissemination and a wider impact of our publications.

The book as a whole is distributed by MDPI under the terms and conditions of the Creative Commons license CC BY-NC-ND.

Contents

About the Editors ix

Massimo Esposito, Giovanni Luca Masala, Aniello Minutolo and Marco Pota
Special Issue on "Natural Language Processing: Emerging Neural Approaches and Applications"
Reprinted from: *Appl. Sci.* **2021**, *11*, 6717, doi:10.3390/app11156717 1

Viera Maslej-Krešňáková, Martin Sarnovský, Peter Butka and Kristína Machová
Comparison of Deep Learning Models and Various Text Pre-Processing Techniques for the Toxic Comments Classification
Reprinted from: *Appl. Sci.* **2020**, *10*, 8631, doi:10.3390/app10238631 7

Chirawan Ronran, Seungwoo Lee and Hong Jun Jang
Delayed Combination of Feature Embedding in Bidirectional LSTM CRF for NER
Reprinted from: *Appl. Sci.* **2020**, *10*, 7557, doi:10.3390/app10217557 35

Xinyu Chen, Liang Ke, Zhipeng Lu, Hanjian Su and Haizhou Wang
A Novel Hybrid Model for Cantonese Rumor Detection on Twitter
Reprinted from: *Appl. Sci.* **2020**, *10*, 7093, doi:10.3390/app10207093 57

Gabriela R. Roldan-Molina, Jose R. Mendez, Iryna Yevseyeva and Vitor Basto-Fernandes
Ontology Fixing by Using Software Engineering Technology
Reprinted from: *Appl. Sci.* **2020**, *10*, 6328, doi:10.3390/app10186328 69

Nour Jnoub, Fadi Al Machot and Wolfgang Klas
A Domain-Independent Classification Model for Sentiment Analysis Using Neural Models
Reprinted from: *Appl. Sci.* **2020**, *10*, 6221, doi:10.3390/app10186221 85

Andraž Pelicon, Marko Pranjić, Dragana Miljković, Blaž Škrlj and Senja Pollak
Zero-Shot Learning for Cross-Lingual News Sentiment Classification
Reprinted from: *Appl. Sci.* **2020**, *10*, 5993, doi:10.3390/app10175993 99

Xiaojun Kang, Bing Li, Hong Yao, Qingzhong Liang, Shengwen Li and Junfang Gong et al.
Incorporating Synonym for Lexical Sememe Prediction: An Attention-Based Model
Reprinted from: *Appl. Sci.* **2020**, *10*, 5996, doi:10.3390/app10175996 121

Shengwen Li, Renyao Chen, Bo Wan, Junfang Gong, Lin Yang and Hong Yao
DAWE: A Double Attention-Based Word Embedding Model with Sememe Structure Information
Reprinted from: *Appl. Sci.* **2020**, *10*, 5804, doi:10.3390/app10175804 135

Injy Sarhan and Marco Spruit
Can We Survive without Labelled Data in NLP? Transfer Learning for Open Information Extraction
Reprinted from: *Appl. Sci.* **2020**, *10*, 5758, doi:10.3390/app10175758 155

Adrián Javaloy and Ginés García-Mateos
Preliminary Results on Different Text Processing Tasks Using Encoder-Decoder Networks and the Causal Feature Extractor
Reprinted from: *Appl. Sci.* **2020**, *10*, 5772, doi:10.3390/app10175772 171

Marco Pota, Massimo Esposito, Giuseppe De Pietro and Hamido Fujita
Best Practices of Convolutional Neural Networks for Question Classification
Reprinted from: *Appl. Sci.* **2020**, *10*, 4710, doi:10.3390/app10144710 . . . . **181**

Adrián Javaloy and Ginés García-Mateos
Text Normalization Using Encoder–Decoder Networks Based on the Causal Feature Extractor
Reprinted from: *Appl. Sci.* **2020**, *10*, 4551, doi:10.3390/app10134551 . . . . **209**

Sandra Rizkallah, Amir F. Atiya and Samir Shaheen
A Polarity Capturing Sphere for Word to Vector Representation
Reprinted from: *Appl. Sci.* **2020**, *10*, 4386, doi:10.3390/app10124386 . . . . **233**

Ivan Boban, Alen Doko and Sven Gotovac
Improving Sentence Retrieval Using Sequence Similarity
Reprinted from: *Appl. Sci.* **2020**, *10*, 4316, doi:10.3390/app10124316 . . . . **255**

Sheng Xu, Xingfa Shen, Fumiyo Fukumoto, Jiyi Li, Yoshimi Suzuki and Hiromitsu Nishizaki
Paraphrase Identification with Lexical, Syntactic and Sentential Encodings
Reprinted from: *Appl. Sci.* **2020**, *10*, 4144, doi:10.3390/app10124144 . . . . **267**

Asmaa M. Aubaid and Alok Mishra
A Rule-Based Approach to Embedding Techniques for Text Document Classification
Reprinted from: *Appl. Sci.* **2020**, *10*, 4009, doi:10.3390/app10114009 . . . . **285**

Seongsik Park and Harksoo Kim
Dual Pointer Network for Fast Extraction of Multiple Relations in a Sentence
Reprinted from: *Appl. Sci.* **2020**, *10*, 3851, doi:10.3390/app10113851 . . . . **307**

Kang-moon Park, Donghoon Shin and Yongsuk Yoo
Evolutionary Neural Architecture Search (NAS) Using Chromosome Non-Disjunction for Korean Grammaticality Tasks
Reprinted from: *Appl. Sci.* **2020**, *10*, 3457, doi:10.3390/app10103457 . . . . **319**

Md. Mostafizer Rahman, Yutaka Watanobe and Keita Nakamura
Source Code Assessment and Classification Based on Estimated Error Probability Using Attentive LSTM Language Model and Its Application in Programming Education
Reprinted from: *Appl. Sci.* **2020**, *10*, 2973, doi:10.3390/app10082973 . . . . **329**

Shuyu Lei, Xiaojie Wang and Caixia Yuan
Cooperative Multi-Agent Reinforcement Learning with Conversation Knowledge for Dialogue Management
Reprinted from: *Appl. Sci.* **2020**, *10*, 2740, doi:10.3390/app10082740 . . . . **351**

Changqin Quan, Zhiwei Luo and Song Wang
A Hybrid Deep Learning Model for Protein–Protein Interactions Extraction from Biomedical Literature
Reprinted from: *Appl. Sci.* **2020**, *10*, 2690, doi:10.3390/app10082690 . . . . **367**

Ubaid Ur Rehman, Dong Jin Chang, Younhea Jung, Usman Akhtar, Muhammad Asif Razzaq and Sungyoung Lee
Medical Instructed Real-Time Assistant for Patient with Glaucoma and Diabetic Conditions
Reprinted from: *Appl. Sci.* **2020**, *10*, 2216, doi:10.3390/app10072216 . . . . **381**

Heewoong Park and Jonghun Park
Assessment of Word-Level Neural Language Models for Sentence Completion
Reprinted from: *Appl. Sci.* **2020**, *10*, 1340, doi:10.3390/app10041340 . . . . **403**

Youngjin Jang and Harksoo Kim
Reliable Classification of FAQs with Spelling Errors Using an Encoder-Decoder Neural Network in Korean
Reprinted from: *Appl. Sci.* **2019**, *9*, 4758, doi:10.3390/app9224758 . . . . **421**

Qicai Wang, Peiyu Liu, Zhenfang Zhu, Hongxia Yin, Qiuyue Zhang and Lindong Zhang
A Text Abstraction Summary Model Based on BERT Word Embedding and Reinforcement Learning
Reprinted from: *Appl. Sci.* **2019**, *9*, 4701, doi:10.3390/app9214701 . . . . **431**

Jintae Kim, Shinhyeok Oh, Oh-Woog Kwon and Harksoo Kim
Multi-Turn Chatbot Based on Query-Context Attentions and Dual Wasserstein Generative Adversarial Networks
Reprinted from: *Appl. Sci.* **2019**, *9*, 3908, doi:10.3390/app9183908 . . . . **451**

Haihong E, Siqi Xiao and Meina Song
A Text-Generated Method to Joint Extraction of Entities and Relations
Reprinted from: *Appl. Sci.* **2019**, *9*, 3795, doi:10.3390/app9183795 . . . . **459**

Jianliang Yang, Yuenan Liu, Minghui Qian, Chenghua Guan and Xiangfei Yuan
Information Extraction from Electronic Medical Records Using Multitask Recurrent Neural Network with Contextual Word Embedding
Reprinted from: *Appl. Sci.* **2019**, *9*, 3658, doi:10.3390/app9183658 . . . . **473**

Qin Li, Shaobo Li, Sen Zhang, Jie Hu and Jianjun Hu
A Review of Text Corpus-Based Tourism Big Data Mining
Reprinted from: *Appl. Sci.* **2019**, *9*, 3300, doi:10.3390/app9163300 . . . . **489**

Xiaohu Du, Jie Yu, Zibo Yi, Shasha Li, Jun Ma and Yusong Tan et al.
A Hybrid Adversarial Attack for Different Application Scenarios
Reprinted from: *Appl. Sci.* **2020**, *10*, 3559, doi:10.3390/app10103559 . . . . **517**

About the Editors

Massimo Esposito

Massimo Esposito is senior researcher at the Institute for High Performance Computing and Networking of the National Research Council of Italy. He received a M.Sc. in Computer Science Engineering (Cum Laude) in 2004, a 1st level Master degree in 2007, and a Ph.D. degree in Information Technology Engineering in 2011. Since 2012, he has been a contract professor of Informatics at the University of Naples Federico II. His current research interests are focused on Artificial Intelligence algorithms and techniques, mixing deep learning and knowledge-based technologies, for building intelligent systems able to converse, understand natural language and answer to questions, with emphasis on the distributional neural representation of text, and on specific natural language tasks such as part of speech tagging, sentence classification and open information extraction. He has been involved in different national and European projects, has been on the program committee of many international conferences, and is member of the editorial board of some international journals. He authored over 100 peer-reviewed papers on international journals and conference proceedings.

Giovanni Luca Masala

Dr. Giovanni Masala is Senior Lecturer in Computer Science at the University of Kent and Leader of the Robotics Lab. Dr. Masala has a Ph.D. in Applied Physics (AI in medical applications) and a Laurea (MSc+BSc) in Electronic Engineering (AI) both at the University of Cagliari, Italy.

Dr. Masala has published widely on ranked journals in AI topics. Dr. Masala is a member of several program committees in international conferences, and he is a Guest Editor in AI topics in a number of journals. In the field of natural language understanding, he was part of a small group of international researchers, who developed a very large-scale neural network of cognitive and language processing, called ANNABELL. The publication in PLoS One in 2015 (1) received high impact both scientifically and in the media. The main interests are brain-inspired architecture for natural language, robotics, human-robot interaction, machine learning on medical applications, and medical imaging.

Aniello Minutolo

Aniello Minutolo received the M.Sc. degree in computer science engineering from the University of Naples Federico II and the Ph.D. degree in information technology engineering from the University of Naples Parthenope. Since 2018, he has been a Contract Professor of informatics with the Faculty of Engineering, University of Naples Federico II. He is currently a Researcher with the Institute for High Performance Computing and Networking, National Research Council (ICARCNR), Italy. His current research interests include artificial intelligence, decision support systems, dialog systems, knowledge management, and modeling and reasoning. He has been involved in different national and European projects and on the program committee of some international conferences and workshops. Moreover, he is also a member of the editorial board of some international journals.

Marco Pota

Marco Pota is researcher at the Institute for High Performance Computing and Networking of the National Research Council of Italy. He received M.Sc. in Chemical Engineering in 2004, and a Ph.D. degree in Multiscale Modelling, Computational Simulation and Characterization for Materials and Life Sciences in 2010. Since 2018, he has been a contract professor of Informatics at the University of Naples Federico II. His current research interests are focused on Artificial Intelligence algorithms and techniques, based on deep learning and knowledge-based technologies, for building predictive models and solving specific natural language processing tasks. He has been involved in different national projects, in the organization of many international conferences, and is guest editor of some international journals. He has authored many peer-reviewed papers on international journals and conference proceedings.

Editorial

Special Issue on "Natural Language Processing: Emerging Neural Approaches and Applications"

Massimo Esposito [1,*], Giovanni Luca Masala [2], Aniello Minutolo [1] and Marco Pota [1]

1. Institute for High Performance Computing and Networking—National Research Council of Italy (ICAR-CNR), 80131 Naples, Italy; aniello.minutolo@icar.cnr.it (A.M.); marco.pota@icar.cnr.it (M.P.)
2. Department of Computing and Mathematics, Manchester Metropolitan University (MMU), Manchester M15 6BH, UK; g.masala@mmu.ac.uk
* Correspondence: massimo.esposito@icar.cnr.it

Citation: Esposito, M.; Masala, G.L.; Minutolo, A.; Pota, M. Special Issue on "Natural Language Processing: Emerging Neural Approaches and Applications". *Appl. Sci.* **2021**, *11*, 6717. https://doi.org/10.3390/app11156717

Received: 25 June 2021
Accepted: 27 June 2021
Published: 22 July 2021

Publisher's Note: MDPI stays neutral with regard to jurisdictional claims in published maps and institutional affiliations.

Copyright: © 2021 by the authors. Licensee MDPI, Basel, Switzerland. This article is an open access article distributed under the terms and conditions of the Creative Commons Attribution (CC BY) license (https://creativecommons.org/licenses/by/4.0/).

Nowadays, systems based on artificial intelligence are being developed, leading to impressive achievements in a variety of complex cognitive tasks, matching or even beating humans [1–4]. Natural language processing (NLP) is a field where the use of deep learning (DL) models in the last five years has allowed AI to advance toward human levels in translation and reading comprehension, as well as other real-world NLP applications, such as question answering and conversational systems, information retrieval, sentiment analysis, and recommender systems.

However, due to the difficulties associated with natural language understanding and generation, which are human capabilities among the least understood by computer systems from a cognitive perspective, and despite the remarkable success of DL in different NLP tasks, this is still a field of research of increasing interest [5–7]. In order to improve DL methods, current models have been scaled up, but their complexity has grown toward directions assumed by empirical engineering solutions [8–11]. Moreover, they are not applicable to languages without extensive datasets [12], and the lack of explainability inhibits further improvements [13].

This Special Issue highlights the most recent research being carried out in the NLP field to discuss these open issues, with a particular focus on both emerging approaches for language learning, understanding, production, and grounding interactively or autonomously from data in cognitive and neural systems, as well as on their potential or real applications in different domains.

There are 30 contributions selected for this Special Issue representing progress and potential applications in the NLP area from original contributions of researchers with a broad expertise in various fields: NLP, cognitive science and psychology, artificial intelligence and neural networks, computational modeling and neuroscience covering the whole range of theoretical and practical aspects, technologies, and systems.

This collection includes one review paper, which focuses on text corpus-based tourism big data mining [14]. Li et al. summarized and discussed different text representation strategies, text-based NLP techniques for topic extraction, text classification, sentiment analysis, and text clustering in the context of tourism text mining, as well as their applications in tourist profiling, destination image analysis, and market demand, among others. Their work also provides guidelines for constructing new tourism big data applications and outlines promising research areas in this field for the coming years.

One letter is also included in this issue, employing evolutionary a neural architecture search for Korean grammaticality tasks [15].

Regarding the other 28 research papers, the following NLP areas are specifically addressed:

Natural language understanding, generation, and grounding: In [16], Ontology-Fixer is presented, a web-based tool that supports a methodology to build, assess, and improve the quality of Ontology Web Language (OWL) ontologies. Another paper [17] addresses the problem of paraphrase identification and presents an approach for leveraging contextual features with a neural-based learning model based on lexical, syntactic, and sentential encodings, incorporating relational graph convolutional networks (R-GCNs) to make use of different features from local contexts (e.g., word encoding, position encoding, and full dependency structures). In addition, in [18], the authors revisited the recurrent neural network (RNN) language model, achieving highly competitive results with the appropriate network structure and hyperparameters.

Universal language models: In [19], Javaloy and the co-author used a method recently proposed, called the causal feature extractor (CFE), for encoder-decoder models on different text processing tasks. The same authors applied this method to text normalization in [20], which is a ubiquitous problem that appears as the first step of many text-to-speech (TTS) systems.

Conversational systems or interfaces and question answering: The authors in [21] proposed the best practices for question classification in different languages using convolutional neural networks (CNNs), finding the optimal settings depending on the language and validating their transferability. The authors in [22] addressed the time-consuming development of manual user simulator policy and introduced a multi-agent dialogue model, where an end-to-end dialogue manager and a user simulator are optimized simultaneously for dialogue management by cooperative multi-agent reinforcement learning. Moreover, in [23], the authors proposed a Medical Instructed Real-time Assistant (MIRA) that listens to the user's chief complaint and predicts a specific disease, thus referring the user to a nearby appropriate medical specialist. Furthermore, in [24], the authors presented a multi-turn chatbot model in which the preceding utterances are exploited in response generation by using different weights.

Sentiment analysis, emotion detection, and opinion mining: The study in [25] investigated a comparison of various DL models used to identify the toxic comments in Internet discussions. Moreover, in [26], the authors proposed a novel hybrid model XGA (namely an XLNet-based bidirectional gated recurrent unit (BiGRU) network with an attention mechanism) for Cantonese rumor detection on Twitter, taking advantage of both semantic and sentiment features for detection. Furthermore, the authors of [27] proposed an intensive study regarding a domain-independent classification model for sentiment analysis using neural models, showing high performance when using different evaluation metrics compared with the state-of-the-art results. Another study in [28] tested different approaches for handling long documents and proposed a novel technique for sentiment enrichment of the Bidirectional Encoder Representations from Transformers (BERT) model as an intermediate training step. In [29], Rizkallah et al. proposed an embedding approach that is designed to capture the polarity issue for sentiment analysis.

Document analysis, information extraction, and text mining: In [30], Ronran et al. evaluated the combination of different types of embedding features in a bidirectional long short-term memory (Bi-LSTM) conditional random field (CRF) model for named entity recognition (NER). The authors in [31] investigated the transferability of the features from an open information extraction (OIE) domain to another and applied the approach for relation extraction (RE). The authors in [32] proposed a rule-based approach for text document classification. The study in [33] proposed an RE model based on a dual pointer network with a multi-head attention mechanism to address the association of multiple entities in a sentence according to various relations. The work in [34] investigated an RE method to solve the possible overlapping among multiple relational triples contained in a sentence. Another topic was introduced by the authors of [35], who introduced a novel hybrid model of extractive-abstractive text summarization to combine BERT word embedding with reinforcement learning. Two contributions to this special issue are focused on medical information extraction. The authors in [36] compared different architectures of DL models, including CNNs, LSTM, and hybrid models. Furthermore, they proposed a hybrid architecture for protein–protein interaction extraction from the biomedical literature.

The authors in [37] developed a multitask attention-based Bi-LSTM–CRF model with pre-trained embeddings from language models (ELMo) in order to achieve improved performance in clinical NER.

Search and information retrieval: In [38], Boban et al. adapted language modeling-based methods for sentence retrieval to test the partial matching of terms through combining sentence retrieval with sequence similarity. This method allows for matching words that are similar but not identical. The authors of [39] proposed a reliable sentence classification model based on an encoder-decoder neural network to resolve lexical disagreement problems between queries and frequently asked questions (FAQs).

Trustworthy and explainable artificial intelligence: Two contributions [40,41] considered "sememe", the smallest semantic unit for describing real-world concepts, which improve the interpretability of NLP systems. In particular, the study in [40] proposed a novel model to improve the performance of sememe prediction by introducing synonyms. On the other hand, the work in [41] implicitly synthesized the structural features of sememes into word embedding models through an attention mechanism. The work proposes a novel double attention word-based embedding (DAWE) model that encodes the characteristics of sememes into words with a "double attention" strategy.

Applications in science, engineering, medicine, healthcare, finance, business, law, education, transportation, retailing, telecommunication, and multimedia: The authors in [42] proposed a hybrid adversarial attack method to generate examples with the aim to explore the vulnerabilities and security aspects of deep learning systems in different application scenarios. An application in programming education was considered in [43]. In this study, the source code assessment and its classification were developed by a sequential language model that used an attention mechanism through an LSTM neural network and based on the estimated error probability.

In summary, this Special Issue contains a series of excellent research works on NLP, covering a wide range of topics. The collection of 30 contributions is highly recommended, and it will benefit readers in various aspects.

Acknowledgments: We would like to thank all the authors, the dedicated referees, the editor team of applied sciences for their valuable contributions, making this special issue a success.

Conflicts of Interest: The authors declare no conflict of interest.

References

1. Ferrucci, D.; Brown, E.; Chu-Carroll, J.; Fan, J.; Gondek, D.; Kalyanpur, A.A.; Lally, A.; Murdock, J.W.; Nyberg, E.; Prager, J.; et al. Building Watson: An Overview of the DeepQA Project. *AI Mag.* **2010**, *31*, 59–79. [CrossRef]
2. Silver, D.; Huang, A.; Maddison, C.; Guez, A.; Sifre, L.; van den Driessche, G.; Schrittwieser, J.; Antonoglou, I.; Panneershelvam, V.; Lanctot, M.; et al. Mastering the game of Go with deep neural networks and tree search. *Nature* **2016**, *529*, 484–489. [CrossRef] [PubMed]
3. Newborn, M. *Kasparov Versus Deep Blue*; Springer: Berlin, Germany, 1997.
4. Baughman, A.; Chuang, W.; Dixon, K.; Benz, Z.; Basilico, J. DeepQA Jeopardy! Gamification: A Machine-Learning Perspective. *Comput. Intell. AI Games IEEE Trans.* **2014**, *6*, 55–66. [CrossRef]
5. Yadav, A.; Vishwakarma, D.K. Sentiment analysis using deep learning architectures: A review. *Artif. Intell. Rev.* **2019**, *53*, 4335–4385. [CrossRef]
6. Yuan, S.; Zhang, Y.; Tang, J.; Hall, W.; Cabotà, J.B. Expert finding in community question answering: A review. *Artif. Intell. Rev.* **2020**, *53*, 843–874. [CrossRef]
7. Wang, Y.; Wang, M.; Fujita, H. Word Sense Disambiguation: A comprehensive knowledge exploitation framework. *Knowl. Based Syst.* **2020**, *190*, 105030. [CrossRef]
8. Laha, A.; Raykar, V. An Empirical Evaluation of various Deep Learning Architectures for Bi-Sequence Classification Tasks. In Proceedings of the COLING 2016, the 26th International Conference on Computational Linguistics: Technical Papers, Osaka, Japan, 11–16 December 2016; pp. 2762–2773.
9. Nguyen, V.H.; Cheng, J.S.; Yu, Y.; Thai, V.T. An architecture of deep learning network based on ensemble empirical mode decomposition in precise identification of bearing vibration signal. *J. Mech. Sci. Technol.* **2019**, *33*, 41–50. [CrossRef]
10. Guo, Q.; Chen, S. An Empirical Study towards Characterizing Deep Learning Development and Deployment across Different Frameworks and Platforms. *arXiv* **2019**, arXiv:1909.06727v1. Available online: https://arxiv.org/pdf/1909.06727.pdf (accessed on 20 July 2021).

11. Pota, M.; Marulli, F.; Esposito, M.; De Pietro, G.; Fujita, H. Multilingual POS tagging by a composite deep architecture based on character-level features and on-the-fly enriched Word Embeddings. *Knowl. Based Syst.* **2019**, *164*, 309–323. [CrossRef]
12. Cherry, C.A. EMNLP Workshop on Deep Learning for Low-Resource NLP. 20 June 2019, China, Association for Computational Linguistics. Available online: https://sites.google.com/view/deeplo19 (accessed on 20 July 2021).
13. Zohuri, B.; Moghaddam, M. Deep Learning Limitations and Flaws. *Mod. Approaches Mater. Sci. Short Commun.* **2020**, *2*, 241–250.
14. Li, Q.; Li, S.; Zhang, S.; Hu, J.; Hu, J. A Review of Text Corpus-Based Tourism Big Data Mining. *Appl. Sci.* **2019**, *9*, 3300. [CrossRef]
15. Park, K.-M.; Shin, D.; Yoo, Y. Evolutionary Neural Architecture Search (NAS) Using Chromosome Non-Disjunction for Korean Grammaticality Tasks. *Appl. Sci.* **2020**, *10*, 3457. [CrossRef]
16. Roldan-Molina, G.R.; Mendez, J.R.; Yevseyeva, I.; Basto-Fernandes, V. Ontology Fixing by Using Software Engineering Technology. *Appl. Sci.* **2020**, *10*, 6328. [CrossRef]
17. Xu, S.; Shen, X.; Fukumoto, F.; Li, J.; Suzuki, Y.; Nishizaki, H. Paraphrase Identification with Lexical, Syntactic and Sentential Encodings. *Appl. Sci.* **2020**, *10*, 4144. [CrossRef]
18. Park, H.; Park, J. Assessment of Word-Level Neural Language Models for Sentence Completion. *Appl. Sci.* **2020**, *10*, 1340. [CrossRef]
19. Javaloy, A.; García-Mateos, G. Preliminary Results on Different Text Processing Tasks Using Encoder-Decoder Networks and the Causal Feature Extractor. *Appl. Sci.* **2020**, *10*, 5772. [CrossRef]
20. Javaloy, A.; García-Mateos, G. Text Normalization Using Encoder–Decoder Networks Based on the Causal Feature Extractor. *Appl. Sci.* **2020**, *10*, 4551. [CrossRef]
21. Pota, M.; Esposito, M.; De Pietro, G.; Fujita, H. Best Practices of Convolutional Neural Networks for Question Classification. *Appl. Sci.* **2020**, *10*, 4710. [CrossRef]
22. Lei, S.; Wang, X.; Yuan, C. Cooperative Multi-Agent Reinforcement Learning with Conversation Knowledge for Dialogue Management. *Appl. Sci.* **2020**, *10*, 2740. [CrossRef]
23. Rehman, U.U.; Chang, D.J.; Jung, Y.; Akhtar, U.; Razzaq, M.A.; Lee, S. Medical Instructed Real-Time Assistant for Patient with Glaucoma and Diabetic Conditions. *Appl. Sci.* **2020**, *10*, 2216. [CrossRef]
24. Kim, J.; Oh, S.; Kwon, O.-W.; Kim, H. Multi-Turn Chatbot Based on Query-Context Attentions and Dual Wasserstein Generative Adversarial Networks. *Appl. Sci.* **2019**, *9*, 3908. [CrossRef]
25. Maslej-Krešňáková, V.; Sarnovský, M.; Butka, P.; Machová, K. Comparison of Deep Learning Models and Various Text Pre-Processing Techniques for the Toxic Comments Classification. *Appl. Sci.* **2020**, *10*, 8631. [CrossRef]
26. Chen, X.; Ke, L.; Lu, Z.; Su, H.; Wang, H. A Novel Hybrid Model for Cantonese Rumor Detection on Twitter. *Appl. Sci.* **2020**, *10*, 7093. [CrossRef]
27. Jnoub, N.; Al Machot, F.; Klas, W. A Domain-Independent Classification Model for Sentiment Analysis Using Neural Models. *Appl. Sci.* **2020**, *10*, 6221. [CrossRef]
28. Pelicon, A.; Pranjić, M.; Miljković, D.; Škrlj, B.; Pollak, S. Zero-Shot Learning for Cross-Lingual News Sentiment Classification. *Appl. Sci.* **2020**, *10*, 5993. [CrossRef]
29. Rizkallah, S.; Atiya, A.F.; Shaheen, S. A Polarity Capturing Sphere for Word to Vector Representation. *Appl. Sci.* **2020**, *10*, 4386. [CrossRef]
30. Ronran, C.; Lee, S.; Jang, H.J. Delayed Combination of Feature Embedding in Bidirectional LSTM CRF for NER. *Appl. Sci.* **2020**, *10*, 7557. [CrossRef]
31. Sarhan, I.; Spruit, M. Can We Survive without Labelled Data in NLP? Transfer Learning for Open Information Extraction. *Appl. Sci.* **2020**, *10*, 5758. [CrossRef]
32. Aubaid, A.M.; Mishra, A. A Rule-Based Approach to Embedding Techniques for Text Document Classification. *Appl. Sci.* **2020**, *10*, 4009. [CrossRef]
33. Park, S.; Kim, H. Dual Pointer Network for Fast Extraction of Multiple Relations in a Sentence. *Appl. Sci.* **2020**, *10*, 3851. [CrossRef]
34. Xiao, S.; Song, M. A Text-Generated Method to Joint Extraction of Entities and Relations. *Appl. Sci.* **2019**, *9*, 3795. [CrossRef]
35. Wang, Y.; Liu, P.; Zhu, Z.; Yin, H.; Zhang, Q.; Zhang, L. A Text Abstraction Summary Model Based on BERT Word Embedding and Reinforcement Learning. *Appl. Sci.* **2019**, *9*, 4701. [CrossRef]
36. Quan, C.; Luo, Z.; Wang, S. A Hybrid Deep Learning Model for Protein–Protein Interactions Extraction from Biomedical Literature. *Appl. Sci.* **2020**, *10*, 2690. [CrossRef]
37. Yang, J.; Liu, Y.; Qian, M.; Guan, C.; Yuan, X. Information Extraction from Electronic Medical Records Using Multitask Recurrent Neural Network with Contextual Word Embedding. *Appl. Sci.* **2019**, *9*, 3658. [CrossRef]
38. Boban, I.; Doko, A.; Gotovac, S. Improving Sentence Retrieval Using Sequence Similarity. *Appl. Sci.* **2020**, *10*, 4316. [CrossRef]
39. Jang, Y.; Kim, H. Reliable Classification of FAQs with Spelling Errors Using an Encoder-Decoder Neural Network in Korean. *Appl. Sci.* **2019**, *9*, 4758. [CrossRef]
40. Kang, X.; Li, B.; Yao, H.; Liang, Q.; Li, S.; Gong, J.; Li, X. Incorporating Synonym for Lexical Sememe Prediction: An Attention-Based Model. *Appl. Sci.* **2020**, *10*, 5996. [CrossRef]
41. Li, S.; Chen, R.; Wan, B.; Gong, J.; Yang, L.; Yao, H. DAWE: A Double Attention-Based Word Embedding Model with Sememe Structure Information. *Appl. Sci.* **2020**, *10*, 5804. [CrossRef]

42. Du, X.; Yu, J.; Yi, Z.; Li, S.; Ma, J.; Tan, Y.; Wu, Q. A Hybrid Adversarial Attack for Different Application Scenarios. *Appl. Sci.* **2020**, *10*, 3559. [CrossRef]
43. Rahman, M.M.; Watanobe, Y.; Nakamura, K. Source Code Assessment and Classification Based on Estimated Error Probability Using Attentive LSTM Language Model and Its Application in Programming Education. *Appl. Sci.* **2020**, *10*, 2973. [CrossRef]

Article

Comparison of Deep Learning Models and Various Text Pre-Processing Techniques for the Toxic Comments Classification

Viera Maslej-Krešňáková, Martin Sarnovský *[ID], Peter Butka and Kristína Machová

Department of Cybernetics and Artificial Intelligence, Faculty of Electrical Engineering and Informatics, Technical University of Košice, 040 01 Kosice, Slovakia; viera.maslej.kresnakova@tuke.sk (V.M.-K.); peter.butka@tuke.sk (P.B.); kristina.machova@tuke.sk (K.M.)
* Correspondence: martin.sarnovsky@tuke.sk

Received: 16 October 2020; Accepted: 27 November 2020; Published: 2 December 2020

Abstract: The emergence of anti-social behaviour in online environments presents a serious issue in today's society. Automatic detection and identification of such behaviour are becoming increasingly important. Modern machine learning and natural language processing methods can provide effective tools to detect different types of anti-social behaviour from the pieces of text. In this work, we present a comparison of various deep learning models used to identify the toxic comments in the Internet discussions. Our main goal was to explore the effect of the data preparation on the model performance. As we worked with the assumption that the use of traditional pre-processing methods may lead to the loss of characteristic traits, specific for toxic content, we compared several popular deep learning and transformer language models. We aimed to analyze the influence of different pre-processing techniques and text representations including standard TF-IDF, pre-trained word embeddings and also explored currently popular transformer models. Experiments were performed on the dataset from the Kaggle Toxic Comment Classification competition, and the best performing model was compared with the similar approaches using standard metrics used in data analysis.

Keywords: natural language processing; toxic comments; classification; deep learning; neural networks

1. Introduction

Nowadays, the World Wide Web is an environment where the users can create and share the information with almost minimal restrictions. The majority of the users use the web responsibly and effectively. However, there is a group of users, which act with the type of behaviour, that could be described as anti-social. Numerous definitions of the anti-social behaviour currently exist [1], but there are two major types of such behaviour present:

- Misinformation spreading—this type of actions usually include creation and sharing of misleading content in various forms, e.g., hoaxes, fake or biased news, fake reviews, etc.
- User reactions—this type of behaviour usually occurs in user conversations and has many different forms, e.g., discussion manipulation, cyber-bullying, hate speech, trolling, spamming and other.

Both forms of anti-social behaviour present a serious issue, as their consequences can be significant, also in the real-world. Internet users often communicate with each other in real-time; the discussions usually involve a considerable number of users. Such massive communication supported by modern technologies which enable partial anonymity also leads to the new threats in form non-proper user reactions. Anti-social user reactions in online discussions are often related to the use of abusive language. There are numerous different definitions of such behaviour and it could be difficult to find the exact definition of such phenomenon and is even a more significant challenge to do so in the online environment [2]. However, toxic comments in an online discussion, in general, can be defined as a response in an aggressive way, which forces the offended participants to abandon it (e.g., personal attacks, verbal bullying) [3]. As the vast majority of those data are in the form of text, various techniques of natural language processing (NLP) can be utilized to their processing.

With a growing number of textual data generated in online environments, there is a strong need to detect and eliminate the various forms of anti-social behaviour effectively. Currently, manual techniques are still frequently used in the detection of such behaviour in online communities (discussion forums, social networks, etc.). Using human moderators responsible for finding and revealing the anti-social behaviour in online environments can be very time consuming and also biased by moderators themselves. In general, there is a strong need to design and implement the new methods able to detect the anti-social behaviour from the content automatically using the NLP, machine learning and artificial intelligence techniques. The overall goal of these approaches is to utilize the results of such methods for both, prevention and elimination of negative impacts of anti-social behaviour in online communities, for example by enabling the fully-automated detection and prediction of different types of anti-social behaviour from the user-created content. However, ML and NLP methods can still suffer from learning from the data which are often human-labelled. Measurement and mitigation of unintended bias is a non-trivial problem, which has been also studied in the area of toxicity detection [4,5].

The work presented in this paper focuses on exploring the use of currently popular deep learning architectures to predict the toxicity in the comments. While several studies were dealing with the problem of using deep learning to predict the toxicity of the comments, they are inconsistent in terms of pre-processing, model application and evaluation. Toxic comments are often written in specific language and style from both perspectives, content and form. Texts are relatively short, written using non-standard language, often using offensive language with a lot of grammatical and spelling errors and punctuation marks. Some of them represent just the common typos, but many of them are written purposely by their authors, to avoid the automatic on-line filtering of the abusive language [6]. In other sentiment analysis tasks, the effect of the pre-processing is well studied and proven, that the right selection of pre-processing may lead to performance improvement [7–9]. In this particular domain, we can assume, that it would require minimal pre-processing techniques to ensure that the information contained in the comment text and form would be preserved. On the other hand, there are word embeddings, as a way of text representations, which are currently frequently being used when training deep learning models. Those embeddings are usually pre-trained using various sets of text corpora. Some of the pre-trained embeddings are built using mostly clean, regular words and are more suitable for processing of standard texts while other ones fit better to short on-line communication. In the toxic comments classification task, it would also be interesting to train the word embeddings from scratch using the dataset related to the task. Therefore, in this research, we aimed to compare multiple currently popular deep learning methods and transformer language models and study the effects of different text representations and basic pre-processing techniques applied in the data preparation.

The paper is organized as follows: Section 2. provides an overview of the abusive language and toxic comments field and application of different machine learning methods to their detection. Section 3 describes the deep learning methods used for text classification. The following section presents the data used in the experiments and their preparation; Section 5 then describes the performance metrics used in the experiments, followed by the section describing implemented models and their settings. The next section is dedicated to the experimental evaluation and describes achieved results.

2. Toxic Comments Classification

Sentiment analysis in general considered a research area which combines NLP and text mining to automatically detect and identify the opinions contained in the text and determine the writer's opinion or attitude with regards to a particular topic [10]. Although multiple approaches have been applied in this field, most of them are based on the application of machine learning methods. A specific sub-section of sentiment analysis is a detection of abusive language in the conversational content. Use of aggressive or offensive language in online discussions may occur in various forms. Various studies address different aspects of the abusive language in the online discussions, often differentiated by the types of aggression expressed. Therefore, when considering the abusive language detection from the texts, various related tasks are explored, including detection of cyber-bullying, hate or hate speech, online harassment, flaming, toxic comments, extremism, etc. Those tasks are often not clearly distinguishable, often are overlapping, and despite the differences between the concepts, often similar methods are utilized to tackle those problems [11]. However, there are studies trying to establish the common typology of the different abusive language detection tasks [12].

Toxic comments detection can be considered as a specific sub-task of approaches mentioned above, which aims to detect and identify the toxicity in the conversational text. It is usually solved as a text classification task, where the input features are extracted from the piece of text. As multiple types of toxicity could be contained in the text (e.g., insults, obscene language, hate, etc.), therefore toxic comments detection is usually considered as a multi-class classification task where the target class describe the particular type of the toxicity contained in the text. In this case, the problem of unbalanced data is a common issue, as the frequency of occurrence of the different toxicity types may vary.

Recently, the essential source of the data used to build the toxicity detection models come from social networks. Data are usually extracted from the discussions, comments or social network posts and typically represent the user reactions to a particular topic [13]. During recent years, several datasets became publicly available, containing labelled data from different social platforms and areas, e.g., Twitter dataset [14] contains 25,000 manually annotated tweets containing hate speech. Youtube dataset [15] consists of 3221 manually labelled comments from YouTube discussions [16] or very popular Wikipedia talk page corpus also used in this work. However, different datasets are often labelled non-consistently, which could be the effect of the different problem understanding and will require a more integrated approach when collecting the data in the future [17].

To detect the toxicity in the conversational data, both traditional machine learning methods, as well as advanced deep learning techniques, have been utilized. Traditional machine learning approaches include the use of various classifiers, e.g., Decision Trees [18], Logistic Regression [19], Support Vector Machine models [15] or Ensemble Models [20]. Traditional machine learning models are frequently used and popular in the detection of other types of anti-social behaviour, such as fake reviews detection. For example, work Naive Bayes and Random Forests have been used in the detection of the fake reviews obtained from Amazon [21] using data describing the seller, website, product, reviewer and review content. Authors in [22] answered interesting questions, if the performance of the classification methods for fake reviews filtering are affected when they are used in real-world scenarios that require online learning. Regarding the toxicity detection, authors in [23] monitored and analyzed the most recently published comments to detect whether an aggressive action emerges in a discussion thread. The authors experimented with various forms of representations of input texts in combination with Radial Basis Function, Support Vector Machines and Hidden Markov Model classifiers. The work [24] is focused on fake reviews detection and the influence of a length of the text data on a measure of the effectiveness of the learned models. The results of experiments showed that the models learned from the whole body of texts are more effective than models learned only from the headlines. Similarly, in [25] authors have examined the influence of a length of the text data on the effectiveness of machine learning models trained for recognition of authors of toxic posts. The paper describes an approach to suspicious authors identification based on the training a specialized dictionary of the toxic author and also the training of Naive Bayes and Support Vector Machine models.

However, recently, deep learning techniques proved to be successful in the detection of various types of anti-social behaviour on the web. For example, deep neural networks were used to detect the cyber-bullying within the user posts on the Twitter [26]. Multiple topologies of Convolutional

Neural Networks (CNN) were evaluated to find the most suitable model when handling this task [27]. Besides tweets, other data sources can be utilized to train the cyber-bullying detectors. Authors in [28] used transfer learning within different datasets of conversational data (e.g., Wikipedia, Twitter) and then compared the performance of deep learning models. Multiple deep networks were successfully used also in hate speech detection [29], including deep learning ensemble models [30]. Multi-label toxic comments classification was also addressed by different deep learning models [31]. In [32], authors used CNN for multi-label classification of the comments and experimented with different word embeddings, in [33], authors compared the performance of CNN to Long Short-Term Memory (LSTM) network, and authors in [34] presented the capsule network approach. When monitoring social networks, an interesting aspect would be tracking the temporal aspects of toxicity in the comments. In [35] authors present the CNN model able to detect the toxic tweets. Authors also utilize the hashtags from the tweets related to toxic tweets and also are able to monitor the toxicity propagation over time. Several previous works approached toxicity detection as the binary classification problem. However, deep learning models are also used in more complex, ensemble approaches. In [36] an ensemble model consisting of CNN, BiLSTM and GRU is presented, which determines whether the text is toxic or not in the first step and then classifies the toxic comments into a more specific category representing the particular type of the toxicity.

3. Deep Learning Methods for Text Processing

Neural networks are considered to be one of the best-performing machine learning algorithms. They have brought great success in the field of artificial intelligence, such as in the field of computer vision, where their task is image processing and pattern recognition, and, for example, in sound processing and speech recognition. In this section, we took a closer look at how neural networks can be used to work with the textual data.

3.1. Feedforward Neural Network

Deep forward neural networks known as the feedforward neural networks (FFNN) or multilayer perceptrons are basic models of deep learning. Feedforward networks became popular in 1986 when Rumelhart, Hinton, and Williams introduced a method of training forward neural networks using the error back-propagation [37]. The goal of feedforward neural networks is to approximate the function f^*. For example, the function $y = f^*(x)$ maps the input x to the value y. FFNN defines the mapping $y = f(x;\theta)$ and finds the value of the parameters θ, which leads to the best approximation of the function. The flow of information in FFNN is forward; in practice, this means that the computational model represents an acyclic graph.

The basic model of a neuron is called perceptron. The perceptron receives input signals $\bar{x} = (x_1, x_2, \ldots, x_{n+1})$ via synaptic weights, which form the vector $\bar{w} = (w_1, w_2, \ldots, w_{n+1})$. The perceptron output is given as the scalar product of the input vectors transformed using the activation function f, to which the bias is added. Bias b is a constant that does not depend on the input parameters and serves to influence the activation function [38,39].

$$output = f(\bar{w} \cdot \bar{x}) = f\left(\sum_{i=1}^{n+1} w_i x_i\right) + b. \qquad (1)$$

For the best classifiers in our work are used following hyper-parameters and settings:

- Activation function on input and hidden layers: ReLU:

    In proposed solution we used ReLU (Rectified Linear Unit) [40] activation function. ReLU belongs to one of the most frequently used activation functions applied in deep networks. It is defined as:

$$f(x) = \max(0, x) \qquad (2)$$

which means, that it transforms negative inputs to 0 and leaves positive inputs without transformation.
- Loss function: binary cross entropy

Error function is used to estimate the error of the model during the training. Using the error backpropagation [41], the neuron weights in particular layer are updated in such manner, that the error rate decreases in following evaluation. We used Binary Cross-Entropy (BCE), which can be defined as:

$$\text{BCE} = -\left(y \log\left(\hat{y}\right)(1-y)\log\left(1-\hat{y}\right)\right), \tag{3}$$

where y represents the ground truth and $\hat{y}$ represents predicted value.
- Optimization: Adam

To minimize the error rate of the model in the prediction, optimization function is used. We used Adam (Adaptive Moment Estimation) [42]. Adam is an optimization function, which computes the learning estimation for each parameter. In addition to storing an exponentially decaying average of past squared gradients $v(t)$ like RMSprop [43], Adam also keeps an exponentially decaying average of past gradients $m(t)$, similar to momentum [44]. Both moving averages are initialized to 0, which leads to the moments' estimation biased towards zero. Such situation occurs mostly during the initial phases when decay parameters ($\beta 1$, $\beta 2$) have values close to 1. Such biased can be removed using modified estimations $\hat{m}_t$ a $\hat{v}_t$:

$$\hat{m}_t = \frac{m_t}{1-\beta_1^t} \qquad \hat{v}_t = \frac{v_t}{1-\beta_2^t}, \tag{4}$$

The parameters are updated according to the formula:

$$\theta_{t+1} = \theta_t \frac{\alpha}{\sqrt{\hat{v}_t}+\epsilon} \cdot \hat{m}_t. \tag{5}$$

Default setting for the parameter β_1 is 0.9 and $\beta_2 = 0.999$, learning rate $\alpha = 0.001$ and 10^{-8} for the ϵ parameter. Adam is considered as a suitable optimization method in practical tasks. When comparing Adam to other methods, its advantage is faster convergence and training speed is also higher. It also removes certain issues of other optimization techniques, such as slow convergence, or high variance of the parameters, which could lead to variations in the error function.
- Regularization: dropout

The main idea of the dropout is the random removal of specific neurons (along with their connections) from the neural network during the model training [45]. Ignoring, or "dropping-out" of specific neurons can prevent their over-adaptation, which could lead to over-fitting. In each iteration, a new sub-network is created, which contains different neurons than during the previous iteration. The output of such a process is a set of sub-networks, which have a higher chance to capture the random phenomena in the data compared to the single robust network. While using this technique, it is necessary to set the parameter defining the probability of selection of a number of neurons, which will be dropped out from the network.
- Output activation function: sigmoid

Sigmoid function is a bounded, differentiable real function. It is defined for all real values and has a non-negative derivative in each point [39]. It is mostly used because of its non-linearity and simplicity of the computation. The function is defined as:

$$f(x) = \frac{1}{1+e^{-x}} \tag{6}$$

The output of the sigmoid activation function is in the range between 0 and 1, which makes it suitable for use in the classification tasks.

3.2. Convolutional Neural Network

Convolutional neural networks (CNN) represent a specific type of forward neural networks, which contain a layer of neurons for the convolution operation. The inspiration for the architecture of this network was the function of the ocular nerve. Neurons respond to the input of the surrounding neurons' activations according to a specified size of the convolutional kernel, also called filter. Convolution consists of shifting the convolution kernel over the whole set of values. In this case, the convolution operation represents the multiplication of the convolution kernel and input values (see Figure 1) [38].

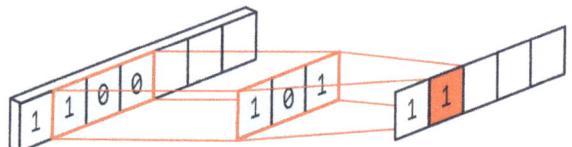

Figure 1. One-dimensional convolutional process. Input data is located on the (**left**), the filter in the middle, and the convolution output on the (**right**).

Pooling layers in convolutional networks are designed to reduce the number of outputs, to reduce the computational complexity, and to prevent the network over-fitting. The sampling layers are usually applied just behind the convolution layers, as the duplicate data are created when the convolution kernels are shifting through the individual inputs. Excess data is removed using the pooling layers.

In our work, we use the Global pooling layer, in which we distinguish between the Global average pooling layer and the Global max pooling layer. These layers work according to the same principle as the traditional average pooling (max pooling) layer. The difference is, that the average (maximum) is not calculated only for a given area, but for the entire input.

3.3. Long Short-Term Memory

Long Short-Term Memory (LSTM) [46] is a type of a recurrent neural network. LSTM has a more complex structure, which makes it suitable to deal with the vanishing gradient problem. Using the LSTM in any sequential task will ensure that long-term information and context is maintained (see Figure 2).

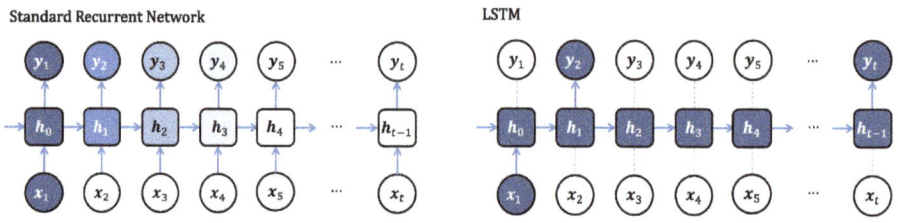

Figure 2. The first figure shows the standard recurrent neural network and the vanishing gradient problem, which results in the loss of context. In contrast, the second figure shows the preservation of information and context in LSTM [47].

Comparing to other types of neural networks, the LSTM network does not consist of interconnected neurons, but of memory blocks that are connected in layers. The block contains gateways that manage the state and output of the block and the flow of information. Gateways can learn which data in a sequence is important and needs to be preserved. There are four memory block elements performing the following functions (see Figure 3):

- Input gate—it is used to control the entry of information into the memory block.
- Cell state—it is used to store long-term information.
- Forget gate—it is used is to decide what information will be discarded and what information will be kept.
- Output gate—based on the input and the memory unit it is used is to decide what operation to perform on the output.

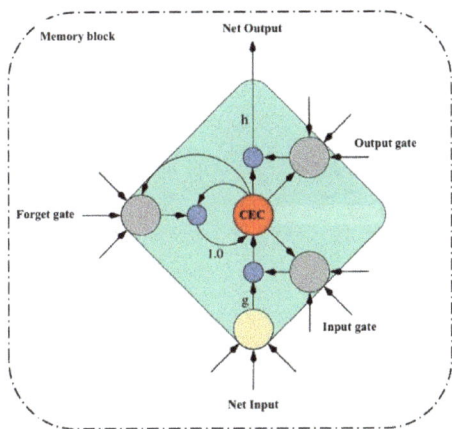

Figure 3. LSTM network memory block. The block has a recurrent connection with the weights set to 1.0. The three gateways collect input from the rest of the network and check the status of the memory block via three multiplicate units (marked in blue). The letters g and h depict the application of a nonlinear function [48].

Bidirectional Long Short-Term Memory network (BiLSTM) represents a specific type of LSTM network. BiLSTMs consists of two individual hidden layers. The first layer is used to process the input sequence forward, and on the other hand, the second hidden layer is used to process the sequence backwards. The hidden layers merge in the output layer, thanks to that the output layer can access to each point's past and the future context in the sequence. LSTM and their bidirectional variants proved to be very suitable. They can learn how and when they can forget certain information and also they can learn not to use some gateways in their architecture. Faster learning rate and better performance are the advantages of a BiLSTM network [49].

3.4. Gated Recurrent Unit

Cho et al. [50] also tried to solve the vanishing gradient problem described in Section 3.3 in the publication, where they presented the recurrent neural network called Gated Recurrent Unit (GRU). GRU can be considered as a variation of the LSTM network because both are designed in a similar fashion. GRU solves the vanishing gradient problem using an update and reset gates. The update gate helps the model to determine, how much of the previous information (from the previous time steps) needs to be used in the future, and the reset gate determines, how much of that information will be discarded. We also used a bidirectional variant of the GRU network (BiGRU) in our experiments.

3.5. Transformer Models

Transformer models are currently very popular methods used to solve various NLP tasks such as question answering, language understanding or summarization, but has been successfully used in text classification tasks [51]. BERT (Bidirectional Encoder Representations from Transformers) is a language transformation model introduced by Google [52]. BERT is is "deeply bidirectional", which means, it learns the deep representation of texts by considering both, left and right contexts. It is a method used for training of general-purpose language models on very large corpuses and then using that model for the NLP tasks. So there are two steps involved in using BERT: pre-training and fine-tuning. During the pre-training phase, the BERT model is trained on unlabelled data. Then, the model is initialized with the pre-trained parameters and fine-tuned for specific NLP task. Fine-tuning of the BERT model is much less expensive on the computational resources. BERT uses the same architecture in different tasks. BERT is built using the Transformers [53]. The model comes in two variants, BERT-base and BERT-large. BERT-base consists of 12 Transformer blocks, hidden size of 768 and 12 self-attention heads, BERT-large consists of 24 Transformer blocks, hidden size of 1024 and 16 self-attention heads. There are several BERT variations currently introduced, such as DistilBERT which aims to reduce the size of the BERT model, while retaining the performance [54], RoBERTa, which optimizes BERT hyper-parameters to improve the performance [55] or XLNet learns the bidirectional contexts over all permutations of the factorization order [56].

4. Data Understanding and Preparation

4.1. Dataset Description

In the experiments, we used the Toxic Comment Classification Challenge (Available online: www.kaggle.com/c/jigsaw-toxic-comment-classification-challenge) competition dataset, as it presents an interesting challenge, widely used in training of the toxicity detection models. It consists of Wikipedia comments, which contain the comment (id) and textual content of the comment (comment_text feature). Each comment is marked with a specific type of toxicity. Each type of the toxicity is represented by a particular label: *toxic, severe_toxic, obscene, threat, insult* and *identity_hate*. The comments can be labelled with multiple types of toxicity. Figure 4 depicts a sample of the training data. As we can see from the figure, toxic comments are often written using an explicit language, written in all caps, using numerous punctuation marks.

comment_text	toxic	severe_toxic	obscene	threat	insult	identity_hate
shut the fuck up bastard	1	1	1	0	1	0
Fucking lying nigger, fes up you peice of shit211.28.54.73	1	1	1	0	1	1
YOU ADMINISTRATE LIKE SHIT ANYWAY, YOU FUCCIN ASSHOLE! ( )	1	1	1	0	1	0
Total Asshole bitches like you just need to get the fuck off. Motherfucking Shithole. Eat your dick.	1	1	1	0	1	0
Go fuck yourself this ain't any of your business and i fucking know what tor is. Asshole.	1	1	1	0	1	0
Who are YOU to tell ME??!! I'll do WHAT I like WHEN I like...cocksucker!!	1	1	1	0	1	0
i hope you feel like shit for deleting my post. go fuck yourself	1	1	1	0	1	0
DOOSH DOOSH DOOSH DOOSH DOOSH FUCKING COCK SUCKER QUEIR BATE ASS WIPE DONT TELL ME WHAT THE FUCK TO WRITE	1	1	1	0	1	0
SuPeRTROLL WiLL LiVe FoReVeR! IF You DoN'T ReSPeCT THe SuPeRTROLL You WiLL Die You PaTHeTiC Foo...	1	0	1	1	1	0
WHY THE FUCK DO U EDIT MY CONTRIB. TO WIKI ABOUT THE IRANIAN ARMY...	1	0	1	1	1	1
EVERYONE WANTS TO KILL BILL GOD DAM GATES HE IS A NERD WHY NOT.??	1	0	0	1	1	0
That's it. Remember last time you fucked with me... the dildo, yo...	1	0	1	1	0	0
Who gives a shit? Anthony Bourdain is a tool. I just wish he had ...	1	0	1	0	0	0
What the fuck does a dumb Canadian polock like you know about Sta...	1	0	1	0	1	1
These hoe's lame on here on leaving this site yall gay and shit	1	0	1	0	1	1
MAYBE ITS BECAUSE YOU ARE A GAY	1	0	0	0	1	1
you need to go to Oz to get a fucking brain	1	0	1	0	1	1

Figure 4. Sample of training data Toxic Comment Challenge.

Dataset is divided into the training and testing set. Training data consists of 159,751 samples. The models were evaluated on the independent testing set consisting of totally 153,164 records. However, to prevent the effect of the hand-labelling of the dataset, the testing set contained comments to be not included in scoring (labelled by −1). After removal of these record, testing set used for evaluation consisted of 63,978 records. Table 1 shows the number of samples in the training and test set for each class. Please note that most of the toxic comments are labelled with more than one type of toxicity. Non-toxic comments have not assigned a specific label, but are not assigned with any of the toxic labels ("clear" comments in the Table 1).

Table 1. Type of toxicity occurrences in training and testing dataset.

Toxicity	Training Set	Testing Set
toxic	15,294	6090
severe toxic	1595	367
obscene	8449	3691
threat	478	211
insult	7877	3427
identity hate	1405	712
"clear"	143,346	5773

The average comment consisted of 394 characters. Figure 5 depicts the number of comments depending on the length of the comment within each class. In our experiments, we worked with an average comment length of 200 characters.

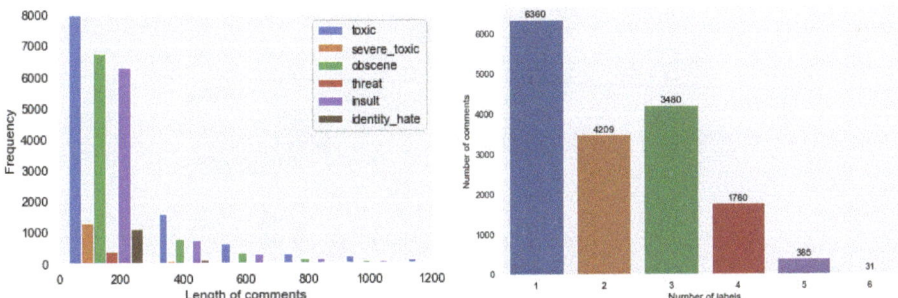

Figure 5. The first graph depicts the length of the comments in respective categories. The second one depicts the number of the comments belonging with multiple categories.

Comments in the data may belong to multiple classes (e.g., toxic comments may contain various types of toxicity). On the contrary, the initial data exploration showed, that certain comments labelled as an obscene, threat, insult, or identity hate, may not be considered as toxic (see Table 2). We decided to keep such comments in the dataset, even though they are not considered as toxic, they could be considered as anti-social from a different perspective.

Table 2. A comparison of the occurrence and frequency of individual categories with the toxic category.

Category	Frequency
severe toxic AND toxic	1595
obscene AND toxic	7926
threat AND toxic	449
insult AND toxic	7344
identity hate AND toxic	1302
severe toxic but NOT toxic	0
obscene but NOT toxic	523
threat but NOT toxic	29
insult but NOT toxic	533
identity hate but NOT toxic	103

Figure 6 shows the correlation between the target variables. The highest levels of correlation can be observed between the obscene, toxic its and insult classes.

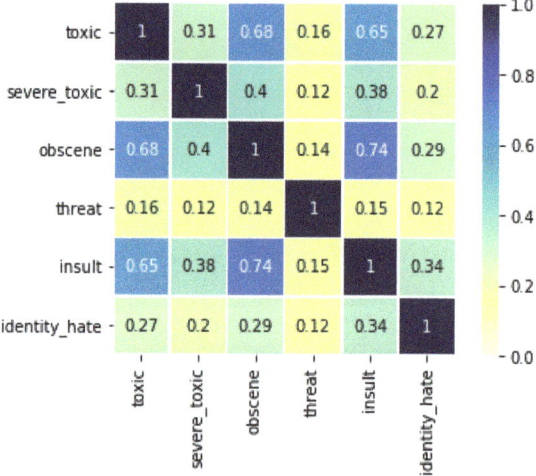

Figure 6. Correlation of features and targets.

4.2. Data Pre-Processing

The initial step after the data understanding is the preparation of the data to the form suitable for the classifier training. When working with the textual documents, data pre-processing usually involves a series of tasks of text cleaning, formatting and creation of its representation used in the model training. Notably, in this case, the texts contain slang expressions, emoticons, incomplete words, typos, etc.; which are usually addressed in the pre-processing. However, in case of abusive language/toxic comments detection from the social media (as well as other similar tasks), it should be noticed, that abusive/toxic content is often associated with non-standard textual content (e.g., slang, upper case letters, emoticons, etc.). Authors in [6] point out, that in a domain such as antisocial behaviour detection on the Internet, it is essential and useful to keep the data in their original form as much as possible. Application of standard pre-processing methods such as lowercasing, stopwords removal or stemming could lead to the loss of the individuality and specific features of both, the content of the message that the author wants to submit and also for the author himself. By using the standard pre-processing methods, in this case, we may lose important traits, crucial in the process of extracting features. In our experiments, one of our primary motivation was to explore this hypothesis.

We decided to compare the models performance also from the aspect of standard pre-processing techniques used in the process and compared on the data pre-processed in a standard manner and on the data with no traditional pre-processing at all.

During the experiments, where we used the data pre-processing, we studied the effect of the standard techniques commonly used in the textual data preparation:

- Tokenization—splitting of strings into a tokens, representing the lexical units (e.g., words);
- Lowercasing—conversion of the entire text to lowercase (words with different cases map to the same lowercase form);
- Punctuation removal—removal of all punctuation marks within the sentence;
- Stop words removal (stop words—words with minimum information value, e.g., conjunctions, prepositions, confusions, etc.).

4.3. Features Representation

We also used the different text representation methods. We used the standard vector space representation using TF-IDF (Term Frequency-Inverse Document Frequency) weighting [57], special tokenizers of popular transformers models (BERT, DistilBERT and XLNet tokenizer) and the representation of the text documents using the following word embeddings:

- word2vec— provides direct access to vector representations of words. It is a combination of two techniques, two neural networks—Continuous bag of words (CBOW) and Skip-gram model [58].
- GloVe—is one of the newest methods for calculating the vector representation of words. However, this approach does not use the whole corpus. It is learned only based on global statistics on the occurrence of words in a current context. The method captures various linguistic patterns and can successfully solve problems based on the principle of analogy [59].
- fastText—is a library created by Facebook's research team to learn and calculate the word representation and sentence classification. Its principle is to assign a vector representation to n-grams of characters that contain individual words [60].

We used GloVe embeddings pre-trained on Common Crawl (300 dimensions) and Twitter (200 dimensions), for the fastText we used pre-trained word vectors for 157 languages, trained on Common Crawl and Wikipedia (also in dimension 300).

Compared to word embeddings, BERT model includes an attention mechanism which is able to learn contextual relations between words in text. BERT consists of an encoder which processes the text input and decoder used to perform the prediction. Since BERT's goal is to generate a language model, only the encoder mechanism is necessary. BERT, which uses the Transformer encoder is able to learn the context of a word based on its entire surrounding (both left and right context of the words). When comparing to other directional models, that read the text input sequentially, transformer models read it as an entire sequence at once (from that point of view, it can be considered as non-directional). We used following tokenizers from Transformers (https://huggingface.co/transformers/:

- BERT tokenizer —bert-base and bert-large cased/uncased tokenizer—based on word piece;
- DistilBERT Tokenizer—distilbert-base-cased tokenizer—is identical to BertTokenizer and runs end-to-end tokenization: punctuation splitting and wordpiece;
- XLNet tokenizer—xlnet-base-cased tokenizer—based on sentence piece.

5. Performance Metrics

To evaluate the models, we decided to use the standard metrics used in classification, e.g., accuracy, precision, recall and F1 score. Such metrics are easy and straightforward to obtain for a binary classification problems and can be computed as:

- Accuracy = TP + TN/TP + FP + FN + FP

- Precision = TP/TP + FP
- Recall = TP/TP + FN
- F1 score = 2 * (Precision * Recall) / Precision + Recall,

where:

- TP—True Positive examples are predicted to be positive and are positive;
- TN—True Negative examples are predicted to be negative and are negative;
- FP—False Positive examples are predicted to be positive but are negative;
- FN—False Negative examples are predicted to be negative but are positive.

To apply such metrics in the multi-label classification, those metrics could be computed for each class (one-vs-rest approach). Usually, we need to compute the confusion matrix (see Figure 7) for each class $c_i \in C = \{1, ..., K\}$. For each class c_i, the i-th class is considered as positive, while the rest of other classes as a negative class. Then, to summarize the performance of the classifier on all classes, metrics can be micro or macro averaged [61]. The use of micro or macro averaging is dependent on the particular use case. In the following formulas, we will use TP_i, FP_i, and FN_i as the true positive, false positive, and false-negative rates associated with the class i.

Micro-averaging at first computes the confusion matrix for all classes and then calculates the overall metrics. Micro-averaging may be preferred in case of class imbalance present in the data. Micro-averaged precision and recall metrics are computed as:

- $Precision_{micro} = \frac{\sum_{i=1}^{|C|} TP_i}{\sum_{i=1}^{|C|} TP_i + FP_i}$

- $Recall_{micro} = \frac{\sum_{i=1}^{|C|} TP_i}{\sum_{i=1}^{|C|} TP_i + FN_i}$

- $F1\ score_{micro} = 2 * \frac{Precision_{micro} * Recall_{micro}}{Precision_{micro} + Recall_{micro}}$

On the other hand, macro-averaging is based on the computation of precision and recall for each class and then averaging the overall metrics:

- $Precision_{macro} = \frac{\sum_{i=1}^{|C|} Precision_i}{|C|}$

- $Recall_{macro} = \frac{\sum_{i=1}^{|C|} Recall_i}{|C|}$

- $F1\ score_{macro} = 2 * \frac{Precision_{macro} * Recall_{macro}}{Precision_{macro} + Recall_{macro}}$

To compare the models, we also used the Area Under Curve (AUC) score to evaluate the models. AUC score computes the area under the Receiver Operating Characteristic (ROC) curve. Although the AUC score is not an ideal metric to compare the models trained on highly-imbalanced data, we used it to compare the models with other models from the relevant literature. The reason behind this is the fact, that the most studies use the AUC score, as it was specified as a criterion in the Toxic Comments Classification Challenge competition.

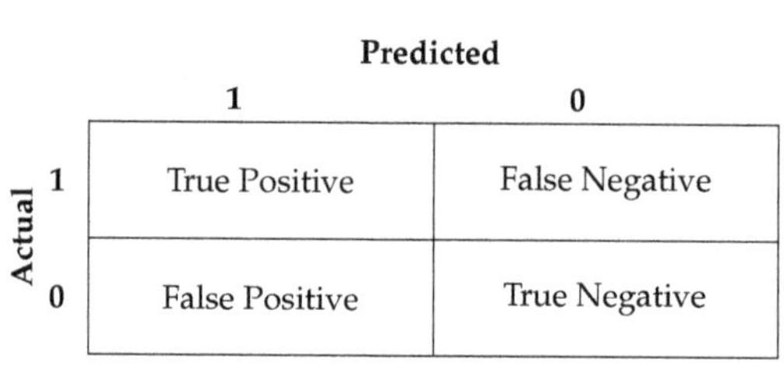

		Predicted	
		1	0
Actual	1	True Positive	False Negative
	0	False Positive	True Negative

Figure 7. Confusion matrix.

6. Models and Settings

6.1. Deep Learning Models

To choose the most suitable model, we performed an initial set of experiments to evaluate the different neural network architectures. We have considered multiple architectures, from simple feedforward to composed models and implemented selected deep neural network architectures-FFNN, CNN, GRU, LSTM, and a combination of bidirectional GRU/LSTM and convolutional layer in order to choose the best performing model for the following experiments with pre-processing techniques.

We used the following deep learning models:

- FFNN with three fully connected layers with 32, 64, 128 neurons, and a 20% dropout regularization
- CNN with one-dimensional convolutional layer with 64 filters, kernel size 3, max-pooling layer with window size 2, a flatten layer and fully-connected layer of 128 neurons, 20% dropout regularization
- GRU, in which we replaced the convolution block with a GRU layer with 128 units
- LSTM, in which we replaced the convolution block with a LSTM layer with 128 units.

Besides the mentioned neural network architectures, we implemented two composed architectures:

- The first architecture includes an embedding layer, a following bidirectional LSTM layer with 128 units, a 1D convolution layer with kernel size 3, and global max and average pooling layers. These pooling layers are concatenated, following with the fully connected layer with 64 neurons. In the bidirectional layer, we used recurrent dropout 10%, and other 20% in a separate layer.
- The second composed architecture, we replaced the LSTM layer with a GRU layer with the same parameters. Figure 8 shows the architecture of the LSTM layer.

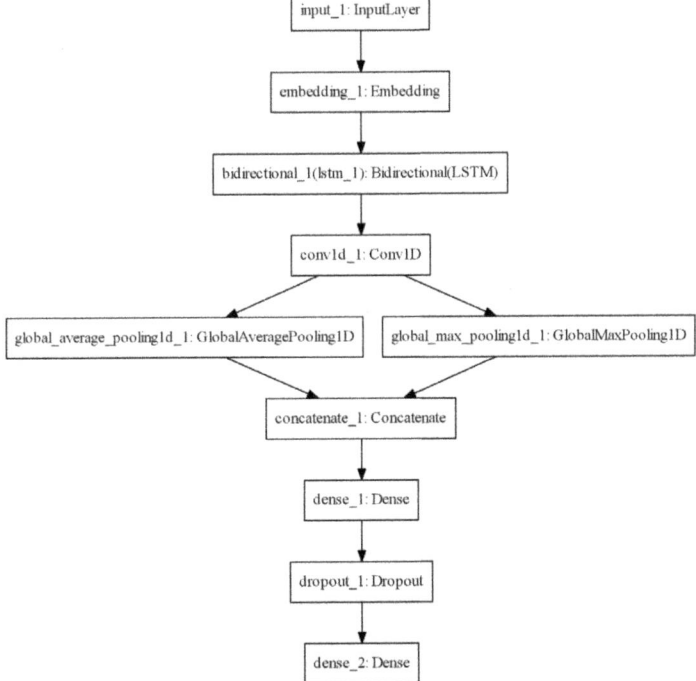

Figure 8. Architecture of the composed BiLSTM + CNN model for multi-label classification.

6.2. Transformer Models

We compared the composed architecture with some recent popular language models. We used a dedicated tokenizer belonging to each of the models. To obtain the desired classification result, we connected each transformer model's output to a feedforward neural network—a fully connected layer with 128 neurons and regularisation layer dropout (15%). The last fully-connected layer represents the output layer of the neural network and consists of six output class (toxicity type in the input text). The architecture of this setup is depicted in the Table 3.

Table 3. Architecture of the pre-trained transformer models.

Layer	Parameters
Input 1	input_shape = (,128)
Input 2	input_shape = (,128)
Transformer model	training = False
Dense	128 neurons, activation ReLU
Dropout	15%
Dense	6 neurons, activation Sigmoid

- BERT : we used BERT tokenizer, and following pre-trained models:

    - BERT model (Cased/Uncased): we used a pre-trained BERT model for sequence classification, which contains a sequence classification/regression head on top (a linear layer on top of the pooled output). In this model, the transformer is pre-trained, and the sequence classification head is only initialized and has to be trained. We used only BERT-base pre-trained model, with BERT-large, we experienced the stability issues with its training. Output of the classification head was used and fed into the FF network for classification.
    - Bare BERT (Cased/Uncased): in this case, we used pre-trained BERT model transformer, which is outputting raw hidden-states without any specific head on top. We used BERT-base and BERT-large versions of the model, both cased and uncased versions. We used pooled output of the model for the classification.

- DistilBERT: we used distilbert-base tokenizer, and we created DistilBERT model (Cased/Uncased) based on the architecture shown in Table 3. We used model with a sequence classification/regression head on top (a linear layer on top of the pooled output).
- XLNet: we used xlnet-base-cased tokenizer, and we created XLNet model based on the architecture shown in Table 3. We used model with a sequence classification/regression head on top (a linear layer on top of the pooled output). XLNet model doesn't provide a pre-trained and uncased version.

7. Experiments

During the experiments, we aimed to compare the effect of different pre-processing techniques on the classification of the toxic comments. In comparison, we used the composed architecture model with different pre-processing methods applied to the data. We aimed to compare the models' performance using:

- TFIDF representation with standard pre-processing;
- TFIDF representation without standard pre-processing;
- Pre-trained embeddings with standard pre-processing (GloVe, fastText);
- Pre-trained embeddings without standard pre-processing (GloVe, fastText);
- Custom-trained embeddings with standard pre-processing (word2vec);
- Custom-trained embeddings without standard pre-processing (word2vec);
- Pre-trained BERT language representations;

- Fine-tuning BERT language representations;
- Pre-trained DistilBERT language representations;
- Pre-trained XLNet language representations.

Figure 9 depicts the workflow of the experiments. It is important to note that due to extreme computational intensiveness of the models training, not every possible combination of the pre-processing and model was explored. Instead, we followed a methodology of the initial evaluation of the models using default settings to choose the best-performing model. Then, we followed with the optimization of hyper-parameters of the best-performing model using grid-search and cross-validation. And finally, we evaluated the fine-tuned model using different combinations of pre-processing and text representations techniques. A more detailed description of the particular steps will be described in the following subsections.

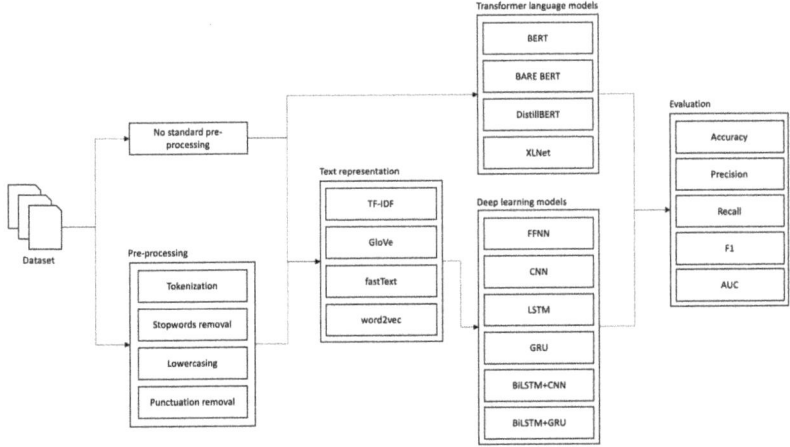

Figure 9. Overall schema of the experiments setup.

7.1. Selection of Best Deep Learning Model

Initial experiments were aimed to select the most suitable method to explore the pre-processing impact. To do so, we compared the described NN architectures on commonly used embeddings (GloVe). When comparing the particular architectures, we obtained the accuracy performance of each model, cross-validated on the training set and evaluated on the testing set; the results are shown in Table 4.

To compute the metrics (accuracy and loss), we transformed the class probabilities (output of the neural networks) into the crisp class predictions using a simple rule, which assigned the sample to a class if a probability of a given category was higher than 0.5. During this phase, we worked with this simplistic approach, in further evaluations of the best performing model, we also adopted a more advanced technique to identify the optimal threshold for each class.

Table 4. Initial evaluation of the models.

	FFNN	CNN	GRU	LSTM	BiLSTM + CNN	BiGRU + CNN
Accuracy	0.878	0.886	0.872	0.873	0.890	0.884
F1 score—micro avg	0.63	0.64	0.66	0.65	0.67	0.67
F1 score—macro avg	0.34	0.42	0.56	0.55	0.53	0.47

The training phase of the deep learning models on the used dataset is very demanding on computational resources. The training process is very time-consuming, even on recent GPUs. We decided to optimize the hyper-parameters of the best model on 10% stratified sample of the dataset. We performed the fine-tuning of the hyper-parameters using a grid search with cross-validation. We tuned the best-performing model (biLSTM-CNN), which we used with the obtained parameters as the starting architecture for further experiments. Considered parameters used for the grid search are shown in Table 5.

Table 5. Hyper-parameters used in grid search for the BiLSTM + CNN model.

Hyper-Parameters	Values
Activation	'relu', 'than'
Batch Size	[16, 32, 64]
Optimizer	['SGD', 'RMSProp', 'Adam'
Dropout rate	[0.1, 0.2]

We achieved the best results using the regularisation dropout 0.2, activation function ReLU, Adam optimizer and batch size 32. The complete results of this experiment are stored on a GitHub (https://github.com/VieraMaslej/toxic_comments_classification/blob/main/result_gridsearch.txt).

To gain a better understanding of the learning process and more importantly, to estimate the learning variance, we performed 10-fold cross-validation of the best performing model on the training data. Table 6 summarizes the results of the particular folds during the cross-validation of the BiLSTM + CNN model. This step was important to estimate the learning variance. As we can observe that the overall variance of the learning is acceptable, we will not use the cross-validation during further experiments with pre-processing. This enabled us to reduce the total time needed to train and test all evaluated combinations of the pre-processing and text representation methods.

Table 6. Cross-validation of the BiLSTM + CNN model.

Model	1	2	3	4	5	6	7	8	9	10	avg
Loss	0.047	0.045	0.045	0.045	0.047	0.047	0.045	0.046	0.045	0.043	0.046
Accuracy	0.991	0.994	0.994	0.971	0.991	0.991	0.994	0.994	0.994	0.994	0.991

All models were implemented in Python language using Tensorflow [62] and Keras [63] libraries. The source codes are available on GitHub (https://github.com/VieraMaslej/toxic_comments_classification). The experiments were conducted on a PC equipped with a 4-core Intel Xeon processor clocked at 4 GHz and NVIDIA Tesla K40c GPU with 12 GB memory.

7.2. Analysis of Text Representation and Pre-Processing Influence on Deep Learning Models

From the initial set of experiments, we selected a composed BiLSTM network architecture in combination with a convolution layer to be the most suitable to explore the effects of different pre-processing. During the following experiments, we focused on using different text representation and pre-processing settings. We computed commonly used metrics in classification, including accuracy, AUC score, precision, recall and F1. Interesting is an F1 score as it expresses the harmonic mean of precision and recall and describes the overall performance of the model better. We compared the performance of the model with a standard pre-processed text corpus and without pre-processing (only using simple tokenization). We also decided to compare different text representations, which we described in Section 4.

In the first step, we explored how the model performs when using the TF-IDF data representation. Table 7 summarizes the results of the experiments. Basic document vector representation using TF-IDF did not prove to be very suitable for this task. The performance of the model using this representation suffered from poor recall. Although accuracy and AUC values gain reasonable values, those metrics are not very useful in imbalanced classes. To better understand the classifier performance, precision and recall provide better insight. In this case, it is clear that the minor classes failed to learn completely. On the other hand, we can observe that the standard pre-processing improves the classification (contrary to the expectations). In TF-IDF, the pre-processing may improve the created vector representation, as it is created from the corpus itself (not from pre-trained vectors, such embeddings).

Table 8 depicts the BiLSTM + CNN model performance using the word2vec embeddings. In both cases (with and without pre-processing), word2vec representations were trained from the dataset. word2vec representation brings massive improvement in comparison to TF-IDF, rapidly improving the performance metrics (both, micro and macro averaged). The results also demonstrate the influence of the pre-processing techniques applied in text preparation. The model gained slightly better performance on the not processed text, improving recall values (most importantly, macro-averaged recall).

Table 7. Performance of the composed BiLSTM + CNN model with TF-IDF text documents representation.

	Accuracy	AUC Score		Precision	Recall	F1 Score
TF-IDF	0.8971	0.8437	micro avg.:	0.60	0.05	0.09
			macro avg.:	0.33	0.02	0.03
TF-IDF + PP	0.9038	0.8533	micro avg.:	0.70	0.23	0.35
			macro avg.:	0.35	0.13	0.19

Table 8. Performance of the composed BiLSTM + CNN model with gensim word2vec embeddings.

	Accuracy	AUC Score		Precision	Recall	F1 Score
word2vec	0.8835	0.9791	micro avg.:	0.62	0.74	0.67
			macro avg.:	0.58	0.53	0.51
word2vec + PP	0.8787	0.9769	micro avg.:	0.61	0.71	0.65
			macro avg.:	0.59	0.45	0.46

Table 9 summarizes the model performance using pre-trained word embeddings, both with standard text pre-processing and a model with no pre-processing. We used two different GloVe pre-trained embeddings, Common Crawl (840 B tokens, 2.2 M vocab) and Twitter (2 B tweets, 27 B tokens). The model performer very similar using different GloVe and fastText embeddings. Although the averaged F1 metrics are very similar, we can observe some differences, how the models perform on precision and recall metrics. Skipping of the pre-processing in case of the CC GloVe embeddings causes recall drop and improvement of the precision, while in case of the Twitter GloVe embeddings it is otherwise. The difference may be caused by either size of the tokes, or how the embeddings were trained. It is possible that the Twitter embeddings are built using the data closer to the domain (as tweets may be similar to the comments). We used F1 metric to select the best performing model, Twitter GloVe embeddings without pre-processing was the best method from that point of view.

Table 9. Performance of the composed BiLSTM + CNN model with pre-trained GloVe and fastText embeddings.

	Accuracy	AUC Score		Precision	Recall	F1 Score
Common Crawl GloVe	0.8904	0.9796	micro avg.:	0.63	0.72	0.67
			macro avg.:	0.60	0.52	0.53
Common Crawl GloVe + PP	0.8621	0.9766	micro avg.:	0.54	0.79	0.64
			macro avg.:	0.47	0.55	0.46
Twitter GloVe	0.8787	0.9798	micro avg.:	0.59	0.77	**0.67**
			macro avg.:	0.57	0.59	**0.56**
Twitter GloVe + PP	0.8903	0.9771	micro avg.:	0.65	0.67	0.66
			macro avg.:	0.63	0.51	0.54
fastText	0.8839	0.9787	micro avg.:	0.61	0.73	0.66
			macro avg.:	0.58	0.52	0.51
fastText + PP	0.8947	0.9749	micro avg.:	0.63	0.70	0.67
			macro avg.:	0.49	0.44	0.43

7.3. Selection of Best Transformer Model

Table 10 compares the performance of BERT model, bare BERT and its DistilBERT and XLNet variants. We compared the performance of these models with BiLSTM + CNN architecture. Regarding the pre-processing, it was a little bit different in this case. As the transformer models are available pre-trained on the text corpora in two different versions-cased and uncased (except the XLNet model, that doesn't come with the uncased version). Furthermore, we used the BERT tokenizer, in which we used lowercasing of the input text (in cased versions) or did not use it (in uncased versions). As described in Section 6.2, we trained two BERT-base for sequence classification models, two bare BERT-base models, two bare BERT-large models, two DistilBERT models and a single XLNet model. We used default hyper-parameters as depicted in Table 11.

Table 10. Performance of the transformer models.

	Accuracy	AUC Score		Precision	Recall	F1 Score
BERT-base (cased)	0.8884	0.9624	micro avg.:	0.66	0.64	0.65
			macro avg.:	0.34	0.34	0.34
BERT-base (uncased)	0.8798	0.9700	micro avg.:	0.61	0.71	0.65
			macro avg.:	0.31	0.38	0.34
bare BERT-base (cased)	0.8998	0.9802	micro avg.:	0.69	0.68	0.69
			macro avg.:	0.63	0.51	0.51
bare BERT-base (uncased)	0.8841	0.9839	micro avg.:	0.60	0.78	**0.68**
			macro avg.:	0.60	0.58	**0.57**
bare BERT-large (cased)	0.8795	0.9801	micro avg.:	0.62	0.73	0.67
			macro avg.:	0.53	0.51	0.51
bare BERT-large (uncased)	0.8921	0.9806	micro avg.:	0.67	0.68	0.67
			macro avg.:	0.60	0.41	0.42
DistilBERT (cased)	0.8866	0.9649	micro avg.:	0.63	0.68	0.66
			macro avg.:	0.34	0.37	0.34
DistilBERT (uncased)	0.8649	0.9781	micro avg.:	0.59	0.73	0.65
			macro avg.:	0.48	0.39	0.34
XLNet (cased)	0.9630	0.9530	micro avg.:	0.60	0.70	0.65
			macro avg.:	0.30	0.37	0.33

Table 10 summarizes the model's performances using the cased and uncased version. We also tried to use a BERT-large version of the BERT sequence classification models, but it is probable that those models were over-fitting in the first epoch and the results were worse than in BERT-base version.

Based on the previous experiment, the BERT-base uncased model provided the best results among the transformer models. Following the initial experiments, we proceed with the fine-tuning of the model. We optimized the values of the hyper-parameters summarized in Table 12. Optimization of the hyper-parameters did not lead to a significantly improved performance, however, for the combination of the accuracy and AUC metrics, the best combination of hyper-parameters turned out to be the settings: learning rate = 0.00002, batch size = 16, dropout = 0.15. The results of the fine-tuned model are shown in Table 13. This model also achieved the best micro-averaged F1 metrics.

Table 11. Hyper-parameters used for transformer models from Table 10.

Hyper-Parameters	Values
Batch size	32
Learning rate	0.00003
Dropout rate	0.15

Table 12. Explored combination of the bare BERT-base hyper-parameters during the fine-tuning.

Hyper-Parameters	Values
Dropout rate	[0.1, 0.15]
Learning rate	[0.00002, 0.00003]
Batch Size	[16, 32]

Table 13. Bare BERT-base uncased model performance after the fine-tuning.

	Accuracy	AUC Score		Precision	Recall	F1 Score
bare BERT-BASE uncased	0.8971	0.9842	micro avg.:	0.67	0.72	0.69
			macro avg.:	0.69	0.51	0.55

7.4. Evaluation

From the experiment results with deep learning models, we can consider the GloVe pre-trained embeddings without standard pre-processing as the most suitable representation. The results proved that omitting the traditional pre-processing techniques improve the classification results. This is especially important in the case of macro-averaged metrics, which are more informative in classification tasks with highly imbalanced data. Another important aspect (besides the improvement of the performance metrics) is the demand on resources and computational intensiveness-the pre-processing techniques represent a step in the overall data analysis process and skipping them can reduce the time of the total data preparation phase. On the other hand, pre-processing usually leads to the reduction of the training data dimensionality. When we leave out such a step, we could expect the more resource-demanding training of the models. Another crucial aspect is the deployment of the models in real-world scenarios, where the training time of the model is not essential. In such a case, the ability to process the data and prediction time is essential. Without pre-processing, it is sufficient to create word tokens from the text and apply a trained model to obtain the prediction.

Tables 14–16 depict the BiLSTM + CNN model (with GloVe Twitter and word2vec embeddings) and bare BERT-base uncased model performance on particular classes. In this task, the class imbalance is present and heavily influences the classification. Minor classes (e.g., *severe_toxic* or *threat*) presented a real challenge to learn from the training data. Much better picture about the real quality of the classification into the particular classes is given by the Matthews Correlation Coefficient (MCC) [64]. When considering this metric, both models perform in a similar fashion. Both models struggle with minor classes, with a model trained using GloVe Twitter embeddings performing better on a *severe_toxic* class, while bare BERT handling better the *threat* category. For some models (e.g., for BERT), the lack of training samples from minor classes may present a problem, as some of the BERT modifications were not able to learn some of the minor classes at all. Composed architecture with embeddings was able to learn minor classes; however, in both cases, with at least one metric severely lacking. There may be more reasons why most of the models fail to perform well, even in minor classes. For example analysis of the misclassifications revealed possible problems in the labelling of the data, where numerous comments labelled as *toxic* did not fall into the proper definition of the toxic comments [11]. Besides the questionable labelling, which may have influenced the evaluation of the trained patterns, several NLP-related phenomena may influence the classification, e.g., toxic comments written without any explicit language or written in ordinary style, comments containing sarcasm, irony or metaphors which require the deeper understanding of the content.

To further improve the best performing models, we fine-tuned the thresholds used to convert class probabilities to crisp values. The unbalanced number of samples in individual classes can have an impact on the resulting metrics when transforming the probabilities for each class in a similar manner. Therefore, to improve the model, we used optimization to find the best threshold for each class we trained a separate classifier, to find the optimal set of thresholds for the probabilities, specific for each class. We used the optimization implemented in scipy library, selected F1 as an optimization criterion. After then, we computed the overall metrics and metrics for particular classes. Tables 17 and 18 show how the performance metrics improved after fine-tuning of the probability thresholds.

Table 14. Results of the individual toxicity classes of biLSTM + CNN model with custom-trained word2vec embeddings without standard pre-processing.

Class	Precision	Recall	F1 Score	MCC	Support
toxic	0.58	0.85	0.69	0.66	6090
severe_toxic	0.35	0.50	0.41	0.42	367
obscene	0.66	0.75	0.71	0.69	3691
threat	0.48	0.07	0.12	0.18	211
insult	0.67	0.68	0.68	0.66	3427
identity_hate	0.73	0.33	0.46	0.49	712

Table 15. Results of the individual toxicity classes of biLSTM + CNN model with pre-trained GloVe Twitter embeddings without standard pre-processing.

Class	Precision	Recall	F1 Score	MCC	Support
toxic	0.56	0.88	0.68	0.66	6090
severe_toxic	0.37	0.46	0.41	0.41	367
obscene	0.61	0.79	0.69	0.67	3691
threat	0.47	0.26	0.34	0.35	211
insult	0.65	0.71	0.68	0.66	3427
identity_hate	0.76	0.42	0.54	0.56	712

Regarding the interpretability of the trained models, we further explored, how the classifiers performed when predicting the actual class labels. We focused on examination of particular comments, especially those, which were classified correctly in multiple categories and on the other hand, the comments that were misclassified. Many comments were categorized correctly, based on the grammar and language used, e.g., the comment "u are a gigantic faggot" was correctly predicted as toxic, obscene, insult, and identity hate. On the other hand, we observed an inconsistency in comments labelling, which is a frequent issue in many hand-labelled datasets. For example, the comment "Bull... Your mom kicking your ass for not studying is influence of Custom. but then again, without all that comic mischief (such as a dead guy and a crying ilha), life would be pretty fukin boring ..." was predicted by the models as toxic and obscene, because of using an explicit language. However, in the testing data, the comment was assigned just with the toxic label. In similar fashion, a comment "oh, shutup, you douchey Wikipedia rent-a-cop" is clearly an insult and was correctly predicted as toxic and insult, but in the testing data was assigned only with the first label.

Table 16. Results of the individual toxicity classes of bare BERT uncased model after fine-tuning.

Class	Precision	Recall	F1 Score	MCC	Support
toxic	0.58	0.87	0.70	0.67	6090
severe_toxic	0.40	0.23	0.29	0.30	367
obscene	0.60	0.80	0.69	0.67	3691
threat	0.63	0.37	0.47	0.48	211
insult	0.66	0.73	0.69	0.67	3427
identity_hate	0.73	0.51	0.60	0.61	712

Table 17. Results of the individual toxicity classes of **optimized** biLSTM + CNN model with pre-trained GloVe Twitter embeddings without standard pre-processing.

Class	Precision	Recall	F1 Score	MCC	Support
toxic	0.59	0.85	0.70	0.67	6090
severe_toxic	0.33	0.66	0.44	0.46	367
obscene	0.61	0.78	0.69	0.67	3691
threat	0.47	0.26	0.34	0.35	211
insult	0.69	0.68	0.68	0.66	3427
identity_hate	0.76	0.43	0.55	0.56	712

Table 18. Results of the individual toxicity classes of optimized and fine-tuned bare BERT uncased model.

Class	Precision	Recall	F1 Score	MCC	Support
toxic	0.64	0.81	0.71	0.69	6090
severe_toxic	0.30	0.64	0.41	0.43	367
obscene	0.67	0.75	0.71	0.69	3691
threat	0.60	0.39	0.47	0.48	211
insult	0.64	0.75	0.69	0.67	3427
identity_hate	0.60	0.71	0.65	0.64	712

7.5. Comparison with Other Models from State-of-the-Art

To compare the models' performance with other similar approaches presented in the literature, we have to consider several aspects. There are numerous studies, in which authors transformed the Kaggle toxic comments competition dataset labels to the binary values (representing toxic and non-toxic values) and solved the binary classification task of toxicity detection [35,65]. On the other hand, when solving the task as a multi-label classification, comparison of these approaches could still be inconsistent, as the evaluation of the models in the literature is not coherent, as multiple studies using different data for evaluation, e.g., a subset of training data (split to 80/20 train/test ratio), or separate labelled testing data, which became available later. Therefore, to compare with the different models, different evaluation of the models had to be implemented. To compare with the results presented in [11,36], we needed to compute the averaged precision and recall values for each class (as a separate classification problems, contrary to multi-label evaluation in previous experiments), and then compute the F1 metric. Overall performance of our approach is compared with several similar approaches using the accuracy, precision, recall, F1 score. Table 19 summarizes the evaluation metrics of the models.

Table 19. Comparison of the performance metrics of the proposed approaches with similar models.

Model	Precision	Recall	F1
BiGRU (GloVe) [11]	0.73	0.85	0.772
BiGRU + Attention (GloVe) [11]	0.73	0.87	0.779
BiGRU + Attention (fastText) [11]	0.74	0.87	0.783
Ensemble model [11]	0.74	0.88	0.791
BiLSTM + CNN + GloVe(Twitter) + No PP	0.78	0.79	0.789
BiLSTM + CNN + GloVe(CC) + No PP	0.75	0.84	0.796
bare BERT-BASE uncased	0.78	0.83	0.801

To analyze how well the models perform on a particular class, we compared the results with other similar approaches described in [66]. Table 20 summarizes and compares our best-performing model with the best performing related models. This time, to be able to compare with the models from the study, we used the accuracy score computed for the specific categories. Please note that the table contains the results presented in one-vs-all approach (e.g., each class compared to the rest of the others), computed from individual confusion matrices for each specific category.

Table 20. Comparison of the accuracy of the BiLSTM + CNN and bare BERT with other similar models (using Intel300, fastText300, GloVe300, word2vec300 embeddings) from paper [66].

	BiLSTM + CNN	bare BERT	Intel300 [66]	fastText300 [66]	GloVe300 [66]	word2vec300 [66]
toxic	0.9238	0.9382	0.95	0.95	0.93	0.93
severe_toxic	0.9943	0.9894	0.96	0.95	0.96	0.96
obscene	0.9609	0.9644	0.95	0.96	0.96	0.95
threat	0.9970	0.9971	0.96	0.96	0.97	0.96
insult	0.9674	0.9641	0.96	0.96	0.96	0.96
identity_hate	0.9919	0.9914	0.97	0.96	0.96	0.96
averaged	0.9725	0.9741	0.96	0.96	0.96	0.95

8. Conclusions

In work presented in this paper, we aimed to compare and evaluate different current state-of-the-art models for multi-label toxic comments classification. We experimentally evaluated the performance of deep learning models, including composed architectures with different methods of text representation and pre-processing. On top of that, currently, popular transformer language models, such as BERT and its modifications were compared as well. We aimed to explore the assumption that in tasks such as detection of anti-social behaviour in the online environments, the application of traditional pre-processing techniques could lead to loss of particular specific information characteristic for such behaviour. We aimed to explore the influence of different pre-processing and representation methods on the deep learning and transformer models also in multi-label task aimed to detect the specific type of anti-social behaviour (in this case, toxic comments). We experimentally evaluated composed architecture of BiLSTM + CNN network with different text representations, pre-trained embeddings and compared it with BERT and its variants.

Further evaluation of the various data preparation techniques confirmed the assumption, that in this type of task, using standard pre-processing may lead to influence the classifier performance. When comparing the network performance using different word embeddings, the results showed, that the application of traditional text preparation techniques does not bring any significant benefit in terms of evaluation metrics. When comparing the standard classification performance metrics, we face the problem of the class imbalance. The models often struggle to perform well in the minority classes. If the collection of more samples from such classes is not straightforward, more advanced approaches or using data augmentation techniques may be required. One of the possible strategies could be represented by the hierarchical ensemble model. In such an approach, different classifiers could be combined to either address the specific classes, or even to perform the classification on a different level of target attribute generalization. The particular model then could be used to distinguish between the toxic and non-toxic comments and particular toxicity type prediction could be handled by separate models. The class imbalance could be addressed by various techniques, e.g., weighting schemes in the ensemble.

It is also important to note that the presented comparison was carried out on a single dataset. Another limitation of the study is the use of pre-trained word embeddings and pre-trained transformer language models (except word2vec embeddings). Usually, pre-trained embeddings are build using corpora consisting of standard, clean forms of the words. Such representations do not cover the entire vocabulary used in the abusive comments, which results in the loss of information. In future work, we would like to focus on embedding custom-training for this particular domain. A very similar situation is with transfer learning models. In most of the NLP tasks, those models outperform the deep learning models. Pre-trained models may represent not an ideal solution in this case, and their further re-training may lead to superior results. Another factor is the computational intensiveness of the deep and transformer models training which practically prevents the ultimate comparison of all models, with all pre-processing settings, hyper-parameter fine-tuning using cross-validation technique. In our experiments, we decided to evaluate the models' performance using standard, commonly used settings, then fine-tune the hyper-parameters of the best-performing architecture using grid search on sampled data. Similarly, we assumed the learning variance during the initial experiment using 10-fold cross-validation and did not perform the cross-validation of an entire set of pre-processing experiments, which would result in extreme time and resource-consuming setup.

Author Contributions: Conceptualization, M.S. and V.M.-K.; methodology, M.S.; software, V.M.-K.; validation, V.M.-K.; formal analysis, P.B.; investigation, V.M.-K. and K.M.; resources, M.S.; writing—original draft preparation, V.M.-K. and M.S.; writing—review and editing, V.M.-K., M.S. and P.B.; supervision, P.B.; All authors have read and agreed to the published version of the manuscript.

Funding: This work was partially supported by the Slovak Research and Development Agency under the contracts No. APVV-16-0213 and No. APVV-17-0267.

Conflicts of Interest: The authors declare no conflict of interest.

Abbreviations

The following abbreviations are used in this manuscript:

BERT	Bidirectional Encoder Representations from Transformers
CNN	Convolutional Neural Network
GRU	Gated Recurrent Unit
LSTM	Long Short-Term Memory
FFNN	FeedForward Neural Network
NLP	Natural Language Processing
CBOW	Continuous Bag of Words
BCE	Binary Cross Entropy
ReLU	Rectified Linear Unit
AUC	Area Under Curve
ROC	Receiver Operating Characteristic

References

1. Cheng, J.; Danescu-Niculescu-Mizil, C.; Leskovec, J. Antisocial behavior in online discussion communities. In Proceedings of the 9th International Conference on Web and Social Media, University of Oxford, Oxford, UK, 26–29 May 2015,.
2. Elizabeth, B. *Making People Behave: Anti-Social Behaviour, Politics and Policy*, 2nd ed.; Willan Publishing: Cullompton, UK, 2013, doi:10.4324/9781843927112.

3. Risch, J.; Krestel, R. Toxic Comment Detection in Online Discussions. In *Deep Learning-Based Approaches for Sentiment Analysis*; Algorithms for Intelligent Systems; Springer: Singapore, 2020, doi:10.1007/978-981-15-1216-2_4.
4. Dixon, L.; Li, J.; Sorensen, J.; Thain, N.; Vasserman, L. Measuring and Mitigating Unintended Bias in Text Classification. In Proceedings of the 2018 AAAI/ACM Conference on AI, Ethics, and Society, New Orleans, USA, 2–3 February 2018, doi:10.1145/3278721.3278729.
5. Morzhov, S. Avoiding Unintended Bias in Toxicity Classification with Neural Networks. In Proceedings of the Conference of Open Innovation Association, Yaroslavl, Russia, 20–24 April 2020, doi:10.23919/FRUCT48808.2020.9087368.
6. Mohammad, F. Is preprocessing of text really worth your time for online comment classification? *arXiv* **2018**, arXiv:1806.02908.
7. Singh, T.; Kumari, M. Role of Text Pre-processing in Twitter Sentiment Analysis. *Procedia Comput. Sci.* 2016, 89, 549–554, doi:10.1016/j.procs.2016.06.095.
8. Shelar, A.; Huang, C.Y. Sentiment analysis of twitter data. In Proceedings of the 2018 International Conference on Computational Science and Computational Intelligence, Las Vegas, NV, USA, 13–15 December 2018, doi:10.1109/CSCI46756.2018.00252.
9. Wang, S.; Manning, C.D. Baselines and bigrams: Simple, good sentiment and topic classification. In Proceedings of the 50th Annual Meeting of the Association for Computational Linguistics, Jeju Island, Korea, 8–14 July 2012.
10. Feldman, R. Techniques and applications for sentiment analysis. *Commun. ACM* **2013**, 56, 82–89, doi:10.1145/2436256.2436274.
11. van Aken, B.; Risch, J.; Krestel, R.; Löser, A. *Challenges for Toxic Comment Classification: An In-Depth Error Analysis*; In Proceedings of the 2nd Workshop on Abusive Language Online (ALW2), Brussels, Belgium, 31 October 2018, doi:10.18653/v1/w18-5105.
12. Waseem, Z.; Davidson, T.; Warmsley, D.; Weber, I. Understanding Abuse: A Typology of Abusive Language Detection Subtasks. **2017**, doi:10.18653/v1/w17-3012.
13. Sarnovský, M.; Butka, P.; Bednár, P.; Babič, F.; Paralič, J. Analytical platform based on Jbowl library providing text-mining services in distributed environment. In Proceedings of the Information and Communication Technology, Daejeon, Korea, 4–7 October 2015, doi:10.1007/978-3-319-24315-3_32.
14. Davidson, T.; Warmsley, D.; Macy, M.; Weber, I. Automated hate speech detection and the problem of offensive language. In Proceedings of the 11th International Conference on Web and Social Media, Montréal, QC, Canada, 15–18 May 2017.
15. Salminen, J.; Almerekhi, H.; Milenković, M.; Jung, S.G.; An, J.; Kwak, H.; Jansen, B.J. Anatomy of online hate: Developing a taxonomy and machine learning models for identifying and classifying hate in online news media. In Proceedings of the 12th International AAAI Conference on Web and Social Media, Stanford, CA, USA, 25–28 June 2018.
16. Almerekhi, H.; Jansen, B.J.; Kwak, H.; Salminen, J. Detecting toxicity triggers in online discussions. In Proceedings of the 30th ACM Conference on Hypertext and Social Media, Hof, Germany, 17–20 September 2019, doi:10.1145/3342220.3344933.
17. Fortuna, P.; Soler, J.; Wanner, L. Toxic, Hateful, Offensive or Abusive? What Are We Really Classifying? An Empirical Analysis of Hate Speech Datasets. In *Proceedings of the 12th Language Resources and Evaluation Conference*; European Language Resources Association: Marseille, France, 11–16 May 2020; pp. 6786–6794.
18. Shtovba, S.; Shtovba, O.; Petrychko, M. Detection of social network toxic comments with usage of syntactic dependencies in the sentences. In Proceedings of the Second International Workshop on Computer Modeling and Intelligent Systems, Zaporizhzhia, Ukraine, 15–19 April 2019.
19. Saif, M.A.; Medvedev, A.N.; Medvedev, M.A.; Atanasova, T. Classification of online toxic comments using the logistic regression and neural networks models. *AIP Conference Proc.* **2018**, 2048, 060011. doi:10.1063/1.5082126.
20. Haralabopoulos, G.; Anagnostopoulos, I.; McAuley, D. Ensemble deep learning for multilabel binary classification of user-generated content. *Algorithms* **2020**, 13, 83, doi:10.3390/A13040083.
21. Chowdhary, N.; Pandit, A.A. Fake Review Detection using Classification. *Int. J. Comput. Appl.* **2018**, 180, 16–21.

22. Cardoso, E.F.; Silva, R.M.; Almeida, T.A. Towards automatic filtering of fake reviews. *Neurocomputing* **2018**, *309*, 106–116, doi:10.1016/j.neucom.2018.04.074.
23. Ventirozos, F.K.; Varlamis, I.; Tsatsaronis, G. Detecting aggressive behavior in discussion threads using text mining. In *Proceedings Computational Linguistics and Intelligent Text Processing*; Springer: Cham, Switzerland, 2018, doi:10.1007/978-3-319-77116-8_31.
24. Machová, K.; Mach, M.; Demková, G. Modelling of the Fake Posting Recognition in On-Line Media Using Machine Learning. *SOFSEM 2020: Theory and Practice of Computer Science*; Chatzigeorgiou, A., Dondi, R., Herodotou, H., Kapoutsis, C., Manolopoulos, Y., Papadopoulos, G.A., Sikora, F., Eds.; Springer International Publishing: Cham, Switzerland, 2020; pp. 667–675.
25. Machova, K.; Staronova, P. *Selecting the Most Probable Author of Asocial Posting in Online Media*; In Proceedings of 17th International Conference on Emerging eLearning Technologies and Applications (ICETA), Starý Smokovec, Slovakia, 21–22 November 2019; pp. 480–485, doi:10.1109/ICETA48886.2019.9040096.
26. Anindyati, L.; Purwarianti, A.; Nursanti, A. Optimizing Deep Learning for Detection Cyberbullying Text in Indonesian Language. In Proceedings of the 2019 International Conference on Advanced Informatics: Concepts, Theory, and Applications, Yogyakarta, Indonesia, 20–22 September 2019, doi:10.1109/ICAICTA.2019.8904108.
27. Al-Ajlan, M.A.; Ykhlef, M. Deep Learning Algorithm for Cyberbullying Detection. *Int. J. Adv. Comput. Sci. Appl.* **2018**, *9*, doi:10.14569/IJACSA.2018.090927.
28. Agrawal, S.; Awekar, A. Deep learning for detecting cyberbullying across multiple social media platforms. In *Advances in Information Retrieval*; Lecture Notes in Computer Science; Springer: Cham, Switzerland, 2018, doi:10.1007/978-3-319-76941-7_11.
29. Ranasinghe, T.; Zampieri, M.; Hettiarachchi, H. BRUMS at HASOC 2019: Deep Learning Models for Multilingual Hate Speech and Offensive Language Identificati on. In *FIRE (Working Notes)*; CEUR-WS: Kolkata, India, 12–15 December 2019.
30. Zimmerman, S.; Fox, C.; Kruschwitz, U. Improving hate speech detection with deep learning ensembles. In Proceedings of the LREC 2018—11th International Conference on Language Resources and Evaluation, Miyazaki, Japan, 7–12 May 2019.
31. Krešňáková, V.M.; Sarnovský, M.; Butka, P. Deep learning methods for Fake News detection. In Proceedings of the 2019 IEEE 19th International Symposium on Computational Intelligence and Informatics and 7th IEEE International Conference on Recent Achievements in Mechatronics, Automation, Computer Sciences and Robotics (CINTI-MACRo), Szeged, Hungary, 14–16 November 2019; pp. 000143–000148.
32. Mestry, S.; Singh, H.; Chauhan, R.; Bisht, V.; Tiwari, K. Automation in Social Networking Comments with the Help of Robust fastText and CNN. In Proceedings of the 1st International Conference on Innovations in Information and Communication Technology, India, 25–26 April 2019, doi:10.1109/ICIICT1.2019.8741503.
33. Anand, M.; Eswari, R. Classification of abusive comments in social media using deep learning. In Proceedings of the 3rd International Conference on Computing Methodologies and Communication, New Jersey, NJ, USA, 27–29 March 2019, doi:10.1109/ICCMC.2019.8819734.
34. Srivastava, S.; Khurana, P.; Tewari, V. Identifying Aggression and Toxicity in Comments using Capsule Network. In Proceedings of the First Workshop on Trolling, Aggression and Cyberbullying (TRAC-2018), Santa Fe, NM, USA, 25 August 2018.
35. Georgakopoulos, S.V.; Vrahatis, A.G.; Tasoulis, S.K.; Plagianakos, V.P. Convolutional neural networks for toxic comment classification. In Proceedings of the ACM International Conference Proceeding Series, Patras, Greece, 9–12 July 2018, doi:10.1145/3200947.3208069.
36. Ibrahim, M.; Torki, M.; El-Makky, N. Imbalanced Toxic Comments Classification Using Data Augmentation and Deep Learning. In Proceedings of the 17th IEEE International Conference on Machine Learning and Applications, Orlando, FL, USA, 17–20 December 2018, doi:10.1109/ICMLA.2018.00141.
37. Rumelhart, D.E.; Hinton, G.E.; Williams, R.J. Learning representations by back-propagating errors. *Nature* **1986**, *323*, 533–536, doi:10.1038/323533a0.
38. Goodfellow, I.; Bengio, Y.; Courville, A. *Deep Learning*; MIT Press: Cambridge, MA, USA,2016.
39. Leshno, M.; Lin, V.Y.; Pinkus, A.; Schocken, S. Multilayer feedforward networks with a nonpolynomial activation function can approximate any function. *Neural Netw.* **1993**, *6*, 861–867.
40. Nair, V.; Hinton, G.E. Rectified linear units improve Restricted Boltzmann machines. In Proceedings of the ICML 2010 27th International Conference on Machine Learning, Haifa, Israel, 21–24 June 2010.

41. Rumelhart, D.E.; Hinton, G.E.; Williams, R.J. *Neurocomputing: Foundations of Research*; Chapter Learning Representations by Back-Propagating Errors; MIT Press: Cambridge, MA, USA, 1988; pp. 696–699.
42. Kingma, D.; Ba, J. Adam: A Method for Stochastic Optimization. In Proceedings of the International Conference on Learning Representations, San Diego, CA, USA, 7–9 May 2015.
43. Hinton, G.E.; Srivastava, N.; Krizhevsky, A.; Sutskever, I.; Salakhutdinov, R. Improving neural networks by preventing co-adaptation of feature detectors. *arXiv* **2012**, arXiv:1207.0580.
44. Polyak, B. Some methods of speeding up the convergence of iteration methods. *Ussr Comput. Math. Math. Phys.* **1964**, *4*, 1–17, doi:10.1016/0041-5553(64)90137-5.
45. Srivastava, N.; Hinton, G.; Krizhevsky, A.; Sutskever, I.; Salakhutdinov, R. Dropout: A simple way to prevent neural networks from overfitting. *J. Mach. Learn. Res.* **2014**, *15*, 1929–1958.
46. Hochreiter, S.; Schmidhuber, J. Long short-term memory. *Neural Comput.* **1997**, *9*, 1735–1780, doi:10.1162/neco.1997.9.8.1735.
47. Graves, A. Supervised sequence labelling. In *Supervised Sequence Labelling with Recurrent Neural Networks*; Springer: Berlin/Heidelberg, Germany, 2012; pp. 5–13.
48. Tavcar, R.; Dedic, J.; Bokal, D.; Zemva, A. Transforming the LSTM Training Algorithm for Efficient FPGA-Based Adaptive Control of Nonlinear Dynamic Systems; *Journal of Microelectronics, Electronic Components and Materials* **2013**, *43*, pp. 131–138.
49. Schuster, M.; Paliwal, K.K. Bidirectional recurrent neural networks. *IEEE Trans. Signal Process.* **1997**, *45*, 2673–2681, doi:10.1109/78.650093.
50. Cho, K.; Merrienboer, B.; Gülçehre Ç.; Bougares, F.; Schwenk, H.; Bengio, Y. Learning Phrase Representations using RNN. In Proceedings of the 2014 Conference on Empirical Methods in Natural Language Processing (EMNLP), Doha, Qatar, 25–29 October 2014.
51. Sun, C.; Qiu, X.; Xu, Y.; Huang, X. How to Fine-Tune BERT for Text Classification? In Proceedings of the Lecture Notes in Computer Science (Including Subseries Lecture Notes in Artificial Intelligence and Lecture Notes in Bioinformatics), Cham, Switzerland, 13 October 2019, doi:10.1007/978-3-030-32381-3_16.
52. Devlin, J.; Chang, M.W.; Lee, K.; Toutanova, K. BERT: Pre-training of deep bidirectional transformers for language understanding. In Proceedings of the NAACL HLT 2019—2019 Conference of the North American Chapter of the Association for Computational Linguistics: Human Language Technologies, Minneapolis, MI, USA, June 2019.
53. Vaswani, A.; Shazeer, N.; Parmar, N.; Uszkoreit, J.; Jones, L.; Gomez, A.N.; Kaiser, Ł.; Polosukhin, I. Attention is all you need. *Adv. Neural Inf. Process. Syst.* **2017**, *30*, 5998–6008.
54. Sanh, V.; Debut, L.; Chaumond, J.; Wolf, T. DistilBERT, a distilled version of BERT: Smaller, faster, cheaper and lighter. *arXiv* **2020**, arXiv:1910.01108.
55. Liu, Y.; Ott, M.; Goyal, N.; Du, J.; Joshi, M.; Chen, D.; Levy, O.; Lewis, M.; Zettlemoyer, L.; Stoyanov, V. RoBERTa: A Robustly Optimized BERT Pretraining Approach. *arXiv* **2019**, arXiv:1907.11692.
56. Yang, Z.; Dai, Z.; Yang, Y.; Carbonell, J.; Salakhutdinov, R.; Le, Q.V. XLNet: Generalized Autoregressive Pretraining for Language Understanding. *arXiv* **2020**, arXiv:1906.08237.
57. Sammut, C.; Webb, G.I.; (Eds.) TF–IDF. In *Encyclopedia of Machine Learning*; Springer: Boston, MA, USA, 2010; pp. 986–987, doi:10.1007/978-0-387-30164-8_832.
58. Mikolov, T.; Chen, K.; Corrado, G.; Dean, J. Efficient estimation of word representations in vector space. *arXiv* **2013**, arXiv:1301.3781.
59. Pennington, J.; Socher, R.; Manning, C.D. Glove: Global vectors for word representation. In Proceedings of the 2014 Conference on Empirical Methods in Natural Language Processing (EMNLP), Doha, Qatar, 25–29 October 2014; pp. 1532–1543.
60. Bojanowski, P.; Grave, E.; Joulin, A.; Mikolov, T. Enriching Word Vectors with Subword Information. *arXiv* **2016**, arXiv:1607.04606.
61. Asch, V.V. *Macro-and Micro-Averaged Evaluation Measures*; CLiPS: Antwerpen, Belgium, 2013.
62. Abadi, M.; Barham, P.; Chen, J.; Chen, Z.; Davis, A.; Dean, J.; Devin, M.; Ghemawat, S.; Irving, G.; Isard, M.; et al. Tensorflow: A system for large-scale machine learning. In Proceedings of the 12th USENIX Symposium on Operating Systems Design and Implementation (OSDI 16), Savannah, GA, USA, 2–4 November 2016; pp. 265–283.
63. Gulli, A.; Pal, S. *Deep Learning with Keras*; Packt Publishing Ltd.: Birmingham, UK, 2017.

64. Matthews, B.W. Comparison of the predicted and observed secondary structure of T4 phage lysozyme. *Biochim. Biophys. Acta* **1975**, *405*, 442–451, doi:10.1016/0005-2795(75)90109-9.
65. Rastogi, C.; Mofid, N.; Hsiao, F.I. Can We Achieve More with Less? Exploring Data Augmentation for Toxic Comment Classification. *arXiv* **2020**, arXiv:2007.00875.
66. Saia, R.; Corriga, A.; Mulas, R.; Reforgiato Recupero, D.; Carta, S. A Supervised Multi-Class Multi-Label Word Embeddings Approach for Toxic Comment Classification. In Proceedings of the 11th International Joint Conference on Knowledge Discovery, Knowledge Engineering and Knowledge Management (IC3K 2019), Vienna, Austria, 17–19 September 2019, doi:10.5220/0008110901050112.

Publisher's Note: MDPI stays neutral with regard to jurisdictional claims in published maps and institutional affiliations.

© 2020 by the authors. Licensee MDPI, Basel, Switzerland. This article is an open access article distributed under the terms and conditions of the Creative Commons Attribution (CC BY) license (http://creativecommons.org/licenses/by/4.0/).

Article

Delayed Combination of Feature Embedding in Bidirectional LSTM CRF for NER

Chirawan Ronran [1,2], Seungwoo Lee [1,2,*] and Hong Jun Jang [2]

1. Department of Big Data Science, University of Science and Technology (UST), Daejeon 34113, Korea; chirawan@kisti.re.kr
2. Korea Institute of Science and Technology Information (KISTI), Daejeon 34113, Korea; hongjunjang@kisti.re.kr
* Correspondence: swlee@kisti.re.kr; Tel.: +82-42-869-1784

Received: 30 July 2020; Accepted: 21 October 2020; Published: 27 October 2020

Abstract: Named Entity Recognition (NER) plays a vital role in natural language processing (NLP). Currently, deep neural network models have achieved significant success in NER. Recent advances in NER systems have introduced various feature selections to identify appropriate representations and handle Out-Of-the-Vocabulary (OOV) words. After selecting the features, they are all concatenated at the embedding layer before being fed into a model to label the input sequences. However, when concatenating the features, information collisions may occur and this would cause the limitation or degradation of the performance. To overcome the information collisions, some works tried to directly connect some features to latter layers, which we call the delayed combination and show its effectiveness by comparing it to the early combination. As feature encodings for input, we selected the character-level Convolutional Neural Network (CNN) or Long Short-Term Memory (LSTM) word encoding, the pre-trained word embedding, and the contextual word embedding and additionally designed CNN-based sentence encoding using a dictionary. These feature encodings are combined at early or delayed position of the bidirectional LSTM Conditional Random Field (CRF) model according to each feature's characteristics. We evaluated the performance of this model on the CoNLL 2003 and OntoNotes 5.0 datasets using the F1 score and compared the delayed combination model with our own implementation of the early combination as well as the previous works. This comparison convinces us that our delayed combination is more effective than the early one and also highly competitive.

Keywords: delayed combination; CNN dictionary; named entity recognition; deep learning NER; bidirectional LSTM CRF; CoNLL; OntoNotes

---

1. Introduction

Named entity recognition (NER) has received much attention in a wide range of natural language processing (NLP) tasks, such as question and answering, information extraction, and machine translation. NER techniques can be classified into four main streams: (1) a rule-based approach based on hand-crafted rules, (2) an unsupervised learning approach that relies on an algorithm without label data, (3) a feature-based supervised learning approach focused on a supervised learning algorithm with feature engineering, and (4) deep learning approaches that automatically detect the result from raw inputs [1].

Recently, along with the development of a deep learning (DL) model, a neural network model has been successfully used for NER tasks. In general, the DL-based NER has used various input representations (e.g., word embedding, character-level, word-level) to learn how to encode a word and its context in input sequence and predict a word's entity label. Most researchers have commonly employed bidirectional Long Short-Term Memory (LSTM) Conditional Random Field (CRF) as a basic DL architecture to encode contextual information and find the best label sequence:

- Lample et al. [2], used hierarchical bidirectional LSTM CRF set up with pre-trained word embedding and character-level LSTM-based word encoding.
- Ma and Hovy [3], also employed the bidirectional LSTM CRF but combined the character-level CNN-based word encoding with pre-trained word embedding to get the final result.
- Rei et al. [4] also used the bidirectional LSTM CRF but applied attention-based weighted sum, instead of concatenation, when combining character-level LSTM-based word encoding with the pre-trained word embedding.
- Chiu and Nichols [5] used the bidirectional LSTM and addition with Log-Sotfmax to get the output and employed word-level pattern-based word encoding and gazetteer-based word encoding in addition to the pre-trained word embedding and character-level Convolutional Neural Network (CNN)-based word encoding.

These works employed various input representations and combined all the representations at the embedding layer of their models (we call it early combination) and passed it through the main model block, bidirectional LSTM.

In contrast, Huang et al. [6] delayed the combining position of some features' encoding until the output of the bidirectional LSTM is ready. They passed only the pre-trained word embedding through the bidirectional LSTM and this output was combined with additional word encodings based on word spelling, contexts of word, Part-Of-Speech (POS) and chunk, and gazetteer. This delayed combination technique was used to avoid a potential feature collision, which may occur during passing the bidirectional LSTM block. However, they did not provide any comparison between delayed combination and early combination.

In this paper, we adapt the delayed combination approach and analyze its effectiveness by comparing it to the existing, commonly used, early combination approach, inspired by Huang et al., 2016. We adapt character-level CNN or LSTM-based word encoding and recent contextualized word embedding and designed CNN-based sentence encoding using a named entity dictionary as supplementary feature encodings, in addition to the common pre-trained word embedding. We pass the pre-trained word embedding and the contextualized word embedding through the separate bidirectional LSTM blocks, respectively, and then we combine the outputs with the CNN or LSTM-based word encoding and the CNN-based sentence encoding. This combined encoding is finally fed into the CRF to find the best named entity label sequence.

We compare the delayed combination model with the early combination model by evaluating our own implementation of the two approaches and also compare our result to the previous works having similar model architecture and features to show the effectiveness of the delayed combination model. The main differences between the two models are as follows:

1. The early combination model concatenates representations at the embedding layer and then passes them through the bidirectional LSTM CRF. During passing through the bidirectional LSTM blocks, some useful but less-dominant encoded information may be mixed and collide with others and, as a result, fail to be propagated to the output layer.
2. The delayed combination model is designed to preserve some feature representations until the last layer by bypassing the bidirectional LSTM blocks, considering the characteristics of each feature (more details are given in Section 3). The comparison result shows that the delayed combination is able to boost the performance of the model.

The rest of the paper is organized as follows. Related works are described in Section 2. We present the proposed model architecture in Section 3. The experimental setup is shown in Section 4. The results are presented and discussed in Section 5. Finally, we conclude in Section 6.

2. Related Work

Recently, deep learning has become a dominant model to achieve the state-of-the-art results in NER task. The crucial advantage is its ability to undertake representation learning. Most deep learning-based NER approaches have designed and utilized various features to encode input sequence, such as (1) pre-trained word embedding, (2) contextual word embedding, (3) character-level CNN or LSTM-based word encoding, (4) word-level pattern-based encoding, and (5) dictionary-based word encoding. These representations were combined and passed through the bidirectional LSTM CRF network to learn further contextual information. In this section, we explore various representations used for encoding the input sequence and how to combine and feed them into the network.

2.1. Distributed Representations for Input

The concept of distributed representations refers to the representation of a word or a sentence by mapping it to a numerical vector. The vector is used to capture the semantic and grammatical properties of words. We review the following four types of distributed representations that have been popularly used in the previous works.

2.1.1. Pre-Trained Word Embedding

Pre-trained word embedding is the main element for most NLP tasks, including NER. Typically, embedding is trained over a large corpus, such as Wikipedia, Common Crawl, or the Reuters RCV-1 corpus. In this section, we describe different algorithms for computing word representations.

1. Word2vec: Word2vec can be implemented in two methods: a continuous bag of words (CBOW) and a Skip-gram method [7–12]. Both are log-linear models that are very useful for discovering the degree of word similarity [13]. In particular, CBOW provides slightly better accuracy for frequent words, whereas Skip-gram represents rare words well.
2. GloVe: GloVe was developed at Stanford [14]. This process begins by going through the text in a corpus, after which it counts the occurrences of word couples that are close to each other in a given window size. The information is stored in a matrix called an occurrence matrix. This matrix is used to build word embedding by minimizing the cosine distance between words to ensure a high co-occurrence probability [15].
3. FastText: FastText [16] was made available by Facebook. This model suggests an NLP improvement over the Skip-gram model, which learns by n-gram embedding. The rationale behind this approach relies on the morphology and information encoding in a subword. This information can be used to generate an unseen and rare word [17].

2.1.2. Contextual Embedding

One limitation of the pre-trained word embeddings is that a word is represented by a unique single embedding regardless of its context. However, it is very common that a word could have a different meaning in a different context. For example, each 'bank' has a different meaning in 'bank account' and 'river bank'. To avoid fixed embedding for each word, several studies have proposed contextual word representation techniques such as ELMO and BERT. ELMO [18] is a character-based model, while BERT takes input as subwords and learns embeddings from the subwords. BERT has inspired many recent NLP research and language models, for instance XLNet [19], RoBERTa [20], and DistilBERT [21].

2.1.3. Word-Level and Character-Level Representations

The pre-trained word embeddings and contextual embeddings learn the representations from the context of a word in a sentence, but does not consider and learn the character composition of a word, which are very important especially in the NER task because we often can infer the named entity (NE) type of a word from its character composition. To make up for this weak point, two different word representation techniques have been developed: one is word-level pattern-based word encoding and the other is character-level CNN or LSTM-based word encoding.

The former (word-level representation) classifies each word based on the following sub-criteria and learns the encoding during training the deep learning network:

1. A case can be initialized in upper-case, all upper-case, all lower-case, and in a mixed case.
2. Punctuation
3. Digits including all digits, words with digits, cardinal and ordinal numbers
4. Characters, for instance, Greek letters
5. Morphology, e.g., prefixes and suffixes
6. Parts of speech – proper names, verbs, nouns
7. A function such as an n-gram, word, or feature pattern

This technique makes it possible to learn word representation based on patterns of a word and encode words with different literals but same patterns with the same representation [2,3,5,6,22–24]. For example, Collobert et al. [22] used the capitalization information of a word, which was removed before training the word embedding. The method uses a lookup table to add a capitalization feature with the following options: AllCaps, UpperInitial, Lowercase, MixedCaps, Noinfo [5,22]. Huang et al., 2015 also used the spelling information as a word-level feature, which includes: start with a capital letter, all capital letter, all lower-case, mixed case, punctuation, prefixes and suffixes, has apostrophe end ('s), has initial capital letters, letter, non-letter and word pattern.

The latter (character-level representation) is obtained by passing each character encodings within a word through Recurrent Neural Network (RNN) or CNN blocks. CNN-based one is good at extracting dominant character information in a word [3] while (RNN) (Gated Recurrent Unit (GRU) or LSTM)-based one is good at capturing prefixes and suffixes in a word [2,24,25]. These character-level representations also have an advantage in handling the Out-Of-the-Vocabulary (OOV) problem because it is possible to learn almost all character embedding from even small or moderate corpus. In other words, these representations are good at inferring unseen words and sharing information about morpheme-level regularities. To improve the model performance, the pre-trained word embedding have been actively combined with character-level CNN-based word encoding [3] or character-level LSTM-based word encoding [2,24,25].

2.1.4. Dictionary Representation

The dictionary-based method is used to extract a set of features of a token by matching it with entries in a dictionary. Two kinds of matching methods are commonly used. One is a full matching, and the other is a partial matching [26,27].

1. Full matching: a dataset uses an n-gram to match an entire dictionary entry. If there are multiple matches found in the dictionary, the longest one is preferred [28]. Using this match, the correct word type is assigned as long as the n-gram overlaps the ground truth [1]. However, a longer match requires more bits to classify a word type and the coverage is very low in general [29].
2. Partial matching: a dataset utilizes an n-gram to match part of a dictionary entry. The coverage could be improved further through the application of an existing lexicon. On the other hand, some research forgoes this partial matching dictionary because it can produce many false matches [5,28].

Both methods have their own disadvantage and it is not trivial to collect dictionary entries having high coverage. To deal with this limitation, we design CNN-based sentence encoding using a dictionary, which could achieve high coverage by reducing the negative effect by false matches. (More details will be explained in Section 3.1).

2.2. Model Architecture for NER Task

The most common model architecture used for NER task in previous works is the bidirectional LSTM CRF [2–4,6,23,30–35]. Except for the works of Huang et al., 2015 and Jie and Lu, 2019, all these previous works combined various feature encodings like pre-trained word embedding, contextual word embedding, word or character-level representations and dictionary-based representation at the embedding layer to feed them into the bidirectional LSTM CRF network. These early combination models combined many feature encodings by just concatenating into one long embedding vector except Rei et al., 2016 suggested a weighted sum based on attention mechanism instead of concatenation.

In contrast, Huang et al., 2015, and Jie and Lu, 2019, bypassed some feature encodings and combined them with the output of the bidirectional LSTM blocks. We call these models delayed combination in contrast with the early combination models. Huang et al., 2015, passed the pre-trained word embedding through the bidirectional LSTM blocks and then concatenated the output with additional word encodings based on word spelling, n-gram context of word, POS and chunk, and gazetteer. Jie and Lu, 2019 first combined pre-trained word embedding with dependency encoding at the embedding layer and then passed it through dependency-guided bidirectional LSTM blocks. They secondly combined the output of the blocks with ELMO embedding just before the CRF layer.

When the features are combined, the feature collision may occur (Mikolov et al. [36]) and this could cause that some important information may disappear after combination. This may limit the performance improvement to be obtained from various feature encodings. Huang et al., 2015 also suggested that this delayed combination could accelerate the training process with similar performance.

However, Huang et al., 2015 and Jie and Lu, 2019 did not provide and analyze any comparison between their delayed combination approach and the common early combination approach to show how effective the delayed combination is.

In this paper, we compare the delayed combination model with the early combination model by evaluating our own implementation of the two approaches and also compare our result to the previous works having similar model architecture and features to show the effectiveness of the delayed model.

3. Delayed Combination of Encoded Features

Our objective is to build a new architecture based on a deep learning technique which uses the delayed combination model to improve the accuracy for two benchmark datasets, i.e., CoNLL 2003 and OntoNotes 5.0.

The main idea of our work is the bidirectional language model (BLM), to which is given as an input, a sequence of tokens $(t_1, t_2, ..., t_n)$ that is passed through forward and backward a language model (LM) [37]. The forward pass of the LM computes the sequence probability according to Equation (1). The backward pass is similar to the forward pass, expect it runs over the reverse sequence to predict the previous token according to the Equation (2).

$$P(t_1, t_2, ..., t_N) = \prod_{k=1}^{N} P(t_k | t_1, t_2, ..., t_{k-1}) \quad (1)$$

$$P(t_1, t_2, ..., t_N) = \prod_{k=1}^{N} P(t_k | t_{k+1}, t_{k+2}, ..., t_N). \quad (2)$$

The forward and backward sequence has two separate, hidden states to capture both past and future information. Each result of forward and backward is concatenated to obtain the result vector before being passed to the CRF layer. For the CRF computation, we denote X as the matrix of the score output from the bidirectional LSTM to predict the tag sequence $Y = y_1, y_2, ..., y_n$ with the probability of the ground truth for a tag of each word shown determined by Equation (3) [31]:

$$P(y|X, \lambda) = \frac{1}{Z(X)} exp \sum_{i=1}^{N} \sum_{j} \lambda_j f_i(X, i, y_{i-1}, y_i). \quad (3)$$

Here, λ is the feature function weight, which is learned by the corresponding algorithm, and $Z(X)$ is the normalization factor according to $Z(X) = \sum_{y \in Y} \sum_{i=1}^{N} \sum_j \lambda_j f_i(X, i, y_{i-1}, y_i)$.

The bidirectional LSTM CRF technique was used for our experiment on the NER task. We first select the most promising features for the NER task from the previous works and also design a novel CNN-based sentence encoding using a dictionary. Then we suggest the delayed combination of the promising features by considering the characteristics of each feature.

3.1. Feature Encodings

1. Pre-trained word embedding: We compared GloVe 840B embedding, trained from Common Crawl using GloVe3 [14], with FastText [16] cc.en.300 embedding, trained on Wikipedia and Common Crawl. Chiu et al. [5] described GloVe improves significantly over available embedding in CoNLL 2003 than Word2vec.

However, GloVe poses to be a limitation with languages having unseen words which may occur a lot in different corpora. On the other hand, FastText was build on the limitation of GloVe and can handle OOV by extending subword information. This information allows the model to create vectors for unseen words. So, we evaluated the performance of GloVe and FastText and then selected FastText as word embedding which significantly increases the performance of our model (More detail in Appendix A).

2. Embeddings from Language Model (ELMO): ELMO, developed by Allen NLP, is one of the pre-trained contextual embedding models, which is available on the TensorFlow Hub (https://tfhub.dev/google/elmo/3). We tokenized each sentence into words for inputting to the embedding layer of ELMO. The ELMO embedding is obtained by weighted sum and scaling of output encodings of the three layers of ELMO [18].

There are other contextual embedding models developed recently, but we selected ELMO by considering the limitation of available hardware and the performance. We also tested BERT-Base but it was not better than ELMO in our preliminary experiments.

The contextual word embedding like ELMO is better than other pre-trained word embeddings in the NER task but the pre-trained embeddings are not still replaceable because they could give further improvement when combined with contextual embeddings. So, we used both of them in our NER model with delayed combination.

3. Character-level CNN or LSTM-based word encoding: Several studies incorporate character representations with pre-trained word embedding for handling the OOV problem [38]. Therefore, we also select these representations due to the same reason as well as the importance of character information in NER task. There are two standard architectures for learning word encoding based on character embedding: CNN and LSTMs.

Ma and Hovy [3] fed the character embeddings into the CNN with 30 filters of size three followed by global max pooling to get the encoding of the corresponding word. Lample et al. [2] passed the character embeddings through forward and backward LSTMs and concatenated each outputs to get the encoding of the corresponding word, as shown in Figure 1.

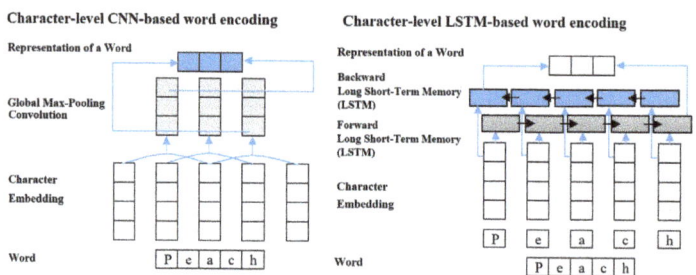

Figure 1. Character-level CNN or LSTM-based word encoding.

We adapted hyper-parameter values such as the number of filters, filter size, max word length and word encoding dimension from the previous works and the detailed values are given in Section 4.2.

4. CNN-based Dictionary Representation: We first build up two versions of the NE dictionary for partial matching: one distinguishes the begin and inside words in a named entity and the other does not distinguish them. The process of dictionary creation consists of four sequential steps, as follows: (1) we gather named entities of eleven types—Person, Location, Norp, Facility, Organization, Product, Event, Work of art, Law, Language and a geopolitical entity (GPE)—from Wikipedia, Kaggle, and Geonames. Then, (2) we additionally generate all upper-cased names and initial upper cased names from the collected names. As a result, we could reduce mismatches when we apply a cased match. Subsequently, (3) we duplicate the dictionary and tokenize these entries, as follows.

- Dictionary without a Begin-Inside Tag: We tokenize each word in the vocabularies and classify each word into an entity type based on the datasets (CoNLL 2003, OntoNotes 5.0).
- Dictionary with a Begin-Inside Tag: we tokenize each names in the list and classify each word based on the word position as well as the entity types. The first word in an entity has 'Begin-tag' along with the entity type and the other words in the entity have 'Inside-tag' along with the entity type.

Now, we obtain two kinds of dictionaries with tokenized words. Finally, (4) we merge entity types along with Begin-Inside tags for each word and construct a matrix of word to possible entity types using binary notation. That is, we set to 1 when a word occurred at least once as that type in the list of names and set to 0 otherwise, as shown in Figure 2.

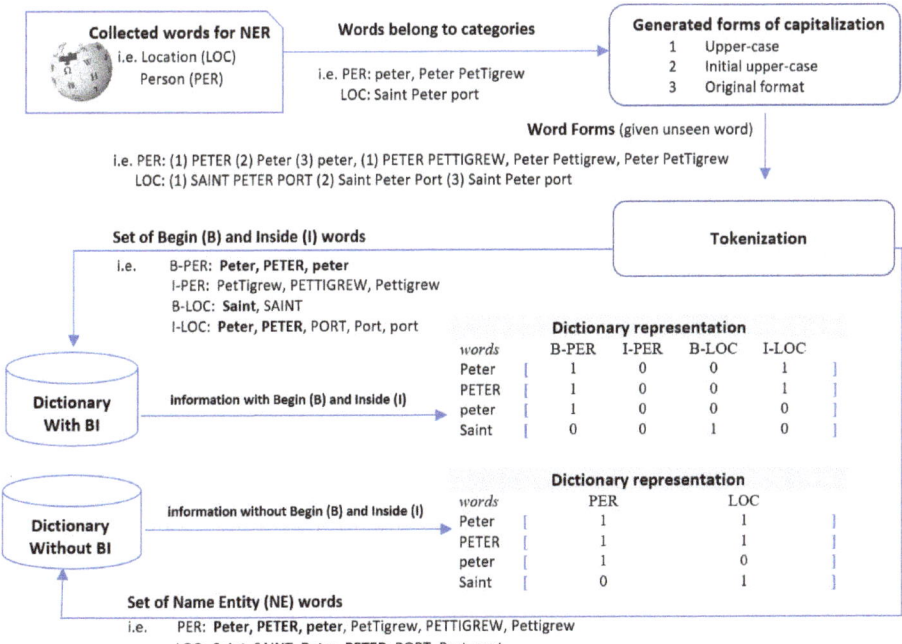

Figure 2. The process of dictionary building: (1) gather named entities from various sources, (2) generate capitalization variants of each names, (3) tokenize and classify with types and word positions, and (4) construct a dictionary using binary notation. The numbers 0 and 1 denote the status of found (1) and not found (0) in each category.

This dictionary is used for encoding each sentence by the CNN with 30 filters of size three and followed by global max pooing. Our dictionary employs partial match strategy, which may cause many false matches and give negative effect on the performance. To soften this problem, we applied CNN-based sentence encoding, as shown in Figure 3, and combined this with the output of the bidirectional LSTM blocks, instead of early combining with other feature encodings at the embedding layer.

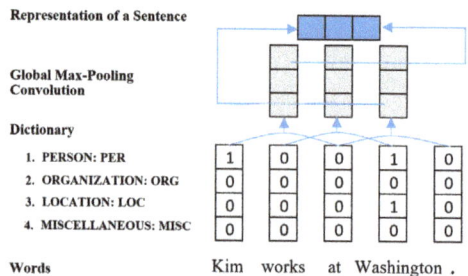

Figure 3. CNN-based sentence encoding using dictionary

This representation also has the advantage in dealing with ungrammatical or non-contextual short sentences, which often occur in the dataset due to incorrect sentence segmentation but could not be correctly predicted using only context.

3.2. Delayed Combination

We selected or designed four kinds of feature encodings, which are promising for NER task: pre-trained word embedding, contextual embedding, character-level CNN/LSTM-based word encoding and CNN-based sentence encoding using a dictionary. These feature encodings are combined at suitable positions of the bidirectional LSTM CRF network according to the characteristics of each feature encoding.

The pre-trained word embedding and contextual embedding were learned from the context of each word. That is, their major role is to maintain and propagate the contextual information of each word to the latter layers. So we decided to pass both of them through each separate bidirectional LSTM blocks to further learn or fine-tune the contextual information from the training data as shown in Figure 4.

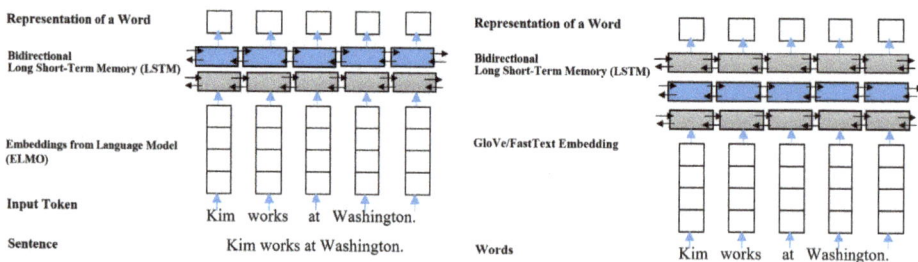

Figure 4. The pre-trained word embedding and contextual embedding passed through its own bidirectional LSTM blocks.

On the contrary, character-level CNN/LSTM-based word encoding is better to bypass the bidirectional LSTM blocks because this word encoding learns only the character compositions within a word, not contextual information of a word. Passing this encoding through the bidirectional LSTM blocks may cause loss of character composition information in that encoding. Early combination of this encoding with other pre-trained feature encodings at the embedding layer may disturb correct learning of that encoding because in general dominant features (i.e., pre-trained ones) are first propagated to the latter layers.

Our dictionary representation is also not passed through the bidirectional LSTM blocks. The representation is obtained by employing a partial match strategy and passing through word CNN. This partial match may cause many false matches and give a negative effect on the performance. To soften this problem, we employed CNN-based sentence encoding. As a result, we combine (i.e., concatenate) the above feature encodings at the fully-connected layer directly after the bidirectional LSTM blocks. The combined encoding further passes fully-connected layer and CRF layer to find the best chainable label sequences. A graphical illustration of our delayed combination model is given in Figure 5.

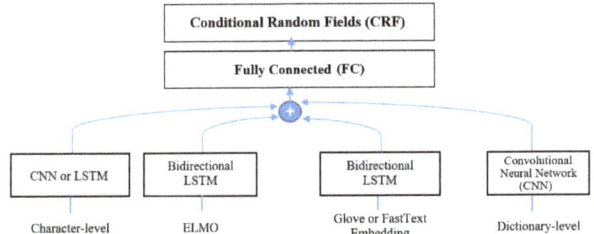

Figure 5. The delayed combination of feature encodings.

The early combination may cause some useful information to mix or collide with other encodings and, as a result, disappear before the output layer. The graphical difference between the early combination and the delayed combination is depicted in Figure 6.

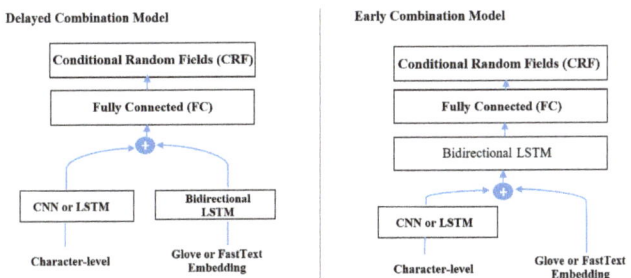

Figure 6. The comparison between delayed and early combinations

Both the delayed combination and early combination models are used for comparison in experiments, as explained in the next section.

4. Experimental Setup

4.1. Datasets

The experiment begins by exploring the NER datasets. The CoNLL 2003 dataset (English language) [39], was taken from Reuters news corpus between August 1996 and 1997. This dataset consists of four types of named entities (i.e., person, location, organization, and miscellaneous). The number of occurrences of each type of named entity is shown in Table 1. The dataset consisted of three parts: a training set, a development set, and a test set. To be specific, the training and development datasets were collected from the news at the end of August of 1996, while the test dataset was obtained from the news in December of 1996.

OntoNotes 5.0 is made up of 300 K Arabic, 900 K Chinese, and 1745 K English text data instances and covers six types of documents such as newswire, websites, broadcasting news, broadcasting conversation, magazine and telephone conversation [40]. It consists of eleven types of named entity and seven types of values and we use the English data and follow the train–validate–test split by [40]. We excluded the telephone conversation section when evaluating our model because it has quite noisy annotations. The detailed statistics of this dataset are given in Table 2.

Table 1. Statistics of named entities in CoNLL 2003 found in the training, development, and test sets. The highest proportion in CoNLL 2003 is location, followed by person, organization, and miscellaneous in that order.

Named Entity	Train Set	Valid Set	Test Set
Location	8297	2094	1925
Organization	10,025	2092	2496
Person	11,128	3149	2773
Malicious	4593	1268	918

Table 2. Statistics of named entities in OntoNotes 5.0 found in the training, development, and test sets. In OntoNotes 5.0, the highest proportion is organization, followed by person and Geopolitical Entity (GPE).

Named Entity	Train Set	Valid Set	Test Set
Person	37,393	5354	3646
Norp	9956	13.45	1152
Facility	3089	363	392
Organization	56,954	8964	4705
Product	1812	471	160
Event	3096	504	250
Work of art	4513	639	516
Law	1657	239	162
Language	372	36	22
Location	4143	596	417
GPE	27,354	4555	3263
Money	15,130	2287	1103
Percentage	8989	1504	992
Ordinal	2151	333	204
Cardinal	13,813	2141	1318
Quantity	3123	522	415
Date	40,077	6527	3793
Time	3505	731	451

We selected these two datasets for benchmarking our model because they have been most actively used for evaluating and comparing NER models until now even though they are a little old. Especially, CoNLL 2003 is a little small and so takes less time to train a model. So, it is suitable for testing and tuning model feasibility at the early stage.

On the contrary, OntoNotes 5.0 is quite large (about five times the size of CoNLL 2003 in the number of sentences in the training set) and has manymore types of named entities. So, it is suitable for testing model extensibility at the latter stage.

4.2. Hyperparameter Setup

As preliminary experiments, we explored the optimal values of several major hyper-parameters such as dropout, optimizer with learning rate, and the number of bidirectional LSTM layers and also tested several versions of the popular pre-trained word embeddings including GloVe and FastText (More detailed information is given in the Appendix A). The other hyper-parameter values were borrowed from the earlier works [2–5,33]. Table 3 shows the hyper-parameter values used in our experiments. The hyper-parameter values are nearly identical between CoNLL 2003 and OntoNotes 5.0, except for the maximum word length and character embedding dimension, which were borrowed from the earlier studies [2,5], respectively.

Table 3. The hyper-parameter values used in our experiments.

Layer	Hyper-Parameter	CoNLL 2003	OntoNotes 5.0
Character-level CNN	Filter size	3	3
	Number of filters	30	30
	Max word length	25	30
	Character embedding dimension	100	30
Character-level LSTM	Max word length	60	97
	Character embedding dimension	100	30
	Hidden units	128	128
CNN with dictionary	Filter size	3	3
	Number of filters	30	30
	Max sentence length	100	100
	Character embedding dimension (With BI tags)	8	22
	Character embedding dimension (Without BI tags)	4	11
BiLSTM with ELMo	ELMO embedding (Dim)	1024	-
	Number of bidirectional LSTM layers	2	2
	Hidden units	128	-
BiLSTM with FastText	Word embedding (Dim)	300	300
	Number of bidirectional LSTM layers	3	3
	Hidden units	128	128
	Dropout	0.5	0.5
	Optimizer	Nadam	Nadam
	Learning rate	0.002	0.001
	Mini-batch size	200	200
	Epochs	200	120

4.3. Model Setup

When training our models, we used two different numbers of iterations without early stopping: (1) 200 epochs for all model variants except the model with ELMo and (2) 120 epochs for the model with ELMo. This is because the performance of the model with ELMo was rarely improved but the model took quite a long time in training at each epoch when further increasing the number of epochs.

We evaluated our model after every epoch with the F1 score on the validation set and selected the best validation F1 scored model within the number of epochs, which was used for evaluating the test set. Due to the randomness, we did the same experiments five times and averaged them. The following equation calculates the F1 score:

$$F1\ score = \frac{2 \times Precision \times Recall}{(Precision + Recall)} \quad (4)$$

Here, precision refers to the ratio of correct named entities found in the NER system, and recall is the ratio of named entities that are retrieved by the NER system. Our goal is to show the effectiveness of the delayed combination and the CNN-based sentence encoding using the dictionary. To achieve this goal, we organized three groups of experiments as follows:

1. The experiments for comparison between the delayed and the early combinations of FastText (FT) and character-level CNN or LSTM word encoding (we refer to these as Delayed-BiLSTM-CRF (FT + CNN or LSTM) and Early-BiLSTM-CRF (FT+ CNN or LSTM), respectively). The results are given in Section 5.1.
2. The experiments with the model equipped with our dictionary representation (we refer to this model as Delayed-BiLSTM-CRF (FT + CNN or LSTM + Dic)). The results are given in Section 5.2.

3. The experiments with the model additionally equipped with ELMo encoding (we refer to this model as Delayed-BiLSTM-CRF (FT + CNN or LSTM + Dic + ELMo)). The results are given in Section 5.3.

5. Results and Discussion

5.1. Comparison between the Delayed and Early Combination Models

In this experiment, we first compared the delayed combination to the early combination by evaluating our own implementations of both combinations on CoNLL 2003 and OntoNotes 5.0. We used FastText for the pre-trained word embedding and character-level CNN-based word encoding. In the early combination, both were concatenated at the embedding layer, and then fed into the bidirectional LSTM blocks. On the contrary, in the delayed combination, only the FastText encoding was passed through the bidirectional LSTM blocks and then the output was concatenated with the character-level CNN-based word encoding. The results are shown in Table 4.

Table 4. Comparison between the delayed and early combination models.

Model	F1 Score in CoNLL 2003		F1 Score in OntoNotes 5.0	
Early-BiLSTM-CRF (FT + CNN)	88.60		84.47	
Delayed-BiLSTM-CRF (FT + CNN)	90.56	(+1.96)	87.87	(+3.40)

We can see that the delayed combination (Delayed-BiLSTM-CRF (FT + CNN)) gives consistently and significantly higher scores than the early combination (Early-BiLSTM-CRF (FT + CNN)) on both datasets. This could convince us that the delayed combination could effectively propagate the useful character composition information to the output layer by bypassing the bidirectional LSTM blocks. The bidirectional LSTM blocks are very good at learning contextual information but the character composition information may diminish or disappear when it passes through the bidirectional LSTM blocks. Furthermore, at the early stage of the training, the pre-trained word embedding has more dominant values than the character-level word encoding, which is randomly initialized. This means that the early combination of feature encodings having different characteristics could hinder the model from learning the less dominant feature encodings especially at the early stage of the training.

Reimer et al. [41] described the difference between character-level CNN-based and LSTM-based word encoding approaches. According to this work, the CNN approach takes only the trigram value into account but cannot distinguish the positions of trigrams, i.e., whether it is at the beginning, inside, or at the end of a word. In contrast, the LSTM approach takes all characters of a word into account and can distinguish between characters at the beginning and end of a word.

Referring to this work [41], we compared the two kinds of character-based word encoding approaches in our delayed combination model. The result is given in Figure 7. On the CoNLL 2003 dataset, the LSTM approach was distinctly better (about +0.23%) than the CNN approach. However, on the OntoNotes 5.0 dataset, the CNN approach was very slightly better (about +0.03%) than the LSTM approach. This means that we cannot say which one is definitely better than the other. This result coincides with the results from the previous works [30]. We also checked the computation time in the training of each approach. The LSTM approach took about 1.75 times longer training time than the CNN approach. This means that the CNN approach has advantage in the view of the training speed. From these results, we decided to fix the approach for character-level word encoding to LSTM on the CoNLL 2003 dataset and CNN on the OntoNotes 5.0 dataset, respectively.

To show the feasibility of our own model, we show in Table 5 the comparison between the results of our models and the results of the previous works having similar model architecture and combining features at the embedding layer. Our delayed model with LSTM-based word encoding, Delayed-BiLSTM-CRF (LSTM), could achieve a better F1 score than the results from Rei et al., 2016, Ghaddar and Langlais, 2018 and Le and Burtsev, 2019, but worse F1 score than the original results from Lample et al., 2016, Ma and Hovy, 2016 and Chiu and Nichols, 2016 on the CoNLL 2003 dataset. However, when comparing to the re-implementation results by DeLFT [42] of the latter three works, our results were not worse. On the OntoNotes 5.0 dataset, our model was also better than the results from Ghaddar and Langlais, 2018 and Chiu and Nichols, 2016. We did not tune the most hyper-parameter values and just borrowed from the previous works. We think our model is open to be further improved by thoroughly tuning the hyper-parameter values [41].

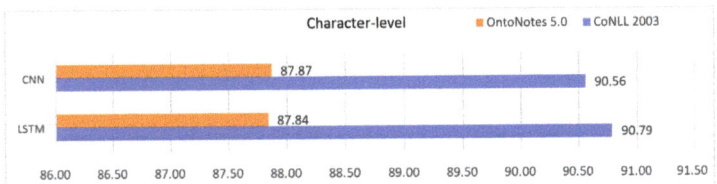

Figure 7. The comparison between the character-level CNN-based and LSTM-based word encodings in our delayed combination model. The result shows that the LSTM approach is better on the CoNLL2003 while the CNN approach is very slightly better on the OntoNotes5.0.

Table 5. Comparison between our work and previous early combination model with the pre-trained word embedding and the character-level word encoding.

Work		Model (Character-Level)	F1 CoNLL 2003	F1 DeLFT's	F1 OntoNotes 5.0
Lample et al.	[2]	BiLSTM-CRF(CNN)	90.94	90.75	-
Ma and Hovy	[3]	BiLSTM-CRF (LSTM)	91.21	90.73	-
Chiu and Nichols	[5]	BiLSTM (CNN)	90.91 !*	89.23	86.28 !*
Rei et al.	[4]	BiLSTM (LSTM)	84.09	-	-
Liu et al.	[30]	BiLSTM (LSTM)	91.71	-	-
Ghaddar and Langlais	[33]	BiLSTM (CNN)	90.52	-	86.57
Le and Burtsev	[34]	BiLSTM (CNN)	90.60	-	-
Ours		BiLSTM-CRF (LSTM)	90.79	-	87.84 *
		BiLSTM-CRF (CNN)	90.56	-	87.87 *

! Chiu and Nichols, 2016 incorporated incorporated the development set as a part of training data. Consequently, the result cannot be directly compared with our model. * indicates that the model used additional preprocessing on the dataset before training and testing.

5.2. The Model Equipped with Our Dictionary Representation

Before evaluating our model with dictionary representation, we first checked the coverage of the collected list of named entities on the two target datasets to assess whether collected names are enough or not for the datasets. The coverages by each named entity (NE) type of CoNLL 2003 and OntoNotes 5.0 are given in Tables 6 and 7, respectively.

Table 6. The coverage of the dictionary on the CoNLL2003 dataset.

CoNLL 2003	Begin-Tag	Inside-Tag
Person	84.19%	94.91%
Organization	86.64%	76.56%
Location	76.45%	89.78%
Miscellaneous	6.57%	2.40%

The percentage in the tables indicates that those ratios of named entity tokens of each type were found in the collected dictionary. On the CoNLL 2003, the dictionary covers well the first three types of names but only a small ratio of miscellaneous typed entities is covered. On the OntoNotes 5.0 dataset, only four types of names such as Person, Facility, Organization and GPE are well covered (i.e., over 50%).

Table 7. The coverage of the dictionary on the OntoNotes5.0 dataset.

OntoNotes 5.0	Begin-Tag	Inside-Tag
Person	61.59%	78.85%
Norp	15.35%	19.64%
Facility	69.87%	76.72%
Organization	76.32%	86.32%
Product	23.14%	48.39%
Event	42.77%	47.17%
Work of art	52.36%	71.92%
Law	28.00%	54.72%
Location	75.57%	48.59%
GPE	70.09%	77.20%
Language	46.65%	0.00 %

As explained in Section 3.1, we built up two kinds of dictionaries: one distinguishes begin and inside tokens in a named entity while the other does not. After combining this dictionary feature with our model at the delayed position, we evaluated our model to show the effectiveness of the dictionary feature.

Table 8 shows the comparison of our models with and without the CNN-based dictionary representation and also compares the two kinds of dictionaries with or without Begin-Inside (BI) tags. On the CoNLL 2003, both of the two dictionary representations (with and without BI tags) could improve significantly the F1 score by +0.34% and +0.45%, respectively. On the OntoNotes 5.0, the dictionary without BI tags could improve the F1 score by +0.20% although the dictionary representation with BI tags rather lowered the F1 score by −0.30%.

Table 8. The comparison of our models with and without dictionary representation.

Model	Dataset	Without Dic	Dictionary With BI Tags	Without BI Tags
Delayed-BiLSTM-CRF (FT + LSTM + DIC)	CoNLL 2003	90.79	91.13	91.24
Delayed-BiLSTM-CRF (FT + CNN + DIC)	OntoNote 5.0	87.87	87.57	88.07

From this result, we could say that the CNN-based dictionary representation could improve the F1 score. Further analysis lets us find that our dictionary effectively classified the type of a word especially when the context of the word is not sufficient. For example, the named entities in one-word sentences (e.g., 'England'), which are often found on CoNLL 2003 dataset, cannot be correctly predicted only using the Recurrent Neural Network (RNN)-typed network because they have no contextual information [43]. However, our CNN-based dictionary representation could predict them correctly.

Commonly on the two datasets, we can notice that the dictionary without BI tags shows a better F1 score. We think this result might be caused by the following two reasons: tag mismatches and many ambiguous words. First, the 'tag mismatches' are very often found in between the dictionary with BI tags and the CoNLL 2003 dataset, especially for Person. We may think that a given name of a person is generally classified with a begin tag, whereas a family name is typically assigned with an inside tag. However, in the dataset of real text, it is very common to refer to a person by only his/her family name without giving a given name. So, family names are assigned both begin and inside tags in the dataset. The most collected names were in the full form of names and the dictionary made from them often caused such tag mismatches and, as a result, degraded the performance.

Secondly, the 'ambiguous words' are very often found in the dictionary with BI tags for OntoNotes 5.0. For example, 'Hong' is a word found in various named entities, such as FACILITY: 'Hong Kong International Airport', GPE: 'Hong Kong', EVENT: 'Hong Kong Jewish Film Festival', WORK_OF_ART: 'Hong Kong Garden', PERSON: 'Hong Chang', 'Chin Hong Goh', LOCATION: 'Disney Hong Kong'. When building the dictionary with BI tags up, 'Hong' is classified with B-FACILITY, B-GPE, B-EVENT,

B-WORK_OF_ART, B-PERSON, I-PERSON, and I-LOCATION tags. This information is used to create a dictionary representation of the word 'Hong'. Like this, many ambiguous words are incorrectly encoded into dictionary representations, among which some adjacent dictionary representations may form unseen patterns that never occurred in the training set but that could be found in the test set. As a result, those representations may pose a problem in that they drastically reduce the performance. This result is similar to that in the earlier work [44].

We also compared our model to the previous similar dictionary-enabled works to show the feasibility of our model. The comparison is given in Table 9. On the CoNLL 2003, our model could achieve a better F1 score than that of Huang et al., 2015 and Wu et al., 2018 but was worse than that of Chiu and Nichols, 2016 and Ghaddar and Langlais, 2018. However, Chiu and Nichols, 2016 trained their model by merging the validation data with the training data and this could lead to improve the F1 score. Ghaddar and Langlais, 2018 used the lexical similarity (LS) embedding which was pre-trained from fined-grained named entity list and Wikipedia text. The LS embedding was well-organized than the existing dictionaries and could lead to improve the F1 score by +1.21%.

In contrast, the OntoNotes 5.0 dataset, our model could achieve better F1 score than those of Chiu and Nichols, 2016 and Ghaddar and Langlais, 2018 even though Chiu and Nichols, 2016 used both training and validation data for training their model and Ghaddar and Langlais, 2018 applied the LS embedding.

Table 9. The comparison of our model with the previous similar dictionary-enabled works.

Work	Pre-Trained Embedding	Character Level	Word Level	Hybrid	Model	F1 CoNLL 2003	F1 OntoNotes 5.0
Huang et al.	[6] SENNA	-	Spelling, n-gram	Gazetteers	-	90.10	-
Chiu and Nichols	[5] SENNA	CNN	CAP	Lexicons	Softmax	91.62 [!*]	86.36 [!*]
Wu et al.	[32] GloVe 6B-300D	CNN	POS	Gazetteers	Neural CRF	91.06	-
Wu et al.	[32] Glove 6B-300D	CNN	POS, SpaCy (CAP)	Gazetteers	Neural CRF	91.89	-
Ghaddar and Langlais	[33] SSKIP and LS representation	LSTM	CAP	Lexical Similarity Vector	BiLSTM CRF	91.73	87.95
Ours	FastText	LSTM	-	CNN dictionary	BiLSTM CRF	91.24	-
	FastText	CNN	-	CNN dictionary	BiLSTM CRF	-	88.07 *

! Chiu and Nichols, 2016 incorporated the development set as a part of training data. Consequently, the result cannot be directly compared with our model. * indicates that the model used additional preprocessing on the dataset before training and testing.

5.3. The Model Additionally Equipped with the ELMO Encoding

Our model is finally combined with the separate bidirectional LSTM network of the ELMo embedding at the delayed position (The OntoNotes5.0 dataset couldn't be used for training our model with ELMo encoding because high-end GPUs like V100 were not available within a limited duration.). On the CoNLL 2003 dataset, we checked the effect of the ELMo encoding on all variants of our model according to all possible combinations with the two kinds of character-level word encodings and the two kinds of dictionary representations.

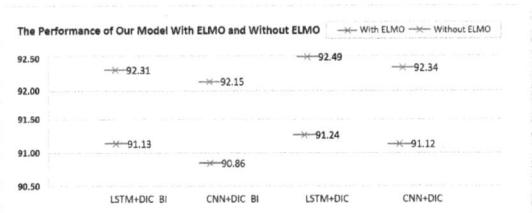

Figure 8. The performance of our model when combined with the ELMo network at the delayed position.

The result is shown in Figure 8. Our model could achieve the highest F1 score, 92.49%, when we combined our model with LSTM-based word encoding, dictionary representation without BI tags, and the bidirectional LSTM-based ELMo encoding. The bidirectional LSTM-based ELMo encoding could consistently improve the F1 score of all four variants of our model by the range of [+1.12%, +1.29%].

We also compared our model equipped with the ELMo encoding to the previous works having contextual embedding as features of their models. This is given in Table 10. Our model could achieve a better F1 score than all the previous works used ELMo as one of their features, such as Peter et al., 2018, Han et al., 2019, Xia et al., 2018, and Jie and Lu, 2018. This result could convince us that our delayed combination model is effective in NER task. Our model still shows a little higher F1 score than the model used BERT-Base (Devlin et al., 2019) but other previous works used BERT-Large or further tuned LM embedding still outperform our model. We think that our model can be further improved by combining with BERT-Large or fine-tuned LM embeddings instead of ELMo.

Table 10. The comparison of our model with the previous works having contextual embeddings (ELMO and BERT) as their features.

Work	Pre-Trained Embedding	Character Level	Word Level	Hybrid	Model	F1 CoNLL 2003	F1 OntoNotes 5.0
Peter et al.	[18] ELMO	-	-	-	BiLSTM CRF	92.22	-
Han et al	[45] ELMO (DELTA)	-	-	-	-	92.20	-
Xia et al.	[46] Word Emb, ELMO	-	POS	-	MGNER	92.28	-
Jie and Lu	[35] GloVe 6B-100D, ELMO	-	-	Dependency	DGLSTM CRF	92.40	88.52
Devlin et al.	[47] BERT-BASE	-	-	-	-	92.40	-
Devlin et al.	[47] BERT-LARGE	-	-	-	-	92.80	-
Luo et al.	[48] BERT	-	-	-	Hierarchical	93.37	90.30
Li et al.	[49] BERT	-	-	-	MRC+DSC	93.33	92.07
Baevski et al.	[50] Cloze-style LM embedding	CNN	-	-	CNN Large and fine-tune	93.50	-
Ours	FastText, ELMO	LSTM	-	CNN dictionary	BiLSTM CRF	92.49	-

6. Conclusions and Future Works

For the success of various deep-learning methods in NER task, most researchers have tested various feature-encoding techniques such as pre-trained word embedding, contextual embedding, character-level CNN or LSTM-based word encoding, word pattern-based encoding and dictionary-based encoding, and incorporated them into the deep learning networks. When more than one feature encoding is used, most previous works combined them at the embedding layer and then passed through the deep neural network to find the best label sequences in the output layer. However, when such an early combination of various feature encodings passes through the deep neural networks like RNN, much useful information could be mixed or shrunk by other more-dominant information and this could consequently limit the improvement in performance.

To avoid such limitations, we introduced the delayed combination model of various promising feature encodings. This model selected FastText as the pre-trained word embedding, ELMo as the contextual embedding and character-level CNN or LSTM word encoding, and designed CNN-based sentence encoding using a dictionary, for feature encoding. We also selected the most common bidirectional LSTM network for learning contextual information from the train set. Among those feature encodings, FastText and ELMo embeddings were passed through its own separate bidirectional LSTM blocks while the remaining feature encodings were bypassed and combined with the outputs of the bidirectional LSTM blocks.

Through several experiments, we showed that our delayed combination model outperforms the early combination one and also showed the feasibility of our model by comparing our results with the corresponding previous works.

As future work, we intend to extend this model by (1) building up a dictionary better-organized and learned from the external resources, (2) incorporating BERT-Large or other fine-tuned LM embeddings into our model, and applying to other non-English languages as well as other fine-grained NER task.

Author Contributions: Conceptualization, S.L. and C.R.; methodology, C.R.; software, C.R.; validation, S.L., H.J.J. and C.R. ; formal analysis, C.R.; investigation, H.J.J.; resources, H.J.J and C.R.; data curation, C.R.; writing—original draft preparation, C.R; writing—review and editing, S.L. and H.J.J; visualization, C.R.; supervision, S.L.; project administration, S.L.; funding acquisition, S.L. All authors have read and agreed to the published version of the manuscript.

Funding: This research was funded by Government-wide R&D Fund project for infectious disease research (GFID), Korea, under grant number HG18C0093.

Conflicts of Interest: The authors declare no conflict of interest.

Appendix A. The Hyperparameters Tuning

Reimer et al. [41] noted that there is a high impact of hyper-parameters (dropout, optimizer, word embedding, and a number of stacked layers) on the accuracy of the bidirectional LSTM CRF. We used the two-stacked bidirectional LSTM CRF model to find optimal hyper-parameters of dropout, optimizer, and word embedding. Hyper-parameter tuning is discussed in the four subsections below.

1. Dropout

   Dropout is a technique that can be used to reduce over-fitting and to improve the model's performance [51–53]. Brownlee [54] suggested that "normally, a small dropout value of 0.2–0.5 of neurons gives a good starting point." For our dropout experiment, dropouts were applied to three positions: (1) **inside** the bidirectional LSTM layer within a recurrence loop, (2) **after** the last output values of the bidirectional LSTM layer, and (3) **before** the outputs are passed through the CRF layer.

   The Figure A1 shows the experiment with different dropout sets. We repeat the experiment five times with different random seeds seeds and averaged them. The dropout value 0.5 of neurons provides our best result. The resulting rate is similar to that in the earlier work by Srivastava et al., 2014 [51], suggesting that the 0.5 dropout is be close to the optimal value for a wide range of neural networks and multiple tasks.

   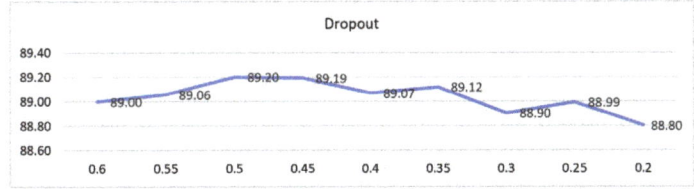

   Figure A1. F1 score on NER with difference dropouts. The dropout value of 0.5 achieves the best score in this task (CoNLL 2003).

2. Optimizer with learning Rate

   The optimizer determines the impact of the gradients on the parameter that we study the optimizers [55] (SGD, Adam, Nadam, RMSProp, and Adagrad) with variant learning rates that are derived from default values provided by Keras (https://keras.io/api/optimizers). In particular, we utilize the set of 0.009, 0.01, 0.02, 0.03, 0.04 for SGD and Adagrad and the set of 0.0009, 0.001, 0.002, 0.003, 0.004 for Adam, Nadam, RMSprop and Adamax. Table A1 shows the optimizers' performance with various learning rates on the CoNLL 2003 and OntoNotes 5.0 datasets. The dropout was fixed at 0.5.

For CoNLL 2003, the average performances of Nadam and Adagrad are first and second highest and achieve rates 89.321% and 89.316%, respectively. In another observation, Adamax(lr = 0.001) shows the best rate at 89.50%. However, it is only 0.01 different from Nadam(lr = 0.002). Earlier work [41] claims that Nadam converges most rapidly. It requires only a small training epoch to achieve better performance. Therefore, we used Nadam with a learning rate of 0.002 and a 0.5 dropout value for the next experiment on the CoNLL 2003 dataset.

Table A1. Five times F1 scores of the optimizer, in this case SGD, Adam, Nadam, RMSprop, Adagrad, and Adamax.

Dataset	Mini-Batch	Optimizer (α)	\multicolumn{5}{c}{Learning Rate Multiplied by Alpha (α)}	Average	SD *
			0.09	0.1	0.2	0.3	0.4		
Conll 2003	200	SGD (α =0.1)	89.40	89.18	89.34	89.12	89.12	89.232	0.13
		Adam (α =0.01)	89.17	89.23	89.45	89.17	88.94	89.190	0.18
		Nadam (α =0.01)	89.17	89.39	**89.49**	89.34	89.22	**89.321**	0.13
		RMSprop (α =0.01)	89.09	89.11	89.30	89.30	89.06	89.172	0.12
		Adagrad (α =0.1)	89.14	89.48	89.40	89.23	89.34	89.316	0.13
		Adamax (α =0.01)	89.24	**89.50**	89.27	89.34	89.21	89.313	0.12
OntoNotes 5.0	200	Nadam (α =0.01)	86.78	**87.08**	86.83	86.28	86.03	86.599	0.43

* Standard deviation (SD or Std Dev) is a measure of variation between values in a set of data.

An earlier experimental result [41] related to our CoNLL 2003 experiment recommends Nadam as an optimal hyper-parameter. For OntoNotes 5.0, we study the effect of Nadam with various learning rates. From the result in Table A1 the 0.001 learning rate provided our best F1 score. Accordingly, we chose Nadam(lr = 0.001) as an optimal hyper-parameter for the next experiment on the OntoNotes 5.0 dataset.

3. Pre-trained Word Embedding

We compared the GloVe 840B embedding and FastText–cc.en.300.vec and cc.en.300.bin. For FastText, the experiment used two options: (1) cc.en.300.vec (without subwords), (2) cc.en.300.bin (with subwords).

In this experiment, each pre-trained embedding was used to convert any word from the target dataset for representation and to pass it through the two-stacked bidirectional LSTM CRF model for predicting the named entity tags. Table A2 shows the experimental results of CoNLL 2003 and OntoNotes 5.0.

Table A2. Five times F1 scores of the pre-trained word embedding with two-stacked bidirectional LSTM. From the result, we achieve the best F1 score when using FastText with subwords.

Dataset	Mini-Batch	Embedding	\multicolumn{5}{c}{Five Times Validation}	Average	SD
			1	2	3	4	5		
Conll 2003	200	GloVe	89.96	89.90	89.94	90.26	90.24	90.06	0.18
		FastText Vec	89.44	89.70	89.79	89.44	89.93	89.66	0.22
		FastText Bin	90.05	90.30	90.20	89.97	90.17	**90.14**	0.13
OntoNotes 5.0	200	GloVe	87.12	87.44	87.42	87.42	87.61	87.40	0.18
		FastText Vec	87.49	87.49	87.44	87.52	87.40	87.47	0.05
		FastText Bin	87.68	87.43	87.74	87.58	87.58	**87.60**	0.12

The results from the CoNLL 2003 dataset show that the average F1 score of FastText (90.14%) with subwords higher than that of the GloVe (90.06%) experiment. For OntoNotes 5.0 experiment, the result is similar to that of CoNLL 2003. The F1 score (at 87.60%) is increased when using FastText with subwords.

Owing to the similar result on the two datasets, we assume that the model performance is improved when (1) the vocabulary in word embedding matches the word in the dataset, and (2) the subword (n-gram) of FastText is used to generate embeddings for rare words.

4. Number of bidirectional LSTM layers

    Currently, the stacked LSTMs are used as a standard technique for challenging sequence predictions [56]. Some previous works [57–59] present the multiple stacked bidirectional LSTMs in a neural network. They show that the classification performance can be improved when using this technique. Furthermore, there is some related theoretical support: a deep hierarchical model is more effective at representing than a shallow model [30,60]. Due to the stacked processes, when the first bidirectional LSTM layer provides an output vector, this output vector provides more complex patterns for the next layer, enabling us to capture information on a different scale.

    Cai et al. [57] suggests the appropriate amount of multi-layer bidirectional LSTM help to understand the relationship between words and words at a deep level. However, when the representation flows through stacked layers, the risk arises that the representation information will be lost [61], and it may also reduce the model performance. Hence, we examined two or three-stacked bidirectional LSTM to find the number of layers most suitable for our model. The comparative of F1 score results are shown in Figure A2 the model shows higher performance when using the three-stacked bidirectional LSTM. Consequently, we assume that three stacks are able to capture more information for our model.

    In contrast, two-stacked bidirectional LSTMs are applied in earlier experiments [2,23,35]. However, these experiments used different batch sizes, optimizers and lower dimensional word embedding compared to our model. Accordingly, we assume that the number of bidirectional layers depends on the hyper-parameters, especially the input size, batch size, optimization and hidden unit [62] of each model.

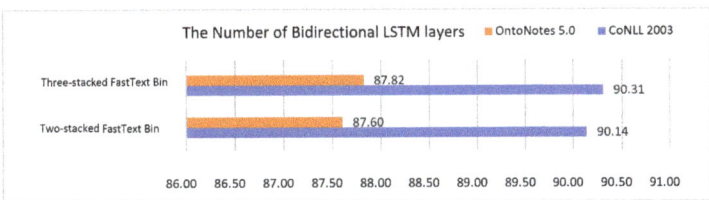

Figure A2. Comparison between two and three stacked bidirectional LSTM CRFs. The results show that three stacked bidirectional LSTM CRFs perform well on both CoNLL 2003 and OntoNotes 5.0.

References

1. Li, J.; Sun, A.; Han, J.; Li, C. A Survey on Deep Learning for Named Entity Recognition. *arXiv* **2018**, arXiv:1812.09449.
2. Lample, G.; Ballesteros, M.; Subramanian, S.; Kawakami, K.; Dyer, C. Neural architectures for named entity recognition. *arXiv* **2016**, arXiv:1603.01360.
3. Ma, X.; Hovy, E. End-to-end sequence labeling via bi-directional lstm-cnns-crf. *arXiv* **2016**, arXiv:1603.01354.
4. Rei, M.; Crichton, G.K.; Pyysalo, S. Attending to characters in neural sequence labeling models. *arXiv* **2016**, arXiv:1611.04361.
5. Chiu, J.P.; Nichols, E. Named entity recognition with bidirectional LSTM-CNNs. *Trans. Assoc. Comput. Linguist.* **2016**, *4*, 357–370. [CrossRef]
6. Huang, Z.; Xu, W.; Yu, K. Bidirectional LSTM-CRF models for sequence tagging. *arXiv* **2015**, arXiv:1508.01991.
7. Khattak, F.K.; Jeblee, S.; Pou-Prom, C.; Abdalla, M.; Meaney, C.; Rudzicz, F. A survey of word embeddings for clinical text. *J. Biomed. Inform. X* **2019**, *4*, 100057. [CrossRef]
8. Mikolov, T.; Chen, K.; Corrado, G.; Dean, J. Efficient estimation of word representations in vector space. *arXiv* **2013**, arXiv:1301.3781.
9. Le, Q.; Mikolov, T. Distributed representations of sentences and documents. *arXiv* **2014**, arXiv:1405.4053.
10. Levy, O.; Goldberg, Y. Linguistic regularities in sparse and explicit word representations. In Proceedings of the Eighteenth Conference on Computational Natural Language Learning, Baltimore, MD, USA, 26–27 June 2014; pp. 171–180.

11. Mikolov, T.; Sutskever, I.; Chen, K.; Corrado, G.S.; Dean, J. Distributed representations of words and phrases and their compositionality. *arXiv* **2013**, arXiv:1310.4546.
12. Mikolov, T.; Yih, W.t.; Zweig, G. Linguistic regularities in continuous space word representations. In Proceedings of the 2013 Conference of the North American Chapter of the Association for Computational Linguistics: Human Language Technologies, Atlanta, Georgia, 9–14 June 2013; pp. 746–751.
13. Sugawara, H.; Takamura, H.; Sasano, R.; Okumura, M. Context representation with word embeddings for wsd. In Proceedings of the Conference of the Pacific Association for Computational Linguistics, Bali, Indonesia, 19–21 May 2015; pp. 108–119.
14. Pennington, J.; Socher, R.; Manning, C.D. Glove: Global vectors for word representation. In Proceedings of the 2014 Conference on Empirical Methods in Natural Language Processing (EMNLP), Doha, Qatar, 25–29 October 2014, pp. 1532–1543.
15. Du, M.; Vidal, J.; Al-Ibadi, Z. Using Pre-trained Embeddings to Detect the Intent of an Email. In Proceedings of the ACIT 2019: Proceedings of the 7th ACIS International Conference on Applied Computing and Information Technology, Honolulu, HI, USA, 29–31 May 2020; doi:10.1145/3325291.3325357. [CrossRef]
16. Bojanowski, P.; Grave, E.; Joulin, A.; Mikolov, T. Enriching word vectors with subword information. *Trans. Assoc. Comput. Linguist.* **2017**, *5*, 135–146. [CrossRef]
17. Almeida, F.; Xexéo, G. Word embeddings: A survey. *arXiv* **2019**, arXiv:1901.09069.
18. Peters, M.E.; Neumann, M.; Iyyer, M.; Gardner, M.; Clark, C.; Lee, K.; Zettlemoyer, L. Deep contextualized word representations. *arXiv* **2018**, arXiv:1802.05365.
19. Yang, Z.; Dai, Z.; Yang, Y.; Carbonell, J.; Salakhutdinov, R.R.; Le, Q.V. Xlnet: Generalized autoregressive pretraining for language understanding. *arXiv* **2019**, arXiv:1906.08237.
20. Liu, Y.; Ott, M.; Goyal, N.; Du, J.; Joshi, M.; Chen, D.; Levy, O.; Lewis, M.; Zettlemoyer, L.; Stoyanov, V. Roberta: A robustly optimized bert pretraining approach. *arXiv* **2019**, arXiv:1907.11692.
21. Sanh, V.; Debut, L.; Chaumond, J.; Wolf, T. DistilBERT, a distilled version of BERT: Smaller, faster, cheaper and lighter. *arXiv* **2019**, arXiv:1910.01108.
22. Collobert, R.; Weston, J.; Bottou, L.; Karlen, M.; Kavukcuoglu, K.; Kuksa, P. Natural language processing (almost) from scratch. *J. Mach. Learn. Res.* **2011**, *12*, 2493–2537.
23. Zhai, Z.; Nguyen, D.Q.; Verspoor, K. Comparing CNN and LSTM character-level embeddings in BiLSTM-CRF models for chemical and disease named entity recognition. *arXiv* **2018**, arXiv:1808.08450.
24. Yang, Z.; Salakhutdinov, R.; Cohen, W. Multi-task cross-lingual sequence tagging from scratch. *arXiv* **2016**, arXiv:1603.06270.
25. Liu, L.; Shang, J.; Ren, X.; Xu, F.F.; Gui, H.; Peng, J.; Han, J. Empower sequence labeling with task-aware neural language model. In Proceedings of the Thirty-Second AAAI Conference on Artificial Intelligence, New Orleans, LA, USA, 2–7 February 2018.
26. Eftimov, T.; Koroušić Seljak, B.; Korošec, P. A rule-based named-entity recognition method for knowledge extraction of evidence-based dietary recommendations. *PLoS ONE* **2017**, *12*, e0179488. [CrossRef]
27. Jonnagaddala, J.; Jue, T.R.; Chang, N.W.; Dai, H.J. Improving the dictionary lookup approach for disease normalization using enhanced dictionary and query expansion. *Database* **2016**, *2016*, baw112. [CrossRef] [PubMed]
28. Song, C.H.; Lawrie, D.; Finin, T.; Mayfield, J. Gazetteer generation for neural named entity recognition. In Proceedings of the Thirty-Third International Flairs Conference, North Miami Beach, FL, USA, 17–20 May 2020.
29. Tsuruoka, Y.; Tsujii, J. Improving the performance of dictionary-based approaches in protein name recognition. *J. Biomed. Inform.* **2004**, *37*, 461–470. [CrossRef] [PubMed]
30. Liu, Z.; Yang, M.; Wang, X.; Chen, Q.; Tang, B.; Wang, Z.; Xu, H. Entity recognition from clinical texts via recurrent neural network. *BMC Med. Inform. Decis. Mak.* **2017**, *17*, 67. [CrossRef] [PubMed]
31. Gridach, M. Character-level neural network for biomedical named entity recognition. *J. Biomed. Inform.* **2017**, *70*, 85–91. [CrossRef] [PubMed]
32. Wu, M.; Liu, F.; Cohn, T. Evaluating the utility of hand-crafted features in sequence labelling. *arXiv* **2018**, arXiv:1808.09075.
33. Ghaddar, A.; Langlais, P. Robust lexical features for improved neural network named-entity recognition. *arXiv* **2018**, arXiv:1806.03489.
34. Le, T.; Burtsev, M. A deep neural network model for the task of Named Entity Recognition. *Int. J. Mach. Learn. Comput.* **2019**, *9*, 8–13.

35. Jie, Z.; Lu, W. Dependency-guided LSTM-CRF for named entity recognition. *arXiv* **2019**, arXiv:1909.10148.
36. Mikolov, T.; Deoras, A.; Povey, D.; Burget, L.; Černocký, J. Strategies for training large scale neural network language models. In Proceedings of the 2011 IEEE Workshop on Automatic Speech Recognition & Understanding, Waikoloa, HI, USA, 11–15 December 2011; pp. 196–201.
37. Ilić, S.; Marrese-Taylor, E.; Balazs, J.A.; Matsuo, Y. Deep contextualized word representations for detecting sarcasm and irony. *arXiv* **2018**, arXiv:1809.09795.
38. Dong, G.; Liu, H. *Feature Engineering for Machine Learning and Data Analytics*; CRC Press: New York, NY, USA, 2018.
39. Sang, E.F.; De Meulder, F. Introduction to the CoNLL-2003 shared task: Language-independent named entity recognition. *arXiv* **2003**, arXiv:cs/0306050.
40. Pradhan, S.; Moschitti, A.; Xue, N.; Ng, H.T.; Björkelund, A.; Uryupina, O.; Zhang, Y.; Zhong, Z. Towards Robust Linguistic Analysis using OntoNotes. In Proceedings of the Seventeenth Conference on Computational Natural Language Learning, Sofia, Bulgaria, 8–9 August 2013; Association for Computational Linguistics: Sofia, Bulgaria, 2013; pp. 143–152.
41. Reimers, N.; Gurevych, I. Optimal hyperparameters for deep lstm-networks for sequence labeling tasks. *arXiv* **2017**, arXiv:1707.06799.
42. DeLFT. 2018–2020. Available online: https://github.com/kermitt2/delft (accessed on 30 July 2020).
43. Frank, S.L. Strong systematicity in sentence processing by an echo state network. In Proceedings of the International Conference on Artificial Neural Networks; Berlin/Heidelberg, Germany, 10–14 September 2006; pp. 505–514.
44. Ponomareva, N.; Thelwall, M. Biographies or blenders: Which resource is best for cross-domain sentiment analysis? In Proceedings of the International Conference on Intelligent Text Processing and Computational Linguistics, New Delhi, India, 11–17 March 2012; pp. 488–499.
45. Han, K.; Chen, J.; Zhang, H.; Xu, H.; Peng, Y.; Wang, Y.; Ding, N.; Deng, H.; Gao, Y.; Guo, T.; et al. DELTA: A DEep learning based Language Technology plAtform. *arXiv* **2019**, arXiv:1908.01853.
46. Xia, C.; Zhang, C.; Yang, T.; Li, Y.; Du, N.; Wu, X.; Fan, W.; Ma, F.; Yu, P. Multi-grained named entity recognition. *arXiv* **2019**, arXiv:1906.08449.
47. Devlin, J.; Chang, M.W.; Lee, K.; Toutanova, K. Bert: Pre-training of deep bidirectional transformers for language understanding. *arXiv* **2018**, arXiv:1810.04805.
48. Luo, Y.; Xiao, F.; Zhao, H. Hierarchical Contextualized Representation for Named Entity Recognition. *arXiv* **2019**, arXiv:1911.02257.
49. Li, X.; Sun, X.; Meng, Y.; Liang, J.; Wu, F.; Li, J. Dice Loss for Data-imbalanced NLP Tasks. *arXiv* **2019**, arXiv:1911.02855.
50. Baevski, A.; Edunov, S.; Liu, Y.; Zettlemoyer, L.; Auli, M. Cloze-driven pretraining of self-attention networks. *arXiv* **2019**, arXiv:1903.07785.
51. Srivastava, N.; Hinton, G.; Krizhevsky, A.; Sutskever, I.; Salakhutdinov, R. Dropout: A simple way to prevent neural networks from overfitting. *J. Mach. Learn. Res.* **2014**, *15*, 1929–1958.
52. Gal, Y.; Ghahramani, Z. A theoretically grounded application of dropout in recurrent neural networks. *arXiv* **2016**, arXiv:1512.05287.
53. Brownlee, J. Machine Learning Mastery with Python: Understand Your Data, Create Accurate Models and Work Projects End-To-End. 2016. Available online: https://machinelearningmastery.com/machine-learning-with-python (accessed on 30 July 2020).
54. Brownlee, J. Deep Learning for Natural Language Processing: Develop Deep Learning Models for Your Natural Language in Python. 2017. Available online: https://machinelearningmastery.com/deep-learning-for-nlp (accessed on 30 July 2020).
55. Ruder, S. An overview of gradient descent optimization algorithms. *arXiv* **2016**, arXiv:1609.04747.
56. Brownlee, J. Long Short-Term Memory Networks with Python: Develop Sequence Prediction Models with Deep Learning. 2017. Available online: https://https://machinelearningmastery.com/lstms-with-python (accessed on 30 July 2020).
57. Cai, L.; Zhou, S.; Yan, X.; Yuan, R. A stacked BiLSTM neural network based on coattention mechanism for question answering. *Comput. Intell. Neurosci.* **2019**, *2019*, 9543490. [CrossRef] [PubMed]
58. Wang, C.; Yang, H.; Meinel, C. Image captioning with deep bidirectional LSTMs and multi-task learning. *ACM Trans. Multimed. Comput. Commun. Appl. (TOMM)* **2018**, *14*, 1–20. [CrossRef]

59. Liu, T.; Yu, S.; Xu, B.; Yin, H. Recurrent networks with attention and convolutional networks for sentence representation and classification. *Appl. Intell.* **2018**, *48*, 3797–3806. [CrossRef]
60. Bengio, Y. *Learning Deep Architectures for AI*; Now Publishers Inc.: Boston, MA, USA, 2009.
61. Godin, F.; Dambre, J.; De Neve, W. Improving language modeling using densely connected recurrent neural networks. *arXiv* **2017**, arXiv:1707.06130.
62. Ding, Z.; Xia, R.; Yu, J.; Li, X.; Yang, J. Densely connected bidirectional lstm with applications to sentence classification. *arXiv* **2017**, arXiv:1802.00889.

Publisher's Note: MDPI stays neutral with regard to jurisdictional claims in published maps and institutional affiliations.

© 2020 by the authors. Licensee MDPI, Basel, Switzerland. This article is an open access article distributed under the terms and conditions of the Creative Commons Attribution (CC BY) license (http://creativecommons.org/licenses/by/4.0/).

Article

A Novel Hybrid Model for Cantonese Rumor Detection on Twitter

Xinyu Chen [†], Liang Ke [†], Zhipeng Lu [†], Hanjian Su [†] and Haizhou Wang [*]

College of Cybersecurity, Sichuan University, Chengdu 610064, China; 2017141531040@stu.scu.edu.cn (X.C.); 2017141531066@stu.scu.edu.cn (L.K.); 2017141491001@stu.scu.edu.cn (Z.L.); 2017141531010@stu.scu.edu.cn (H.S.)
* Correspondence: whzh.nc@scu.edu.cn
† These authors contributed equally to this work.

Received: 31 July 2020; Accepted: 26 August 2020; Published: 12 October 2020

Abstract: The development of information technology and mobile Internet has spawned the prosperity of online social networks. As the world's largest microblogging platform, Twitter is popular among people all over the world. However, as the number of users on Twitter increases, rumors have become a serious problem. Therefore, rumor detection is necessary since it can prevent unverified information from causing public panic and disrupting social order. Cantonese is a widely used language in China. However, to the best of our knowledge, little research has been done on Cantonese rumor detection. In this paper, we propose a novel hybrid model XGA (namely XLNet-based Bidirectional Gated Recurrent Unit (BiGRU) network with Attention mechanism) for Cantonese rumor detection on Twitter. Specifically, we take advantage of both semantic and sentiment features for detection. First of all, XLNet is employed to produce text-based and sentiment-based embeddings at the character level. Then we perform joint learning of character and word embeddings to obtain the words' external contexts and internal structures. In addition, we leverage BiGRU and the attention mechanism to obtain important semantic features and use the Cantonese rumor dataset we constructed to train our proposed model. The experimental results show that the XGA model outperforms the other popular models in Cantonese rumor detection. The research in this paper provides methods and ideas for future work in Cantonese rumor detection on other social networking platforms.

Keywords: online social networks; rumor detection; Cantonese; XGA model

1. Introduction

With the rapid development of the Internet, social media have provided a convenient online platform for users to obtain information, express opinions, and communicate with each other. As one of the most popular social networks and microblogging platforms, Twitter has attracted more and more people to publish and share their opinions. As more and more people participate in discussions about hot topics and exchange their opinions on social networks, many rumors appear on Twitter. A rumor refers to a story or statement in general circulation without confirmation or certainty as to facts. Due to the large number of users and easy access to social networks, rumors can spread widely and quickly on Twitter, causing public panic and disrupting social order, even endangering national security [1]. Therefore, it is necessary to detect rumors and stop them from spreading widely on Twitter. There are some fact-checking websites, such as Snopes [2] and PolitiFact [3], that provide information and reports for rumor analysis and checking. However, these websites rely heavily on manual labor to track and debunk rumors, and the verified rumors are often limited to specific topics.

In this case, automatic rumor detection methods should be proposed for saving human effort and debunking rumors more efficiently.

There has been a lot of work related to rumor detection on Twitter concerning English and Chinese [4–7], but Cantonese rumors are seldomly studied. Cantonese is a branch of Chinese and it is mostly used in Guangdong Province and Hong Kong in China. Although Cantonese is widely used in speaking, it is in increasing use for informal communication like in forums or blogs. However, due to the complexity of Cantonese semantics and the lack of benchmark datasets, Cantonese rumor detection is a challenging task.

To address the problem of Cantonese rumor detection, we have proposed a novel hybrid model XGA and conducted experiments to evaluate its performance. The main contributions of this paper are summarized as follows:

- To cope with the complexity of Cantonese semantics and extract the deep features of Cantonese, we take both semantic and sentiment features into account for rumor detection. An XLNet model is used to produce text-based and sentiment-based embeddings. We perform joint learning of character and word embeddings to better fit in with the structre of Cantonese.
- A novel hybrid model XGA is proposed to improve the performance of Cantonese rumor detection, which takes advantage of XLNet, BiGRU and the attention mechanism. The Cantonese rumor dataset we constructed before is used to train our proposed model. The evaluation results show that XGA significantly outperforms other widely used rumor detection approaches in the Cantonese rumor detection.

The rest of this paper is organized as follows. Section 2 introduces related work on rumor detection. Section 3 elaborates the proposed model. Section 4 describes the experimental setup and gives out evaluation results. Section 5 concludes the research in this paper and discusses future work.

2. Related Work

Currently, most rumor detection methods are supervised. The literature related to rumor detection has been reviewed by several comprehensive surveys [8–10]. In our work, we briefly review some significant works based on deep learning methods.

Deep learning has been the most revolutionary development in artificial intelligence, which is widely used in the field of rumor detection. The two most popular deep learning models are Recurrent Neural Network (RNN) and Convolutional Neural Network (CNN).

For identifying rumors, Ma et al. [4] utilized RNN to learn continuous representations of microblog events, which captured the variation of contextual information of relevant posts over time. Then, in [11], the authors improved this approach by combining the attention mechanism with RNN to focus on textual features with different attentions. Recently, Ma et al. [12] employed the adversarial learning method to improve the performance of the rumor classifier, where the discriminator was used as a classifier and the corresponding generator improved the discriminator by generating conflicting noises. In addition, a multi-task learning approach was proposed by Kochkina et al. [13] to solve the problem of rumor classification. To be specific, they implemented a multi-task learning framework with an LSTM layer shared among all tasks, as well as a number of task-specific layers. In [14], Sumeet et al. designed a Tree LSTM model for rumor and stance detection that converted the propagation tree into a binarized constituency tree structure. The model applied convolution units in Tree LSTMs, which were better at learning patterns in features and employed the multi-task learning to propagate the useful stance signal up in the tree at the root node. But RNN was not qualified for the early detection of misinformation and had a bias towards the latest input elements.

So in [15], Yu et al. proposed a method based on CNN to learn key features scattered among an input sequence and shape high-level interactions among significant features. What's more, Qian et al. [16] introduced a Two-Level CNN with User Response Generator (TCNN-URG) where TCNN captured underlying semantic information at word and sentence levels, and URG generated user responses to new articles with the assistance of historical user responses. Furthermore, a mixture of RNNs and CNNs was exploited in recent works. Liu et al. [6] incorporated both RNN and CNN to get the user features based on time series. In addition, a model of Credible Early Detection (CED) was presented by Song et al. [17] to detect rumors on social media based on repost information. CNN was leveraged to obtain feature vectors of original microblogs and repost sequence. Then, the repost sequence was sent into RNN. What's more, in [18], the authors proposed a multi-modal network comprising CNN and Long Short-Term Memory (LSTM) with the attention mechanism. It jointly learned representations of textual contents and social contexts in rumors. However, these methods were inefficient to learn the features of the propagation structure, and they ignored the global structural features of rumor dispersion.

So, to focus on the differences between the characteristics in propagation of real and false information, Ma et al. [7] proposed models based on top-down and bottom-up tree-structured Recursive Neural Networks (RvNN), which deeply integrated the structural and textual features of tweets for detecting rumors at early stages from propagation trees or networks. Based on this, they designed discriminative attention mechanisms for the RvNN-based models to selectively attend on the subset of evidential posts during the bottom-up/top-down recursive composition [19]. Moreover, in [20], the authors built a model based on Bi-Directional Graph Convolutional Network (Bi-GCN) to explore characteristics by operating on both top-down and bottom-up propagation of rumors. But these methods only detected rumors based on the meaning of text and ignored the sentiment of it. In [21], authors designed a hybrid framework to analyze the data from social media based on sentiment analysis. Inspired by this, we proposed a hybrid model that took both semantic and sentiment features into account for Cantonese rumor detection.

3. The Proposed Model

In this work, we propose a novel deep neural network-based model XGA to detect Cantonese rumors on Twitter. The XGA takes advantage of semantic and sentiment features for detection. To be specific, XLNet is used to produce text-based and sentiment-based embeddings. In addition, BiGRU and the attention mechanism are involved to extract important semantic features. The structure of the XGA model is shown in Figure 1.

3.1. Input Layer

In this work, we use the Cantonese Rumor Dataset (CR-Dataset) [22] we constructed before. It contains 13,000 tweets, including 6377 rumors and 6623 non-rumors. As shown in *Input Layer* in Figure 1, the input of the model $I = \{I_1, I_2, ..., I_n\}$ is a pre-processed tweet. Since the maximum length of a tweet written in Cantonese is 140, the maximum sequence length is set to 140 to cover the input. Then we use tokens to represent each of the characters in the tweet and feed them into XLNet-Text and XLNet-Sentiment, respectively.

3.2. Embedding Layer

As shown in *Embedding Layer* in Figure 1, the model generates text-based and sentiment-based embeddings to extract the semantic and sentiment features of the tweet. In addition, we combine the character embeddings produced by XLNet with Cantonese word embeddings to learn the contextual information and internal structures of the words, so as to make the model more suitable for the Cantonese rumor detection.

XLNet is a generalized Autoregressive (AR) pre-training method that combines the advantages of AR and Autoencoder (AE) methods. The architecture of XLNet is developed to work seamlessly with the AR objective, including integrating Transformer-XL and the design of the two-stream attention mechanism. Experimental results show that XLNet achieves substantial improvement over previous pre-training methods on various tasks [23]. In this study, we use XLNet to create embeddings and pre-train the XLNet-Base [24] which contains 12-layer, 768-hidden, and 12-heads.

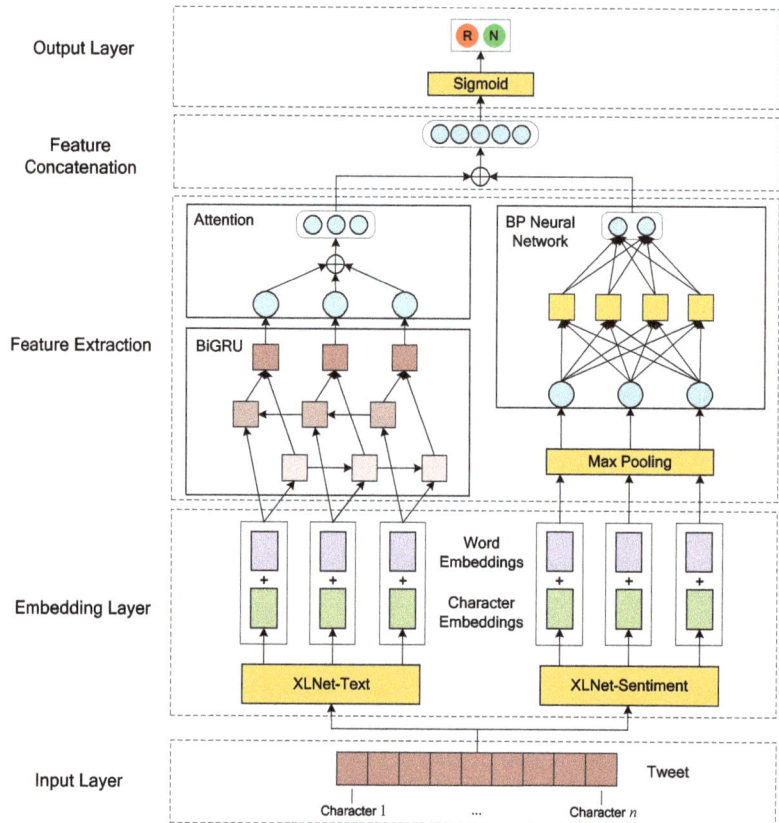

Figure 1. Structure of the XLNet-based BiGRU network with Attention mechanism (XGA) model.

3.2.1. Text-based Embeddings

Firstly, in order to capture the features of Cantonese, we construct a multi-domain Cantonese corpus, which includes new articles/blogs, the entities on Encyclopedia of Virtual Communities in Hong Kong (EVCHK) [25], restaurant reviews, forum threads, etc. Then, XLNet-Base is pre-trained on the corpus and fine-tuned using our constructed CR-Dataset. Specifically, the tokens of all the characters in the tweet are fed into the XLNet model and we get 768-dimensional vectors $C_t = \{C_{t_1}, C_{t_2}, ..., C_{t_n}\}$, which are the outputs of the last hidden layer. In order to obtain the words' external contexts and internal structures, we present an addition operation for semantic features between $C_t = \{C_{t_1}, C_{t_2}, ..., C_{t_n}\}$ (character embeddings) and Cantonese word embeddings $W = \{W_1, W_2, ..., W_n\}$ that provided by fastText [26]. The n denotes the number of characters in the tweet. Finally, we take the results of the addition operation as text-based embeddings $E_t = \{E_{t_1}, E_{t_2}, ..., E_{t_n}\}$ and then feed them into the BiGRU model. E_t is calculated by

$$E_{t_i} = C_{t_i} + W_i, \tag{1}$$

where E_{t_i} represents the text-based embedding of ith character in the tweet, C_{t_i} represents the character embedding of ith character in the tweet, and W_i represents the word embedding of ith character in the tweet.

3.2.2. Sentiment-based Embeddings

Compared to non-rumors, rumors are more inflammatory and deceptive. Therefore, the sentiment polarity of most rumors tends to be negative. For example, a rumor on Twitter is that "顏色水根本唔系水！系化學毒劑，令皮膚很灼熱刺痛！唔好被政府誤導，唔好叫顏色水！請大家以後叫它「化學毒劑」或「化武車」！化學毒劑傷害民眾，殘留毒物污染社區，已經瘋狂失控！" (Color water is not water at all! It is a chemical poison that makes the skin very burning and stinging! Don't be misled by the government and don't call it color water! Please call it "chemical toxic agent" or "chemical weapon vehicle"! This chemical toxic agent hurts people and the residual poisons pollute the community. It is out of control!). The probability that the sentiment polarity of this rumor to be negative is 73%, which is given by the sentiment analysis of Baidu AI [27]. Since the text-based embeddings focus on the semantic features of tweets, it is difficult for them to capture much information about sentiment. So we propose a model to create sentiment embeddings and extract sentiment features of tweets.

In most cases, supervised machine learning approaches are used to train a sentiment classifier with labeled data. But in this research, no data annotation indicating the sentiment polarity of tweets has done on CR-Dataset. Thus, we fine-tune a pre-trained model on a Cantonese dataset with sentiment polarity to solve this problem.

Similar to the work in Section 3.2.1, we first pre-train the XLNet-Base using a multi-domain Cantonese corpus. The pre-trained XLNet is then fine-tuned by the openrice-senti dataset [28], which contains random reviews of restaurants from OpenRice Hong Kong Section [29]. Then the tweet in CR-Dataset is fed into the pre-trained XLNet. We add the outputs of the last hidden layer, which are the character embeddings $C_s = \{C_{s_1}, C_{s_2}, ..., C_{s_n}\}$, with the word embeddings $W = \{W_1, W_2, ..., W_n\}$. The sentiment-based embeddings $E_s = \{E_{s_1}, E_{s_2}, ..., E_{s_n}\}$ are calculated by

$$E_{s_i} = C_{s_i} + W_i, \tag{2}$$

where E_{s_i} represents the sentiment-based embedding of ith character in the tweet, C_{s_i} represents the character embedding of ith character in the tweet, and W_i represents the word embedding of ith character in the tweet.

3.2.3. Joint Learning of Character and Word Embeddings

Most word embedding methods take a word as a basic unit and learn embeddings according to words' external contexts, ignoring the internal structures of words. However, in Cantonese, a word is usually composed of several characters and contains rich internal information [30]. The semantic meaning of a word is also related to the meanings of its composing characters. In some cases, a single character in Cantonese is very ambiguous and may be composed of multiple words. If a character is used as a semantic unit, it cannot accurately represent the current contextual information. As an example, "鬼唔知咩" means that who doesn't know. "鬼" has different meanings in Cantonese. For instance, it can be used as a metaphor for people with various characteristics. But in this word, it serves as the subject as an interrogative pronoun. This example shows that we cannot use a single character as a semantic unit. So, in this part, we introduce internal character information into word embedding methods to alleviate excessive reliance on external information.

3.3. Feature Extraction

In this work, we take the text-based embeddings as the inputs of BiGRU. Then, the attention mechanism is used to focus on the important words in the tweet and output a 150-dimensional vector which indicates the semantic features of the tweet. In addition, we perform the max-pooling step on the sentiment-based embeddings to map the features to a lower-dimensional space. Then, we make use of the Back Propagation (BP) neural network to learn the implicit relationship between features and obtain a 50-dimensional vector which indicates the sentiment features of the tweet.

3.3.1. Bidirectional Gated Recurrent Unit

Gated Recurrent Units (GRU) model consists of two gates: update gate and reset gate. The update gate controls whether the status of GRU is updated or how many units are updated. The reset gate determines how much previous information should be ignored. We use BiGRU for two reasons. One is to solve the problem of vanishing gradients. The other is to obtain contextual information.

Specifically, the model feeds the text-based embeddings $E_t = \{E_{t_1}, E_{t_2}, ..., E_{t_n}\}$ into the BiGRU network to learn the contextual features of the tweet. The output $H = \{h_1, h_2, ..., h_k\}$ is a 150-dimensional vector. k is the number of hidden units in the network. $H = \{h_1, h_2, ..., h_k\}$ is given by

$$\vec{h}_i = GRU(E_{t_i}, \vec{h}_{i-1}), \tag{3}$$

$$\overleftarrow{h}_i = GRU(E_{t_i}, \overleftarrow{h}_{i+1}), \tag{4}$$

$$h_i = \vec{h}_i \oplus \overleftarrow{h}_i, \tag{5}$$

where $\vec{h}_{i-1}$ is the state generated in the previous step of GRU, $\overleftarrow{h}_{i+1}$ is the state generated in the next step of GRU, and h_i is the output of BiGRU. The $\oplus$ denotes the concatenation of two vectors.

3.3.2. Attention

Our model uses the attention mechanism to automatically discover the typical words in the rumor detection and capture the most important semantic information from each tweet. In addition, the input sentence in this research is long. If all the semantic information is represented by an intermediate vector, it would lead to the loss of many details. So it is necessary to introduce the attention mechanism which can give higher weights to the words related to rumors and improve the accuracy of rumor detection.

Specifically, we use the attention mechanism to assign different weights to the outputs of BiGRU $H = \{h_1, h_2, ..., h_k\}$ according to their importance. The 150-dimensional vector F_t that indicates semantic features is described by

$$F_t = Attention(H). \tag{6}$$

3.3.3. Back Propagation Neural Network

We add a max pooling layer to obtain new sentiment-based embeddings with smaller dimensions, which are then mapped to a 50-dimensional vector through a BP neural network.

Pooling is a technique of reducing spatial dimensions. It can reduce the number of parameters to learn and the amount of computation performed in the network. The max pooling layer in our model is to take the maximum value of each dimension of the vectors [7]. To be specific, the size of sentiment-based embeddings E_s is turned from $13,000 \times 140 \times 768$ to $13,000 \times 768$ through the max pooling layer. The output of the max pooling layer E'_s is described by

$$E'_s = Pooling(E_s). \tag{7}$$

Then, E'_s is mapped to a 50-dimensional vector F_s through the fully connected layer of the BP neural network. The F_s indicates the sentiment features of the tweet, which is given by

$$F_s = f(w_s \cdot E'_s + b_s), \tag{8}$$

where $f()$ is the activation function, w_s is a weight matrix in the trained detection model, and b_s is the bias term.

3.4. Feature Concatenation

The semantic and sentiment features of the tweet are distinguishing in the task of rumor detection. So we concatenate F_t and F_s to obtain a 200-dimensional vector F, which indicates all the features extracted for Cantonese rumor detection. F is given by

$$F = F_t \oplus F_s. \tag{9}$$

3.5. Output Layer

The vector F is passed into the *Sigmoid* function to obtain the result of classification, which is given by

$$p = Sigmoid(F), \tag{10}$$

$$y = \begin{cases} 0, p \in [0, 0.5) \\ 1, otherwise \end{cases}, \tag{11}$$

where p is the possibility that the tweet is a rumor, and $p \in [0, 1]$. The y is the classification result. In this binary classification task, $y = 1$ indicates a rumor, and $y = 0$ indicates a non-rumor.

4. Experiments and Evaluation

In this section, we evaluate the performance of the proposed XGA model based on CR-Dataset. All experiments were undertaken on a workstation with two Tesla-V100 32G GPUs. In the experiments, we held out 80% of CR-Dataset for training, 10% for validation, and 10% for testing. The results shown in this section are the average value of each experiment that was repeated ten times independently.

Four metrics are used to evaluate the performance of the embedding layer and the proposed detection model, including *Accuracy, Precision, Recall*, and *F-score*. The *True Positive (TP)* is the number of rumors that are correctly detected, the *False Negative (FN)* is the number of rumors that are incorrectly detected, the *False Positive (FP)* is the number of non-rumors that are incorrectly detected, and the *True Negative (TN)* is the number of non-rumors that are correctly detected. *Accuracy, Precision, Recall*, and *F-score* can be computed by

$$Accuracy = \frac{TP + TN}{TP + TN + FP + FN}, \tag{12}$$

$$Precision = \frac{TP}{TP + FP}, \tag{13}$$

$$Recall = \frac{TP}{TP + FN}, \tag{14}$$

$$F - score = \frac{2 \times Precision \times Recall}{Precision + Recall}. \tag{15}$$

In addition, we plot a Receiver Operating Characteristic (ROC) curve based on *True Positive Rate (TPR)* and *False Positive Rate (FPR)* and compute the Area Under Curve (AUC) score to evaluate the performance of our proposed model. *TPR* and *FPR* can be computed by

$$TPR = \frac{TP}{TP + FN}, \tag{16}$$

$$FPR = \frac{FP}{FP + TN}. \tag{17}$$

4.1. Evaluation of the Embeddings

We use XLNet as the embedding extractor in the XGA model. To evaluate the effectiveness of XLNet, we compare it with the other five popular word embedding models. Note that the structures of the other parts in the model remain unchanged. The performance of models with different embeddings is shown in Table 1.

Table 1. The performance of models with different embeddings.

Embedding	Accuracy	Precision	Recall	F-Score
BERT	0.9119	0.9099	0.9102	0.9101
GPT	0.9099	0.9092	0.9063	0.9076
ELMo	0.9048	0.9048	0.9046	0.9047
fastText	0.9030	0.9031	0.9028	0.9029
Word2vec	0.9079	0.9056	0.9063	0.9060
XLNet	0.9200	0.9224	0.9142	0.9176

In this study, we have pre-trained and fine-tuned the XLNet model on Cantonese data to achieve a better performance of rumor detection. The XLNet used in this experiment is the original XLNet-Base for the fairness of the experiment. As shown in Table 1, XLNet outperforms Bidirectional Encoder Representations from Transformers (BERT) [31], Generative Pre-Training (GPT), and Embeddings from Language Models (ELMo) [32]. This is because XLNet leverages the best of both AR language modeling and AE while avoiding their limitations. Specifically, since an AR language model (e.g., ELMo, GPT) is only trained to encode a uni-directional context, it is not effective at modeling deep bidirectional contexts, which are often required in the downstream language understanding tasks. In comparison, an AE pre-training method (e.g., BERT) is allowed to utilize bidirectional contexts. However, the artificial symbols like [MASK] used by BERT during pre-training are absent from real data at fine-tuning, resulting in a pretrain-finetune discrepancy [23]. In addition, XLNet is better than fastText and Word2vec. This is because XLNet generates contextualized embeddings, which are computed for a word based on its context by pre-trained models, while fastText and Word2vec produce embeddings for each word regardless of its context. Therefore, XLNet achieves the best result among all the models.

4.2. Ablation Study

There are two kinds of features used in our model for rumor detection, i.e., semantic features and sentiment features. In addition, the attention mechanism and word embeddings play an important role in the model. To evaluate the contributions of these significant components to the model, we take turns to exclude them from the model:

- XGA-SF-1: Only the semantic features are used.
- XGA-SF-2: Only the sentiment features are used.
- XG: The attention mechanism is removed.
- XGA-CE: The word embeddings are removed and only the character embeddings are used.
- XGA: Full model.

The results of the ablation study are shown in Table 2. We can see that both semantic and sentiment features improve the performance of the model. Moreover, semantic features are more effective than sentiment features in the detection. This is because the sentiment polarity of some tweets is unclear. In addition, since the attention mechanism can give greater weights to typical rumor vocabulary, XGA performs better than XG. What's more, we compare XGA-CE with XGA and find that performing joint learning of character and word embeddings is useful because it can obtain both the words' external contexts and internal information. In conclusion, XGA outperforms all the other models, and all of these components make great contributions to the detection.

Table 2. The results of ablation study.

Model	Accuracy	Precision	Recall	F-Score
XGA-SF-1	0.9175	0.9176	0.9178	0.9175
XGA-SF-2	0.8794	0.8820	0.8784	0.8789
XG	0.9157	0.9158	0.9161	0.9157
XGA-CE	0.9030	0.9031	0.9028	0.9029
XGA	0.9281	0.9259	0.9276	0.9267

4.3. Evaluation of the XGA Model

We compare the proposed XGA model with other widely used approaches in rumor detection, including TextCNN, RNN, LSTM, att-BiGRU (BiGRU with the attention mechanism), and BERT. We use *Accuracy, Precision, Recall,* and *F-score* as the evaluation metrics of the detection approaches. The performance of different deep learning approaches and XGA is shown in Figure 2. The ROC curve is shown in Figure 3.

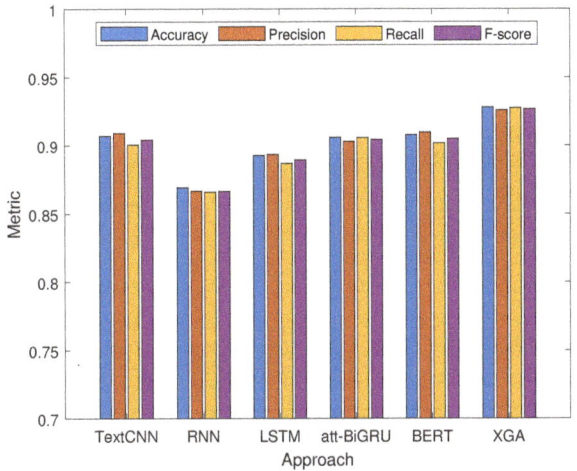

Figure 2. The performance of different deep learning approaches and XGA.

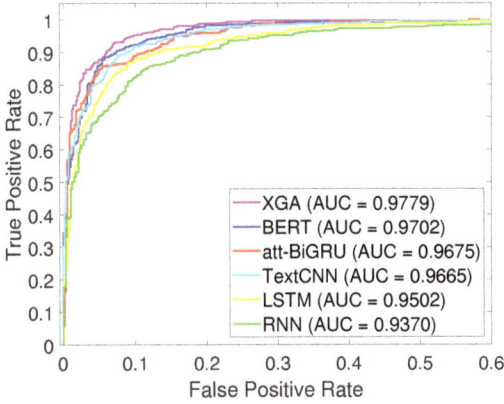

Figure 3. The ROC curve.

As shown in Figure 2, we can see that the XGA model achieves the F-score of 0.9267 on CR-Dataset and shows the best result in all the four metrics. This is because XLNet uses Transformer-XL as its feature extractor, which has better performance than CNN (used by TextCNN), RNN (used by RNN, LSTM, and att-BiGRU), and Transformer [33] (used by BERT) on semantic feature extraction. In addition, the AUC score shown in Figure 3 proves that att-BiGRU performs better than TextCNN, RNN, and LSTM, which indicates that BiGRU and the attention mechanism have an advantage of extracting features, and that is why we use them in the XGA model to create semantic feature vectors for Cantonese tweets. What's more, the XGA model outperforms att-BiGRU by a margin of 2%, which proves the effectiveness of XLNet and sentiment views involved in our model. In conclusion, compared with other deep learning approaches, the proposed XGA model using XLNet, BiGRU, and the attention mechanism is more effective in Cantonese rumor detection. In the experiment, among the test set which includes 1300 tweets, non-rumors are misclassified 55 times, and rumors 41 times. In some cases, a non-rumor is posted to refute a certain rumor and often contains reasoning or turns. For example, a non-rumor may first explain an existing rumor, and use examples or reasoning to prove that the rumor is false in the subsequent text. So, the final detection result of the non-rumor will be affected by the rumor with negative emotional tendencies. That is the reason why some non-rumors cannot be detected correctly. Moreover, the sentiment polarity of some rumors is unclear, which results in the misclassification of rumors. In the future, to reduce the misclassification, we can optimize our model to make it learn the mutual negation between paragraphs in the tweet.

5. Conclusions and Future Work

In this paper, we have proposed a novel hybrid model called XGA for detecting Cantonese rumors, which takes advantage of XLNet, BiGRU, and the attention mechanism. To be specific, we extracted both semantic and sentiment features for the detection. The XLNet, which was pre-trained and fine-tuned on Cantonese data, was used to produce text-based and sentiment-based embeddings. In addition, we combined the character embeddings extracted by XLNet with Cantonese word embeddings to learn the words' external contexts and internal structures. Furthermore, we made use of BiGRU and the attention mechanism to obtain the important semantic features, which were then concatenated with sentiment features to get the final classification results. We performed two experiments to evaluate the effectiveness of our model and came to the following conclusions: the XLNet performed better than other word embedding models, and the XGA model we designed achieved the F-score of 0.9267 in Cantonese rumor detection and outperformed other widely used detection models in all metrics.

In the future, we plan to conduct further research on Cantonese word segmentation to improve the performance of word embeddings. In addition, we will try to discover more effective features for the Cantonese rumor detection and make use of them in our model.

Author Contributions: Conceptualization, H.W., X.C., L.K., H.S. and Z.L.; methodology, H.W., X.C., and L.K.; validation, X.C. and L.K.; formal analysis, X.C. and L.K.; investigation, X.C. and L.K.; data curation, X.C., L.K., Z.L. and H.S.; writing—original draft preparation, X.C. and L.K.; writing—review and editing, X.C., L.K., H.W., Z.L. and H.S.; supervision, H.W.; project administration, X.C. All authors have read and agreed to the published version of the manuscript.

Funding: This research received no external funding.

Acknowledgments: This work was completed under the guidance of Haizhou Wang of Sichuan University, China.

Conflicts of Interest: The authors declare no conflicts of interest.

References

1. Liang, G.; He, W.; Xu, C.; Chen, L.; Zeng, J. Rumor identification in microblogging systems based on users' behavior. *IEEE Trans. Comput. Soc. Syst.* **2015**, *2*, 99–108. [CrossRef]
2. Snopes. Available online: https://www.snopes.com (accessed on 28 August 2020).
3. PolitiFact. Available online: https://www.politifact.com (accessed on 28 August 2020).

4. Ma, J.; Gao, W.; Mitra, P.; Kwon, S.; Jansen, B.J.; Wong, K.F.; Cha, M. Detecting rumors from microblogs with recurrent neural networks. In Proceedings of the 25th International Joint Conference on Artificial Intelligence, New York, NY, USA, 9–15 July 2016; pp. 3818–3824.
5. Vaswani, A.; Shazeer, N.; Parmar, N.; Uszkoreit, J.; Jones, L.; Gomez, A.N.; Kaiser, Ł.; Polosukhin, I. CSI: A hybrid deep model for fake news detection. In Proceedings of the 26th 2017 ACM on Conference on Information and Knowledge Management, Singapore, 6–10 November 2017; pp. 797–806.
6. Liu, Y.; Wu, Y.F.B. Early detection of fake news on social media through propagation path classification with recurrent and convolutional networks. In Proceedings of the 32nd AAAI Conference on Artificial Intelligence, New Orleans, LA, USA, 2–7 February 2018; pp. 354–361.
7. Ma, J.; Gao, W.; Wong, K.F. Rumor Detection on Twitter with Tree-structured Recursive Neural Networks. In Proceedings of the 56th Annual Meeting of the Association for Computational Linguistics, Melbourne, Australia, 15–20 July 2018; pp. 1980–1989.
8. Bondielli, A.; Marcelloni, F. A survey on fake news and rumour detection techniques. *Inf. Sci.* **2019**, *497*, 38–55. [CrossRef]
9. Meel, P.; Vishwakarma, D.K. Fake news, rumor, information pollution in social media and web: A contemporary survey of state-of-the-arts, challenges and opportunities. *Expert Syst. Appl.* **2020**, *153*, 112986. [CrossRef]
10. Zubiaga, A.; Aker, A.; Bontcheva, K.; Liakata, M.; Procter, R. Detection and resolution of rumours in social media: A survey. *ACM Comput. Surv.* **2018**, *51*, 1–36. [CrossRef]
11. Chen, T.; Li, X.; Yin, H.; Zhang, J. Call attention to rumors: Deep attention based recurrent neural networks for early rumor detection. In Proceedings of the 22nd Pacific-Asia Conference on Knowledge Discovery and Data Mining, Melbourne, Australia, 3–6 June 2018; pp. 40–52.
12. Ma, J.; Gao, W.; Wong, K.F. Detect rumors on twitter by promoting information campaigns with generative adversarial learning. In Proceedings of the 28th The World Wide Web Conference, San Francisco, CA, USA, 13–17 May 2019; pp. 3049–3055.
13. Kochkina, E.; Liakata, M.; Zubiaga, A. All-in-one: Multi-task Learning for Rumour Verification. In Proceedings of the 27th International Conference on Computational Linguistics, Santa Fe, NM, USA, 20–26 August 2018; pp. 3402–3413.
14. Kumar, S.; Carley, K.M. Tree lstms with convolution units to predict stance and rumor veracity in social media conversations. In Proceedings of the 57th Annual Meeting of the Association for Computational Linguistics, Florence, Italy, 28 July–2 August 2019; pp. 5047–5058.
15. Yu, F.; Liu, Q.; Wu, S.; Wang, L.; Tan, T. A convolutional approach for misinformation identification. In Proceedings of the 26th International Joint Conference on Artificial Intelligence, Melbourne, Australia, 19–25 August 2017; pp. 3901–3907.
16. Qian, F.; Gong, C.; Sharma, K.; Liu, Y. Neural user response generator: Fake news detection with collective user intelligence. In Proceedings of the 27th International Joint Conference on Artificial Intelligence, Stockholm, Sweden, 13–19 July 2018; pp. 3834–3840.
17. Song, C.; Yang, C.; Chen, H.; Tu, C.; Liu, Z.; Sun, M. CED: Credible early detection of social media rumors. *IEEE Trans. Knowl. Data Eng.* **2019**, *1*. [CrossRef]
18. Jin, Z.; Cao, J.; Guo, H.; Zhang, Y.; Luo, J. Multimodal fusion with recurrent neural networks for rumor detection on microblogs. In Proceedings of the 25th ACM International Conference on Multimedia, Mountain View, CA, USA, 23–27 October 2017; pp. 795–816.
19. Ma, J.; Gao, W.; Joty, S.; Wong, K.F. An Attention-based Rumor Detection Model with Tree-structured Recursive Neural Networks. *ACM Trans. Intell. Syst. Technol.* **2020**, *11*, 42. [CrossRef]
20. Bian, T.; Xiao, X.; Xu, T.; Zhao, P.; Huang, W.; Rong, Y.; Huang, J. Rumor Detection on Social Media with Bi-Directional Graph Convolutional Networks. In Proceedings of the 34th AAAI Conference on Artificial Intelligence, New York, NY, USA, 7–12 February 2020; pp. 549–556.
21. Dashtipour, K.; Gogate, M.; Li, J.; Jiang, F.; Kong, B.; Hussain, A. A hybrid Persian sentiment analysis framework: Integrating dependency grammar based rules and deep neural networks. *Neurocomputing* **2020**, *380*, 1–10. [CrossRef]
22. Cantonese Rumor Dataset. Available online: https://github.com/cxyccc/CR-Dataset (accessed on 28 August 2020).

23. Yang, Z.; Dai, Z.; Yang, Y.; Carbonell, J.; Salakhutdinov, R.R.; Le, Q.V. Xlnet: Generalized autoregressive pretraining for language understanding. In Proceedings of the 33rd Conference on Neural Information Processing Systems, Vancouver, BC, Canada, 8–14 December 2019; pp. 5753–5763.
24. XLNet-Base. Available online: https://github.com/zihangdai/xlnet (accessed on 28 August 2020).
25. Encyclopedia of Virtual Communities in Hong Kong. Available online: https://evchk.wikia.org/zh/wiki/ (accessed on 28 August 2020).
26. FastText Pre-trained Vectors. Available online: https://fasttext.cc/docs/en/pretrained-vectors (accessed on 28 August 2020).
27. Sentiment Analysis of Baidu AI. Available online: https://ai.baidu.com/tech/nlp_apply/sentiment_classify (accessed on 28 August 2020).
28. Openrice-senti Dataset. Available online: https://github.com/toastynews/openrice-senti (accessed on 28 August 2020).
29. OpenRice Hong Kong Section. Available online: https://www.openrice.com/zh/hongkong (accessed on 28 August 2020).
30. Chen, X.; Xu, L.; Liu, Z.; Sun, M.; Luan, H. Joint learning of character and word embeddings. In Proceedings of the 24th International Joint Conference on Artificial Intelligence, Buenos Aires, Argentina, 25–31 July 2015; pp. 1236–1242.
31. Devlin, J.; Chang, M.W.; Lee, K.; Toutanova, K. BERT: Pre-training of Deep Bidirectional Transformers for Language Understanding. In Proceedings of the 17th Conference of the North American Chapter of the Association for Computational Linguistics: Human Language Technologies, Minneapolis, MN, USA, 2–7 June 2019; pp. 4171–4186.
32. Peters, M.; Neumann, M.; Iyyer, M.; Gardner, M.; Clark, C.; Lee, K.; Zettlemoyer, L. Deep Contextualized Word Representations. In Proceedings of the 16th Conference of the North American Chapter of the Association for Computational Linguistics: Human Language Technologies, New Orleans, LA, USA, 1–6 June 2018; pp. 2227–2237.
33. Vaswani, A.; Shazeer, N.; Parmar, N.; Uszkoreit, J.; Jones, L.; Gomez, A.N.; Kaiser, Ł.; Polosukhin, I. Attention is all you need. In Proceedings of the 31st Conference on Neural Information Processing Systems, Long Beach, CA, USA, 19 May 2017; pp. 5998–6008.

© 2020 by the authors. Licensee MDPI, Basel, Switzerland. This article is an open access article distributed under the terms and conditions of the Creative Commons Attribution (CC BY) license (http://creativecommons.org/licenses/by/4.0/).

Article

Ontology Fixing by Using Software Engineering Technology

Gabriela R. Roldan-Molina [1], Jose R. Mendez [1,2,3,*], Iryna Yevseyeva [4] and Vitor Basto-Fernandes [5]

1. Department of Computer Science, University of Vigo, ESEI-Escuela Superior de Ingeniería Informática, Edificio Politécnico, Campus Universitario As Lagoas s/n, 32004 Ourense, Spain; groldan@uvigo.es
2. CINBIO-Biomedical Research Centre, University of Vigo, Campus Universitario Lagoas-Marcosende, 36310 Vigo, Spain
3. SING Research Group, Galicia Sur Health Research Institute (IIS Galicia Sur), SERGAS-UVIGO, 36312 Vigo, Spain
4. Cyber Technology Institute, School of Computer Science and Informatics, Faculty of Computing, Engineering & Media, De Montfort University, Gateway House, The Gateway, Leicester LE1 9BH, UK; iryna@dmu.ac.uk
5. Instituto Universitário de Lisboa (ISCTE-IUL), University Institute of Lisbon, ISTAR-IUL, Av. das Forças Armadas, 1649-026 Lisboa, PT, Portugal; vitor.basto.fernandes@iscte-iul.pt
* Correspondence: moncho.mendez@uvigo.es; Tel.: +34-988-387-015

Received: 31 July 2020; Accepted: 9 September 2020; Published: 11 September 2020

Abstract: This paper presents OntologyFixer, a web-based tool that supports a methodology to build, assess, and improve the quality of ontology web language (OWL) ontologies. Using our software, knowledge engineers are able to fix low-quality OWL ontologies (such as those created from natural language documents using ontology learning processes). The fixing process is guided by a set of metrics and fixing mechanisms provided by the tool, and executed primarily through automated changes (inspired by quick fix actions used in the software engineering domain). To evaluate the quality, the tool supports numerical and graphical quality assessments, focusing on ontology content and structure attributes. This tool follows principles, and provides features, typical of scientific software, including user parameter requests, logging, multithreading execution, and experiment repeatability, among others. OntologyFixer architecture takes advantage of model view controller (MVC), strategy, template, and factory design patterns; and decouples graphical user interfaces (GUI) from ontology quality metrics, ontology fixing, and REST (REpresentational State Transfer) API (Application Programming Interface) components (used for pitfall identification, and ontology evaluation). We also separate part of the OntologyFixer functionality into a new package called OntoMetrics, which focuses on the identification of symptoms and the evaluation of the quality of ontologies. Finally, OntologyFixer provides mechanisms to easily develop and integrate new quick fix methods.

Keywords: ontologies; fixing ontologies; quick fix; quality metrics

---

1. Introduction and Motivation

Ontologies are knowledge representations, in which concepts and categories of a certain domain are stored together with their properties and the relations between them. Currently, ontologies are used to represent knowledge from a large number of domains in order to solve different problems and improve the experience of users in different contexts. For example, in the Semantic Web, they are used to describe terms, retrieve information, and interconnect web services. Due to the increasing use of ontologies, a large number of models and languages have been introduced to manage them, including resource description framework (RDF) [1], resource description framework schema (RDFS) [2], and ontology web language (OWL) [3], among others. However, it is necessary to be able to evaluate the quality of the creation of these ontologies in order to guarantee good performance, and take advantage of the benefits they offer. Currently, ontologies facilitate aspects such as communication, interoperability, and automatic reasoning [4–7]. Ontologies allow us to represent and share knowledge using a common vocabulary, and to exchange data between different systems and contexts [8].

Furthermore, ontologies are very useful to facilitate automatic reasoning. On the basis of inferencing, a reasoning engine can use the ontology data (categories, concepts, relations, and properties) to reach conclusions. On the other hand, the use of ontologies allows knowledge engineers to organize and structure the information so that software agents can interpret their meaning, and, consequently, search and integrate data much better. Using the knowledge stored in ontologies, applications can automatically extract data from web pages, process them, draw conclusions, make decisions, and negotiate with other agents or people [9,10].

A significant number of ontologies are manually generated or created by taking advantage of applications, and implementing the extraction of information from natural language text [11]. The use of these tools in conjunction with the natural inconsistencies of human languages can lead to the appearance of errors, inconsistencies, or bad designs that require further debugging or repair processes. The process of detecting and fixing errors or bad design symptoms is a difficult task and should be done as an iterative process, where each step should include the evaluation of the state of the ontology, selecting the most appropriate change for the current situation and evaluating whether the changes made are appropriate.

The detection of ontology errors, inconsistencies, and flaws can be made using tools such as OOPS! [12], a web application that detects bad practices when modelling ontologies. This tool provides mechanisms for automatically detecting potential errors, called pitfalls, in order to help developers during the validation process. However, some pitfalls are detected semi-automatically, such as "Creating synonyms as classes" or "Creating unconnected ontology elements", among others [13]. Each pitfall provides the following information: title, description, elements affected, and importance level. A recent study [14] showed a method for finding errors in apparently coherent and consistent ontologies, but these may contain contradictions in the axiom statements and provide incorrect information. The approach uses knowledge from other knowledge bases that debug ontology modelling errors. Moreover, some frameworks have been introduced for measuring the quality of ontologies, most notably OquaRE [15], which implements several quality metrics based on the SQuaRE (system and software quality requirements and evaluation) [16] software quality standard. This framework provides a guide to evaluate the quality of ontologies in diverse dimensions, such as reliability, operability, maintainability, compatibility, transferability, and functional adequacy. Although some tools for error detection and/or quality evaluation of ontologies are available, the process of aiding the debugging/fixing of ontologies has not been addressed in a global form. Particularly, we found that these tools could be combined to create a tool to fix errors, and improve the global quality of ontologies. Additionally, taking advantage of quick fix schemes used in integrated development environments (IDEs), the fixing tool could suggest appropriate solutions to address each detected trouble, to simplify the fixing process. In this study, we developed a software tool implementing the proposed solution for ontology fixing, detailing its architecture, functionality, and usage. The software integrates a wide amount of software technology that has been successfully adapted to the context of knowledge engineering (OQuaRE, pitfalls, quick fix schemes, etc.). The result is the creation of the OntologyFixer tool, which can be successfully downloaded from GitHUB (Available at https://github.com/gabyluna/OntologyFixer) and is available on http://ontologyfixer.online.

The remainder of the paper is structured as follows: Section 2 presents the state of the art in the context of repairing ontologies. Section 3 presents the architecture of the developed software in detail. Section 4 shows the main features of the generated software. Finally, Section 5 shows the main conclusions, and future developments to complement this work.

2. State of the Art

Given the increased use among software and knowledge engineering communities of ontologies to represent knowledge, their quality and correctness have become two key aspects to consider. Quality evaluation assists in finding design defects, inconsistencies, errors, or limitations in stored knowledge. Moreover, the correction of an ontology implies the detection of a problem, the exploration of possible ways to fix it, and the application of the selected correction. This section compiles previous studies that have introduced algorithms and techniques to implement these functionalities, which are key to the implementation of OntologyFixer.

The evaluation of ontology quality has been addressed in previous resources including (ordered from most to least recent): (i) OquaRE [15], (ii) Foval [17], (iii) OntoQA [18], and (iv) OntoClean [19].

OQuaRE is a method of evaluating the quality of ontologies that emerged as an adaptation of the SQuaRE (system and software quality requirements and evaluation) standard (ISO/IEC 25000) to the context of knowledge engineering, comprising evaluation support, evaluation processes, and quality metrics. OQuaRE uses different metrics to assess the quality of the ontologies with regard to different dimensions, including reliability, operability, maintainability, compatibility, transferability, and functional adequacy. Most quality sub-characteristics suggested by SQuaRE (system and software quality requirements and evaluation) [20] were also adopted in OQuaRE. Additionally, OQuaRE includes the structural characteristic, which is important in evaluating ontologies.

FOval provides an evaluation model to select ontologies that best fit the user needs (requirements), while OntoQA is a suite of metrics that evaluates the quality of ontologies in different dimensions, including schemas, knowledge base, and class metrics. Finally, OntoClean is a methodology for the validation of the ontological adequacy and logical consistency of taxonomic relationships. All of these works provide interesting measures to assess different aspects of quality including (i) lexical, (ii) hierarchy, (iii) other semantic relationships, (iv) context, (v) syntactic, and (vi) structure, as recommended in a previous study [21].

As in the case of OQuaRE, software engineering domain technology has inspired some proposals that aid in the detection of the potential troubles of ontologies. Particularly, pitfall, code smells, or simply smells, were popular forms of symptoms of software design troubles [22]. A recent study [12] introduced how the same concept (pitfall) can be applied to the context of knowledge engineering, to address the detection of design troubles. Given the success of the application of these software engineering technologies, we suggest the possibility of using quick-fix schemes to improve some knowledge engineering design processes. Introducing these concepts, in the context of ontologies, and combining them with current technology will lead to new, and better, ontology fixing tools (OntologyFixer).

The next section describes how quick-fix support has been included in our proposal, to be used as an aid in fixing and improving the quality of ontologies.

3. System Overview

OntologyFixer diagnoses the quality of the ontologies, and also allows for the detection and correction of errors. For the diagnosis, OntologyFixer applies different metrics that allow measuring different aspects of the quality of ontologies, such as structure, logic, and semantics, among others. Table 1 shows the measures we have selected for the evaluation of ontologies.

Table 1. Quality Metrics.

Metric	Description
ANOnto	Measures annotation richness
CBOnto	Determines coupling between Objects
CROnto	Assess Class Richness
INROnto	Number of relationships per class
LCOMOnto	Measures the lack of Cohesion in Methods
NOMOnto	Finds the number of properties per class
RCOnto	Instances distributed across classes
RFCOnto	Determines the response measure for a class
RROnto	Assess relationship richness

Most of the selected metrics are available in the OQuaRE framework except for RCOnto, which is provided by the OntoQA framework. Assuming the selected measures should be maximized, we represent them in a radar chart, and compute the area of the polygon formed using the measures evaluated as vertices. OntologyFixer supports the loading of an additional ontology (as a reference), to compare its quality with that of the ontology being corrected. Figure 1 shows an example of a diagnosis generated by the application.

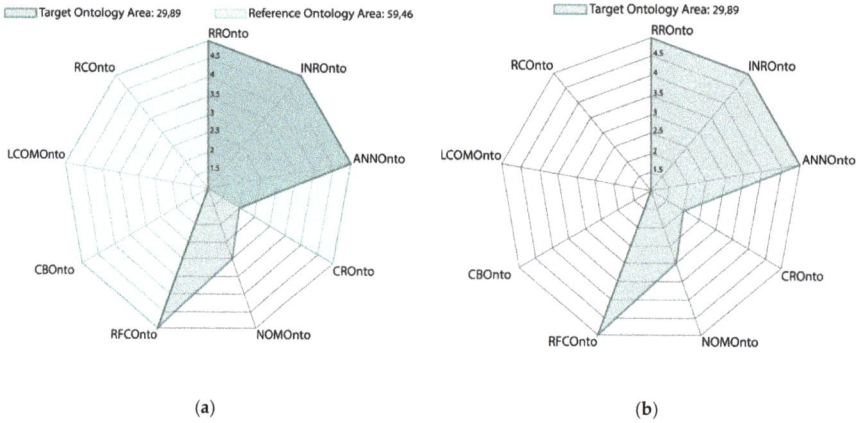

Figure 1. Ontology quality assessment result: (a) Quality comparison with a reference ontology, (b) Quality evaluation of an ontology.

As shown in Figure 1, the application can also compare a model ontology with the ontology to be evaluated (Figure 1a), allowing the user to better visualize the weaknesses of the ontology that is being fixed. However, it is also possible to visualize the diagnosis of the quality of the ontology without the need to load a reference ontology (Figure 1b).

Additionally, OntologyFixer integrated OOPS! [12], to detect errors or pitfalls. OOPS! is a framework that detects pitfalls, and prioritizes them according to their importance. OntologyFixer implements a quick fix strategy to automate the correction of ontologies. Using OOPS!, OntologyFixer is able to provide complete information about the errors of an ontology.

Currently, only two quick fixes were implemented in the first version of the application: (i) RM_INVOLVED_ELEMENTS and (ii) RM_SIMILAR_ELEMENTS. The former removes some (or all) ontology elements (classes, object properties, or data properties) that are causing troubles. The latter searches and removes similar elements caused by typos (and the use of ontology automatic generation tools) that are causing a pitfall in the ontology. To carry out this process, we applied the Levenshtein algorithm [23] to find the lexical distance between two words. This quick fix removes elements having a distance lower than, or equal to, 1. For example, when comparing the elements "action" and "actions", which could cause circularity in the ontology, the distance calculated between them is 1; that is, there is a similarity between the terms so that when the RM_SIMILAR_ELEMENTS quick fix is applied, one of the elements is removed from the ontology in conjunction with the axioms related to it.

When the available quick fixes are not adequate, OntologyFixer allows downloading of the current status of the ontology for manual editing. This allows users to modify the ontology using their favourite ontology editor (e.g., Protégé), and to then upload the resulting ontology again.

Another functionality of OntologyFixer is the possibility of performing a rollback of the ontology; that is, the application has a history of versions with the possibility of returning to an earlier version, which allows undoing changes, with respect to a quick fix previously applied. To this end, OntologyFixer stores ontology snapshots before applying any operation (quick fix or manual edition). Nevertheless, before applying a quick fix, OntologyFixer shows a detailed description of the actions that are going to be performed to ensure the user agrees with the action.

One notable advantage of OntologyFixer is the evaluation and correction of errors without needing to use multiple applications. Another advantage, is the possibility of integrating new quality metrics and quick fix schemes, due to the scalable and decoupled nature of the tool's design.

The following subsections provide a brief description of the architecture of the application (Section 3.1), the integration with frameworks and APIs (Section 3.2), and the metrics adopted for the research project (Section 3.3).

3.1. General Architecture

OntologyFixer was designed following a web-based client/server scheme. This section shows the design of the architecture in detail as well as the main features of the application. Figure 2 shows the interaction of web browsers (clients) with OntologyFixer, which was deployed in a J2EE Application Server.

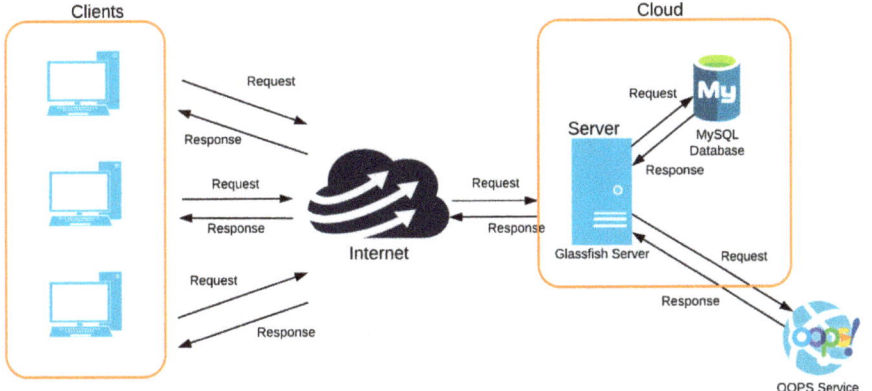

Figure 2. Application architecture.

As shown in Figure 2, user interaction takes place through a web browser, sending HTTPS requests to a Glassfish application server running in the cloud. Persistence is supported by a Spring ORM (object relational mapping) implementation that transparently manages the information stored in a MySQL database engine. Additionally, the external RESTful Web Service (OOPS!) [24] API is used for the evaluation and detection of errors in the ontologies. Figure 3 shows a set of technologies separated into different layers, in order to delegate specific functions for each of them, promoting the software development single responsibility principle [25]. Each of the technologies was specially selected for the development of OntologyFixer, for its ease of integration, robustness, and availability as open source software.

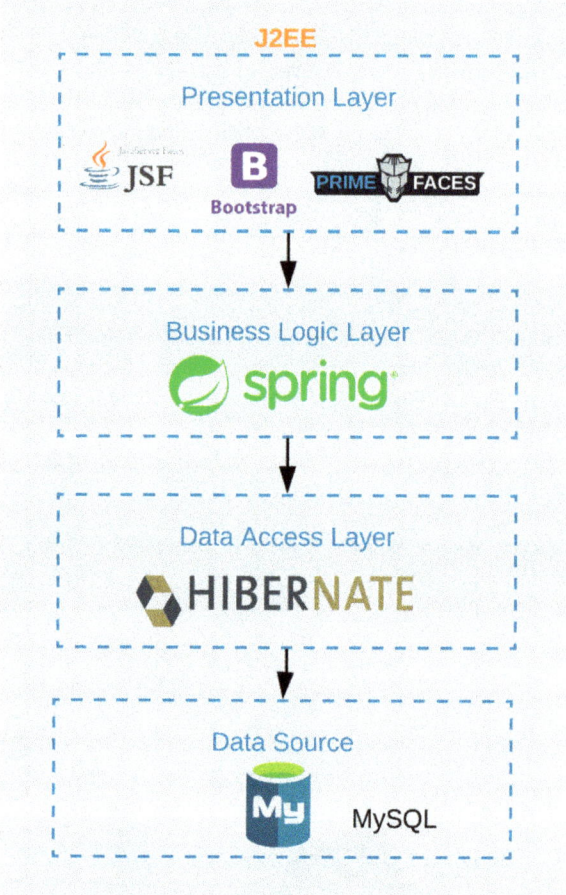

Figure 3. Layered architecture.

As shown in Figure 3, OntologyFixer implements a multiple-layer design in which the functionalities defined in the lower layers provide access to resources or services to the upper layers. The main advantage of this type of architecture is the ability to build scalable applications that favor the integration of other components, software maintenance, and evolution. The presentation layer uses web technologies such as JSF (Java Server Faces) version 2.2 [26]. JSF is a user-interface framework implementing the MVC (model view controller) architecture pattern, which facilitates the development and maintenance of web applications. Additionally, PrimeFaces framework version 5.3, which provides open source visual components for JSF 2.2 and Bootstrap [27], was adopted to provide a responsive interface design that can be easily used in a wide range of computing devices. Finally, for ontology visualization, we took advantage of the WebVOWL (Web-based Visualization of Ontologies) (Available at http://vowl.visualdataweb.org/webvowl.html) external web application.

The business logic layer was implemented using Spring framework because of its relevant features (i.e., "Dependency Injection" or "Inversion of Control"). Currently, Spring provides a wide variety of functionalities in the form of modules, including Spring Security, Spring AOP, Spring JPA, etc.

Spring JPA and Hibernate were used for the development of the persistence and access layer of OntologyFixer. These frameworks allowed the transparent access to the data stored in a MySQL database. The next subsection introduces the main design patterns that were used in the development of OntologyFixer and its main purpose.

3.2. Software Design Details

The MVC [28] design pattern was adopted for the software development, as it presents well-known robust properties and software quality attributes. MVC separates business logic with respect to the data (model) and the user interface (view/GUI). It allows independent changes in each component without affecting the others. In other words, changes in the graphical user interface (GUI) do not affect data handling, and data can be reorganized without changing the user interface. Figure 4 shows the components that are part of the model.

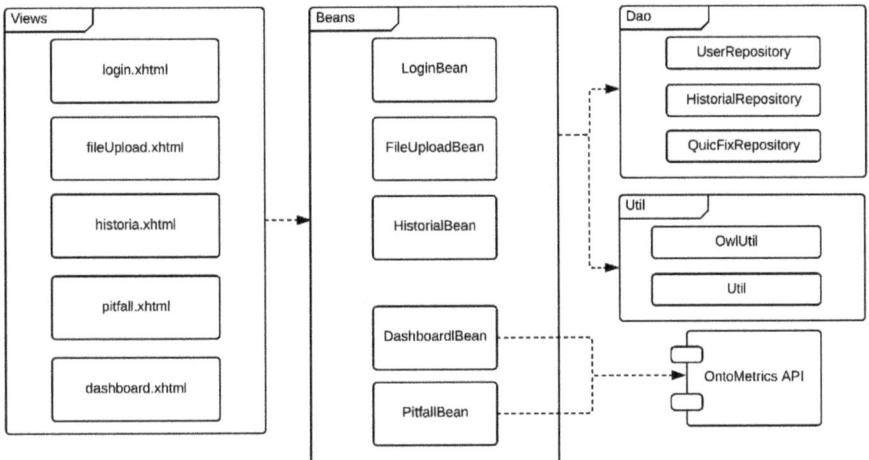

Figure 4. Model View Controller design.

In the Views component shown in Figure 4 we can see the user interface for each functionality. The controller uses Beans (one per view) that are responsible for making the connection between the view and the application logic. Finally, the model component uses Spring JPA to access the data layer, i.e., to make the call to the persistence layer that communicates with the MySQL database. To do so, Spring uses the DAO (data access object) objects [29], which are design patterns, in which a data access object provides an abstract interface to some type of database or other persistence technology. DAOs provide some specific data operations without exposing database data model details (i.e., create, update, or delete).

Additionally, OntologyFixer integrates an external OntoMetrics API, developed in the context of this research for computing the different metrics used to evaluate the quality of the ontologies. This API was integrated as a Maven dependency in the OntologyFixer project. OntoMetrics were structured into three modules: basic metrics, quality metrics, and symptom identification methods.

The development of this API involved the use of some design patterns that facilitate software comprehension, maintenance, and evolution. The behavior pattern strategy [30] was used to define a family of algorithms, each of them in separate classes, making their objects interchangeable. Figure 5 shows the design of the OntoMetrics API package.

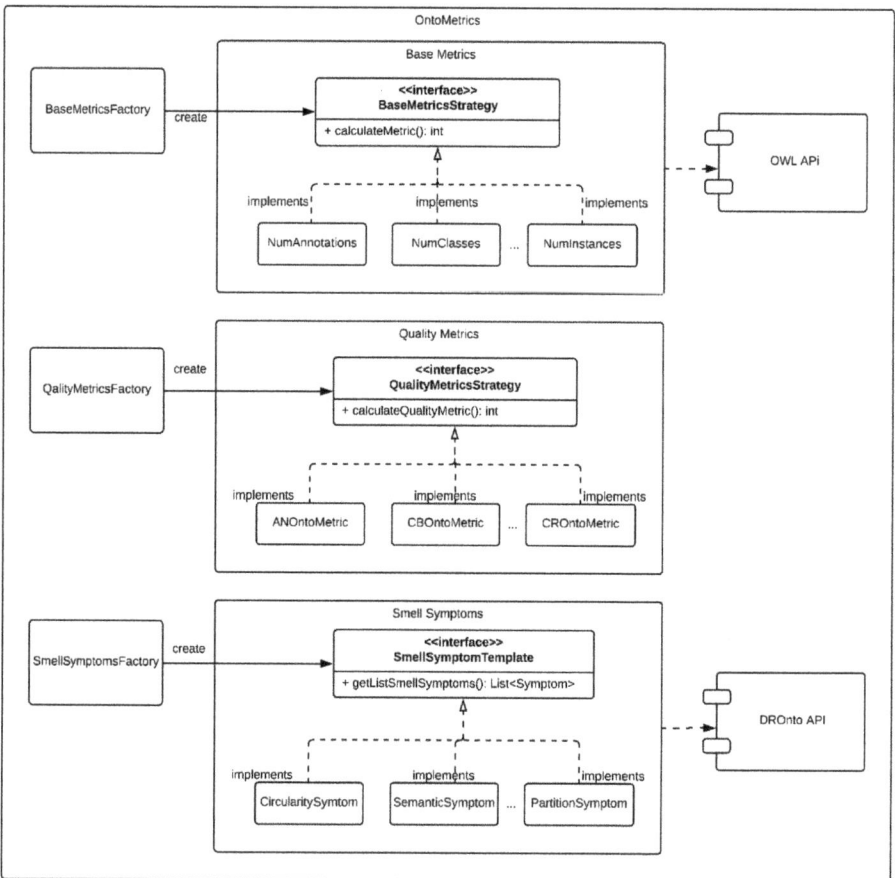

Figure 5. OntoMetrics design.

As shown in Figure 5, the implementation of the package includes a Strategy interface, implemented by strategy classes for basic and quality metrics. Moreover, the Template pattern [30] was used to implement smell symptom identification. Finally, we used the Factory design pattern [30] for creating objects, without having to specify their exact class. This Creational pattern avoids close coupling between the creator and concrete products. In addition, it complies with the principle of sole responsibility because it can move the product creation code to a specific place (the Factory class) in the program, making the code easier to maintain. In addition, by combining the selected patterns, the use of the metrics is clearly easier for developers. Figure 6 shows different examples of using the metrics included in the library.

```
01  //Example BaseMetrics (Number of annotations of ontology)
02  BaseMetricsStrategy baseMetricsStrategy;
03  baseMetricsStrategy = BaseMetricsFactory.getBaseMetric(BaseMetricEnum.ANNOTATIONS);
04  int annotations = baseMetricsStrategy.calculateMetric(ontology);
05
06  //Example QualityMetrics
07  QualityMetricsStrategy qualityMetricsStrategy;
08  QualityMetricFactory qualityMetricFactory = new QualityMetricFactory();
09  qualityMetricsStrategy = qualityMetricFactory.getQualityMetric(indexMetric);
10  resultMetric = qualityMetricsStrategy.calculateQualityMetric(metricsOntology);
11
12  //Example SmellSymptoms
13  SmellSymptomTemplate circularitySymptomTemplate =
14      SmellSymptomFactory.getSmellError(SmellSymptom.CIRCULARITY);
15  List<Symptoms> listCircularitySymptoms =
16      circularitySymptomTemplate.getListSmellSymptoms(pathOntology);
```

Figure 6. Example of using different kinds of metrics from the package OntoMetrics.

Another of the main features of OntologyFixer is the possibility of applying quick fixes. The application was designed with an architecture that allows for the easy addition of new quick fixes, to improve ontologies. Figure 7 shows the QuickFixInterface interface, which specifies the methods that should be implemented to develop additional quick fixes.

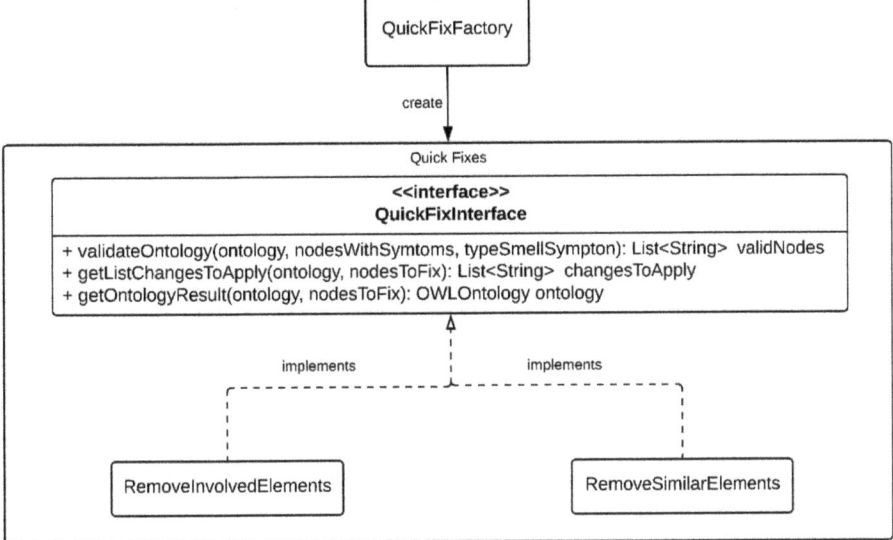

Figure 7. QuickFix interface.

In order to develop a new quick fix scheme, three methods should be implemented. The first one (validateOntology) determines which nodes of an ontology that have a problem can be fixed by applying the quick fix. Moreover, getListChangesToAppy finds the list of changes that are required for fixing certain nodes of the ontology using the quick fix. Finally, the getResult method allows the quick fix to be applied to certain nodes of an ontology. Currently, two quick fix methods (RemoveInvolvedElements and RemoveSimilarElements) are supported by OntologyFixer. However, the inclusion of new quick fix schemes can be easily added to the design by implementing the QuickFixInterface and registering the implementation in the QuickFixFactory class. The simplification and extensible design of the architecture ensures new quick solutions can be easily added to OntologyFixer.

The next subsection compiles the metrics that were included in the OntoMetrics package.

3.3. Implemented Metrics and Symptoms Detection

This subsection provides a complete list of the smell symptoms detection mechanisms and the metrics (basic and quality) implemented by OntoMetrics API, as well as some of the implementation details.

To compute basic metrics, we used the OWL API [31], which manages the ontologies and provides components for the manipulation of ontological structures in different formats, such as OWL and RDF (resource description framework) among others. In addition, we also used reasoning engines. Eight basic metrics were implemented. Table 2 describes each of the basic metrics.

Table 2. Basic metrics implemented in OntologyFixer.

Metric	Description
Number of annotations	Indicates the total entries that exist in the ontology.
Number of classes	Finds how many classes exist in ontology.
Number of classes with individuals	Shows the number of classes that have at least one individual.
Number of instances	Computes the number of instances of the ontology.
Number of properties	Indicates the number of properties contained in the ontology.
Number of relations of Thing	Stands for the relationships that exist towards "Thing".
Number of subclasses	Counts the total subclasses that exist in the ontology.
Number of superclasses	Identifies the number of superclasses that exist in the ontology.

The implementation of quality metrics was based on the OQuaRE (framework described in Section 2), which provides a guide to evaluate the quality of ontologies in diverse dimensions, such as reliability, operability, maintainability, compatibility, transferability, and functional adequacy. Nine quality metrics (see Table 1) were implemented to assess the quality of ontologies by using some basic metrics.

Finally, for identifying smell symptoms, the web service that provides OOPS! [24] was used. The service takes a file with an OWL extension of the ontology as input, evaluates it, and returns a list of smell errors, with additional fields to identify the level of criticality it represents in the ontology. The smell symptoms described in Table 3 were implemented for the project.

Table 3. Smell Symptoms ("ONTOLOGICAL ERRORS—Inconsistency, Incompleteness, and Redundancy" 2008).

Smell Symptom	Description
CircularitySymptoms	Detects cycles between two (or more) classes
IncompletenessSymptoms	The symptom entails not representing all the knowledge that could be included in the ontology.
PartitionSymptoms	Detects symptoms when disjoint decomposition exists. There are three types: Common Instances and Classes in Disjoint, Decomposition and Partitions.
SemanticSymptoms	The symptom entails problems in the logic between elements and relationships of the ontology.

The next subsection presents the outcomes that emerged from the development of the tool.

3.4. Lessons Learned

This subsection identifies the main outcomes achieved by carrying out this study. The most important conclusions are related to the successful testing and validation of software engineering approaches, methods, and technologies, adapted and applied to knowledge engineering problems. After their incorporation into the domain, the identification of bad design symptoms (smells), or the use of quality metrics (OOPS!), we were able to successfully adapt quick fix mechanisms, included in popular integrated development environments (IDEs), to improve the quality of the ontologies.

Additionally, the combination of quality metrics, errors or smell symptoms detection, and quick fix for developing an ontology fixing tool seems to be very reliable, as demonstrated in this study. However, at the moment there is no quick fix tools for ontology-based knowledge representation available, and we have to implement them following strategies similar to those used by software IDEs.

As a part of this study, we provided a collection of ontology quality metrics, the error detection, and the identification of bad design symptoms for the OntoMetrics library. This facilitates the use of these metrics, by providing a uniform way to access these functionalities. For the evaluation of quality, OntoMetrics takes advantage of the metrics defined in the OQUARE framework. In the case of symptom detection, OOPS! was integrated into our OntoMetrics library, to take advantage of DrontoAPI to detect smells in analyzed ontologies. DrontoAPI functionalities are provided through a web service which incorporates methods to find the elements of the ontology that are affected by any type of symptom (circularity, incompleteness, semantics).

Finally, from a more technical perspective, we also employed different tools including Spring, an open source application development framework for the Java platform. Spring is based on different design patterns including DAO (data access object). This pattern is used to encapsulate data access logic, thus avoiding mixing it with business logic. Spring also provides a consistent approach to data access, either JDBC (Java DataBase Connectivity), or through some data access frameworks, such as Hibernate, iBatis, JDO, or TopLink, among others, and allows changing the framework used for persistence without affecting the code already written. For the construction of OntologyFixer we used PrimeFaces, a library of visual components for Java Server Faces (JSF) providing a large number of elements, to make the development of the presentation layer easier. A notable advantage of using this library is the Ajax support for updating the components and achieving a better user experience. Furthermore, to enhance the interface, we used Bootstrap, which embeds technologies such as JavaScript and CSS (Cascading Style Sheets) in order to help developers quickly and efficiently design a responsive website, and to make the design correct and usable both for conventional and tactile devices (responsive web design). The combination of these tools makes the application more robust and scalable over time, with the possibility of adding or changing new technologies that fit the needs of the project.

The functionality of the resulting application is shown in the next section. Particularly, it highlights some interface details and operations by using some screenshots and providing a detailed description of the inner operation of OntologyFixer.

4. System Use

OntologyFixer was designed with a user friendly and easy to use graphical interface. It allows a user to (i) upload an ontology, (ii) evaluate ontology quality, (iii) apply fixes to the ontology, and (iv) use the changes history to restore a previous state when needed. An ontology can be evaluated by applying two different strategies: performing a metrics-based quality evaluation, and finding possible troubles (errors or symptoms of bad design) that may lead to ontology inconsistencies. Figure 8 shows the interface details for both functionalities.

As shown in Figure 8a, the evaluation of the quality of Ontologies is made in the form of a radial chart combining different quality measures. The quality is shown in a dashboard which includes "Base Metrics" (located at the top of the figure), which include the number of classes, subclasses, properties, instances, and annotations of the ontology to evaluate and compare with the reference ontology (optional). The bottom of the dashboard contains a quality evaluation chart that perceives the quality of the ontology at a simple glance. The chart represents RROnto, INROnto, ANNOnto, CROnto, NOMOnto, RFCOnto, CBOOnto, LCOMOnto, and RCOnto scores (see Table 2), achieved by the ontology. Additionally, the area of the figure described by the representation of these measurements (that is also shown) could be used to assess the global quality of the ontology. Finally, the knowledge engineer can graphically visualize the ontology itself if desired.

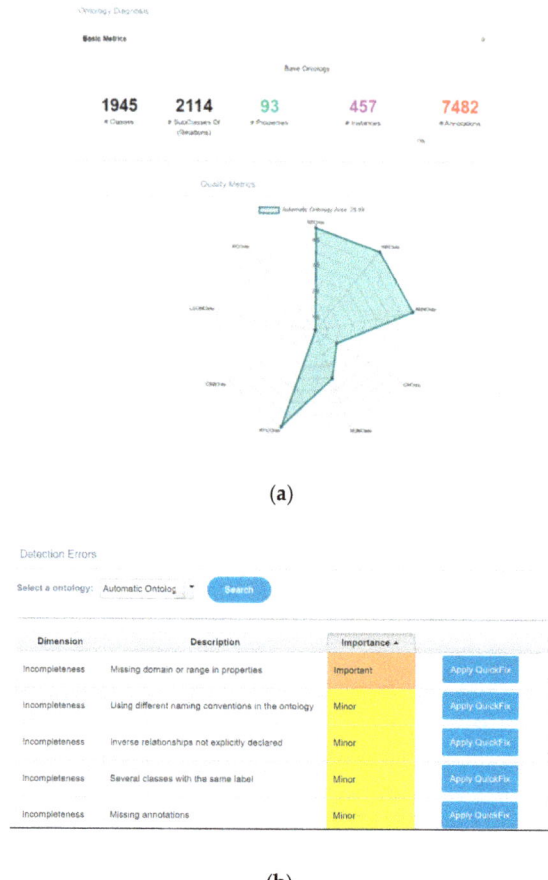

Figure 8. Different forms of ontology diagnosis implemented in OntologyFixer. (**a**) Quality evaluation. (**b**) Errors and smells detection.

As shown in Figure 8b, the features allowing the detection of errors and smells enable the knowledge engineer to identify and address specific troubles found in the ontology. The results table included in Figure 8b details the trouble found in the ontology (circularity, incompleteness, and semantics), a brief description for it, and its level of importance. The level of importance (which is assessed by using the OOPS! framework) is highlighted using different background colors. Specifically, critical errors are highlighted in red, important troubles are marked in orange, and finally, minor issues are represented with a yellow background.

Once the main weaknesses and errors of the ontology have been identified, OntologyFixer supports the application of a quick-fix and the upload of a new version of the ontology. Additionally, OntologyFixer stores snapshots of the ontology each time a modification is made; this ensures that an older version of the ontology can be restored. These snapshots are stored in a local database but also in a Git repository (if configured) to ensure the versions of the ontology are shared according to the preferences of the user. Figure 9 shows capabilities of the application for fixing ontologies.

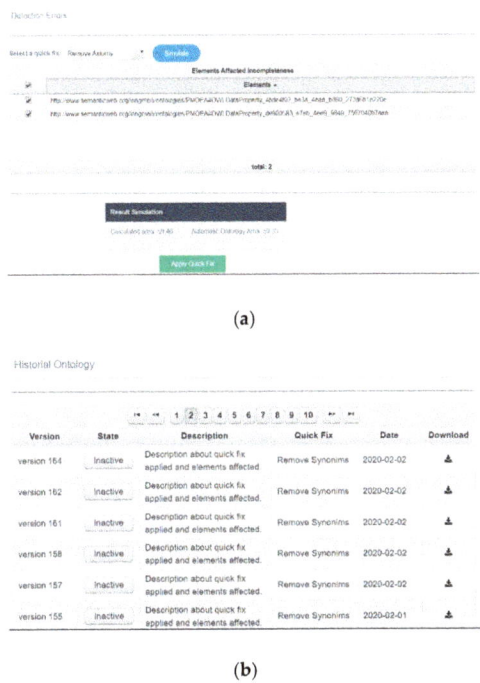

Figure 9. Fixing errors in ontologies. (**a**) Applying a quick fix. (**b**) History of modifications.

Figure 9a shows the "Apply Quick Fix" button, which allows the execution of a quick fix to those elements of the ontology (instances, classes, relationships) affected by some type of issue. This button is used to compute the list of all affected items for an error. As shown in Figure 9a, OntologyFixer users can select one or more elements found, and apply one of the quick fixes described in Section 3. One of the functionalities of OntologyFixer is the possibility of simulating the results of applying a quick fix, which is useful for deciding whether to apply a certain solution. The simulation result shows a value for the current area and the new area calculated after applying the quick fix in the ontology (Figure 9a). Finally, the "Apply Quick Fix" button shown in Figure 9a will generate a new version of the ontology and store it as a new version in history.

As described in Section 3, one of the advantages of the application is the possibility of performing a rollback in the ontology editions (Figure 9b). The button included in the "Status" column can be used to return to an earlier version of the ontology. This action allows us to activate an older version of the ontology, re-analyze, and fix it by applying a new quick fix. In addition, the rollback function included in OntologyFixer offers the possibility of downloading each of the versions to which changes were applied (button located at "Download" column). The next section presents the main conclusions extracted from this work and outlines future research directions.

5. Conclusions and Future Work

This work introduces OntologyFixer, a tool for assisting users in improving the quality of ontologies and fixing their troubles, by using software engineering inspired techniques. The functionality of OntologyFixer was achieved by combining some recently introduced techniques that are inspired by software engineering (e.g., quality evaluation frameworks, such as OQUARE, or smell symptoms detection, such as OOPS!), and others that are being introduced and used for the first time in this study (quick fix for ontologies). OntologyFixer combines 17 measures to assess the quality of an ontology and supports the detection of four types of bad design symptoms (smells). This group of functionalities was encapsulated into an external library (OntoMetrics) to standardize their invocation. Additionally, the application was developed by incorporating recent and innovative frameworks (Spring, PrimeFaces, Bootstrap) to ensure robustness, usability, and ease of maintenance.

The use of quick fix technology, extracted from popular IDEs for developing software, provides an easy to use and customizable mechanism to fix ontologies more easily. Particularly, the application of quick fix methods implies developing several methods that (i) determine which issues can be fixed by using the quick fix, (ii) provide a list of changes that will be made through applying the quick fix, and (iii) apply the changes. OntologyFixer functionalities were integrated into a graphical interface that allows the user to identify those elements that present a symptom, also allowing one of the quick solutions to be applied to one or more elements of the ontology that presents problems. One of the more noteworthy advantages of the proposal is the possibility for the user to simulate the application of a quick fix in order to determine whether the result is favorable, before applying it permanently. However, after applying a quick solution there is the possibility of consulting/downloading/restoring the different earlier versions generated by OntologyFixer.

OntologyFixer also defines a graphical method to represent the quality of an ontology (Figure 8a), ensuring the user can get an overview of its quality at a glance. Additionally, the application supports the detection of errors and smell symptoms that will guide the application of quick fixes. Finally, the application of quick fixes can be rolled back if the ontology does not achieve the desired level of quality (Figure 9b).

The number of implemented OntologyFixer quick fixes is expected to be developed as future work in a short period of time.

Additionally, we believe that the tool could benefit from the use of multi-objective optimization algorithms to implement a semi-automatic ontology fixing scheme. OntologyFixer multi-objective optimization features will provide support to address the improvement of multiple ontology quality metrics simultaneously, by searching and identifying the optimal subset of quick fix actions to be applied to the ontology, and the optimal order of their application.

Although quality improvements of the ontology by the means of automatic and optimal fixing decisions reduce the effort required by the knowledge engineer, the automatic decisions might favor some quality attributes that do not correspond to the knowledge engineer's preferences. Therefore, the optimization process must consider the benefits and costs of the automatic decision, i.e., decrease the efforts of the knowledge engineer by an automatic decision that generally improves the ontology quality, or forward a diverse subset of optimal alternatives for the knowledge engineer to select, according to his/her preferences.

The set of actions to be considered by the optimization process are dependent on the detected pitfalls, e.g., annotation pitfalls that refer to the lack of information in the ontology can be fixed by identifying the classes of greatest relevance in the ontology, and by asking the user to add the comments or annotations that are pertinent to improve the understanding of the ontology and its elements. Reasoning pitfalls may include relations incorrectly defined as inverse, which can be solved by checking that they have a domain and range. If this were not the case, the tool could suggest possible options for domains and ranges or suggest removing them. The OntologyFixer optimization process will identify an optimal sequence of actions (quick fixes such as RM_INVOLVED_ELEMENTS and/or RM_SIMILAR_ELEMENTS) to improve the ontology and will present alternative sequences of actions (with the corresponding ontology quality attributes impact) to apply the one that best fits the knowledge engineer's preferences. The number of decisions to be forwarded to the knowledge engineer must also be considered as criteria to be minimized in the optimization process.

Author Contributions: Conceptualization, G.R.R.-M., J.R.M. and V.B.-F.; methodology, G.R.R.-M. and V.B.-F.; software, G.R.R.-M.; validation, I.Y.; formal analysis, I.Y. and V.B.-F.; investigation, G.R.R.-M., J.R.M., I.Y. and V.B.-F.; resources, G.R.R.-M., J.R.M. and V.B.-F.; data curation, G.R.R.-M. and V.B.-F.; writing—original draft preparation, G.R.R.-M., J.R.M. and V.B.-F.; writing—review and editing, J.R.M., I.Y. and V.B.-F.; visualization, G.R.R.-M., J.R.M., I.Y. and V.B.-F.; supervision, J.R.M. and V.B.-F.; project administration, J.R.M. and V.B.-F.; funding acquisition, J.R.M. and V.B.-F. All authors have read and agreed to the published version of the manuscript.

Funding: This research was funded by the Spanish Ministry of Economy, Industry and Competitiveness (SMEIC), State Research Agency (SRA) and the European Regional Development Fund (ERDF) under the project Semantic Knowledge Integration for Content-Based Spam Filtering, grant number TIN2017-84658-C2-1-R". This research was funded by FCT—Fundação para a Ciência e a Tecnologia, I.P., grant numbers UIDB/04466/2020 and UIDP/04466/2020.

Acknowledgments: SING group thanks CITI (Centro de Investigación, Transferencia e Innovación) from University of Vigo for hosting its IT infrastructure.

Conflicts of Interest: The authors declare no conflict of interest.

References

1. RDF Working Group RDF—Semantic Web Standards. Available online: https://www.w3.org/RDF/ (accessed on 26 March 2020).
2. RDF Working Group RDFS—Semantic Web Standards. Available online: https://www.w3.org/2001/sw/wiki/RDFS (accessed on 26 March 2020).
3. OWL Working Group OWL—Semantic Web Standards. Available online: https://www.w3.org/2001/sw/wiki/OWL (accessed on 26 March 2020).
4. Köhler, S.; Bauer, S.; Mungall, C.J.; Carletti, G.; Smith, C.L.; Schofield, P.; Gkoutos, G.V.; Robinson, P.N. Improving ontologies by automatic reasoning and evaluation of logical definitions. *BMC Bioinform.* **2011**, *12*, 418. [CrossRef] [PubMed]
5. Ali, N.; Hong, J.-E. Failure Detection and Prevention for Cyber-Physical Systems Using Ontology-Based Knowledge Base. *Computers* **2018**, *7*, 68. [CrossRef]
6. Munir, K.; Sheraz Anjum, M. The use of ontologies for effective knowledge modelling and information retrieval. *Appl. Comput. Inform.* **2018**, *14*, 116–126. [CrossRef]
7. Arch-int, N.; Arch-int, S. Semantic Ontology Mapping for Interoperability of Learning Resource Systems using a rule-based reasoning approach. *Expert Syst. Appl.* **2013**, *40*, 7428–7443. [CrossRef]
8. Zhang, J.; Zhao, W.; Xie, G.; Chen, H. Ontology- Based Knowledge Management System and Application. *Procedia Eng.* **2011**, *15*, 1021–1029. [CrossRef]
9. Uschold, M.; Gruninger, M. Ontologies: Principles, methods and applications. *Knowl. Eng. Rev.* **1996**, *11*, 93–136. [CrossRef]
10. Gruber, T.R. A translation approach to portable ontology specifications. *Knowl. Acquis.* **1993**, *5*, 199–220. [CrossRef]
11. Storey, V.C.; Chiang, R.; Chen, G.L. Ontology Creation: Extraction of Domain Knowledge from Web Documents. In Proceedings of the 2005 24th Conference on Conceptual Modelling, Klagenfurt, Austria, 24–28 October 2005; pp. 256–269.
12. Poveda-Villalón, M.; Gómez-Pérez, A.; Suárez-Figueroa, M.C. OOPS! (OntOlogy Pitfall Scanner!). *Int. J. Semant. Web Inf. Syst.* **2014**, *10*, 7–34. [CrossRef]
13. Poveda-Villalón, M. OOPS!—OntOlogy Pitfall Scanner!—Pitfall Catalogue. Available online: http://oops.linkeddata.es/catalogue.jsp (accessed on 26 March 2020).
14. Teymourlouie, M.; Zaeri, A.; Nematbakhsh, M.; Thimm, M.; Staab, S. Detecting hidden errors in an ontology using contextual knowledge. *Expert Syst. Appl.* **2018**, *95*, 312–323. [CrossRef]
15. Duque-Ramos, A.; Fernández-Breis, J.T.; Iniesta, M.; Dumontier, M.; Egaña Aranguren, M.; Schulz, S.; Aussenac-Gilles, N.; Stevens, R. Evaluation of the OQuaRE framework for ontology quality. *Expert Syst. Appl.* **2013**, *40*, 2696–2703. [CrossRef]
16. Bøegh, J. A New Standard for Quality Requirements. *IEEE Softw.* **2008**, *25*, 57–63. [CrossRef]
17. Bachir Bouiadjra, A.; Benslimane, S.-M. FOEval: Full ontology evaluation. In Proceedings of the 2011 7th International Conference on Natural Language Processing and Knowledge Engineering, Tokushima, Japan, 27–29 November 2011; IEEE: Piscataway, NJ, USA; pp. 464–468.

18. Tartir, S.; Arpinar, I.B. Ontology Evaluation and Ranking using OntoQA. In Proceedings of the International Conference on Semantic Computing (ICSC) 2007, Irvine, CA, USA, 17–19 September 2007; IEEE: Piscataway, NJ, USA; pp. 185–192.
19. Guarino, N.; Welty, C.A. An Overview of OntoClean. In *Handbook on Ontologies*; Springer: Berlin/Heidelberg, Germany, 2009; pp. 201–220.
20. International Organization for Standardization Systems and Software Engineering—Systems and Software Quality Requirements and Evaluation (SQuaRE)—Guide to SQuaRE 2014. Available online: https://www.iso.org/standard/64764.html (accessed on 26 March 2020).
21. Brank, J.; Grobelnik, M.; Mladenić, D. A Survey of Ontology Evaluation Techniques. In Procroceedings of the 8th International Multi-Conference Information Society, Ljubljana, Slovenia, 17 October 2005; pp. 166–169.
22. Tufano, M.; Palomba, F.; Bavota, G.; Oliveto, R.; Di Penta, M.; De Lucia, A.; Poshyvanyk, D. When and Why Your Code Starts to Smell Bad. In Proceedings of the 2015 IEEE/ACM 37th IEEE International Conference on Software Engineering, Florence, Italy, 16–24 May 2015; IEEE: Piscataway, NJ, USA; pp. 403–414.
23. Haldar, R.; Mukhopadhyay, D. Levenshtein Distance Technique in Dictionary Lookup Methods: An Improved Approach. *arXiv* **2011**, arXiv:1101.1232.
24. Poveda, M.; Delgado García, M.Á. OOPS!—OntOtology Pitfall Scanner! RESTFul Web Service 2013. Available online: http://oops.linkeddata.es/webservice.html (accessed on 26 March 2020).
25. Martin, R.C. *Agile Software Development, Principles, Patterns, and Practices*; Prentice Hall: Upper Saddle River, NJ, USA, 2003; ISBN 978-0135974445.
26. JSR-314 (JSF 2.0) Expert Group JavaServer Faces.org 2004. Available online: https://jcp.org/en/jsr/detail?id=314 (accessed on 26 March 2020).
27. GrayGrids Inc. Gentelella—Free Bootstrap Admin Template 2019. Available online: https://graygrids.com/templates/gentelella-free-bootstrap-admin-template/ (accessed on 26 March 2020).
28. Grove, R.F.; Ozkan, E. THE MVC-WEB DESIGN PATTERN. In Proceedings of the 7th International Conference on Web Information Systems and Technologies, SciTePress—Science and and Technology Publications, Setúbal (Portugal), Noordwijkerhout, The Netherlands, 6–9 May 2011; pp. 127–130.
29. Baeldung SRL The DAO Pattern in Java 2020. Available online: https://www.baeldung.com/java-dao-pattern (accessed on 26 March 2020).
30. Edwin, N.M. Software Frameworks, Architectural and Design Patterns. *J. Softw. Eng. Appl.* **2014**, *07*, 670–678. [CrossRef]
31. Horridge, M.; Bechhofer, S. The OWL API: A Java API for OWL Ontologies. *Semant. Web* **2011**, *2*, 11–21. [CrossRef]

© 2020 by the authors. Licensee MDPI, Basel, Switzerland. This article is an open access article distributed under the terms and conditions of the Creative Commons Attribution (CC BY) license (http://creativecommons.org/licenses/by/4.0/).

Article

A Domain-Independent Classification Model for Sentiment Analysis Using Neural Models

Nour Jnoub [1,*], Fadi Al Machot [2] and Wolfgang Klas [1]

1. Faculty of Computer Science, University of Vienna, 1040 Vienna, Austria; wolfgang.klas@univie.ac.at
2. Research Center Borstel—Leibniz Lung Center, 23845 Borstel, Germany; falmachot@fz-Borstel.de
* Correspondence: nour.jnoub@univie.ac.at

Received: 31 July 2020; Accepted: 28 August 2020; Published: 8 September 2020

Abstract: Most people nowadays depend on the Web as a primary source of information. Statistical studies show that young people obtain information mainly from Facebook, Twitter, and other social media platforms. By relying on these data, people may risk drawing the incorrect conclusions when reading the news or planning to buy a product. Therefore, systems that can detect and classify sentiments and assist users in finding the correct information on the Web is highly needed in order to prevent Web surfers from being easily deceived. This paper proposes an intensive study regarding domain-independent classification models for sentiment analysis that should be trained only once. The study consists of two phases: the first phase is based on a deep learning model which is training a neural network model once after extracting robust features and saving the model and its parameters. The second phase is based on applying the trained model on a totally new dataset, aiming at correctly classifying reviews as positive or negative. The proposed model is trained on the IMDb dataset and then tested on three different datasets: IMDb dataset, Movie Reviews dataset, and our own dataset collected from Amazon reviews that rate users' opinions regarding Apple products. The work shows high performance using different evaluation metrics compared to the stat-of-the-art results.

Keywords: sentiment analysis; natural language processing; deep learning

1. Introduction

Sentiment analysis is the task of recognizing positive and negative opinions of users regarding different purposes, e.g., users' opinions about movies, products, music albums, and many other fields. To provide a better definition, the sentiment is referred to as a judgement, opinion, attitude, or emotional state prompted by feeling. Sentiment analysis is an automated process in which, by using the natural language processing (NLP), the subjective information is computationally identified, analyzed, and classified into positive, negative, or neutral to specify the sentiment of that text which is the result of its author's attitude [1]. There are different types of sentiment analysis, the most popular types are classified and described in the following:

1. Grained Sentiment Analysis: The results in this type are more than binary classification results where two labels (positive, negative) are presented. It is achieved in fine-grained granularity varying from strong negative, weakly negative, neutral, weakly positive to strong positive based on the determined polarity, mainly used when the polarity precision is highly important and binary results like negative or positive could not be useful and may provide incorrect classifications [2].
2. Emotion detection: It classifies different emotions in the text such as fear, anger, sadness, joy, disgust, etc. Sophisticated machine learning algorithms [3] are used to detect emotions for different goals.

3. Aspect-based Sentiment Analysis: The results in this type are achieved after splitting the text into different aspects and then assign each aspect a corresponding sentiment. For instance, the result of aspect-based sentiment analysis on a special product's review "It is so easy to use but Insanely Expensive" would be (a) Ease of use: positive and (b) Price: negative due to the nature of this type, it is mostly utilized in customer-centric businesses to have a deeper understanding of customer's requirements [4].

The sentiment analysis field has many applications. For example, in businesses and organizations, they need to find consumer or public opinions regarding their products and services. Individual consumers may also need to know the evaluation of other users of a product before purchasing it. Moreover, they might be interested in others' opinions concerning political candidates before making a voting decision in a political election. Furthermore, nowadays data are published enormously and freely on the Web, but with no data quality assurance, it is left to the readers to decide whether they believe it or not. This results in high demand for advanced fact checking techniques and applications that contribute to the assurance of data quality. In particular, users surfing the Web are more often inflicted with harm/damage by inconsistent information. In addition, designing and developing such fact checking systems need robust models of sentiment analysis. This task for fact checking detection can be fulfilled when fact checking systems are provided by a general or universal model that can be trained once and then applied to other reviews. Surely, this model should show high performance to increase the accuracy of such fact checking systems.

Hussein in [5] discussed the importance and effects of the challenges in sentiment analysis is the domain-dependence. Moreover, the author concluded that the nature of the topic and the review structure determine the suitable challenges for the evaluation of sentiment reviews. Hence, building a generalized model is a challenge that should be considered by researchers in this research field.

This work focuses on providing a generalized model for sentiment analysis. It has two main contributions: (a) it shows that convolutional neural networks (CNN) combined with our review to vector algorithm can lead to design models that can be trained once and work well using other types of data that might even be related to a different domain and (b) it shows high performance using different precision metrics compared to other approaches from the state of the art that use same datasets for evaluation. We believe that this is one of the few works that address the generalization capabilities of deep models w.r.t. domain-Independence.

The remainder of this paper is organized as follows: Section 2 outlines a set of related works. In Section 3, we present the proposed approach. Section 4 lists datasets that are used for evaluation purposes. In Section 5, we cover experimental results. Section 6 illustrates a detailed discussion containing the major contribution of the paper. Section 7 concludes the paper and gives an overview of future work.

2. Related Works

Although linguistics and natural language processing (NLP) have a long history of research, few works were published concerning sentiments before the year 2000 [6]. After 2000, the field has attracted the attention of researchers and many research groups to work on.

To provide an example, [7] studies the prediction of every review for being negative or positive in the aspect-oriented opinion in the opinion mining domain at the sentence level. The authors of this work propose groups of selected models based on conditional random fields (CRFs) with an added multi-label presentation that not only models the opinion in a review, but also models set of opinions in a single review. In [8], authors suggest a sentiment analysis system that is able to identify and relate the sentiment to every rated product or item in the reviews. They present a probabilistic model to investigate the structure of each review and to which cluster each of them is related to, where it represents a specific sentiment.

In [9], the researchers offer a flexible automated classification system that uses supervised machine learning techniques using Markov Logic for sentiment classification on a sub sentence level and incorporates polarity differentiations from different origins.

Furthermore, in [10], enhanced latent aspect rating analysis model is presented. This model does not require predefined keywords that are associated with specific aspects. This work investigates the reviews in order to define the topical aspects, the ratings of the individual aspect and assigning weights that differentiate depending on the aspects from a reviewer point of view. [11] proposes a simple hierarchical clustering approach (unsupervised model) for product aspects extraction, clustering, and also defining the relations between aspects (relevant and irrelevant). In [12], the authors introduce a novel supervised approach for joint topic aspects for choosing specific reviews that are considered to be helpful among a set of reviews.

Moreover, in [13], an employee dataset is created and a novel ensemble model for sentiment analysis is proposed on aspects level. In [14], a sentiment analysis is conducted on movie reviews. New features are extracted that have influence on determining the polarity scores of the opinion more accurately. Natural language processing approaches are applied using the impact of the unique extracted features. In [15], supervised and semi-supervised approaches are investigated for text classification.

Additionally, deep learning is also used for sentiment analysis. Authors of convolutional neural networks for sentence classification use CNN to classify users' reviews for movies. Others, as in [15], use bidirectional long-short term memory models which is applied to the IMDb dataset.

Table 1 shows a summary of the state-of-the-art approaches for sentiment analysis. More information regarding the performance of different approaches can be found in Section 6.

Table 1. A summary of the state-of-the-art approaches for sentiment analysis.

Paper	Dataset	Labels	Approach
[7]	Hotel Reviews	Multi-labels	Supervised machine learning techniques using conditional random fields models for aspect detection sentiment analyzing.
[8]	Multiple datasets (Restaurant reviews, medical descriptions, Yelp)	Two labels	Unsupervised machine learning technique using probabilistic topic modeling approaches for sentiment content clustering.
[9]	Product reviews	Two labels	Supervised machine learning techniques using Markov logic for sentiment classification.
[10]	Hotel Reviews and MP3 player product review from Amazon	5 star rating	Unsupervised machine learning techniques for Latent Aspect Rating Analysis Model.
[11]	Chinese product reviews	Two labels	A hierarchical clustering approach for product aspects extraction and clustering.
[12]	Companies employee reviews	Ratings	A novel supervised joint topic model approach to select helpful reviews among a set of reviews.
[13]	Different products reviews	Ratings	A novel hybrid approach to implement aspect-level sentiment analysis that assigns sentiment labels to the reviews.
[14]	IMDb	Two labels	N-grams followed by a random forest classifier.
[15]	IMDb	Two labels	Bidirectional LSTM.
[16]	IMDb	Two labels	Maximum entropy classification combined with support vector machines using unigrams and bigrams.
[17]	IMDb	Two labels	Lexical filtering.
[18]	IMDb	Two labels	Context-Free Grammars (CFGs).
[19]	Movie Review	Two labels	Convolutional Neural Networks (CNN).
[20]	Movie Review	Two labels	Novel machine learning frame-work based on recursive autoencoders.
[21]	Movie Review	Two labels	Multiple classifiers—a hybrid approach.

Based on the previous works, this research has started to be one of the highlights for scientific contributions because: (a) it has different applications for recommender systems and fact checking systems, and (b) it contains several challenging research problems that motivate researchers to work and improve their works on them.

3. Approach

In this section, we present the preprocessing, the review to vector algorithm and the design details of the proposed neural models for sentiment analysis, and then the evaluation metrics and the overall evaluation. We aim at training a neural model once using a batch of IMDb dataset and test it on other reviews' datasets to see how far the generalization is possible.

3.1. Review to Vector

Before features extraction, we removed the stop words from the given dataset, e.g., "the", "a", "an", and "in". Then, the next step includes removing punctuation. In this step, we extracted feature elements from a batch of IMDb dataset for positive and negative reviews. The batch size has been determined using grid search (see Section 5). We formulated a function which works like a dictionary where the keys are the words in the text and the values are the count associated with that word. The output is saved in *word_features*.

Algorithm 1 illustrates the procedure of converting reviews to vectors. It takes two inputs and returns the input vectors for all reviews saved in *all_features*. The output vectors will be fed later into our proposed neural models The input parameters are *word_features* which is the first 4900 words after calculating the frequency distribution of each word from both training data, mainly the positive and negative reviews. The number 4900 words have been selected after applying grid search using different lengths which give the highest performance. The second input parameter is the *reviews*. The summary of the algorithm is as follows: for each review in the reviews, the function *word_tokenize* splits the current review into sub-strings (words). After that, for each word in *word_features*, it should be checked whether that word is a word in the current review. If yes, 1 is added to the features list or 0 is added if it is not. Finally, the function returns *all_features*, which is a matrix.

The vectors of the review to vector algorithm (see Algorithm 1) are used for training different classification models (see Section 3.2).

3.2. Classification

3.2.1. Convolutional Neural Network (CNN)

To perform the sentiment classification task, we propose a neurocomputing-based approach. A CNN is a kind of feed-forward network structure that consists of multiple layers of convolutional filters followed by subsampling filters and ends with a fully connected classification layer. The classical LeNet-5CNN was first proposed by LeCun et al. [22], which is the basic model of different CNN applications for object detection, localization, and prediction. First, the output vectors of the review to vector Algorithm 1 are converted to matrices where the goal is to make the application of CNN model possible. As illustrated in Figure 1, the proposed CNN model has one convolutional layer, one subsampling layer, and an output layer.

The convolutional layers generate feature maps using five (2×2) filters followed by a Scaled Exponential Linear Units (SELU) [23] as an activation function. Additionally, in the subsampling layers, the generated feature maps are spatially dissembled. In our proposed model, the feature maps in layers are subsampled to a corresponding feature map of size 2×2 in the subsequent layer.

The final layer, which is a fully CNN model that performs the classification process, consists of three layers. The first layer is the input layer which has 6125 nodes and the second that has five nodes. Each SELU activation function.

The final layer is the softmax output layer. The result of the mentioned layers is a 2D representation of extracted features from input feature map(s) based on the input features for the reviews.

Algorithm 1

1: **Input:** *word_features, Reviews*
2:
3: **function** REVIEW_TO_VECTOR(Reviews)
4:
5:     *all_features* = [ ]
6:
7:     **for** review in reviews **do**
8:
9:         words = word_tokenize(review)
10:
11:         features =[ ]
12:
13:         **for** w in word_features **do**
14:
15:             **if** (w in words) **then**
16:
17:                 Features[w] = 1
18:
19:             **else**
20:
21:                 Features[w] = 0
22:
23:             **end if**
24:
25:         **end for**
26:
27:         all_features+=[Features]
28:
29:     **end for**
30:     **return** *all_features*
31: **end function**
32:

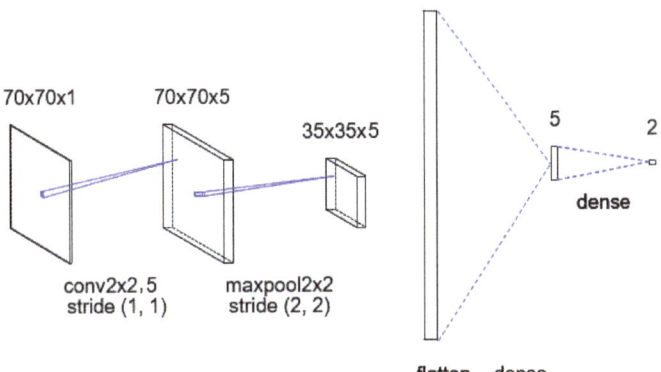

Figure 1. The proposed CNN model.

The proposed CNN consists of one convolutional layer and a max-pooling layer is because the small size of our input dimension does not require additional layers to extract features/patterns. The reason for using SELU is due to the fact that (a) SELUs performed better than Rectified Linear Units (RELUs), (b) SELUs offer self-normalization [23], and (c) they never lead to vanishing gradients problem. Since the dropout is a regularization technique to avoid over-fitting in neural networks based on preventing complex co-adaptations on training data [24], our dropout for each layer was 0.75, which is related to the fraction of the input units to drop.

The proposed CNN model has been trained on IMDb. Then, the model has been saved to be tested on other datasets. The length of the considered feature vectors is 4900 words that are converted to matrices of size (70 × 70).

The parameters of CNN are selected by using grid search from a scikit-learn library considering different settings. Table 2 shows parameters used for all the layers of the proposed CNN model.

Table 2. Parameters used for all the layers of the proposed CNN model.

Layer	Kernel, Units	Other Layers Parameters
Convolution	(2 × 2), 5	Activation = Selu, Strides = 1
Max Pooling	(2 × 2)	Strides = 2
Dropout	0.75	
Fully Connected		Units = 5, Activation = Selu
Softmax	-	NumbrOfClasses = 2

3.2.2. Shallow Neural Network (SNN)

To perform the sentiment classification task, we use a neural model [25,26]. First, the output vectors of the review to vector algorithm are fed into the neural model to the hidden layer which consists of three neurons and a hyperbolic activation function; then, the final layer is the output layer which consists of a softmax activation function, Adam optimizer [27], and a cross entropy loss function. The parameters are selected by using a grid search from scikit-learn library (https://scikit-learn.org, see Figure 2), where the optimizer is Adam and the loss function is the binary cross entropy.

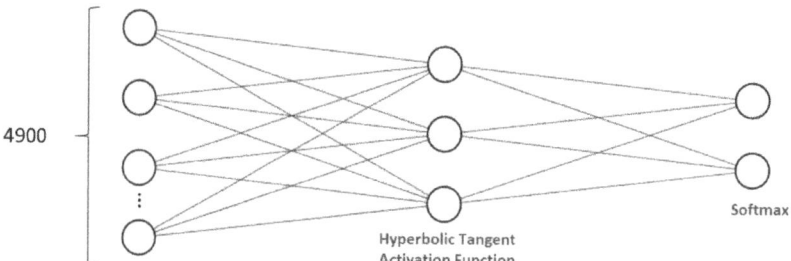

Figure 2. The proposed SNN model.

The proposed neural network model has been trained on a batch of IMDb datasets. Then, the model has been saved to be tested on other datasets. Table 3 shows parameters used for all the layers of the proposed CNN model.

Table 3. Parameters used for all the layers of the proposed SNN model.

Layer	Units	Other Layers' Parameters
Hidden layer	3	Activation = Hyperbolic tangent activation (tanh)
Output layer	2	Activation = softmax

3.2.3. Other Classifiers

Additionally, we examine several classifiers to compare the performance of the existing models and the proposed ones, particularly Support Vector Machines (SVM) [28], K–Nearest Neighbor (KNN) [29], Naive Bayes [30], and Random Forest [31]. In addition, selecting the previous classifiers has different advantages such as the objective of random forests that they consider a set of high-variance, low-bias decision trees, and the ability to convert them into a model that has both low variance and low bias. On the other hand, K-nearest neighbors is an algorithm which stores all the available cases and classifies new cases based on a similarity measure (e.g., distance functions). Therefore, KNN has been applied in statistical estimation and pattern recognition from the beginning of 1970s on as a non-parametric technique [29]. SVM are well-known in handling non linearly separable data based on their nonlinear kernel; e.g., SVM with a polynomial kernel (SVM (poly)) and the SVM with a radial basis kernel (SVM (rbf)). Therefore, we classify the reviews data using three types of SVMs; the standard linear SVM (SVM (linear)), SVM (poly), and SVM (rbf). Finally, we used a simple probabilistic model which is the Naive Bayes. The purpose of using such a probabilistic model is to show how it behaves w.r.t. different contexts.

Table 4 shows values of parameters for the proposed SNN, CNN, and all other classifiers.

Table 4. Values of parameters of proposed CNN, SNN, and other classifiers.

Model	Parameters
SVM (poly)	Degree of the polynomial kernel function = 3, $\gamma = \frac{1}{number of features}$
SVM (rbf)	$\gamma = \frac{1}{number of features}$
Random Forest	Number of estimators estimators =10 trees, criterion = Gini impurity, The minimum number of samples required to split an internal node = 2
Naive Bayes	Prior = probabilities of the classes
Proposed (CNN)	Loss = Softmax, optimizer = Adamax, batch_size =1000, epochs = 30
Proposed (SNN)	Loss = cross entropy, optimizer = Adam, batch_size =128, epochs = 40, lr = 0.001, $beta_1$ = 0.9, $beta_2$ = 0.999, epsilon = 0.01, decay = 0.0

3.3. Evaluation Metrics and Validation Concept

To evaluate the overall performance of the classifiers, we consider several performance metrics. In particular, we use precision, recall, f-measure, and accuracy, as in [32].

Equations (1)–(4) show mathematical expressions of the metrics accuracy, precision, recall, and f-measure, respectively, where TP, TN, FP, and FN refer respectively to "True Positives", "True Negatives", "False Positives", and "False Negatives", respectively:

$$Accuracy = \frac{TP + TN}{TP + FP + FN + TN} \quad (1)$$

$$Precision = \frac{TP}{TP + FP} \quad (2)$$

$$Recall = \frac{TP}{TP + FN} \quad (3)$$

$$F1 = \frac{2 \cdot precision \cdot recall}{precision + recall} \quad (4)$$

Regarding the evaluation scenarios, we consider two cases: the domain-dependent and domain–independent cases. Domain-dependent means training and testing have been performed for each dataset. Domain–independent means the training has been performed on a IMDb datasets of subjects and testing has been performed on a totally new datasets. The reason for training on IMDb is due to its large size and thus can support a better generalized model if the training has been preformed and regularized properly.

4. Datasets

4.1. IMDb Dataset

ACL-IMDb [33] dataset is a collection of reviews that are taken from Internet Movie Database (IMDb). The dataset size is 50 K and contains highly polar movie reviews annotated as positive or negative review, which makes it widely used for a binary classification tasks. The average length of a document in the training set is 25 k for training and 25 k for testing. The dataset also contains an additional bag of words formats and raw texts (http://ai.stanford.edu/~amaas/data/sentiment/).

4.2. Movie Reviews (MR)

Movie Reviews (MR) is a small sized dataset (https://www.cs.cornell.edu/people/pabo/movie-review-data/) [34] (5 k positive and 5 k negative reviews) that contains reviews in the form of labeled sentences, which can be specified as objective or subjective. Furthermore, the selected sentences have been gathered from IMDb and Rotten Tomatoes websites (https://www.rottentomatoes.com/), each selected sentence contains at least 10 words. The sentiments of these sentences have been classified as positive or negative.

4.3. Amazon Dataset (Amazon)

Reviews data from iPhone wireless earphones on Amazon were collected. Overall, we collected 480 negative reviews and 480 positive ones in order to use the data to check the overall performance of the proposed model. We annotated the data with 0 or 1 where every positive review is annotated or labeled by 1 and the negative reviews were annotated by 0.

5. Results

In this section, we want to demonstrate the performance of the proposed approach. The prototype is implemented in Python. In order to gain sufficient information and prove the applicability of our approach, the following libraries have been used: NLTK (https://www.nltk.org/) library for natural language processing, Keras (https://keras.io/) (Deep learning) and scikit-learn (https://scikit-learn.org/stable/) (machine learning), which is mainly used for testing the performance of the other classifiers. We applied 10-fold cross-validation for performance evaluation. The neural models have been trained on a GeForce GTX 1080-NVIDIA (https://www.nvidia.com/de-de/geforce/products/10series/geforce-gtx-1080/).

In order to conduct experimental results and check the performance of the proposed approach, we tested the algorithm using the extracted features based on three datasets, namely IMDb, Movie Reviews, and Amazon reviews.

To evaluate the overall performance of the classifiers, we consider several performance metrics. In particular, we use precision, recall, f1, and accuracy, as in [32].

Regarding the evaluation scenarios, we used the trained model in Section 3.2.

Tables 5–7 present the precision, the recall, and the f-measure using IMDb, Movie Reviews, and Amazon datasets, respectively.

Table 5. Performance metrics for IMDb, where SVM (poly): Support Vector Machine using a polynomial kernel, SVM (rbf): Support Vector Machine using a radial basis function kernel.

Classifier	Precision	Recall	F-Measure	Accuracy
Random Forest	0.73	0.73	0.73	0.73
Naive Bayes	0.64	0.59	0.56	0.59
SVM (poly)	0.24	0.29	0.33	0.49
SVM (rbf)	0.24	0.29	0.33	0.49
Proposed SNN	0.87	0.87	0.87	0.87
Proposed CNN	0.81	0.81	0.81	0.81

Table 6. Performance metrics for MR, where SVM (poly): Support Vector Machine using a polynomial kernel, SVM (rbf): Support Vector Machine using a radial basis function kernel.

Classifier	Precision	Recall	F-Measure	Accuracy
Random Forest	0.67	0.66	0.65	0.66
Naive Bayes	0.58	0.58	0.57	0.58
SVM (poly)	0.23	0.48	0.31	0.48
SVM (rbf)	0.75	0.61	0.55	0.48
Proposed SNN	0.82	0.82	0.82	0.82
Proposed CNN	0.75	0.75	0.75	0.75

Table 7. Performance metrics for Amazon reviews, where SVM (poly): Support Vector Machine using a polynomial kernel, SVM (rbf): Support Vector Machine using a radial basis function kernel.

Classifier	Precision	Recall	F-Measure	Accuracy
Random Forest	0.80	0.80	0.80	0.80
Naive Bayes	0.71	0.67	0.67	0.67
SVM (poly)	0.31	0.55	0.40	0.55
SVM (rbf)	0.31	0.55	0.40	0.55
Proposed SNN	0.77	0.76	0.74	0.74
Proposed CNN	0.67	0.67	0.67	0.68

In all tables, the proposed neural models show the highest performance compared to random forest which is hereby the next best classifier. However, the support vector machine using a radial basis function kernel also performs well for the IMDb dataset, but the Naive Bayes classifier performs much better using our own Amazon dataset.

Additionally, it is remarkable to realize that the proposed shallow neural network performs better than the proposed convolutional neural network model. However, random forest and our proposed neural models show a robust behavior regarding sentiment classification.

Moreover, it should be realized that some classifiers show high precision and low recall or vice versa where high precision relates to a low false positive rate, and high recall relates to a low false negative rate. This reflects the complexity of this classification task and shows the robust performance of the proposed neural models.

Furthermore, the trained neural models are applied on different datasets that are not related to each other (see Table 8). Despite of this fact, it still behaves well and, consequently, it can be extended for different applications in the research field of sentiment analysis.

Table 8. Performance metrics for Amazon reviews and MR reviews using the pretrained neural models on the IMDb dataset.

Classifier	Precision	Recall	F-Measure	Accuracy
SNN (Amazon)	0.66	0.65	0.64	0.64
CNN (Amazon)	0.65	0.64	0.64	0.64
SNN (MR)	0.82	0.82	0.82	0.82
CNN (MR)	0.80	0.80	0.80	0.80

Figures 3 and 4 show the 10-folds cross-validation results for the trained CNN and SNN models, respectively. In addition, they show the mean accuracy and the standard deviation for each fold. We can observe a reasonable symmetric distribution and that the mean captures the central tendency well. The cross-validation results belong to the pre-trained model which has been applied to calculate the results in Table 8.

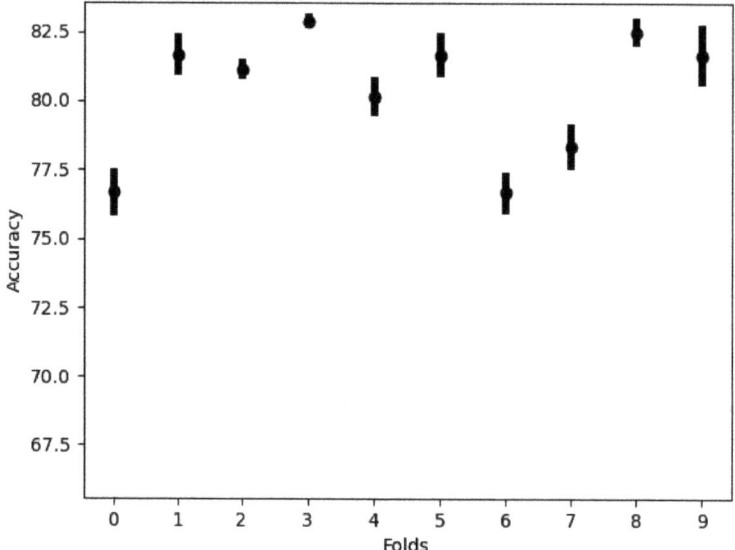

Figure 3. The cross-validation results for the trained CNN model using IMDb model, which has been used on MR and Amazon datasets.

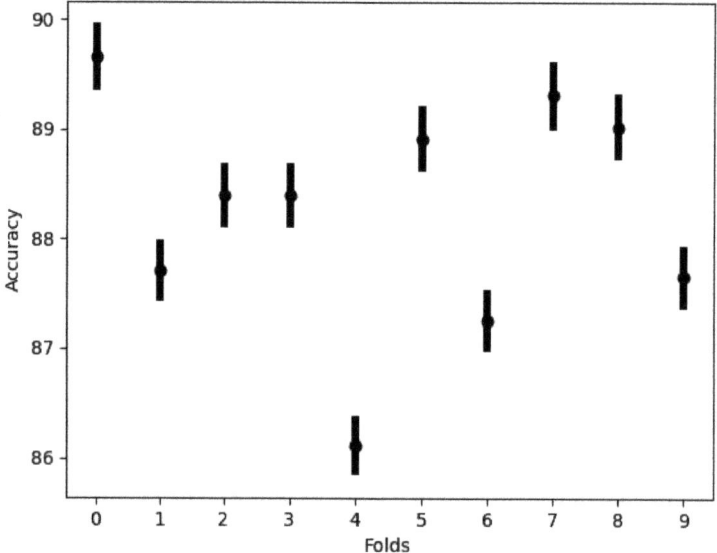

Figure 4. The 10-fold cross-validation results for the trained SNN model using the IMDb model, which has been used on the MR and Amazon datasets.

6. Discussion

Based on our results, we could demonstrate the following points:

1. Summarizing the final opinion in some words might lead to the problem that the extracted features did not take that sentence as a feature of interest. For example, a reviewer might have a

positive opinion about acting and the overall story of a movie, but he was not satisfied by the music in certain scenes.
2. Sentiments can be expressed in different forms that might be even indirect expressions. Therefore, they require common sense reasoning techniques to be classified. In addition, it is challenging to analyze sentiments with complex structures of sentences, especially when negations do exist.
3. Some reviewers may use expressions that have negative connotations, but at the end of the review, they summarize their overall opinion clearly. Consequently, this makes the classification a tough task.
4. Feature engineering suffers from overcoming the previous problems.
5. Sentiment analysis requires analyzing large units of individual words to capture the context in which those words appear.
6. Table 8 shows that SNN shows a better generalization performance using the MR dataset compared to CNN. The results of other approaches are listed in Tables 9 and 10 for movie review data and IMDb, respectively. Some of the proposed approaches perform better; however, they do not consider the domain-independent sentiment classification. It means that the results are obtained for training and testing on the same dataset.

Table 9. A summary of state-of-the-art performance metrics for MR, where DCNN: Dynamic Convolutional Neural Network, SVM: Support Vector Machine.

Paper	Classifier Used	Accuracy
[19]	CNN	0.81
[20]	Autoencoders	0.77
[35]	SVM	0.77
[36]	DCNN	0.86

Table 10. A summary of the state-of-the-art precision metrics for IMDb, where SVM: Support Vector Machine.

Paper	Classifier Used	Accuracy
[16]	SVM	0.82
[17]	Markov Model	0.80
[14]	Random Forest	0.88
[18]	statistical approach	0.87

We can observe that this work is:

1. Able to classify binary reviews very well, especially, domain-independent reviews.
2. The first building block toward the generalization of sentiment classification where a model can be trained once and tested on totally new datasets that even may come from different contexts.
3. It inherits the advantages of neural models which is nowadays able to classify hundreds of objects using a pre-trained model.

This is due to the fact that CNN can overcome many challenges of sentiment analysis that have been highlighted previously. For example, words in a specific region are more likely to be related than words far away. Thus, CNN can automatically and adaptively extract spatial hierarchies of features out of written reviews that may capture different writing styles of users.

7. Conclusions

In this work, we proposed a sentiment analysis generalized approach that is able to classify the sentiments of different datasets robustly. Additionally, the proposed approach showed promising results in the context of domain-independent sentiment analysis. This is due to the fact that neural models can extract robust features when reviews are converted to proper input vectors using our proposed review for vector algorithms. Furthermore, it shows a high performance regarding generalization. The proposed model has been trained once and tested on three different datasets from different domains. The model could perform very well compared to other works that used the same datasets and showed a generalization capability for sentiment classification w.r.t. different domains. Furthermore, the paper covered a wide range of sentiment analysis approaches from the state of the art and compared the results obtained to the performance of the proposed neural models.

Additionally, in our future work, we will integrate the implemented version of the algorithm into different browsers and platforms aiming at using the power of this approach for fact checking purposes.

Author Contributions: Conceptualization: N.J.; Methodology: N.J. and F.A.M.; Supervision: F.A.M. and W.K.; Formal analysis: N.J., F.A.M., and W.K. All authors have read and agreed to the published version of the manuscript.

Funding: This research received no external funding

Conflicts of Interest: The authors declare no conflict of interest. The authors ensure that there are no personal circumstances, interest, or sponsors that may be perceived as inappropriately influencing the representation or interpretation of reported research results.

References

1. Cambria, E.; Das, D.; Bandyopadhyay, S.; Feraco, A. *A Practical Guide to Sentiment Analysis*; Springer: Berlin/Heidelberg, Germany, 2017.
2. Wang, Z.; Chong, C.S.; Lan, L.; Yang, Y.; Ho, S.B.; Tong, J.C. Fine-grained sentiment analysis of social media with emotion sensing. In Proceedings of the 2016 Future Technologies Conference (FTC), San Francisco, CA, USA, 6–7 December 2016; pp. 1361–1364.
3. Suhasini, M.; Srinivasu, B. Emotion Detection Framework for Twitter Data Using Supervised Classifiers. In *Data Engineering and Communication Technology*; Springer: Berlin/Heidelberg, Germany, 2020; pp. 565–576.
4. Zainuddin, N.; Selamat, A.; Ibrahim, R. Discovering Hate Sentiment within Twitter Data through Aspect-Based Sentiment Analysis. In *Journal of Physics: Conference Series*; IOP Publishing: Bristol, UK, 2020; Volume 1447, p. 012056.
5. Hussein, D.M.E.D.M. A survey on sentiment analysis challenges. *J. King Saud Univ. Eng. Sci.* **2018**, *30*, 330–338. [CrossRef]
6. Liu, B. Sentiment analysis and opinion mining. *Synth. Lect. Hum. Lang. Technol.* **2012**, *5*, 1–167. [CrossRef]
7. Marcheggiani, D.; Täckström, O.; Esuli, A.; Sebastiani, F. Hierarchical multi-label conditional random fields for aspect-oriented opinion mining. In *European Conference on Information Retrieval*; Springer: Berlin/Heidelberg, Germany, 2014; pp. 273–285.
8. Sauper, C.; Barzilay, R. Automatic aggregation by joint modeling of aspects and values. *J. Artif. Intell. Res.* **2013**, *46*, 89–127. [CrossRef]
9. Zirn, C.; Niepert, M.; Stuckenschmidt, H.; Strube, M. Fine-grained sentiment analysis with structural features. In Proceedings of the 5th International Joint Conference on Natural Language Processing, Chiang Mai, Thailand, 8–13 November 2011; pp. 336–344.
10. Wang, H.; Lu, Y.; Zhai, C. Latent aspect rating analysis without aspect keyword supervision. In *Proceedings of the 17th ACM SIGKDD International Conference on Knowledge Discovery and Data Mining*; ACM: New York, NY, USA, 2011; pp. 618–626.
11. Zhao, Y.; Qin, B.; Liu, T. Clustering product aspects using two effective aspect relations for opinion mining. In *Chinese Computational Linguistics and Natural Language Processing Based on Naturally Annotated Big Data*; Springer: Berlin/Heidelberg, Germany, 2014; pp. 120–130.

12. Hai, Z.; Cong, G.; Chang, K.; Liu, W.; Cheng, P. Coarse-to-fine review selection via supervised joint aspect and sentiment model. In *Proceedings of the 37th International ACM SIGIR Conference on Research & Development in Information Retrieval*; ACM: Berlin/Heidelberg, Germany, 2014; pp. 617–626.
13. Bajpai, R.; Hazarika, D.; Singh, K.; Gorantla, S.; Cambria, E.; Zimmerman, R. Aspect-Sentiment Embeddings for Company Profiling and Employee Opinion Mining. *arXiv* **2019**, arXiv:1902.08342.
14. Sahu, T.P.; Ahuja, S. Sentiment analysis of movie reviews: A study on feature selection & classification algorithms. In Proceedings of the 2016 International Conference on Microelectronics, Computing and Communications (MicroCom), Durgapur, India, 23–25 January 2016; pp. 1–6.
15. Sachan, D.S.; Zaheer, M.; Salakhutdinov, R. Revisiting LSTM Networks for Semi-Supervised Text Classification via Mixed Objective Function. *Proc. AAAI Conf. Artif. Intell.* **2019**, 6940–6948. [CrossRef]
16. Pang, B.; Lee, L.; Vaithyanathan, S. Thumbs Up? Sentiment Classification Using Machine Learning Techniques. In *Proceedings of the ACL-02 Conference on Empirical Methods in Natural Language Processing—Volume 10 (EMNLP '02)*; Association for Computational Linguistics: Stroudsburg, PA, USA, 2002; pp. 79–86. [CrossRef]
17. Salvetti, F.; Lewis, S.; Reichenbach, C. Automatic Opinion Polarity Classification of Movie Reviews. *Colo. Res. Linguist.* **2004**, *17*. [CrossRef]
18. Dong, L.; Wei, F.; Liu, S.; Zhou, M.; Xu, K. A statistical parsing framework for sentiment classification. *Comput. Linguist.* **2015**, *41*, 293–336. [CrossRef]
19. Kim, Y. Convolutional neural networks for sentence classification. *arXiv* **2014**, arXiv:1408.5882.
20. Socher, R.; Pennington, J.; Huang, E.H.; Ng, A.Y.; Manning, C.D. Semi-supervised recursive autoencoders for predicting sentiment distributions. In *Proceedings of the Conference on Empirical Methods in Natural Language Processing*; Association for Computational Linguistics: Stroudsburg, PA, USA, 2011; pp. 151–161.
21. Tsutsumi, K.; Shimada, K.; Endo, T. Movie review classification based on a multiple classifier. In Proceedings of the 21st Pacific Asia Conference on Language, Information and Computation, Seoul, Korea, 1–3 November 2007; pp. 481–488.
22. LeCun, Y.; Bengio, Y. Convolutional networks for images, speech, and time series. *Handb. Brain Theory Neural Netw.* **1995**, *3361*, 1995.
23. Klambauer, G.; Unterthiner, T.; Mayr, A.; Hochreiter, S. Self-normalizing neural networks. In *Advances in Neural Information Processing Systems*; Curran Associates Inc: Red Hook, NY, USA, 2017; pp. 971–980.
24. Hinton, G.E.; Srivastava, N.; Krizhevsky, A.; Sutskever, I.; Salakhutdinov, R.R. Improving neural networks by preventing co-adaptation of feature detectors. *arXiv* **2012**, arXiv:1207.0580.
25. Hornik, K.; Stinchcombe, M.; White, H. Multilayer feedforward networks are universal approximators. *Neural Netw.* **1989**, *2*, 359–366. [CrossRef]
26. Funahashi, K.I. On the approximate realization of continuous mappings by neural networks. *Neural Netw.* **1989**, *2*, 183–192. [CrossRef]
27. Kingma, D.P.; Ba, J. Adam: A method for stochastic optimization. *arXiv* **2014**, arXiv:1412.6980.
28. Cortes, C.; Vapnik, V. Support-vector networks. *Mach. Learn.* **1995**, *20*, 273–297. [CrossRef]
29. Altman, N.S. An introduction to kernel and nearest-neighbor nonparametric regression. *Am. Stat.* **1992**, *46*, 175–185.
30. Webb, G.I. Naïve Bayes. In *Encyclopedia of Machine Learning and Data Mining*; Springer: Berlin/Heidelberg, Germany, 2017; pp. 895–896.
31. Breiman, L. Random forests. *Mach. Learn.* **2001**, *45*, 5–32. [CrossRef]
32. Powers, D.M. Evaluation: From precision, recall and F-measure to ROC, informedness, markedness & correlation. *J. Mach. Learn. Technol.* **2011**, *2*, 37–63. [CrossRef]
33. Maas, A.L.; Daly, R.E.; Pham, P.T.; Huang, D.; Ng, A.Y.; Potts, C. Learning word vectors for sentiment analysis. In *Proceedings of the 49th Annual Meeting of the Association for Computational Linguistics: Human Language Technologies—Volume 1*; Association for Computational Linguistics: Portland, OR, USA, 2011; pp. 142–150.
34. Pang, B.; Lee, L. A Sentimental Education: Sentiment Analysis Using Subjectivity Summarization Based on Minimum Cuts. *arXiv* **2004**, arXiv:cs/0409058.

35. Yessenalina, A.; Yue, Y.; Cardie, C. Multi-level structured models for document-level sentiment classification. In *Proceedings of the 2010 Conference on Empirical Methods in Natural Language Processing*; Association for Computational Linguistics: Stroudsburg, PA, USA, 2010; pp. 1046–1056.
36. Kalchbrenner, N.; Grefenstette, E.; Blunsom, P. A convolutional neural network for modelling sentences. *arXiv* **2014**, arXiv:1404.2188.

© 2020 by the authors. Licensee MDPI, Basel, Switzerland. This article is an open access article distributed under the terms and conditions of the Creative Commons Attribution (CC BY) license (http://creativecommons.org/licenses/by/4.0/).

Article

Zero-Shot Learning for Cross-Lingual News Sentiment Classification

Andraž Pelicon [1,2,*], Marko Pranjić [2,3], Dragana Miljković [1], Blaž Škrlj [1,2] and Senja Pollak [1,*]

1 Jožef Stefan Institute, 1000 Ljubljana, Slovenia; dragana.miljkovic@ijs.si (D.M.); blaz.skrlj@ijs.si (B.Š.)
2 Jožef Stefan International Postgraduate School, 1000 Ljubljana, Slovenia; marko.pranjic@styria.ai
3 Trikoder d.o.o., 10010 Zagreb, Croatia
* Correspondence: Andraz.Pelicon@ijs.si (A.P.); senja.pollak@ijs.si (S.P.)

Received: 31 July 2020; Accepted: 25 August 2020; Published: 29 August 2020

Abstract: In this paper, we address the task of zero-shot cross-lingual news sentiment classification. Given the annotated dataset of positive, neutral, and negative news in Slovene, the aim is to develop a news classification system that assigns the sentiment category not only to Slovene news, but to news in another language without any training data required. Our system is based on the multilingual BERT model, while we test different approaches for handling long documents and propose a novel technique for sentiment enrichment of the BERT model as an intermediate training step. With the proposed approach, we achieve state-of-the-art performance on the sentiment analysis task on Slovenian news. We evaluate the zero-shot cross-lingual capabilities of our system on a novel news sentiment test set in Croatian. The results show that the cross-lingual approach also largely outperforms the majority classifier, as well as all settings without sentiment enrichment in pre-training.

Keywords: sentiment analysis; zero-shot learning; news analysis; cross-lingual classification; multilingual transformers

1. Introduction

Sentiment analysis is one of the most popular applications of natural language processing (NLP) and has found many areas of applications in customers' product reviews, survey textual responses, social media, etc. It analyzes users' opinions on various topics, such as politics, health, education, etc. In sentiment analysis, the goal is to analyze the author's sentiments, attitudes, emotions, and opinions [1]. Traditionally, such analysis was performed towards a specific entity that appears in the text [2]. A less researched, but nevertheless prominent field of research in sentiment analysis is to shift the focus from analyzing sentiment towards a specific target to analyzing the intrinsic mood of the text itself. Several works try to model feelings (positive, negative, or neutral) that readers feel while reading a certain piece of text, especially news [3,4]. In Van de Kauter et al. [5], the authors claimed that the news production directly affects the stock market as the prevalence of positive news boosts its growth and the prevalence of negative news impedes it. In the context of news media analytics, the sentiment of news articles has been used also as an important feature in identifying fake news [6] and biases in the media [7]. Rambaccussing and Kwiatkowski [8] explored the change in sentiment of news articles from major U.K. newspapers with respect to current economic conditions. Bowden et al. [9] took a step further and tried to improve the forecasting of three economic variables, inflation, output growth, and unemployment, via sentiment modeling. They concluded that, using sentiment analysis, out of the three variables observed, the forecasting can be effectively improved for unemployment.

In the last year, the use of pre-trained Transformer models has become standard practice in modeling text classification tasks. Among the first such models was the BERT (Bidirectional Encoder Representations from Transformers) model developed by [10], which achieved state-of-the-art performance on several benchmark NLP tasks, as well as in real-world applications, e.g., Google search engine [11] and chatbots [12]. The initial model was however pre-trained only on English corpora and could consequently be used only for modeling textual data in the English language. A new version of the BERT model, titled multilingual BERT or mBERT, soon followed. This model was pre-trained on unlabeled data in 104 languages with the largest Wikipedias using a joint vocabulary. Several studies noted the ability of the mBERT model to work well in multilingual and cross-lingual contexts even though it was trained without an explicit cross-lingual objective and with no aligned data [13,14].

In the context of sentiment analysis of news articles, we however identified two potential drawbacks of the mBERT model. The first is that the model accepts the inputs of a fixed length where the length is determined by the length of the context window, i.e., the maximum length of the input sequence during the pre-training phase. Since the training becomes computationally more expensive with the size of the context window, several standard implementations of the mBERT model have the context window set to a maximum length [15]. The standard solution for longer documents is therefore to cut the inputs to the length of the context window [16]. This method however potentially causes the loss of important information that could be present in the later parts of the document. Another potential drawback is that the input representations produced by the Transformer models may encode only a small amount of sentiment information. The pre-training objectives, namely the masked language modeling and next sentence prediction, are designed to focus on encoding general syntactic and certain semantic features of a language. The only explicit sentiment signal the models get is during the fine-tuning phase, when the models are generally trained on a much smaller amount of data.

The paper presents the advances achieved in the scope of the European project H2020 EMBEDDIA (www.embeddia.eu, duration 2019–2021), which focuses on the development of cross-lingual techniques to transfer natural language processing tools to less-resourced European languages with applications to the news media industry. In this paper, we present our approach to cross-lingual news sentiment analysis, where given an available sentiment-annotated dataset of news in Slovene [3], we propose a news sentiment classification model for other languages. In this paper, we focus on Croatian, where the news dataset is provided by 24sata, one of the leading portals in Croatia, and was labeled with the same sentiment annotation scheme as the Slovenian dataset in order to allow comparison in a zero-shot learning setting where no annotations in the target language are expected.

We identify three main contributions of this paper focusing mainly on the cross-lingual zero-shot learning setting. First, we gathered a sentiment-annotated corpus of Croatian news, where the annotation guidelines follow the annotation scheme of the Slovenian sentiment-annotated news dataset [3], therefore enabling cross-lingual zero-shot learning sentiment evaluation. Second, we tested several document representation techniques to overcome one of the shortcomings of the BERT models of not being capable of efficiently processing longer text documents. Last, but not least, we propose a novel intermediate training step to directly enrich the BERT model with sentiment information in order to produce input representations of better quality for sentiment classification tasks. These representations were then tested both in a monolingual setting, as well as in the zero-shot cross-lingual setting, where the model was tested on a different language without any additional target language training. Our experiments show that these representations improve the results in the monolingual setting and achieve a substantially better result than the majority baseline classifier in the cross-lingual setting.

The article is structured as follows. In Section 2, we first present the related work upon which our study builds. In Section 3, we present two datasets of news articles that are manually labeled in terms of sentiment: the existing Slovenian dataset [3] and the newly constructed Croatian test set. Section 4, where we present the methodology, is followed by Section 5, explaining the experimental setup, with the training regime applied and the evaluation method. Section 6 presents the results of the experiments and discusses their impact, which is followed by qualitative inspection of the models in Section 7. Section 9 presents the conclusions of this work and ideas for future research.

2. Related Work

Traditionally, sentiment analysis was modeled through the use of classical machine learning methods, where especially learners such as support vector machines combined with the TF-IDF text representations proved to be widely successful [17,18]. Lately, however, deep neural networks have become more frequent for sentiment analysis and started outperforming the classical approaches. Mansar et al. [19] used convolutional neural networks (CNN), a variant of neural networks, which are heavily utilized for computer vision. With the help of the convolutional layer, they acquired word-level representations of individual news articles from the learning corpus and combined them with the sentiment score of the individual article, which was obtained with a simple, rule-based model. The attributes were used as input to the fully connected NN. Their model showed the best performance on the SemEval2017 challenge (Task 5, Subtask 2). Moore and Rayson [20] used two models for analyzing sentiment in financial news titles, a support vector machine and a bidirectional LSTM (Long-Short Term Memory) neural network. They reported the LSTM neural network to outperform the SVM modelsby 4–6%.

Several recent works also explored the problem of cross-lingual sentiment analysis. One of the earlier studies [21] employed machine translation to translate a large corpus of sentiment-annotated English training data for the development of a Chinese sentiment classifier. These translated data were then used in addition to the original Chinese data to train an SVM-based classifier. While machine translation can be a good solution for cross-lingual modeling, a quality machine translation system for a particular language pair may not exist or may be expensive to train. Furthermore, machine learning systems struggle with distant language pairs [22]. Zhou et al. [23] developed a cross-lingual English-Chinese attention-based neural architecture for sentiment classification. It utilizes a two-level hierarchical attention mechanism. The first layer of the model encodes each sentence separately by finding the most informative words. Then, the second layer produces the final document representation from lower-level sentence representations. The downside of their work is that the model uses aligned data in two languages, which are not readily available for every language pair. Ref. [24] proposed a representation learning method that utilizes emojis as an instrument to learn language-independent sentiment-aware text representations. The approach is however limited to text types where emojis regularly appear. The cross-lingual sentiment classification approaches presented above also do not address news analysis, but focus on shorter social media texts, where there is no need for adaptation to longer text sequences and they do not leverage cross-lingual Transformer models, such as mBERT, that have been recently introduced as the state-of-the-art for cross-lingual classification tasks. In this paper, we will bridge this gap by proposing a novel approach where we not only leverage standard transfer learning where pretrained language models are fine-tuned for specific classification tasks (in the same or another language), but introduce a novel intermediate training step for sentiment enrichment of BERT models.

The need for labeled data is seen as one of the main obstacles in developing robust cross-lingual systems for natural language processing, especially for low-resource languages. For this reason, research has been focused lately on models that can work in a zero-shot setting, i.e., without being explicitly trained on data from the target language or domain. This training paradigm has been utilized with great effect for several popular NLP problems, such as cross-lingual document retrieval [25], sequence labeling [26], cross-lingual dependency parsing [27], and reading comprehension [28]. More specific to classification tasks, Ye et al. [29] developed a reinforcement learning framework for cross-task text classification, which was tested also on the problem of sentiment classification in a monolingual setting. Jebbara and Cimiano [30] developed models for cross-lingual opinion target extraction, which were tested in a zero-shot setting, similar to ours. Their approaches rely on the alignment of static monolingual embeddings into the shared vector space for input representation. Fei and Li [31] trained a multi-view cross-lingual sentiment classifier based on the encoder-decoder architecture used for unsupervised machine translation. Their systems showed state-of-the-art performance on several benchmark datasets. The difference from our work is that the datasets used are all product review datasets, which contain considerably shorter texts. Furthermore, as described in Section 1, product reviews contain the target of the modeled sentiment in the text, while news articles generally do not, which makes the two problems different on a more fundamental level.

Novel research has also been done on better input text representation techniques for classification tasks. Tan et al. [32] proposed a clustering method for words based on their latent semantics. The vectors composing the same clusters were then aggregated together into cluster vectors. The final set of cluster vectors was then used as the final text representations. This novel text representation technique showed improvement on five different datasets. Pappagari et al. [33] proposed a modification to the BERT model for long document classification in a monolingual setting. They utilized a segmentation approach to divide the input text sequences into several subsequences. For each subsequence, they obtained a feature vector from the Transformer, which they then aggregated into one vector by applying another LSTM- or Transformer-based model over it. This work has inspired part of our current research for obtaining better Transformer-based representation of long text sequences. Ref. [34] recently presented a Transformer architecture, which is able to produce input representations from long documents in an efficient manner. However, the model they produced based on this architecture was pre-trained only on English data.

3. Datasets

In this section, we present in detail the two datasets of sentiment-labeled news that were used in this experiment.

3.1. SentiNews Dataset in Slovene

We used the publicly available SentiNews dataset (available at https://www.clarin.si/repository/xmlui/handle/11356/1110) [3], which is a manually sentiment-annotated Slovenian news corpus. The dataset contains 10,427 news texts mainly from the economic, financial, and political domains from Slovenian news portals (www.24ur.com, www.dnevnik.si, www.finance.si, www.rtvslo.si, www.zurnal24.si), which were published between 1 September 2007 and 31 December 2013. The texts were annotated by two to six annotators using the five-level Likert scale on three levels of granularity, i.e., on the document, paragraph, and sentence level. The dataset contains information about average sentiment, standard deviation, and sentiment category, which correspond to the sentiment allocation according to the average sentiment score. The dataset statistics are:

- 10,427 documents;
- 89,999 paragraphs;
- 168,899 sentences.

For our news classification experiments, we used the document-level annotations, with 10,427 news articles and an imbalanced distribution of 3337 (32%) negative, 5425 (52%) neutral, and 1665 (16%) positive news, where the sentiment category corresponds to the sentiment allocation according to the average sentiment score. For intermediate training, we also leveraged paragraph-level annotations.

3.2. Croatian Sentiment Dataset

The Croatian dataset was annotated in the scope of project EMBEDDIA and for the purposes of testing cross-lingual classification; therefore, the annotation procedure fully matched the Slovenian dataset [3].

The data came from 24sata, one of the leading media companies in Croatia with the highest circulation newspaper. The 24sata news portal is one of the most visited websites in Croatia, and it consists of a portal with daily news and several smaller portals covering news from specific topics such as automotive news, health, culinary content, and lifestyle advice. Portals included in the dataset are www.24sata.hr (daily news content, the majority of the dataset), as well as miss7.24sata.hr, autostart.24sata.hr, joomboos.24sata.hr, miss7mama.24sata.hr, miss7zdrava.24sata.hr, www.express.hr, and gastro.24sata.hr.

The dataset statistics are:

- 2025 documents;
- 12,032 paragraphs;
- 25,074 sentences.

As in [3], the annotators chose the sentiment score on the Likert [35] scale (corresponding to the question: Did this news evoke very positive/positive/neutral/negative/very negative feelings?), but for the final dataset, the average annotations were then three classes (positive, negative, and neutral). Annotations were done on three levels: document, paragraph, and sentence level. The distribution of positive, negative and neutral news texts of the document-level annotations used in this study is as follows: 303 (15.1%) positive, 439 (21.5%) negative, and 1283 (63.4%) neutral. They will be made available under a CC license upon acceptance of the paper. More details about inter-annotator agreement and annotation procedure are available in the Appendix A of this paper.

As one of the contributions of this paper is the evaluation of representation learning for long articles, we also provide the statistics of both datasets in terms of length. Table 1 compares the Slovenian and Croatian news datasets in terms of the length of annotated articles. It presents the average number of tokens per article, as well as the length of the longest and shortest articles in the respective datasets. We present the lengths in terms of the standard tokenization procedure where each word and punctuation mark counts as a separate token. However, the BERT model uses a different form of tokenization, namely the WordPiece tokenization [36]. Using this tokenization process, each word is broken into word pieces, which form the vocabulary of the tokenizer. The vocabulary is obtained using a data-driven approach: given a training corpus G and a number of word pieces D, the task is to select D word pieces such that the segmented corpus G contains as much unsegmented words as possible. The selected word pieces then form the vocabulary of the tokenizer. This approach is proven to handle the out-of-vocabulary words better than standard tokenization procedures. Since the inputs to the BERT model have to be tokenized according to this algorithm in order for the model to properly learn, we present the length statistics in terms of BERT's WordPiece tokenization model as well in the column "BERT tokens". We may observe that the average length of the articles in both datasets is relatively long in terms of the BERT tokens. Especially in the Slovenian dataset, which is used for training in this experiment, the average length of an article surpasses the maximum window size of the BERT model, which is set to 512 tokens in the implementation we are using for this work.

Table 1. Length of the articles in the Slovenian and Croatian datasets in terms of the number of tokens. The row "Tokens" presents the length in terms of the standard tokenization procedure, and the row "BERTtokens" presents the length of the articles in terms of BERT's WordPiece tokenization.

	Slovenian			Croatian		
	Min	Max	Mean	Min	Max	Mean
Tokens	10	2833	350	155	515	273
BERT tokens	19	4961	648	256	816	456

4. Methodology

We tested two approaches, one focusing on techniques for long document representation and the second one on improving the performance on the sentiment analysis task through intermediate pre-training.

In this work, we model sentiment in news articles, which are frequently longer than the BERT context windows, as discussed in Section 1. Therefore, in our first approach, we experiment with several methods for representing longer documents.

The second approach, presented in Section 4.4, proposes a novel technique for sentiment enrichment of mBERT. In standard BERT architectures, the pre-training phase of BERT consists of masked language modeling and next sentence prediction tasks, which are robust, but not necessarily relevant for sentiment classification, as discussed in Section 1. Therefore, we add an intermediate training step where, aside from masked language modeling, the sentiment classification is used as a learning objective. This model is then used for final fine-tuning. The role of intermediate training for BERT is still unexplored in NLP, with some initial experiments presented in [37].

4.1. Beginning of the Document

In the first experimental setting, we produced the document representations by using only the beginning part of the document. We first tokenized the document with the pre-trained multilingual BERT tokenizer. We then took the sequence of 512 tokens from the beginning of the document and fed them to the BERT language model. As proposed in Devlin et al. [10], we used the representation of the [CLS] token produced by the language model as the document representation. The [CLS] token is a special token prepended to every input of the BERT model, which, after fine-tuning, is used to represent the input sequence for classification tasks. We then sent this representation to the classification head composed of a single linear layer. This experiment mimics the usual usage of the BERT pre-trained models for text classification tasks and is included in this work for better benchmarking of other proposed text representation methods.

4.2. Beginning and End of the Document

For the second setting, we tried to produce the document representations by using the beginning and end of the document. The length of the input sequence was retained at 512 tokens. For sequences longer than 512 tokens after tokenization, we took 256 tokens from the beginning of the text and 256 tokens from the end of the text and concatenated them. We then fed the sequence to the BERT language model and used the [CLS] token vector from the last layer as the document representation. This document representation was then fed to the classification head composed of a linear layer.

4.3. Using Sequences from Every Part of the Document

In the third setting, we tried to compose our document representation by using information in the whole document.

For the language model fine-tuning phase, we tokenized each document and broke it into sequences of 512 tokens. We then used a sliding window that moved over all the subsequences in the order they appeared in the original sequence. Each subsequent window would overlap the first fifty tokens from the previous window. This way, we hoped our model would capture the relationships across sentence boundaries. We attached the document sentiment label to each of the subsequences from the same document. Such an oversampled dataset was then used to fine-tune the multilingual BERT language model with the attached linear layer for classification. This method is graphically presented in Figure 1.

After finetuning we again prepared each document in the dataset as described above and sent every subsequence of a particular document to the fine-tuned BERT model. We extracted the [CLS] vector representations from the last layer and combined them into a final document representation. This approach is inspired by the work of Pappagari et al. [33]. The main difference of our study is in the way the subsequence representations are merged into a document representation. In this work, we tested three different ways of combining the output vector representations into the final document representation.

- Using the most informative subsequence representation:

    In this approach, we tried to identify the most informative subsequence for the task at hand. As the BERT language model was fine-tuned on the sentiment classification task, we assumed some notion of the importance of different parts of the text was encoded directly into the vector representations. Using this line of thought, we defined the most informative subsequence as the subsequence with the highest euclidean vector norm. Formally, from the set of ordered subsequence representations: $S = \{x_1, x_2, \ldots x_n\}$ we chose: $x = argmax(||x||_2 : x \in S)$. We then used only this representation as the final vector representation and discarded the rest. The document representation is then sent into a two-layer fully connected neural network, which produces the final predictions.

- Averaging the representations of all subsequences:

    As the first approach is based on a strong assumption and it does not actually utilize the data from the whole document, here we combine all the vector representations of subsequences into one final document representation. We used a relatively naive approach of simply averaging all the vector representations to produce the final document embedding. The document representation is then sent into a two-layer fully connected neural network, which produces the final predictions.

- Using convolutional layers:

    In this approach, we extracted the most informative parts of the document with the use of 1D convolutional neural layers. We used a convolutional filter of size 2 with stride 2 that runs over the produced subsequence representations. This way, the convolutional filter processes the subsequences in pairs and extracts the most informative features from each pair of subsequences from each part of the document. Since we have documents of variable lengths that may be represented by a variable number of subsequences, all the representations were padded with zero vectors up to the maximum length of 6. We used 128 filters to produce 128 feature maps. We then mapped these maps to a final 128-dimensional document vector representation using a max pooling operation. The final embedding is then sent into a linear layer that produces the classification.

The advantage of the first two mapping operations is that, in comparison to the methods proposed in Pappagari et al. [33], they are more computationally efficient as we need to perform simple vector norm and averaging calculations to produce the final document representations. The third mapping operations uses a convolutional layer to map the different subsequences into one document representation. The convolutional networks have proven in the past to be competitive with other text-processing approaches in NLP [38]; therefore, our approach presents an alternative to the LSTM and Transformer-based sequence aggregation.

4.4. Sentiment Enrichment of the mBERT Model

In this approach, the aim is to to induce sentiment information directly into the vectorized document representations that are produced by the multilingual BERT model. To do so, we added an intermediate training step for the mBERT model before the fine-tuning phase. The intermediate training phase consists of jointly training the model on two tasks. The first task we used was the masked language modeling task as described in the original paper by Devlin et al. [10]. We left this task unchanged in hopes that the model would better capture the syntactic patterns of our training language and domain.

For the second task, we used the sentiment classification task, which mirrors the fine-tuning task, but is trained using a different set of labeled data. With this task, we tried to additionally constrain the model to learn sentiment-related information before the actual fine-tuning phase. The task was formally modeled as a standard classification task where we tried to learn a predictor that would map the documents to a discrete number of classes:

$$\gamma : x \rightarrow C$$

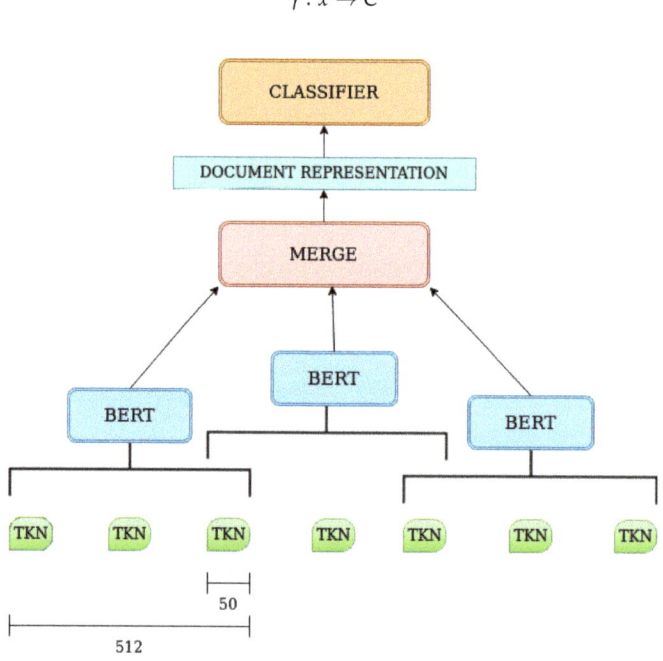

Figure 1. The document representation approach using a sliding window over the whole input sequence. Each subsequence is embedded using a fine-tuned BERT model, and all the subsequences are then merged into a final document representation, which is sent further as the input to the classifier. The length of the sliding window is 512 tokens. The first 50 tokens of each subsequent sliding window overlap with the last 50 tokens of the previous sliding window.

For each document x_i in the training set $S = \{x_1, x_2, \ldots, x_n\}$, we produced a document representation $d \in R^{1 \times t}$, where t is the dimension of the representation, by encoding the document with the mBERT model and taking the representation of the [CLS] token from the last layer. We sent this representation through a linear layer and a softmax function to map it to one of the predefined classes $C = \{y_1, y_2, \ldots, y_n\}$.

$$h = Linear(d, W) \qquad (1)$$
$$\hat{y} = Softmax(h) \qquad (2)$$

We calculated the loss of the sentiment classification task: $\mathcal{L}_s$ at the end using the negative log likelihood loss function

$$\mathcal{L}_s = -\log(\hat{y}_i)$$

where $\hat{y}_i$ is the probability of the correct class.
The final loss $\mathcal{L}$ is computed as:

$$\mathcal{L} = \mathcal{L}_{mlm} + \mathcal{L}_s$$

where $\mathcal{L}_{mlm}$ represents the loss from the masked language modeling task. The model is then jointly trained on both tasks by backpropagating the final loss through the whole network.

The original mBERT model is pre-trained on another task, namely next sentence prediction, which, according to the authors, helps the model learn sentence relationships. During training, the input for this task is treated as belonging to two separate sequences and the model has to decide if the two sequences follow one another in the original text or not. This information is useful for a variety of downstream tasks such as question answering. Since in this experiment we are dealing with a classification task, where the input is treated as being a part of the same sequence, we felt the additional training using the next sentence prediction task would not add much relevant information to the model so we omitted it in the intermediate training phase.

5. Experimental Setup

This sections describes the setup that we used to perform the experiments. It is divided into three subsections: the first subsection describes the regime we used for the fine-tuning phases; the second subsection describes the regime we used for the intermediate training phase; and the third subsection presents the evaluation of the trained models.

5.1. Fine-Tuning Phase

For the fine-tuning phase, we used the Slovenian news dataset [3] annotated on the document level (see Section 3), as the goal of our classification is to assign the sentiment label to a news article. We followed the suggestions in the original paper by Devlin et al. [10] for fine-tuning. We used the Adam optimizer with the learning rate of $2E-5$ and learning rate warmup over the first 10% of the training instances. For regularization purposes, we used the weight decay set to 0.01. We reduced the batch size from 32 to 16 due to the high memory consumption during training, which was the result of a long sequence length. For benchmarking purposes, we used the k-fold cross-validation training regime for the fine-tuning phase, where we split the dataset into k folds. In each cross-validation step, the k-1 folds are used as the training set, while the k-th fold is used as the testing set. The models in each cross-validation step were trained for 3 epochs. To avoid overfitting, we split the training folds into smaller training and development sets. After each epoch, we measured the performance on the development set and saved the new model parameters only if the performance of the model on the development set increased. For the document representation methods, described in Sections 4.1 and 4.2, the fine-tuning of the language model and the training of the classification head were performed end-to-end, while for the methods, described in Section 4.3, the classification heads were trained after the fine-tuning phase was completed. Otherwise, the training regime and the chosen hyperparameters were the same for all the experiments.

5.2. Intermediate Training Phase Regime

For the intermediate training phase, we utilized the proposed modified modeling objectives, described in Section 4.4. We used the Slovenian news dataset with annotations on the paragraph level. The annotations on this level of granularity were used because we wanted to perform the intermediate training phase on a different dataset than the one used for fine-tuning, but containing information relevant for the document-level sentiment classification task.

Since the annotated paragraphs were part of the same documents we used for the fine-tuning step, we took measures to prevent any form of data leakage. As described in Section 5.1, the fine-tuning phase was performed using 10-fold cross-validation. We performed the intermediate training in each cross-validation step, but excluded the paragraphs that were part of the documents in the k-th testing fold of the fine-tuning step from the dataset. We split the remaining data into a training and development set and trained the language model for a maximum of five epochs. At the end of each epoch, we calculated the perplexity score of the model on the development set and saved the new weights only if perplexity improved in the previous epoch. If perplexity did not improve for three consecutive epochs, we stopped the training early. For this phase, we used the same hyperparameter settings as for the fine-tuning phase.

5.3. Evaluation

All the models were first trained and evaluated on the Slovenian dataset using 10-fold cross-validation as described in Sections 5.1 and 5.2. Next, the performance of the models from each fold was additionally tested on the Croatian test set to check the performance in the zero-shot learning setting (i.e., without any Croatian data used in training). The performances from each fold on the Croatian test set were then averaged and reported as a final result. The results for this set of experiments are presented in Table 2. The performance of the models was summarized using a standard classification metric, namely the macro-averaged F1 score, which is the appropriate measure given the highly imbalanced nature of the dataset (dominant neutral class). For completeness, we also separately report the precision and recall, both macro-averaged over all classes. Additionally, we also report the average F1 score performance of the model on the Slovenian and Croatian test sets. The performance of our models was compared to the baseline majority classifiers for both the Slovenian and Croatian datasets.

Table 2. Results of the document representation approaches. The first column shows the performance of models in the Slovenian 10-fold cross-validation setting; the second column is the average zero-shot performance on the Croatian test set; and the last column presents the average F1 score of the results on the Slovenian and Croatian datasets. Best results are marked in bold.

Model	Slovenian Cross-Validation			Croatian Test Set			Average
	Precision	Recall	F1	Precision	Recall	F1	F1
Majority classifier	17.34	33.33	22.76	0.20	0.33	25.00	/
Beginning of the document	65.45 ± 2.61	**62.83 ± 2.46**	63.34 ± 2.29	57.74 ± 1.20	**53.91 ± 2.41**	52.06 ± 2.64	57.70
Beginning and end of the document	64.72 ± 2.82	62.67 ± 2.69	63.33 ± 2.56	**59.00 ± 1.62**	53.53 ± 3.64	**52.41 ± 2.58**	57.87
Sequences from every part of the document							
Most informative subsequence	64.42 ± 2.44	62.09 ± 2.27	63.00 ± 2.34	57.87 ± 1.32	53.23 ± 2.82	52.30 ± 2.86	57.65
Averaging subsequence representations	**66.50 ± 3.13**	62.00 ± 2.45	**63.39 ± 2.42**	57.53 ± 1.14	52.95 ± 3.38	51.55 ± 3.93	57.47
1D CNN	63.96 ± 10.02	60.91 ± 5.22	61.58 ± 7.78	54.96 ± 5.48	53.31 ± 3.62	50.28 ± 4.65	55.93

6. Results

This section presents the results of the experiments conducted in the course of this study. We first present the results of the document representation approaches. The results are presented in Table 2. Next, for the best performing representation approach, we test our newly introduced technique for sentiment classification with intermediate training, and the results with and without the intermediate training objective are compared in Table 3. We also compare our results with the previous sate-of-the-art SVM and Naive Bayes models on the Slovenian dataset from [3], as well as with the neural network model based on LSTMs and TF-IDF from [39]. We note, however, that the testing regime in these experiments was not the same. In [3], the authors tested their models using five times 10-fold cross-validation, while in [39], the model was trained and tested on a random train-test split of the whole dataset with an 80:20 train-test split ratio. For this reason, the results are not directly comparable.

Table 3. Performance of the model using our intermediate sentiment classification training approach compared to the model without intermediate training. Additionally, we include the reported results from the related work using the same dataset. Best results are marked in bold.

Model	Slovenian			Croatian			Average
	Precision	Recall	F1	Precision	Recall	F1	F1
Majority classifier	17.34	33.33	22.76	0.20	0.33	25.00	/
Reported results from related studies							
SVM (from Bučar et al. [3]) 5 × 10 CV	/	/	63.42 ± 1.96	/	/	/	/
NBM (from Bučar et al. [3]) 5 × 10 CV	/	/	65.97 ± 1.70	/	/	/	/
LSTM+TF-IDF (from Pelicon [39]) train-set split	/	/	62.5	/	/	/	/
Results from the current study							
Beginning of the document	65.45 ± 2.61	62.83 ± 2.46	63.34 ± 2.29	57.74 ± 1.20	53.91 ± 2.41	52.06 ± 2.64	57.70
Beginning and end of the document with sentiment intermediate training	**67.19 ± 2.67**	**66.00 ± 3.00**	**66.33 ± 2.60**	56.32 ± 1.88	**54.90 ± 2.36**	**54.77 ± 1.39**	**60.55**

As shown in Table 2, all the models using one of the tested document representation methods in this experiment performed better than the majority baseline classifier by a substantial margin. The best performing model on the Slovenian dataset (in terms of F1 score) utilizes document representations formed by simple averaging of the subsequence representations. The different document representation methods that were tested in this work do not seem to impact the model performance much as the performances of all our models differed only by a small margin when tested on the Slovenian data.

As far as absolute performance, we can see that the tested methods achieved F1 scores in the sixties for this particular Slovenian dataset with the best F1 score of 63.39 with averaging subsequence representations. When these models were tested on the Croatian test set in a zero-shot setting, the performance additionally dropped for approximately 11% with best the F1 scores achieving the low fifties. The best performing representation on the Croatian dataset uses the beginning and end of the document. Interestingly, the best performing model on the Slovenian dataset also saw the highest drop on the Croatian dataset of 11.84%. We additionally observed high variance of the CNN model compared to the other models.

Since the three best performing document representation techniques were within a 0.06% difference on the Slovenian dataset, for experiments with intermediate training for sentiment enrichment, we opted for the document representation that used the beginning and ending of the input document as its average performance on the test sets of both Slovenian and Croatian languages was the highest. The results for the intermediate training experiment (Table 3) show that the model with the additional intermediate training step outperforms the model without the intermediate training step when using the same document representation technique. The results show three points better average performance on the Slovenian dataset and 2.68 points average improvement on the Croatian dataset in terms of the F1 score. Our model also manages to outperform the previous state-of-the-art models on the Slovenian dataset, achieving a 0.36 point increase in terms of F1 score, however this should be taken with precaution as the two evaluation settings differ.

7. Qualitative Exploration of the Models: Behavior of the Attention Space

With the increasing use of neural language models, in recent years, the methodology aimed at the exploration of the human-understandable patterns, emerging from trained models, has gained notable attention. Models, such as BERT [40] and similar ones, can consist of hundreds of millions of parameters, which carry little useful information in terms of studying which parts of the model input were of relevance when making a prediction. To remedy this shortcoming, visualization methodologies are actively developed and researched for the task of better understanding the associations between the input token space and the constructed predictions.

The existing toolkits that offer the exploration of attention have been actively developed in recent years [41,42] and are widely used to better understand a given model's behavior. In this section, we exploit the recently introduced, freely available AttViz [43], an online toolkit for the exploration of the self-attention space of trained classifiers (http://attviz.ijs.si/). The tool is used to explore the behavior of the self-attention when considering positive, negative, and neutral classifications. The original tool was developed for instance-based exploration. In addition, we introduce a novel functionality of the tool aimed at the analysis of global attention values (per class analysis on the token collection level).

In the remainder of this section, we fist present a collection of selected examples, offering insight into the trained model's behavior. We begin by discussing selected positive instances, followed by neutral and negative ones. All the visualizations were done with the sentiment-enriched model that we trained in the course of this study. The main aim of this section is to explore the currently available means of inspecting trained neural language models. A positive example is shown in Figure 2.

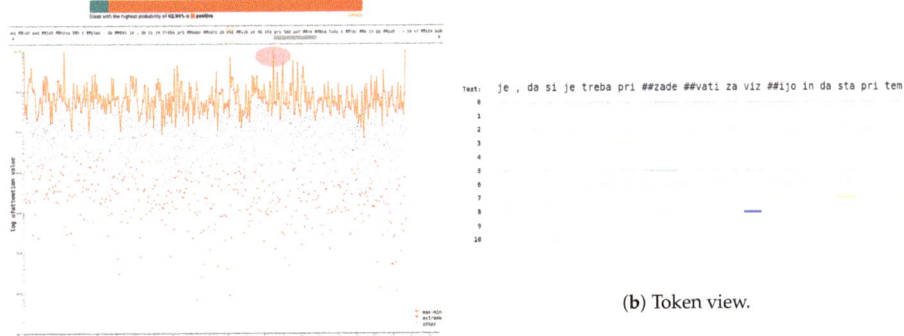

(a) Sequence view.

(b) Token view.

Figure 2. Positive Example No. 41. The red ellipse (**a**) highlights one of the tokens (byte pairs) with the highest (normalized) self-attention—the token is part of the word "vizija" (translation: vision) (**b**). Note also the peaks at the beginning and the end; these peaks refer to the special tokens (e.g., [CLS]]).

The positive example was selected as it has a very high probability of being positive class and it showcases two main patterns that can be observed throughout the space of positively classified examples: first, only a handful of tokens are emphasized (if any), and second, there appears to be strong bias towards the first and the last token, indicating the potential effect of pre-training.

Next, we considered some of the examples classified as negative sentiment (see the example in Figures 3 and 4).

Figure 3. Negative Example No. 62. In this example, one of the highest attention values was around the token "izdaje" (translation: treason), which could be one of the carriers of the negative sentiment. Note that individual lines represent attention values for each of the ten attention heads. The document was classified with 87.45% probability.

The attention (highlighted red circle) peaks at the discussed token (translated as treason and negotiations respectively) can be observed, indicating that the neural language model picked up a signal at the token level during the association of the byte-paired inputs with outputs. Furthermore, we observed a similar pattern related to the starting [CLS] token, as well as the ending [SEP] token, i.e., token defining the end of the sentence. The pattern was consistent also throughout the neutral examples.

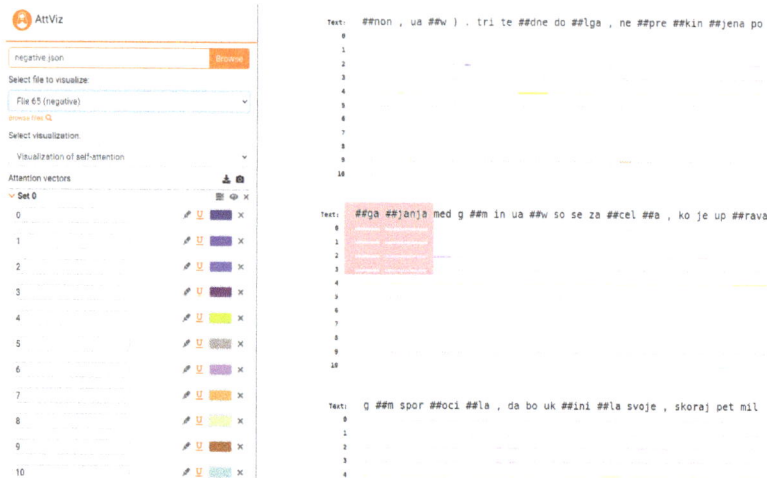

Figure 4. Negative Example No. 65. The highlighted region (red) corresponds to the term "pogajanja" (translation: negotiations), which appears to be associated with the classification of the observed text into the negative class.

The considered attention spaces offered insight into two main aspects of the trained model. First, the self-attention space, i.e., the space of the attention values alongside the attention matrix diagonals, offers relatively little insight into what the model learned. There are at least two main reasons for the observed behavior, as it appears to deviate from the reported explanations [43]. First, the considered documents are relatively long. Such documents give rise to a higher spread of the self-attention, smoothing out the individual peaks. Second, the wider spread of the attention could also be to the morphology-rich language considered (Slovene).

We next discuss the behavior of the global attention values both at the token, as well as the distribution level. The top 15 tokens according to the mean attention values are shown in Figure 5.

The presented results confirm the initial finding (e.g., Figure 2) that most of the attention space has high variability and, as such, does not directly offer interpretable insights; however, some meaningful results are also observed, e.g., the token with the greatest attention value for the positive class is sport. The final analysis we conducted was at the level of the global attention distributions. Here, we plotted the kernel density estimates of raw attention values across different types of instances. The results are shown in Figure 6.

The distribution visualization indicates that the main differences emerge when considering the minimum value, a given token ever achieved; this result, albeit unexpected, potentially indicates that the attention is for classification of negative texts focused on a more particular subset of tokens, yielding a lower average subject to a skewed distribution. We finally offer quantile-quantile plots in Figure 7.

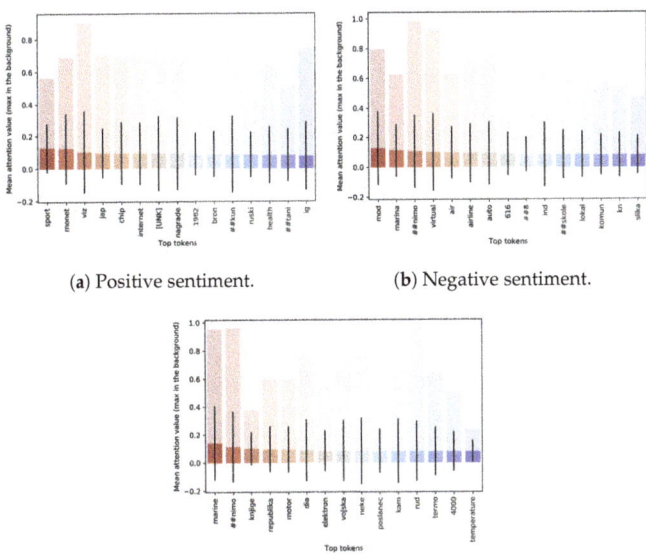

(a) Positive sentiment.

(b) Negative sentiment.

(c) Neutral sentiment.

Figure 5. Visualization of token level attention. The figures represent the top 15 tokens according to the mean attention values. In the background, the maximum attention for a given token is also plotted. Note that the high standard deviation indicates little emphasis on the individual tokens.

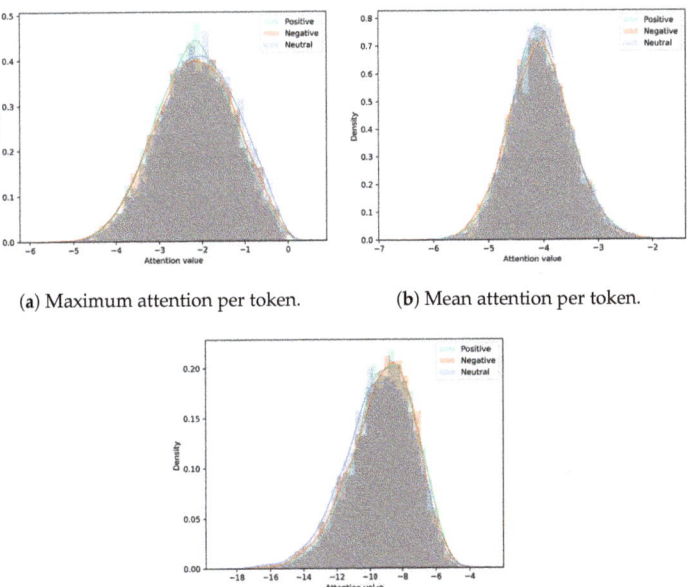

(a) Maximum attention per token.

(b) Mean attention per token.

(c) Minimum attention per token.

Figure 6. Visualization of attention (log-transformed) distributions. It can be observed that the largest differences emerge when considering minimum attention. There, the negative texts' distribution is the most skewed. When considering maximum and mean distributions, however, no notable differences emerge.

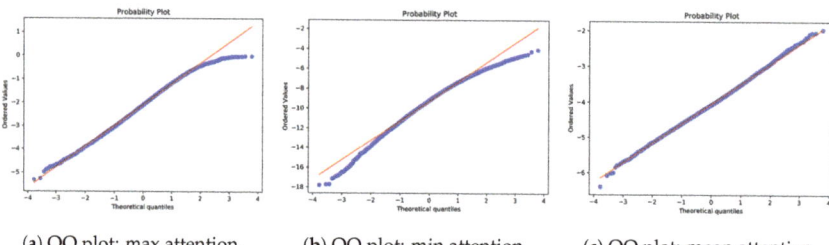

(a) QQ plot: max attention.   (b) QQ plot: min attention.   (c) QQ plot: mean attention.

Figure 7. The quantile-quantile fits of the three considered attention distributions. It can be observed that the min and max attention distributions are skewed, indicating the presence of more extreme values.

The considered QQ-plots further confirm the observation that the skewed distribution of attention can be observed when considering min-max values; however, on average, the log transform could be interpreted to behave as a normal distribution; however, additional tests, such as Pearson's sample skewness (computed as $\frac{n^{-1}\sum_{i=1}^{n}(x_i-\bar{x})^3}{(n^{-1}\sum_{i=1}^{n}(x_i-\bar{x})^2)^{3/2}}$, where x_i is the i-th value out of n samples) could be conducted to further quantify the attention behavior.

8. Availability

The croatian news dataset with document-level sentiment annotations is available on the CLARIN repository under the Creative Commons license (CC-BY-NC-ND) (http://hdl.handle.net/11356/1342). The code for all the experiments is available on GitHub (https://github.com/PeliconA/crosslingual_news_sentiment.git).

9. Conclusions and Future Work

In this work, we addressed the task of sentiment analysis in news articles performed in a zero-shot cross-lingual setting. The goal was to successfully train models that could, when trained on data in one language, perform adequately also on data in another language. For this purpose, we used publicly available data of Slovenian news manually labeled for sentiment to train our models. Additionally, we gathered a new dataset of Croatian news and labeled it according to the guidelines for the annotation of the Slovenian dataset. This new dataset served as a test set for the zero-shot cross-lingual performance of our models.

We based our models on the multilingual Transformer-based model BERT, which has shown remarkable multilingual and cross-lingual performance. We however identified two potential drawbacks with the BERT model. The input window of the BERT model is fixed and relatively short. A widespread approach to this limitation is to shorten the input before sending it to the model for processing. While this approach is adequate for shorter texts, with longer documents, like news articles, it may cause severe information loss. The second drawback is that while BERT is pre-trained on a large collection of data, the only explicit sentiment signal it gets is during the fine-tuning phase on a usually small collection of labeled data.

To remedy the first potential drawback, we first tested several techniques for producing more informative long document representations. The techniques, which were described in detail, were partially inspired by earlier work, but to the best of our knowledge, they have not yet been tested in a cross-lingual setting. Our results show that all the techniques outperform the majority baseline classifier by a large margin, even when applied to the Croatian test set in a zero-shot setting where the model is not fine-tuned on Croatian data.

For the second identified limitation of the BERT model, we proposed a novel intermediate learning phase that encompasses the masked language modeling task and sentiment classification task. This phase is performed before the fine-tuning phase using a training set with separate annotations. The goal of this phase is to induce the sentiment-related information directly into the BERT representations before the fine-tuning begins on the target task data. Results show that after fine-tuning, the sentiment-enriched model outperforms the models without the intermediate training phase both on the Slovenian dataset and on the Croatian test set in a zero-shot setting. Additionally, it slightly outperforms the current state-of-the-art on the Slovenian dataset, as reported in [3].

In the future, we plan to further test our proposed intermediate sentiment-enrichment phase with masked language modeling and sentiment classification tasks. Currently, the fine-tuning and the intermediate training phases share the dataset, but use labels on different levels of granularity: we used document-level labels for fine-tuning and paragraph-level labels for intermediate training. We would like to test how using training data from a very different training set would impact the performance of the proposed intermediate training step. We will also test the general transferability of this phase. Given a large enough corpus of sentiment-labeled instances that can be used for the intermediate training step, we would like to see if a Transformer-based model enriched with our proposed method can work well on sentiment tasks in different target languages and from different domains. Another interesting research area would be using topic modeling as a supplementary method for the news-related sentiment classification task. Such research would also test the underlying assumption that there is a positive correlation between the topic of a news article and the sentiment that a news article evokes in the readers. Even though the news articles in the datasets used for this work are not explicitly labeled for topics, they nevertheless deal with varying content and could support such research.

Author Contributions: A.P. and S.P. designed the study and developed its methodology. M.P. and D.M. provided the data for the study and guided the annotation process. Formal analysis of the study was done by A.P. Software for the experiments was written by A.P. Visualization of the trained models was done by B.Š. Validation of the results and supervision of the study was done by S.P. A.P., M.P., D.M., B.Š. and S.P. cotributed to the writing, reviewing and editing of the paper. All authors have read and agreed to the published version of the manuscript.

Funding: This research is supported by the European Union's Horizon 2020 research and innovation program under Grant Agreement No. 825153, project EMBEDDIA (Cross-Lingual Embeddings for Less-Represented Languages in European News Media). The work of A.P. was funded also by the European Union's Rights, Equality and Citizenship Programme (2014–2020) project IMSyPP (Innovative Monitoring Systems and Prevention Policies of Online Hate Speech, Grant No. 875263). We acknowledge also the funding by the Slovenian Research Agency (ARRS) core research program Knowledge Technologies (P2-0103). The results of this publication reflect only the authors' views, and the Commission is not responsible for any use that may be made of the information it contains.

Acknowledgments: We would like to thank 24sata, especially Hrvoje Dorešić and Boris Trupčević, for making the data available. We thank Jože Bučar for leading the annotation process.

Conflicts of Interest: The authors declare no conflict of interest.

Appendix A. Appendix A. Details on Croatian Dataset Construction

For the selection of articles, the time period was specified: approximately half of the articles were selected from the period from 1 September 2007 to 31 December 2013 in order to match the Slovenian dataset, while the other half were recent articles from last five years. From the initial set of articles, short and medium length articles were kept, leading to final selection. The articles were then cleaned and preprocessed, and the quality was checked (automatically and manually). The final dataset consisted of 2025 news articles. The sentiment annotation task was performed on three levels: document, paragraph, and sentence level.

For the selection of annotators, the condition of being native speakers was imposed, and we also considered the candidate's interest in the task.

The annotator were trained in two phases:

- In the first phase, we introduced the project EMBEDDIA and its goals. A referee introduced the web application for the annotation task. The annotators received basic guidelines, which were explained to them in detail by a referee. This was followed by the annotation of five articles, which were annotated together on the three levels (sentence, paragraph, and document level). Using a five-level Likert scale: [35] (1—very negative, 2—negative, 3—neutral, 4—positive, and 5—very positive), the annotators annotated each article according to the following question: "Did this news evoke very positive/positive/neutral/negative/very negative feelings? (Please specify the sentiment from the perspective of an average Croatian web user)". Together with a referee, they discussed the individual instances, every single decision, and the annotation grade and resolved possible issues and doubts.

- In the second phase, all annotators annotated the same 25 articles individually. Afterwards, we analyzed the results of the annotation. The agreement (Cronbach's alpha measure) between the annotators on the document level was 0.816, which was a very good achievement with only 25 articles. We planned to achieve a 0.8 threshold. If the annotators had not achieved the planned threshold, they would repeat the second phase until they achieved it. The instances with lower agreement were discussed, and the issues were resolved.

Since a satisfying inter-annotator agreement was reached, the rest of the 2000 were annotated by different numbers of annotators. They followed the instructions they were given in the first and second phases.

To evaluate the process of annotation, we explored correlation coefficients using various measures of inter-annotator agreement at three levels of granularity, as shown in Table A1. The first three internal consistency estimates of reliability for the scores, shown in Table A1, normally range between zero and one. The values closer to one indicate more agreement, when compared to the values closer to zero. Cronbach's alpha values indicated a very good internal consistency at all levels of granularity. Normally, we refer to a value greater than 0.8 as a good internal consistency and above 0.9 as an excellent one [44]. The value of Krippendorff's alpha [45] at the document level of granularity implied a fair reliability test, whereas its values at the paragraph level and sentence level were lower. Fleiss' kappa values illustrated a moderate agreement among the annotators at all levels of granularity. In general, a value between 0.41 and 0.60 implies a moderate agreement, above 0.61 a substantial agreement, and above 0.81 an almost perfect agreement [46]. Kendall's values indicated a fair level of agreement between the annotators at all levels of granularity. Correspondingly, the Pearson and Spearman values range from −1 to 1, where 1 refers to the total positive correlation, 0 to no correlation, and −1 to the total negative correlation. The coefficients showed moderate positive agreement among the annotators, but their values decreased when applied to the paragraph and the sentence level. Usually, the values above 0.3 refer to a weak correlation, above 0.5 to a moderate correlation, and above 0.7 to a strong correlation [47].

Table A1. Results of dataset annotation: level of inter-rater agreement for document, paragraph, and sentence levels.

	Document Level				Paragraph Level			Sentence Level		
a_c	0.927				0.888			0.881		
a_k	0.671				0.565			0.548		
k	0.527				0.489			0.441		
	min	max	avg	min	max	avg	min	max	avg	
r_p	0.544	0.824	0.682	0.488	0.719	0.572	0.425	0.706	0.558	
r_s	0.557	0.762	0.669	0.474	0.702	0.548	0.42	0.696	0.54	
W	0.508	0.73	0.625	0.449	0.656	0.513	0.389	0.649	0.504	

Our results support the claim by [48] that it can be more difficult to accurately annotate sentences (or even phrases). In general, the sentiment scores by different annotators were more consistent at the document level than at the paragraph and sentence level.

The final sentiment of an instance is defined as the average of the sentiment scores given by the different annotators (as in the Slovenian news set). An instance was labeled as:

- negative, if the average of given scores was less than or equal to 2.4,
- neutral, if the average of given scores was between 2.4 and 3.6,
- positive, if the average of given scores was greater than or equal to 3.6.

References

1. Beigi, G.; Hu, X.; Maciejewski, R.; Liu, H. An overview of sentiment analysis in social media and its applications in disaster relief. In *Sentiment Analysis and Ontology Engineering*; Springer: Cham, Switzerland, 2016; pp. 313–340.
2. Mejova, Y. *Sentiment Analysis: An Overview*; University of Iowa, Computer Science Department: Iowa City, IA, USA, 2009.
3. Bučar, J.; Žnidaršič, M.; Povh, J. Annotated news corpora and a lexicon for sentiment analysis in Slovene. *Lang. Resour. Eval.* **2018**, *52*, 895–919.
4. Liu, B. Sentiment Analysis and Opinion Mining. *Synth. Lect. Hum. Lang. Technol.* **2012**, *5*, 1–167. doi:10.2200/s00416ed1v01y201204hlt016.
5. Van de Kauter, M.; Breesch, D.; Hoste, V. Fine-Grained Analysis of Explicit and Implicit Sentiment in Financial News Articles. *Expert Syst. Appl.* **2015**, *42*, 4999–5010. doi:10.1016/j.eswa.2015.02.007.
6. Bhutani, B.; Rastogi, N.; Sehgal, P.; Purwar, A. Fake news detection using sentiment analysis. In Proceedings of the IEEE 2019 Twelfth International Conference on Contemporary Computing (IC3), Noida, India, 8–10 August 2019; pp. 1–5.
7. El Ali, A.; Stratmann, T.C.; Park, S.; Schöning, J.; Heuten, W.; Boll, S.C. Measuring, understanding, and classifying news media sympathy on twitter after crisis events. In Proceedings of the 2018 CHI Conference on Human Factors in Computing Systems, Montreal, QC, Canada, 21–26 April 2018; pp. 1–13.
8. Rambaccussing, D.; Kwiatkowski, A. Forecasting with news sentiment: Evidence with UK newspapers. *Int. J. Forecast.* **2020**. doi:10.1016/j.ijforecast.2020.04.002.
9. Bowden, J.; Kwiatkowski, A.; Rambaccussing, D. Economy through a lens: Distortions of policy coverage in UK national newspapers. *J. Comp. Econ.* **2019**, *47*, 881–906.
10. Devlin, J.; Chang, M.W.; Lee, K.; Toutanova, K. Bert: Pre-training of deep bidirectional transformers for language understanding. *arXiv* **2018**, arXiv:1810.04805.
11. Schwartz, B. Google's Latest Search Algorithm to Better Understand Natural Language. Search Engine Land. 25 October 2019. Available online: https://searchengineland.com/welcome-bert-google-artificial-intelligence-for-understanding-search-queries-323976 (accessed one 28 August 2020).
12. Albarino, S. Does Google's BERT Matter in Machine Translation? Slator. 17 October 2019. Available online: https://slator.com/machine-translation/does-googles-bert-matter-in-machine-translation/ (accessed one 28 August 2020).
13. Pires, T.; Schlinger, E.; Garrette, D. How multilingual is Multilingual BERT? *arXiv* **2019**, arXiv:1906.01502.
14. Karthikeyan, K.; Wang, Z.; Mayhew, S.; Roth, D. Cross-lingual ability of multilingual bert: An empirical study. In Proceedings of the International Conference on Learning Representations, Scottsdale, AZ, USA, 2–4 May 2019.
15. Wolf, T.; Debut, L.; Sanh, V.; Chaumond, J.; Delangue, C.; Moi, A.; Cistac, P.; Rault, T.; Louf, R.; Funtowicz, M.; Brew, J. HuggingFace's Transformers: State-of-the-art Natural Language Processing. *arXiv* **2019**, arXiv:1910.03771.
16. Xie, Q.; Dai, Z.; Hovy, E.; Luong, M.T.; Le, Q.V. Unsupervised data augmentation for consistency training. *arXiv* **2019**, arXiv:1904.12848.
17. Lin, K.Y.; Yang, C.; Chen, H.H. Emotion Classification of Online News Articles from the Reader's Perspective. In Proceedings of the 2008 IEEE/WIC/ACM International Conference on Web Intelligence and Intelligent Agent Technology, Sydney, Australia, 9–12 December 2009; Volume 1, pp. 220–226. doi:10.1109/WIIAT.2008.197.
18. Li, X.; Xie, H.; Chen, L.; Wang, J.; Deng, X. News Impact on Stock Price Return via Sentiment Analysis. *Knowl. Based Syst.* **2014**, *69*. doi:10.1016/j.knosys.2014.04.022.

19. Mansar, Y.; Gatti, L.; Ferradans, S.; Guerini, M.; Staiano, J. Fortia-FBK at SemEval-2017 Task 5: Bullish or Bearish? Inferring Sentiment towards Brands from Financial News Headlines. In *Proceedings of the 11th International Workshop on Semantic Evaluation (SemEval-2017)*; Association for Computational Linguistics: Vancouver, BC, Canada, 2017; pp. 817–822. doi:10.18653/v1/S17-2138.
20. Moore, A.; Rayson, P. Lancaster A at SemEval-2017 Task 5: Evaluation metrics matter: predicting sentiment from financial news headlines. In *Proceedings of the 11th International Workshop on Semantic Evaluation (SemEval-2017)*; Association for Computational Linguistics: Vancouver, BC, Canada, 2017; pp. 581–585. doi:10.18653/v1/S17-2095.
21. Wan, X. Co-training for cross-lingual sentiment classification. In Proceedings of the Joint Conference of the 47th Annual Meeting of the ACL and the 4th International Joint Conference on Natural Language Processing of the AFNLP, Singapore, 2–7 August 2009; pp. 235–243.
22. Guzmán, F.; Chen, P.J.; Ott, M.; Pino, J.; Lample, G.; Koehn, P.; Chaudhary, V.; Ranzato, M. The FLoRes evaluation datasets for low-resource machine translation: Nepali-english and sinhala-english. *arXiv* **2019**, arXiv:1902.01382.
23. Zhou, X.; Wan, X.; Xiao, J. Attention-based LSTM network for cross-lingual sentiment classification. In Proceedings of the 2016 Conference on Empirical Methods in Natural Language Processing, Austin, TX, USA, 1–5 November 2016; pp. 247–256.
24. Chen, Z.; Shen, S.; Hu, Z.; Lu, X.; Mei, Q.; Liu, X. Emoji-powered representation learning for cross-lingual sentiment classification. In Proceedings of the World Wide Web Conference, San Francisco, CA, USA, 13–17 May 2019; pp. 251–262.
25. Funaki, R.; Nakayama, H. Image-mediated learning for zero-shot cross-lingual document retrieval. In Proceedings of the 2015 Conference on Empirical Methods in Natural Language Processing, Lisbon, Portugal, 17–21 September 2015; pp. 585–590.
26. Rei, M.; Søgaard, A. Zero-shot sequence labeling: Transferring knowledge from sentences to tokens. *arXiv* **2018**, arXiv:1805.02214.
27. Wang, Y.; Che, W.; Guo, J.; Liu, Y.; Liu, T. Cross-lingual BERT transformation for zero-shot dependency parsing. *arXiv* **2019**, arXiv:1909.06775
28. Hsu, T.Y.; Liu, C.L.; Lee, H.Y. Zero-shot Reading Comprehension by Cross-lingual Transfer Learning with Multi-lingual Language Representation Model. *arXiv* **2019**, arXiv:1909.09587
29. Ye, Z.; Geng, Y.; Chen, J.; Chen, J.; Xu, X.; Zheng, S.; Wang, F.; Zhang, J.; Chen, H. Zero-shot Text Classification via Reinforced Self-training. In Proceedings of the 58th Annual Meeting of the Association for Computational Linguistics, Seattle, WA, USA, 5–10 July 2020; pp. 3014–3024.
30. Jebbara, S.; Cimiano, P. Zero-Shot Cross-Lingual Opinion Target Extraction. *arXiv* **2019**, arXiv:1904.09122
31. Fei, H.; Li, P. Cross-Lingual Unsupervised Sentiment Classification with Multi-View Transfer Learning. In Proceedings of the 58th Annual Meeting of the Association for Computational Linguistics, Seattle, WA, USA, 5–10 July 2020; pp. 5759–5771.
32. Tan, X.; Yan, R.; Tao, C.; Wu, M. Classification over Clustering: Augmenting Text Representation with Clusters Helps! In *Proceedings of the CCF International Conference on Natural Language Processing and Chinese Computing*; Springer: Cham, Switzerland, 2019; pp. 28–40.
33. Pappagari, R.; Zelasko, P.; Villalba, J.; Carmiel, Y.; Dehak, N. Hierarchical Transformers for Long Document Classification. In Proceedings of the 2019 IEEE Automatic Speech Recognition and Understanding Workshop (ASRU), Singapore, 14–18 December 2019; pp. 838–844.
34. Beltagy, I.; Peters, M.E.; Cohan, A. Longformer: The long-document transformer. *arXiv* **2020**, arXiv:2004.05150.
35. Likert, R. A Technique for the Measurement of Attitudes. *Arch. Psychol.* **1932**, *140*, 5–55.
36. Wu, Y.; Schuster, M.; Chen, Z.; Le, Q.V.; Norouzi, M.; Macherey, W.; Krikun, M.; Cao, Y.; Gao, Q.; Macherey, K.; et al. Google's neural machine translation system: Bridging the gap between human and machine translation. *arXiv* **2016**, arXiv:1609.08144
37. Pruksachatkun, Y.; Phang, J.; Liu, H.; Htut, P.M.; Zhang, X.; Pang, R.Y.; Vania, C.; Kann, K.; Bowman, S.R. Intermediate-Task Transfer Learning with Pretrained Models for Natural Language Understanding: When and Why Does It Work? *arXiv* **2020**, arXiv:2005.00628.

38. He, C.; Chen, S.; Huang, S.; Zhang, J.; Song, X. Using Convolutional Neural Network with BERT for Intent Determination. In Proceedings of the IEEE 2019 International Conference on Asian Language Processing (IALP), Shanghai, China, 15–17 November 2019; pp. 65–70.
39. Pelicon, A. Zaznavanje sentimenta v novicah z globokimi nevronskimi mrežami. In Proceedings of the Conference on Language Technologies and Digital Humanities 2020 (to appear), Ljubljana, Slovenia 17–20 March 2020.
40. Vaswani, A.; Shazeer, N.; Parmar, N.; Uszkoreit, J.; Jones, L.; Gomez, A.N.; Kaiser, Ł.; Polosukhin, I. Attention is all you need. In Proceedings of the Advances in Neural Information Processing Systems, Long Beach, CA, USA, 4–9 December 2017; pp. 5998–6008.
41. Vig, J. Visualizing Attention in Transformer-Based Language Representation Models. *arXiv* **2019**, arXiv:1904.02679.
42. Vig, J.; Belinkov, Y. Analyzing the structure of attention in a transformer language model. *arXiv* **2019**, arXiv:1906.04284.
43. Škrlj, B.; Eržen, N.; Sheehan, S.; Luz, S.; Robnik-Šikonja, M.; Pollak, S. AttViz: Online exploration of self-attention for transparent neural language modeling. *arXiv* **2020**, arXiv:2005.05716.
44. George, D.; Mallery, P. *SPSS for Windows Step-by-Step: A Simple Guide and Reference, 14.0 Update*, 7th ed.; Allyn and Bacon, Inc.: Boston, MA, USA, 2006.
45. Krippendorff, K. *Content Analysis: An Introduction to Its Methodology*, 2nd ed.; Sage Publications: Thousand Oaks, CA, USA, 2004.
46. Landis, J.R.; Koch, G.G. The Measurement of Observer Agreement for Categorical Data. *Biometrics* **1977**, *33*, 159–174.
47. Rumsey, D.J.; Unger, D. *U Can: Statistics for Dummies*; John Wiley: Hoboken, NJ, USA, 2015.
48. O'Hare, N.; Davy, M.; Bermingham, A.; Ferguson, P.; Sheridan, P.; Gurrin, C.; Smeaton, A. Topic-dependent sentiment analysis of financial blogs. In Proceedings of the TSA 2009—1st International CIKM Workshop on Topic-Sentiment Analysis for Mass Opinion Measurement, Hong Kong, China, 6 November 2009; TSA: Arlington County, VA, USA, 2009; pp. 9–16, ISBN 978-1-60558-805-6.

© 2020 by the authors. Licensee MDPI, Basel, Switzerland. This article is an open access article distributed under the terms and conditions of the Creative Commons Attribution (CC BY) license (http://creativecommons.org/licenses/by/4.0/).

Article

Incorporating Synonym for Lexical Sememe Prediction: An Attention-Based Model

Xiaojun Kang [1], Bing Li [1], Hong Yao [1], Qingzhong Liang [1], Shengwen Li [2,3], Junfang Gong [2,4] and Xinchuan Li [1,*]

1. School of Computer Science, China University of Geosciences, Wuhan 430074, China; kangxj@cug.edu.cn (X.K.); 20141002431@cug.edu.cn (B.L.); yaohong@cug.edu.cn (H.Y.); qzliang@cug.edu.cn (Q.L.)
2. School of Geography and Information Engineering, China University of Geosciences, Wuhan 430074, China; swli@cug.edu.cn (S.L.); jfgong@cug.edu.cn (J.G.)
3. National Engineering Research Center for Geographic Information System, China University of Geosciences, Wuhan 430074, China
4. Key Laboratory of Urban Land Resources Monitoring and Simulation, Ministry of Natural Resources, Shenzhen 518034, China
* Correspondence: lixinchuan@cug.edu.cn; Tel.: +86-27-67883716

Received: 29 July 2020; Accepted: 27 August 2020; Published: 29 August 2020

Abstract: Sememe is the smallest semantic unit for describing real-world concepts, which improves the interpretability and performance of Natural Language Processing (NLP). To maintain the accuracy of the sememe description, its knowledge base needs to be continuously updated, which is time-consuming and labor-intensive. Sememes predictions can assign sememes to unlabeled words and are valuable work for automatically building and/or updating sememeknowledge bases (KBs). Existing methods are overdependent on the quality of the word embedding vectors, it remains a challenge for accurate sememe prediction. To address this problem, this study proposes a novel model to improve the performance of sememe prediction by introducing synonyms. The model scores candidate sememes from synonyms by combining distances of words in embedding vector space and derives an attention-based strategy to dynamically balance two kinds of knowledge from synonymous word set and word embedding vector. A series of experiments are performed, and the results show that the proposed model has made a significant improvement in the sememe prediction accuracy. The model provides a methodological reference for commonsense KB updating and embedding of commonsense knowledge.

Keywords: natural language processing; knowledge base; commonsense; sememe prediction; attention model

1. Introduction

In the field of Natural Language Processing (NLP), knowledge bases (KBs) play an important role in many NLP tasks. They provide rich semantic information for downstream tasks such as semantic disambiguation using WordNet's categorical information [1], bilingual embedded learning based on a multilingual KB [2]. Besides, recent researches have demonstrated that the introducing of KBs, especially commonsense KBs, not only improves the interpretability and performance of natural language processing task but also reduces the training time for machine learning [3–5].

In the commonsense KB of natural language, sememe denotes a single basic concept represented by words in Chinese and English. Linguists pointed out a long time ago that sememes are finer-grained semantic units than words [6], and a similar point is made in the theory of the universals of language [7]. For example, sememe is used as a basic representation object to reveal the relationship between concepts and properties they possess in HowNet, which is a well-known Chinese general KB [8]. HowNet employs linguists to artificially define some 2000 sememes as the smallest, most basic units of meaning that cannot be subdivided. It uses these sememes to annotate over 100,000 words and phrases. So far, HowNet has been successfully applied to a variety of NLP tasks, such as word similarity computation [9], semantic disambiguation [10], sentiment analysis [11], and improving word vector quality [12], and evaluating the semantic reasonableness of sentences [13].

The continued emergence of new words and the semantic evolution of words, facilitated by the increase in human communication capabilities and methods, has made it necessary to frequently enrich and update KBs. However, manually labeling sememes of words is a time-consuming and labor-intensive process. Besides, it can also suffer from inconsistent annotation results if the peoples who label sememes are not a domain knowledge expert. Benefiting the semantic information contained in the pre-trained word vectors, Xie, R., et al. [14,15] proposed a series of automatic labeling methods based on word vectors. These methods model the association between word vector representations by collaborative filtering or matrix decomposition methods, achieving automatic assigning sememes into unseen words.

However, there still remain challenges in accurately predicting sememes of unlabeled words. One of the challenges is that the performance of the model is highly dependent on the quality of the pre-trained word embedding vector. Furthermore, the word vector model is relatively simple, and the word vectors it constructs may not fully represent the senses of words in the real world. Table 1 illustrates a real-world example of the word "Shen Xue (申雪)", which means "redress an injustice". In Table 1, the similar words of the word "Shen Xue (申雪)" in the word embedding vector space are more similar to skating, because there is a famous skater named "Shen Xue (申雪)". That is to say, sometimes a word's embedding vector does not capture its semantics well. This may be due to the fact that most language models learn vectors based on the assumption that co-occurrence words are similar. We argue that the obtained word-embedding vectors mainly present correlations between words, rather than similarities between words.

Table 1. Comparison of the synonyms words and the top similar words in embedding space of "Shen Xue (申雪)".

Metric	Words	Similarity in Embedding Space
Top similar words in embedding vector	Skating (滑冰)	0.617
	winter Olympics (冬奥会)	0.573
	Speedskating (速滑)	0. 536
	Ice Arena (冰场)	0. 471
	Gymnastics (体操)	0.466
Synonyms	complain of an injustice (叫屈)	0.136
	appeal for justice (申冤)	0.122
	cry out for justice (喊冤)	0.036
	exonerate (昭雪)	0.057
True sememes	Corrections (改正), result (结果), error (误)	

To address the problem, we propose to use synonyms to improve the performance of the sememe prediction. Compared to word embedding vectors, synonyms are more consistent with human cognition, thus providing more solid references for predicting sememe. More importantly, synonym acquisition does not require a lot of training like word embedding training. Assigning synonyms of words does not require specialized knowledge, thus it can be done by volunteers.

This study aims to improve the prediction accuracy of the sememes of unlabeled words by introducing synonyms. Our original contributions include: (1) By introducing synonym knowledge, a sememe prediction model is explored from the perspective of word similarities rather than word correlations. (2) An attention-based sememe prediction model that incorporates information on synonym sets and word embeddings is developed to optimize the prediction effect through an attention strategy.

The rest of this paper is organized as follows. In Section 2, we review the related works and illustrate the limitations that remain. Section 3 details how the proposed model works. The dataset and evaluation experiments are presented in Section 4. We discuss several major factors that may affect model performance in Section 5. Section 6 concludes our work.

2. Related Work

Many KBs have been built recently for understanding the processes of NLP and improving the performance of NLP. One type of KB is known as commonsense KB, such as WordNet [16], HowNet [8], and BabelNet [17]. Compared to other types of KBs, such as Freebase [18], DBPedia [19], and YAGO [20], those manually defined commonsense KBs are richer in human knowledge and provide promising backing for various NLP tasks.

Considering that commonsense knowledge is increasing and evolving, it is important to update the commonsense KB, such as sememes of words, by automated approaches. The core of the automated process is to build intelligent algorithms that can accurately predict the sememes of unlabeled words or evolved words. To obtain higher accuracy, the algorithms may need to leverage all available knowledge.

One line of work that predicts sememes of unlabeled words was initiated using word embedded vectors. It assumes that similar words in word vector space should share the same sememes, thus sememes of unlabeled words can be inferred with pre-trained words embedded vector [21,22]. Sememe Prediction with Word Embeddings (SPWE) model first retrieves words that are similar to the vector representation of the word to be predicted and then recommends these words to the unlabeled word to be predicted, which in turn leads to the sememe prediction [14]. The paper also developed models based on matrix decomposition strategy to learn semantics and semantic relationships between words, including Sememe Prediction with Sememe Embeddings (SPSE) model and Sememe Prediction with Aggregated Sememe Embeddings (SPASE) model, and consequently predict the sememes of unlabeled words. LD-seq2seq treats sememe prediction as a weakly ordered multi-label task to label new words [23]. The models above, however, are limited by the quality of the word embedding vector, and it remains a challenge to obtain higher prediction accuracy.

To improve sememe prediction accuracy, various data have been introduced into existing prediction models. By introducing the internal structural features of words to solve the out-of-vocabulary (OOV) problem, Character-enhanced Sememe Prediction (CSP) model improves the prediction accuracy of the low-frequency words [15]. The method can alleviate the problem of large errors in the word vectors for words with fewer frequencies in the corpus. Based on the complementarity of different languages, Qi, F., et al. [24] establishes the association between semantics and cross-lingual words in the low-dimensional semantic space, and thus improves the ability of semantics prediction. Although the above work is very innovative, the employed knowledge is not very closed with sememes, and there is still a gap between the predicted results and the sememes that should be assigned.

Recently, the Sememe Prediction with Sentence Embedding and Chinese Dictionary (SPSECD) model have been proposed, which incorporates a dictionary as auxiliary information and predicts the sememe through the Recurrent Neural Network [25]. The model can account for the fact that some words have multiple senses, achieving the improvement of prediction accuracy. However, both the senses of new words and newly evolved sense of existing words cannot be presented by a dictionary in time, because it also needs time for updating. Especially, the word item in dictionaries is a very accurate expression, thus it needs more time to carefully revise new items by professional people.

3. Methodology

In our approach, we follow the basic idea of SPWE model, an assumption that similar words will share sememes. However, we argue that although word vectors can represent some semantic relatedness between words, it is not sufficient to represent the similarity of words in the real world, and thus are limited for accurately predicting the sememes of unlabeled words. Therefore, we employ synonyms, which embed a more accurate and richer human knowledge, to achieve sememe prediction.

3.1. Score Sememes from Synonyms

In the study, words with similar semantics are grouped into the same set, which we refer to here as synonym set, $T = \{w_1, w_2, \ldots, w_i, \ldots, w_j, \ldots, w_n\}$, where w_i denotes a word. Any two words, w_i and w_j, in the same synonym set are synonymous.

A score function is defined to score all the candidate sememes of unlabeled word w, in which high-scored sememes will be predicted as the sememes of w. For incorporating the knowledge in pre-trained word vectors, the distance of words in the pre-trained vector space is employed in the function. The function, using synonyms, can be formulated as Equation (1):

$$Score_{SPS}(s_j, w) = \sum_{w_i \in T} \cos(w, w_i) \cdot M_{ij} \cdot c^{r_i} \quad (1)$$

where M is the matrix representing the relationship between words and sememes, and can be calculated as

$$M_{ij} = \begin{cases} 1 & s_j \text{ is sememe of } w_i \\ 0 & \text{otherwise} \end{cases} \quad (2)$$

and $\cos(w, w_i)$ presents the cosine distance between the embedding vector of w and that of w_i. Different from the classic collaborative filtering in recommendation systems, sememes of most unrelated words do not include the true sememes of w in sememe prediction task. Therefore, the score function should give significantly large weight to the most similar words. To increase the influences of a few top words that are similar to w, a declined confidence factor c^{r_i} for each word w_i is assigned, where r_i the similarity rank of the word is w_i. to the word w in embedding space.

3.2. Attention-Based Sememe Prediction

Although synonyms can more accurately depict semantic similarity between two words than word embedding vector, the number of words existing in the synonym dataset is far fewer than the number of words represented in the pre-trained word vector dataset, such as Glove [26]. For words that are not included in synonym datasets, the above score function does not yet fully support the task of sememe prediction. Besides, prediction accuracy may also be impaired for words with fewer synonyms. Therefore, we combine synonym sets and pre-trained word vectors to depict the semantic similarity between words. A straightforward model can be derived, which score recommendation sememes by summing the scores of the two models using a coefficient of weight, as shown in Equation (3).

$$Score_{SPSW}(s_j, w) = \alpha Score_{SPS}(s_j, w) + (1 - \alpha) Score_{SPWE}(s_j, w) \quad (3)$$

where α is a hyperparameter, which denotes the weight of the SPS model's score.

Actually, we found that the predicted sememes based on synonym and based on word vectors, such as SPWE, were significantly different for different words. Using Equation (2) weights presented by the hyperparameter α is relatively straightforward, it is not flexible enough to make full use of knowledge from both the synonym and word embedding.

The study assumes that the weights of different knowledge should vary for different unlabeled words that are to be predicted. Inspired by [27], this study introduces an attention mechanism to obtain those weights. One of the benefits of attention mechanisms is that they allow for dealing with variable inputs, focusing on the most relevant parts of the input to make decisions [28]. An attention function can be described as mapping a query and a set of key-value pairs to an output [27], where the query and keys are word vectors; output is the weights of related words. Thus, an attention-based model, named ASPSW (Attention-based Sememe Prediction combining Synonym and Word embedding), is derived, and its score function can be calculated as Equation (4):

$$Score_{ASPSW}(s_j, w) = Attn(s_j, w, W) = \sum_{W_i \in Y}^{n} a_i^{Attn} Score(s_j, w) \qquad (4)$$

where a_i^{Attn} denotes the weights of contributions to different knowledge for different sememes in the joint model. The difference can be adjusted according to the distance in the word embedding space. Based on this, the weights of the contributions of different knowledge can be calculated by dynamically adjusting the score weights of the knowledge from Synonym and pre-trained word vector:

$$a_i^{Attn} = \begin{cases} \dfrac{1}{2 - \log(|Sim_{we} - Sim_{sy}|)} & if\ w_i \in W \\ \dfrac{1 - \log(|Sim_{we} - Sim_{sy}|)}{2 - \log(|Sim_{we} - Sim_{sy}|)} & if\ w_i \in T \end{cases} \qquad (5)$$

$$Sim_{we} = \frac{1}{K} \sum_{w_i \in W} cos(w, w_i) \qquad (6)$$

$$Sim_{sy} = \frac{1}{N} \sum_{w_i \in T} cos(w, w_i) \qquad (7)$$

where T is the synonym set of word w; W presents the top K similar words set of w in embedding space respectively, where K is a hyperparameter; Sim_{we} and Sim_{sy} represent the average semantic similarity between new words and similar words in word embedding and synonyms, respectively; $cos(w, w_i)$ is the cosine similarity between w and w_i according to their embedding vectors.

4. Experiment and Results

4.1. Dataset

HowNet: HowNet is a commonsense KB, in which approximately 2,000 sememes are manually defined. Those sememes serve as the smallest unit of meaning that is not easily re-divided, and more than 100,000 words and phrases are annotated with these sememes. The structure of HowNet is illustrated in Figure 1. The example in the figure shows the word "草根" explained in terms of sememes. The word consists of two senses in Chinese. One is "Grass root", which means a certain organ of a plant, and the other is "Grass roots", which generally refers to people at the bottom level or entrepreneurs starting from scratch. The former is explained by sememes, "part", "base" and "flowerGrass", and the latter consists of sememes, "human" and "ordinary". To reduce the noises from low-frequency sememes, the study removed the low-frequency sememes following the approach in [14] and experimented with only 1,400 remaining sememes.

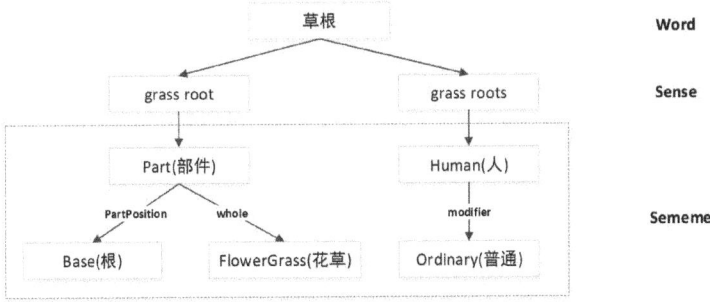

Figure 1. The sememes of Word "草根" in a commonsense database.

Sogou-T: The Sogo-T Corpus is an Internet corpus developed by Sogou and its corporate partners, which contains a variety of original web pages from the Internet, with a total of about 2.7 billion words.

Synonym dictionary: There are several available synonym data sources, such as the synonym dictionary ABC Thesaurus, the Chinese Dictionary, HIT IR-Lab Tongyici Cilin from Harbin Institute of Technology Social Computing and Information Retrieval Research Center, China. In the experiment, we selected HIT IR-Lab Tongyici Cilin (Extended) as a data source of the synonym set. It contains a total of 77,343 words. All words are organized together in a tree-like hierarchy with a total of five layers, as shown in Figure 2. For each layer, each category corresponds to a different code, e.g., "Evidence", "Proof" belong to the same category with code "Db03A01". The lower the layer, the finer the granularity of the category and the more similar the sense of words under the same node. The study uses only the lowest layer to construct synonym sets.

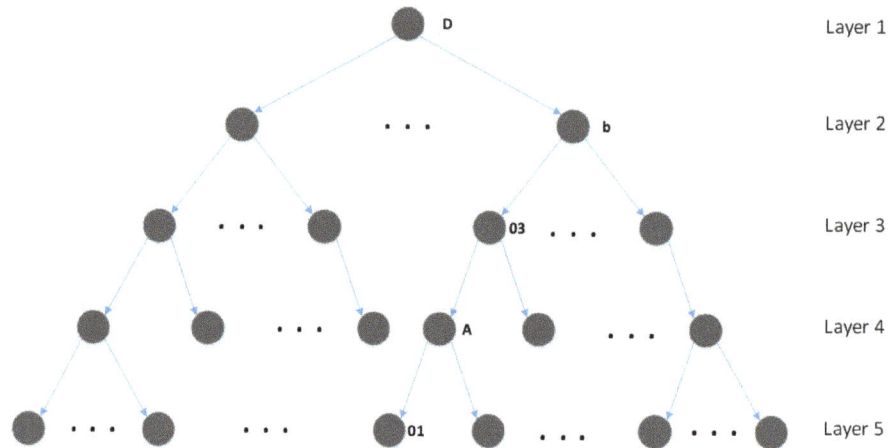

Figure 2. The five layers in HIT IR-Lab Tongyici Cilin.

4.2. Experimental Settings

The study employs Glove [26] to obtain the word embedding vectors of all words in the Sogou-T corpus. To keep data alignment, we removed words that were not contained in the pre-trained word vectors or not listed in the synonym sets. In the end, we selected a total of 44,556 words from HowNet. Ten percent of the words are selected for the test, and the rest 90% words are for training.

Models in three state-of-the-art works are selected as baseline models. The first work [14] includes five models, SPWE, SPSE, SPASE, SPWE+SPSE, and SPWE+SPASE. The second group models are proposed in [15], including five models variants: SPWCF (Sememe Prediction with Word-to-Character Filtering); SPCSE (Sememe Prediction with Character and Sememe Embeddings); SPWCF+SPCSE models that use only the internal information of words and both internal and external information for the original meaning; and the integrated framework of prediction CSP (Character-enhanced Sememe Prediction), respectively. The model in the last group is LD-seq2seq (Label Distributed seq2seq) that treats the sememe prediction as a weakly ordered multi-label task [23].

Follow the settings in [14], all the dimension sizes of word vectors, sememe vectors, and character vectors are set to 200. For the baseline model, in the SPWE model, the hyperparameter c that controls the contribution weight of different words is set to 0.8. The number of semantically similar words in the word vector space is set to $K=100$, which is the same as the setting in work [14]. In the SPSE model, the probability of decomposing zero elements in the matrix of word-sememe is set to 0.5%, the initial learning rate is set to 0.01, and the learning rate drops after iteration, and $\lambda_{SPWE}/\lambda_{SPSE}$ is set to 2.1 in its joint model, where λ_{SPWE} and λ_{SPSE} represent the weights of the SPWE and SPSE models, respectively.

For models from [15], we use cluster-based character embedding [29] to learn pre-trained character embeddings; the probability of decomposing zero elements in the matrix of word-sememe is set to 2.5%. For the joint model, we set the weight ratio of SPWCF and SPCSE to 4.0, the r weight ratio of SPWE and SPSE is 0.3125, and the weight ratio of internal and external models is 1.0. For LD-seq2seq [23] model, the dimension size of all hidden layers is set to 300, and its training batch size is set to 20. For SPSW model, we argue the contributions from SPS and SPWE are approximately equivalent, so α is set to 0.5.

4.3. Results

Since a large number of words have multiple sememes, the sememe prediction task can be considered as a multi-label classification task. The study uses the Mean Average Precision (MAP) as a metric, which is the same as previous work [14], to evaluate the accuracy of predicting sememe. For each unlabeled word in the test set, our model and the baseline models ranked all candidate sememes. Their MAPs are calculated by ranked results on the test dataset and are reported in Table 2.

Table 2. Prediction accuracy: Mean Average Precision (MAP); the best result is in bold-faced.

Model	MAP
SPWE [14]	0.5610
SPSE [14]	0.3916
SPASE [14]	0.3538
SPWE+SPSE [14]	0.5690
SPWE+SPASE [14]	0.5684
SPCSE [15]	0.3105
SPWCF [15]	0.4529
SPWCF+SPCSE [15]	0.4849
CSP [15]	0.6408
LD-seq2seq [23]	0.3765
SPS	0.5818
SPSW	0.6578
ASPSW	**0.6774**

Table 2 shows the accuracy of the sememe prediction accuracies of the baselines model and the proposed models in the study, where SPS, SPSW, and ASPSW are three models that employ Equation (1), (2), and (3) as score function, respectively.

The results suggest the proposed models ASPSW had made significant improvements compared to SPWE model. This experimental result further supports our idea that synonym sets, compared to word vectors, can more accurately characterize the sememe correlated relationships between words. The SPSW model has a larger gain than the SPS model, which shows that although the synonymy forest can provide more accurate semantic similarity, the synonyms provided by the synonymy forest are limited and rare, so the semantic information provided by the word vector can be combined to further improve the accuracy of the prediction of sememes. The ASPSW, using attention strategy to dynamic weigh model significantly, outperforms the fixed weights, which shows that the proposed attention mechanism is effective in predicting the semantics for different unlabeled words and can effectively adjust the effects of different knowledge for words to be predicted.

5. Discussion

5.1. The Two Ways of Combining Synonyms and Word Embedding Vectors

Two score functions are introduced in Section 3.2 for combining knowledge from synonyms and word embedding vector. One is the static SPSW, as shown in Equation (2), and the other is attention-based ASPSW, as shown in Equation (3). The former score function combines the knowledge between synonyms and from pre-trained word vector by the hyperparameters, α, and the later score function dynamically balances two kinds of knowledge using an attention strategy. To examine the performance of two models, we performed experiments with a different value on static SPSW, and listed the results in Table 3.

Table 3. The prediction accuracy of different α; the best result is in bold-face.

α	MAP
0.1	0.5820
0.2	0.6023
0.3	0.6222
0.4	0.6416
0.5	0.6578
0.6	0.6718
0.7	**0.6787**
0.8	0.6764
0.9	0.6674
ASPSW	0.6774

As shown in Table 3, the values of α have made a significant effect on the prediction accuracy. When it was set to 0.7, the model SPSW achieved the best results, and the ASPSW obtained the second-best results. Despite an appropriately selected α value, static SPSW achieves better results, the best and the second results are a little different. Considering the robustness of methods, we argue that ASPSW is a more promising model for sememe prediction.

To observe the difference caused by models, we performed experiments on random-selected 100 words with three typical models (score function), SPWE, SPS, and ASPSW. The scores of the three models are recorded and plotted in Figure 3. The figure shows that some of the scores of the SPS model are close to 0, which may be because the knowledge in the synonym dictionary is incomplete. For a new word, SPS can rarely find a valid synonym for inferring sememes. In most cases, the prediction score of the ASPSW model is higher than that of the SPWE model and the SPS model, indicating that the dynamical weights in the joint model can make full use of different knowledge and avoid false predictions due to incompleteness or inaccuracy in a single type of knowledge.

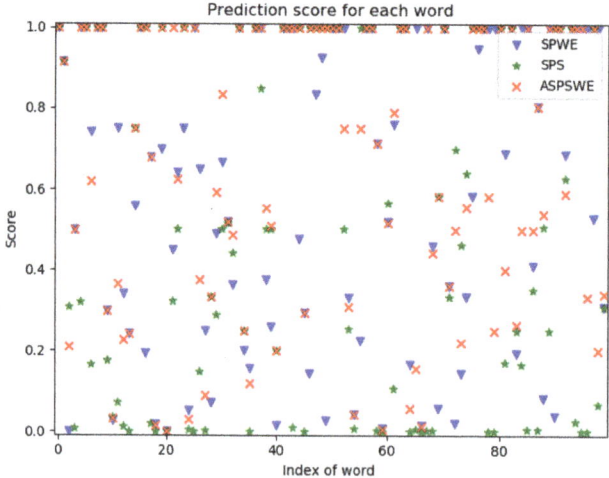

Figure 3. Randomly select 100 words and test their sememes prediction score (MAP value) of the SPWE, SPS, and ASPSW models.

5.2. Impact of the Value of K

The parameter K is the number of similar words in the word vector space used to select candidate sememe. As a hyperparameter, the size of K may affect the prediction accuracy of the proposed model. To examine the effect of the value of K, we set the value K from 10 to 100. The accuracies of SPWE and the proposed model, ASPSW, are listed in Table 4.

Table 4. Prediction accuracy of the SPWE and ASPSW models under setting different values of k;the best results are in bold-face.

Nearest Word Number	SPWE	ASPSW
10	0.5478	0.6724
20	0.5566	0.6762
30	0.5587	0.6773
40	0.5597	**0.6778**
50	0.5602	**0.6778**
60	0.5605	0.6776
70	0.5606	0.6775
80	0.5608	0.6777
90	0.5609	0.6777
100	0.5610	0.6774

As shown in Table 2, ASPSW provides great prediction accuracy; even the value of K is set to small values. When K is set to larger than 20, the prediction results tend to be stable, indicating that the model has good robustness. From this, it suggests that smaller numbers of the most similar words will cover the semantics of the words, thus achieving a quite accurate prediction of sememes. The results further confirm that in Table 1, although the synonym KB provides a few synonyms, it is still possible to reach an accuracy that exceeds the baseline. As the values of K increase, the prediction accuracy of the model improves. In the process, the prediction accuracy of the ASPSW model is kept well above the accuracy of the baseline model, SPWE, demonstrating the validity of the ASPSW model.

5.3. Calculation Performance Analysis

In the experiment, we examined the time efficiency of different models on predicting the sememes of unlabeled words. As shown in Table 5, we randomly selected 5000 words as a test task for predicting their sememes with different models and recorded the time consumption of the training process and prediction, respectively.

Table 5. Time consumption for predicting sememes of 5000 unlabeled words.

Method	Training Costs (s)	Predicting Costs(s)	Total (s)
SPWE	NA	2129	2129
SPSE	6510	40	6550
SPWE+SPSE	6510	2195	8705
SPCSE	41,191	2031	43,222
SPWCF	NA	334	334
SPWCF+SPCSE	41,191	2417	43,608
CSP	47,701	4656	52,357
SPS	NA	22	22
SPSW	NA	2169	2169
ASPSW	NA	2639	2639

Table 5 shows that the SPSY model takes the least amount of time to accomplish this task. It benefited from the fact that the model does not contain training the process of the reference words, synonym, and thus, it does not need to calculate word similarities with word vectors. Actually, all the models without the training process spend less time than the models that contain a training process, because the training process is very time-consuming. Although the SPS model based on matrix decomposition and SPWCF model based on internal character features of words can complete the prediction process in a relatively short time, their prediction accuracy still remains lower.

In addition, compared with SPSE and SPCSE models, the SPSW and ASPSW model does not require additional time for training. The SPSW model based on fixed weights is similar to the SPWEA model based on word embedding in time consumption. The ASPSW model based on an attention mechanism can also improve the prediction accuracy of sememes without significantly increasing time consumption.

5.4. Case Study

In the case study, we give further analysis by detailed examples to explain the effectiveness of our model.

Table 6 lists the results of some of the SPWE model and ASPSW model sememe predictions. Each word shows its top five predicted sememes, in which the true sememes are in bold. As it can be seen from the table, ASPSW predicts the true sememes in their top positions, thus showing that the finding of semantically similar words is crucial for the sememe prediction of words. In the SPWE model using the word vector only, the corrected predicted sememe of words such as "saber" and "pull, social connections" do not rank in top positions. For the word "saber", the vector-based model focuses more on the semantics of the simultaneous occurrence of the word "knife", so that sememe "tools" and "cutting" rank higher than the correct sememe "army" and "weapon". With the introduction of the synonym set, the ASPSW model can compensate for the inability of word embedding to accurately define semantics and make the recommended sememe for "saber" more biased towards the sememes of "army" and "weapon". In addition, for words such as "appease" and "old woman", the SPWE model failed to predict correct sememes. For example, the SPWE model does not capture the semantic information of the word "appease", and the recommended sememe is all semantics that is not closed to "appease". The introduction of the ASPSW model with a synonym set achieves good prediction results, which further demonstrates that word embedding has a significant gap in the capture of semantic information from the synonym set.

Table 6. Comparison of sememe prediction examples for the SPWE and ASPSW models, the sememes in bold font are the true sememes for each word.

Words	Top 5 Sememes with SPWE	Top 5 Sememes with ASPSW	True Sememes
Saber (军刀)	tools, Cutting, Breaking, **Army, Weapons** (用具, 切削, 破开, 军, 武器)	**army, weapons**, tools, cutting, **piercing** (军, 武器, 用具, 切削, 扎)	Army, Weapons, Piercing (军, 武器, 扎)
Kindergarten (幼儿园)	**place**, education, teaching, learning, **people** (场所, 教育, 教, 学习, 人)	**place, people, children, care**, education, people (场所, 人, 少儿, 照料, 教育)	people, place, children, care (人, 场所, 少儿, 照料)
special column (专栏)	Chinese, **books**, publishing, news, time (语文, 书刊, 出版, 新闻, 时间)	**book, special**, Chinese, publishing, news (书刊, 特别, 语文, 出版, 新闻)	Parts, Books, special (部件, 书刊, 特别)
appease (息怒)	person, be kind, answer, sit, emperor (人, 善待, 答, 坐蹲, 皇)	**emotion, angry, stop**, person, be kind (情感, 生气, 制止, 人, 善待)	emotion, angry, stop (情感, 生气, 制止)
pull, social connections (门路)	rich, become, **method**, **person**, **intimate** (富, 成为, 方法, 人, 亲疏)	**method, person, intimate**, success, road (方法, 人, 亲疏, 成功, 道路)	person, method, intimate (人, 方法, 亲疏)
old woman (妪)	crying, poultry, shouting, diligent, surname (哭泣, 禽, 喊, 勤, 姓)	**person, elderly, female**, crying, poultry (人, 老年, 女, 哭泣, 禽)	person, elderly, female (人, 女, 老年)

To better illustrate the difference effect over different words, we took two more words as an example, and distinguish their similar words by whether they contain correct sememes in the pre-trained word vector space. As shown in Figure 4a, the top similar words to word "申雪" in the vector space do not contain the sememe that should recommend the word "申雪". For the unlabeled word "便士", as shown in Figure 4b, the words which contain the same sememe with it are clustered around it in the vector space. The two examples show that there is a very clear deviation in the distribution of similar words in word vector; this may be caused by the fact that the language model of generating word embedding vectors is inferred from word co-occurrence instead of similar semantics. To overcome those deviations, we suggest again that it is very necessary to combine the synonym and pre-trained word vector for better understanding word embedding vectors and improving the performances of various downstream tasks.

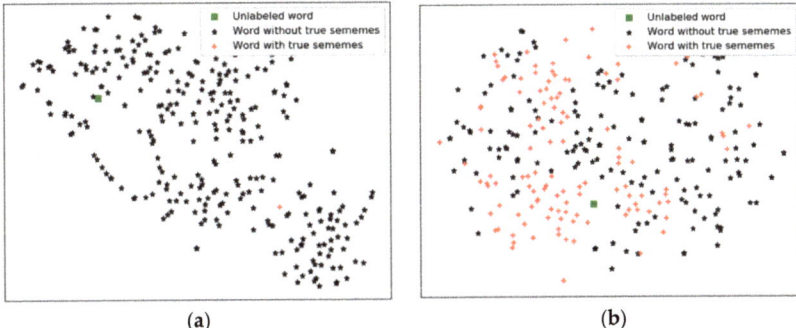

Figure 4. Top 300 similar words of the unlabeled word (a) "申雪" (b) "便士" in the word vector space, where "+" means that the sememes can be recommended for the unlabeled word because the word contains the true sememe of the unlabeled word; "*" presents a word that it is impossible to recommend the true sememe for unlabeled word because the word and the unmarked word do not contain the same sememes.

6. Conclusions and Future Work

In this study, we propose to predict the sememes of unlabeled words by introducing a synonym. An attention-based model, ASPSW, is developed that incorporates similar relationships in the synonym set into the sememe prediction decisions. A series of experiments are performed, and the results show that the proposed model has made a significant improvement in the sememe prediction accuracy. This study suggests that the dynamical fusion of knowledge from different sources is expected to enhance the ability to perform NLP tasks, especially in the absence of training samples.

In our future work, we will make the following efforts: (1) There is a tree-like hierarchy structure in HowNet dataset, and we plan to merge the hierarchical relationships between the sememes into future prediction models, which may improve the accuracy of sememe prediction; (2) more synonym datasets, including WordNet, will be combined to improve the performance of sememe prediction.

Author Contributions: Conceptualization, X.K. and X.L.; methodology, X.K., X.L. and B.L.; software, B.L.; resources, H.Y.; writing—original draft preparation, B.L. and S.L.; writing—review and editing, X.K., Q.L., S.L., H.Y. and J.G.; funding acquisition, H.Y. All authors have read and agreed to the published version of the manuscript.

Funding: This research was supported by the NSF of China (Grant No. 61972365, 61673354, 61672474, 41801378), and Open Fund of Key Laboratory of Urban Land Resources Monitoring and Simulation, Ministry of Natural Resources (grant number: KF-2019-04-033).

Acknowledgments: In this section you can acknowledge any support given which is not covered by the author contribution or funding sections. This may include administrative and technical support, or donations in kind (e.g., materials used for experiments).

Conflicts of Interest: The authors declare no conflict of interest.

References

1. Aouicha, M.B.; Taieb, M.A.H.; Marai, H.I. WordNet and Wiktionary-Based Approach for Word Sense Disambiguation. In *Transactions on Computational Collective Intelligence XXIX*; Springer: Cham, Switzerland, 2018; pp. 123–143.
2. Artetxe, M.; Labaka, G.; Agirre, E. Learning bilingual word embeddings with (almost) no bilingual data. In Proceedings of the 55th Annual Meeting of the Association for Computational Linguistics, Vancouver, BC, Canada, 30 July–4 August 2017; Volume 1, pp. 451–462.
3. Chen, Y.; Luo, Z. A Word Representation Method Based on Hownet. *Beijing Da Xue Xue Bao* **2019**, *55*, 22–28.
4. Peng-Hsuan, L. CA-EHN: Commonsense Word Analogy from E-HowNet. *arXiv* **2019**, arXiv:1908.07218.
5. Iqbal, F.; Fung, B.C.M.; Debbabi, M.; Batool, R.; Marrington, A. Wordnet-based criminal networks mining for cybercrime investigation. *IEEE Access* **2019**, *7*, 22740–22755. [CrossRef]
6. Bloomfield, L. A set of postulates for the science of language. *Language* **1926**, *2*, 153–164. [CrossRef]
7. Goddard, C.; Wierzbicka, A. *Semantic and Lexical Universals: Theory and Empirical Findings*; John Benjamins Publishing: Amsterdam, The Netherlands, 1994; Volume 25.
8. Dong, Z.; Dong, Q. *Hownet and the Computation of Meaning*; World Scientific: Singapore, 2006; pp. 1–303.
9. Liu, Q.; Li, S. Word similarity computing based on Hownet. *Comput. Linguist. Chin. Lang. Process.* **2002**, *7*, 59–76.
10. Duan, X.; Zhao, J.; Xu, B. Word sense disambiguation through sememe labeling. In Proceedings of the International Joint Conference on Artificial Intelligence, Hyderabad, India, 6–12 January 2007; pp. 1594–1599.
11. Huang, M.; Ye, B.; Wang, Y.; Chen, H.; Cheng, J.; Zhu, X. New word detection for sentiment analysis. In Proceedings of the 52nd Annual Meeting of the Association for Computational Linguistics, Baltimore, MD, USA, 22–27 June 2014; Volume 1, pp. 531–541.
12. Yang, L.; Kong, C.; Chen, Y.; Liu, Y.; Fan, Q.; Yang, E. Incorporating Sememes into Chinese Definition Modeling. *IEEE/ACM Trans. Audio Speech Lang. Process.* **2019**, *28*, 1669–1677. [CrossRef]
13. Liu, S.; Xu, J.; Ren, X. Evaluating semantic rationality of a sentence: A sememe-word-matching neural network based on hownet. In Proceedings of the CCF International Conference on Natural Language Processing and Chinese Computing, Dunhuang, China, 9–14 October 2019; pp. 787–800.
14. Xie, R.; Yuan, X.; Liu, Z.; Sun, M. Lexical sememe prediction via word embeddings and matrix factorization. In Proceedings of the 26th International Joint Conference on Artificial Intelligence, Melbourne, Australia, 19–25 August 2017; pp. 4200–4206.
15. Jin, H.; Zhu, H.; Liu, Z.; Xie, R.; Sun, M.; Lin, F.; Lin, L. Incorporating Chinese Characters of Words for Lexical Sememe Prediction. In Proceedings of the 56th Annual Meeting of the Association for Computational Linguistics, Melbourne, Australia, 15–20 July 2018; Volume 1.
16. Miller, G.A. WordNet: A Lexical Database for English. *Commun. ACM* **1995**, *38*, 39–41. [CrossRef]
17. Navigli, R.; Ponzetto, S.P. BabelNet: The automatic construction, evaluation and application of a wide-coverage multilingual semantic network. *Artif. Intell.* **2012**, *193*, 217–250. [CrossRef]
18. Bollacker, K.; Evans, C.; Paritosh, P.; Sturge, T.; Taylor, J. Freebase: A collaboratively created graph database for structuring human knowledge. In Proceedings of the ACM SIGMOD International Conference on Management of Data, Vancouver, BC, Canada, 10–12 June 2008; pp. 1247–1249.
19. Auer, S.; Bizer, C.; Kobilarov, G.; Lehmann, J.; Cyganiak, R.; Ives, Z. DBpedia: A nucleus for a Web of open data. In *Lecture Notes in Computer Science (including subseries Lecture Notes in Artificial Intelligence and Lecture Notes in Bioinformatics)*; Springer: Berlin/Heidelberg, Germany, 2007; Volume 4825 LNCS, pp. 722–735.
20. Hoffart, J.; Suchanek, F.M.; Berberich, K.; Weikum, G. YAGO2: A spatially and temporally enhanced knowledge base from Wikipedia. *Artif. Intell.* **2013**, *194*, 28–61. [CrossRef]
21. Rizkallah, S.; Atiya, A.F.; Shaheen, S. A Polarity Capturing Sphere for Word to Vector Representation. *Appl. Sci.* **2020**, *10*, 4386. [CrossRef]
22. Devlin, J.; Chang, M.-W.; Lee, K.; Toutanova, K. BERT: Pre-training of Deep Bidirectional Transformers for Language Understanding. In Proceedings of the NAACL-HLT, Minneapolis, MN, USA, 2–7 June 2019.
23. Li, W.; Ren, X.; Dai, D.; Wu, Y.; Wang, H.; Sun, X. Sememe prediction: Learning semantic knowledge from unstructured textual wiki descriptions. *arXiv* **2018**, arXiv:1808.05437.

24. Qi, F.; Lin, Y.; Sun, M.; Zhu, H.; Xie, R.; Liu, Z. Cross-lingual Lexical Sememe Prediction. In Proceedings of the 2018 Conference on Empirical Methods in Natural Language Processing, Brussels, Belgium, 31 October–4 November 2018; pp. 358–368.
25. Bai, M.; Lv, P.; Long, X. Lexical Sememe Prediction with RNN and Modern Chinese Dictionary. In Proceedings of the 2018 14th International Conference on Natural Computation, Fuzzy Systems and Knowledge Discovery (ICNC-FSKD), Huangshan, China, 28–30 July 2018; pp. 825–830.
26. Pennington, J.; Socher, R.; Manning, C.D. GloVe: Global vectors for word representation. In Proceedings of the 2014 Conference on Empirical Methods in Natural Language Processing (EMNLP), Doha, Qatar, 25–29 October 2014; pp. 1532–1543.
27. Vaswani, A.; Shazeer, N.; Parmar, N.; Uszkoreit, J.; Jones, L.; Gomez, A.N.; Kaiser, Ł.; Polosukhin, I. Attention is all you need. In Proceedings of the Advances in Neural Information Processing Systems, Long Beach, CA, USA, 4–9 December 2017; pp. 5998–6008.
28. Veličković, P.; Cucurull, G.; Casanova, A.; Romero, A.; Lio, P.; Bengio, Y. Graph attention networks. In Proceedings of the 6th International Conference on Learning Representations, ICLR 2018-Conference Track, Vancouver, BC, Canada, 30 April–3 May 2018.
29. Chen, X.; Xu, L.; Liu, Z.; Sun, M.; Luan, H. Joint learning of character and word embeddings. In Proceedings of the Twenty-Fourth International Joint Conference on Artificial Intelligence, Buenos Aires, Argentina, 25–31 July 2015.

© 2020 by the authors. Licensee MDPI, Basel, Switzerland. This article is an open access article distributed under the terms and conditions of the Creative Commons Attribution (CC BY) license (http://creativecommons.org/licenses/by/4.0/).

Article

DAWE: A Double Attention-Based Word Embedding Model with Sememe Structure Information

Shengwen Li [1,2], Renyao Chen [1], Bo Wan [1,2], Junfang Gong [1], Lin Yang [1,2] and Hong Yao [3,*]

1. School of Geography and Information Engineering, China University of Geosciences, Wuhan 430074, China; swli@cug.edu.cn (S.L.); cryao@cug.edu.cn (R.C.); wanbo@cug.edu.cn (B.W.); jfgong@cug.edu.cn (J.G.); yanglin@cug.edu.cn (L.Y.)
2. National Engineering Research Center for Geographic Information System, University of Geosciences, Wuhan 430074, China
3. School of Computer Science, China University of Geosciences, Wuhan 430074, China
* Correspondence: yaohong@cug.edu.cn; Tel.: +86-27-67883716

Received: 15 July 2020; Accepted: 19 August 2020; Published: 21 August 2020

Abstract: Word embedding is an important reference for natural language processing tasks, which can generate distribution presentations of words based on many text data. Recent evidence demonstrates that introducing sememe knowledge is a promising strategy to improve the performance of word embedding. However, previous works ignored the structure information of sememe knowledges. To fill the gap, this study implicitly synthesized the structural feature of sememes into word embedding models based on an attention mechanism. Specifically, we propose a novel double attention word-based embedding (DAWE) model that encodes the characteristics of sememes into words by a "double attention" strategy. DAWE is integrated with two specific word training models through context-aware semantic matching techniques. The experimental results show that, in word similarity task and word analogy reasoning task, the performance of word embedding can be effectively improved by synthesizing the structural information of sememe knowledge. The case study also verifies the power of DAWE model in word sense disambiguation task. Furthermore, the DAWE model is a general framework for encoding sememes into words, which can be integrated into other existing word embedding models to provide more options for various natural language processing downstream tasks.

Keywords: natural language processing; word representation learning; word2vec; sememes; attention mechanism; structural information

---

1. Introduction

The basis of applying deep learning to solve natural language processing (NLP) tasks is to obtain high-quality representations of words from large amounts of text data [1]. Traditionally, words are represented in a sparse high-dimensional space using count-based vectors in which each word in a vocabulary is represented by a single dimension [2]. In contrast, word embedding aims to map words into continuous low-dimensional semantic space; in this way, each word is represented by a real-valued vector, namely word vector, often composed tens or hundreds of dimensions [3]. Word embedding assumes that words used in similar ways should have similar representations, thereby naturally capturing their meaning. Word vectors obtained from word embedding have been widely used in many applications: text summarization, sentiment analysis, reading comprehension, machine translation, etc.

In a great deal of word embedding-related works that have emerged in recent years, the Word2Vec [3] model strikes a good balance between efficiency and quality. In the training process of Word2vec, words are mapped to the same vector space. For words that share a similar context in the corpus, their corresponding vectors should be close to each other in the vector space [4]. During the training process, the vector assignments of the words are repeatedly adjusted until the values are close enough to each other, if they are adjacent in the text corpus. As a result, the low-frequency words in corpus cannot be accurately represented in Word2Vec model because the training process of such words is not sufficient.

Recently, studies have shown that taking external knowledge as the complement of text corpus can effectively improve the quality of word embeddings [5–10]. Among them, the "word–sense–sememe" (Figure 1) knowledge is an intuitive form of organizing words and their senses that are easily organized and understood [11]. By synthesizing the "word–sense–sememe" knowledge, Niu et al. [7] proposed the sememe-encoded word representation learning (SE-WRL) model that made significant performance in word embedding.

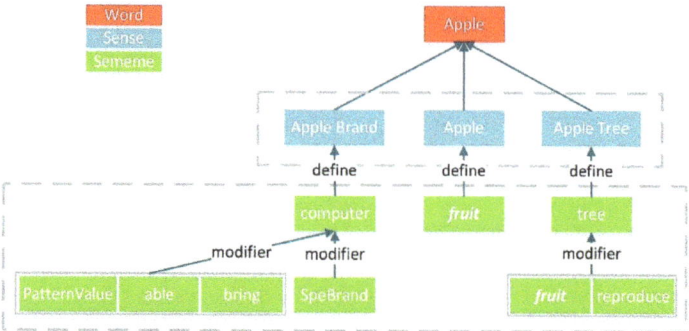

Figure 1. An example of the word–sense–sememe structure, where sememes are defined as minimum units of word meanings. There exists a limited close set of sememes to compose the open set of word meanings (i.e., word sense). For instance, the word (the first layer) "Apple" contains three senses (the second layer): "Apple Brand" (a famous computer brand), "Apple" (a sort of fruit) and "Apple Tree". The third layer is those sememes explaining each sense. The sememes of sense "Apple Brand" are "computer", "PatternValue", "able", "bring" and "SpeBrand (specific brand)". The sememe of sense "Apple" is "fruit". The sememes of sense "Apple Tree" are "fruit", "reproduce" and "tree".

SE-WRL model believes that contributions of each sememe under a sense are equivalent. However, the nature of sememes determines that different sememes under a sense may be different, which means the contributions of each sememe to the sense should be varied depending on the particular case. The inequality may be caused by two main reasons: (1) Different senses correspond to the different hierarchical structures of sememes. The sememes are organized into a hierarchical structure, such as the sememes in the sense "Apple brand" in Figure 1. Because of the hierarchical structure, there is fusion among sememes, which means that sememes at different branches of different levels are usually not equivalent. For example, the sememe "computer" in the sense "Apple brand" can be presented by its under-layer sememes ("PatternValue", "able", "bring" and "SpeBrand (specific brand)"). Furthermore, sememes at the same level are not equivalent in most cases. (2) The context of sememes is varied. The meaning of a word needs to be reflected in a special context, so the sememes are also affected by the context of the word. As shown in Figure 2, when the word "Apple" appears in the context "I am going to the ~ store now.", the meaning of "Apple" should be close to the sense "Apple brand". At this point, the sememe "SpeBrand" should have a higher weight than other sememes of the sense "Apple brand". Therefore, the weights of sememes in a sense should change dynamically with different contexts.

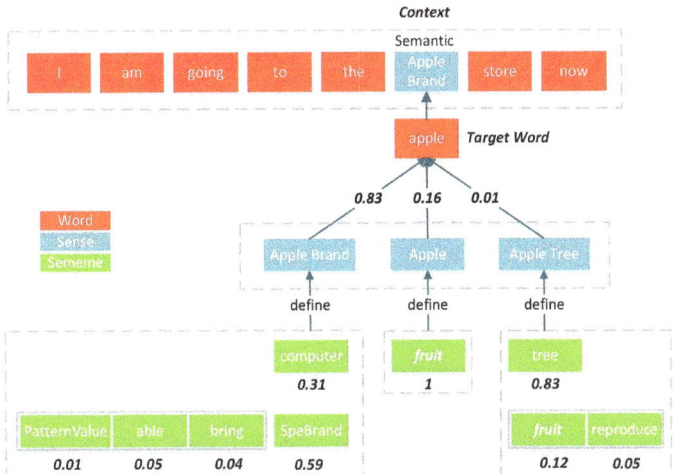

Figure 2. Interpretation of weight changes of sense and sememe. Sense means the meaning that exists within the word and does not change with the context, but its semantic contribution to the word is different in different contexts. For example, the word "Apple" has three different "senses": "Apple Brand", "Apple (Fruit)" and "Apple Tree". In the context "I am going to the ~ store now.", the semantic of the word "apple" tends to the sense "Apple Brand". The sememe's contribution to the sense should be different.

To fill this gap, a "double attention" mechanism is proposed to capture the inequality of sememes, thereby the meanings of words can be more accurately represented. Specifically, we derive a double attention-based word embedding (DAWE) model. This model uses senses as a bridge in the process of encoding sememes into words, in which the word can be represented as a fusion of their different senses and a sense can be represented as the weighted sum of the sememes of the sense.

The original contributions of this work can be summarized as follows: (1) The proposed "double attention" mechanism captures the weight changes of the different sememes of a sense with context, as well as the weight changes of the different senses within the word with context so that the obtained word vectors can be represented completely and accurately by sememes. (2) Two specific word training models are derived by combining the DAWE word encoding model with context-aware semantic matching. The experimental results of both word similarity task and word analogy reasoning task on the standard datasets show that the proposed models outperform previous models. (3) The proposed DAWE model is a general framework of encoding sememes into words and can be integrated with other existing word embedding models to provide more methods for word embedding.

2. Notation and Definition

The symbolic conventions that are used below are given here: W, S and X represent word set, sense set and sememe set, respectively. For each word $w \in W$, there are multiple senses $s_i^{(w)} \in S^{(w)}$, and $S^{(w)}$ represents the sense set corresponding to the word w; for each sense $s_i^{(w)}$, corresponding to several different sememes $x_j^{(s_i)} \in X_i^{(w)}$, $X_i^{(w)}$ represents the sememe set of the ith sense corresponding to the word w and $C(w)$ represents the context word set corresponding to the word w. We use the bold form $w/s/x \subset \mathbb{R}^D$ corresponding to w/s/x to represent the vectors of word/sense/sememe, where D is the dimension of those vectors.

Definition 1. *Word Embedding.*

As shown in Figure 3, for the text corpus C, word embedding maps each word w ∈ W to a continuous low-dimensional space $\mathbb{R}^D$, while ensuring that the final embeddings (vectors) can represent the semantic relevance between words in the original text corpus C.

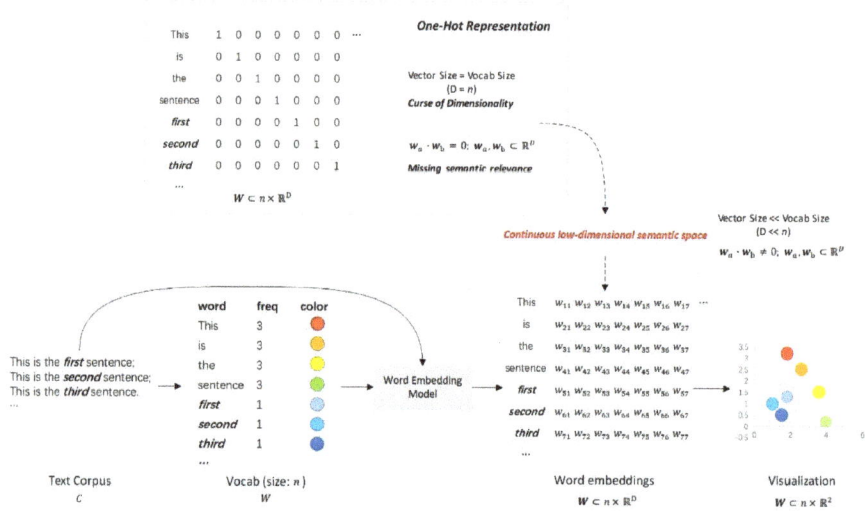

Figure 3. Word embedding workflow.

Definition 2. *Encoding Words with Sememes.*

It is a process of using sememes as a semantic supplement to encode words. In the process, word embedding can be simplified as the encoding of words from sememes to words, which means word vectors can be obtained by encoding corresponding sememes of words:

$$w = f_{X \to w}(X^{(w)}, \theta_{X \to w}), \tag{1}$$

where $\theta_{X \to w}$ represents the parameters when encoding sememe set $X^{(w)}$ to its corresponding word w. $f_{X \to w}(X^{(w)}, \theta_{X \to w})$ can be a simple encoding function, such as sum operation ($f_{X \to w}(X^{(w)}, \theta_{X \to w}) = \sum_{i=1}^{|X^{(w)}|} x_i^{(w)}$) or average operation ($f_{X \to w}(X^{(w)}, \theta_{X \to w}) = \frac{1}{|X^{(w)}|} \sum_{i=1}^{|X^{(w)}|} x_i^{(w)}$), or $f_{X \to w}(X^{(w)}, \theta_{X \to w})$ be neural networks, such as $f_{X \to w}(X^{(w)}, \theta_{X \to w}) = \sigma(W \cdot X^{(w)} + b)$, where σ denotes the activation function, W is the weight matrix and b is the bias.

Definition 3. *Encoding Words with Sememes through Senses.*

As shown in Figure 1, a word may consist of many different senses, each of which is described by several sememes. Therefore, this "word–sense–sememe" structure allows us to achieve the encoding process from sememes to words using senses as a semantic bridge, that is, the encoding process of the word w is represented as a mapping function of all its corresponding senses $S^{(w)}$. The formalization is as follows:

$$w = f_{S \to w}(S^{(w)}, \theta_{S \to w}), \tag{2}$$

for each sense $s_i^{(w)} \in S^{(w)}$, it is encoded by all its corresponding sememes $X_i^{(w)}$:

$$s_i^{(w)} = f_{X \to s}\left(X_i^{(w)}, \theta_{X \to s}\right), \tag{3}$$

where $\theta_{S \to w}$ and $\theta_{X \to s}$ denote the trainable parameters.

The objective of this study is to find the $f_{S \to w}$ function and the $f_{X \to s}$ function in Equation (2) and Equation (3), while taking full advantage of the structure of the sememes.

3. Related Works

In this section, we mainly introduce the works related to this study, including classical word embedding models and the word embedding models that introduce internal semantic information of words and external semantic information (image, knowledgebase, etc.). These works are illustrated in Figure 4.

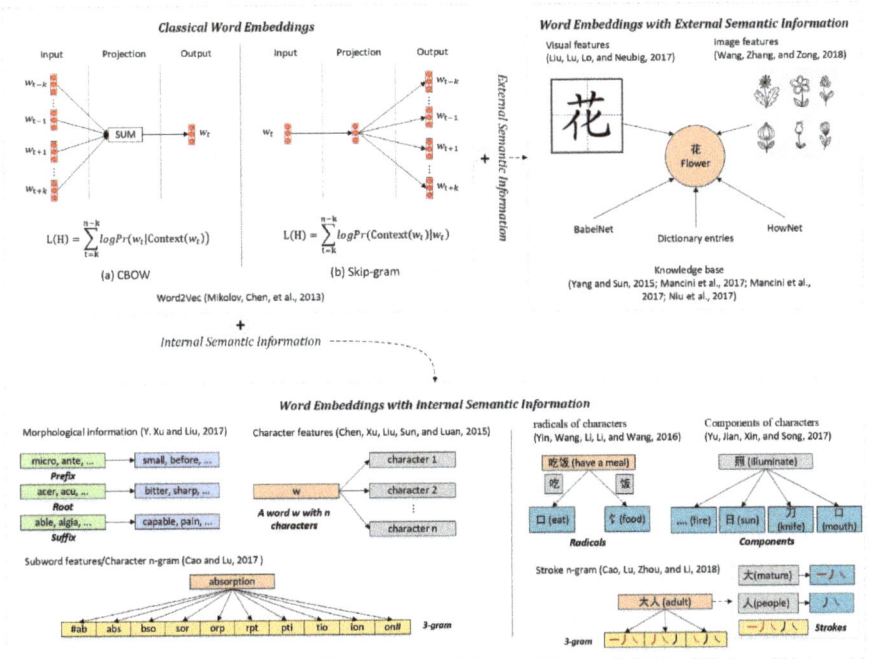

Figure 4. Several typical works of word embeddings.

3.1. Classical Word Embeddings

Word embedding aims to embed words into continuous low-dimensional, high-density semantic space. Early models usually use an NLM (neural language model) to generate word vectors (word-level word embedding vectors). The typical representative of them is the Word2Vec, which includes a CBOW model (continuous bag-of-words model) and a Skip-gram model (continuous skip-gram model), as shown in Figure 4. The key idea of Word2Vec is that the words with similar text contexts (or those words appearing in the same window that slides through the text with a size of k) should be close to each other in the semantic space, that is, their word vectors should be similar. As shown in Figure 3, the words "first", "second" and "third" are close to each other in the semantic space because they have the same context "This is the ~ sentence".

Skip-gram is a model which predicts the context words (surrounding words) given a target word (the center word). It intends to maximize the likelihood function as follows:

$$L(H) = \sum_{t=k}^{n-k} \log P(w_{t-k}, \ldots, w_{t+k} | w_t) \cong \sum_{t=k}^{n-k} \log \prod_{w_c \in C(w_t)} P(w_c | w_t). \qquad (4)$$

where n is the size of the text corpus, that is, the number of words contained in the corpus. $P(w_{t-k}, \ldots, w_{t+k} | w_t)$ denotes the probability of the context $[w_{t-k}, \ldots, w_{t+k}]$ being predicted by the target word w_t, $[w_{t-k}, \ldots, w_{t+k}]$ is the set of the first and last k words of the current word w_t in the text sequence and k is the size of the context window. For example, for the text sequence, "I twisted an apple off the tree," when the target word is "apple" and k = 2, then $[w_{t-k}, \ldots, w_{t+k}]$ = [twisted, an, off, tree]. Based on the assumption of context independence, the probability of predicting context $[w_{t-k}, \ldots, w_{t+k}]$ by the target word w_t can be converted to the product of the probability of predicting each word w_c in the context (the co-occurrence probability of the target word and the context word): $P(w_{t-k}, \ldots, w_{t+k} | w_t) \cong \prod_{w_c \in C(w_t)} P(w_c | w_t)$, where $C(w_t) = [w_{t-k}, \ldots, w_{t+k}]$.

By introducing the negative sampling [12] method, the co-occurrence probability of each context word and the target word can be formalized by the following:

$$P(w_c | w_t) \cong \sigma(w_c^T \cdot w_t) \prod_{w_t' \in NEG(w_t)} \left(1 - \sigma(w_c^T \cdot w_t')\right), \qquad (5)$$

where $\sigma(\cdot)$ denotes the sigmoid function and $NEG(w_t)$ is the negative word set for the target word w_t. The objective of negative sampling is to make the context word w_c as close as possible to the target word w_t in the semantic space and as far away as possible from the negative sample w_t'. It aims to make the co-occurrence probability of w_c and w_t ($\sigma(w_c^T \cdot w_t)$) greater than w_c and w_t' ($\sigma(w_c^T \cdot w_t')$). Although Word2Vec strikes a good balance between efficiency and quality, the representation of low-frequency words remains a challenge on due to the lack of adequate training for sparse words.

3.2. Word Embeddings with Internal Semantic Information

In addition to the word co-occurrence, the internal features of words have also been shown to contribute to word embedding. Related works can be roughly divided into three categories: models based on morphological information, models based on character information and models based on subword information. Examples of "morphological information", "character information" and "subword information" are illustrated in Figure 4, where morphological information mainly refers to the features from components (i.e., prefix, root and suffix) of the word. Bian, Gao and Liu [1] utilized morphological (prefix, root and suffix), syntactic and semantic knowledge to achieve high-quality word embeddings. Chen et al. [13] and Sun et al. [14] performed character-level embedding and word embeddings obtained by fusing character features and word features. Xu et al. [15] also used a character-level embedding, and the weight information of different characters was taken into account in the fusion process. Cao and Lu [16] combined both the morphological information of the word and the information of the character-level and captured the structure information of the context by adding the subword information (character n-gram, root/affix and inflections). To better discover the laws of language for word embedding, Li et al. [17] tried to discover the relationship between morphology and semantics in language expression and summarized 68 implicit morphological relationships and 28 display semantics relationships.

Actually, in Chinese, characters are not the smallest granularity units, but strokes. On top of this, there are structures such as radicals and components. Shi et al. [18] and Yin et al. [19] added the features of radicals of the characters inside target words to CBOW model. Yu et al.'s [20] method, regarded as a more refined version of those of Shi, Zhai, Yang, Xie and Liu [18] and Yin, Wang, Li, Li and Wang [19], captured not only the radical information but also other components inside the character. To better exploit the structural information inside the character, Cao et al. [21] proposed to use the set of Stroke n-gram information of characters to supplement the semantics of characters.

The methods mentioned above only use the semantic information of the word itself, such as from word-level embeddings to character-level embeddings or other more fine-grained embeddings. However, the semantic information obtained from the word is limited. Besides, the models are influenced by the formation of language, the characteristics of language, etc., thus it is difficult to generalize to other languages.

3.3. Word Embeddings with External Semantic Information

A lot of semantic information related to words is now emerging, such as images with text labels, as well as some semantic knowledge bases including WordNet [22], BabelNet [23], ConceptNet [24] and HowNet [11]. These semantic data should help us improve the accuracy of word vectors.

A large and growing body of literature has researched on joining external semantic information for word embedding. Liu et al. [25] proposed a character-level embedding model that attempts to capture the common structure between characters from visual features by using morphological images corresponding to characters. Wang, Zhang and Zong [26] proposed a word-level embedding model, which uses images from the real world as a complement to text semantics, rather than directly replacing text semantic information with visual feature information. In terms of considering external semantic knowledge base, Yang and Sun [9] used Tongyici Cilin [27] whose purpose is to make the words with the same semantic classification in the Tongyici Cilin close to each other (Tongyici Cilin is a Chinese semantic knowledge base based on synonym sets, which can classify words according to their semantics). Mancini, Camacho-Collados, Iacobacci and Navigli [6] used BabelNet to annotate the different senses of words and then performed joint learning to get word and sense embeddings. Tissier, Gravier and Habrard [8] introduced the concepts of "strong pairs" and "weak pairs" from dictionary entries, so as to better distinguish the relative intensity of word pairs in the semantic space. Liu et al. [28] proposed a knowledge-enabled language representation model with knowledge graphs (KGs), in which KG triples are injected into the sentences as domain knowledge. Niu, Xie, Liu and Sun [7] proposed the sememe-encoded word representation learning (SE-WRL) model. The SE-WRL model embeds words by encoding sememe in word–sense–sememe knowledge of HowNet. Since the word–sense–sememe is an intuitive form of organizing words, it is easily organized and interpretable [11] and has a wide range of potential uses.

Specifically, three SE-WRL models are mentioned: simple sememe aggregation model (SSA), sememe attention over context model (SAC) and sememe attention over target model (SAT).

(1) The SSA model simply represents vector w of each word as the average of all its sememe vectors, as shown in Equation (6).

$$w = \frac{1}{m} \sum_{s_i^{(w)} \in S^{(w)}} \sum_{x_j^{(s_i)} \in X_i^{(w)}} x_j^{(s_i)},\qquad(6)$$

where m is the number of sememes of the word w.

(2) Based on the SSA model, Niu, Xie, Liu and Sun [7] developed a SAC model and a SAT model that can distinguish different word meanings:

$$att\left(s_j^{(w_u)}, w_v\right) = \frac{\exp\left(w_v \cdot \hat{s}_j^{(w_u)}\right)}{\sum_{k=1}^{|S^{(w_u)}|} \exp\left(w_v \cdot \hat{s}_k^{(w_u)}\right)}.\qquad(7)$$

In the above formula, if w_v represents the target word w_t and w_u represents the context w_c, then it is SAC model, while, if w_v represents context w_c and w_u represents the target word w_t, then it is the SAT model.

In this study, we used both sememe and word–sense–sememe structure as external supplements to refine the process of word embedding. Different from SE-WRL, our model captures the weight changes of different sememes under the same sense over different contexts, while using sememe to encode words.

4. Methodology

The proposed double attention-based word embedding (DAWE) model is derived from SE-WRL, where "double attention" refers to sense-level attention and sememe-level attention. The model assumes that the meaning of a word in a sentence is composed of senses with different weights, and each sense is composed of different sememes with different weights. In addition, the study assumes that a better way to disambiguate the senses of words in different contexts is to carefully design the process of constituting senses from sememes.

DAWE model, introduced in Section 4.1, is a general framework for encoding sememes into words. Double attention over context model (DAC) introduced in Section 4.2 and double attention over target model (DAT) introduced in Section 4.3 are two specific word training models that are obtained by integrating the DAWE model through context-aware semantic matching.

4.1. Double Attention-Based Word Embedding Model

To encode the semantics of sememes into words through the "word–sense–sememe" structure, a DAWE model is developed, as shown in Figure 5.

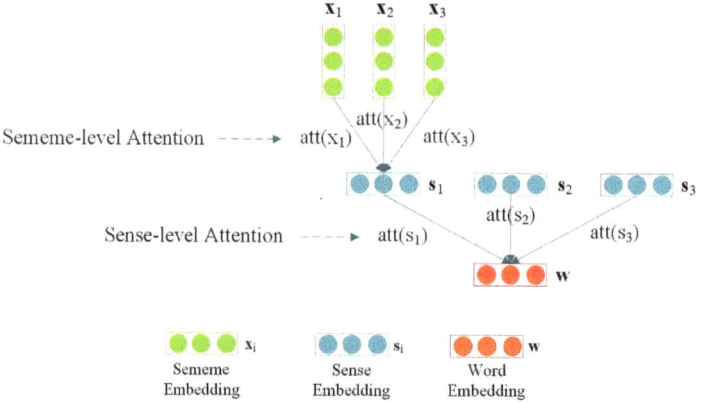

Figure 5. DAWE model.

In the DAWE model, a "double attention" architecture is adopted: (1) Sense-level attention is to capture senses weight changes with context. A word may have different meanings in different contexts, but those meanings are not isolated. We argue that the meaning of a word in a specific context should be a fusion of different senses. As the context changes, the fusion weight of the senses also changes accordingly. (2) Sememe-level attention is to capture the weight change of sememes with context. In the SE-WRL model, each weight of sememes that constitutes the senses is thought as equivalent. Actually, when a sense presents different meanings, the weights of sememes under a sense should be different.

As shown in Figure 5, DAWE is a word embedding model based on the word–sense–sememe structure, as well as a word sense disambiguation (WSD) model. In DAWE, sememes constitute the different senses of a word, and then different senses reconstitute into word meanings that are relevant to the textual context.

The purpose of word embedding is to keep semantic relevance of words while words are embedded into a unified semantic space. However, word embedding has the semantic confusion defect of representing all the meanings of a word in the same vector. To remedy such deficiencies, the different meanings of words need to be modeled separately to overcome the chaos of word embedding. The research suggests that better decomposition of word meanings combined with context leads to better representations of word meanings. WSD is to distinguish the different senses of words in different contexts, which can be roughly divided into unsupervised methods and knowledge-based methods. DAWE uses a knowledge-based approach to disambiguate the different senses of words in context using weighted sememes for the presenting of senses under a word. As a word embedding model based on knowledge, the objective of DAWE is the same as conventional approaches based on knowledge, which is to have words with the same semantics close to each other and words with different semantics away from each other [29].

According to the location of the object of the "attention", DAWE models can be extended to double attention over context model (DAC) and double attention over target model (DAT). Figures 6 and 7 illustrate the relationships and differences between the two models.

4.2. Double Attention over Context Model

As shown in Figure 6, DAC consists of two parts: encoding part and training part, which correspond to the DAWE encoding framework and Skip-gram training framework respectively.

For each context word $w_c \in C(w)$ ($C(w) = [w_{t-k}, \ldots, w_{t-1}, w_{t+1}, \ldots, w_{t+k}]$, where k is the size of the context window), we have:

$$w_c = \sum_{i=1}^{|S^{(w_c)}|} att\left(s_i^{(w_c)}, w_t\right) \cdot s_i^{(w_c)}, \quad (8)$$

where $att\left(s_i^{(w_c)}, w_t\right)$ denotes that the target word w_t is used as attention to calculating the weight of the ith sense of the context word w_c, as follows:

$$att\left(s_i^{(w_c)}, w_t\right) = \frac{\exp\left(\hat{s}_i^{(w_c)} \cdot w_t\right)}{\sum_{j=1}^{|S^{(w_c)}|} \exp\left(\hat{s}_j^{(w_c)} \cdot w_t\right)}, \quad (9)$$

where $\hat{s}_i^{(w_c)}$ denotes the value used in the calculation of weight, which is obtained by the sememe embeddings of the sememe set $X_i^{(w_c)}$ corresponding to the sense $s_i^{(w_c)}$. It can be formalized by the following:

$$\hat{s}_i^{(w_c)} = \sum_{j=1}^{|X_i^{(w_c)}|} att\left(x_j^{(s_i)}, w_t\right) \cdot x_j^{(s_i)}. \quad (10)$$

Similar to $att\left(s_i^{(w_c)}, w_t\right)$, $att\left(x_j^{(s_i)}, w_t\right)$ indicates that the target word w_t is used as attention to calculating the weight of the jth sememe in the ith sense of the context word w_c, as follows:

$$att\left(x_j^{(s_i)}, w_t\right) = \frac{\exp\left(x_j^{(s_i)} \cdot w_t\right)}{\sum_{k=1}^{|X_i^{(w_c)}|} \exp\left(x_k^{(s_i)} \cdot w_t\right)}. \quad (11)$$

DAWE is a two-layer encoding framework. The first layer is sense encoding, which corresponds to Equation (10) and Equation (11). In the first layer, the sememe embeddings are used as input, and then the sense embeddings are obtained through sememe-level attention. The second layer is word encoding, corresponding to Equation (8) and Equation (9). In the second layer, the sense embeddings obtained by Equation (10) are used as input, and then the word embeddings are obtained through sense-level attention. In DAC, the target word w_t is used to guide the generation of word vectors of context words. Under this attention mechanism, if the sememe vectors and sense vectors of the context word are more relevant to the target word vectors, the corresponding sememes and senses will get higher weight. This is similar to the idea in Word2Vec that the more similar words are closer in the semantic space. In this way, the different senses of context words can be disambiguated too.

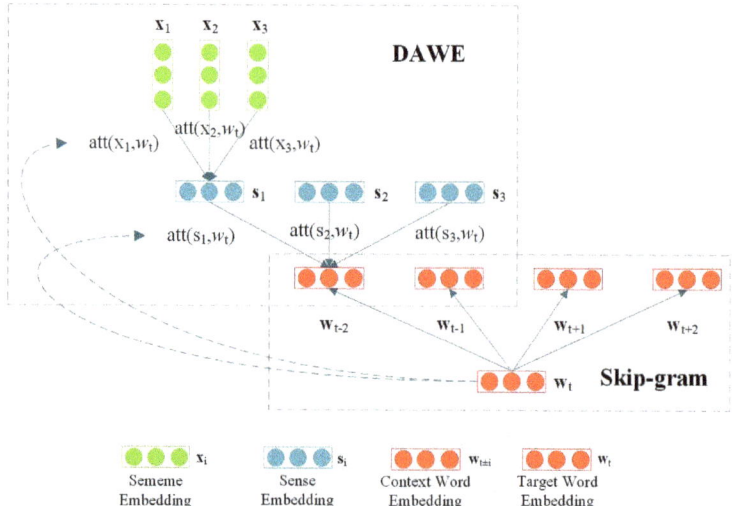

Figure 6. Double attention over context model (DAC).

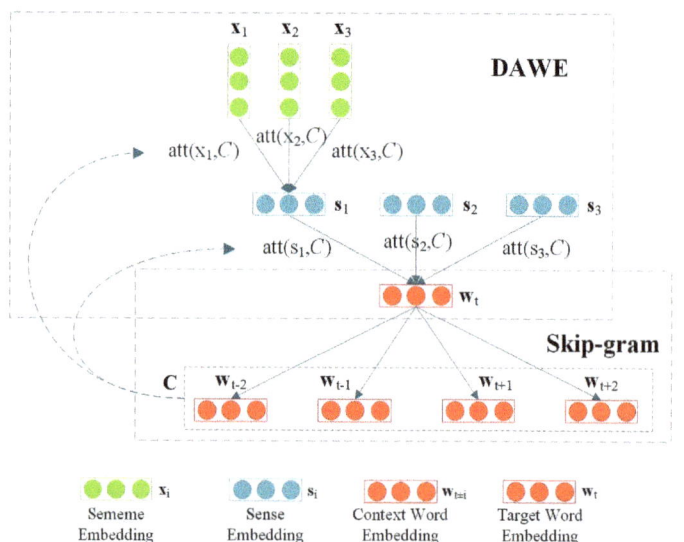

Figure 7. Double attention over target model (DAT).

4.3. Double Attention over Target Model

DAT is a variant of DAC, and word vectors are also encoded by the DAWE model and trained by the Skip-gram model. In contrast to DAC, DAT takes context embedding as attention to guide the generation of the word vector of the target word. The model structure of DAT is shown in Figure 7.

For each target word $w_t \in W$, we have:

$$w_t = \sum_{i=1}^{|S^{(w_t)}|} \text{att}\left(s_i^{(w_t)}, C(w_t)\right) \cdot s_i^{(w_t)}, \qquad (12)$$

where $\text{att}\left(s_i^{(w_t)}, w_{\text{context}}\right)$ denotes that the context word set $C(w_t)$ is used as attention to calculating the weight of ith sense of w_t, as follows:

$$\text{att}\left(s_i^{(w_t)}, w_{\text{context}}\right) = \frac{\exp\left(\hat{s}_i^{(w_t)} \cdot C(w_t)\right)}{\sum_{j=1}^{|S^{(w_t)}|} \exp\left(\hat{s}_i^{(w_t)} \cdot C(w_t)\right)}, \qquad (13)$$

The calculation of $\hat{s}_i^{(w_t)}$ is similar to DAC (Equation. (10) and Equation (11)), which is the weighted sum of all sememe embeddings of sememe set $X_i^{(w_t)}$ corresponding to sense $s_i^{(w_t)}$, where $C(w_t)$ denotes the context, and its corresponding word vector is obtained by the average of all context word vectors in the context window. It is formalized by the following:

$$C(w_t) = \frac{1}{2K} \sum_{j=t-k}^{j=t+k} w_j, \; j \neq t, \qquad (14)$$

where k is the size of the context window.

DAT uses context as attention and is richer in contextual semantics than DAC, hence it should be more conducive to the choice of sememes and senses.

4.4. Optimization

This section takes DAT as an example to illustrate the training process of the proposed model. As shown in Figure 8, in DAT's pre-processing phase, each word in the vocab needs to be annotated according to "word–sense–sememe" knowledge (association is established among sememe, sense and word). Then, in DAWE framework, the target word w_t is encoded through the "double-attention" mechanism. In DAT, the context (Equation (14)) is used to guide the encoding of the target word (see Section 4.3 for details). The objective of the optimization is the same as classical Skip-gram (Equation (4)); however, the parameters that need to be optimized include not only word embeddings but also sense embeddings and sememe embeddings:

$$\begin{cases} w_t := w_t + \alpha \cdot \Delta w_t \\ w_{t\pm i} := w_{t\pm i} + \alpha \cdot \Delta w_{t\pm i} \\ S^{(w_t)} := S^{(w_t)} + \alpha \cdot \Delta S^{(w_t)} \\ X^{(w_t)} := X^{(w_t)} + \alpha \cdot \Delta X^{(w_t)} \end{cases}, i = \{1, 2, \ldots, k\}. \qquad (15)$$

where α denotes the learning rate; k is the size of the context window (in Figure 8, k = 2); $S^{(w_t)}$ denotes the vector set of senses corresponding to w_t; and $X^{(w_t)}$ denotes the sememe vector set corresponding to w_t.

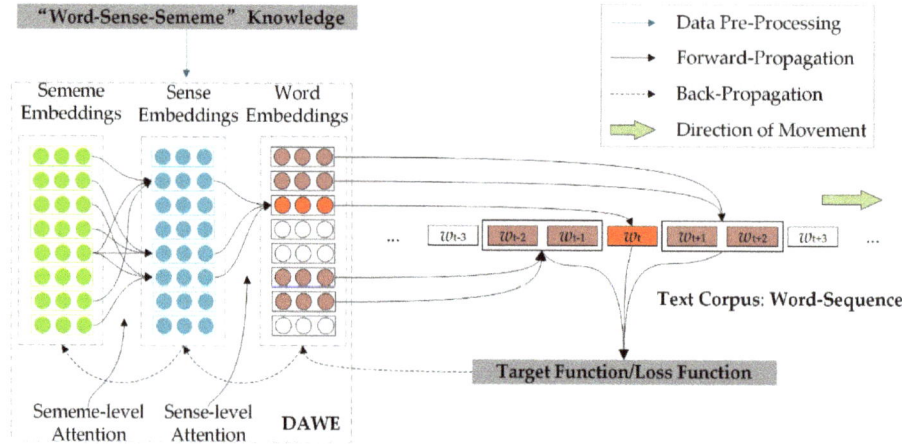

Figure 8. Training with DAT.

The optimization process of DAC is similar to DAT, and is not be elaborated upon in this paper.

5. Experiments and Results

Our experiments were conducted on a Chinese word embedding task. Model performances were examined with two tasks: the word similarity task and the word analogy task. In this section, we first introduce the experimental datasets, including the training set and the evaluation set in the two evaluation tasks. Next, we introduce the experimental settings, including the selection of baselines and the setting of parameters. Finally, we present the metrics and results of the two evaluation tasks.

5.1. Datasets

For training, HowNet annotated text corpus Clean-SogouT1 [7] was selected to train our model. Each word in the vocab of Clean-SogouT1 dataset is annotated in this form: (word w, sense num (s), sememe number of first sense, sememe set of first sense $X_1^{(w)}$, ..., sememe number of the sth sense, sememe set of sth sense $X_s^{(w)}$). The example of "Apple" in Figure 1 can be represented as ("Apple", 3, 5, ("computer", "PatternValue", "able", "bring", "SpeBrand (specific brand)"), 1, ("fruit"), 3, ("fruit", "reproduce", "tree")). The basic statistics of the dataset are shown in Table 1. Table 1 shows that more than 60% of the words in the dataset have more than two senses, which suggests that dynamic sense disambiguation is necessary for improving word embedding models. Following Niu, Xie, Liu and Sun [7], this study removed words from the vocab set with word frequency under 50.

Table 1. Text corpus statistics. AS/PW, average senses/per word; AS/PS, average sememes/per sense; PWMS, percentage of words that have multiple senses.

Text Corpus	Words	Vocab Size	Sememes	AS/PW	AS/PS	PWMS
Clean-SogouT1	1.8B	350K	1889	2.683	1.701	60.78%

For evaluation, we chose the Chinese word similarity (CWS) dataset and the Chinese word analogy (CWA) dataset provided by Niu, Xie, Liu and Sun [7] to evaluate the performance of the models in the word similarity task and the word analogy reasoning task. The CWS datasets Wordsim-240 and Wordsim-297 contain 240 similar word pairs and 297 similar word pairs, respectively, and each word pair in the CWS dataset has its corresponding similarity score, e.g., "consumer, customer, 8.4". Each entry in the CWA dataset is composed of four words "w_1, w_2, w_3, w_4". The form of word analogy is: $w_2 - w_1 \cong w_4 - w_3$, such as the classic example: $w_{king} - w_{man} \cong w_{queen} - w_{woman}$. The bold form $\mathbf{w} \subset \mathbb{R}^D$ denotes the embedding of the word w. The statistics of the CWA dataset used in this study is shown in Table 2.

Table 2. Chinese word analogy dataset, which contains three analogy types: capitals of countries (Capital), e.g., $w_{London} - w_{England} \cong w_{Beijing} - w_{China}$; cities in states (City), e.g., $w_{Jacksonville} - w_{Florida} \cong w_{Francisco} - w_{California}$; and family relationships (Relationship), e.g., $w_{Father} - w_{Mather} \cong w_{Son} - w_{Dauther}$.

Capital	City	Relationship	All
677	175	272	1124

5.2. Experimental Settings

In the experiments, we chose Skip-gram (the basic training framework of our models), CBOW (another model in Word2Vec, for comparison with Skip-gram) and GloVe [30] (different from the calculation method of Skip-gram in the local context window, Glove obtains the word embeddings by global matrix decomposition) as the comparison models. We also chose the SSA model (encoding words with sememes without attention mechanism), SAC (for comparison with DAC) and SAT (for comparison with DAT) proposed in Niu, Xie, Liu and Sun [7] as our baselines.

Following Niu, Xie, Liu and Sun [7], the vector dimensions of word embeddings, sense embeddings and sememe embeddings were set to 200; the size of the context window was set to 8; the initial learning rate was 0.025; and the number of negative samples was set to 25 in the negative sampling method. For the SAT and DAT, we set the context embedding window size to 2.

Our DAWE models were implemented based on the code of the SE-WRL model (https://github.com/thunlp/SE-WRL). The benchmark models and our models were trained on the same machine.

5.3. Word Similarity

In this section, this study examine the quality of word embeddings through the performance of the proposed models in word similarity tasks. In the evaluation of the word similarity tasks, we used the cosine value between the vectors of two words as their similarity scores to obtain the similarity ranking of all pairs of words in the benchmark datasets (Wordsim-240 and Wordsim-297). By calculating the Spearman correlation coefficient between the similarity ranking obtained by our models and the similarity ranking in the benchmark datasets, we could evaluate the performance of the model in word similarity tasks. The higher the Spearman correlation coefficient is, the better the model performs in the word similarity task.

Table 3 shows the evaluation results on word similarity tasks. (1) On the Wordsim-240 dataset and Wordsim-297 dataset, our models performed better compared to the baseline models. This shows that distinguishing the sememes within the senses can help us to present different senses of the word more accurately and deeply. (2) DAT performed better than DAC. DAT takes context embedding as attention to guide the semantic generation to the target words, thus it can better capture contextual semantic information. Therefore, when the training of words is sufficient, the results of DAT will be better than DAC.

Table 3. Evaluation results of word similarity tasks.

Model	Wordsim-240	Wordsim-297
CBOW	57.987	62.063
GloVe	57.618	57.107
Skip-gram	55.279	60.565
SSA	60.410	60.167
SAC	57.574	57.825
SAT	60.480	62.280
DAC	57.157	59.671
DAT	61.162	63.327

5.4. Word Analogy

In this section, we examine the quality of word embeddings by the performance of the models in the word analogy reasoning task. In the Chinese word analogy reasoning task, each analogy sample consists of two-word pairs (w_1, w_2) and (w_3, w_4), which satisfy: $w_2 - w_1 \cong w_4 - w_3$, ie $w_2 - w_1 + w_3 \cong w_4$. Therefore, in the word analogy reasoning task, the score of the candidate word is calculated by replacing w_4 with the candidate word w and by the following formula:

$$S_A(w) = \cos(w_2 - w_1 + w_3, w). \tag{16}$$

After obtaining the ranking of all candidate words, the experiment chose top-ranked words and evaluated the performance of the model by calculating accuracy and mean rank metrics. The higher is the accuracy and the lower is the mean rank, the better is the model.

The results of the word analogy reasoning task are shown in Table 4. From the evaluation results of the word analog task, we can conclude that:

Table 4. Evaluation results of word analogy task.

Model	Accuracy				Mean Rank			
	Capital 677	City 175	Relationship 272	All 1124	Capital 677	City 175	Relationship 272	All 1124
CBOW	45.05	86.85	84.19	61.03	60.28	1.43	41.87	46.66
GloVe	62.03	83.42	82.35	70.28	17.09	1.77	14.28	14.02
Skip-gram	60.26	96.00	77.57	70.01	78.67	1.05	2.98	48.27
SSA	72.67	80.00	74.63	74.28	21.05	7.21	2.74	14.45
SAC	66.24	92.28	71.87	71.66	40.86	5.74	2.56	13.51
SAT	71.64	87.14	74.44	74.73	14.79	2.07	2.34	9.80
DAC	68.53	93.14	72.24	73.26	14.10	1.15	2.74	9.34
DAT	74.00	91.42	75.36	77.04	8.87	1.71	2.58	6.23

(1) In the word analogy reasoning task, our models are significantly better than the previous models. The accuracy of DAC is 2% higher than that of SAC, and the accuracy of DAT is 3% higher than that of SAT. DAC has increased more than 4% compared to the SAC model and DAT has increased more than 3% compared to the SAT model of mean rank. The experimental results show that both DAC and DAT are more conducive to the accurate description of senses by distinguishing the internal sememes.

(2) Our models perform well in the class of Capital, which is the collection of groups of capital and country around the world. Most of the words of the capital names have distinct meanings in various contexts, such as the word "Washington" may be the name of a capital city, a state, a university, a hotel, or a people. In the training process, the proposed model can dynamic adjustment the weights of both senses and sememes by the "double-attention" mechanism, hence offering more powerful ability on the embedding of those words.

(3) Although the performances of our models are not the best in the classes of City and Relationship, our models are more robust in the overall performance of accuracy and mean rank.

(4) DAWE models are significantly improved in the performance of the word analogy reasoning task, but only a small increase in performance in the word similarity task. Since Skip-gram trains word vectors based on context, the more similar the context is, the closer the word vector is in the semantic space. Thus, with sufficient training, there is no significant difference among the performance of these Skip-gram-based models for the word similarity task. By adding sememe-level attention, our models can more accurately express the sense of the word, resulting in better results in the word analogy reasoning task requiring higher semantic accuracy.

6. Discussions

6.1. Case Study

To illustrate the dynamic semantic generation of our models, we select some specific cases for analysis. Tables 5–7 lists the relative weights of the different senses of the word "Apple" (Sense 1: "Apple Brand" (Sememe: "computer", "PatternValue", "able", "bring" and "SpeBrand (specific brand)"); Sense 2: "Apple" (Sememe: "fruit"); Sense 3: "Apple Tree" (Sememe: "fruit", "reproduce" and "tree")) in a specific context and the relative weights of different sememes within the senses. Those weights are calculated by sense-level attention and sememe-level attention of DAT. Tables 5–7 show that: (1) Our model correctly distinguishes the different senses of "Apple" from different contexts. This shows the power of our model in word sense disambiguation (WSD). (2) In the sense "Apple Brand", the sememe "SpeBrand" gets a large weight. This is consistent with our description in the Introduction. In the process of sense construction, the distribution of weights between sememes should be unequal. (3) When the meanings of "Apple" changing with different contexts (the meaning of "Apple" changes when the sentence changes), both the sense items of the word and the sememe items in each sense of the word do not change, what changes with the context are the weights of those senses and the weights of those sememes. The model of this paper is trained on the large text corpus Clean-SogouT1, and the learned word vectors and model parameters are consistent with the feature distribution of the entire corpus. As a result, the sense representation inside the words will tend to be stable, that is, the weight distribution of sememes inside the senses will also be stable (sememe consists of sense, sense and then word).

Table 5. "You can like apple (**Apple Brand**) computers, just don't vilify other brands."

Senses	Sememes					
Apple Brand 1.91	bring 5.15	PatternValue 0.00	SpeBrand 6.77	computer 0.31	able 8.06
Apple 0.86			fruit 0.00		
Apple Tree 0.00		tree 19.93	fruit 21.28	reproduce 0.00	

Table 6. "I just hit you with an apple (**Apple**) core."

Senses	Sememes					
Apple Brand 0.00	bring 4.22	PatternValue 0.00	SpeBrand 6.94	computer 1.20	able 4.55
Apple 3.06			fruit 0.00		
Apple Tree 0.08		tree 14.55	fruit 20.18	reproduce 0.00	

Table 7. "There are many kinds of high-quality apple (**Apple Tree**) seedlings in southeast Asia."

Senses			Sememes		
Apple Brand 0.00	bring 4.50	PatternValue 0.00	SpeBrand 5.58	computer 1.85	able 5.97
Apple 0.05			fruit 0.00		
Apple Tree 0.08		tree 12.60	fruit 12.30	reproduce 0.00	

In the above cases, we take the word "Apple (Apple/Apple Brand/Apple Tree)" as an example to examine the weight distribution of sememes and verify the effectiveness of our model in WSD. We take the word "Notebook (Notebook/ Laptop Computer)" as an example to study the impact of sememe's weight distribution in a specific context. As shown in Table 8, when the meaning of word "Notebook" in the context tends to the sense "Laptop Computer", we observe the following:

Table 8. The impact of context on the weight of sememes. The values in this table represent relative weights and the relative weight of the sense "Notebook" is 0. Word: "Notebook" (Sense 1: "Notebook" (Sememe: "account"); Sense 2: "Laptop Computer" (Sememe: "bring", "PatternValue", "computer" and "able")).

Context	Sememes			
	Bring	PatternValue	Computer	Able
Laptop Computer (0.57): Those who want to buy a notebook (Laptop Computer) can write down my contact information	4.69	0.00	1.82	5.62
Laptop Computer (4.59): HP business notebook (Laptop Computer) has industry-leading security technology	5.85	0.00	2.07	4.49
Laptop Computer (1.21): Our shop can provide you with notebook (Laptop Computer) repair service	4.88	0.00	1.98	4.10
Laptop Computer (4.53): There are two notebook (Laptop Computer) computers in the computer room. They are very old and slow	5.82	0.82	0.00	6.63
Laptop Computer (8.73): Everyone has the chance to get refrigerator, notebook (Laptop Computer) computer, LCD TV, etc	5.82	0.98	0.00	4.97
Laptop Computer (6.77): This notebook (Laptop Computer) computer with a strong display is a real eye-opener	5.20	0.43	0.00	6.20

(1) When the word "Notebook" and the word "Computer" appear together, that is, "Notebook Computer", the weight of the sememe "computer" is the lowest among all the sememes of the sense "Laptop Computer". It can be explained that, when "Notebook Computer" appear together, "Notebook" is mainly used as a modifier of "Computer" to indicate that "Computer" is light, thin and portable. Therefore, "Notebook" will have less "computer" meaning.

(2) When "Notebook" appears alone, sememe "computer" has more weight than when "Notebook Computer" appear together. At this point, "Notebook" no longer appears as a modifier of "Computer" but as a separate entity, thus it should cover the semantics that tends to favor "computer".

(3) When "Notebook" appears alone, the weight of the sense "Laptop Computer" is generally lower than when "Notebook Computer" appear together because, when "Notebook Computer" appear together, the context carries more semantics that tends to the sense "Laptop Computer", thus "Laptop Computer" is generally weighted more heavily. (Note the second example of Table 8, where the weight

of "Laptop Computer" reached 4.59. This is because "HP" is a computer brand, which results in the "Laptop Computer" weight more than the other case of "Notebook" appearing alone).

The results in Table 8 also show the effectiveness of our model. In the DAWE model, the representation of words depends on senses, the weight distribution of the sememes cannot directly determine the final representation of words. As the word "Notebook" appears alone, the weight of the sense "Laptop Computer" is lower than that when "Notebook Computer" appear together, although the weight of the sememe "Computer" is higher than when "Notebook Computer" appear together.

In summary, in the training process of word embeddings, the semantics of words are affected not only by the semantic accumulation in corpus, but also by the context in the current slide window. (1) The impact of semantic accumulation is mainly reflected in the gradual stabilization of the representation of the inherent senses within the word. As shown in the examples in Tables 5–7, the weight distribution of the sememes used to represent the internal senses of the word "Apple" is consistent in different contexts. (2) The current context is mainly used to select the appropriate senses and can affect the weight distribution of sememes. As shown in Tables 5–7, although the representation of the inherent senses inside the word "Apple" tends to stable, the weight of these senses is varied in different sentences. Besides, the senses of the target word "Notebook" and the weights of their sememes in Table 8 also illustrate this point.

6.2. Integrating DAWE with Other Models

DAWE is a general encoding framework. In this paper, we integrate and train DAWE based on the Skip-gram model. DAWE can be extended for other models many by the following steps:

(1) Data pre-processing. Using "word–sense–sememe" knowledge to annotate text corpus.

(2) Determine the encoding "target" of DAWE. For example, in DAC, the "target" is the context, while, in DAT, the "target" is the target word.

(3) Determine the "object" of "double-attention". For example, in DAC, the "object" is the target word, while, in DAT, the "object" in the context.

(4) Forward propagation (encoding). According to the "target" and "object" determined in Steps 2 and 3, in the DAWE framework, "object" is used to guide the encoding of the "target" through the "double-attention" mechanism.

(5) Back propagation. Model parameters (word embeddings, sense embeddings and sememe embeddings) are updated according to the model optimization objective.

Among them, Steps 1 and 5 are relatively easy to implement. The core step is Step 4, which depends on Steps 2 and 3. Therefore, in expanding DAWE, the parts that are difficult and require careful design are Steps 2 and 3. Once Steps 2 and 3 are established, DAWE can be easily extended to other models.

7. Conclusion and Future Work

In this paper, double attention-based word embedding (DAWE) model is proposed to encode sememes into words by a "double attention" mechanism, resulting in going deep into the senses of a word to describe the word. Our proposed DAWE model is a general framework that can be applied to other existing word embedding training frameworks, such as Word2Vec. In this paper, we extend the DAWE model to get two specific training models. In the experiments of word similarity task and word analogy task, the validity of our models was demonstrated. To further explore the models proposed in this paper, some cases were analyzed in the experiment. The results show that word semantics are not only affected by the global semantic accumulation, but also by the context of a word. Experimental results show that DAWE models can effectively capture the semantic changes of words through dynamic semantic generation, which means that our model is also effective in word sense disambiguation. The findings of this study suggest it could get performance improvement of NLP tasks if words are processed in a more fine-grained perspective.

A limitation of this study is that the DAWE model requires more training time than baseline models because it increases training parameters as it integrates the "double attention" mechanism. Additionally, the values of hyperparameters in this study are set following previous research; further experimental investigations are needed to estimate the impacts of those hyperparameters.

Author Contributions: Conceptualization, S.L. and H.Y.; methodology and software, R.C.; writing—original draft preparation, R.C.; and writing—review and editing, S.L., H.Y., B.W., J.G. and L.Y. All authors have read and agreed to the published version of the manuscript.

Funding: This research was supported by the NSF of China (Grant Nos. 61972365, 61673354, 41801378 and 61672474), and Open Fund of Key Laboratory of Urban Land Resources Monitoring and Simulation, Ministry of Natural Resources (Grant No. KF-2019-04-033).

Conflicts of Interest: The authors declare no conflict of interest.

References

1. Bian, J.; Gao, B.; Liu, T.-Y. *Knowledge-Powered Deep Learning for Word Embedding*; Springer: Berlin/Heidelberg, Germany, 2014; pp. 132–148.
2. Cao, S.; Lu, W. *Improving Word Embeddings with Convolutional Feature Learning and Subword Information*; AAAI: San Francisco, CA, USA, 2017; pp. 3144–3151.
3. Mikolov, T.; Sutskever, I.; Chen, K.; Corrado, G.; Dean, J. Distributed representations of words and phrases and their compositionality. In Proceedings of the 26th International Conference on Neural Information Processing Systems, Sydney, Australia, 12–15 December 2013; Volume 2, pp. 3111–3119.
4. Mikolov, T.; Chen, K.; Corrado, G.; Dean, J. Efficient Estimation of Word Representations in Vector Space. In Proceedings of the International Conference on Learning Representations, Scottsdale, Arizona, 2–4 May 2013.
5. Goikoetxea, J.; Soroa, A.; Agirre, E. Bilingual embeddings with random walks over multilingual wordnets. *Knowl. Based Syst.* **2018**, *150*, 218–230. [CrossRef]
6. Mancini, M.; Camacho-Collados, J.; Iacobacci, I.; Navigli, R. Embedding Words and Senses Together via Joint Knowledge-Enhanced Training. In Proceedings of the 21st Conference on Computational Natural Language Learning (CoNLL 2017), Vancouver, BC, Canada, 3–4 August 2017; pp. 100–111.
7. Niu, Y.; Xie, R.; Liu, Z.; Sun, M. Improved word representation learning with sememes. In Proceedings of the 55th Annual Meeting of the Association for Computational Linguistics, Vancouver, BC, Canada, 30 July–4 August 2017; Volume 1, pp. 2049–2058.
8. Tissier, J.; Gravier, C.; Habrard, A. Dict2vec: Learning Word Embeddings using Lexical Dictionaries. In Proceedings of the Conference on Empirical Methods in Natural Language Processing (EMNLP 2017), Copenhagen, Denmark, 7–11 September 2017; pp. 254–263.
9. Yang, L.; Sun, M. Improved learning of chinese word embeddings with semantic knowledge. In *Chinese Computational Linguistics and Natural Language Processing Based on Naturally Annotated Big Data*; Springer: Guangzhou, China, 13–14 November 2015; pp. 15–25.
10. Zhang, Z.; Han, X.; Liu, Z.; Jiang, X.; Sun, M.; Liu, Q. ERNIE: Enhanced Language Representation with Informative Entities. In Proceedings of the 57th Annual Meeting of the Association for Computational Linguistics, Florence, Italy, 28 July–2 August 2019; pp. 1441–1451.
11. Dong, Z.; Dong, Q. Hownet-a hybrid language and knowledge resource. In *Proceedings of the International Conference on Natural Language Processing and Knowledge Engineering, Proceedings 2003*; IEEE: Piscataway, NJ, USA, 2003; pp. 820–824.
12. Mikolov, T.; Sutskever, I.; Chen, K.; Corrado, G.S.; Dean, J. Distributed representations of words and phrases and their compositionality. In *Advances in Neural Information Processing Systems*; The MIT Press: Cambridge, MA, USA, 2013; pp. 3111–3119.
13. Chen, X.; Xu, L.; Liu, Z.; Sun, M.; Luan, H. Joint learning of character and word embeddings. In Proceedings of the Twenty-Fourth International Joint Conference on Artificial Intelligence, Buenos Aires, Argentina, 25–31 July 2015.
14. Sun, F.; Guo, J.; Lan, Y.; Xu, J.; Cheng, X. Inside out: Two jointly predictive models for word representations and phrase representations. In Proceedings of the Thirtieth AAAI Conference on Artificial Intelligence, Phoenix, AZ, USA, 12–17 February 2016.

15. Xu, J.; Liu, J.; Zhang, L.; Li, Z.; Chen, H. Improve chinese word embeddings by exploiting internal structure. In Proceedings of the 2016 Conference of the North American Chapter of the Association for Computational Linguistics: Human Language Technologies, San Diego, CA, USA, 12–17 June 2016; pp. 1041–1050.
16. Cao, S.; Lu, W. Improving word embeddings with convolutional feature learning and subword information. In Proceedings of the Thirty-First AAAI Conference on Artificial Intelligence, San Francisco, CA, USA, 4–9 February 2017.
17. Li, S.; Zhao, Z.; Hu, R.; Li, W.; Liu, T.; Du, X. Analogical reasoning on chinese morphological and semantic relations. In Proceedings of the 56th Annual Meeting of the Association for Computational Linguistics, Melbourne, Australia, 15–20 July 2018; Volume 2, pp. 138–143.
18. Shi, X.; Zhai, J.; Yang, X.; Xie, Z.; Liu, C. Radical embedding: Delving deeper to chinese radicals. In Proceedings of the 53rd Annual Meeting of the Association for Computational Linguistics and the 7th International Joint Conference on Natural Language Processing, Beijing, China, 26–31 July 2015; Volume 2, pp. 594–598.
19. Yin, R.; Wang, Q.; Li, P.; Li, R.; Wang, B. Multi-granularity chinese word embedding. In Proceedings of the 2016 Conference on Empirical Methods in Natural Language Processing, Austin, TX, USA, 1–4 November 2016; pp. 981–986.
20. Yu, J.; Jian, X.; Xin, H.; Song, Y. Joint embeddings of chinese words, characters, and fine-grained subcharacter components. In Proceedings of the 2017 Conference on Empirical Methods in Natural Language Processing, Copenhagen, Denmark, 9–11 September 2017; pp. 286–291.
21. Cao, S.; Lu, W.; Zhou, J.; Li, X. Cw2vec: Learning chinese word embeddings with stroke n-gram information. In Proceedings of the Thirty-Second AAAI Conference on Artificial Intelligence, New Orleans, LA, USA, 2–7 February 2018.
22. Miller, G.A. Wordnet: A lexical database for english. *Commun. ACM* **1995**, *38*, 39–41. [CrossRef]
23. Navigli, R.; Ponzetto, S.P. Babelnet: The automatic construction, evaluation and application of a wide-coverage multilingual semantic network. *Artif. Intell.* **2012**, *193*, 217–250. [CrossRef]
24. Speer, R.; Chin, J.; Havasi, C. Conceptnet 5.5: An open multilingual graph of general knowledge. In Proceedings of the Thirty-First AAAI Conference on Artificial Intelligence, San Francisco, CA, USA, 4–9 February 2017.
25. Liu, F.; Lu, H.; Lo, C.; Neubig, G. Learning character-level compositionality with visual features. In Proceedings of the 55th Annual Meeting of the Association for Computational Linguistics, Vancouver, BC, Canada, 30 July–4 August 2017; Volume 1, pp. 2059–2068.
26. Wang, S.; Zhang, J.; Zong, C. Learning multimodal word representation via dynamic fusion methods. In Proceedings of the Thirty-Second AAAI Conference on Artificial Intelligence, New Orleans, LA, USA, 2–7 February 2018.
27. Mei, J.; Zhu, Y.; Gao, Y.; Yin, H. *Tongyici Cilin (Dictionary of Synonymous Words)*; Shanghai Cishu Publishing: Shanghai, China, 1983.
28. Liu, W.; Zhou, P.; Zhao, Z.; Wang, Z.; Ju, Q.; Deng, H.; Wang, P. K-Bert: Enabling Language Representation with Knowledge graph; AAAI: New York, NY, USA, 7–12 February 2020; pp. 2901–2908.
29. Camacho-Collados, J.; Pilehvar, M.T. From word to sense embeddings: A survey on vector representations of meaning. *J. Artif. Intell. Res.* **2018**, *63*, 743–788.
30. Pennington, J.; Socher, R.; Manning, C. Glove: Global vectors for word representation. In Proceedings of the 2014 conference on empirical methods in natural language processing (EMNLP), Doha, Qatar, 25–29 October 2014; pp. 1532–1543.

© 2020 by the authors. Licensee MDPI, Basel, Switzerland. This article is an open access article distributed under the terms and conditions of the Creative Commons Attribution (CC BY) license (http://creativecommons.org/licenses/by/4.0/).

Article

Can We Survive without Labelled Data in NLP? Transfer Learning for Open Information Extraction

Injy Sarhan [1,2,*] and Marco Spruit [2]

[1] Department of Computer Engineering, Arab Academy for Science, Technology and Maritime Transport (AAST), Alexandria 21500, Egypt
[2] Department of Information and Computing Sciences, Utrecht University, Princetonplein 5, 3584 CC Utrecht, The Netherlands; m.r.spruit@uu.nl
* Correspondence: injy.sarhan@aast.edu or i.a.a.sarhan@uu.nl

Received: 29 July 2020; Accepted: 18 August 2020; Published: 20 August 2020

Abstract: Various tasks in natural language processing (NLP) suffer from lack of labelled training data, which deep neural networks are hungry for. In this paper, we relied upon features learned to generate relation triples from the open information extraction (OIE) task. First, we studied how transferable these features are from one OIE domain to another, such as from a news domain to a bio-medical domain. Second, we analyzed their transferability to a semantically related NLP task, namely, relation extraction (RE). We thereby contribute to answering the question: can OIE help us achieve adequate NLP performance without labelled data? Our results showed comparable performance when using inductive transfer learning in both experiments by relying on a very small amount of the target data, wherein promising results were achieved. When transferring to the OIE bio-medical domain, we achieved an F-measure of 78.0%, only 1% lower when compared to traditional learning. Additionally, transferring to RE using an inductive approach scored an F-measure of 67.2%, which was 3.8% lower than training and testing on the same task. Hereby, our analysis shows that OIE can act as a reliable source task.

Keywords: transfer learning; open information extraction; relation extraction; recurrent neural networks; word embeddings

1. Introduction

In deep learning for natural language processing (NLP), the collection of labelled data necessary for training and building models is expensive. This has further highlighted the urgency towards transfer learning research. The aim of transfer learning is to benefit from information gathered from previous training data in directly making predictions in the target task by utilizing the extracted information. Deep learning approaches in NLP did not start until the early 2000s [1]. Recently, there has been an exponential increase in the number of scientific publications in neural networks in various NLP tasks [1].

Open information extraction (OIE) is a challenging task of extracting relation tuples from an unstructured corpus. Its main objective is to generate structured information from unstructured data in the form of a relation triple, <Argument 1> <Relation> <Argument 2>, without the need of predefining the relation between the two arguments. The extracted tuples can be binary, ternary, or n-ary, where the relationship is expressed between more than two entities such as the Person–Location–BornIn–BornOn relation (Jack Adams, Michigan, California, 1975).

Relation extraction (RE)—also classified as a category of information extraction—is the processes of identifying semantic relationships between entities. Contrary to OIE, RE requires predefining the relation prior to extraction. Similar to OIE, the extracted relation can either be a binary relation, for instance, Located-In (Berlin, Germany), or a higher order relation (n-ary), for instance, a 3-ary relation between Employee–Position–Company (Adam Smith, Marketing Manager, XYZ Company). Examples of both OIE and RE triples can be found in Table 1.

Table 1. Open information extraction and relation extraction example.

Sentence	John Lennon Was Born on 9 October 1940, in Liverpool and Gained Worldwide Fame as the Founder of the Beatles.
OIE Tuples	< John Lennon, Born, 9 October 1940> < John Lennon, Born, Liverpool> < John Lennon, founder, Beatles>
RE Tuples	Person-Born-On: < John Lennon, Born, 9 October 1940> Person-Born-In: < John Lennon, Born, Liverpool > Person-Organization: < John Lennon, founder, Beatles>

OIE is a crucial NLP task, and thus it was chosen as a source task to transfer to other NLP tasks due to its various potential applications in information retrieval, information extraction, text summarization, and question answering [2]. While various OIE algorithms have been developed in the past decade, only a small number employ deep learning techniques.

In recent years, researchers have increasingly been showing interest towards model generalization in deep learning due to the lack of labelled data. In this paper, we investigated the ability to transfer OIE to other NLP tasks, ranging from domain–adaptation (news domain to bio-medical) to RE as a semantically related task. RE task was chosen because of the nature of both OIE and RE, and our choice was backed up by the semantic overlap between both tasks. Throughout our research, we also compared and experimented with the use of different word embeddings.

This work aimed to measure how OIE can assist in other NLP tasks. Our primary objective was to conduct a fair comparison of different methods and settings with respect to OIE transfer learning effects to other NLP tasks. Therefore, we did not focus on outperforming state-of-the-art results in the target tasks.

The remainder of the paper is structured as follows. Section 2 presents a brief overview of transfer learning, while Section 3 surveys previous work in both OIE and RE. The neural network architecture is explained in Section 4, and experimental setup is explained in Section 5. Results and evaluation are discussed in Section 6. Finally, Section 7 concludes the paper and discusses future work.

2. Transfer Learning in NLP

Formerly, there was a misconception that a machine learning framework will achieve the desirable results only if the testing data and training data have similar distribution and feature space. Thus, a new framework was required for data with different distribution properties and features, making the collection of labelled training data expensive and difficult. Transfer learning lessens the demand of gathering an immense amount of labelled training data by reemploying the knowledge gained from a different task to tackle new tasks faster and constructively.

Pan and Yang introduced a transfer learning taxonomy [3]. Additionally, they categorized transfer learning into three classes:

Inductive transfer learning: labelled data are accessible in source and target domain.

Transductive transfer learning: labelled data are only available in the source domain.

Unsupervised transfer learning: No labelled data are both source and target domain.

Transfer learning has been implemented in various different machine learning tasks, achieving notable results, for instance, textual summarization [4], named entity recognition [5], question answering [6,7], and text classification [8].

BERT (Bidirectional Encoder Representations from Transformers) [9] was a breakthrough in transfer learning on a range of language-based tasks, not only due to the fact that BERT was pretrained on an immense dataset, but also because it has a substantial number of transformer blocks (encoder layers) and feed-forward networks. Later on, many transfer learning models built on BERT were introduced, for example ULMFiT [10] and OpenAI transformer [11]. This novel development also affected the way words are encoded, with more elaboration being found in Section 4.2.

As shown in Figure 1, in our work, two transductive transfer learning experiments were carried out. The first one transfers knowledge learned from the OIE news domain to the OIE bio-medical domain—this is referred to as domain adaptation. In contrast to transfer learning, domain adaption entails adapting a model trained on one domain to other different domains on the same task. The default process of supervised domain adaptation for neural models involves pre-training the network on data from the source domain followed by fine-tuning hyperparameters on data from the target domain. The second experiment transfers information from the OIE news domain to the RE news domain. Moreover, a small percentage of OIE bio-medical data were added to OIE news data to experiment with inductive transfer learning. Similarly, a small amount of RE training data were inputted to the neural model along with OIE news corpus, with both experiments being referred to as multi-task learning.

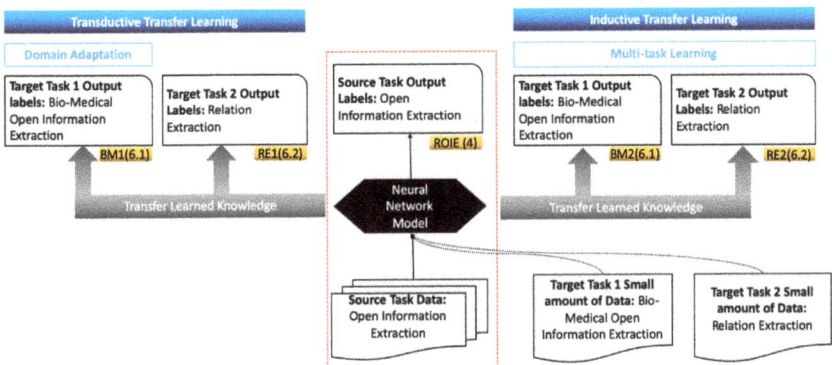

Figure 1. Open information extraction (OIE) transfer learning assessment. A total of four transfer learning experiments were carried out in our work. Left: the two transductive transfer learning experiments (BM1 and RE1). Right: illustration of the two experiments using inductive approaches (BM2 and RE2). Middle: the red dotted line represents the original model (ROIE), in which we tested our proposed neural model by testing and training on OIE news data, which is discussed in Section 4. The experiments' ID and the section they are discussed in are encapsulated in the yellow rectangles.

3. Related Work

In this section, we focus on previous works performed on OIE and RE relation extraction in the literature.

3.1. State-of-the-Art Open Information Extraction

OIE can be portrayed in three broad categories [12]: (a) machine learning classifier approaches, (b) hand-crafted rules approaches, and (c) neural network approaches. The first two categories can be further divided into two sub-categories: shallow syntactic analysis and dependency parsing. Below we discuss state-of-the-art work in each of these categories.

3.1.1. Machine Learning Classifiers Approaches

OIE systems that are built on machine learning classifier techniques require automatically generated data to train the classifier. In 2007, Banko et al. introduced the first OIE system based on shallow syntactic analysis, TextRunner [13]. It implements extraction in three main phases. It starts with a self-supervised learner that depends mainly on a conditional random field (CRF) classifier that utilizes unlexicalized features required for relation extraction, followed by a single pass extractor that extracts any potential relation triple and classifies each as either trustworthy or not. Finally, a redundancy-based assessor that re-ranks the extracted relations and assigns a confidence score to each extracted tuple is implemented. Not only did the authors of TextRunner facilitate domain-independent detection of relations from a corpus but their work triggered researchers towards developing OIE systems. For instance, the WOE (Wikipedia-based Open Extractor) [14] system is built on TextRunner, having two modes of operation: WOE^{Pos} and WOE^{Parse}. The main hypothesis behind WOE is the automated assembly of training samples by heuristically pairing Wikipedia info box values with corresponding texts, hence improving TextRunner's performance. WOE^{Pos} exploits the CRF classifier trained with shallow syntactic proprieties to extract specific words between two noun phrases that represents a relation.

An example of an OIE approach that utilizes dependency parsing is WOE^{Parse}; it exploits a rich dictionary of dependency path patterns acquired from Wikipedia extractions. While the OLLIE (Open Language Learning for Information Extraction) approach [15] relies on the bootstrapping concept, it learns semi-lexicalized pattern templates using dependency parses by bootstrapping a plentiful amount of training data that results in surpassing WOE's performance.

3.1.2. Hand-Crafted Rules Approaches

REVERB, introduced by Fader et al. [16], extracts tuples by singling out relation phrases that satisfy syntactic and lexical constraints; for each relation phrase, a pair of noun phrase arguments are identified. REVERB then uses logistic regression trained on 1000 sentences from the web with shallow syntactic features to assign a confidence score to each extracted relation triple. The R2A2 approach [17] upgrades REVERB by adding ARGLEARNER, an argument identifier that makes use of patterns as features to identify the left and right boundaries of each argument.

KRAKEN [18] is one of the few OIE system that is able to capture N-ary relations. It utilizes hand-crafted patterns to identify relation phrases and their correlated arguments over typed dependency parsers. As a further matter, KRAKEN is able to detect completeness and correctness of the extracted facts, thus increasing the quality of the extracted information. Del Corro and Gemulla proposed ClausIE (Clause-based Open Information Extraction) [19], which locates clauses in input sentences by making use of linguistic information of the English language's grammar by computing a dependency parse tree of the input phrase to determine its syntactical structure. Each clause is later classified to be compatible with the grammatical function of its constituents. Unlike the aforementioned OIE systems, ClausIE does not exploit any training data.

3.1.3. Neural Network Approaches

Recently, as a result of their successfulness in a diverse NLP tasks [1], deep neural networks paved the way to the OIE task. A recurrent neural network (RNN) encoder–decoder OIE framework was proposed by Cui et al. [20]. A fluctuating length sequence is sent to the network's encoder as a sole input. The encoder then generates a compressed representation vector to transfer to the decoder in order to produce the output sequence. A three-layer long short-term memory (LSTM) [21] is the internal structure of both the encoder and the decoder. Stanovsky et al. [22] presented a neural OIE paradigm that trains a bidirectional LSTM (bi-LSTM) transducer to label each word, verifying that supervised learning can have a positive effect on OIE performance.

3.2. State-of-the-Art Relation Extraction

RE research falls mainly under one of the following approaches: supervised, semi-supervised, distant supervision, and unsupervised. As always, the main issue of supervised techniques is the necessity of having a large amount of labelled data, which is difficult to gather [23]. Semi-supervised approaches mainly depend on bootstrapping techniques. Distant supervision techniques merge both semi-supervised and unsupervised approaches. However, popularity of unsupervised techniques declined due to the fact that the learner is provided unannotated data, and for that reason, evaluation becomes demanding at a large scale. We limited our discussion to supervised, semi-supervised, and distant supervision approaches. Neural approaches appear as a subclass in all the aforementioned classes.

3.2.1. Supervised Approaches

RE is treated as a multi-class classification task in supervised approaches. Supervised categories can be classified into kernel-based approaches and feature-based approaches. An example of the latter is the work of [24], who merged diverse features of lexical, syntactic, and semantic knowledge by employing a support vector machine (SVM) to extract relations, proving the effectiveness of base phrase chunking information. Authors of [25] introduced a kernel-based RE paradigm that incorporates term generalization techniques—word clustering and latent semantic analysis—with structured kernels to enhance RE results in different domains. Moreover, a neural approach based on adversarial training was proposed by Peng Su and K. Vijay-Shanker [26], aiming to boost RE task performance through various adversarial examples and adding perturbation on all input features of the model. Adversarial learning is built on the basis that similar data instances are assigned the same label.

3.2.2. Semi-Supervised Approaches

The first bootstrapping algorithm was DIPRE (Dual Iterative Pattern Relation Expansion) [27], which employs a pattern-matching model as classifier by using a set of seeds to extract patterns from the dataset in order to extract new candidate relations. The DualRE model [28] was proposed to overcome the problem of semantic drift associated with bootstrapping approaches. The key idea behind DualRE is training a retrieval module along a relation prediction module, hereby mutually improving the quality of one another through labelling data to use as auxiliary training data. In [29], a convolutional neural network (CNN) RE architecture was proposed that employs graph-structured data where label knowledge is smoothed over the graph by means of explicit graph-based regularization.

3.2.3. Distant Supervision Approaches

The traditional distant supervision RE approaches claim that if a sentence consists of two related entities then the same relation lies between those two entities. Nevertheless, Sebastian et al. proposed an RE model that supports a different claim, "if two entities participate in a relation, then at least one sentence that mentions those two entities might express that relation" [30], by utilizing a factor graph to aid in determining if two entities are related or not. Additionally, a learning algorithm is employed to train this graphical framework by structuring distant supervision as an instance of constraint-driven semi-supervision.

A piecewise CNN RE technique was proposed by [31], not only to overcome the noise generated from the feature extraction phase, but also to address the issue of handling distant relation extraction as a multi-instance task, which leads to lack of certainty of instance labels. By designing a convolutional framework with piecewise max pooling as an alternative to feature engineering to automatically learn related features, the authors of [31] were able to overcome the aforementioned problems.

4. ROIE: A Recurrent Neural Network Model for Open Information Extraction

Our recurrent neural network (RNN) model is based on our work in [32] by tackling the OIE task as a sequencing labeling problem resulting in the extraction of multiple, overlapping tuples for each sentence.

4.1. Neural Model Architecture

Throughout the back-propagation process, RNNs are prone to vanishing and exploding gradient descent complications, making RNN training challenging. Thus, LSTMs and gated recurrent units

(GRUs) were established to address the issues related to the unstable gradient. When the gradient becomes too big or simply disappears, killing the learning process, LSTMs and GRUs aid by using the relevant gates to allow the gradient to flow backward through time, freely and effectively keeping long-term dependencies [33].

Both LSTMs and GRUs are able to train on long word contexts and connect information using cell states. LSTM has three gates (*input, output,* and *forget*), contrary to GRU, which couples *input* and *forget gates* in one gate—*update gate*, in addition to *reset gate*, which determines how to incorporate previous memory with the current input. As a result, our model employs GRUs instead of LSTMs, since GRUs are less complex with only two gates, and hereby they require less training parameters and utilize less memory, effectively making GRU faster than LSTM.

The default operation in RNN captures context in a single direction, which may lead to comprehending issues; for instance, consider the following two sentences:

"Second place is not as prestigious as first place."

"Second is the standard international unit of time."

In these sentences, the word "second" carries different meanings, which traditional RNNs will not be able to comprehend, since it is the first word in the sentence; nevertheless, bidirectional RNNs support learning from both ends. A bidirectional GRU (Bi-GRU) was employed in our model to learn forward and backward lexical semantics of each word in a given sentence. There are two different methods to implement a bidirectional network; either by having two RNNs operating in opposite directions or within the internal architecture of the RNN itself. In our ROIE framework, we implemented the latter approach.

4.2. Word Embeddings

Recently, several types of word embeddings have been introduced; nevertheless, they all serve the same purpose of mapping words to low-dimensional vector representations. The aforementioned OIE and RE deep learning-based approaches in Sections 3.1.3 and 3.2, respectively, utilized one of the traditional word embeddings, either GloVe [34] or Word2Vec [35].

In our work, we incorporated the novel contextualized word embeddings. Due to their ability to capture complex syntactic and semantic features of a word, deep contextualized word embeddings have proven to be successful in various NLP tasks when compared to the traditional word embeddings. The main concept behind contextualized word embeddings is that a word's representation varies according to its neighboring words, and thus the same word can have different representations depending on its adjacent words.

Table 2 shows the word embeddings we employed in our experiment, along with the dimensionality of each embedding and the data they are trained on. We picked one traditional non-contextualized embedding, GloVe, and three contextualized embeddings with different dimensionalities: BERT [9], XLNet [36], and XLM-RoBERTa [37]. XLNet is trained on data much larger than Google's BERT training data, and thus it outperforms BERT on 20 different NLP tasks [36]. Facebook's XLM-RoBERTa depends on the masked language model objective and is effective in text processing from 100 different languages.

Table 2. Word embeddings employed in our work.

Embedding	Dimensionality	Trained On
GloVe [34]	100	Aggregated global word–word co-occurrence statistics from a corpus.
BERT [9]	3072	Wikipedia and +10,000 books of different genres.
XLNet [36]	2048	Over 130 GB of textual data.
XLM-RoBERTa [37]	1024	2.5 TB of filtered CommonCrawl data.

Flair [38] is a simple framework that offers a unified interface for conceptually varying types of word and document embeddings, which we utilized in our experiments.

4.3. Work Flow

The embedded sentence—composed of a fixed-length vector—is sent as an input to our ROIE neural network framework. Specifically, predicates—the part of a sentence or clause containing a verb and stating something about the subject—are regarded as the building blocks of most languages, as they denote significant actions that are deemed extremely efficient in extracting relations of interest. Therefore, in line with the work of [22,32], the predicate in each sentence is presumed to be the relation that links the tuple; consequently, the predicate is inputted to the neural network framework as a feature vector alongside the part of speech (POS) tag of the input sentence obtained using the NLTK toolkit [39], as shown in Figure 2.

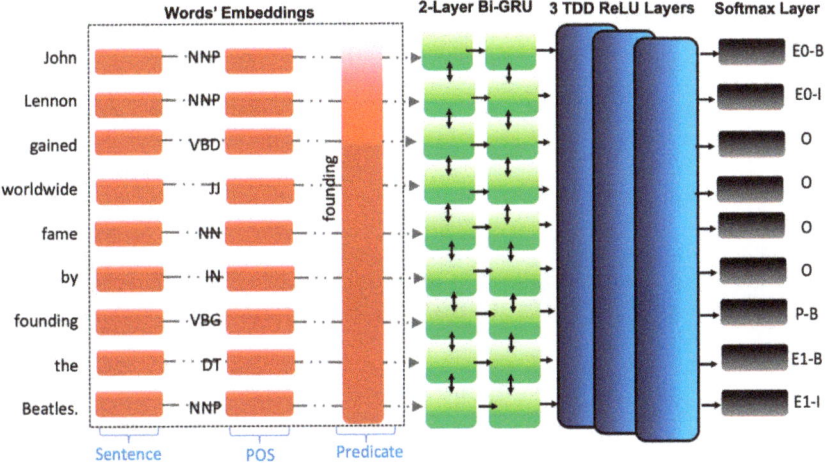

Figure 2. Our ROIE transferable neural model architecture.

After embedding the three aforementioned inputs, we concatenated them all to form our feature vector of shape *(3, length of sentence, embedding size)*; the feature vector is defined as follows:

$$\text{Feature Vector} = \text{Embedded Word} \oplus \text{Embedded POS} \oplus \text{Embedded Predicate} \quad (1)$$

The generated feature vector is then passed to the two-layer Bi-GRU, which in turn outputs a tensor that is progressed to three-layer time distributed dense (TDD) layers, which is finally passed to the SoftMax layer for label prediction.

4.4. Sequence Labelling

In NLP, sequence labelling is the task of identifying and assigning a label to each word, for instance the POS task, where each word is tagged to a particular POS. Sequencing labelling achieved more promising results when compared to traditional statistical techniques among a diverse array of NLP tasks [22]. In our work, we used BIO tags (Begin-Intermediate-Outside) [40] to indicate the word's location in the sentence and label it accordingly. The SoftMax output layer assigns the probability score to each word to determine its corresponding label, as shown in Figure 2. Our proposed ROIE paradigm is only able to capture binary relations. If a sentence contains more than one predicate, another instance of that sentence is created to capture any possible relation. However, if a sentence has no relations, only the predicate is labelled "P-B" (Predicate-Begin), "P-I" (Predicate-Intermediate), while label "O" (Outside) is assigned to the remaining words in the sentence, without assigning any "E" (Entity) labels.

4.5. Dataset

To train and test our OIE neural framework, we used the Wikipedia News Corpus (WikiNews) [41]. Our dataset was split into a training set to train the network, a development set for validation purposes and a test set to assess the performance of our ROIE framework on a 60/20/20 ratio. An overview of the dataset is shown in Table 3.

Table 3. WikiNews dataset overview.

Dataset	No. of Sentences	No. of Tuples
Train set	1174	2906
Development set	392	946
Test set	393	993

4.6. Hyperparameter Settings

Our ROIE neural framework was implemented using the Keras framework [42] with a TensorFlow backend [43]. Table 4 shows our model's hyperparameter configurations that achieved the best results when training and testing on OIE. As shown, our framework was trained on 20 epochs and the training dataset was split into 100 batches. For regularization purposes, in order to avoid over-fitting, the dropout rate was set to 0.1. Furthermore, early stopping was utilized to terminate training when the training performance stopped improving. Both bidirectional GRU layers and the three TDD layers had an identical number of units, 128 units. Additionally, rectified linear unit (ReLU) [44] was the chosen activation function in the three TDD layers, while the Adam optimizer [45] was utilized to train our framework.

Table 4. Hyperparameter settings used in ROIE.

Hyperparameter	Value
Epochs	20
Batches	100
Bidirectional GRU	128 units
TDD activation function	ReLU
TDD units	128 units
Dropout rate	0.1
Optimizer	Adam

4.7. Results of our ROIE Model

It should be emphasized that our ROIE neural model outperformed other state-of-the-art neural OIE approaches, as documented in [32], while using ELMo word embeddings [46], also a deep contextualized word embedding that models both complex syntactic and semantic features of a word.

Better results were attained after XLNet was substituted for ELMo [46] when compared to our results in [32]; the results are reported in Table 5. An exhaustive grid search was performed to single out the best batch–epoch pair for each word embedding. Our batches and epochs ranged from 20 to 120 and 1 to 50, respectively, both with increments of 5. GloVe achieved an F-measure of 56.1%, while BERT and XLM-RoBERTa achieved a F-measure of 61.1% and 61.5%, respectively. Nevertheless, XLNet surpassed all the other embeddings—including ELMo's 59% F-measure—and achieved 65%.

Table 5. Results of the ROIE model using different word embeddings. Both training and testing were done on the OIE WikiNews dataset. Recall (R), precision (P), and F-measure (F) were used as evaluation metrics.

Source Task (Train)	Target Task (Test)	Word Embeddings	Hyper Parameters (Batches–Epochs)		Results (R–P–F)		
OIE (news)	OIE (news)	GloVe	100	5	58.2%	54.1%	56.1%
		BERT	100	5	64.3%	58.2%	61.1%
		XLNet	100	20	68.1%	62.2%	65.0%
		XLM-RoBERTa	100	5	65.4%	58.1%	61.5%

5. Materials and Methods

In this section, we explain the experiments carried out and dataset utilized in our two main tasks, transferring to OIE bio-medical domain and transferring to RE task. In the source task, the aforementioned WikiNews training set [41] was utilized.

5.1. Transfering to OIE: Bio-Medical Domain

A classifier trained on a news corpus would observe an altered distribution if employed to classify bio-medical data. Therefore, domain adaptation methods are deployed in transfer learning in such scenarios. In the transductive learning task, specifically domain adaptation, we handle our pretrained model as a feature extractor; in our case, the pretrained model was trained on the news domain, where there is a characteristic shift in distribution of the data between source and target domains that necessitates adjustments to effectively transfer knowledge.

DDIExtraction 2013 [47] is a bio-medical dataset mainly specialized in the subject of drug–drug interactions. The dataset was structured from the DrugBank database [48] and MEDline abstracts [49] related to drug–drug interactions. We utilized the DDIExtraction as a test set in the following experiments. In our work, the performance of the following three experiments were compared against each other:

Transductive transfer learning: transferring knowledge learnt from the OIE news domain to the OIE bio-medical domain.

Inductive transfer learning: a small amount of bio-medical data also from DDIExtraction is fed to the neural network alongside news data to train the neural network.

Traditional learning: both training and testing on bio-medical data.

5.2. Transfering to Relation Extraction

The OIE and RE tasks are both subclasses of information extraction, making the two tasks similar in semantics. The dataset used in the RE task for training, testing, and validation is Semeval-2010 Task 8 [50]. The nine predefined relations in the dataset are shown in Table 6. The training set consists of 8000 sentences, however, for a fair comparison we trained our neural network on the same number of relation tuples available in the OIE training set; thus, 2906 tuples were randomly selected from the training set. Similarly, the same experiments were compared against each other when transferring from the OIE news domain to RE:

Transductive transfer learning: transferring knowledge learnt from the OIE news domain to the RE news domain.

Inductive transfer learning: a small percentage of the RE corpus is fed into the neural framework along OIE news data to train the neural network.

Traditional learning: both training and testing on the RE news domain.

In all the above-mentioned experiments in both tasks, we used bio-medical OIE and RE, a development set containing 946 tuples composed of the same structure as the source task, for validation purposes.

Table 6. List of predefined relations in the Semeval-2010 corpus and their number of occurrences.

Relations.	Number of Instances	
	Train Set	Test Set
1. Cause–Effect	485	228
2. Instrument–Agency	245	156
3. Product–Producer	320	231
4. Entity–Origin	398	258
5. Entity–Destination	392	252
6. Component–Whole	209	110
7. Content–Container	118	102
8. Member–Collection	345	233
9. Message–Topic	394	261
Total	2906	1831

6. Results and Evaluation

The following measures were used to measure the effect of transferring knowledge learnt from our ROIE framework: Recall (R), Precision (P), and F-measure (F). All the aforementioned evaluation metrics were expressed as percentages throughout the experiments, with the F-measure being the determining performance measure. All hyperparameters—shown previously in Table 4—except for epochs and batches were fixed throughout our experiments. Contextual embeddings were highly sensitive to changes in hyperparameters, specifically with respect to number of epochs and batches. Steep falls and rises were noticed when the number of epochs and batches were changed.

It is worth noting that the dimensionality of the word embeddings refers to the length of the vector; in theory the size of the vector is directly proportional to the information it can store, which allows NLP systems to perform better. However, in practice, there was not much benefit with the embeddings with higher dimensionality when compared with lower dimensionality embeddings.

6.1. Results of Transferring to OIE: Bio-Medical Domain

In order to properly evaluate transfer learning results, we compared it with training and testing on the target task. Detailed results of the experiments can be found in Table 7, indicating the source task (training set) and the target task (testing set). The hyperparameters that achieved the highest scores are the ones reported in Table 7.

OIE: Bio-Medical Domain Results Discussion

Our system achieved the highest results using XLM-RoBERTa in all three experiments: transductive transfer learning, inductive transfer learning, and traditional learning, outperforming all other word embeddings.

When our training set was composed entirely of news data, XLM-RoBERTa scored the highest F-measure of 64.4%, with 100 batches and 5 epochs. XLNet and GloVe achieved the same F-measure of 62.9% using the same number of batches and epochs, 100 and 5, respectively. Nevertheless, BERT achieved the lowest F-measure of 60%.

In inductive transfer learning, a small amount of bio-medical data were inputted to the neural framework by sampling a random batch from the DDIExtraction 2013 training data using a 4:1 ratio, with bio-medical data having the lower ratio. A significant increase in the F-measure of 13.6% was attained in inductive transfer learning when comparing to transductive transfer learning. Using both XLM-RoBERTa and XLNet, our inductive transfer approach realized an F-measure of approximately 78%, with XLM-RoBERTa's precision surpassing XLNet's by 0.9%. BERT came in third and achieved 75.2%, while GloVe scored an F-measure of 73.7%.

Table 7. Domain adaptation results by transferring from the OIE news domain to the OIE bio-medical domain using four different word embeddings. Bold values indicate the highest achieved F-measure in each of the three experiments (transductive transfer learning, inductive transfer learning, traditional learning).

	Source Task (Train)	Target Task (Test)	Word Embeddings	Hyperparameters (Batches–Epochs)		Results (R–P–F)		
Transductive Transfer Learning (BM1)	OIE (news)	OIE (bio-medical)	GloVe	100	5	68.2%	58.4%	62.9%
			BERT	50	10	72.4%	51.3%	60.0%
			XLNet	100	5	68.4%	58.3%	62.9%
			XLM-RoBERTa	100	5	**71.0%**	**59.0%**	**64.4%**
Inductive Transfer Learning (BM2)	OIE (news) + OIE (bio-medical)	OIE (bio-medical)	GloVe	100	15	69.8%	78.2%	73.7%
			BERT	100	5	71.9%	78.9%	75.2%
			XLNet	100	10	73.6%	82.9%	77.9%
			XLM-RoBERTa	100	5	**73.0%**	**83.8%**	**78.0%**
Traditional Learning	OIE (bio-medical)	OIE (bio-medical)	GloVe	100	5	70.8%	71.7%	71.2%
			BERT	100	15	73.1%	85.9%	78.9%
			XLNet	100	15	72.9%	84.2%	78.1%
			XLM-RoBERTa	100	15	**72.5%**	**86.9%**	**79.0%**

The results scored using traditional learning by training entirely on bio-medical data were only 1% higher than the results achieved using the inductive transfer learning technique. Once again, XLM-RoBERTa outperformed the other embeddings by scoring an F-measure of 79% using 100 batches and 15 epochs. Additionally, BERT achieved roughly the same F-measure as XLM-RoBERTa of 78.9%, using the same number of epochs and batches; however, it achieved a lower precision of 85.9%. It is notable that GloVe achieved a higher F-measure in inductive transfer learning than traditional learning. Our interpretation is that adding news training data to the biomedical tasks resulted in a higher performance with GloVe embeddings. This could correlate with the original training data of the GloVe model used in our experiments. Thus, our results show that using a small percentage from the target task while training our neural network results in a proximate outcome when compared to traditional learning.

6.2. Results of Transfering to Relation Extraction

Equally, in order to establish a fair comparison in the following three experiments, we fixed the training set size to 2906 relation instances. Results of both transductive and inductive transfer learning were compared against the results achieved by traditional learning. Results are reported in Table 8.

Relation Extraction Results Discussion

Firstly, in transductive transfer learning, with 50 batches and 10 epochs, BERT was able to achieve an F-measure of 54.4%. Both XLNet and XLM-RoBERTa scored the same F-measure of 49.1%, which was nearly 4.6% higher than the F-measure achieved using GloVe.

With inductive transfer learning, we found an improvement of 12.8% when compared to transductive learning also using a 4:1 ratio, with the OIE news dataset overtaking the higher ratio. Using XLM-RoBERTa, a 67.2% F-measure was attained when the network was trained on 15 epochs and the training dataset was divided into 100 batches. BERT and XLNet did not fall far behind XLM-RoBERTa, as they achieved F-measures of 66.3% and 65.4%, respectively. GloVe achieved the lowest F-measure of 59.9%.

Table 8. Results of transferring from OIE to RE using four different word embeddings. Bold values indicate the highest achieved F-measure in each of the three experiments (transductive transfer learning, inductive transfer learning, traditional learning).

	Source Task (Train)	Target Task (Test)	Word Embeddings	Hyperparameters (Batches–Epochs)		Results (R–P–F)		
Transductive Transfer Learning (RE1)	OIE (news)	RE (news)	GloVe	100	5	55.9%	37.0%	44.5%
			BERT	**50**	**10**	**62.2%**	**48.4%**	**54.4%**
			XLNet	50	5	58.8%	42.1%	49.1%
			XLM-RoBERTa	100	15	53.2%	45.6%	49.1%
Inductive Transfer Learning (RE2)	OIE (news) + RE (news)	RE (news)	GloVe	100	10	52.8%	69.3%	59.9%
			BERT	100	5	61.7%	73.0%	66.3%
			XLNet	100	15	59.7%	72.2%	65.4%
			XLM-RoBERTa	**100**	**15**	**59.7%**	**76.9%**	**67.2%**
Traditional Learning	RE (news)	RE (news)	GloVe	100	15	57.6%	77.1%	65.9%
			BERT	**100**	**15**	**62.4%**	**82.3%**	**71.0%**
			XLNet	100	5	61.6%	81.3%	70.5%
			XLM-RoBERTa	100	15	59.8%	79.9%	68.4%

When employing default learning settings, where we train on our target task, there was a 3.8% enhancement in the F-measure. Once again, BERT outperformed by scoring an F-measure of 71%, only 0.5% higher than XLNet, and 2.6% higher than XLM-RoBERTa. Consistently, GloVe scored the lowest F-measure of 65.9%, hereby proving the notable effect in the model's performance when using contextualized word embeddings in contrast with traditional word embeddings.

Table 9 summarizes the best results of the three main experiments acquired in our work: ROIE model, transferring to bio-medical domain, and transferring to RE. As seen in Table 9, we could not single out a particular contextualized word embedding to utilize, as the use of word embedding may vary according to the various reasons: type of task (OIE, RE, or sentiment analysis), dataset domain (news, bio-medical data, or financial data), and the computational power available to the user. This is also in agreement with other papers that extensively compared embeddings in various tasks and found that the most suitable one is highly dependent on the task and data nature [51,52].

Table 9. Summary of the best result obtained in each experiment by different systems described in the paper: original ROIE model, transferring from OIE to bio-medical OIE (transductive transfer learning, inductive transfer learning, traditional learning), and transferring from OIE to (transductive transfer learning, inductive transfer learning, traditional learning).

Source Task (Train)	Target Task (Test)	Word Embeddings	Hyperparameters (Batches–Epochs)		Results (R–P–F)		
OIE (news)	OIE (news)	XLNet	100	20	68.1%	62.2%	65.0%
OIE (news)	OIE (bio-medical)	XLM-RoBERTa	100	5	71.0%	59.0%	64.4%
OIE (news) + OIE (bio-medical)	OIE (bio-medical)	XLM-RoBERTa	100	5	73.0%	83.8%	78.0%
OIE (bio-medical)	OIE (bio-medical)	XLM-RoBERTa	100	15	72.5%	86.9%	79.0%
OIE (news)	RE (news)	BERT	50	10	62.2%	48.4%	54.4%
OIE (news) + RE (news)	RE (news)	XLM-RoBERTa	100	15	59.7%	76.9%	67.2%
RE (news)	RE (news)	BERT	100	15	62.4%	82.3%	71.0%

To further elaborate that the choice of the word embedding is dependent upon the task and nature of data, XLNet outperformed all the other word embeddings when training and testing on the news dataset. However, on bio-Medical data, XLM-RoBERTa performed better in all three experiments: transductive transfer learning, inductive transfer learning, and traditional learning. It is worth noting that XLM-RoBERTa outperformed in four out of a total seven experiments in our work. Thus, we were motivated to compare and experiment with the use of different word embeddings.

7. Conclusions and Future Work

Can we survive without labelled data in NLP? On the basis of our findings: yes! Nevertheless, employing labelled data in NLP tasks still results in better performance. However, the process of collection of labelled data is demanding and, in some cases, inaccessible. In this paper, we utilized training on OIE to diminish the complication of insufficient training data of neural network models in various NLP tasks and encourage model generalization. Since OIE plays a fundamental role in turning massive, unstructured data into factual information that can be used as a foundation to many NLP tasks, we favored OIE as our source task, thereby ensuring our work is useful and beneficial to the NLP community.

In the domain adaptation experiment, we transferred information learnt from one domain to the other on the same task. The neural model was trained on the OIE news domain and tested on the bio-medical domain. Results obtained from the inductive approach indicated that our ROIE neural model can play a fundamental role in domain adaptation.

Moreover, our research also covered the transferability to a semantically related task. Results achieved from transferring from the OIE to RE followed the same pattern as transferring from the OIE news domain to the bio-medical domain. Inductive transfer learning achieved promising and comparable results with traditional learning. Thus, our work demonstrates that OIE can act as a reliable source task, not only in domain adaptation but also when transferring to related tasks.

In the future, we intend to expand our work beyond sequence labelling tasks and experiment with multi-transfer learning thoroughly on several NLP tasks, specifically tasks that are not semantically related to OIE such as sentiment analysis. Additionally, we intend to investigate different transferring mechanisms to study how to leverage knowledge acquired from pre-trained models in varied ways.

Author Contributions: Conception and design of the experiments, I.S. and M.S.; data curation, I.S.; methodology, I.S.; software, I.S.; supervision, M.S.; validation, M.S.; writing—original draft, I.S.; writing—review and editing, M.S. All authors have read and agreed to the published version of the manuscript.

Funding: This work was made possible with funding from the European Union's Horizon 2020 research and innovation program under grant agreement no. 883588 (GEIGER). The opinions expressed and arguments employed herein do not necessarily reflect the official views of the funding body.

Conflicts of Interest: The authors declare no conflict of interest.

References

1. Otter, D.W.; Medina, J.R.; Kalita, J. A Survey of the Usages of Deep Learning for Natural Language Processing. *arXiv* **2019**, arXiv:1807.10854. [CrossRef] [PubMed]
2. Mausam, M. Open Information Extraction Systems and Downstream Applications. In Proceedings of the Twenty-Fifth International Joint Conference on Artificial Intelligence, New York, NY, USA, 15 July 2016.
3. Yang, Q.; Zhang, Y.; Dai, W.; Pan, S. Foundations of transfer learning. In *Transfer Learning*; Cambridge University Press: Cambridge, UK, 2020; pp. 1–2.
4. Keneshloo, Y.; Ramakrishnan, N.; Reddy, C.K. Deep Transfer Reinforcement Learning for Text Summarization. In Proceedings of the 2019 SIAM International Conference on Data Mining, Calgary, AB, Canada, 2–4 May 2019; pp. 675–683.
5. Bhatia, P.; Arumae, K.; Celikkaya, E.B. Dynamic transfer learning for named entity recognition. In *Social Networks: A Framework of Computational Intelligence*; Springer: Cham, Switzerland, 2019; pp. 69–81.
6. Min, S.; Seo, M.; Hajishirzi, H.; Barzilay, R.; Kan, M.Y. Question answering through transfer learning from large fine-grained supervision data. *arXiv* **2017**, arXiv:1702.02171.
7. Yu, J.; Qiu, M.; Jiang, J.; Huang, J.; Song, S.; Chu, W.; Chen, H. Modelling Domain Relationships for Transfer Learning on Retrieval-based Question Answering Systems in E-commerce. In Proceedings of the Eleventh ACM International Conference on Multimedia—MULTIMEDIA'03, Berkeley, CA, USA, 7 November 2003; pp. 682–690.
8. Chuong, D.B.; Andrew, N.Y. Transfer learning for text classification. *Adv. Neural Inf. Process. Syst.* **2006**, 299–306.

9. Devlin, J.; Chang, M.W.; Lee, K.; Toutanova, K. BERT: Pre-training of deep bidirectional transformers for language understanding. *arXiv* **2018**, arXiv:1810.04805.
10. Howard, J.; Ruder, S. Universal language model fine-tuning for text classification. *arXiv* **2018**, arXiv:1801.06146.
11. Radford, A.; Karthik, N.; Salimans, T.; Sutskever, I. Improving Language Understanding by Generative Pre-Training. 2018. Available online: https://www.cs.ubc.ca/~{}amuham01/LING530/papers/radford2018improving.pdf (accessed on 20 August 2020).
12. Sarhan, I.; Marco, S. Uncovering algorithmic approaches in open information extraction: A literature review. In Proceedings of the 30th Benelux Conference on Artificial Intelligence, Hertogenbosch, The Netherlands, 8–9 November 2018.
13. Etzioni, O.; Banko, M.; Soderland, S.; Weld, D. Open information extraction from the web. In Proceedings of the Twentieth International Joint Conference on Artificial Intelligence, Hyderabad, India, 6–12 January 2007; Volume 7, pp. 2670–2676.
14. Wu, F.; Weld, D.S. Open information extraction using Wikipedia. In Proceedings of the 48th Annual Meeting of the Association for Computational Linguistics, Uppsala, Sweden, 11–16 July 2010; pp. 118–127.
15. Schmitz, M.; Bart, R.; Soderland, S.; Etzioni, O. Open language learning for information extraction. In Proceedings of the 2012 Joint Conference on Empirical Methods in Natural Language Processing and Computational Natural Language Learning; Association for Computational Linguistics, Jeju Island, Korea, 12–14 July 2012.
16. Fader, A.; Soderland, S.; Etzioni, O. Identifying relations for open information extraction. In Proceedings of the Conference on Empirical Methods in Natural Language Processing, Association for Computational Linguistics (ACL), Edinburgh, UK, 11 July 2011.
17. Christensen, J.; Soderland, S.; Etzioni, O. An analysis of open information extraction based on semantic role labeling. In Proceedings of the K-CAP'2011: Knowledge Capture Conference, Banff, AB, Canada, 25–29 June 2011; Volume 11, pp. 3–10.
18. Akbik, A.; Löser, A. Kraken: N-ary facts in open information extraction. In Proceedings of the Joint Workshop on Automatic Knowledge Base Construction and Web-scale Knowledge Extraction, Montreal, QC, Canada, 7–8 June 2012; pp. 52–56.
19. Del Corro, L.; Gemulla, R. ClausIE: Clause-based open information extraction. In Proceedings of the 22nd International Conference on WWW, Rio de Janeiro, Brazil, 13–17 May 2013; pp. 355–366.
20. Cui, L.; Wei, F.; Zhou, M. Neural open information extraction. *arXiv* **2018**, arXiv:1805.04270.
21. Hochreiter, S.; Schmidhuber, J. Long short-term memory. *Neural Comput.* **1997**, *9*, 1735–1780. [CrossRef]
22. Stanovsky, G.; Michael, J.; Zettlemoyer, L.; Dagan, I. Supervised Open Information Extraction. In Proceedings of the 2018 Conference of the North American Chapter of the Association for Computational Linguistics: Human Language Technologies, New Orleans, LA, USA, 1–6 June 2018; Volume 1.
23. Sarhan, I.; El-Sonbaty, Y.; El-Nasr, M.A. Arabic relation extraction: A survey. *Int. J. Comput.* **2016**, *5*, 430–437.
24. Guodong, Z.; Jian, S.; Jie, Z.; Min, Z. Exploring various knowledge in relation extraction. In Proceedings of the 43rd Annual Meeting, Ann Harbour, MI, USA, 25–30 June 2005.
25. Plank, B.; Moschitti, A. Embedding semantic similarity in tree kernels for domain adaptation of relation extraction. In Proceedings of the 51st Annual Meeting of the Association for Computational Linguistics, Sofia, Bulgaria, 4–9 August 2013.
26. Su, P.; Vijay-Shanker, K. Adversarial learning for supervised and semi-supervised relation extraction in bio-medical literature. *arXiv* **2020**, arXiv:2005.04277.
27. Brin, S. Extracting patterns and relations from the world wide web. In *The World Wide Web and Databases*; Springer: Berlin, Germany, 1999; pp. 172–183.
28. Lin, H.; Yan, J.; Qu, M.; Ren, X. Learning Dual Retrieval Module for Semi-supervised Relation Extraction. In Proceedings of the World Wide Web Conference on—WWW '19, San Fransisco, CA, USA, 13–17 May 2019; pp. 1073–1083.
29. Kipf, T.N.; Welling, M. Semi-supervised classification with graph convolutional networks. *arXiv* **2016**, arXiv:1609.02907.
30. Riedel, S.; Yao, L.; McCallum, A. Modeling Relations and Their Mentions without Labeled Text. In Proceedings of the Joint European Conference on Machine Learning and Knowledge Discovery in Databases, Heidelberg, Germany, 16–20 September 2010.

31. Zeng, D.; Liu, K.; Chen, Y.; Zhao, J. Distant Supervision for Relation Extraction via Piecewise Convolutional Neural Networks. In Proceedings of the 2015 Conference on Empirical Methods in Natural Language Processing, Lisbon, Portugal, 19–23 September 2015.
32. Sarhan, I.; Spruit, M.R. Contextualized Word Embeddings in a Neural Open Information Extraction Model. In Proceedings of the International Conference on Applications of Natural Language to Information Systems, Salford, UK, 26–28 June 2019.
33. Pascanu, R.; Tomas, M.; Yoshua, B. On the Difficulty of Training Recurrent Neural Networks. In Proceedings of the International Conference on Machine Learning, Atlanta, GA, USA, 16–21 June 2013.
34. Pennington, J.; Socher, R.; Manning, C. Glove: Global Vectors for Word Representation. In Proceedings of the 2014 Conference on Empirical Methods in Natural Language Processing (EMNLP), Doha, Qatar, 19–25 October 2014; pp. 1532–1543.
35. Mikolov, T.; Sutskever, I.; Chen, K.; Corrado, G.; Dean, J. Distributed representations of words and phrases and their compositionality. *arXiv* **2013**, arXiv:1310.4546.
36. Yang, Z.; Dai, Z.; Yang, Y.; Carbonell, J.; Salakhutdinov, R.; Le, Q.V. XLNet: Generalized autoregressive pretraining for language understanding. *Adv. Neural Inf. Process. Syst.* **2019**, *32*, 5753–5763.
37. Conneau, A.; Khandelwal, K.; Goyal, N.; Chaudhary, V.; Wenzek, G.; Guzmán, F.; Grave, E.; Ott, M.; Zettlemoyer, L.; Stoyanov, V. Unsupervised cross-lingual representation learning at scale. *arXiv* **2019**, arXiv:1911.02116.
38. Akbik, A.; Bergmann, T.; Blythe, D.; Rasul, K.; Schweter, S.; Vollgraf, R. FLAIR: An Easy-to-Use Framework for State-of-the-Art NLP. In Proceedings of the 2019 Annual Conference of the North American Chapter of the Association for Computational Linguistics (Demonstrations), NAACL, Princeton, MI, USA, 2–7 June 2019.
39. Loper, E.; Bird, S. NLTK: The natural language toolkit. *arXiv* **2002**, arXiv:cs/0205028.
40. Ramshaw, L.; Mitchell, A.; Marcus, P. *BIO Labels: Text Chunking Using Transformation-Based Learning. Natural Language Processing Using Very Large Corpora*; Springer: Dordrecht, The Netherlands, 1999; pp. 157–176.
41. Stanovsky, G.; Dagan, I. Creating a Large Benchmark for Open Information Extraction. In Proceedings of the 2016 Conference on Empirical Methods in Natural Language Processing, Austin, TX, USA, 2–6 November 2016; pp. 2300–2305.
42. Franois, C. Keras. 2015. Available online: https://github.com/fchollet/keras (accessed on 20 March 2020).
43. Abadi, M. Tensorflow: A system for large-scale machine learning. In Proceedings of the 12th {USENIX} Symposium on Operating Systems Design and Implementation ({OSDI} 16), Savannah, GA, USA, 2–4 November 2016.
44. Nair, V.; Hinton, G.E. Rectified linear units improve restricted Boltzmann machines. In Proceedings of the 27th International Conference on Machine Learning (ICML-10), Haifah, Isreal, 21–24 June 2010.
45. Kingma, D.P.; Ba, J. Adam: A method for stochastic optimization. *arXiv* **2014**, arXiv:1412.6980.
46. Peters, M.; Neumann, M.; Iyyer, M.; Gardner, M.; Clark, C.; Lee, K.; Zettlemoyer, L. Deep contextualized word representations. *arXiv* **2018**, arXiv:1802.05365.
47. Segura-Bedmar, I.; Martínez, P.; De Pablo-Sánchez, C. Using a shallow linguistic kernel for drug–drug interaction extraction. *J. Biomed. Inform.* **2011**, *44*, 789–804. [CrossRef]
48. Wishart, D.S. DrugBank: A comprehensive resource for in silico drug discovery and exploration. *Nucleic Acids Res.* **2006**, *34*, D668–D672. [CrossRef]
49. Bethesda, M.D. National Library of Medicine (US). 2013. Available online: https://medlineplus.gov/ (accessed on 29 March 2020).
50. Hendrickx, I.; Kim, S.N.; Kozareva, Z.; Nakov, P.; Séaghdha, D.Ó.; Padó, S.; Pennacchiotti, M.; Romano, L.; Szpakowicz, S. SemEval-2010 Task 8: Multi-way classification of semantic relations between pairs of nominals. *arXiv* **2019**, arXiv:1911.10422.
51. Tawfik, N.S.; Spruit, M.R. Evaluating sentence representations for biomedical text: Methods and experimental results. *J. Biomed. Inform.* **2020**, *104*, 103396. [CrossRef]
52. Perone, C.S.; Silveira, R.; Paula, T.S. Evaluation of sentence embeddings in downstream and linguistic probing tasks. *arXiv* **2018**, arXiv:1806.06259.

 © 2020 by the authors. Licensee MDPI, Basel, Switzerland. This article is an open access article distributed under the terms and conditions of the Creative Commons Attribution (CC BY) license (http://creativecommons.org/licenses/by/4.0/).

Article

Preliminary Results on Different Text Processing Tasks Using Encoder-Decoder Networks and the Causal Feature Extractor

Adrián Javaloy [1] and Ginés García-Mateos [2,*]

1 Max Planck Institute for Intelligent Systems, 72076 Tübingen, Germany; adrian.javaloy@tuebingen.mpg.de
2 Department of Computer Science and Systems, University of Murcia, 30100 Murcia, Spain
* Correspondence: ginesgm@um.es; Tel.: +34-868-888-530

Received: 28 July 2020; Accepted: 18 August 2020; Published: 20 August 2020

Abstract: Deep learning methods are gaining popularity in different application domains, and especially in natural language processing. It is commonly believed that using a large enough dataset and an adequate network architecture, almost any processing problem can be solved. A frequent and widely used typology is the encoder-decoder architecture, where the input data is transformed into an intermediate code by means of an encoder, and then a decoder takes this code to produce its output. Different types of networks can be used in the encoder and the decoder, depending on the problem of interest, such as convolutional neural networks (CNN) or long-short term memories (LSTM). This paper uses for the encoder a method recently proposed, called Causal Feature Extractor (CFE). It is based on causal convolutions (i.e., convolutions that depend only on one direction of the input), dilatation (i.e., increasing the aperture size of the convolutions) and bidirectionality (i.e., independent networks in both directions). Some preliminary results are presented on three different tasks and compared with state-of-the-art methods: bilingual translation, LaTeX decompilation and audio transcription. The proposed method achieves promising results, showing its ubiquity to work with text, audio and images. Moreover, it has a shorter training time, requiring less time per iteration, and a good use of the attention mechanisms based on attention matrices.

Keywords: natural language processing; deep neural networks; causal encoder; bilingual translation; speech-to-text; LaTeX decompilation

---

1. Introduction

Deep neural networks (DNN) are going through a golden era, demonstrating great effectiveness and high ubiquity to be used in different areas of research, specifically in natural language processing (NLP) tasks. Presently, hardware capabilities have been multiplied and dataset sizes have also grown to the point of having millions of entries in problems such as bilingual translation, audio transcription or LaTeX decompilation. For example, recently Yang et al. [1] presented an interesting survey of the state of the art in bilingual translation or, in general, neural machine translation (NMT) problems. The existing approaches are divided into recurrent and non-recurrent models; between them, the Transformer model by Vaswani et al. [2] achieved remarkable improvements by exploiting the idea of fully attention-based models. Some works, such as the ConvS2S model by Gehring et al. [3], address NMT problems in a fully convolutional approach, obtaining results that are comparable to the state of the art. This methodology has also been applied to speech recognition in audio, such as the work by Kameoka et al. [4]. Concerning the problem of LaTeX decompilation, it can also be understood as an NMT task, in this case from image to text [5]. Deng et al. [6] proposed a convolutional solution to this problem using a hierarchical attention mechanism called coarse-to-fine, which produced significant improvements over previous systems with simpler attention models.

However, this progress in DNN applied in NMT has also translated into a more competitive research environment, promoting some bad habits that have been built over the years. As stated by Lipton and Steinhardt [7], these include claiming hypothesis as true even when they have not been proved, not clearly differentiating between speculations and facts, or flooding their written works with unnecessary mathematical formulas with the aim of showing expertise.

In this paper, a novel type of encoder recently proposed [8], called Causal Feature Extractor (CFE), is assessed for different NLP tasks. It is based on the causal convolutional neural networks introduced by Oord et al. [9], and it is used as the encoder in an encoder-decoder architecture, a commonly used model in MNT tasks. Specifically, this encoder-decoder model is applied to a variety of NLP problems which have something in common: all of them take a sequence as input, and output another sequence that depends on the input. Thus, the main goal of this work is to test the new encoder in different types of input, making use of statistical tests, giving them a strong basis that supports all the conclusions based on the obtained results. A particularity of the selected MNT tasks is that they have different types of input, while the output is always a text sequence: in bilingual translation problem (in our case, from English to German) the input is a text; in LaTeX decompilation, the input is given by the image of an equation; and in audio transcription, the input is a one-dimensional audio signal which is transformed into a spectrogram. CFE is able to work in all these cases, achieving promising results.

2. Materials and Methods

2.1. Encoder-Decoder Architecture

Presently, the predominant technique for implementing deep neural networks in the field of MNT is the encoder-decoder architecture. A great number of variations have been proposed in the literature, offering solutions that make up the state of the art in different tasks [10]. It consists of two parts that collaborate with each other. On the one hand, there is an encoder that, from the input vector $\mathbf{X} = x_1, x_2 \ldots x_l$, generates an intermediate vector $\mathbf{Z} = z_1, z_2 \ldots z_l$ of the same length as $\mathbf{X}$, where each column z_i describes the characteristics of the environment around the i-th value of the input. On the other hand, the decoder acts sequentially and, at each instant t, it takes the i-th input of the intermediate vector, z_i, and the output produced by itself at the previous instant, y_{t-1}. It computes the output at the current instant, y_t, thus forming the output vector $\mathbf{Y} = y_1, y_2 \ldots y_{l'}$, with length l', that can be different from l. The output ends when the decoder produces a special "end of string" symbol.

An interesting complementary technique working in conjunction with the encoder-decoder architecture is the attention mechanism, which was introduced by Bahdanau et al. [11]. It is an effective method that allows the decoder to decide the most interesting parts of the input, i.e., what parts of $\mathbf{Z}$ are used at each instant. This technique has proven to be effective on problems such as audio textual interpretation [12] and other problems [13]. Figure 1a shows a graphical overview of the encoder-decoder architecture with an attention mechanism.

In our case, the attention model is a fully connected neural network (FCNN) with 1 hidden layer and l output values, where l is the size of the input. The input to this part is the intermediate code of the encoder, $\mathbf{Z}$, and the vector of hidden states of the decoder in the previous step, h_{t-1}.

Additional techniques are used to improve the effectiveness of the system, such as dropout [14,15] (randomly removing some neurons with a given probability), weight normalization [16] (regularizing the weights of the neuron layers), gradient clipping [17] (limiting the norm of the gradient to a maximum value), and random search of the hyperparameters [18] (performing different executions of the process to find the optimal configuration of the hyperparameters of the network).

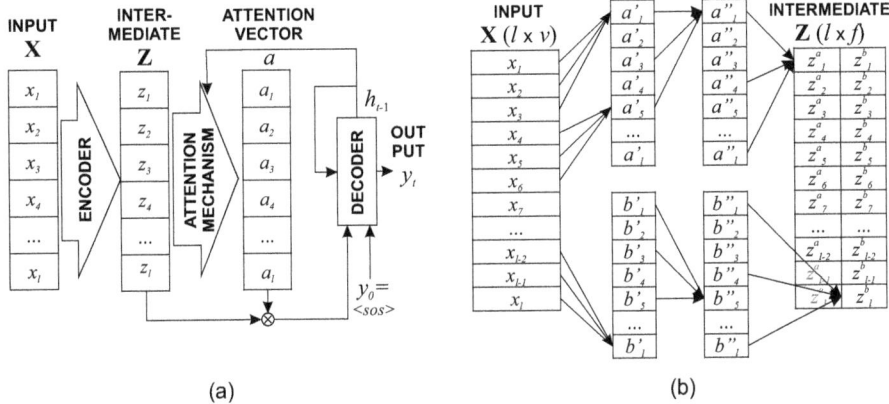

Figure 1. Scheme of the proposed neural network architecture. (**a**) Global scheme of the encoder-decoder architecture including the attention mechanism. The input matrix, **X**, which contains l vector elements $(x_1, x_2 \ldots x_l)$, is transformed into an intermediate code, $\mathbf{Z} = z_1, z_2 \ldots z_l$. Then, the attention mechanism selects the importance, a, of each tuple at each time, t. Using both values, the decoder produces the output at each instant, y_t. The hidden state of the decoder at the previous instant, h_{t-1}, is fed into the attention mechanism and into the decoder. <sos> means "start of sequence". (**b**) Outline of the proposed Causal Feature Extractor for the part of the encoder, in this case with 3 layers. The input is matrix **X**, with l vectors of size v. There are two independent sub-nets (upper and lower), each of which generates $f/2$ features for each input vector. They are convolutional NNs which are causal (a uses the previous values, and b uses the later values) and dilated (the step in the 1st layer is 1, in the 2nd layer 2, and in the 3rd layer 4). The output is the code **Z**, with f features for each input vector.

2.2. Causal Feature Extractor

In the encoder-decoder architecture, both the encoder and the decoder are independent modules that can be implemented in different ways. For example, they can consist of Convolutional Neural Networks (CNN) [19], which is a typical selection method in images. In the case of sequential data, Long Short-Term Memories (LSTM) [20] are more frequently found.

As mentioned before, the purpose of this study is to analyze the feasibility of a new type of layer for the encoder, called Causal Feature Extractor (CFE) [8]. This method is inspired by the Dilated Convolutional Neural Networks and the Causal Convolutional Neural Networks, introduced by Oord et al. [9]. The proposed model, depicted in Figure 1b, is built under three main ideas:

- First, in order to extend the receptive field of the convolutions without requiring large kernels, several convolutional neural layers are stacked, and each one has two times the dilation of the previous one. That is, in the first layer, the convolution for position t depends on $t, t-1, t-2\ldots$; in the second layer, it depends on $t, t-2, t-4\ldots$; in the third layer, $t, t-4, t-8\ldots$, and so on.
- Second, with the aim of making a better use of the attention mechanisms in comparison with CNNs, these stacked convolutional layers are turned into causal convolutions, meaning that the output at one position will depend on the inputs previous or next to that position, but never both. This is the same idea as the Causal CNN proposed by Oord et al. [9].
- Third, considering that the use of causal layers means the misuse of one part of the input, two stacks of causal convolution layers are used, each one taking into account a different direction of the input (the previous or the subsequent input values). The same idea of bidirectionality has also been applied to LSTMs [21].

The main hyperparameters that define the structure of the CFE encoder are the CNN kernel width, the desired receptive field, and the number of features to generate, f. The first hyperparameter indicates the width of the kernels of the convolutions. Along with the second parameter, they determine the number of layers of the CNN. For example, if the kernel width is 5 and the desired receptive field is 20, then there would be 3 convolutional layers (since the dilations are multiplied by 2, the receptive fields of the 1st, 2nd and 3rd layers would be 5, 10 and 20, respectively). Other hyperparameters that are used during the training process are the size of the batches applied in the input, the way of normalizing the weights of the convolutions, the maximum norm of the gradient, and the dropout rate applied to the neurons; there is also the possibility of including or not the position of the input values in the encoder.

In the previous work [8], CFE was applied in the encoder of a text normalization problem (i.e., given a text with symbols, producing a text without symbols as it should be read by a text-to-speech system), achieving a good effectiveness in this NLP problem. The accuracy of the result ranged from 83.5% to 96.8% depending on the training datasets. In the present paper, it is further applied to audio and images; in the second case, the concept of causality considers an order of the pixels from top to bottom and from left to right.

2.3. Language Processing Tasks

The proposed CFE encoder can be applied to any task that requires transforming an input sequence into an output sequence. Thus, the experiments have been focused on the three following well-known computational linguistic problems:

- *Text translation* or *bilingual translation*. This is one of the first and most studied problems in machine NLP, so it is an interesting test bed for the proposed method. Given a text in one language, the output is an equivalent phrase in another language. The difficulty of this task is that there may be words and idioms that do not have a direct translation, or phrases that can be translated into different ways, being all of them valid. The state-of-the-art system used for comparison is given by the Transformer model introduced by Vaswani et al. [2] which overcame the results of other popular machine translation systems such as the GMT model (used in Google Translate). It uses an encoder-decoder architecture and new iterations and improvements of the attention mechanism. We also included in the comparison an encoder-decoder model with LSTM networks in the decoder.

  In the experiments, we used the dataset for the translation from English to German provided in the ACL 2016 Conference on Machine Translation (http://www.statmt.org/wmt16/). The training set of this resource contains near two million parallel sentences (English-German), with a total about 48 million words in English and 45 million words in German. The validation set contains 3000 sentences, and the test set also 3000 sentences. The parameter used to measure the quality of the result is the well-known Bilingual Evaluation Understudy (BLEU) [22]. Another interesting parameter is the perplexity [23], that is used during the training process in the validation set to check the network progress. It is defined as 2 raised to the cross entropy of the empirical distribution of the actual data and the distribution of the predicted values, so that a lower value indicates a better result.

- *LaTeX decompilation*. This problem, which is useful in tasks such as digitization of scientific texts, can also be seen as a particular case of automatic translation. In this case, the input is an image containing a mathematical formula, and the output is a LaTeX command that must produce the same formula as generated by a LaTeX engine. It combines computer vision and neural machine translation, so it is interesting for studying the effectiveness of the proposed CFE model into images. As before, the solution is not necessarily unique, since multiple LaTeX commands can produce the same result.

  The current state-of-the-art model used for comparison is the system presented by Deng et al. [6]. Again, it is based on an encoder-decoder architecture; the encoder consists of two steps, a CNN and a recurrent network, while the decoder is a recurrent network. The method introduces a specific attention mechanism called coarse-to-fine attention. The experiments have been done with the dataset available in [6], which contains over 103,000 training samples, 9300 validation samples and 10,300 test samples. Some of these samples are shown in Figure 2. The accuracy measures are also the BLUE and the perplexity.

$$\widetilde{\gamma}_{\rm hopf} \simeq \sum_{n>0} \widetilde{G}_n \frac{(-a)^n}{2^{2n-1}}$$
(a)

$$(\mathcal{L}_a g)_{ij} = 0, \quad (\mathcal{L}_a H)_{ijk} = 0,$$
(b)

```
\widetilde\gamma_{\rm
hopf}\simeq\sum_{n>0}\widetilde{G}
_n{(-a)^n\over2^{2n-1}}\label{H4}
```
(c)

```
({\cal L}_a g)_{ij} = 0, \\ \\ \\
({\cal L}_a H)_{ijk} = 0 ,
```
(d)

Figure 2. Two sample images of the dataset for the LaTeX decompilation task. (a) and (b) Input images. (c) and (d) Output LaTeX commands corresponding to the images. Information extracted from the public dataset: http://lstm.seas.harvard.edu/latex/.

- *Audio transcription.* The task of audio transcription is another well studied problem, which can also be understood as a type of translation, from audio to text. In this way, the main types of input have been analyzed: text, audio, and images. This problem is used both in online services and in out-of-line transcription of multimedia content. The defining characteristic, with respect to the other problems, is the possible existence of noise in the audio.

  The state of the art of this problem is given by models that do not follow an encoder-decoder architecture, but techniques based on hidden Markov models. Nevertheless, there are good encoder-decoder transcription systems which can be used for comparison. In particular, we used the Listen-Attend-Spell model from Chan et al. [12] to compare the results of the proposed CFE. The dataset is the AN4 set from CMU (http://www.speech.cs.cmu.edu/databases/an4/), which contains more than 1000 recordings of dates, names, numbers, etc. Concreting, the training set includes 1018 samples and the test set 140. The accuracy measures are the word error rate (WER) defined as the correctly identified words over the total, and the perplexity.

3. Results and Discussion

3.1. Experimental Setup

For the execution of the experiments, OpenNMT (https://opennmt.net/) was used. It is an open source ecosystem for neural machine translation using Python. We used the implementation based on PyTorch (https://pytorch.org/) deep learning framework. Apart from the library functions, it also offers useful implementations of some recent methods for different problems. In the bilingual translation problem, it includes the Transformer method Vaswani et al. [2], and an alternative encoder-decoder model using LSTM in the encoder. For the LaTeX decompilation problem, the model called Im2Text Deng et al. [6] was used for the comparison; and in the speech-to-text problem, the Listen-Attend-Spell model by Chan et al. [12].

The computer used in the experiments is a PC with an Intel(R) Core(TM) i7-5930K processor with 12 threads (6 with hyperthreading) at a frequency of 3.50 GHz; it has 3 NVIDIA GeForce GTX1080 GPUs and 600 Gb of SSD hard disk, although only one GPU is used in each execution.

For the configuration of the hyperparameters of the networks, two alternatives were tested: a manual adjustment of the parameters; and a random search of the hyperparameters space. In the second case, 30 random combinations of the hyperparameters were tested in a reduced execution of

1 h for each test, selecting the combination with the least error. The resulting structure of the networks using both methods is presented in Table 1. As indicated in this table, in all the cases the encoder is a CFE network, the decoder is a recurrent neural network (RNN), and there can be a dense neural network (or bridge) between them or not.

Table 1. Hyperparameters of the encoder-decoder networks used in the three problems of interest. Bridge: add a dense layer between encoder and decoder. Global attention: score function used in the attention model. Position encoding: add position information in the encoding. RNN layers: number of layers in the RNN of the decoder. RNN size: number of units in each layer of the RNN. CNN kernel width: size of the convolution filters in CFE. Receptive field: selected receptive field for the CFE. Normalization: method used to normalize the gradients. Batch size: size of the batches used in the training. Max grad. norm.: maximum allowed norm of the gradient. Dropout: dropout rate used. Learning rate decay: value applied to reduce the learning rate.

Hyperparameter Method	Text Translation		LaTeX Decompilation		Audio Transcription	
	Manual	Random	Manual	Random	Manual	Random
Bridge	no	yes	no	yes	no	yes
Global attention	general	concat	general	dot	general	dot
Position encoding	no	yes	no	no	yes	no
RNN layers	3	4	2	1	2	1
RNN size	512	238	500	414	500	126
CNN kernel width	5	3	5	11	5	7
Receptive field	20	13	20	16	20	17
Normalization	tokens	sents	sents	sents	sents	tokens
Batch size	64	16	20	12	16	9
Max grad. norm.	1	14.12	20	28.68	20	3.79
Dropout	0.3	0.71	0.3	0.2	0.3	0.52
Learning rate decay	0.5	0.654	0.5	0.576	0.5	0.465

Finally, to validate the statistical significance of the results, the approximate randomization test of Riezler and Maxwell [24] was applied. This test is used to prove that the outputs produced by two prediction systems are statistically distinguishable.

3.2. Accuracy Performance Results

Table 2 summarizes the results obtained by the encoder-decoder networks using CFE configured with both methods, manual and random search, and the alternative state-of-the-art methods, for the three problems of interest.

Table 2. Experimental results for the proposed CFE model and other architectures. BLEU/WER: accuracy measures for the test set, bilingual evaluation understudy (text translation and LaTeX decompilation) and word error rate (audio transcription), respectively; ACC and PER: accuracy and perplexity obtained for the validation set, respectively. The total number of iterations applied for each problem in the training process is indicated.

Problem	Method	BLEU/WER %	ACC %	PER
Text translation 75,000 iterations	CFE Manual	23.34	62.73	13.59
	CFE Random	27.80	63.02	13.39
	LSTM	36.48	69.64	11.52
	Transformer	34.95	67.78	14.30
LaTeX decompilation 25,000 iterations	CFE Manual	77.57	96.55	1.24
	CFE Random	75.82	96.56	1.24
	Im2Text	80.46	96.78	1.13
Audio transcription 60,000 iteration	CFE Manual	53.12	60.13	8.84
	CFE Random	55.05	59.13	22.4
	Lis.-Att.-Spell	43.14	70.98	5.37

Figure 3 contains a graphical representation of the training process for these problems, showing the cross entropy of the models throughout the iterations applied.

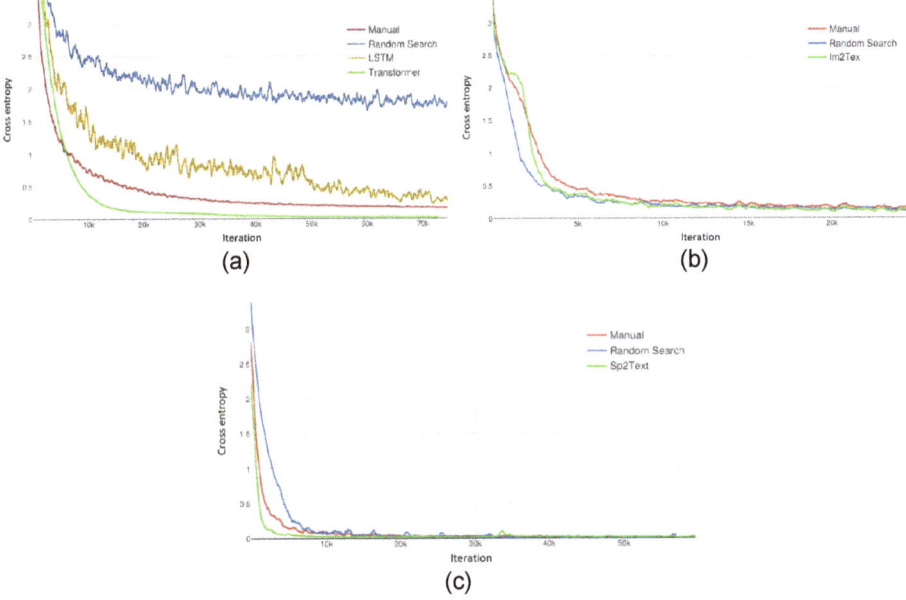

Figure 3. Evolution of the training errors (cross entropy) of the different models compared, for the three problems of interest. (**a**) Text translation. (**b**) LaTeX decompilation. (**c**) Audio transcription.

3.3. Discussion of the Results

In general, the proposed CFE encoder is able to achieve very promising results, near those that are in the state of the art. The evolution of the CFE models in Figure 3 shows a behavior that is very similar to the other systems used for comparison. In any case, these tests should be considered to be preliminary results, needing further experiments and improvements to achieve its full potential. For example, new adaptations could be studied for the decoder network, which was not the purpose of the present work.

These are the main findings of the experiments:

- The proposed CFE models are not able to overcome the results of the state-of-the-art methods used for comparison, as it can be seen in Table 2, although they are very close in many cases. These differences between methods have been confirmed by the approximate randomization tests, indicating that the differences of the predictors are statistically significant. However, it must be observed that these alternative methods are specifically designed for each problem, while the proposed method has shown to be generic, being able to work with text, audio and images, with minimal adaptations for each problem.
- In all the experiments, the number of iterations of the learning process was fixed for each problem (as indicated in Table 2). However, it has to be considered that the average time per iteration is not the same for all the methods. In fact, the proposed CFE encoder is approximately 1.7 times faster than the other alternatives. Thus, for a fixed learning time, the proposed solution could overcome the other methods in some cases. This can be observed in the validation measures (ACC and PER). For example, using the same learning time in the LaTeX decompilation task, CFE achieves an ACC of 96.5%, while Im2Text achieves 96.1%. In other words, Im2Text method needs around

70% more time to achieve its optimum result. A special case is the Transformer method for the problem of bilingual translation, whose average time per iteration is 4 times greater than the time of CFE; so, for the same training time, the performance achieved by CFE would be higher.
- It was observed that the proposed CFE encoder makes a better usage of the attention mechanisms [8]. The attention matrices obtained by CFE are *sharper* than those obtained for the other methods, i.e., they present a bigger different between the elements of interest and those that are not interesting for the decoder. This effect can be observed in the attention matrices shown in Figure 4 for the bilingual translation problem. This is a very positive aspect, since it indicates that future improvements of the proposed method could benefit more from the attention mechanisms.

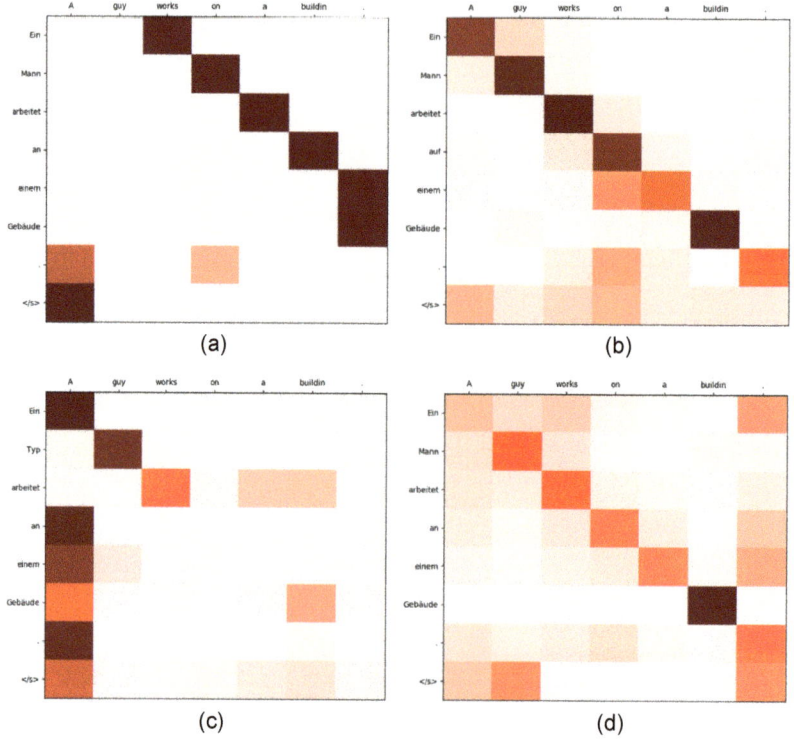

Figure 4. Attention matrices produced by the attention mechanism in the problem of bilingual translation, for the translation of the sentence (horizontal axis) "A guy works on a building". (**a**) Attention matrix for manual CFE, the output (vertical axis) is "Ein Mann arbeitet an einem Gebäude". (**b**) Attention matrix for random CFE, the output is "Ein Mann arbeitet auf einem Gebäude". (**c**) Attention matrix for Transformer model, the output is "Ein Typ arbeitet an einem Gebäude". (**d**) Attention matrix for LSTM, the output is "Ein Mann arbeitet an einem Gebäude".

4. Conclusions

In this paper, we analyzed the feasibility of a novel type of encoder, the Causal Feature Extractor, as a part of an encoder-decoder deep neural network, in different problems of machine neural translation. The results obtained are very promising, achieving a 63.0% accuracy in bilingual translation, 96.6% in LaTeX decompilation and 60.1% in audio transcription. However, the best solution is always the specifically designed system, that has been adjusted and fine-tuned by the corresponding research groups over the years, with improvements of 6.6%, 0.2% and 10.8% in the cited problems, respectively.

Therefore, the results obtained by our approach are close to that of other works that constitute the state of the art, especially in the image processing problem of LaTeX decompilation.

Furthermore, the proposed model has the inherent advantages of convolutional networks with respect to recurrent and LSTM networks. On the one hand, it is a generic architecture that can be adapted to a large number of scenarios, while the use of recurrent networks is more restricted. On the other hand, convolutional networks are known for being parallelizable and highly optimized for training using GPUs, so improving the implementation of this architecture should be much faster than recurrent networks. This was observed in the average execution times per iteration, which is considerably faster for CFE than for the specific models. Those solutions require on average 70% more time than the proposed approaches.

Clearly, there is still ample room for improvement in the application of CFE to the problems of natural language processing. For example, more complex attention mechanisms (such as multi-head attention or local attention) could be combined with the proposed CFE architecture. Also, elimination or relaxation of the use of dilations in the CFE architecture, which could be diluting the influence of the input data too much, could be beneficial. Finally, since the proposed CFE model is very generic, it could be interesting to analyze its application in other areas of computational learning.

Author Contributions: Conceptualization, A.J. and G.G.-M.; methodology, A.J. and G.G.-M.; software, A.J.; validation, A.J. and G.G.-M.; formal analysis, A.J.; investigation, A.J. and G.G.-M.; resources, A.J.; data curation, A.J.; writing—original draft preparation, A.J.; writing—review and editing, A.J. and G.G.-M.; visualization, A.J.; supervision, G.G.-M. All authors have read and agreed to the published version of the manuscript.

Funding: This research was funded by Spanish Ministry of Science, Innovation and Universities, FEDER funds, under grant RTI2018-095855-B-I00 (G.G.-M.).

Acknowledgments: Adrián wants to acknowledge support from the Max Planck Institute for Intelligent Systems.

Conflicts of Interest: The authors declare no conflict of interest. The funders had no role in the design of the study; in the collection, analyses, or interpretation of data; in the writing of the manuscript, or in the decision to publish the results.

Abbreviations

The following abbreviations are used in this manuscript:

ACC	Accuracy
BLEU	Bilingual evaluation understudy
CFE	Causal feature encoder
CNN	Convolutional neural networks
FCNN	Fully connected neural network
LSTM	Long short-term memory
MNT	Machine neural translation
NLP	Natural language processing
PER	Perplexity
WER	Word error rate
RNN	Recurrent neural network

References

1. Yang, S.; Wang, Y.; Chu, X. A Survey of Deep Learning Techniques for Neural Machine Translation. *arXiv* **2020**, arXiv:2002.07526.
2. Vaswani, A.; Shazeer, N.; Parmar, N.; Uszkoreit, J.; Jones, L.; Gomez, A.N.; Kaiser, Ł.; Polosukhin, I. Attention is all you need. Advances in Neural Information Processing Systems (NIPS), Long Beach, CA, USA, 4–9 December 2017; pp. 5998–6008.
3. Gehring, J.; Auli, M.; Grangier, D.; Yarats, D.; Dauphin, Y.N. Convolutional sequence to sequence learning. *arXiv* **2017**, arXiv:1705.03122.
4. Kameoka, H.; Tanaka, K.; Kwaśny, D.; Kaneko, T.; Hojo, N. ConvS2S-VC: Fully Convolutional Sequence-to-Sequence Voice Conversion. *IEEE/ACM Trans. Audio Speech Lang. Process.* **2020**, *28*, 1849–1863. [CrossRef]

5. Daudaravicius, V. Textual and Visual Characteristics of Mathematical Expressions in Scholar Documents. In Proceedings of the Workshop on Extracting Structured Knowledge from Scientific Publications (ESSP), Minneapolis, MN, USA, 6 June 2019; pp. 72–81.
6. Deng, Y.; Kanervisto, A.; Ling, J.; Rush, A.M. Image-to-markup generation with coarse-to-fine attention. In Proceedings of the 34th International Conference on Machine Learning (ICML), Sydney, Australia, 7–9 August 2017; pp. 980–989.
7. Lipton, Z.C.; Steinhardt, J. Troubling trends in machine learning scholarship. *Queue* **2019**, *17*, 45–77.
8. Javaloy, A.; García-Mateos, G. Text Normalization Using Encoder–Decoder Networks Based on the Causal Feature Extractor. *Appl. Sci.* **2020**, *10*, 4551. [CrossRef]
9. Oord, A.v.d.; Dieleman, S.; Zen, H.; Simonyan, K.; Vinyals, O.; Graves, A.; Kalchbrenner, N.; Senior, A.; Kavukcuoglu, K. Wavenet: A generative model for raw audio. *arXiv* **2016**, arXiv:1609.03499.
10. Shrestha, A.; Mahmood, A. Review of deep learning algorithms and architectures. *IEEE Access* **2019**, *7*, 53040–53065. [CrossRef]
11. Bahdanau, D.; Cho, K.; Bengio, Y. Neural machine translation by jointly learning to align and translate. *arXiv* **2014**, arXiv:1409.0473.
12. Chan, W.; Jaitly, N.; Le, Q.; Vinyals, O. Listen, attend and spell: A neural network for large vocabulary conversational speech recognition. In Proceedings of the 2016 IEEE International Conference on Acoustics, Speech and Signal Processing (ICASSP), Shanghai, China, 20–25 March 2016; pp. 4960–4964.
13. Galassi, A.; Lippi, M.; Torroni, P. Attention, please! a critical review of neural attention models in natural language processing. *arXiv* **2019**, arXiv:1902.02181.
14. Srivastava, N.; Hinton, G.; Krizhevsky, A.; Sutskever, I.; Salakhutdinov, R. Dropout: A simple way to prevent neural networks from overfitting. *J. Mach. Learn. Res.* **2014**, *15*, 1929–1958.
15. Baldi, P.; Sadowski, P. The dropout learning algorithm. *Artif. Intell.* **2014**, *210*, 78–122. [CrossRef] [PubMed]
16. Salimans, T.; Kingma, D.P. Weight normalization: A simple reparameterization to accelerate training of deep neural networks. In Proceedings of the Advances in Neural Information Processing Systems (NIPS), Barcelona, Spain, 5–10 December 2016; pp. 901–909.
17. Pascanu, R.; Mikolov, T.; Bengio, Y. On the difficulty of training recurrent neural networks. In Proceedings of the International Conference on Machine Learning (ICML), Atlanta, GA, USA, 16–21 June 2013; pp. 1310–1318.
18. Bergstra, J.; Bengio, Y. Random search for hyper-parameter optimization. *J. Mach. Learn. Res.* **2012**, *13*, 281–305.
19. LeCun, Y.; Haffner, P.; Bottou, L.; Bengio, Y. Object recognition with gradient-based learning. In *Shape, Contour and Grouping in Computer Vision*; Springer: Berlin/Heidelberg, Germany, 1999; pp. 319–345.
20. Hochreiter, S.; Schmidhuber, J. Long short-term memory. *Neural Comput.* **1997**, *9*, 1735–1780. [CrossRef] [PubMed]
21. Zhou, P.; Shi, W.; Tian, J.; Qi, Z.; Li, B.; Hao, H.; Xu, B. Attention-based bidirectional long short-term memory networks for relation classification. In Proceedings of the 54th Annual Meeting of the Association for Computational Linguistics (Volume 2: Short Papers), Berlin, Germany, 7–12 August 2016; pp. 207–212.
22. Papineni, K.; Roukos, S.; Ward, T.; Zhu, W.J. BLEU: A method for automatic evaluation of machine translation. In Proceedings of the 40th Annual Meeting on Association for Computational Linguistics, Philadelphia, PA, USA, 7–12 July 2002; pp. 311–318.
23. Nabhan, A.R.; Rafea, A. Tuning statistical machine translation parameters using perplexity. In Proceedings of the IRI-2005 IEEE International Conference on Information Reuse and Integration, Las Vegas, NV, USA, 15–17 August 2005; pp. 338–343.
24. Riezler, S.; Maxwell, J.T. On some pitfalls in automatic evaluation and significance testing for MT. In Proceedings of the ACL Workshop on Intrinsic and Extrinsic Evaluation Measures for Machine Translation and/or Summarization, Ann Arbor, MI, USA, 29 June 2005; pp. 57–64.

© 2020 by the authors. Licensee MDPI, Basel, Switzerland. This article is an open access article distributed under the terms and conditions of the Creative Commons Attribution (CC BY) license (http://creativecommons.org/licenses/by/4.0/).

Article

Best Practices of Convolutional Neural Networks for Question Classification

Marco Pota [1,*], Massimo Esposito [1], Giuseppe De Pietro [1] and Hamido Fujita [2,3,4]

1. Institute for High Performance Computing and Networking—National Research Council of Italy (ICAR-CNR), 80131 Naples, Italy; massimo.esposito@icar.cnr.it (M.E.); giuseppe.depietro@icar.cnr.it (G.D.P.)
2. Faculty of Information Technology, Ho Chi Minh City University of Technology (HUTECH), Ho Chi Minh City 720000, Vietnam; hfujita-799@acm.org
3. Andalusian Research Institute in Data Science and Computational Intelligence (DaSCI), University of Granada, 18010 Granada, Spain
4. Faculty of Software and Information Science, Iwate Prefectural University, Iwate 020-0693, Japan
* Correspondence: marco.pota@icar.cnr.it

Received: 16 June 2020; Accepted: 3 July 2020; Published: 8 July 2020

Abstract: Question Classification (QC) is of primary importance in question answering systems, since it enables extraction of the correct answer type. State-of-the-art solutions for short text classification obtained remarkable results by Convolutional Neural Networks (CNNs). However, implementing such models requires choices, usually based on subjective experience, or on rare works comparing different settings for general text classification, while peculiar solutions should be individuated for QC task, depending on language and on dataset size. Therefore, this work aims at suggesting best practices for QC using CNNs. Different datasets were employed: (i) A multilingual set of labelled questions to evaluate the dependence of optimal settings on language; (ii) a large, widely used dataset for validation and comparison. Numerous experiments were executed, to perform a multivariate analysis, for evaluating statistical significance and influence on QC performance of all the factors (regarding text representation, architectural characteristics, and learning hyperparameters) and some of their interactions, and for finding the most appropriate strategies for QC. Results show the influence of CNN settings on performance. Optimal settings were found depending on language. Tests on different data validated the optimization performed, and confirmed the transferability of the best settings. Comparisons to configurations suggested by previous works highlight the best classification accuracy by those optimized here. These findings can suggest the best choices to configure a CNN for QC.

Keywords: question classification; multilingual; convolutional neural networks; Natural Language Processing (NLP); deep learning

1. Introduction

Nowadays, intelligent systems able to interact with users in natural language are being developed. However, due to the difficulties associated with natural language understanding by computer systems, this is still a field of research of increasing interest [1–3].

In particular, question answering systems should be able to answer automatically to questions presented in natural language. In order to accomplish this task, a number of operations are required, in order to eventually translating from spoken to written text, to process natural language (tokenization, part-of-speech tagging, dependency parsing), to analyze the question (entity extraction, question classification, query formulation), and to consult the information corpora (information retrieval and answer extraction).

This work concerns the Question Classification (QC) module, which is of primary importance [4,5], since it is in charge of distinguishing different types of questions, corresponding to the expected Lexical Answer Type, enabling the correct extraction of the answer [6].

The function of the QC module is accomplished by a model, trained on a set of already labelled questions. This model classifies textual fragments according to a pre-defined taxonomy. Different types of characteristics, i.e., morphological [7,8], syntactic [4,5], and semantic [9,10], should be considered to interpret text correctly.

However, QC differs from other text classification problems, like sentiment analysis and document categorization, due to the interrogative form and the length that are peculiar of questions. As a consequence, the best performing approach for QC should be chosen peculiarly, and eventually by adopting a different design with respect to methods used for other text classification tasks.

In addition, the ability to classify questions optimally could be accomplished differently, depending on the language [9]. Indeed, syntax rules are different, e.g., English has a more rigid word order to mark the difference between subjects and objects, with respect to Italian. This means that one could have to consider differently sized sets of words together, to catch the same meaning in different languages. Moreover, from the morphological point of view, some languages, like Italian, are richer than others, like English, with impoverished inflection in nouns and verbs; e.g., a single verb in Italian could be inflected in up to 50 different words, while this number is maximum 8 for English. As a consequence, different approaches could be more useful to represent words, depending on the morphological richness of languages.

Various approaches were employed in research literature to tackle short-text classification [11–14] and for QC task in particular [15,16]. However, with respect to classical machine learning approaches, which need the extraction of a big number of features from the text by Natural Language Processing (NLP) methods [17], most recently, great improvements are gained by using neural networks, both from the points of view of the speed of the model and of the classification performance. The text is typically represented by a relatively small number of features obtained by the Word Embedding (WE) process [18], performed by means of a technique chosen among different existing ones. The most common architecture used for text classification by the state-of-the-art solutions was to implement Convolutional Neural Networks (CNNs), since they allow to obtain outstanding results [19,20]. The details of the convolutional architecture and of the learning procedure have been chosen by researchers mainly based on subjective choices. However, as written above, a peculiar solution should be individuated for QC task, probably also depending on the language and on the dataset size.

This work aims at suggesting best practices for using CNNs for QC, with the aim of improving the results of the best existing approaches. However, instead of proposing a different architecture, the basic CNN architecture is implemented with freely adjustable settings, to have insights about their influence and thus choosing the best configuration for the QC problem. Enough numerous experiments, consisting in training and testing the neural network, are executed, to be able to perform a multivariate analysis and evaluate the influence of all the factors and some of their interactions. In particular, words representation, architectural characteristics and hyperparameters, detailed in the following, are all examined as factors, with regard to their potential influence on the QC performance. The expected result consists in the possibility of designing the most performing settings for classifying questions depending on the language.

To the best of our knowledge, with respect to previous similar research [19,21,22], this work is the first one focused on QC, that analyses all the factors involved in the model construction, and their influence on classification performance depending on the language.

More in detail, the main contribution of this work consists in the analysis and optimization of all the factors involved in the CNN design potentially contributing to the improvement of the QC performance and of their interactions:

1. Regarding the text representation, the following approaches are compared here: The inclusion or deletion of punctuation, the use of a well-established pre-trained WE model or of random

vectors for words representation, the use of null vectors or of random vectors for representing Out-Of-Vocabulary (OOV) words, the embedding dimension, and the possibility of fine-tuning WE vectors during learning or keeping them constant;

2. regarding the CNN architecture, which uses filters to extrapolate features relative to sets of consecutive words, the following characteristics are tuned here: Filter region size, number of filters, and the activation function, while only the pooling strategy is fixed; and

3. regarding the learning hyperparameters, for training network weights and eventually the WE vectors, the following are analyzed: Batch size, learning method, learning rate, and regularization terms, while the number of epochs is chosen for each run to ensure convergence.

Moreover, the proposed procedure is performed and settings are tuned for two languages, English and Italian, in order to evaluate differences of the contribution of each factor between languages having different morphological richness, and to demonstrate that a system optimized by the proposed approach can be employed successfully in a multilingual context.

The analysis and the subsequent application of the optimized QC model is performed for two datasets of labelled questions made available in both English and Italian languages by a task presented at Text Retrieval Conferences (TREC) 2002 and 2003 (https://trec.nist.gov/, accessed 1 July 2020). In addition, a widely used dataset of English labelled questions (http://cogcomp.cs.illinois.edu/Data/QA/QC/, accessed 1 July 2020) is employed to check transferability.

Finally, the optimal CNN configurations found here are compared with those found in the most relevant previous similar works, [19,21].

The paper is structured as follows. The following part of this section summarizes related works, while in Section 2 describes the data, formalizes the general QC approach comprising the CNN, and plan the model optimization. The experimental plan with results and their discussion are presented in Section 3. Finally, Section 4 draws conclusions of the work.

Related Works

QC, and more generally speaking sentence classification, is a crucial task for NLP [1,2,16]. Natural language sentences, in both affirmative and interrogative forms, have complicated structures, both sequential and hierarchical, that must be handled to allow their comprehension. Thanks to their ability to capture local relations of temporal or hierarchical structures, CNNs have emerged as a relatively simple yet powerful class of models for sentence modelling and classification, since characterized by remarkably strong performances, with different shallow or deep architectures proposed in the recent years.

The first CNN for sentence classification with end-to-end training is proposed in [23,24]. In this seminal work, one convolutional layer is used together with a new global max-pooling operation, resulting to be very effective for text. Moreover, multiple deep models are co-trained on many tasks to transfer task-specific information. Starting from the results of this work, a simpler architecture with slight modifications have been presented in [21], achieving state-of-the-art performances even on many small datasets. In particular, one convolutional layer with multichannel representation and variable-size filters are employed, where fine-tuned or pre-trained word embeddings are combined in multi-channels, convolutions allow determining high-level abstract features, and multiple linear filters are used to effectively extract different n-gram features. Both the CNN architectures proposed in [23,24] and in [21] make use of max-pooling to keep the most important information to represent the sentence. Moreover, the pooling operation helps the network deal with variable sentence lengths. In [25] a further variant of multi-layer CNN architecture was proposed, with a dynamic k-max-pooling, where k depends on the length of the sentence and can be dynamically set as a part of the network. This allows detecting the k most relevant features occurring into a sentence, independent of their specific position and preserving their relative order. In [26], a multichannel variable-size CNN architecture for sentence classification was described, further exploring the capabilities of multichannel and variable size feature detectors. In particular, it combines diverse versions of pre-trained word embeddings and extracts features of multi-granular phrases with variable-size convolution filters.

All of CNNs presented in these works are based on word input tokens, encoded as distributed representations in the form of WE vectors [27]. Moreover, they are rather shallow (two layers in most of them), if compared to those successfully proposed to face computer vision problems, due to the reduced length, in terms of number of words, of typical sentences and paragraphs.

Later, a first attempt of CNN jointly using character-level, word-level, and sentence-level representations to perform sentence classification is described in [28], with a shallow architecture made of two convolutional layers to extract relevant features from words and sentences of any size. More recently, a deep CNN architecture, with up to 6 convolutional layers, was proposed in [29], able to automatically learn the notions of words and sentences on texts operating directly at a character level, without any pre-processing, not even tokenization. Convolutional kernels of size 3 and 7 were used, as well as simple max-pooling layers. Another interesting aspect of this work is the usage of several large-scale data sets for text classification. In [30], a new deep CNN architecture, with up to 29 convolutional layers, was proposed for text classification, operating directly at character level and using only small convolutions and pooling operations.

More specifically with respect to QC, in [20], a CNN was used to classify Italian questions. In particular, different solutions regarding the CNN architecture have been tested, and, according to literature advices, the best settings have been searched in the proper ranges, in order to maximize the classification power for the particular case of Italian questions dataset. In [31], an extended CNN architecture is proposed, able to first classify a question into a broader category, and, successively, based on the prior knowledge, assign to it a more specific category. This solution was tested on an English questions dataset with pre-trained word embeddings, showing results on par or improved with respect to other classical methods. In [32], a simple and effective method for QC is presented, which increases generalization, by replacing entities with placeholders, and diversity of sentence features, by reading sentence vectors from both forward and reverse directions. This approach has shown better performance than many other complex CNN models, also proving its effectiveness applied to question answering systems. Finally, in [33], a QC approach based on word embedding using subword information and CNN is outlined, in order to improve classification accuracy. In particular, a comparison between English and Italian languages is reported, by highlighting eventual improvements obtained by initializing word embeddings with advanced vectors learned in an unsupervised manner and comprising character-based information.

Summarizing, all the presented approaches based on CNNs for sentence classification, and specifically for QC, are characterized by models, whose structure is designed by hand by experts, thus requiring considerable skill and experience to select suitable hyperparameters such as the learning rate, the size of convolutional filters, the number of layers and so on. Moreover, these hyperparameters have internal dependencies, which make them particularly expensive for tuning and can depend on the specific classification task considered. Even though some recent works have shown that there exists much room to improve current optimization techniques for learning deep CNN architectures [34], fundamental working principles and behaviors of CNN models when specifically applied to QC have not been extensively investigated.

The most relevant works addressing these issues are generally tested for text classification. In [21], different strategies for words representation are compared, by employing in turn, singularly or combined in a multi-channel way, differently initialized, and eventually fine-tuned WE vectors. On the basis of [21] model, a sensitivity analysis of CNNs is proposed in [19], summarizing the influences of various hyperparameters, i.e., WE vectors, filter size, number of filters, activation function, pooling strategy, and regularization. Both these works, for the QC task considered among the others, found different best settings with respect to the other tasks.

However, to the best of our knowledge, related research considered only few settings, and without reference to possible interactions among them. Moreover, (i) QC was only considered as an instance of text classification; (ii) the possible relation with the language not taken into account.

Thus, this work constitutes the first attempt of considering hyperparameters in a comprehensive way, examining different possibilities with respect to morphologically different languages, to study the problem of configuring the appropriate CNN architecture for QC.

2. Materials and Methods

2.1. Data

QC aims at associating each question to a class comprised in a given set. This is made accordingly to a number of examples of labelled questions, used to train and test the model.

Different datasets are available, particularly for English language. The main example is the TREC dataset provided by [35], used in various previous works, comprising [21], which is particularly big. However, in order to study questions in different languages, multilingual data are rare and less extensive.

In order to compare English and Italian languages, the chosen data are made of the union of two datasets presented at TREC conferences 2002 and 2003, each comprising 500 training questions and labelled according to the same taxonomy. The same 1000 questions are available in English and Italian, among the other languages. For example, a row of the joint dataset is made of four attributes (coarse class, fine class, question in English, question in Italian), as follows: "FACTOID—LOCATION—What is Africa's largest country?—Qual è il paese più vasto dell'Africa?".

In Table 1, the two-levels taxonomy is reported.

Table 1. Taxonomy of question classes.

Coarse Classes	Fine Classes
Definition	Location, Person, Other.
Factoid	Acronym, How, Location, Material, Measure, Person, Time, Title, Other.
List	Location, Person, Title, Other.

Since the aim of the approach is the single (not hierarchical) classification task, coarse classes were not considered in this work. On the other hand, all the questions were included, and the union of fine classes for any of the three coarse classes is considered, which results in the following 9 labels: "Acronym", "How", "Location", "Material", "Measure", "Person", "Time", "Title", "Other".

Each experiment is performed by 10-fold cross-validation. Therefore, the runs are performed with a number of examples for training $Ntrain = 900$, and a number of examples for testing $Ntest = 100$.

Moreover, the dataset provided by (Li and Roth 2002), available online, is also used, to compare results with those of other state-of-the-art best convolutional architectures. It is already divided into 5452 questions for training and 500 for testing, and is based on a 2-levels taxonomy, whose coarse level, used here, is made of the following 6 classes: "ABBREVIATION", "ENTITY", "DESCRIPTION", "HUMAN", "LOCATION", "NUMERIC".

2.2. Question Classification Model

This section describes the structure of the model employed for classifying questions, and the learning procedure. This model, firstly developed in [23,24], was implemented with variable settings in the open source Python framework TensorFlow (https://www.tensorflow.org/, accessed 1 July 2020). The testing platform consisted of a fold containing data, a main program with subroutines for pre-processing and model architecture and producing the results, and three configuration json files, where the user can manually change all the settings before each run. The variable settings were defined within sets chosen coherently with findings of previous literature and with preliminary experiments. The model general form is schematized in Figure 1. It comprised a pre-processing phase, which allowed translation of the question into a sparse matrix constituting the input layer, the embedding phase, which allowed representation of the question by a matrix with smaller dimension constituting the embedding layer, and a CNN made of convolutional layer, pooling layer, fully connected layer, and output layer, which finally associated each question to a class.

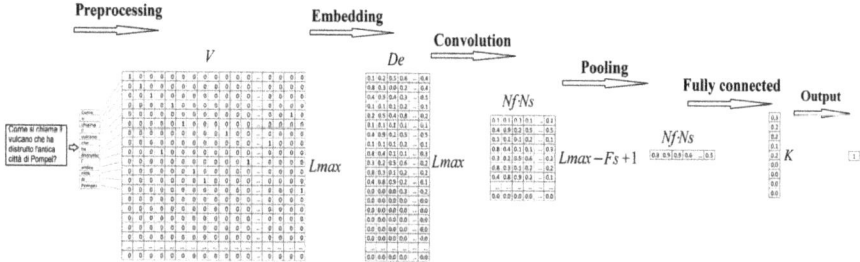

Figure 1. The Question Classification model.

The following subsections describe in detail the pre-processing and WE phases (Section 2.2.1), the CNN architecture (Section 2.2.2), and the procedure for learning network weights (Section 2.2.3). Finally, since this approach is implemented here with freely adjustable settings, Section 2.2.4 summarizes the degrees of freedom considered with respective possible values, and explains the optimization approach.

2.2.1. Question Pre-Processing and Word Embedding

Each question had to be pre-processed, to be divided into a sequence of tokens, and represented as a sparse matrix.

Firstly, special characters, not comprised in the set {A-Za-z0-9(),;.:!?'"} were substituted with spaces. Then, apostrophes and some substrings comprising them were substituted, depending on the language, as reported in Table 2.

Table 2. Substitution of strings comprising apostrophes.

English	
Original Characters	**Substitution**
" (double typewriter apostrophe)	" (quotation marks)
" (double backtick)	" (quotation marks)
've (apostrophe+"ve")	have (space+"have")
n't ("n"+apostrophe+"t")	not (space+"not")
're (apostrophe+"re")	are (space+"are")
's (apostrophe+"s")	's (space added before)
'd (apostrophe+"d")	'd (space added before)
'll (apostrophe+"ll")	'll (space added before)
Italian	
Original Characters	**Substitution**
" (double typewriter apostrophe)	" (quotation marks)
" (double backtick)	" (quotation marks)
'a (apostrophe+"a")	' a (space added between)
'e (apostrophe+"e")	' e (space added between)
'i (apostrophe+"i")	' i (space added between)
'o (apostrophe+"o")	' o (space added between)
'u (apostrophe+"u")	' u (space added between)
a' ("a"+apostrophe)	à ("a" with grave accent)
e' ("e"+apostrophe)	è ("e" with grave accent)
i' ("i"+apostrophe)	ì ("i" with grave accent)
o' ("o"+apostrophe)	ò ("o" with grave accent)
u' ("u"+apostrophe)	ù ("u" with grave accent)

The possibility of eliminating the other standard punctuation symbols {(),,;:!?'"} is a degree of freedom:

$$AvoidPunctuation = \begin{cases} True \\ False \end{cases}. \quad (1)$$

Therefore, if they were eliminated (*AvoidPunctuation* = True), they were substituted with spaces, otherwise (*AvoidPunctuation* = False) a space was added before and after each of them. Finally, sets of consecutive spaces were substituted with only one space. At this point, the text was already divided in tokens by spaces.

Each question was made of L tokens, and the maximum length $Lmax$ was calculated over the whole dataset. Moreover, a vocabulary was assembled by gathering all V different tokens plus an entry <UNK> in the first position corresponding to unknown token. Original tokens are used, instead of lemmatizing them, to be coherent with pre-trained WE.

Once the vocabulary was fixed, each token was represented as a vector with V elements, which were all equal to 0, except the element corresponding to the position of the token in the vocabulary, equal to 1. Therefore, each question was represented as a matrix X with V columns and $Lmax$ rows, composed by vectors x_j, with $j = 1, \ldots, Lmax$, where if $L < Lmax$, last rows were filled with all zeros. This matrix was the input layer of the deep neural network.

The next embedding phase consisted in the linear transformation of X into a matrix with smaller dimension. Each one-hot V-dimensional vector x_j was transformed into a De-dimensional vector corresponding to the representation of the word suggested by the pre-trained WE model or to a random or null vector. In practice, X was multiplied by the embedding matrix W_{emb} with De columns and V rows, to obtain a matrix X_{emb} made of De columns and $Lmax$ rows:

$$X_{emb} = XW_{emb}. \quad (2)$$

The embedding matrix was initialized depending on the choice of the *WEinit* factor:

$$WEinit = \begin{cases} pre-trained \\ random \end{cases}. \quad (3)$$

If pre-trained WE vectors are used (*WEinit* = pre-trained), then the row of W_{emb} corresponding to each known word was initialized as the pre-trained WE vector, while the other rows corresponding to OOV words were initialized with null vectors (*OOVinit* = null). The pre-trained WE representation chosen for this work was based on fastText model, with 300 dimensions ($De = 300$), trained on the Wikipedia corpora (https://fb-public.app.box.com/s/htfdbrvycvroebv9ecaezaztocbcnsdn, accessed 1 July 2020), both in English and Italian languages. This model was chosen for its outstanding characteristics. In fact, it was an evolution of the skip-gram model, which trains the representation of each word by unsupervised learning to predict words that appear in its context, but fastText also measures similarity between words based on character n-grams included in them. Therefore, these vectors encode information regarding syntactic structure of the text and semantic features like the skip-gram model, as well as information regarding the morphology of the words.

On the other hand, if pre-trained vectors were not used (*WEinit* = random), then all the rows of W_{emb} were initialized with random vectors, both for known or unknown words (*OOVinit* = random). This representation was made with a number of dimension which was a further degree of freedom, studied in the following interval:

$$De \in [10, 500]. \quad (4)$$

Since the values assumed by *OOVinit* are coupled with those assumed by *WEinit*, in the following *OOVinit* was omitted.

In both cases, the embedding matrix $\mathbf{W_{emb}}$ could be kept constant or fine-tuned during the network training:

$$WEtuning = \begin{cases} \text{static} \\ \text{dynamic} \end{cases}. \qquad (5)$$

2.2.2. Convolutional Neural Network Architecture

A classical CNN architecture was used here for associating questions with labels. However, here the architecture was not fixed, but was implemented with freely adjustable settings.

A convolution was firstly applied to $\mathbf{X_{emb}}$, by using a single channel, with no padding and stride 1, as recommendable in text classification context. Filters of different sizes may be employed, therefore, if there were Ns different sizes and for each size a number Nf of filters, the total number $Ntot$ of filters was:

$$Ntot = Nf \cdot Ns. \qquad (6)$$

The sizes and the total number of filters were degrees of freedom, and they were considered in the following ranges:

$$Fs \in [1, 10], \qquad (7)$$

$$Ntot \in [50, 500]. \qquad (8)$$

Each filter of a certain size consists in a matrix $\mathbf{W}_{conv}^i$, with $i = 1, \ldots, Ntot$ made of De columns and Fs rows. The result of the convolution was a vector $\mathbf{x}_{conv}{}^i$ with dimension $Lmax - Fs + 1$, whose components $x_{conv}^{i,j}$, with $j = 1, \ldots, Lmax - Fs + 1$, can be written as:

$$x_{conv}^{i,j} = \sum_{jj=1}^{Fs} \sum_{d=1}^{De} \left(\mathbf{X_{emb}}[j + jj - 1][d] \cdot \mathbf{W}_{conv}^i[jj][d] \right). \qquad (9)$$

Then a bias term b_{conv}^i was added to each component, and an activation function f was applied, to get each component $x_{act}^{i,j}$, with $j = 1, \ldots, Lmax - Fs + 1$, of the vector $\mathbf{x}_{act}^i$, which was the final result of the convolution by the given filter $\mathbf{W}_{conv}^i$:

$$x_{act}^{i,j} = f\left(x_{conv}^{i,j} + b_{conv}^i \right). \qquad (10)$$

Of course, vectors $\mathbf{x}_{act}^i$ with the same size were obtained by using filters with the same Fs, while vectors of different sizes were obtained by differently sized filters. However, $Ntot$ vectors were obtained, and they constitute the convolutional layer.

The activation function to use for convolution was a degree of freedom of the proposed implementation. The following functions were used, whose meaning is shown in Figure 2:

$$f = \begin{cases} \text{eLU} \\ \text{Identity} \\ \text{ReLU} \\ \text{sigmoid} \\ \text{softplus} \\ \text{softsign} \\ \tanh \end{cases}. \qquad (11)$$

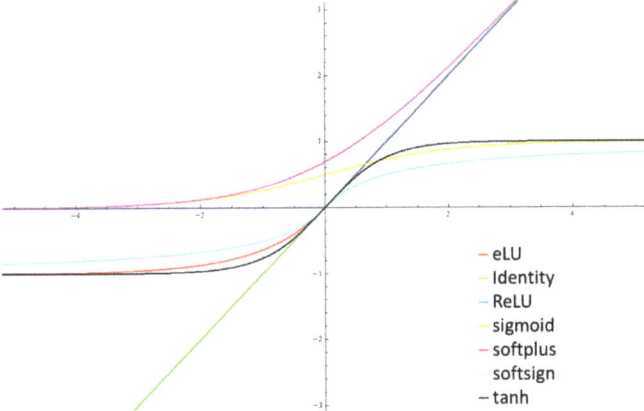

Figure 2. The activation functions employed.

The following operation was the pooling, which was implemented coherently with the common choice, i.e., the 1-max pooling strategy. In fact, using the max function was forced by the padding with zeros the input representation of questions shorter than *Lmax*, and the choice of only one maximum element was certainly enough, due to the big number of filters employed. Therefore, the pooling layer was constituted by a horizontal vector **p** with dimension *Ntot*, whose elements p^i, with $i = 1, \ldots, Ntot$, were:

$$p^i = \max x^i_{act}. \tag{12}$$

The following fully connected layer was constituted by *K* neurons, where *K* was also the number of classes. In the considered case, $K = 9$. The vector of class activations **y** was computed by multiplying **p** by a matrix of weights $\mathbf{W}_{fc}$ with *Ntot* rows and *K* columns, and adding a bias vector $\mathbf{b}_{fc}$:

$$\mathbf{y} = \mathbf{p}\mathbf{W}_{fc} + \mathbf{b}_{fc}. \tag{13}$$

The final output layer was made of only one node, which contains the position of the class with the highest activation:

$$output = \mathrm{argmax}\,\mathbf{y}. \tag{14}$$

2.2.3. Learning Procedure

The described model includes many parameters that were initialized randomly and have to be trained, i.e., $\mathbf{W}^i_{conv}$ with $i = 1, \ldots, Ntot$, b^i_{conv} with $i = 1, \ldots, Ntot$, $\mathbf{W}_{fc}$, and $\mathbf{b}_{fc}$, for a total of $De \cdot Fs \cdot Ntot + Ntot \cdot K + K$. Moreover, $\mathbf{W}_{emb}$ can be initialized by pre-trained WE or randomly, but in both cases they were fine-tuned if *WEtuning* = *Dynamic*, bringing other $V \cdot De$ parameters.

These parameters were adapted on data by a learning procedure summarized as follows.

Firstly, the training dataset was divided in batches composed of a certain number of examples. In this work, the batch size was a degree of freedom, studied in its whole range:

$$batch \in [1, 900]. \tag{15}$$

All examples of a batch were used as input of the model, but during the training, in order to learn separately different parts of the network, the pooling layer was modified by the dropout function, which randomly transforms each component p^i multiplying it by zero with probability $(1 - P_{keep})$, and by $1/P_{keep}$ with probability P_{keep}, so that the expected sum remains unchanged. Here, the dropout was a degree of freedom, variable in the following interval:

$$P_{keep} \in (0.0, 1.0]. \tag{16}$$

For each input b, the loss was calculated by the cross entropy function (19), where p_k (17) was the softmax transform of the kth component of computed vector $\mathbf{y}$, and c_k (18) was 1 for the position of the true label k_{True}, 0 otherwise:

$$p_k = \frac{e^{y_k}}{\sum_{\kappa=1}^{K} e^{y_\kappa}}. \tag{17}$$

$$c_k = \begin{cases} 1 \text{ if } k = k_{True} \\ 0 \text{ otherwise} \end{cases}. \tag{18}$$

$$loss_b = -\sum_{k=1}^{K} c_k \cdot \log(p_k). \tag{19}$$

After a batch, the whole associated loss was calculated as:

$$loss = \frac{1}{batch} \sum_{b=1}^{batch} loss_b + l2 \cdot \left(\frac{|\mathbf{W}_{fc}|^2}{2} + \frac{|\mathbf{b}_{fc}|^2}{2} \right). \tag{20}$$

The regularization parameter $l2$, used to prevent big values of fully connected layer weights, was a degree of freedom here, studied in the following interval:

$$l2 \in [1.0, 5.0]. \tag{21}$$

The loss gradient was used for updating network weights by a backpropagation approach based on Stochastic Gradient Descent (SGD) algorithm, which implies a stochastic approximation [36] of the basic gradient descent algorithm. Since it reduces the computational complexity, achieving faster iterations in trade for a lower convergence rate [37], it was recognized as a very effective learning algorithm in machine learning [38]. A variant of the updating rule was freely chosen among the following ones:

$$optimizer = \begin{cases} \text{Adadelta} \\ \text{Adagrad} \\ \text{Adam} \\ \text{Ftrl} \\ \text{GradientDescent} \\ \text{Momentum} \\ \text{ProximalAdagrad} \\ \text{ProximalGradientDescent} \\ \text{RMSProp} \end{cases}. \tag{22}$$

While in case $optimizer$ = Momentum, the momentum parameter was fixed to 0.1, according to previous findings, the learning rate, which was a further parameter common to all the algorithms, was the last considered degree of freedom, studied in the following wide range, enlarged with respect to previous works [19,21]:

$$\eta \in [0.01, 10]. \tag{23}$$

The intent in this work was to get the best possible model, therefore the number of epochs was not taken as an adjustable setting.

2.2.4. Threats to Validate

Different threats could affect the learning procedure.

First, underfitting could affect results, if the number of epochs chosen for learning was too low. In order to avoid it, a sufficient number of epochs was chosen for different runs. For most of the runs, 2000 epochs result enough to reach convergence, while in some cases (properly compared with the others) 20000 epochs were needed.

Second, a large number of epochs could cause overfitting on training data. In order to avoid it, every 2 epochs, the model was tested on a randomly sampled dev set, and at the end of the epochs, the model presenting the best accuracy on the dev set was chosen.

Finally, the choice of training and testing questions within the dataset could (positively or negatively) influence and distort the results. In order to avoid it, each experiment was performed by stratified 10-fold cross-validation. Therefore, the dataset was randomly divided into 10 subsets of 100 questions with approximately the same rate of labels. Each run was performed with the union of 9 question subsets for training, and the remaining subset for testing, this was repeated 10 times for considering all the examples for testing, and the results of the 10 runs were averaged to obtain the result of the experiment.

2.2.5. Model Optimization

In order to optimize the QC model, its classification accuracy was studied by analyzing different experiments, corresponding to respective configurations of settings (factors).

Since each experiment was the set of 10 training and testing phases constituting a 10-fold cross-validation, the accuracy of an experiment was the average of the accuracies gained by the 10 trained models on the respective test set. The accuracy on a test set was calculated as a percentage, by averaging c_{output}, which was 1 if the network output (14) was equal to the position of the true label associated with the bth input of the test set ($output = k_{True}$), 0 otherwise:

$$Acc = \frac{1}{Ntest} \sum_{b=1}^{Ntest} c_{output} \cdot 100\%. \qquad (24)$$

The factors here considered to analyze their influence on the model accuracy are summarized in Table 3. For categorical factors, all the possible values were considered, while for quantitative ones the considered admitted ranges were based on previous literature findings.

Since considering all the possible interactions among factors would involve an unfeasible experimentation, some factors were analyzed in the following one by one, since they were hypothesized to have negligible interactions with the others, while some sets of factors were studied together to verify potential interactions.

For each factor or set of factors, their individual influences and interactions (effects) were evaluated in a chosen range by performing a set of experiments. Most sets of experiments were planned according to full factorial designs, which comprise all the combinations of factors levels. This approach needs more numerous experiments, but minimizes the risk of confounding different effects. The range of each factor, and the fixed values of other settings, relative to factors not being evaluated in a set of experiments, since were hypothesized to not interact, were chosen according to findings of previous works [19–21,33], or to preliminary experiments.

Table 3. Freely adjustable settings of the Question Classification (QC) model analyzed here and their admitted values.

Setting	Symbol	Set of Admitted Values
Text representation		
Eliminate punctuation	*AvoidPunctuation*	{True,False}
Pre-trained WE vectors for known words and null vectors for OOV words, or random vectors for all the words	*WEinit*	{pre-trained,random}
Embedding dimension	*De*	[10,500]
Fine tuning of WE vectors together with other network weights during training	*WEtuning*	{static,dynamic}
CNN architecture		
Filter size	*Fs*	[1,10]
Total number of filters	*Ntot*	[50,500]
Activation function	*f*	{eLU,Identity,ReLU,sigmoid,softplus,softsign,tanh}
Learning procedure		
Batch size	*batch*	[1,900]
Probability that dropout function keeps a node	P_{keep}	(0.0,1.0]
Parameter of loss regularization	*l2*	[1.0,5.0]
Weights updating rule	*optimizer*	{Adadelta,Adagrad,Adam,Ftrl,GradientDescent,Momentum, ProximalAdagrad,ProximalGradientDescent,RMSProp}
Learning rate	η	[0.01,10]

Due to the random initialization of weights and to some other sources of randomness in the learning procedure (splitting training data in batches, dropout function, and SGD algorithm), each run, and thus each whole experiment, gave different results if repeated. Therefore, some repetitions were performed, to estimate the experimental variance σ^2, which was used to evaluate the experiments reproducibility.

The intrinsic variance in the measurement of the experiment performance implies that a deterministic functional dependence between factors and model accuracy does not exist. Therefore, in order to analyze the effects on the QC accuracy, an approximate function was extrapolated from each set of experimental results:

$$acc = c_0 + c_1 x_1 + c_2 x_2 + c_{12} x_1 x_2 + \ldots \tag{25}$$

where $x_1, x_2, \ldots$ represent the individual factors, $x_1 x_2, \ldots$ represent their interactions, and coefficients $c_0, c_1, c_2, c_{12}, \ldots$ were used to linearly combine these (also nonlinear) effects to predict experimental accuracy.

The significance of effects was evaluated in terms of the respective coefficients [39]. Indeed, each estimated coefficient belongs to a respective confidence interval, corresponding to the interval comprising the true coefficient value with 95% probability, that was calculated as follows. Given the estimated experimental variance σ^2, calculated with a certain number of degrees of freedom, the variance of each coefficient can be estimated as σ^2/N, where N is the number of experiments of the full factorial design. Therefore, the width of the coefficient confidence interval can be calculated as $\sigma/N^{1/2} \cdot t_{0.975}$, where $t_{0.975}$ is the value of a t-student distribution with the same degrees of freedom corresponding to 0.975 cumulative probability (two tails t-test). As a consequence, if the estimated coefficient was lower than the confidence interval semi-width, then the confidence interval comprises the null value, and the hypothesis that the true coefficient value was zero cannot be rejected, and the corresponding effect was not significant.

Moreover, the estimated function (24) comprising significant effects can be used to predict the accuracy, on the basis of the considered factors and their eventual interactions. This allows finding optimal values of factors, corresponding to higher calculated accuracy.

After that all the factors were individually optimized, some repetitions corresponding to the optimal settings were performed, to evaluate the performance of the QC model in optimal conditions. Moreover, optimal conditions were validated on a larger set of data.

3. Results and Discussion

In this section, the results obtained by the QC model are reported and discussed. As described before, the accuracy reported in correspondence of a configuration of settings was obtained by the average of 10 cross-validation runs.

The results were obtained for each configuration by considering questions in both English and Italian languages.

First of all (Section 3.1), repeated experiments using the same configuration are described and discussed. Then, the influence of settings regarding text representation (Section 3.2), network architecture (Section 3.3), and learning procedure (Section 3.4) was evaluated. In addition, Section 3.5 takes into account all the previous findings to individuate the most influencing parameters. Finally, Section 3.6 presents optimal settings obtained for different cases, and evaluates the performance of the associated proposed models, also showing a comparison with baseline models found as optimal in previous literature, on a widely used dataset.

In total, 2404 runs for training and testing the described QC model were performed.

3.1. Repetitions

As explained before, each experiment reported here was made of 10 runs since cross-validation is performed. Therefore, for each experiment, an "internal" variance of the testing accuracy is calculated. Averaging on all the experiments, the "internal" standard deviations found were about 4.0% for English and 3.5% for Italian. These quite low values were due to the robustness of the random stratified splitting of the dataset in folds.

On the other hand, some whole experiments were performed 5 times, to evaluate their reproducibility. In the hypothesis that the system is homoscedastic, the accuracy variance could be estimated in correspondence of only one configuration. Here, this hypothesis is relaxed, due to the structural differences between runs performed by using fixed pre-trained WE vectors or random vectors, and between runs performed with fixed WE vectors or by fine-tuning them. Therefore, the accuracy variance is estimated in correspondence of the combinations of these settings. For each configuration, 5 repetitions of the same experiment were performed. In Table 4, the experimental variance σ^2 calculated over repetitions is reported.

Table 4. Variance of testing accuracy over experiments repetitions [1].

		WEinit\WEtuning	Static	Dynamic
σ^2	English	random	0.37	0.86
		pre-trained	0.14	0.23
	Italian	random	0.32	0.07
		pre-trained	0.72	0.13

[1] Other settings were: AvoidPunctuation = True, De = 300, Fs = {1,2,3}, Ntot = 300, f = ReLU, batch = 900, P_{keep} = 0.5, l2 = 3.0, optimizer = Adadelta, η = 0.1.

Since the estimated variance is itself a random variable, on the basis of results of Table 4, the homoscedasticity can be hypothesized, also with respect to the language; therefore, the experimental variance was estimated by averaging over different configurations the mean pure squared errors of the repetitions. It corresponds to a low standard deviation σ = 0.6% (calculated with 32 degrees of freedom, therefore $t_{0.975}$ = 2.038), and compared to the variance of different experiments, corresponds to a good reproducibility (= 0.90).

3.2. Text Representation

The first setting analyzed here regards the text representation, and in particular, the possibility of eliminating all punctuation symbols from the question during pre-processing. This qualitative factor can assume 2 levels, and it was hypothesized to not interact with others. Therefore, the only 2 experiments for each language reported in Table 5 were performed.

Table 5. Testing accuracy obtained by eliminating or not punctuation from text [1].

	AvoidPunctuation	True	False
Acc (%)	English	88.1	88.3
	Italian	86.6	86.8

[1] Other settings were: $WEinit$ = pre-trained, De = 300, $WEtuning$ = dynamic, Fs = {1,2,3}, $Ntot$ = 300, f = ReLU, batch = 10, P_{keep} = 0.5, $l2$ = 3.0, optimizer = Adadelta, η = 0.1.

Even if for both languages the case $AvoidPunctuation$ = True gives slightly higher accuracy, the differences with the case $AvoidPunctuation$ = False were statistically not significant, since it is comparable to (and even smaller than) the standard deviation of repeated experiments. In other words, if a model describing the accuracy as a function of this variable is constructed, the linear coefficient results 0.1% for both languages, which is smaller than the semi-width of its confidence interval (0.9%), therefore the chance that the true value of the coefficient is zero cannot be discarded.

This finding suggests that, in order to simplify the QC model, punctuation can be eliminated without significant loss of information.

Other two factors regarding the text representation, i.e., the possibility of initializing WE vectors of known words by fastText pre-trained vectors and OOV words by null vectors or initializing all WE vectors randomly, and the possibility of fine-tuning these vectors during training or not, were analyzed together, to evaluate at the same time their effects and eventual interactions. Each of these qualitative factors can assume 2 levels; therefore, 4 configurations for each language were tested. For each configuration, 5 repeated experiments were performed, used to estimate variances reported in Table 4, and whose mean accuracies are reported in Table 6.

Table 6. Testing accuracy obtained by different Word Embedding (WE) initialization and fine-tuning strategy [1].

		WEinit\WEtuning	Static	Dynamic
Acc (%)	English	random	77.6	77.8
		pre-trained	77.6	80.2
	Italian	random	76.1	76.1
		pre-trained	75.2	80.4

[1] Other settings were: $AvoidPunctuation$ = True, De = 300, Fs = {1,2,3}, $Ntot$ = 300, f = ReLU, batch = 900, P_{keep} = 0.5, $l2$ = 3.0, optimizer = Adadelta, η = 0.1.

In this case, the effects of the evaluated factors $WEinit$ and $WEtuning$, and of their interaction, produced significant results. In particular, random or pre-trained WE vectors give equivalent results if they are static, and fine-tuning of random vectors does not improve accuracy, but the combination of $WEinit$ = pre-trained and $WEtuning$ = dynamic gives a contribution to the mean accuracy of about 2.6% for English and 4.3% for Italian. These contributions are greater than the confidence interval semi-width (about 0.6%).

This behavior can be explained by observing that the generally valid information embodied by WE pre-trained vectors was not necessarily the same required by the specific classification task, therefore, if kept static, they could result equivalent to random ones; however, they embody semantic information that allows, if properly fine-tuned, to get closer to optimal, with respect to random ones.

These findings suggest the following considerations:

- It is convenient to employ fastText pre-trained vectors to initialize WE vectors, which embody semantic and morphological information in words representation;

- it is convenient to fine-tune WE vectors, since optimizing the representation of the single words most influencing on QC allows to stress their importance;
- a significant improvement on QC accuracy is gained if these two settings were used at the same time, since the WE vectors of words semantically associated with question classes, already represented by embodying semantic information, can be coherently optimized; and
- all these effects result more relevantly in the Italian language, with respect to English, since all the improvements regarding words representation were more useful for a morphologically rich language.

The last factor taken into account for text representation was the embedding dimension D_e, hypothesized to have no interactions with the others. This quantitative factor was analyzed in the range [10,500], and in particular, in correspondence of the representative levels {10,100,300,500}, to analyze also its nonlinear effects. Therefore, four configurations for each language were tested, and results are reported in Table 7 and shown in Figure 3.

Table 7. Testing accuracy obtained by different embedding dimensions [1].

	D_e	10	100	300	500
Acc (%)	English	54.8	74.0	77.8	78.1
	Italian	41.0	73.7	76.1	75.7

[1] Other settings were: $AvoidPunctuation$ = True, $WEinit$ = random, $WEtuning$ = dynamic, Fs = {1,2,3}, $Ntot$ = 300, f = ReLU, $batch$ = 900, P_{keep} = 0.5, $l2$ = 3.0, $optimizer$ = Adadelta, η = 0.1.

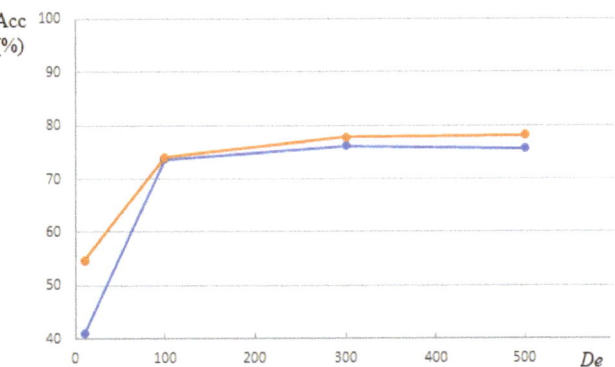

Figure 3. Testing accuracy obtained by different embedding dimensions, for English (red) and Italian (blue).

From results reported in Table 7, a function was fitted for each language to predict accuracy as a quadratic function of D_e in logarithmic scale, and all coefficients result much greater than their confidence interval, therefore, D_e gives significant effects. The fitted function, in accordance with results shown in Figure 3, explains that, as the embedding dimension increases, a great improvement to QC was given, since more semantic, syntactic, and morphological aspects of words were represented. However, for more than some hundreds dimensions, a plateau was reached, and adding other dimensions does not give a significant improvement.

Therefore, also in accordance with most of the previous literature works, and with the majority of the available pre-trained WE vectors, the value D_e = 300 was chosen as optimal here.

3.3. CNN Architecture

The CNN architecture was analyzed firstly in terms of both the filter size (7) and their total number (8), and then with regard to the activation function involved in (10), while their interactions were neglected.

Different filter sizes were experimented in the range [1,10], taking into account all possible sizes. The functions fitted in this whole range to predict accuracy reveal no significant linear or quadratic effect; however, in the restrictions of this range, the experimental results showed significant trends, associated with significant improvements in correspondence of individual filter sizes with respect to the others, as discussed in the following.

Firstly, all filters with the same size were employed. Results for both languages are reported in Table 8 and shown in Figure 4.

Table 8. Testing accuracy obtained by different filter sizes [1].

Fs		1	2	3	4	5	6	7	8	9	10
Acc (%)	English	79.0	81.8	79.4	79.2	78.9	78.3	78.6	79.7	78.3	78.0
	Italian	78.6	81.0	79.3	78.3	79.3	77.6	78.1	76.5	77.2	77.5

[1] Other settings were: AvoidPunctuation = True, WEinit = pre-trained, De = 300, WEtuning = dynamic, $Ntot$ = 300, f = ReLU, batch = 900, P_{keep} = 0.5, $l2$ = 3.0, optimizer = Adadelta, η = 0.1.

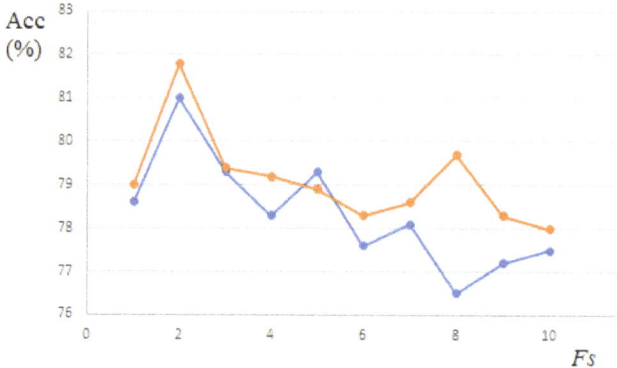

Figure 4. Testing accuracy obtained by different filter sizes, for English (**red**) and Italian (**blue**).

Within the first set of experiments, the best single filter size results Fs = 2, which corresponds to significant improvements with respect to both Fs = 1 and Fs > 2. The trend was similar for both languages, while a misalignment results for Fs = 8, which may be due to experimental variance.

Then, in order to evaluate the possibility of using filters of different sizes at the same time, as suggested by previous works [19,20], 150 filters of size 2 were fixed, while the size of the other 150 was varied in the same interval. Results for both languages are reported in Table 9 and shown in Figure 5.

Table 9. Testing accuracy obtained by different filter sizes [1].

Fs		{2,1}	{2,2}	{2,3}	{2,4}	{2,5}	{2,6}	{2,7}	{2,8}	{2,9}	{2,10}
Acc (%)	English	79.9	81.8	80.9	79.8	81.2	80.8	80.4	80.1	79.9	80.7
	Italian	79.4	81.0	80.6	80.1	79.2	79.0	80.3	78.9	78.3	79.4

[1] Other settings were: AvoidPunctuation = True, WEinit = pre-trained, De = 300, WEtuning = dynamic, $Ntot$ = 300, f = ReLU, batch = 900, P_{keep} = 0.5, $l2$ = 3.0, optimizer = Adadelta, η = 0.1.

These results again allow to individuate Fs = 2 as the best filter size, also in association with other filters of size 2. This corresponds to significant improvements with respect to Fs = 1 and slight improvements with respect to Fs > 2.

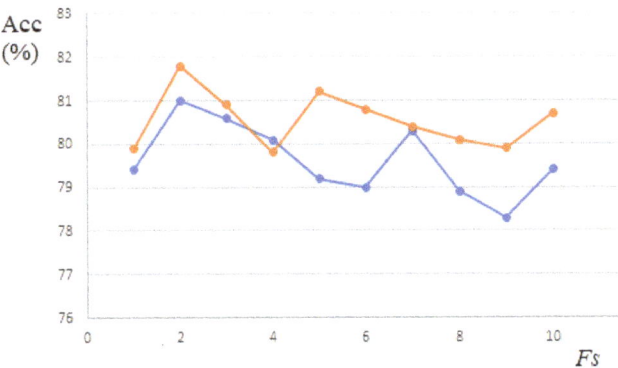

Figure 5. Testing accuracy obtained by different filter sizes apart from 150 filters of size 2, for English (**red**) and Italian (**blue**).

These results mean that substituting 150 filters with others having different sizes does not improve the accuracy. Therefore, further experiments were performed by fixing 200 filters of size 2, while the size of only 100 varies. Results for both languages are reported in Table 10 and shown in Figure 6.

Table 10. Testing accuracy obtained by different filter sizes [1].

Fs		{2,2,1}	{2,2,2}	{2,2,3}	{2,2,4}	{2,2,5}	{2,2,6}	{2,2,7}	{2,2,8}	{2,2,9}	{2,2,10}
Acc (%)	English	80.2	81.8	81.4	81.5	80.4	81.0	80.8	80.8	80.8	80.6
	Italian	79.2	81.0	80.4	79.9	80.3	80.5	79.6	79.6	79.3	80.3

[1] Other settings were: $AvoidPunctuation$ = True, $WEinit$ = pre-trained, De = 300, $WEtuning$ = dynamic, $Ntot$ = 300, f = ReLU, $batch$ = 900, P_{keep} = 0.5, $l2$ = 3.0, $optimizer$ = Adadelta, η = 0.1.

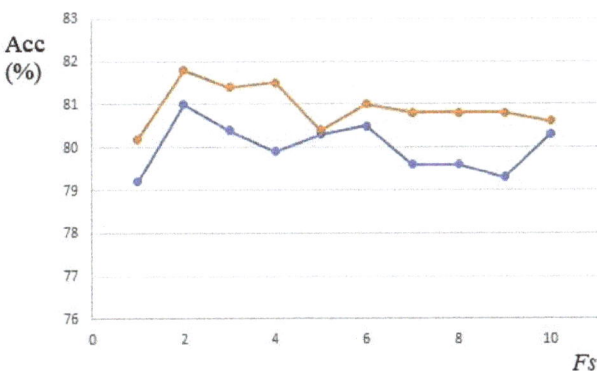

Figure 6. Testing accuracy obtained by different filter sizes apart from 200 filters of size 2, for English (**red**) and Italian (**blue**).

Also in this case, the filter size 2 results the best. However, it corresponds to significant improvements with respect to Fs = 1, while the variations for $Fs \geq 2$ were not significant, since they were comparable with the confidence interval of the linear coefficient of the function approximating this trend (about 0.9%).

This finding of the best filter size corresponding to Fs = 2 can be explained by observing that, while other literature results were inferred for classifying sentences, if questions were considered as in this work, their classification can be done for most of them by considering a sequence of maximum 2 words comprised in them. This is coherent with previous findings, e.g., [4], individuating single words like "head words", or "WH-words" (*why, when, where, ...*), or couples of words (*how much, how long, ...*) as the most informative for QC.

The total number of filters was analyzed as well, within the range [50,500], by considering the following values: {50,100,200,300,400,500}. Results are reported in Table 11 and shown in Figure 7.

Table 11. Testing accuracy obtained by different numbers of filters [1].

	N_{tot}	50	100	200	300	400	500
Acc (%)	English	80.8	81.7	81.5	81.8	81.0	81.3
	Italian	80.5	81.4	81.1	81.0	80.5	79.4

[1] Other settings were: *AvoidPunctuation* = True, *WEinit* = pre-trained, D_e = 300, *WEtuning* = dynamic, F_s = 2, f = ReLU, *batch* = 900, P_{keep} = 0.5, $l2$ = 3.0, *optimizer* = Adadelta, η = 0.1.

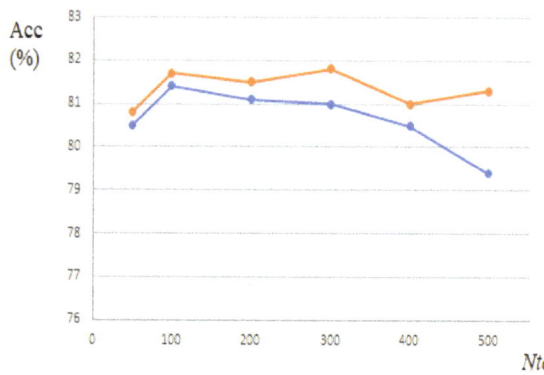

Figure 7. Testing accuracy obtained by different numbers of filters, for English (**red**) and Italian (**blue**).

Also in this case, in the whole considered range, the functions fitted to predict accuracy reveal no significant linear or quadratic effect, but a significant improvement can be detected in correspondence of N_{tot} = 100 with respect to N_{tot} = 100. Moreover, starting from 100 filters, i.e., given that enough filters were used, as this number increases, the positive influence of adding filters disappears. Even if for English the result for 300 filters was slightly better than that with 100, for both languages similar trends can be recognized, therefore this difference can be ascribed to the experimental variance. On the contrary, a decreasing trend of the accuracy can be detected as N_{tot} increases.

These results mean that a minimum of 100 filters should be used, since at least 100 filters were useful to extract different features from text. Moreover, the decreasing trend can be explained by observing that each filter adds 609 weights to the model, therefore adding a great number of filters cause overfitting on training data, and thus a worse accuracy on testing. Therefore, the value N_{tot} = 100 appears the best choice.

As far as the activation function is regarded, those reported in Table 12, together with respective results, are analyzed.

Table 12. Testing accuracy obtained by different activation functions [1].

	f	eLU	Identity	ReLU	Sigmoid	Softplus	Softsign	Tanh
Acc (%)	English	84.9	84.7	85.1	65.6	85.0	79.0	83.4
	Italian	84.1	84.0	83.7	56.7	84.3	79.2	82.9

[1] Other settings were: *AvoidPunctuation* = True, *WEinit* = pre-trained, D_e = 300, *WEtuning* = dynamic, F_s = {1,2,3}, N_{tot} = 300, *batch* = 100, P_{keep} = 1, $l2$ = 3.0, *optimizer* = Adadelta, η = 0.1.

These results, similar for both languages, show that a very low accuracy was obtained by using the sigmoid function. Also with f = softsign the accuracy was significantly lower than the others, while using f = tanh, the accuracy was better, but however, a t-test still reveals that the difference with the others (eLU, Identity, ReLU, softplus) was significant. On the other hand, the activation functions f = eLU, f = Identity, f = ReLU, and f = softplus allow to obtain higher accuracies, with variations among them comparable with the experimental variance. From Figure 2, it can be noticed that these functions giving better results can be distinguished by their characteristic of infinitely increasing trend, with respect to the worse ones that have asymptotic behavior. Since they offer comparable results, one of them can be chosen. For example, f = softplus could be chosen by considering resulting small differences in accuracy, while f = Identity could be preferred in order to design the simplest network architecture.

3.4. Learning Procedure

The first hyperparameter defining the learning procedure considered here was the batch size, i.e., the number of examples considered together to calculate the loss value. Given the training dataset, the variability range was $batch \in [1,900]$, and all the orders of magnitude were considered, i.e., $batch$ = {1,10,100,900}. Results are reported in Table 13 and graphically represented in logarithmic scale in Figure 8.

Table 13. Testing accuracy obtained by different batch sizes [1].

	batch	1	10	100	900
Acc (%)	English	88.1	88.1	85.1	80.2
	Italian	86.4	86.6	83.3	80.4

[1] Other settings were: $AvoidPunctuation$ = True, $WEinit$ = pre-trained, De = 300, $WEtuning$ = dynamic, Fs = {1,2,3}, $Ntot$ = 300, f = ReLU, P_{keep} = 0.5, $l2$ = 3.0, $optimizer$ = Adadelta, η = 0.1.

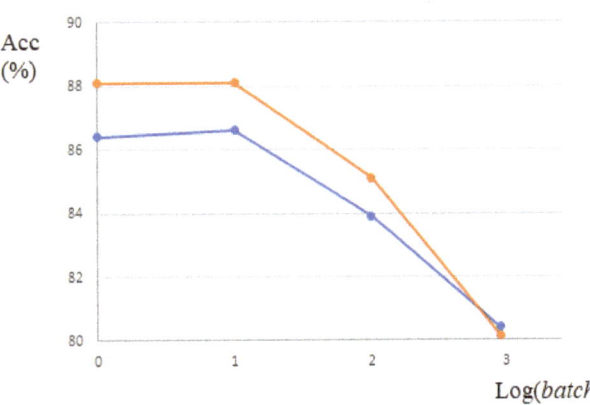

Figure 8. Testing accuracy obtained by different batch sizes, for English (**red**) and Italian (**blue**).

Figure 8 clearly shows that, while the influence of batch size was not significant for sizes between 1 and 10, as the batch size increases, the accuracy clearly decreases, with a very strong effect of this hyperparameter. This finding confirms the usefulness of employing batches instead of summing up the loss function for all the examples. In particular, the smaller the batch size was, the higher accuracy was obtained. However, one should also take into account that smaller batch sizes also cause much longer training time. For this reason, here, in order to choose the best batch size, between 1 and 10, having comparable performances, $batch$ = 10 was chosen.

The dropout was also varied, in the range P_{keep} = (0,1], and in particular, in correspondence of the following representative levels: P_{keep} = {0.1,0.5,0.9,1}. Results are reported in Table 14.

Table 14. Testing accuracy obtained by different dropout [1].

P_{keep}		0.1	0.5	0.9	1.0
Acc (%)	English	82.6	84.8	84.9	84.8
	Italian	81.9	83.5	84.2	84.2

[1] Other settings were: AvoidPunctuation = False, WEinit = pre-trained, De = 300, WEtuning = dynamic, Fs = {1,2,3}, Ntot = 300, f = ReLU, batch = 100, $l2$ = 3.0, optimizer = Adadelta, η = 0.1.

From Table 14, it can be seen that, excepting the case P_{keep} = 0.1, which causes significant accuracy worsening, the other cases were very similar. This means that for this kind of system, and for the considered size of the dataset, dropout was not strictly necessary. Therefore, for the considered dataset, the dropout can be avoided, by choosing P_{keep} = 1.0, or equivalently P_{keep} = 0.9 can be chosen.

The regularization term $l2$ was also considered, at the following levels: $l2$ = {1.0,3.0,5.0}. Results are reported in Table 15.

Table 15. Testing accuracy obtained by different regularization terms [1].

$l2$		1.0	3.0	5.0
Acc (%)	English	86.7	85.1	83.4
	Italian	85.6	83.9	83.5

[1] Other settings were: AvoidPunctuation = True, WEinit = pre-trained, De = 300, WEtuning = dynamic, Fs = {1,2,3}, Ntot = 300, f = ReLU, batch = 100, P_{keep} = 0.5, optimizer = Adadelta, η = 0.1.

From Table 15, a slight but significant decreasing trend of the accuracy can be detected while $l2$ increases. Therefore, $l2$ = 1.0 was chosen.

Finally, the updating rule *optimizer* used to perform weights update by SGD backpropagation algorithm, and the associated learning rate η, were studied together, in order to evaluate also their probable interactions. According to a full factorial design, all the combinations of factors levels were experimented, i.e., all the available updating rules *optimizer* = {Adadelta,Adagrad,Adam,Ftrl, GradientDescent,Momentum,ProximalAdagrad,ProximalGradientDescent,RMSProp} combined with all the magnitude orders in the considered range of the learning rate η = {0.01,0.1,1,10}. Results were reported in Table 16 and shown in Figure 9. In Table 16, some results were not reported ("-"), since the corresponding experiments were not performed, because they make no sense in light of the other experiments. Moreover, the results of some experiments were reported as "<20.0", since in those cases the learning procedure did not offer acceptable accuracy. Some others were reported as "DIV", since the learning procedure gave exceptions due to overflow. The results indicated by an asterisk were obtained by 20,000 epochs instead of 2000; however, results with different numbers of epochs can be compared, because in all the cases the training was stopped after that convergence was reached. For each set of experiments with different learning rates, the best result is reported in bold.

From Table 16, it can be evinced that some updating rules does not work with a too high learning rate, giving overflow problems. In particular, when *optimizer* = {GradientDescent,Momentum, ProximalGradientDescent}, the learning rate η = 1 was already too high. Moreover, when *optimizer* = Ftrl and η = 0.01 (too low η), and when *optimizer* = RMSProp and η = 1 (too high η in this case), the learning procedure does not improve the testing accuracy of the initial random model. Another point to take into account was that experiments obtained by 20000 epochs, necessary to get convergence for some low values of η, need much more computation time. These observations limit the range of the usable values of η, peculiarly for each updating rule.

Table 16. Testing accuracy obtained by different learning updating rules and learning rates [1].

	optimizer\η	0.01	0.1	1	10
Acc (%)	**English**				
	Adadelta	84.9 *	87.2 *	**88.4**	88.2
	Adagrad	85.8 *	**86.1**	55.7	-
	Adam	**85.1**	65.8	50.5	-
	Ftrl	<20.0	**57.4**	53.5	-
	GradientDescent	**87.4 ***	85.7	DIV	-
	Momentum	**87.2 ***	86.4	DIV	-
	ProximalAdagrad	85.4 *	**86.6**	57.1	-
	ProximalGradientDescent	**87.0 ***	85.3	DIV	-
	RMSProp	**87.0**	55.3	<20.0	-
	Italian				
	Adadelta	83.8 *	87.4 *	**88.6**	88.0
	Adagrad	85.2 *	**86.0**	57.0	-
	Adam	**85.9**	67.8	66.4	-
	Ftrl	<20.0	**56.4**	49.8	-
	GradientDescent	**86.2 ***	82.3	DIV	-
	Momentum	**86.2 ***	82.8	DIV	-
	ProximalAdagrad	85.0 *	**85.3**	63.6	-
	ProximalGradientDescent	**86.0 ***	82.5	DIV	-
	RMSProp	**86.4**	57.0	<20.0	-

[1] Experiments not performed reported as "-". Not acceptable accuracy reported as "<20.0". Exceptions due to overflow reported as "DIV". Results obtained by 20,000 epochs instead of 2000 indicated by an asterisk. Best result for each set of experiments with different learning rates reported in bold. Other settings were: *AvoidPunctuation* = True, *WEinit* = pre-trained, *De* = 300, *WEtuning* = dynamic, *Fs* = {1,2,3}, *Ntot* = 300, *f* = softplus, *batch* = 100, P_{keep} = 1.0, *l2* = 3.0.

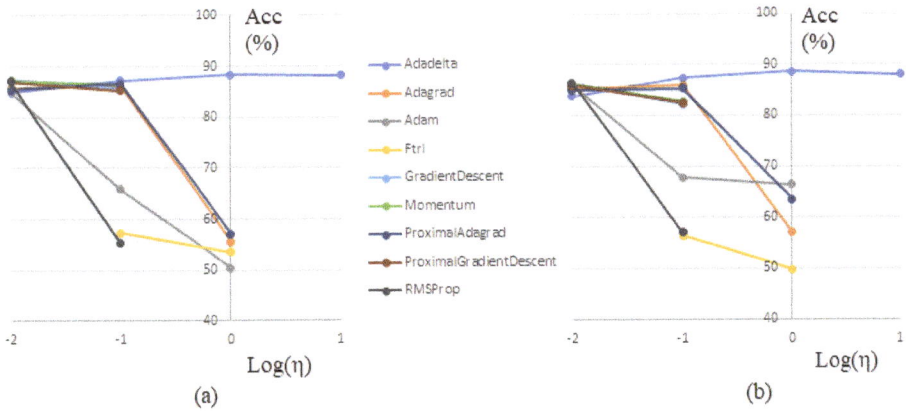

Figure 9. Testing accuracy obtained by different weights updating rules and different learning rates, for English (**a**) and Italian (**b**).

Most updating rules result equivalent for low learning rates, as can be evinced by Figure 9, in correspondence of η = 0.01. In particular, the cases *optimizer* = {GradientDescent, Momentum,ProximalGradientDescent} result equivalent for this dataset in the whole range of η. Moreover, as can be seen in Figure 9, in the acceptable ranges of η for each updating rule, most of them present similar trends, with significantly increasing accuracy values as η decreases. This can be explained by the network behavior of adapting fast to training data for high learning rates, which allows to increase predictivity only during the first few epochs. Therefore, while experimenting lower learning rates was not doable due to too high computation time, the option of higher learning rates was not promising for most of the cases. On the other hand, when *optimizer* = Adadelta, accuracy surprisingly increases with η, even if the differences in the range η = [0.1,10] were comparable with experimental variance, and this allows using high learning rates (e.g., $\eta = 1$), and not too many epochs. Moreover, in correspondence of *optimizer* = Adadelta and $\eta \geq 0.1$, a significant accuracy improvement was gained, with respect to the maximal values of the other algorithms obtained with $\eta = 0.01$. Therefore, the following couple of values of the considered degrees of freedom was chosen as optimal: *optimizer* = Adadelta and $\eta = 1$.

3.5. Most Influencing Hyperparameters

The previous findings can be compared and summarized as follows.

For classifying questions (in 9 classes, using 900 training instances, with a CNN), the influence associated to variations of different settings, relative to text representation, CNN architecture, and learning procedure, was qualitatively described in Table 17.

Table 17. Qualitative description of influence of settings.

Setting	Symbol	Influence
Words representation		
Eliminate punctuation	*AvoidPunctuation*	Not significant
Use of pre-trained and fine-tuned Word Embedding vectors	*WEinit* AND *WEtuning*	Significant
Embedding dimension	*De*	Very strong ($De \leq 100$) – Significant ($100 < De \leq 300$) – Not significant ($300 < De \leq 500$)
CNN architecture		
Filter size	*Fs*	Significant
Total number of filters	*Ntot*	Significant ($Ntot \leq 100$) – Not significant ($Ntot > 100$)
Activation function	*f*	Not significant (among eLU,Identity,ReLU,softPlus) – Significant (vs. softsign,tanh) – Very strong (vs. sigmoid)
Learning procedure		
Batch size	*batch*	Not significant ($batch \leq 10$) – Strong ($batch > 10$)
Dropout	P_{keep}	Significant ($P_{keep} < 0.5$) – Not significant ($P_{keep} \geq 0.5$)
Loss regularization	*l2*	Significant
Weights updating rule	*optimizer*	Not significant (associated with $\eta = 0.01$) – Very strong (associated with $\eta \geq 0.1$)
Learning rate	η	Significant (associated with *optimizer* = Adadelta) – Very strong (otherwise)

From Table 17, the set of possible causes of very bad results can be individuated, i.e., too few embedding dimensions, sigmoid activation function, and a wrong choice of learning rate associated with a certain weights updating rule.

On the other hand, the strongest positive effect on accuracy was associated with a small batch size. Other settings give significant positive effects: Use of pre-trained and fine-tuned WE vectors, minimum 300 embedding dimensions, filter size equal to 2, minimum 100 total number of filters, choice of the activation function among {eLU,Identity,ReLU,softplus}, low loss regularization constant, and low learning rate. On the contrary, the influence of eliminating punctuation, and of the dropout function (given $P_{keep} \geq 0.5$) were not significant.

3.6. Experiments with Optimal Settings

The results reported above allow individuating the best settings, for hopefully obtaining the highest accuracy values, with respect to those reported so far.

Therefore, some experiments were performed in correspondence of the best settings, in CV and with some repetitions, in order to validate the optimization procedure described before. In particular, two different settings were chosen, one (OPT1) comprising one of the best activation functions (f = softplus), the other without the activation function (f = Identity).

Moreover, the results obtained here were compared with those obtained with settings individuated as optimal in previous works [19,21]. For configurations found in previous works, fastText WE pre-trained vectors are used here.

In Table 18, the settings relative to different final experiments are reported, together with respective accuracy on testing.

Table 18. Testing accuracy for optimal settings, averaged on experiments repetitions, and for settings individuated in previous literature.

Symbol	OPT1 (This Work)	OPT2 (This Work)	[21]	[19]
N_{train}/N_{test}		900/100		
Words representation				
AvoidPunctuation	True	True	False	False
WEinit	pre-trained	pre-trained	pre-trained	pre-trained
De	300	300	300	300
WEtuning	dynamic	dynamic	dynamic	dynamic
CNN architecture				
Fs	2	2	{3,4,5}	{2,3,4,5}
Ntot	100	100	300	400
f	softplus	Identity	ReLU	ReLU
Learning procedure				
batch	10	10	50	50
P_{keep}	1	1	0.5	0.7
l2	1.0	1.0	3.0	5.0
optimizer	Adadelta	Adadelta	Adadelta	Adadelta
η	1.0	1.0	0.1	0.1
Performance				
Acc (%) for English	88.8	89.2	85.6	85.7
Acc (%) for Italian	89.0	89.0	85.4	85.0

Results presented in Table 18, firstly validate the optimization performed of the whole model. Indeed, the accuracy values were the highest obtained so far on this dataset.

Moreover, the results obtained by taking into account optimal configurations individuated by [19,21] were significantly worse than those obtained here. The most noticeable differences in the configurations revealed that the model chosen here was much simpler, since it avoids considering punctuation, uses only 100 filters of size 2, and does not use dropout (nor any activation function, for OPT2).

Since [19,21] found their best configurations on a different dataset, the same comparison was performed on the most used dataset provided by [35] for the English language. In Table 19, the settings and the respective accuracy on testing were reported, relative to different final experiments, also on this bigger sized dataset.

Table 19. Testing accuracy on [35] data with optimal settings, and with settings individuated in previous literature.

Symbol	OPT1 (This Work)	OPT2 (This Work)	[21]	[19]
Ntrain/Ntest		5452/500		
Words representation				
AvoidPunctuation	True	True	False	False
WEinit	pre-trained	pre-trained	pre-trained	pre-trained
De	300	300	300	300
WEtuning	dynamic	dynamic	dynamic	dynamic
CNN architecture				
Fs	2	2	{3,4,5}	{2,3,4,5}
Ntot	100	100	300	400
f	softplus	Identity	ReLU	ReLU
Learning procedure				
batch	10	10	50	50
P_{keep}	1	1	0.5	0.7
l2	1.0	1.0	3.0	5.0
optimizer	Adadelta	Adadelta	Adadelta	Adadelta
η	1.0	1.0	0.1	0.1
Performance				
Acc (%) for English	93.0	92.2	91.8	91.0

Among results of Table 19, those obtained with the proposed optimal settings were better than those obtained with settings optimized in previous works for this particular dataset. This confirms the validity and transferability of the optimal text representation, CNN architecture, and learning procedure obtained here for the QC task.

3.7. Limitations

The optimal settings found here were based on a multilingual dataset regarding QC, using the taxonomy explained in Section 2.1. Moreover, they were validated on a further dataset, also regarding QC, presenting a different taxonomy.

However, the optimality of those settings cannot be demonstrated for any taxonomy of question classes. Moreover, it cannot be extended to other sentence classification tasks. For example, if a filter of size 2 was enough to classify some questions by just individuating "How much" sequence of words, the same small filter could be undersized to distinguish more fine-grained question classes or to classify sentiment of affirmative sentences.

4. Conclusions

This paper presented a study performed to analyze the settings of Convolutional Neural Networks for Question Classification, in terms of words representation, network architecture and learning procedure.

Both English and Italian languages were considered, since they have different morphological richness, and training sets made of different number of questions were tested. All experiments were based on questions properly extracted from the same multilingual dataset, in order to check possible dependencies of optimal settings with respect to language.

All the hyperparameters and the most plausible interactions among them were tested in correspondence of wide ranges of variability. For each of them, statistical significance of its influence was evaluated by means of a comparison with intrinsic variability, measured through repetitions of the same experiments.

Results of the huge number of experiments drove to the individuation of optimal settings, which are similar for both languages. They can be summarized as follows. Regarding the text representation, it is better to avoid punctuation, to use pre-trained word embedding vectors with dimension 300, and fine-tune them according to available data; regarding the architecture, 100 filters of size 2 were enough for coarse-grain classification, and an infinitely increasing activation function should be preferred (eLU, ReLU, softplus), or equivalently no activation function (Identity); regarding the learning procedure, using a small batch of 10 gives strong improvements, while choosing it smaller only increases computation time, dropout and loss regularization should be avoided, and the best and fastest optimizer was Adadelta, associated with learning rate 1.0.

The individuated best configuration was tested on the same data and on a different set of questions widely used for QC, and compared to the configurations suggested by the most relevant previous works. These further results validated the optimization performed and confirmed the transferability of the best settings on different data, since in all cases the models optimized here showed significantly better classification accuracy than those suggested before.

Author Contributions: Conceptualization, M.P., M.E. and H.F.; methodology, M.P. and M.E.; software, M.P.; validation, M.E. and H.F.; formal analysis, M.P.; investigation, M.P. and M.E.; resources, G.D.P.; data curation, M.P.; writing—original draft preparation, M.P. and M.E.; writing—review and editing, M.P. and M.E.; visualization, M.P.; supervision, M.E., G.D.P. and H.F.; project administration, G.D.P.; funding acquisition, G.D.P. All authors have read and agreed to the published version of the manuscript.

Funding: This research received no external funding.

Conflicts of Interest: The authors declare no conflict of interest.

References

1. Yadav, A.; Vishwakarma, D.K. Sentiment analysis using deep learning architectures: A review. *Artif. Intell. Rev.* **2019**. [CrossRef]
2. Yuan, S.; Zhang, Y.; Tang, J.; Hall, W.; Cabotà, J.B. Expert finding in community question answering: A review. *Artif. Intell. Rev.* **2020**, *53*, 843–874. [CrossRef]
3. Wang, Y.; Wang, M.; Fujita, H. Word Sense Disambiguation: A comprehensive knowledge exploitation framework. *Knowl. Based Syst.* **2020**, *190*, 105030. [CrossRef]
4. Pota, M.; Fuggi, A.; Esposito, M.; De Pietro, G. Extracting Compact Sets of Features for Question Classification in Cognitive Systems: A Comparative Study. In Proceedings of the 10th International Conference on P2P, Parallel, Grid, Cloud and Internet Computing, 3rd Workshop on Cloud and Distributed System Applications, Krakow, Poland, 4–6 November 2015; IEEE: Piscataway, NJ, USA; pp. 551–556. [CrossRef]
5. Pota, M.; Esposito, M.; De Pietro, G. A forward-selection algorithm for SVM-based question classification in cognitive systems. In Proceedings of the 9th International KES Conference on Intelligent Interactive Multimedia: Systems and Services (KES-IIMSS-16), Tenerife, Spain, 15–17 June 2016; pp. 587–598. [CrossRef]
6. Pota, M.; Esposito, M.; De Pietro, G. Learning to rank answers to closed-domain questions by using fuzzy logic. In Proceedings of the IEEE International Conference on Fuzzy Systems (FUZZ-IEEE), Naples, Italy, 9–12 July 2017; pp. 1–6. [CrossRef]
7. Argamon, S.; Koppel, M.; Pennebaker, J.W.; Schler, J. Automatically profiling the author of an anonymous text. *Commun. ACM* **2009**, *52*, 119–123. [CrossRef]
8. Estival, D.; Gaustad, T.; Pham, S.B.; Radford, W.; Hutchinson, B. Tat: An author profiling tool with application to arabic emails. In Proceedings of the Australasian Language Technology Workshop, Melbourne, Australia, 21–30 December 2007.
9. Franco-Salvador, M.; Rangel, F.; Rosso, P.; Taulé, M.; Martí, M.A. Language variety identification using distributed representations of words and documents. In Proceedings of the CLEF 2015 Conference and Labs of the Evaluation Forum-Experimental IR meets Multilinguality, Multimodality, and Interaction, LNCS, Toulouse, France, 8–11 September 2015; Springer: Berlin/Heidelberg, Germany, 2015; Volume 9283, pp. 24–40.
10. Bayot, R.; Gonçalves, T. Author Profiling using SVMs and Word Embedding Averages—Notebook for PAN at CLEF 2016. In Proceedings of the Working Notes of CLEF'2016—Conference and Labs of the Evaluation forum CLEF 2016 Evaluation Labs and Workshop—Working Notes Papers, Évora, Portugal, 5–8 September 2016.

11. Liu, G.; Guo, J. Bidirectional LSTM with attention mechanism and convolutional layer for text classification. *Neurocomputing* **2019**, *337*, 325–338. [CrossRef]
12. Guo, B.; Zhang, C.; Liu, J.; Ma, X. Improving text classification with weighted word embeddings via a multi-channel TextCNN model. *Neurocomputing* **2019**, *363*, 366–374. [CrossRef]
13. Wang, P.; Xu, B.; Xu, J.; Tian, G.; Liu, C.-L.; Hao, H. Semantic expansion using word embedding clustering and convolutional neural network for improving short text classification. *Neurocomputing* **2016**, *174*, 806–814. [CrossRef]
14. Poria, S.; Peng, H.; Hussain, A.; Howard, N.; Cambria, E. Ensemble application of convolutional neural networks and multiple kernel learning for multimodal sentiment analysis. *Neurocomputing* **2017**, *261*, 217–230. [CrossRef]
15. Xia, W.; Zhu, W.; Liao, B.; Chen, M.; Cai, L.; Huang, L. Novel architecture for long short-term memory used in question classification. *Neurocomputing* **2018**, *299*, 20–31. [CrossRef]
16. Loni, B. *A Survey of State-of-the-Art Methods on Question Classification*; Technical Report; Delft University of Technology: Delft, The Netherlands, 2011.
17. Dale, R. Classical approaches to natural language processing. In *Handbook of Natural Language Processing*; Chapman & Hall/CRC: Boca Raton, FL, USA, 2010.
18. Mikolov, T.; Sutskever, I.; Chen, K.; Corrado, G.S.; Dean, J. Distributed representations of words and phrases and their compositionality. *Adv. Neural Inf. Process. Syst.* **2013**, *26*, 3111–3119.
19. Zhang, Y.; Wallace, B.C. A sensitivity analysis of (and practitioners' guide to) convolutional neural networks for sentence classification. In Proceedings of the 8th International Joint Conference on Natural Language Processing, Taipei, Taiwan, 26–31 July 2015; pp. 253–263.
20. Pota, M.; Esposito, M.; De Pietro, G. Convolutional Neural Networks for Question Classification in Italian Language. In Proceedings of the 16th International Conference on Intelligent Software Methodologies, Tools, and Techniques (SOMET_17), Kitakyushu, Japan, 26–28 September 2017; pp. 604–615. [CrossRef]
21. Kim, Y. Convolutional neural networks for sentence classification. *arXiv* **2014**, arXiv:1408.5882.
22. Qin, P.; Xu, W.; Guo, J. An empirical convolutional neural network approach for semantic relation classification. *Neurocomputing* **2016**, *190*, 1–9. [CrossRef]
23. Collobert, R.; Weston, J. A unified architecture for natural language processing: Deep neural networks with multitask learning. In Proceedings of the 25th International Conference on Machine Learning, New York, NY, USA, 5–9 July 2008; pp. 160–167.
24. Collobert, R.; Weston, J.; Bottou, L.; Karlen, M.; Kavukcuoglu, K.; Kuksa, P. Natural language processing (almost) from scratch. *J. Mach. Learn. Res.* **2011**, *12*, 2493–2537.
25. Kalchbrenner, N.; Grefenstette, E.; Blunsom, P. A convolutional neural network for modelling sentences. In Proceedings of the 52nd Annual Meeting of the Association for Computational Linguistics, Baltimore, MD, USA, 22–27 June 2014.
26. Yin, W.; Schütze, H. Multichannel variable-size convolution for sentence classification. In Proceedings of the 19th Conference on Computational Language Learning, Beijing, China, 30–31 July 2015; pp. 204–214.
27. Bengio, Y.; Ducharme, R.; Vincent, P.; Jauvin, C. A neural probabilistic language model. *J. Mach. Learn. Res.* **2003**, *3*, 1137–1155.
28. Dos Santos, C.N.; Gatti, M. Deep convolutional neural networks for sentiment analysis of short texts. In Proceedings of the 25th International Conference on Computational Linguistics (COLING), Dublin, Ireland, 23–29 August 2014.
29. Zhang, X.; Zhao, J.; LeCun, Y. Character-level convolutional networks for text classification. In Proceedings of the 28th International Conference on Neural Information Processing Systems, Montreal, QC, Canada, 8–13 December 2014.
30. Conneau, A.; Schwenk, H.; Barrault, L.; LeCun, Y. Very deep convolutional networks for natural language processing. *arXiv* **2016**, arXiv:1606.01781.
31. Dachapally, P.R.; Ramanam, S. In-depth Question classification using Convolutional Neural Networks. *arXiv* **2018**, arXiv:1804.00968.
32. Lei, T.; Shi, Z.; Liu, D.; Yang, L.; Zhu, F. A novel CNN-based method for Question Classification in Intelligent Question Answering. In Proceedings of the 2018 International Conference on Algorithms, Computing and Artificial Intelligence, Sanya, China, 21–23 December 2018.

33. Pota, M.; Esposito, M. Question Classification by Convolutional Neural Networks Embodying Subword Information. In Proceedings of the IEEE International Joint Conference on Neural Networks (IJCNN), Rio de Janeiro, Brazil, 8–13 July 2018. [CrossRef]
34. Gu, J.; Wang, Z.; Kuen, J.; Ma, L.; Shahroudy, A.; Shuai, B.; Chen, T. Recent advances in convolutional neural networks. *Pattern Recognit.* **2018**, *77*, 354–377. [CrossRef]
35. Li, X.; Roth, D. Learning question classifiers. In Proceedings of the 19th International Conference on Computational Linguistics (COLING'02), Morristown, NJ, USA, 26–30 August 2002.
36. Robbins, H.; Monro, S. A Stochastic Approximation Method. *Ann. Math. Stat.* **1951**, *22*, 400. [CrossRef]
37. Bottou, L.; Bousquet, O. The Tradeoffs of Large Scale Learning. In *Optimization for Machine Learning*; MIT Press: Cambridge, MA, USA, 2012; pp. 351–368.
38. Bottou, L. Online Algorithms and Stochastic Approximations. In *Online Learning and Neural Networks*; Cambridge University Press: Cambridge, UK, 1998.
39. Neyman, J. Outline of a theory of statistical estimation based on the classical theory of probability. *Philos. Trans. R. Soc. Lond. Ser. A Math. Phys. Sci.* **1937**, *236*, 333–380.

© 2020 by the authors. Licensee MDPI, Basel, Switzerland. This article is an open access article distributed under the terms and conditions of the Creative Commons Attribution (CC BY) license (http://creativecommons.org/licenses/by/4.0/).

Article

Text Normalization Using Encoder–Decoder Networks Based on the Causal Feature Extractor

Adrián Javaloy [1] and Ginés García-Mateos [2,*]

1. Max Planck Institute for Intelligent Systems, 72076 Tübingen, Germany; adrian.javaloy@tuebingen.mpg.de
2. Department of Computer Science and Systems, University of Murcia, 30100 Murcia, Spain
* Correspondence: ginesgm@um.es; Tel.: +34-868-888-530

Received: 9 May 2020; Accepted: 27 June 2020; Published: 30 June 2020

Abstract: The encoder–decoder architecture is a well-established, effective and widely used approach in many tasks of natural language processing (NLP), among other domains. It consists of two closely-collaborating components: An encoder that transforms the input into an intermediate form, and a decoder producing the output. This paper proposes a new method for the encoder, named Causal Feature Extractor (CFE), based on three main ideas: Causal convolutions, dilatations and bidirectionality. We apply this method to text normalization, which is a ubiquitous problem that appears as the first step of many text-to-speech (TTS) systems. Given a text with symbols, the problem consists in writing the text exactly as it should be read by the TTS system. We make use of an attention-based encoder–decoder architecture using a fine-grained character-level approach rather than the usual word-level one. The proposed CFE is compared to other common encoders, such as convolutional neural networks (CNN) and long-short term memories (LSTM). Experimental results show the feasibility of CFE, achieving better results in terms of accuracy, number of parameters, convergence time, and use of an attention mechanism based on attention matrices. The obtained accuracy ranges from 83.5% to 96.8% correctly normalized sentences, depending on the dataset. Moreover, the proposed method is generic and can be applied to different types of input such as text, audio and images.

Keywords: text normalization; natural language processing; deep neural networks; causal encoder

1. Introduction

Research in natural language processing (NLP) has traditionally focused on the resolution of problems such as automatic bilingual translation [1], text summarization [2], automatic text generation [3] and text classification [4]. However, there are also other not so well-known problems that are often overlooked, despite being as difficult to solve as the former ones. In particular, the problem of text normalization is one such case. Its definition is simple: Given an arbitrary text, transform it into its normalized form. This normalized form depends on the context in which we are working. For example, in the context of text-to-speech (TTS) systems—which is the objective of this paper—normalizing a text means rewriting it as it should be read, for example:

I have $20 → I have twenty dollars
It happened in 1984 → It happened in nineteen eighty four
He weights 50kg → He weights fifty kilograms

At first glance, this problem might seem trivial and rather unimportant. Nevertheless, text normalization is a ubiquitous task, present in most NLP problems. The reason is that normalizing the input as a first step significantly decreases the complexity of those subsequent tasks, since equivalent phrases—yet differently written—end up being exactly the same phrase, as illustrated in Figure 1. WaveNet [5] is an example of these systems, where a generative model for TTS is trained with normalized text as input.

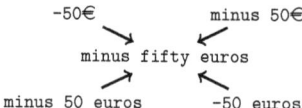

Figure 1. An example of equivalent phrases producing the same normalized output.

Despite its apparent simplicity, this problem entails an interesting challenge. Data-driven approaches, specifically Deep Learning, deserve special attention since: (1) There exists a general belief that Deep Learning can solve any problem; and (2) it is the framework used in this research. Text normalization gathers three main features that make it challenging for this type of techniques, as it has been already discussed by Sproat and Jaitly [6]. In short:

- Non-trivial cases (i.e., those whose output and input differ) are sparse.
- It is context-dependent, for example, a normalized date could change depending on the local variant of the language.
- There is no natural reason for building a text normalization database. Everyone knows that 2 means *two*.

Different models have been developed to tackle this problem. The first attempts date back to the times when researchers were developing the first complete TTS systems, as described by Sproat and Jaitly [6]. Systems based on traditional techniques include finite state automata as well as finite state transducers [7]. The usage of these models has the advantage of being well-known techniques that work (and fail) as expected; yet, these solutions need to be hand-crafted from scratch for each language, suffering from lack of flexibility (which translates into an increase in production costs).

Nowadays, many researchers are moving towards Deep Learning models, that try to learn how to solve the problems from the data itself [6]. However, the amount of information that these models require to work correctly can be prohibitive. In the cases where the target language is low-resourced, that is, a language for which little data is available, rule-based solutions have been attempted [8], as well as Deep Learning models that make use of data augmentation techniques to compensate the lack of samples [9]. In particular, this system is based on an encoder–decoder architecture, using bidirectional recurrent neural networks working at character-level; this is similar to our proposed approach, except for the encoder and other adjustments of the network.

Text normalization is also a very common step in the analysis of social media messages, where the input text is prone to present problems of misspelling, abbreviation, incorrect grammar, etc. For example, Arora and Kansal [10] proposed a system to perform sentiment analysis in Twitter messages using Convolutional Neural Networks (CNN), with text normalization as a preprocessing step. Their method is based on character-level embedding (instead of the most common word-level embedding), with convolutional, max-pooling and fully connected layers, achieving a classification accuracy above 98.1%. However, the normalization step is based on traditional techniques using tokenization, dictionary word replacement, lemmarization and stemming.

The models proposed by Sproat and Jaitly [6] deserve special attention. They are based on Deep Learning techniques and, at each time-step, they read a character and produce an entire word, thus being character-based at the input, and word-based at the output. These models obtained a high accuracy performance (one case achieving a 99.8% on the English test set). Unfortunately, they suffered from the so-called *silly*, undetectable or unrecoverable errors. This means that these errors cannot be detected only looking at the produced output. For example, this is the case when normalizing *I'm 12* as *I am thirteen*, yet the error *Im twenty* could be detected in the subsequent process. Our hypothesis is that these errors could be due to the use of recurrent word-level models, and they could be avoided to a large extent by a character-level approach. More recently, this model was improved in [11], by using a covering grammar for the given language, with the purpose of avoiding those unrecoverable errors. This grammar constrains the execution of the recurrent neural network, with the particularity that these grammars can be learned automatically from the samples.

The present approach has been designed with two main goals in mind. The first one is offering a solution for the text normalization problem that exclusively uses neural networks, taking advantage of the benefits of data-driven solutions. The second goal is to introduce convolutional components in the neural model, substituting its recurrent counterparts and, thus, speeding up the whole process. Moreover, proving the usefulness of such convolutional architecture would help to push even further the idea that CNNs can be used outside of a computer vision framework.

The main contributions of this work are as follows: (1) Proposal of a character-based approach for the text normalization problem which does not suffer from undetectable or unrecoverable errors; (2) introduction of a new general-purpose encoder based on causal convolutions, the Causal Feature Extractor (CFE); and (3) a variation of the traditional attention mechanisms, in which a context matrix is generated, instead of a context vector.

2. Materials and Methods

2.1. Text Normalization Dataset

As stated in Section 1, it can be challenging to obtain a valid database of normalized text. Fortunately, a huge database was built and released to the whole Machine Learning community by Sproat and Jaitly [6]. This dataset occupies a total of 9.1 Gb and contains about 40 million phrases extracted from Wikipedia. It includes 1.1 billion words of English text. The expected output for the input sentences was mostly obtained with a set of hand-built rules used by a finite-state grammar [12].

The database was prepared for their word-level model and, therefore, requires some preprocessing before being suitable for a character-level approach. Particularly, each entry on the original database is a pair of words (or special symbols) plus an additional column describing its semiotic class, as shown in Figure 2. In order to use a character-level approach, each row needs to be composed of all the words belonging to the same phrase, and information regarding each individual word (such as its semiotic class) has to be disregarded.

```
"Semiotic Class","Input Token","Output Token"
"PLAIN","Rosemary,"<self>"
"PLAIN","is","<self>"
"PLAIN","a","<self>"
"PLAIN","plant","<self>"
"PUNCT",".","<sil>"
"<eos>","<eos>",""
"DATE","2006","two thousand six"
"LETTERS","IUCN","i u c n"
```

Figure 2. Sample text from the original dataset (https://github.com/rwsproat/text-normalization-data).

As shown in Figure 2, there are special symbols in the original dataset, namely: (1) <eos>, denoting the end of the current sentence; (2) <sil>, marking a silence (comma, colon, and so on); and (3) <self>, meaning that the output in that entry is the same as the input. Since these symbols cannot be used in a character-level approach (due to the alignment problem), they were removed in the following way: <eos> disappears once the sentence has been recomposed; whereas <sil> and <self> are substituted by the corresponding input.

Other minor changes have been made on the original dataset to speed up the training process, obtaining a new dataset as shown in Figure 3. The process consists of the following steps:

1. Concatenation of the words belonging to the same phrase and removal of special symbols, as mentioned before.
2. Phrases with non-permitted characters are discarded, keeping an alphabet of $v = 127$ characters, including numbers, basic arithmetic symbols, currency, and the English alphabet.
3. Entries with an output longer than 177 characters are discarded as well, which corresponds to removing only 0.01% of the sentences.
4. Entries are sorted in descending order with respect to their output length. This way, the padding introduced in batches is minimized and, as described by Xu et al. [13], convergence speed is increased without a significant loss in accuracy.

```
"Input Token","Output Token"
"Rosemary is a plant.","Rosemary is a plant."
"2006 IUCN.","two thousand six i u c n."
"We all lost.","We all lost."
"vol 6 no","volume six no"
"Rees et al.","Rees et al."
```

Figure 3. Sample entries from the preprocessed dataset.

2.2. Character-Level Encoding

Regarding the actual input and output used in the model, we use a one-hot encoding, i.e., a string $s = s_1 s_2 \ldots s_l$ of size $l \in \mathbb{N}$ is transformed into a matrix $\mathbf{X} \in \mathbb{M}_{v \times l}$, where the i-th column $x_i \in \mathbf{X}$ is set to zero in all positions except the one corresponding to the index of the character s_i, according to the model alphabet. Recall that v is the size of the alphabet (127 in our case).

The advantages and disadvantages of using a character-level model—as opposed to word-level models—have been described by some authors, since it appears as a basic design decision in many NLP problems. Four arguments in favor of character-level approaches are shown, three of them introduced by Chung et al. [14], and the last one given by Lee et al. [15]:

- Out-of-vocabulary issues do not appear, as it could happen in word-level models. We could suffer from out-of-alphabet issues, but these can be easily solved.
- Such approaches are able to model rare morphological variants of a word.
- Input segmentation is no longer required.
- By not segmenting into words, the models have to discover the internal rules and structure of the sentences by themselves.

Since text segmentation is known to be problematic and error-prone, even for well-known languages such as English, removing this step without losing performance is a significant advantage to consider. Moreover, we can provide an additional argument for character-level approaches: If the model uses attention mechanisms, observing the attention matrices after a particular sample gives a better understanding of the system's logic and the language itself. For example, consider the case where the model transforms *2s* into *two seconds*; its attention matrix could potentially show that the last letter was produced by looking at the number.

2.3. Encoder–Decoder Architecture

The encoder–decoder architecture is a common and popular design in recent Neural Machine Translation literature [16]. The model is composed of two parts: (1) An encoder that takes the input $\mathbf{X}$ (in this case, a phrase), and produces an intermediate representation $\mathbf{Z}$ (or code) that highlights its main features; and (2) a decoder that processes that set of features and produces the required output $\mathbf{Y}$ (in this case, a normalized phrase). $\mathbf{Z}$ is a matrix of size $\mathbf{Z} \in \mathbb{M}_{f \times l}$, where f represents the selected number of features to encode for each input value. Figure 4 shows a basic diagram of this model.

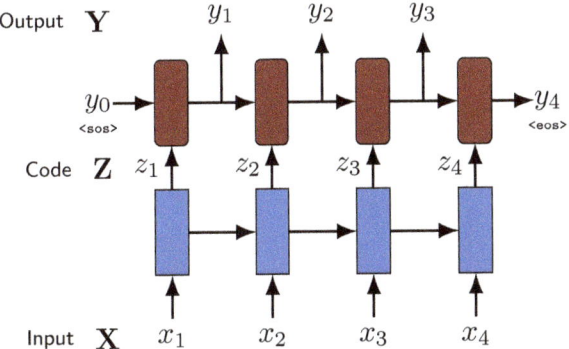

Figure 4. A basic encoder–decoder architecture. Blue: Encoder. Red: Decoder. Given an input sequence, $X = x_1 x_2 \ldots$, the system produces an output sequence, $Y = y_1 y_2 \ldots$ The intermediate code is $Z = z_1 z_2 \ldots$ There are two special symbols: <sos> start of sequence; <eos> end of sequence.

This is a simplified representation of the encoder–decoder architecture, involving that the size of the input, the intermediate representation and the output is the same. This can be the case, for example, of many image processing tasks. Nevertheless, in many NLP problems, they can have different sizes. In our case, the intermediate code always has the same length, l, as the input, but the length of the output can be different. The end of the output is determined by the production of an <eos> symbol. Thus, a more precise diagram of the model is presented in Figure 5.

There is a trend in using Long Short-Term Memory (LSTM) neural networks as encoders and decoders (for example, Sutskever et al. [17]) due to their ability to capture long dependencies among the elements of a sequence. Our proposed model uses an LSTM network as decoder. However, different encoders have been analyzed, including the proposed one, and their performances have been tested and compared.

Besides, some additional techniques that are common in the deep learning field were applied to improve the effectiveness of the system, such as batch processing (processing the input in batches of a certain size), dropout [18,19] (randomly removing some neurons with a given probability), weight normalization [20] (regularizing the weights of the neuronal layers), gradient clipping [21] (limiting the norm of the gradient), and decaying learning rate combined with the Adam optimizer [22] (progressively reducing the learning rate used in the backpropagation algorithm).

Attention Mechanisms

The basic encoder–decoder model is a very powerful and useful architecture, but some key issues arise when it is put into practice. Two of them stand out and are worth mentioning: (1) As shown in Figure 4, at each time step, the decoder only works with the code produced at that moment, hindering the usage of long-term dependencies; and (2) output and input need to have the same length, as previously mentioned, limiting its application to many practical problems.

We overcome these two restrictions by making use of attention mechanisms [23]. The idea behind them, depicted in Figure 5, is simple: First, produce the codes of the whole input sequence at once and, at each time step, let the decoder choose the most interesting elements of the input based on the latest output.

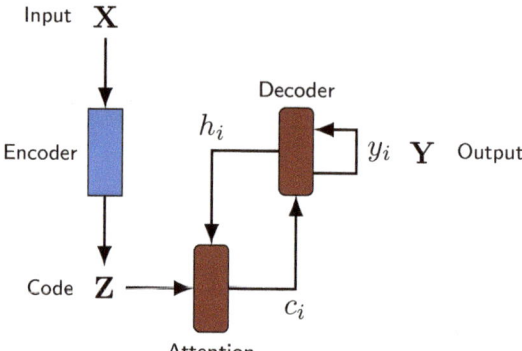

Figure 5. An encoder–decoder architecture with attention mechanism. **X**: Input sequence. **Z**: intermediate code. **Y**: Output sequence. y_i: Output at instant i. c_i: Context coefficients at instant i. h_i: hidden states of the decoder at instant i.

This can be expressed in mathematical terms as follows. Suppose that $Z = z_1 z_2 \ldots z_l$ is the obtained intermediate representation. The attention mechanism consists of a fully connected neural network with one hidden layer, taking as input Z and the vector h_t of the hidden state of the LSTM decoder at each time step t. This network produces a vector of *interesting* features $a \in \mathbb{M}_{f \times 1}$. This vector a describes the characteristics that are expected to be obtained, so it is compared with each column of Z, z_i, using the dot product as a function of similarity. So, a vector $\alpha \in \mathbb{M}_{1 \times l}$ is generated in this way:

$$\alpha = \alpha_1 \alpha_2 \ldots \alpha_l = (a \cdot z_1, a \cdot z_2 \ldots a \cdot z_l) \tag{1}$$

Then, this vector α is transformed into a stochastic vector, i.e., a vector such that $\sum \alpha_i = 1$, via:

$$\alpha'_i = \frac{\exp \alpha_i}{\sum_j \exp \alpha_j} \tag{2}$$

Now, α'_i represents the interest of the decoder with respect to the i-th element of the code, z_i, at the given time step. With this information, a context vector is produced, that is, a vector representing the portion of the input that is actually interesting for the decoder at this instant. Traditionally, this context vector is given by a weighted sum of the elements of z_i, weighted by α', i.e., $c = \sum_i \alpha'_i z_i$. Another possibility is to select only the code z_i corresponding to the highest α'_i. However, we propose a different approach which consists in selecting several codes with the highest α'_i values. Thus, instead of performing a weighted sum or taking the maximum, a new hyperparameter d is introduced to indicate the number of context elements that are considered. In this way, a context matrix $c \in \mathbb{M}_{f \times d}$ is generated at each time step t, where the i-th column, c_i, corresponds to the vector $\alpha'_j z_j$, where α'_j is the i-th largest value of α'. That is, c_1 corresponds to the largest value of α', c_2 to the second largest value, etc. Subsequently, the decoder receives this context matrix, c, instead of just a context vector.

The idea inspiring this modification is that taking the average of the feature vectors involves a significant loss of information. Instead, by using the d greatest elements, the internal semantic of them is preserved.

2.4. Proposed Causal Feature Encoder

In this paper we propose a new type of encoder, the Causal Feature Extractor (CFE), that can be described as a two-step modification of a traditional CNN. The first change is that, instead of using regular convolutions, causal convolutions are applied; this concept was introduced by van den Oord et al. [5]. Figure 6a,b show a basic representation comparing a regular and causal neural network, respectively.

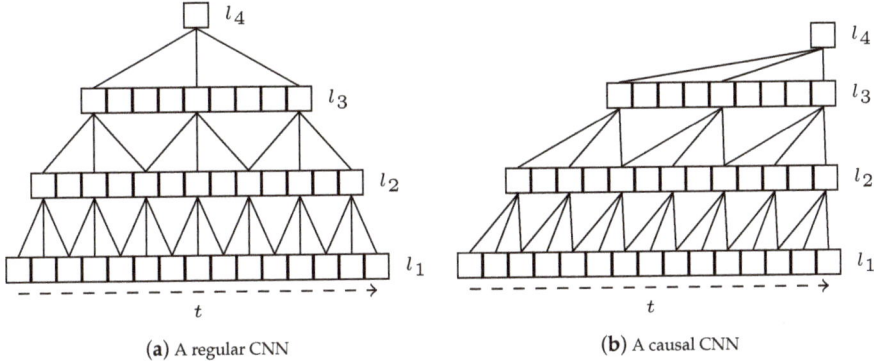

(a) A regular CNN (b) A causal CNN

Figure 6. Comparison between a regular and a causal convolutional neural network, with dilatation coefficient 2. (**a**) Sample regular convolutional neural networks (CNN). (**b**) Sample of the proposed causal CNN. t: Temporal order of the input sequence. l_1: First layer (input sequence). l_2, l_3, l_4: Subsequent convolutional layers.

In a regular one-dimensional convolution, the output for a position t depends on the input values at $\ldots t-2, t-1, t, t+1, t+2 \ldots$ Conversely, in a causal convolution, the output depends only on the inputs previous or posterior to that position, but never both. In other words, the causal convolution for t can use the values $t, t+1, t+2 \ldots$ or $t, t-1, t-2 \ldots$ This idea can be easily extended to images or, in general, to n-dimensional data.

However, a convolution defined in such way only captures dependencies in one direction. To solve this important drawback, we propose a second change. To make the CFE bidirectional, in a similar fashion as it is done with LSTMs. Thereby, it contains two independent models that read the input in each direction, and their outputs are concatenated to produce the encoded representation. We depict this idea in Figure 7.

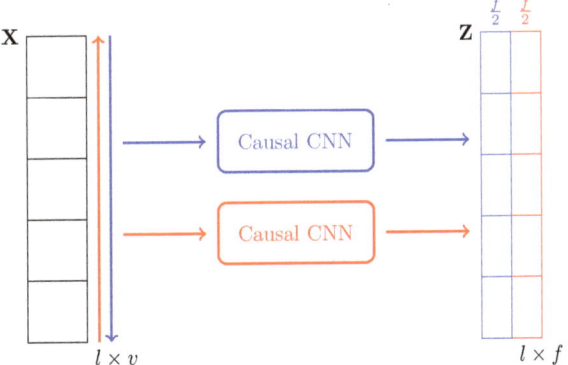

Figure 7. Diagram showing the bidirectionality of the proposed Causal Feature Extractor (CFE) encoder. The intermediate output of the encoder, **Z**, is the concatenation of two causal convolutions in the opposite directions (blue and red), each of them generating $f/2$ features. **X**: Input sequence. l: Length of the input sequence. v: Size of the alphabet in the one-hot encoding. f: Total number of intermediate features.

An additional technique is applied in the proposed encoder. Considering the long sequences that can be found in text normalization (in our datasets, up to 177 characters), we apply dilated convolutions to the convolutional models, as described by van den Oord et al. [5]. This technique consists in doubling the dilatation of each convolutional layer as it goes deeper into the structure, as depicted in Figure 6. So, in the first layer, the convolution for t depends on the input at $t, t-1, t-2\ldots$; in the second layer, it depends on the previous layer at $t, t-2, t-4\ldots$; in the third layer, $t, t-4, t-8\ldots$, and so on. Moreover, the same for the opposite causal direction. By doing that, the actual receptive field of the model (i.e., the initial positions that contribute to the final result) is significantly increased without increasing the number of parameters of the network.

This new encoder has been designed to solve a problem that many applications of CNNs have with attention mechanisms. In previous experiments, it has been observed that CNNs tend to attend the wrong inputs according to our prior intuition. Namely, they choose the $i + C$-th element instead of the i-th element of the input, where C is a certain constant. Our intuition is that this could be caused by the padding introduced in each side of the input. By using causal convolutions, the model is forced to choose the outermost elements if it is interested in those.

2.5. Statistical Significance Test

When comparing the performance of various models, a critical aspect is to ensure that the obtained differences are statistically significant. It must be proved that those differences are significant, and not a mere product of the implicit variance of the training process. This is typically performed using some statistical test that asserts that the differences are actual differences up to some confidence level of probability, usually 95%.

In this paper, we have applied the approximate randomization test [24], also known as random permutation test. This statistical test measures the probability of the outputs of two different models of being indistinguishable, i.e., the probability that, by just looking at the predictions, we cannot tell whether they come from different models. The main reasons for using this method are: (1) It is computationally efficient; (2) it is distribution-free, meaning that it does not make any assumptions on the measured distribution; and (3) it is model-free, that is, the only required resources to perform the test are the actual predictions, making it suitable for any type of model.

Let us assume that the predictions of two different models are the ordered sets $A = \{a_i\}_{i=1}^n$ and $B = \{b_i\}_{i=1}^n$, and we have a function e that measures the similarity of the predictions with respect to the expected values, Y; for example, in our case e is the accuracy measure, defined as the percentage of correctly predicted characters with respect to the length of the output. Then, we can define the function:

$$t(A, B) = e(A, Y) - e(B, Y) \qquad (3)$$

We want to estimate the probability of obtaining an error bigger than $t(A, B)$, assuming that both sets of predictions are indistinguishable, that is $P(X \geq t(A, B) H_0)$, where H_0 is the null hypothesis (i.e., both models are not significantly different).

The algorithm to approximate this value consists in repeating many times the following process: Randomly swap each element of the first set with its counterpart in the second set; and count the number of times that the total error difference, measured by t, is greater or equal than the original one, that is, $t(A, B)$. Figure 8 shows the pseudocode of this algorithm. A small p-value, e.g., below 0.05, 0.02 or 0.01, indicates that the null hypothesis has to be rejected, so the models are significantly different.

In this test, the estimation of the p-value has an error itself, which is given by $\sqrt{p(1-p)/R}$, where p is the obtained p-value, and R is the number of iterations. If this error is too large, the p-value is unreliable; hence, the number of repetitions has to be computed to reduce the error [25]. In order to force the upper bound of the confidence interval of the estimated p being below the decision threshold, we need to find an R such that $l^2 \alpha (1-\alpha)/P^2 \leq R$, where l is the confidence interval. Using P at $\alpha = 0.05$ and requesting a 95% confidence interval, we get $R \geq 7600$. Consequently, that is the number of repetitions used in the tests.

```
A = N predictions from the first model
B = N predictions from the second model

r = 0
from 1 to R:
        X = A
        Y = B
        from i=1 to N:
                swap X[i] and Y[i] with probability 1/2
        if t(X, Y) >= t(A, B):
                r = r + 1

p-value = (r + 1) / (R + 1)
```

Figure 8. Pseudocode of the approximate randomization test. R is the number of repetitions selected. Adapted from [24].

3. Experimental Results

In the following subsections we describe the results obtained in this research, comparing the proposed encoder and other alternative methods. The last subsection is dedicated to the discussion of these results.

3.1. Experimental Setup

Three different experiments have been performed using different subsets of the filtered database, in order to analyze different aspects of the proposed model. The first two datasets are used to test and compare different models, whereas the latter is used to train the final model. Table 1 shows their name, training time, number of training/test/validation samples, and how the samples were selected; *random* means that they were randomly taken, and *shortest* that the elements with shortest outputs were selected. In all the cases, the validation and test size is 1/5 of the training size, and all the sets are disjoint.

Table 1. Description of the datasets used in the experiments. Name: Dataset identifier. Duration: Time used for training the models. Training size: Number of samples used for training. Test/validation size: Number of samples used for test and for validation. Selection: Sample selection criteria.

Name	Duration	Training Size	Test/Validation Size	Selection
E1	1 h	50,000	10,000	shortest
E2	12 h	50,000	10,000	random
E3	22 h	1,000,000	200,000	random

Training time is a key parameter in most deep learning systems, since it can determine the practical feasibility of a given method. Thus, accuracy is closely related with computational efficiency. For this reason, the comparison in the datasets is done by setting the duration of the training process, rather than fixing the number of training iterations or until reaching convergence.

For the execution of the experiments, all the computations were done in a remote server via secure shell and distributed between three NVIDIA GeForce GTX1080 GPUs (each experiment using a single GPU), in a computer with an i7-5930K Intel(R) CPU, 12 effective threads (6 with hyperthreading), and 600GB hard disk drive. Regarding the software, the code was mainly written in Python v.3.6, making use of the Pytorch v0.4 framework to build the neural models [26], as well as OpenNMT [27]. The latest is a neural machine translation toolkit used to speed up the process of solving and testing different problem solutions.

3.2. Proposed Methods and Number of Parameters

As stated before, the presented encoder–decoder architecture for text normalization was implemented in Python, using Pytorch and OpenNMT. In order to analyze whether the proposed CFE achieves a significant improvement, different existing encoders were taken into account. These alternative encoders (and their aliases) are the following:

LSTM   A 3 layer bidirectional LSTM network.

FCNN   A 4 layer fully CNN encoder, where the i-th element is an embedding of the i-th input, i.e., the encoded value only depends on the i-th input value.

    FE   A traditional CNN with dilated convolutions. This is similar to the proposed CFE, but without considering causality.

   CFE   The proposed Causal Feature Extractor encoder.

In all these cases, the only modification on the architecture resides in the the encoder. The decoder and attention mechanism remain always the same, that is, as they were described in the previous section. The hyperparameters of the models were manually tuned by trial and error, trying to obtain the best results. After that, the results presented here are averaged over five repetitions of the same models trained with different random seeds. Table 2 presents the selected hyperparameters.

Table 2. Hyperparameters of the models used in the experiments.

Symbol	Description	Value
b	Batch size	128
f	Number of features produced by the encoder	256
s	Size of the internal hidden vectors of LSTM	128
d	Number of columns of the context matrix	10
ml	Number of neurons of the intermediate dense networks	256
w	Width of the convolutional filters	5
rf	Receptive field to be considered in the input	10
lr	Initial learning rate of Adam algorithm	0.001
β	Multiplier used in the decay of the learning rate	0.85
$step$	Number of iterations before applying the decay	400
p_d	Probability of disabling a neuron in the dropout	0.5
p_t	Probability of substituting a weight by expected value	0.4
$clip$	Upper limit of the norm of the gradient in the clipping	5

The number of parameters of the four models used in the experiments are shown in Table 3. These values correspond to the number of trainable parameters, i.e., the weights of the neural networks of each model, considering the encoder and the whole model. In general, the more parameters, the greater the complexity of the model is (and the greater the memory and time requirements are). So, for a similar performance, simpler models are usually preferred.

Table 3. Number of internal parameters of the models compared (in millions), considering only the encoder and the entire model (encoder + attention mechanism + decoder).

Number of Parameters of	LSTM	FCNN	FE	CFE
Encoder (millions)	1.102	0.285	0.111	0.111
Total (millions)	7.380	6.653	6.479	6.479

It can be observed that LSTM requires nearly 10 times more parameters than FE and CFE, while FCNN requires 2.5 times more parameters. This translates into a lower efficiency and speed of convergence of these models. In any case, the rest of the system (attention and decoder) has a considerably larger number of parameters, with about 6.3 million values that have to be trained. To initialize these parameters, the uniform method of Xavier [28] was used.

3.3. First Experiment

The purpose of this first experiment is to compare the accuracy achieved by the different methods in a reduced setup using the shortest entries containing: 50,000 training samples, 10,000 test samples, and 10,000 validation samples, as presented in Table 1. These values have been chosen so that the number of samples is large enough to train an accurate normalization model, but also small enough to require a reasonable training time that allows multiple repetitions. Specifically, training is limited to only 1 h in all cases. The obtained results are shown in Table 4. Observe that these results are averaged over 5 runs and extracted from the test set, except from the results concerning the training speed, which are taken from the training logs. From left to right, the columns of Table 4 indicate the following parameters:

- Negative Log-Likelihood Loss (NLLLoss). It is the measure optimized by the neural networks during training, since it is the common measure used in classification problems.
- Character Error Rate (CER). It is defined as the mean Levenshtein distance [29] between the prediction and the expected value, that is, the minimum number of character insertions/deletions/substitutions required to change one sentence into the other, for all the test samples.
- Accuracy. It is a basic and well-known measure, defined as the percentage of correct output values, measured at a character level.
- Number of iterations performed during the training phase in the duration of the experiment (in this case 1 h).
- Rate. Number of iterations per second, on average, achieved during training.

Table 4. Results obtained by the four models for the first experiment (E1). Encoder: Name of the encoder used. NLLLoss: Negative log-likelihood loss. CER: Character error rate. Acc (%): Accuracy. No. iters: Number of iterations. Rate: Iterations per second.

Encoder	Test			Validation	
	NLLLoss	CER (%)	Acc (%)	No. Iters	Rate
LSTM	1.352	3.13	95.87	3620	1.005
FCNN	5.035	70.61	28.40	4370	1.214
FE	1.042	2.52	96.46	6980	1.939
CFE	0.952	2.24	96.83	6300	1.750

In order to get an in-depth view of the differences in the training process, Figure 9 shows the evolution of the NLLLoss of the validation samples for each model during training. Table 5 shows the resulting *p*-values after running the approximate randomization test for each pair of models.

In this first experiment, CFE is clearly able to achieve the best results in terms of accuracy, CER and NLLLoss of the test set. It is interesting to observe that, although LSTM, FE and CFE tend to converge to the same NLLLoss values on the validation set, as shown in Figure 9, the differences are more prominent on the test set. Thus, the proposed method has a greater capacity for generalization on previously unobserved samples. Moreover, the statistical tests in Table 5 prove that these differences are significant. The probability that the results from FE and CFE are equivalent is below 2%. FCNN was unable to provide correct results, producing a very large character error rate. Concerning the computational efficiency, FE was able to execute almost 2 iterations per second. CFE is a 10% slower, but it is faster than the remaining methods.

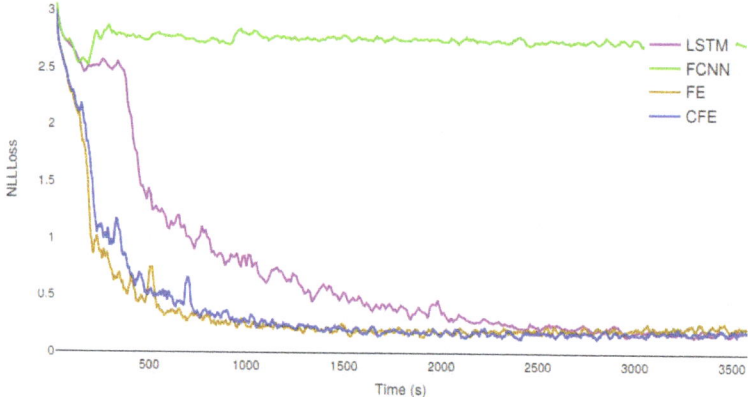

Figure 9. Evolution of the validation error (NLLLoss) during training of the four models on E1.

Table 5. *p*-Values of the first experiment (E1), indicating the probability of the null hypothesis, i.e., the probability that the results of the models are not distinguishable.

p-Value	LSTM	FCNN	FE	CFE
LSTM		0.0001	0.0001	0.0026
FCNN	0.0001		0.0001	0.0001
FE	0.0001	0.0001		0.0184
CFE	0.0026	0.0001	0.0184	

3.4. Second Experiment

The objective of the second experiment is to compare the four encoders in a more complex scenario, where the samples were selected with more varied sizes. The number of samples of the training, test and validation datasets is the same as in the first experiment, but the samples are randomly selected from the whole dataset, with sizes varying at random between 1 and 177 characters (the maximum allowed length of the output, as justified in Section 2.1).

As before, Table 6 presents the accuracy measures obtained by the four encoders for the second experiment. Figure 10 and Table 7 show the evolution of the validation error and the results of the statistical tests, respectively.

Table 6. Results obtained by the four models for the second experiment (E2). Encoder: Name of the encoder used. NLLLoss: Negative log-likelihood loss. CER: Character error rate. Acc (%): Accuracy. No. iters: Number of iterations. Rate: Iterations per second.

Encoder	Test			Validation	
	NLLLoss	CER (%)	Acc (%)	No. Iters	Rate
LSTM	3.310	25.59	71.06	8900	0.206
FCNN	5.396	82.09	17.90	17 750	0.411
FE	2.680	11.93	83.38	36 650	0.848
CFE	2.686	12.69	83.45	36 200	0.838

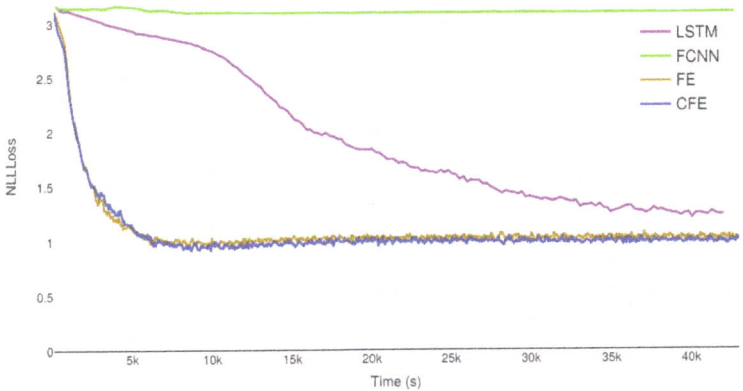

Figure 10. Evolution of the validation error (NLLLoss) during training of the four models on E2.

Table 7. *p*-Values of the second experiment (E2), indicating the probability of the null hypothesis, i.e., the results of the models are not distinguishable.

p-Value	LSTM	FCNN	FE	CFE
LSTM		0.0001	0.0001	0.0001
FCNN	0.0001		0.0001	0.0001
FE	0.0001	0.0001		0.0003
CFE	0.0001	0.0001	0.0003	

Again, FE and CFE are the two best encoders, being able to achieve an accuracy above 83.3%, while LSTM only obtains a 71%. Moreover, FCNN is unable to function properly, with a poor 17.9%. In fact, all the performance measures of FE and CFE are very close, and so are their computational efficiencies. However, the statistical test, which is performed on the accuracy parameter, proves that CFE is significantly better than FE; the probability that they are indistinguishable is only 0.03%. Overall, the obtained results indicate that this experiment is far more complex than E1, which had a best accuracy of 96.8%. Moreover, the training time in E2 is 12 h, while it was only 1 h for E1. Figure 10 suggests that LSTM would need even more time to reach convergence; it not only performs fewer iterations per second, but it requires more iterations to converge.

3.5. Third Experiment

Unlike the other experiments, the purpose of dataset E3 is not to compare the different encoders, but to train the final architecture of the proposed CFE method with a more complete and complex input, in order to compare the obtained results with other state-of-the-art works reported in the literature. Therefore, the training set contains 1 million samples, and the test and validation sets have 200,000 samples each.

The architecture is identical to the one used in the previous experiments, with the hyperparameters presented in Table 2, and five repetitions. Figure 11 depicts the evolution of the training and validation errors during the training phase, and Table 8 shows the accuracy measures obtained for the test set.

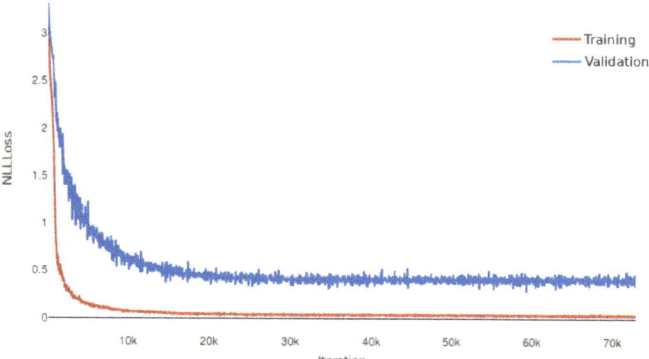

Figure 11. Evolution of the training (red) and validation (blue) errors (NLLLoss) for the proposed CFE encoder using dataset E3. In this case, the horizontal scale represents the number of iterations. The training time was 22 h.

Table 8. Results obtained by the proposed CFE encoder for the third experiment (E3). Encoder: Name of the encoder used. NLLLoss: Negative log-likelihood loss. CER: Character error rate. Acc (%): Accuracy.

	Test		
Encoder	NLLLoss	CER (%)	Acc (%)
CFE	1.701	5.44	92.74

The accuracy measures achieved for E3 are between those obtained for E1 and E2, with a mean accuracy of 92.74% and a CER of 5.44. This indicates that although the test cases are more complex and varied than E2, having a larger training set is beneficial for the system. On the other hand, Figure 11 seems to indicate that convergence was reached long before the 22 h duration of the experiment.

3.6. Attention Matrices

In order to analyze whether the CFE encoder makes a better usage of the attention mechanisms than its non-causal counterpart, it is interesting to observe some actual examples and the attention matrices that they generate. These matrices are a representation of the decoder focus of interest while it was processing the input: The i-th row represents the i-th predicted character, and the j-th column is the model focus while predicting that character, i.e., the values of α'_i (see Equation (2)).

The first case, shown in Table 9, is an example extracted from the test set of the first experiment, E1. The input phrase is "23 Aug 2013". Regarding what would be ideally expected from the attention matrix, it should show three different phases: (1) First, it outputs the day while focusing on its digits; (2) then, the attention is moved towards the month; and (3) it finishes by looking at the year. Figure 12 shows the four attention matrices obtained.

Table 9. Predictions obtained by the four different models for a selected sample case in the experiment E1. The output produced by FCNN is incorrect since it falls in an infinite loop.

Input		23 Aug 2013.
Output		the twenty third of august twenty thirteen .
LSTM	✓	the twenty third of august twenty thirteen .
FCNN	✗	the twent t t eeeeeeeeeeeeeeeeeeee...
FE	✓	the twenty third of august twenty thirteen .
CFE	✓	the twenty third of august twenty thirteen .

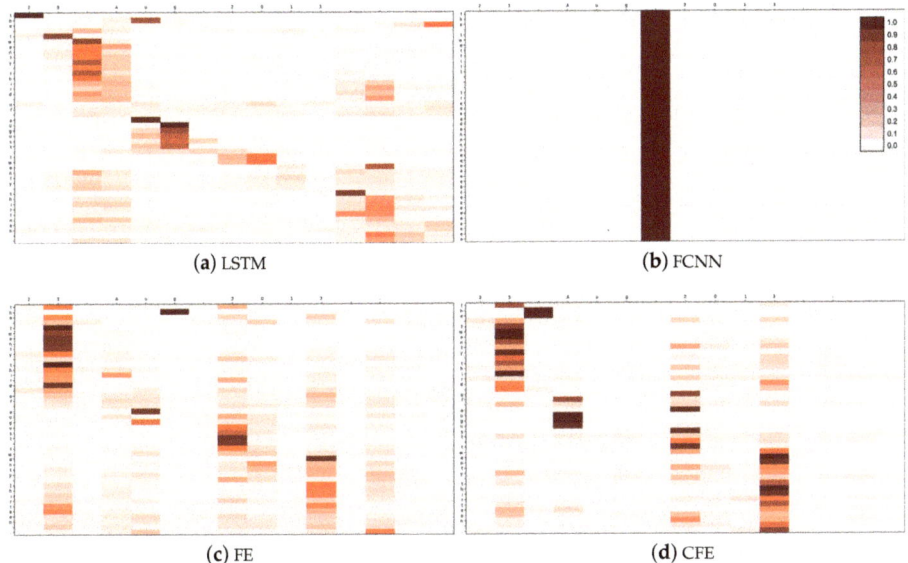

Figure 12. Attention matrices obtained by the four models for the sample selected from E1, shown in Table 9. The input sentence (horizontal axis) is *"23 Aug 2013"*. The values represented are the attention coefficients, α'_i (see Equation (2)); a darker color represents a larger value.

The matrix obtained by CFE (Figure 12d) is the one that most closely resembles what one would expect from a useful attention mechanism. It clearly presents the three phases of this prediction, in which the system selects the day, the month and the year. FE and LSTM also follow this scheme, although not so clearly defined.

The second prediction selected to exemplify the use of the attention mechanism is taken from the test set of the second experiment, E2. It corresponds to the input sentence *"Belpiela is a community in Tamale Metropolitan District in the Northern Region of Ghana."* This sample has been specifically selected because it is a longer case where the input and output are identical; thus, the ideally expected attention matrices should resemble an identity matrix. Table 10 shows the predictions obtained by the four models, whereas Figure 13 depicts the corresponding attention matrices.

Table 10. Predictions obtained by the four different models for a selected sample case in the experiment E2. Only the output obtained by CFE is correct.

Input		*Belpiela is a community in Tamale Metropolitan District in the Northern Region of Ghana.*
Output		*Belpiela is a community in Tamale Metropolitan District in the Northern Region of Ghana.*
LSTM	✗	*Belpiela is a community in Tamale Metropolitan Disire egion te i e ...*
FCNN	✗	*Th ...*
FE	✗	*Belpiela is a community in Tamale Metropolitan District in the Northern Region Region of Ghana .*
CFE	✓	*Belpiela is a community in Tamale Metropolitan District in the Northern Region of Ghana .*

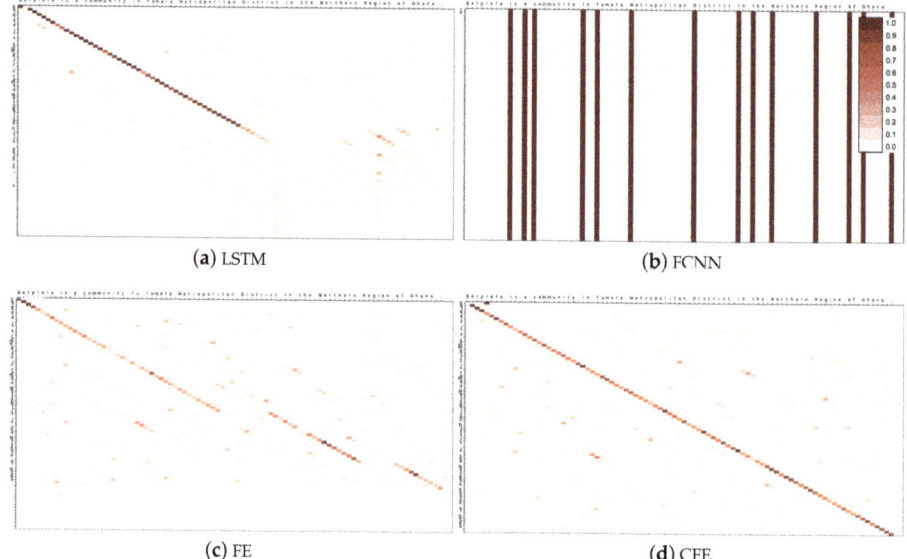

Figure 13. Attention matrices obtained by the four models for the sample selected from E2, shown in Table 10. The input sentence (horizontal axis) is *"Belpiela is a community in Tamale Metropolitan District in the Northern Region of Ghana."* The values represented are the attention coefficients, α'_i (see Equation (2)); a darker color represents a larger value.

Again, CFE is the only model that is able to produce a valid attention matrix, clearly resembling an identity. For this reason, it is the only method that was able to predict the correct output in this case. FE has a similar shape, but it produces some gaps which lead to a repetition of the word "Region" in the output.

3.7. Analysis of the Types of Errors

After analyzing the errors made by the proposed CFE method, we have observed that most of these errors can be classified into a reduced set of types. To get a better understanding of these types, all the incorrect predictions of CFE for the test set of the third experiment, E3, were dumped and classified by hand. Based on these observations, the taxonomy of error types has been defined as follows:

- T1. Infinite loop errors. The attention system of the model gets stuck and the maximum number of printed characters is reached. For example:

    Input   Ruppert, Edward E.; Fox, Richard, S.; Barnes, Robert D. (2004).
    Output   Ruppert, Edward e; Fox, Richard, s; Barnes, Robert d (two thousand four).
    Prediction Ruppert, Edward e; Fox, Richard, s R s , , , , , , , , , , , , , , , , , , , ...

- T2. Coincidental errors. Predictions where only a few isolated characters are wrongly printed. For example:

    Input   The income was $11,091.
    Output   The income was eleven thousand ninety one dollars.
    Prediction The income was fleven thousand ninety one dollars.

- T3. Early stop errors. Errors where the model finishes before processing the whole input. For example:

Input	Parmentier, Bruno (1 May 2000).
Output	Parmentier, Bruno (the first of may two thousand).
Prediction	Parmentier, Bruno (.

- T4. (Finite) jumps. The attention model finds the same pattern in the entry and repeats/oversees a part of it. For example:

Input	According to the 2011 census of India, Bhisenagar has 818 households.
Output	According to the twenty eleven census of India, Bhisenagar has eight hundred eighteen households.
Prediction	According to the twenty eleven census of India, Bhisenagar has eighteen households.

An automatic classification tool has been implemented in order to (approximately) quantify the errors according to their type. The results are shown in Table 11 where *Others* refers to the errors unclassified by the tool. Note that errors produced by jumps are not detected by the tool, since they can have different forms, but they represent a big portion of the unclassified errors.

Table 11. Distribution of the main types of errors made by the proposed CFE encoder for the test set of experiment E3.

Type	T1	T2	T3	Others	Total
Quantity	23,381	7159	50	10,696	41,286
Percentage (%)	56.63	17.34	0.12	25.9	100

As shown, more than half of the errors are produced by infinite loops. These are caused by a malfunction of the attention mechanism, that returns to a previously treated character. The same reason could be inferred for the errors of type T3, but these represent only a 0.12%. On the other hand, the errors of type T2 are most probably due to deficiencies in the decoder. Moreover, the category Others can be due to any component of the system.

Besides these types of errors, it is worth-mentioning that some observed errors were caused by the dataset itself, which contains some examples whose expected output is debatable (or simply incorrect). This was also observed by Sproat and Jaitly in [6], who estimated this error in a 0.1% of the total (although it was done in a manual analysis of only 1000 samples). These come from different sources, for example, from inconsistent rules for normalizing text among different entries, such as spelling or not spelling an acronym:

Input	Uppsala: Sprak och folkminnesinstitutet (SOFI).
Output	Uppsala: Sprak och folkminnesinstitutet (SOFI).
Prediction	Uppsala: Sprak och folkminnesinstitutet (S o f i).

Input	Chloroformic acid has the formula ClCO 2 H.
Output	Chloroformic acid has the formula c l c o two H.
Prediction	Chloroformic acid has the formula ClCO two H.

Or providing a few entries for rare cases that resemble too much to other more common cases:

Input	1980 A engine added to Transporter (T 3).
Output	one nine eight o A engine added to Transporter (T three).
Prediction	nineteen eighty A engine added to Transporter (T three).

Or inconsistencies in the entries (e.g., American vs British English):

Input	The mobilisation was announced by the mayor.
Output	The mobilization was announced by the mayor.

Prediction   The mobilisation was announced by the mayor.

Input   The Robinsons are a family in the soap opera Neighbours.
Output   The Robinsons are a family in the soap opera neighbors.
Prediction   The Robinsons are a family in the soapera Neighbors.

The proposed model also shows special difficulties deciding whether it should maintain capital letters on the predictions or not. This last sample also contains an example of overseeing parts of the input, probably because of the similarities between the words *soap* and *opera*. Another example of such jumps, in this case going backward in the input and thus repeating words, is the following:

Input   The primary east west highway passing through Belmont is interstate 85.
Output   The primary east west highway passing through Belmont is interstate eighty five.
Prediction   The primary east west west west highway passing through Belmont is interstate eighty five.

Which happened because the model confounds the suffix of *west* with the one of *east* as it can be seen on Figure 14. Attention matrices can be displayed for all these errors, shedding light on the underlying attention-related issues, except for the coincidental errors.

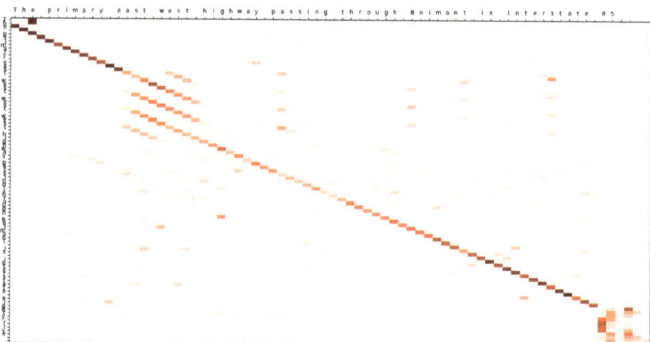

Figure 14. Attention matrix for a backwards finite jump error. The input sentence (horizontal axis) is "The primary east west highway passing through Belmont is interstate 85." and the predicted output (vertical axis) is "The primary east west west west highway passing through Belmont is interstate eighty five."

Finally, is it worth-noting the role of undetectable errors, since they were observed in previous works in the literature [6]. This type of error also appeared in the analyzed cases, as in the example shown for error type T4. However, in all the cases, they are a realization of another type of error that happens to be undetectable by chance, so the source of the error can be explained and solved. For example, the aforementioned error occurs as an occurrence of a jump error where the model confounds the first *8* with the third one of *818* when processing the input.

4. Discussion

This section discusses the results presented in Section 3. More specifically, the main questions raised in Section 1 can be formulated as follows:

1.   Can the problem of text normalization be solved solely by means of neural networks?
2.   Is such a solution viable using convolutional components? Which encoder is better?

Answering the first question, the most obvious result that we can extract based on any of the results from E1 and E2 (for example, Figure 10), is that the FCNN encoder does not work at all. Most probably, this erratic behavior comes from the differentiating feature of FCNN, that is, it extracts information from a single character of the input (instead of a neighborhood of it). This is a clear proof of an expected result: In order to work properly, the decoder cannot act on its own; extracting high level features from the surrounding characters is essential. So, the FCNN model should be discarded.

By looking at the second experiment, we can observe a significant difference between LSTM and its convolutional counterparts. Specifically, Table 6 shows that the accuracy of the convolutional encoders is about 12% higher than the LSTM encoder. Nevertheless, it could be the case that LSTM only needs more time to reach convergence. This leads us to the major differences between them: Number of parameters, convergence time, and iteration time. Three points strengthen this argument:

- Table 3 shows that the number of parameters of the LSTM encoder is ten times bigger than those of the convolutional encoders, making it harder to train and more expensive to use.
- Figures 9 and 10 indicate that the LSTM encoder started to converge in E2 after 2 h 45 min of training, whereas the convolutional encoders were close to their minimum at 1 h 23 min.
- Regarding the iteration speed, Tables 4 and 6 show that, besides being more accurate, the convolutional encoders operate around 2 and 4 times faster than the LSTM encoder, respectively.

This phenomenon can be explained by three reasons: (1) The aforementioned difference in the number of parameters; (2) the existence of recursive connections in LSTM, making it harder to optimize; and (3) the fact that convolutional networks run very fast on GPUs. Hence, this ensures that convolution-based encoders are viable, significantly faster, and statistically distinguishable from recurrent encoders (as proved by the tests in Table 7).

This solves the first part of question 2, whereas the second part concerns the selection of the best convolutional encoder. As show in Table 6, both encoders are quantitatively very similar, even though CFE obtains slightly better results and is distinguishable from FE. Qualitatively, CFE presents some advantages over FE regarding the attention mechanism:

- The first comparative of the attention matrices, Figure 12, shows that the three encoders behave in a similar fashion. However, CFE seems cleaner and more localized, since it knows better where to focus, distinguishing the three phases of this sample: Day, month, and year.
- The second comparative graphic, Figure 13, is even clearer. LSTM did not converge yet, so its prediction is far from the expected result. Regarding the convolutional encoders, CFE gets the example right, its attention matrix seems clean, and it resembles an identity matrix; whereas FE struggles to maintain the focus (many non-diagonal elements have taken attention) and makes erratic leaps (which results in missing words in the prediction, see Table 10).

Thus, it can be concluded that, in this case, CFE is preferable to FE due to its qualitative benefits and, to a lesser extent, its quantitative results. Regarding the undetectable errors reported in Sproat and Jaitly [6], it can be firmly confirmed that they are not an issue in these models as they appear by chance due to solvable errors. Specifically, these errors are highly related with the attention mechanism, as Table 11 shows, since the most common error is getting stuck in an infinite loop. These problems cause the model to lose focus and jump around when confounding similar parts of the input. Therefore, this could be greatly improved by using more sophisticated attention models that, for example, focus on local neighborhoods, take into account the index, or force the model to put more focus in the next character of the input.

Finally, we discuss the results obtained on the third experiment. Figure 11 shows that, during training, the model quickly converged. There is a gap between training and generalization error that the model has not been able to solve. However, the results obtained on the test set are very promising: It achieved 92.74% accuracy and 5.44% CER, against the 99.8% accuracy and 13.43% CER obtained by the models of Sproat and Jaitly [6] and Ikeda et al. [9], respectively. However, this comparison with previous works has to be carefully taken, since there are differences that do not allow a direct comparison. For example, in the case of [6], the dataset contains about 40 million sentences. This is translated into training times between 5 and 10 days using a system with eight GPUs. Compared to that, our method used 1 million sentences from the same dataset, and the training time was 22 h with 1 GPU. The difference is also in the underlying model of the encoder, which is a 4-layer bidirectional LSTM in [6] and the convolutional CFE encoder in our case, both working at character level. Lastly, in order to achieve the best accuracy of 99.8%, an additional finite state filter is applied to guide the decoding, while our method is exclusively based on neural networks.

Considering the second work, by Ikeda et al. [9], it must be noted that it is specific for Japanese text normalization. The system is also based on an encoder–decoder architecture, using bidirectional recurrent neural networks in the encoder, working at character-level. Nevertheless, the corpus is quite different, containing a set of over 200,000 synthesized sentences using 3500 Kanji characters; the training time was not reported.

Consequently, we consider that the results obtained by the proposed CFE are promising, and point out a viable direction to solve the problem of text normalization in a data-driven fashion. It is computationally less expensive than LSTMs, and the analysis of the errors has shown that it not prone to produce undetectable or unrecoverable errors, thus answering question 1.

5. Conclusions

In this paper, a new encoder–decoder architecture with attention mechanisms has been proposed for the problem of text normalization, using a character-level approach and introducing a new type of encoder. This encoder, called Causal Feature Extractor, is a novel technique designed to work properly in cooperation with the attention mechanisms. The experiments have empirically proven that this method is able to achieve very positive results, using the attention matrices more like it would be expected. Besides, it is able to work at least as good as the best of the compared encoders, and it brings all the benefits of using convolutional neural networks (e.g., computational efficiency and fast convergence). The last aspect that distinguishes this encoder from the traditional recurrent encoders is its simplicity to be adapted to other input layouts (for example, sound, images or video). Another contribution is the introduction of a new variation of the attention mechanisms, by using a context matrix instead of a vector.

Regarding previous works, the initial results have shown to be close to the state of the art, with much room for future improvements. Despite getting worse accuracy than the method presented in [6] (92.74% vs. 99.8%), it does not critically suffer from unrecoverable errors, nor it seems to concentrate its errors on any particular semiotic class, since most errors are attention-based; besides, the proposed method is less computationally expensive and does not include additional rule-based filters.

From a general point of view, an interesting result that can be extracted is the empirical proof that empowers the role of encoders in the encoder–decoder architectures. It has been shown that the system does not work correctly if it only takes features of single elements (without considering their neighborhood).

Future research lines could focus on some aspects such as applying the proposed CFE encoder as a general-purpose encoder in different tasks of natural language processing. In particular, applications to audio and images are already being studied. It is also interesting to develop new methods for hyperparameter selection in order to obtain better results. The models have a large number of hyperparameters, and each execution of the system can take several hours. Finally, future works could consider conditioning the model to external factors, for example, to distinguish between British and American English.

Author Contributions: Conceptualization, A.J. and G.G.-M.; methodology, A.J. and G.G.-M.; software, A.J.; validation, A.J. and G.G.-M.; formal analysis, A.J.; investigation, A.J. and G.G.-M.; resources, A.J.; data curation, A.J.; writing–original draft preparation, A.J.; writing–review and editing, A.J. and G.G.-M.; visualization, A.J.; supervision, G.G.-M. All authors have read and agreed to the published version of the manuscript.

Funding: This research was funded by Spanish Ministry of Science, Innovation and Universities, FEDER funds, under grant RTI2018-095855-B-I00 (G.G.-M.).

Acknowledgments: We would like to express our gratitude to Richard Sproat for his useful feedback on this article. Besides, Adrián acknowledges support from the Max Planck Institute for Intelligent Systems.

Conflicts of Interest: The authors declare no conflict of interest.

Abbreviations

The following abbreviations are used in this manuscript:

NLP	Natural language processing
TTS	Text-to-speech
CNN	Convolutional Neural Networks
LSTM	Long Short-Term Memory
FCNN	Fully Convolutional Neural Network
FE	Feature Encoder
CFE	Causal Feature Encoder
NLLLoss	Negative Log-Likelihood Loss
CER	Character Error Rate
Acc	Accuracy

References

1. Dabre, R.; Chu, C.; Kunchukuttan, A. A Comprehensive Survey of Multilingual Neural Machine Translation. *arXiv* **2020**, arXiv:2001.01115.
2. Gambhir, M.; Gupta, V. Recent automatic text summarization techniques: A survey. *Artif. Intell. Rev.* **2017**, *47*, 1–66. [CrossRef]
3. Gatt, A.; Krahmer, E. Survey of the state of the art in natural language generation: Core tasks, applications and evaluation. *J. Artif. Intell. Res.* **2018**, *61*, 65–170. [CrossRef]
4. Minaee, S.; Kalchbrenner, N.; Cambria, E.; Nikzad, N.; Chenaghlu, M.; Gao, J. Deep Learning Based Text Classification: A Comprehensive Review. *arXiv* **2020**, arXiv:2004.03705.
5. Van den Oord, A.; Dieleman, S.; Zen, H.; Simonyan, K.; Vinyals, O.; Graves, A.; Kalchbrenner, N.; Senior, A.W.; Kavukcuoglu, K. WaveNet: A Generative Model for Raw Audio. In Proceedings of the 9th ISCA Speech Synthesis Workshop, Sunnyvale, CA, USA, 13–15 September 2016; p. 125.
6. Sproat, R.; Jaitly, N. RNN Approaches to Text Normalization: A Challenge. *arXiv* **2016**, arXiv:1611.00068.
7. Sproat, R. Multilingual text analysis for text-to-speech synthesis. *Nat. Lang. Eng.* **1996**, *2*, 369–380. [CrossRef]
8. Sodimana, K.; Silva, P.D.; Sproat, R.; Theeraphol, A.; Li, C.F.; Gutkin, A.; Sarin, S.; Pipatsrisawat, K. Text Normalization for Bangla, Khmer, Nepali, Javanese, Sinhala, and Sundanese TTS Systems. In Proceedings of the 6th International Workshop on Spoken Language Technologies for Under-Resourced Languages (SLTU-2018), Gurugram, India, 29–31 August 2018; pp. 147–151.
9. Ikeda, T.; Shindo, H.; Matsumoto, Y. Japanese Text Normalization with Encoder–Decoder Model. In Proceedings of the 2nd Workshop on Noisy User-generated Text, NUT@COLING 2016, Osaka, Japan, 11 December 2016; pp. 129–137.
10. Arora, M.; Kansal, V. Character level embedding with deep convolutional neural network for text normalization of unstructured data for Twitter sentiment analysis. *Soc. Netw. Anal. Min.* **2019**, *9*, 12. [CrossRef]
11. Zhang, H.; Sproat, R.; Ng, A.H.; Stahlberg, F.; Peng, X.; Gorman, K.; Roark, B. Neural models of text normalization for speech applications. *Comput. Linguist.* **2019**, *45*, 293–337. [CrossRef]
12. Roark, B.; Sproat, R.; Allauzen, C.; Riley, M.; Sorensen, J.; Tai, T. The OpenGrm open-source finite-state grammar software libraries. In Proceedings of the ACL 2012 System Demonstrations, Jeju Island, Korea, 10 July 2012; pp. 61–66.
13. Xu, K.; Ba, J.; Kiros, R.; Cho, K.; Courville, A.C.; Salakhutdinov, R.; Zemel, R.S.; Bengio, Y. Show, Attend and Tell: Neural Image Caption Generation with Visual Attention. In Proceedings of the 32nd International Conference on Machine Learning, ICML 2015, Lille, France, 6–11 July 2015; pp. 2048–2057.
14. Chung, J.; Cho, K.; Bengio, Y. A Character-level Decoder without Explicit Segmentation for Neural Machine Translation. In Proceedings of the 54th Annual Meeting of the Association for Computational Linguistics, ACL 2016, Berlin, Germany, 7–12 August 2016; Volume 1: Long Papers.
15. Lee, J.; Cho, K.; Hofmann, T. Fully Character-Level Neural Machine Translation without Explicit Segmentation. *Trans. Assoc. Comput. Linguist.* **2017**, *5*, 365–378. [CrossRef]
16. Cho, K.; Van Merriënboer, B.; Bahdanau, D.; Bengio, Y. On the properties of neural machine translation: Encoder–decoder approaches. *arXiv* **2014**, arXiv:1409.1259.

17. Sutskever, I.; Vinyals, O.; Le, Q.V. Sequence to Sequence Learning with Neural Networks. In Proceedings of the Advances in Neural Information Processing Systems 27: Annual Conference on Neural Information Processing Systems 2014, Montreal, QC, Canada, 8–13 December 2014; pp. 3104–3112.
18. Srivastava, N.; Hinton, G.; Krizhevsky, A.; Sutskever, I.; Salakhutdinov, R. Dropout: A simple way to prevent neural networks from overfitting. *J. Mach. Learn. Res.* **2014**, *15*, 1929–1958.
19. Baldi, P.; Sadowski, P. The dropout learning algorithm. *Artif. Intell.* **2014**, *210*, 78–122. [CrossRef] [PubMed]
20. Salimans, T.; Kingma, D.P. Weight normalization: A simple reparameterization to accelerate training of deep neural networks. In Proceedings of the 30th Conference on Neural Information Processing Systems (NIPS 2016), Barcelona, Spain, 5–10 December 2016; pp. 901–909.
21. Pascanu, R.; Mikolov, T.; Bengio, Y. On the difficulty of training recurrent neural networks. In Proceedings of the International Conference on Machine Learning (ICML 2013), Atlanta, GA, USA, 16–21 June 2013; pp. 1310–1318.
22. Kingma, D.P.; Ba, J. Adam: A method for stochastic optimization. *arXiv* **2014**, arXiv:1412.6980.
23. Bahdanau, D.; Cho, K.; Bengio, Y. Neural Machine Translation by Jointly Learning to Align and Translate. *arXiv* **2014**, arXiv:1409.0473.
24. Riezler, S.; Maxwell, J.T., III. On Some Pitfalls in Automatic Evaluation and Significance Testing for MT. In Proceedings of the Workshop on Intrinsic and Extrinsic Evaluation Measures for Machine Translation and/or Summarization@ACL 2005, Ann Arbor, MI, USA, 29 June 2005; pp. 57–64.
25. Ojala, M.; Garriga, G.C. Permutation tests for studying classifier performance. *J. Mach. Learn. Res.* **2010**, *11*, 1833–1863.
26. Paszke, A.; Gross, S.; Chintala, S.; Chanan, G.; Yang, E.; DeVito, Z.; Lin, Z.; Desmaison, A.; Antiga, L.; Lerer, A. Automatic differentiation in pytorch. In Proceedings of the 31st Conference on Neural Information Processing Systems (NIPS 2017), Long Beach, CA, USA, 4–9 December 2017.
27. Klein, G.; Kim, Y.; Deng, Y.; Senellart, J.; Rush, A.M. Opennmt: Open-source toolkit for neural machine translation. *arXiv* **2017**, arXiv:1701.02810.
28. Glorot, X.; Bengio, Y. Understanding the difficulty of training deep feedforward neural networks. In Proceedings of the Thirteenth International Conference on Artificial Intelligence and Statistics, Sardinia, Italy, 13–15 May 2010; pp. 249–256.
29. Levenshtein, V.I. Binary codes capable of correcting deletions, insertions, and reversals. In *Soviet Physics Doklady*; MAIK Nauka/Interperiodica: Moscow, Rusia, 1966; Volume 10, pp. 707–710.

© 2020 by the authors. Licensee MDPI, Basel, Switzerland. This article is an open access article distributed under the terms and conditions of the Creative Commons Attribution (CC BY) license (http://creativecommons.org/licenses/by/4.0/).

Article
A Polarity Capturing Sphere for Word to Vector Representation

Sandra Rizkallah *, Amir F. Atiya and Samir Shaheen

Faculty of Engineering, Department of Computer Engineering, Cairo University, Giza Governorate 12613, Egypt; amir@alumni.caltech.edu (A.F.A.); sshaheen@eng.cu.edu.eg (S.S.)
* Correspondence: sandrawahid@hotmail.com

Received: 20 May 2020; Accepted: 23 June 2020; Published: 26 June 2020

Abstract: Embedding words from a dictionary as vectors in a space has become an active research field, due to its many uses in several natural language processing applications. Distances between the vectors should reflect the relatedness between the corresponding words. The problem with existing word embedding methods is that they often fail to distinguish between synonymous, antonymous, and unrelated word pairs. Meanwhile, polarity detection is crucial for applications such as sentiment analysis. In this work we propose an embedding approach that is designed to capture the polarity issue. The approach is based on embedding the word vectors into a sphere, whereby the dot product between any vectors represents the similarity. Vectors corresponding to synonymous words would be close to each other on the sphere, while a word and its antonym would lie at opposite poles of the sphere. The approach used to design the vectors is a simple relaxation algorithm. The proposed word embedding is successful in distinguishing between synonyms, antonyms, and unrelated word pairs. It achieves results that are better than those of some of the state-of-the-art techniques and competes well with the others.

Keywords: word to vector; word embeddings; antonymy detection; polarity

1. Introduction

Word vector embeddings seek to model each word as a multi-dimensional vector. There are many distinct benefits to modeling words as vectors. Implementing natural language processing (NLP) algorithms using machine learning models necessitates converting a textual word or sentence to a numeric format. Moreover, this conversion has to be meaningful. For example, words with similar meanings should possess vectors that are in close proximity in the embedded space. This is because such words should produce similar outputs, if applied to a machine learning model. Additionally, a word embedding of a complete dictionary will provide a complete representation of the corpus. In this, each word is assigned to its unique position in the vector space, which reflects its aggregate relations with all other words in one cohesive construct. Word vector spaces have been very useful in many applications; for example, machine translation [1], sentiment analysis [2–5], question answering [6,7], information retrieval [8,9], spelling correction [10], crowdsourcing [11], named entity recognition (NER) [12], text summarization [13–15], and others.

The problem of existing word vector embedding methods is that the polarity of words is not adequately considered. Two antonyms are considered polar opposites, and have to be modeled as such. However, most current methods do not deal with this issue. For example, they do not differentiate in the similarity score between two unrelated words and two opposite words.

In this work we propose a new embedding that takes into account the polarity issue. The new approach is based on embedding the words into a sphere, whereby the dot product of the corresponding vectors represents the similarity in meaning between any two words. The polar nature of the sphere is the main motivation behind such embedding since this way antonymous relations can be captured such that a word and its antonym are placed at opposite poles of the sphere. This polarity capturing feature is essential for some applications such as sentiment analysis. Recently, word embedding methods have started to pervade the sentiment analysis field, at the expense of traditional machine learning algorithms, which rely on sentiment-polarity data that are annotated manually, and expensive feature engineering. Using word embeddings, a sentence can be mapped to a number of features based on the embeddings of its words. However, these embeddings should reflect the polarity of words in order to be able to perform the sentiment analysis task. As mentioned before, this polarity issue is completely addressed in our word embedding approach.

Figure 1 illustrates the concept of the proposed approach. As shown in the figure, the two vectors corresponding to the words "happy" and "joyful" have close similarity because they are synonyms. On the other hand, the vectors corresponding to "happy" and "sad" are on opposite poles and have a similarity score of -1, because they are antonyms. The algorithm can infer a new relation that "joyful" and "sad" are antonyms too, as their corresponding vectors are also placed close to opposite poles of the sphere.

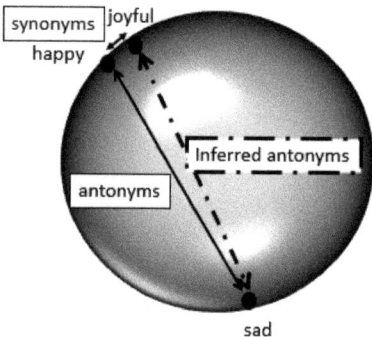

Figure 1. Semi-supervised illustration.

Two words that are similar in meaning are assigned vectors whose similarity measure is 1. Two unrelated words will be assigned a similarity close to zero, and two antonyms are assigned similarity close to -1. In other words, we specifically consider the polarity issue and make a distinction between "opposite" and "unrelated".

The fact that the similarity between opposing words or antonyms is close to -1 is consistent with the logically appealing fact that negation amounts to multiplying by -1. Double negation amounts to multiplying -1 twice, giving a similarity close to one (the antonym of an antonym is a synonym). In our geometry, negation can also be considered as reflection around the origin. Thus, the designed model makes logical sense. Another question to investigate is whether the unrelated words should have similarity close to zero. The answer is yes. It is logical that unrelated words, e.g., "train" and "star", would have their vectors far away from each other, because of our principle that vector similarities or closeness should reflect relatedness. This is consistent with the theory that at a high dimension, the dot product of randomly occurring unit vectors on the sphere is close to zero [16]. The algorithm has a number of beneficial features:

- The proposed algorithm is a very simple relaxation algorithm, and it converges very well and fast. It is simpler than the typically used word to vector design methods, such as neural networks or deep networks.
- We believe that embedding the vectors into a sphere provides a natural representation, unlike distributional models for learning word vector representations and other co-occurrence-based models. Some of these models often fail to distinguish between synonyms and antonyms,

since antonymous words occur in similar context the same way synonymous words do. Other models fail to distinguish between antonymous word pairs and unrelated word pairs.
- The learned word vectors can always be continuously augmented. The database can flexibly be extended to include more words by simply feeding the algorithm with more word pairs with the desired target similarity scores. The algorithm guarantees that these new vectors will be placed correctly with regard to the existing vectors.
- Composite words can also be handled by our algorithm. This is because any word pair with the desired similarity score can be fed into the algorithm . For example, "old-fashioned" is an expression that combines two words: "old" and "fashion"; this combined expression can be given to our algorithm as a synonym to a word that conveys its meaning; e.g., "outdated".
- Generally it is a supervised procedure. The designer typically gives synonyms/antonyms from thesauri or other sources. However, it could also be designed in a semi-supervised setting. This means that in addition to the user-defined similarity scores between the collected words, there could be many more unlabeled pairs that have to be learned from the text pieces available (for example, through co-occurrence arguments). The labeled pairs will provide some anchor around which the unlabeled pairs will organize, and are therefore essential for guiding the correct vector placements. In other words, new relations between word pairs will be inferred from existing ones.

2. Literature Review

One of the earliest word vector embeddings is the work by Mikolov et al. [17], who published the Google word2vec representations of words. Their method relies on the continuous skip-gram model for learning the vectors introduced in [18]. Finding vector representations that predict the surrounding words is the training goal of the skip-gram model. For computational efficiency, the authors have replaced the full softmax with three alternative choices, and evaluated the results for each: hierarchical softmax, noise contrastive estimation, and negative sampling. Moreover, subsampling of frequent words was introduced to speed up the training and leverage the accuracy of word representations.

Pennington et al. [19] have published another approach (called GloVe) of word vector modeling using a method that combines the benefits of the techniques of global matrix factorization and local context window. The authors have suggested the idea of learning the word vector with the ratios of co-occurrence probabilities rather than the probabilities themselves. The result is a new global log-bilinear regression model, where the model directly captures global corpus statistics.

Mikolov et al. [20] developed a model known as fastText that is based on continuous bag-of-words (cbow) used in word2vec [18]. The authors used a combination of known improvements to learn high-quality word vector representations. To obtain higher accuracy, the authors added position-dependent weights and subword features to the cbow model architecture.

Dev et al. [21] developed a technique that aligns word vector representations from different sources such as word2vec [17] and GloVe [19]. The authors extend absolute orientation approaches to work for arbitrary dimensions.

It can be noted that word2vec [17,18], GloVe [19], and fastText [20] are distributional models for learning word vector representations. Words are assigned similarity relations based on co-occurrence in text. The limitation of these models is a weakness in distinguishing antonyms from synonyms because antonymous words such as "good" and "bad" very often occur in similar contexts so their learned vectors will be close. This way it may be hard to figure out whether a pair of words is a pair of synonyms or antonyms. However, such information is crucial for some applications such as sentiment analysis. On the other hand, our approach is a simple relaxation algorithm that takes into account learning word vectors that are able to distinguish between word relations such as synonyms, antonyms, and unrelated words. It is based on embedding the vectors on the sphere. The sphere provides a natural setting for this task, because antonyms can be placed on opposite sides of the sphere. In contrast, most methods embed the vectors in the space R^n, which does not provide a natural way of modeling opposites. The aforementioned models rely on corpus data of huge sizes to guarantee the effectiveness of the generated vectors. In our approach, we make use of the available experts' lexicons, dictionaries, and thesauruses, and so the similarity relations are fairly accurate, because of the expert knowledge used to construct these lexicons.

Other works include Vilnis et al. [22], who introduced density-based distributed embeddings by learning representations in the space of Gaussian distributions. Bian et al. [23] focused on incorporating morphological, syntactic, and semantic knowledge with deep learning to obtain more efficient word embeddings. Zhou et al. [24] used the category information associated with the community question answering pages as metadata. These metadata are fed to the skip-gram model to learn continuous word embeddings, followed by applying Fisher kernel to obtain fixed length vectors.

Some works introduce retrofitting to overcome the deficiencies in distributional models in representing the semantic and relational knowledge between words. Faruqui et al. [25] applied retrofitting to pre-trained word vectors from distributional models. The vectors are refined to account for the information in semantic lexicons. The method used is graph-based learning where the graph is constructed for the relations extracted from the lexicons. Jo [26] proposed extrofitting by extracting the semantic relations between words from their vectors using latent semantic analysis. The author further combined extrofitting with external lexicons for synonyms to obtain improved results.

There have been some attempts at tackling the polarity issue. Mohammad et al. [27] proposed an empirical none-word embedding approach for the detection of antonymous word pairs. The authors' approach relies on the co-occurrence and distributional hypotheses of antonyms, stating that antonymous word pairs occur in similar contexts more often than chance. Nevertheless, these hypotheses are only useful indications but not sufficient conditions to detect antonymous words.

Lobanova [28] proposed pattern-based methods to automatically identify antonyms. The author pointed out how antonyms are useful in many NLP applications, including contradiction identification, paraphrase generation, and document summarization.

Yih et al. [29] derived the word vector representations using latent semantic analysis (LSA), with assigning signs to account for antonymy detection, and devising the polarity inducing LSA (PILSA). Yet the authors pivoted on the fact that words with least cosine similarity are indeed opposites without regard to distinguishing between unrelated word pairs, which also have low cosine similarity, and antonymous word pairs. To embed out-of-vocabulary words, the authors adopted a two stage strategy: first conducting a lexical analysis, and, if no match was found, using semantic relatedness. This strategy weakens the smoothness of extending their approach.

Again, Mohammad et al. [30] devised an empirical method that marks word pairs that occur in the same thesaurus category as synonyms and others that occur in contrasting categories as opposites. They then apply postprocessing rules, since based on their method one word pair may be marked as both synonym and antonym at the same time. The approach devised is a none-word embedding one.

Chang et al. [31] introduced multi-relational latent semantic analysis (MRLSA) that extends PILSA [29], modeling multiple word relations. The authors proposed a 3-way tensor, wherein each slice captures one particular relation. However, the model performance depends on the quality of a pivot slice (e.g., the synonym slice), which MRLSA has to choose. Motivated by this approach, Zhang et al. [32] introduced a Bayesian probabilistic tensor factorization model. Their model combined both thesauri information and existing word embeddings, though their model used pre-trained word embeddings.

Santus et al. [33] devised a new average-precision-based measure to discriminate between synonyms and antonyms. The measure is built on the paradox of "simultaneous similarity and difference between the antonyms." The authors deduced that both synonyms and antonyms are similar in all dimensions of meaning except one. This different dimension can be identified and used for the discrimination task.

Ono et al. [34] trained word embeddings to detect antonyms. They introduced two models: a word embeddings on thesauri information (WE-T) model and a word embeddings on thesauri and distributional information (WE-TD) model. For WE-T, the authors applied an AdaGrad online learning method that uses a gradient-based update with automatically-determined learning rate. For WE-TD, the authors introduce skip-gram with negative sampling (SGNS). However, their model is trained such that synonymous and antonymous pairs have high and low similarity scores respectively. This imposes a challenge in differentiating between antonymous word pairs and unrelated word pairs since both will have low similarity scores.

Nguyen et al. [35] proposed augmenting lexical contrast information to distributional word embeddings in order to enhance distinguishing between synonyms and antonyms. Moreover, the authors extended the skip-gram model to incorporate the lexical contrast information into the objective function.

Motivated by the fact that antonyms mostly lie at close distances in the vector space, Li et al. [36] proposed a neural network model that is adapted to learn word embeddings for antonyms. These embeddings are used to carry out contradiction detection.

In most of these aforementioned antonymy construction methods the problem is that they focus mostly on this task only. For example [29,32,34] only evaluated their vectors on antonymy detection without showing the performance of these vectors on synonyms or unrelated words. The goal in these works has mainly not been to obtain a global word embedding that works for synonyms, antonyms, and unrelated words.

Word embeddings obtain the whole picture, as to the semantic relations of the words in a corpus. As such, they have many applications. For example, Zou et al. [1] proposed a method to learn bilingual embeddings to perform a Chinese–English machine translation task. Moreover, word embeddings methods are applied to sentiment analysis; Maas et al. [2] proposed a model that combines supervised and unsupervised techniques to learn word vectors that capture sentiment content. The goal was to be able to use these vectors in sentiment analysis tasks. The authors used an unsupervised probabilistic model of documents followed by a supervised model that maps a word vector to a predicted sentiment label using a logistic regression predictor that relies on sentiment annotated texts. Tang et al. [3] developed a word embedding method by training three neural networks. The method relies on encoding sentiment information in the continuous representations of words. They evaluated their method on a benchmark Twitter sentiment classification dataset. Dragoni et al. [4] employed word embeddings and deep learning to bridge the gap between different domains, thereby building a multi-domain sentiment model. Deho et al. [5] used word2vec to generate word vectors that learn contextual information. To perform sentiment analysis, the generated vectors were used to train machine learning algorithms in the form of classifiers. Question answering is another application of word embeddings; for example, Liang et al. [6] tackled the rice FAQ (frequently asked question) question-answering system. The authors proposed methods based on word2vec and LSTM (long-short term memory). The core of the system is question similarity computing, which is used to match users' questions and the questions in FAQ. Liu et al. [7] designed a deep learning model based on word2vec to find the best answers to the farmers' questions. Search service also exploits word embeddings; Liu et al. [9] established a model based on word embeddings to improve the accuracy of data retrieval in the cloud. Spelling correction can also be done using word embeddings. Kim et al. [10] proposed a method of correcting misspelled words in Twitter messages by using an improved Word2Vec. The authors in [11] proposed crowdsourcing where the relevance between task and worker is obtained. The proposed model involves the computation of the similarity of word vectors and the establishment of the semantic tags similar matrix database based on the Word2vec deep learning. Habibi et al. [12] proposed a method based on deep learning and statistical word embeddings to recognize biomedical named entities (NER), such as genes, chemicals, and diseases. Word embeddings have also tackled the field of text summarization; to achieve automatic summarization Kågebäck et al. [13] proposed the use of continuous vector representations as a basis for measuring similarity. Rossiello et al. [14] proposed a centroid-based method for text summarization that exploits the compositional capabilities of word embeddings.

Word embeddings have been developed for other languages as well. Zahran et al. [37] compared diverse techniques for building Arabic word embeddings, and evaluated these techniques using intrinsic and extrinsic evaluations. Soliman et al. [38] proposed the AraVec model, a pre-trained distributed word embedding project, which makes use of six different models. The authors described the used resources for building such models and the preprocessing steps involved.

3. The Proposed Method

Let $x_i = (x_{i1}, \ldots, x_{iN})^T$ be an N-dimensional vector of unity length that represents word i; i.e., $\|x_i\| = 1$. The fact that the length of the vector is 1 means that the word is embedded on a sphere. The dot product between two vectors $x_i^T x_j$ represents the similarity between their corresponding words. For example $x_i^T x_j$ for the words *easy* and *simple* would be very high (close to 1). For the words *easy* and *manageable* it would also be high, but a shade lower. For the opposites *easy* and *difficult* it would be close to -1, and for unrelated words, such as *easy* and *cat*, it would be close to zero. It is well known that when picking up any two random vectors on a sphere of high dimension, their dot product will be close to zero. This means that the bulk of the words will have similarity close to zero with the word *easy*. Note also that because of the unit length property, the dot product $x_i^T x_j$ and the distance are related in a one to one way (because $\|x_i - x_j\|^2 = \|x_i\|^2 + \|x_j\|^2 - 2x_i^T x_j = 2[1 - x_i^T x_j]$).

We collect a number of words for which we estimate a similarity number, on a scale from -1 to 1. For example, for a pair of words with corresponding vectors x_i and x_j, let the estimated similarity be s_{ij}. We collect a very large training set, obtained from some well-known synonym and antonym lists. For any word relations that are not covered by these lists, we add a moderately sized but typically not-large training set, mainly labeled by an expert human. The expert-labeled dataset serves as the nucleus that will guide the training using the other larger collected datasets.

We develop an algorithm that estimates the vectors x_i that would yield the similarity numbers as close as possible to the given similarity numbers. We define the following error function:

$$E = \sum_i \sum_j w_{ij} \left[x_i^T x_j - s_{ij} \right]^2$$

subject to $\|x_i\| = 1, i = 1, \ldots, K$ \qquad (1)

where w_{ij} is a weighting coefficient representing the confidence in the similarity estimate s_{ij}. For example, the word pairs labeled by an expert may have higher weighting coefficient than other word pairs in the remaining larger training set. It is hard to solve this large optimization problem if one seeks to obtain all K vectors x_i at once. However, we propose a relaxation algorithm, that tackles one x_i at a time. In this algorithm we focus on some x_k and fix all other x_l's for the time being. Then we optimize E with respect to x_k. This is feasible and gives a close form solution. Then, we move on to the next vector, and fix the others, optimize with respect to that vector. We continue in this manner until we complete all vectors. Then we start another cycle, and re-optimize each x_k, one at a time. We perform a few similar cycles until the algorithm converges.

Consider that we are focusing now on vector x_k, while keeping all other vectors constant. Then we can decompose the objective function in (1) into a component containing x_k and other components that do not have x_k in them, as follows.

$$E = \sum_{i \neq k} \sum_{j \neq k} w_{ij} \left[x_i^T x_j - s_{kj} \right]^2 + 2 \sum_{j \neq k} w_{kj} \left[x_k^T x_j - s_{kj} \right]^2$$

$$= R_k + 2 \sum_{j \neq k} w_{kj} \left[x_k^T x_j - s_{kj} \right]^2 \qquad (2)$$

where R_k is the term not containing x_k. We skipped the term $x_k^T x_k - s_{kk}$ because it equals zero always (the similarity between a vector and itself is 1, and the norm of any vector is enforced as 1 too). The factor 2 in the RHS is to account for the existence of x_k in first summation, and in the second summation. The optimization will now focus on optimizing the second term in the summation. Using a Lagrange multiplier to take into account the unity norm constraint, we formulate the augmented objective function:

$$V = R_k + 2 \sum_{j \neq k} w_{kj} \left[x_k^T x_j - s_{kj} \right]^2 - \lambda (x_k^T x_k - 1) \tag{3}$$

where λ is the Lagrange multiplier. For simplicity, let us redefine quantities in a way to skip the factor of 2 in the equation. Simplifying, we get:

$$\begin{aligned} V &= R_k + \sum_{j \neq k} w_{kj} \left[x_k^T x_j x_j^T x_k - 2 x_j^T s_{kj} x_k + s_{kj}^2 \right] \\ &\quad - \lambda x_k^T x_k + \lambda \\ &= R_k + x_k^T \left(\sum_{j \neq k} w_{kj} x_j x_j^T \right) x_k - \left(2 \sum_{j \neq k} w_{kj} x_j^T s_{kj} \right) x_k \\ &\quad + \sum_{j \neq k} w_{kj} s_{kj}^2 - \lambda x_k^T x_k + \lambda \\ &= R_k + x_k^T A x_k - 2 b^T x_k + c \end{aligned} \tag{4}$$

where we isolated x_k from the terms that do not contain x_k, and the following matrices are defined as:

$$A = \sum_{j \neq k} w_{kj} x_j x_j^T - \lambda I \tag{5}$$

$$b = \sum_{j \neq k} w_{kj} x_j s_{kj} \tag{6}$$

$$c = \sum_{j \neq k} w_{kj} s_{kj}^2 + \lambda \tag{7}$$

Taking the derivative with respect to x_k and equating to zero, we get

$$\frac{dV}{dx_k} = 2 A x_k - 2 b = 0 \tag{8}$$

$$x_k = A^{-1} b \tag{9}$$

To evaluate λ we enforce the condition $x_k^T x_k = 1$.

$$x_k^T x_k = b^T A^{-2} b = 1 \tag{10}$$

where we used the fact that A is a symmetric matrix. We get

$$b^T \left[A' - \lambda I \right]^{-2} b = 1 \tag{11}$$

where

$$A' = \sum_{j \neq k} w_{kj} x_j x_j^T \tag{12}$$

To solve Equation (11), we note that λ is a scalar, so we simply implement a one-dimensional search.

Once we obtain x_k as above, we turn our attention to the next vector, and apply similar analysis. Once we complete all vectors, we perform another cycle through all vectors, and so on. The algorithm converges, in the sense that each step leads to a reduction in the objective function (1), leading to a local minimum (akin to neural network training and other machine learning algorithms). This is proven in the theorem described below.

Theorem 1. *Let the errors before and after applying (9) and (11) be E_1 and E_2 respectively (we mean the errors given by Equation (1)).*
Then

$$E_2 \leq E_1 \qquad (13)$$

The application of the steps with cycling through the vectors one by one, and repeating the cycles several times will lead to a convergence of the attained vectors to some limiting values.

The proof of this assertion, as well as other details of the optimization problem, are given in the Appendix A.

Figure 2 is a graph which empirically shows that the vectors stabilize one cycle after another. Shown in the graph is $\max(|x_k(new) - x_k(old)|)$ against cycle number. The maximum is computed over the components of the vector and over all vectors x_k. One can observe that after around 15 cycles the changes in vectors become very small, indicating their convergence to their particular positions in the space.

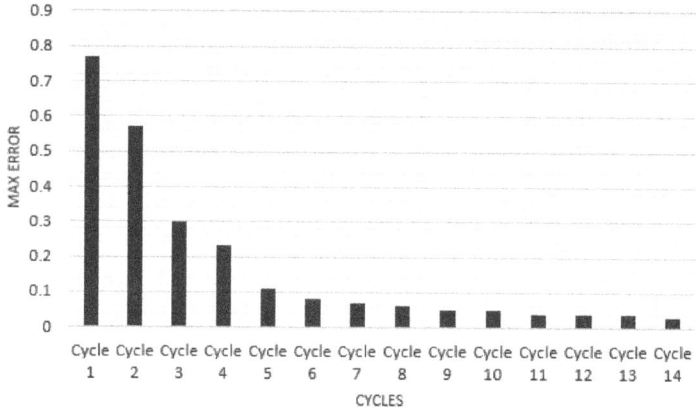

Figure 2. Convergence.

4. Vocabulary and Data Gathering

To design the proposed word embedding, we have collected data in the form of labeled pairs of words from multiple sources. Moreover, we explored the properties of the vocabulary that achieve best results using our algorithm. We model our vocabulary as a graph referred to as the graph of words, such that the words are the vertices and relations between the words are the edges. (graph modeling has been a very useful tool in natural language processing; see [39].) Weights are attached to the edges of the graph, and these weights represent the similarity scores between the two words they each connect. The existence of an edge means that a labeled word pair exists as a part of the vocabulary to train the algorithm. There is, however, a potential problem. The graph could have a number of components that are disconnected from each other; i.e., no sequence of edges can lead from one component to the other. This could lead to potentially multiple solutions for the optimization task. The algorithm would not know where to place the vectors corresponding to the disconnected components with respect to each other. In other words, one can rotate entire connected groups without them affecting the error function (in Equation (1)), because no similarity terms exist between any of the disconnected groups' vertices. This would lead to arbitrarily estimated similarities between the vectors (words) of any two disconnected components.

Venkatesh p. 124 [40] provides an in depth investigation of when a large graph is void of disconnected components; i.e., one large connected component. He proves the following theorem:

Theorem 2. *Consider a graph with n vertices and with probability p that an edge exists between any two vertices. If $p = \frac{\log n}{n} + \frac{c}{n}$, for some constant c, then the probability that the random graph $G(n,p)$ is connected tends to $e^{-e^{-c}}$, as $n \longrightarrow \infty$.*

This theorem essentially says that if $p \gg \log(n)/n$ then the graph is one giant connected component. Since the expected degree of each vertex is $k = np$, this means that the average degree of our graph should be generally higher than $\log(n)$; i.e., $k > \log(n)$. We used this fact as a guide in determining the number of synonym/antonym pairs used to create the training set, since each pair will create an edge in the out graph of words.

At the end of generating the training set, we apply the networkx python algorithm [41] to detect the number of components in a graph. There may still be several disconnected components. In such a case, we manually select pairs of words corresponding to the disconnected components. We seek to connect them by estimating the similarity using our judgment of the word meanings. This essentially draws edges between the disconnected components. Ideally, how many edges should we add between any two disconnected components? The answer is d, the dimension of our vector space. This would essentially anchor the vectors in fixed places with respect to each other. It would also prevent the possibility of rotating a component with respect to another along some remaining degrees of freedom without violating the existing distances or similarities between the vectors as given in the training set.

To collect our vocabulary we have used several sources. This is in order not to rely overly on one single source. We used the following:

- Lists for frequent English words' synonyms and antonyms extracted from the web sites: [42,43].
- Lists for certain categories that we manually constructed; e.g., family, sports, animals, countries, capitals, and others (we added 33 lists). Each list consists of many words, and we assigned a specific similarity score among the words in each list, based on our judgment.
- We collected an extensive amount of words from WordNet [44] and from other sources, such as educational websites and books [45–53]. Subsequently, we created a crawler that would visit the site of thesaurus.com (the premier site for word meanings, synonyms, antonyms, etc.) [54]. The crawler would fetch the synonyms and antonyms of the sought words from the thesaurus. The obtained words would be fed again to the site and more synonyms and antonyms were obtained, and so on. These would then be added to the training set.
- We gathered random word pairs from a site that contains random phrases [55]. We checked these pairs, and selected only the ones that were unrelated. As mentioned before, unrelated pairs should give similarity around zero, and they have the important task of connecting disconnected groups in the graph. In addition to the unrelated pairs, we collected synonyms and antonyms for these selected words using the crawler from thesaurus.com.
- We gathered other unrelated word pairs randomly by pairing words manually in the constructed vocabulary (of course after checking that they are indeed unrelated).
- We manually added some synonyms, antonyms, and unrelated word pairs using other different online dictionaries.

For the collected pairs we have assigned a similarity close to 1 for synonyms and close to -1 for antonyms. This is just the theoretical target function. After convergence it typically yields different similarities. The reason is that there is competition between words to pull the vectors of its synonymous words towards its vector. This results in "middle ground" vector locations that satisfy reasonable contiguity towards its different synonyms. Table 1 shows the structure of the constructed vocabulary while Figure 3 is a histogram for the degree of vertices in the constructed vocabulary.

Table 1. Vocabulary structure.

Number of distinct words (graph vertices)	27770
Number of synonymous pairs	102260
Number of antonymous pairs	38783
Number of unrelated pairs	182287
Number of graph edges	323330
Ratio of number of edges to number of vertices	11.64
Average degree of the graph	23.29
Number of connected components	1

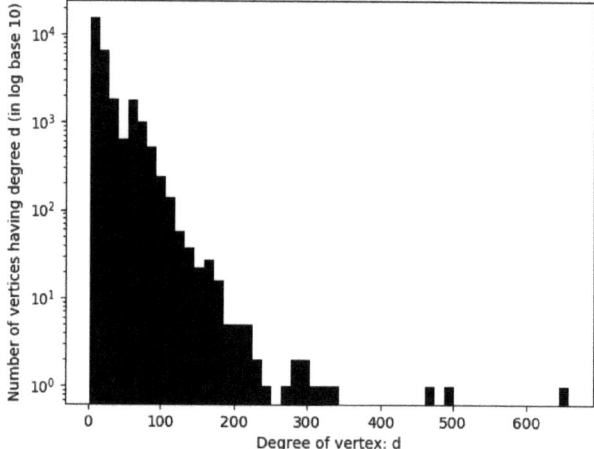

Figure 3. Histogram for the degree of vertices.

5. Results and Discussion

We have tested the proposed word embedding method. After a thorough design, and training using our method, we have performed the following four evaluation experiments in addition to outlining an opinion mining application for hotel reviews:

1. Word Similarity: We present the similarity scores obtained between many selected word pairs, and compare with the scores of other published word vector representations. The comparison of the performances should be done using the judgment of the reader.
2. Human Judged Similarity: We apply our approach and some competing methods on benchmark word pair lists. These lists, published in some papers, have human-judged similarity scores. So this allows comparison with actual numbers.
3. Antonymy Detection: We evaluate our approach on answering closest-opposite questions (extracted from the GRE test), comparing our results with the published ones.
4. Antonym/Synonym Discrimination: We test the performance of our approach in discriminating between antonyms and synonyms. The performance is compared with other published word vector representations.
5. Opinion Mining: We outline the application of our method on an opinion mining task. Moreover, we use other published word vectors to compare the performance on such task.

All used datasets are the same for all the compared models in order to have fair comparisons. In all the conducted experiments, we used the word vectors generated using our implemented algorithm. The training vocabulary used is the one gathered as explained in the previous section. The generated word vector's number of dimensions is 50.

5.1. Word Similarity

Table 2 contains a number of word pairs where the corresponding similarity scores are obtained by the proposed word embedding. The similarity score is computed as the dot product between unit vectors. We have compared our scores with the scores of other published pre-trained word vectors: word2vec [17], GloVe [19], and fastText [20]. The number of dimensions of the vectors in word2vec, GloVe, and fastText is 300, while the dimension of the vectors in our approach is 50. The reason for selecting a number of dimensions of 50 is that more dimensions lead to sparser space, and more overfitting. N/A means that one or both of the words in the given pair have no pre-trained vectors in the method considered. In the table we have included word pairs from different categories:

- Synonyms that occur in the training vocabulary of the proposed method.
- Synonyms that are not part of the training vocabulary of the proposed method (marked with the * symbol in the table).
- Antonyms that are part of the training vocabulary.
- Antonyms that are not included as part of the training vocabulary (also marked with the * symbol).
- Unrelated words that occur in the training vocabulary.
- Unrelated words that are not part of the training vocabulary (marked with the * symbol).
- Word pairs that belong to a certain category (e.g., countries).

Note that the pairs that are not part of the training set constitute an unbiased out of sample test, since the algorithm has not seen them while training.

From Table 2, we can observe several interesting facts:

1. By human judgment, the proposed algorithm seems to be more successful in capturing the similarity between the different words. For example, the pairs "happy–joyful", "amusing–happy" and "district–county" are close synonyms, and our algorithm manages to assign a high similarity. Opposing algorithms give low similarity scores around 0.5 or so.
2. For the antonyms, our algorithm assigns rightly negative numbers. For example, the pairs "modern–outdated" and "unlike–same" are assigned similarities lower than −0.8. The competing algorithms assign similarities in the range of about 0.3 to 0.68, not really signaling that these words are antonyms.
3. For unrelated words, the proposed embedding generally gives them similarities close to zero. For example, the pairs "array–again", "useful–wash" and "decent–morning" are given respectively 0.294, 0.195, and 0.027, which are reasonably close to zero.
4. The competing algorithms are not very successful in differentiating antonyms from unrelated pairs. They give them all comparable scores. For example, the antonyms "modern–outdated" and "unlike–same", and the unrelated pairs "array–again", "useful–wash" and "decent–morning" are given similarities in the same range. It is not clear from the scores whether the pair is an an antonym or an unrelated pair. Additionally the pair "yes–no" is the most basic antonym, and in spite of that, the competing algorithms do not give them a zero score.
5. An antonymous pair such as "happy–unhappy" is given a high similarity score in all the other three competing approaches. Thus it is treated the same as a synonymous pair while it is given a negative similarity score in our approach.

6. An antonymous pair such as "decelerate–speed" is given a low similarity score in all the other three approaches, and thus is treated the same as an unrelated pair while it is given a negative similarity score in our approach.
7. In all the four approaches, the "country–capital" pairs have close similarities.
8. In all the four approaches, the "country–nationality" pairs have close similarities.
9. The pair "Japan–Greece" has a lower similarity score than the pair "Japan–China", although both pairs are country pairs. This is due to the fact that Japan and China have more properties in common (both are Asian countries, and are distance-wise close to each other).
10. A combination such as "African-country" is not found in any of the other three vocabularies. Since the other approaches do not represent such composite words as vectors.
11. We must caution, however, that the competing methods word2vec, GloVe, and fastText are not specifically designed to handle antonyms. Therefore, the comparison presented, which shows clear domination of our method for antonyms, may not be fully due to a particular design or algorithmic outperformance, but also partly due to the fact that the competing methods were not designed to deal with antonyms.

Table 2. Word similarity comparison (* means the pair is not part of the training set for our method).

Word1	Word2	Sphere (Our Approach)	Word2vec [17]	GloVe [19]	FastText [20]
happy	joyful	0.944	0.424	0.598	0.701
amusing	happy	* 0.778	0.27	0.387	0.5
king	queen	* 0.83	0.651	0.76	0.764
boy	girl	* 0.859	0.854	0.825	0.862
male	female	* 0.702	0.841	0.938	0.945
education	student	0.608	0.401	0.682	0.547
movement	motion	0.887	0.231	0.56	0.583
oscillate	move	* 0.828	0.239	0.166	0.354
district	county	* 0.733	0.594	0.651	0.586
district	commune	0.761	0.164	0.367	0.464
friend	partner	0.96	0.37	0.609	0.619
valuable	worthy	0.849	0.351	0.537	0.649
great	tremendous	0.858	0.775	0.668	0.804
joyfulness	joy	* 0.986	0.513	0.362	N/A
France	Paris	0.94	0.555	0.721	0.632
Germany	Berlin	0.949	0.554	0.685	0.673
Egypt	Cairo	0.934	0.602	0.699	N/A
France	French	0.82	0.633	0.686	0.68
Germany	German	0.801	0.681	0.7	0.742
Egypt	Egyptian	0.869	0.602	0.718	0.753
Japan	China	* 0.738	0.315	0.697	0.645
Japan	Greece	* 0.609	0.545	0.494	0.595
african-country	european-country	* 0.88	N/A	N/A	N/A
modern	ongoing	* 0.487	0.129	0.357	0.424
obsolete	outdated	* 0.915	0.743	0.725	0.797
money	shopping	* 0.599	0.166	0.487	0.407
internet	web	0.888	0.597	0.737	0.683
apple	orange	* 0.93	0.392	0.493	0.561
soccer	football	0.926	0.731	0.819	0.804
lion	tiger	* 0.987	0.512	0.621	0.67
giraffe	animal	0.954	0.422	0.436	0.573
light	sun	* 0.612	0.401	0.525	0.558
geology	earth	* 0.701	0.264	0.444	0.531
tenor	opera	* 0.847	0.459	0.395	0.519
unauthorized	simultaneously	* −0.101	0.175	0.237	0.3
bag	country	* 0.061	0.085	0.301	0.367
beach	truck	* 0.448	0.09	0.296	0.421
array	again	* 0.294	-0.011	0.314	0.317
useful	wash	* 0.195	0.073	0.288	0.224
tourism	beach	* 0.513	0.266	0.389	0.459
decent	morning	* 0.027	0.041	0.373	0.253
go	new	* 0.111	0.113	0.564	0.345
yes	no	−1	0.392	0.695	0.549

Table 2. Cont.

Word1	Word2	Sphere (Our Approach)	Word2vec [17]	GloVe [19]	FastText [20]
active	passive	−0.916	0.436	0.577	0.678
happy	unhappy	−0.912	0.613	0.565	0.767
young	old	−0.841	0.417	0.573	0.583
youth	old	* −0.357	0.212	0.384	0.392
youth	elderly	−0.674	0.215	0.39	0.499
valuable	valueless	* −0.912	0.334	0.262	0.614
recall	forget	* −0.907	0.3	0.532	0.567
education	ignorance	−0.854	0.2	0.306	0.487
complex	easy	* −0.769	0.213	0.439	0.453
beginning	deadline	* −0.73	0.22	0.447	0.348
modern	outdated	* −0.933	0.404	0.427	0.528
unlike	same	* −0.957	0.299	0.681	0.482
grow	eradicate	* −0.858	0.241	0.308	0.491
certainty	uncertainty	−0.931	0.492	0.617	0.706
truth	lying	* −0.766	0.237	0.468	0.479
daring	coward	* −0.676	0.196	0.233	0.432
decelerate	speed	* −0.843	0.212	0.22	0.385

5.2. Human Judged Similarity

We considered here datasets from other researchers that attached human-judged similarity scores to the word pairs. This would give an unbiased assessment, as the similarity estimate is performed by different researchers. None of the human-judged similarity scores associated with the pairs in these datasets are included in our training set, in order to have it as an out of sample test.

We considered the labeled data of MC30 [56] and RG [57], which have human-judged similarity measures. There is a third dataset available, namely, the WordSim-353 [58] human-judged dataset, but we did not perform a test using this dataset because they estimated antonyms as similar while in our approach we consider antonyms as opposites. We computed two metrics, the Spearman rank correlation (Sp) and root mean square error (RMSE). Moreover, we have compared the obtained metrics' values with those of word2vec [17], GloVe [19], and fastText [20]. Table 3 shows that we achieve the best results for both metrics on both datasets.

Table 3. Results of human-judged datasets.

Approach	MC30		RG	
	Sp	RMSE	Sp	RMSE
Sphere (our approach)	0.91	0.18	0.9	0.15
word2vec	0.8	0.3	0.76	0.29
GloVe	0.79	0.27	0.82	0.25
fastText	0.83	0.24	0.84	0.22

5.3. Antonymy Detection

We have applied our approach on answering the closest-opposite GRE questions, collected in [27,30]. The GRE, or Graduate Record Examinations, is a worldwide exam needed for admission to graduate schools. The verbal part has a group of multiple choice questions that seek the closest-opposite. The 162 questions of the development set are used as a part of our training vocabulary; i.e., the words together with the correct answers are added to the training vocabulary as antonymous pairs. On the other hand, both the 950 questions and the 790 questions datasets are used as test sets (i.e., their pairs do not exist in our training set).

We applied our word embedding method to compute the similarities between the word in question and all candidate answers, and selected the answer that is closest to −1, signifying an antonym. We have computed the precision, recall, and F-score as given in [27], so that we could make comparisons with the numbers given in the competing methods. They are given by

$$Precision(P) = \frac{\text{Number of questions answered correctly}}{\text{Number of questions attempted}} \quad (14)$$

$$Recall(R) = \frac{\text{Number of questions answered correctly}}{\text{Total number of questions}} \quad (15)$$

$$F\text{-}score = \frac{2 \times P \times R}{P + R} \quad (16)$$

In our case we note that the precision = recall = F-score; this is because our approach attempted all the questions. All the words that exist in the questions and in the candidate answers have corresponding vectors in our word embedding method.

Furthermore, we compared our results with the best results recorded in [27,29–32,34] that use the same dataset. From Table 4, it is shown that we achieved the best precision, recall, and F-score for the development set. We achieved the second best scores in both test sets after [34]; however, the dimension of their vectors is 300 while the dimension of our vectors is only 50. As mentioned earlier, their model is trained such that there is no differentiation between antonymous pairs and unrelated pairs, as both will have low similarity scores. Moreover, we were able to compare our results with [34] only on antonymy detection as the authors did not include the performance of their vectors on synonyms or unrelated words.

Table 4. Results of closest-opposite GRE.

Approach	Development Set			Test Set 950			Test Set 790		
	Precision	Recall	F-Score	Precision	Recall	F-Score	Precision	Recall	F-Score
Sphere (our approach)	0.98	0.98	0.98	0.83	0.83	0.83	0.8	0.8	0.8
Mohammad et al., 2008 [27]	0.76	0.66	0.70	0.76	0.64	0.70	-	-	-
Yih et al., 2012 [29]	0.88	0.87	0.87	0.81	0.80	0.81	-	-	-
Mohammad et al., 2013 [30]	0.79	0.66	0.72	-	-	-	0.77	0.63	0.69
Chang et al., 2013 [31]	0.88	0.85	0.87	0.81	0.77	0.79	-	-	-
Zhang et al., 2014 [32]	0.88	0.88	0.88	0.82	0.82	0.82	-	-	-
Ono et al., 2015 [34]	0.92	0.91	0.91	0.90	0.88	0.89	0.89	0.87	0.88

5.4. Antonym/Synonym Discrimination

In this section, we show using statistical measures how our approach perform in the task of discriminating between antonyms and synonyms. Moreover, our approach's performance is compared to the other published word vectors' models: word2vec [17], GloVe [19], and fastText [20]. The used dataset is introduced by [35]. This dataset considers word pairs in three categories: adjectives, nouns and verbs. The pairs are marked as antonyms or synonyms. Therefore, we have conducted this experiment as a binary classification task with two classes namely, antonyms and synonyms. The classification is done based on the similarity score between the vectors of the word pair. If this similarity score is equal to or greater than a certain threshold (more specifically 0.5), then the pair is classified as synonyms otherwise the pair is classified as antonyms. The used dataset is refined such that pairs that have any non-existent word in any of the models are removed. After this refinement the dataset has the following structure:

- 470 adjectives: (238 antonyms and 232 synonyms);
- 547 nouns: (276 antonyms and 271 synonyms);

- 632 verbs: (311 antonyms and 321 synonyms).

In Tables 5–7 the performance measures are recorded for the four models and for the three categories respectively. The results show that our model outperforms all the other three models in all the categories.

Table 5. Antonym/synonym discrimination results—adjectives.

Approach	Precision	Recall	F-Score	Accuracy
Sphere (our approach)	0.86	0.83	0.83	82.98%
word2vec	0.61	0.56	0.50	55.96%
GloVe	0.65	0.60	0.57	60.43%
fastText	0.67	0.67	0.67	66.81%

Table 6. Antonym/synonym discrimination results—nouns.

Approach	Precision	Recall	F-Score	Accuracy
Sphere (our approach)	0.72	0.72	0.72	72.39%
word2vec	0.65	0.58	0.51	57.77%
GloVe	0.67	0.62	0.58	61.61%
fastText	0.67	0.66	0.65	65.81%

Table 7. Antonym/synonym discrimination results—verbs.

Approach	Precision	Recall	F-Score	Accuracy
Sphere (our approach)	0.83	0.81	0.81	81.49%
word2vec	0.70	0.54	0.43	53.80%
GloVe	0.69	0.59	0.53	59.02%
fastText	0.66	0.63	0.61	62.66%

5.5. Comments on the Results

We can observe that the proposed word embedding approach gives more reasonable similarity scores than some of the major approaches, such as word2vec, GloVe, and fastText. These methods have a particular deficit dealing with antonyms, and distinguishing between antonyms and unrelated words. The failure of some of them in assigning the right similarity score to the pair "yes" and "no" is case in point. Our algorithm also fared better on the two benchmarks tested. It also did well compared to other algorithms that are specifically designed to deal with antonyms, on the GRE antonym dataset. Furthermore, our approach proved its efficiency in discriminating between antonyms and synonyms as compared to other published word vectors' models. Our algorithm can handle composite words (like "fairy tale"). It could potentially also handle words with multiple meanings, such as "bat" (the animal) and "bat" (a club). The way to tackle these is to consider them as different words, like "bat-1" and "bat-2". The challenge facing all word embedding methods is to distinguish words with multiple meanings from the context of the sentence.

5.6. Opinion Mining

Opinion mining application refers to classifying a review as positive or negative. We applied our approach to learn vectors for words that have bias from which sentiments can be inferred. We have begun with a small set of such words then grow our sphere by obtaining synonyms and antonyms for these words. The generated word vectors are used to compute the sentiment that the review reflects. Every word in the review has two sub-scores that are obtained by respectively the dot product between this word and a number of positive words on one hand, and a number of negative words on the other hand, which are specifically collected to gauge sentiment. We applied the approach to 20,000 hotel reviews [59] from "515K Hotel Reviews Data in Europe" dataset [60] that are collected from booking.com where each review is annotated as positive or negative. Furthermore, we used vectors from other models to compare the results. We achieved the highest F-score compared to word2vec [17], GloVe [19], and fastText [20]. The scores obtained are 0.81, 0.79, 0.74, and 0.79 respectively [61].

6. Conclusions

In this work we have devised a new approach for embedding words into a sphere. The algorithm is a simple relaxation one without the need for intensive training phases. The approach is a polarity capturing one in the sense that antonymous word pairs are located at opposite poles of the sphere. Not only antonymy can be detected but also other relations (e.g. unrelated pairs).

We have managed to gather an adequate vocabulary that can flexibly be extended. Moreover, we evaluated our approach using several datasets, showing that the approach competes well with other approaches in the literature. We have successfully proved that our approach does not suffer from the ambiguity in differentiating between various word pair relations such as synonyms, antonyms, and unrelated pairs.

Author Contributions: Conceptualization, S.R. and A.F.A.; methodology, S.R., A.F.A. and S.S.; software, S.R.; validation, S.R.; formal analysis, S.R., A.F.A., and S.S.; investigation, S.R., A.F.A., and S.S.; resources, S.R.; data curation, S.R.; writing—original draft preparation, S.R.; writing—review and editing, S.R. and A.F.A.; visualization, S.R.; supervision, A.F.A. and S.S.; project administration, A.F.A. and S.S. All authors have read and agreed to the published version of the manuscript.

Funding: This research received no external funding.

Acknowledgments: The authors would like to acknowledge the help and the discussions with Professor Aly Aly Fahmy of the Arab Academy of Science and Technology, and Professor William Hager of University of Florida.

Conflicts of Interest: The authors declare no conflict of interest.

Data Availability: The word vectors generated are found at https://github.com/SandraRizkallah/Sphere-Eng-WordVectors.

Appendix A. Proof of Theorem 1: Convergence of the Algorithm

When we consider a particular word, we apply Equations (9) and (11), in order to tune the position of the word's designated vector. To prove that the repeated application of this step (for one word after another) leads to convergence, we show that each application leads to a non-increase of the error function Equation (1). Since this error function is bounded from below by zero, the algorithm converges to some limit of the error function.

This formulation of an optimization falls under the form of optimization of a quadratic function on the sphere, i.e., subject to the solution lying on the sphere $\|x\|^2 = r^2$. It has been studied in detail by [62–65], as it is applied in types of optimization methods called trust region methods of nonlinear optimization.

Let the errors before and after applying (9) be E_1 and E_2 respectively (we mean the errors given by Equation (1)). Since both before and after the update the vector x_k would be normalized to become unit length, we can use V (given in (3), (4)) in place of E. The subtracted term $\lambda(x_k^T x_k - 1)$ will equal zero in both cases, so it will not impact it. Therefore

$$\begin{aligned} E_2 - E_1 &= V_2 - V_1 \\ &= x_k^T A x_k - 2b^T x_k - \left[x_k'^T A x_k' - 2b^T x_k' \right] \end{aligned} \tag{A1}$$

where x_k' is the word vector before the update. After applying Equation (9) it becomes x_k, given by:

$$\begin{aligned} x_k &= A^{-1} b \\ &= (A' - \lambda I)^{-1} b \end{aligned} \tag{A2}$$

where the last step follows from the definitions of A and A' (5) and (12). As mentioned, λ is determined from:

$$b^T [A' - \lambda I]^{-2} b = 1 \tag{A3}$$

According to [62–65] Equation (A3) has at most $2N$ solutions for λ, where N is the dimension of the vector x_k, with the smallest and largest solutions corresponding to respectively the minimum and the maximum of the optimization problem. The solutions in the middle correspond to the saddle points. The smallest solution obeys the condition $\lambda \leq$ all eigenvalues of A' [64], which means that $A' - \lambda I$ is positive semi-definite (because the eigenvalues of $A' - \lambda I$ equal the eigenvalues of A' minus λ). Because of these conditions, the aforementioned works of [62–65] prove that $E_2 - E_1 \leq 0$.

Irrespective of their proof, we formulated a simplified proof, given as follows: Substituting (A2) into (A1), we get

$$\begin{aligned} E_2 - E_1 &= b^T A^{-1} A A^{-1} b - 2 b^T A^{-1} b - \left[x_k'^T A x_k' - 2 b^T x_k' \right] \\ &= -b^T A^{-1} b - \left[x_k'^T A x_k' - 2 b^T x_k' \right] \\ &= -\left[A x_k' - b \right]^T A^{-1} \left[A x_k' - b \right] \end{aligned} \tag{A4}$$

The latter line follows by expanding the two multiplied brackets. We find that it equals the expression in the preceding line. Since the matrix $A = A' - \lambda I$, and the latter is shown to be positive semi-definite,

$$E_2 - E_1 \leq 0 \tag{A5}$$

because any quadratic form $y^T Q y \geq 0$ for any positive semi-definite matrix Q and any vector y. So the error reduces after each iteration, or stays the same. After applying the update for every word, and having a complete cycle where the error does not reduce any more for any of the vectors, convergence of the algorithm is signified.

References

1. Zou, W.Y.; Socher, R.; Cer, D.; Manning, C.D. Bilingual word embeddings for phrase-based machine translation. In Proceedings of the 2013 Conference on Empirical Methods in Natural Language Processing, Seattle, WA, USA, 18–21 October 2013; pp. 1393–1398.
2. Maas, A.L.; Daly, R.E.; Pham, P.T.; Huang, D.; Ng, A.Y.; Potts, C. Learning word vectors for sentiment analysis. In Proceedings of the 49th Annual Meeting of the Association for Computational Linguistics: Human Language Technologies-Volume 1, Portland, OR, USA, 19–24 June 2011; pp. 142–150.
3. Tang, D.; Wei, F.; Yang, N.; Zhou, M.; Liu, T.; Qin, B. Learning sentiment-specific word embedding for twitter sentiment classification. In Proceedings of the 52nd Annual Meeting of the Association for Computational Linguistics (Volume 1: Long Papers), Baltimore, MD, USA, 22–27 June 2014; Volume 1, pp. 1555–1565.
4. Dragoni, M.; Petrucci, G. A neural word embeddings approach for multi-domain sentiment analysis. IEEE Trans. Affect. Comput. 2017, 8, 457–470. [CrossRef]
5. Deho, B.O.; Agangiba, A.W.; Aryeh, L.F.; Ansah, A.J. Sentiment Analysis with Word Embedding. In Proceedings of the 2018 IEEE 7th International Conference on Adaptive Science & Technology (ICAST), University of Ghana, Legon, Accra, Ghana, 22–24 August 2018; pp. 1–4.
6. Liang, J.; Cui, B.; Jiang, H.; Shen, Y.; Xie, Y. Sentence similarity computing based on word2vec and LSTM and its application in rice FAQ question-answering system. J. Nanjing Agric. Univ. 2018, 41, 946–953.
7. Liu, H. Agricultural Q&A System Based on LSTM-CNN and Word2vec. Revis. Fac. Agron. Univ. Zulia 2019, 36, 543–551.
8. Roy, D. Word Embedding based Approaches for Information Retrieval. In Proceedings of the Seventh BCS-IRSG Symposium on Future Directions in Information Access 7, Barcelona, Spain, 5 September 2017; pp. 1–4.

9. Liu, Y.; Fu, Z. Secure search service based on word2vec in the public cloud. *Int. J. Comput. Sci. Eng.* **2019**, *18*, 305–313. [CrossRef]
10. Kim, J.; Hong, T.; Kim, P. Word2Vec based spelling correction method of Twitter message. In Proceedings of the 34th ACM/SIGAPP Symposium on Applied Computing, Limassol, Cyprus, 8–12 April 2019; pp. 2016–2019.
11. Pan, Q.; Dong, H.; Wang, Y.; Cai, Z.; Zhang, L. Recommendation of Crowdsourcing Tasks Based on Word2vec Semantic Tags. *Wirel. Commun. Mob. Comput.* **2019**, *2019*, 2121850. [CrossRef]
12. Habibi, M.; Weber, L.; Neves, M.; Wiegandt, D.L.; Leser, U. Deep learning with word embeddings improves biomedical named entity recognition. *Bioinformatics* **2017**, *33*, i37–i48. [CrossRef]
13. Kågebäck, M.; Mogren, O.; Tahmasebi, N.; Dubhashi, D. Extractive summarization using continuous vector space models. In Proceedings of the 2nd Workshop on Continuous Vector Space Models and Their Compositionality (CVSC), Gothenburg, Sweden, 26–30 April 2014; pp. 31–39.
14. Rossiello, G.; Basile, P.; Semeraro, G. Centroid-based text summarization through compositionality of word embeddings. In Proceedings of the MultiLing 2017 Workshop on Summarization and Summary Evaluation Across Source Types and Genres, Valencia, Spain, 3 April 2017; pp. 12–21.
15. Yang, K.; Al-Sabahi, K.; Xiang, Y.; Zhang, Z. An integrated graph model for document summarization. *Information* **2018**, *9*, 232. [CrossRef]
16. Simard, P.Y.; LeCun, Y.A.; Denker, J.S.; Victorri, B. Transformation invariance in pattern recognition—Tangent distance and tangent propagation. In *Neural Networks: Tricks of the Trade*; Springer: New York, NY, USA, 1998; pp. 239–274.
17. Mikolov, T.; Sutskever, I.; Chen, K.; Corrado, G.S.; Dean, J. Distributed representations of words and phrases and their compositionality. *Adv. Neural Inf. Process. Syst. 26 (NIPS 2013)* **2013**, 3111–3119.
18. Mikolov, T.; Chen, K.; Corrado, G.; Dean, J. Efficient Estimation of Word Representations in Vector Space. *arXiv* **2013**, arXiv:1301.3781.
19. Pennington, J.; Socher, R.; Manning, C. Glove: Global vectors for word representation. In Proceedings of the 2014 Conference on Empirical Methods in Natural Language Processing (EMNLP), Doha, Qatar, 25–29 October 2014; pp. 1532–1543.
20. Mikolov, T.; Grave, E.; Bojanowski, P.; Puhrsch, C.; Joulin, A. Advances in pre-training distributed word representations. *arXiv* **2017**, arXiv:1712.09405.
21. Dev, S.; Hassan, S.; Phillips, J.M. Absolute Orientation for Word Embedding Alignment. *arXiv* **2018**, arXiv:1806.01330.
22. Vilnis, L.; McCallum, A. Word representations via gaussian embedding. *arXiv* **2014**, arXiv:1412.6623.
23. Bian, J.; Gao, B.; Liu, T.Y. Knowledge-powered deep learning for word embedding. In *Joint European Conference on Machine Learning and Knowledge Discovery in Databases*; Springer: New York, NY, USA, 2014; pp. 132–148.
24. Zhou, G.; He, T.; Zhao, J.; Hu, P. Learning continuous word embedding with metadata for question retrieval in community question answering. In Proceedings of the 53rd Annual Meeting of the Association for Computational Linguistics and the 7th International Joint Conference on Natural Language Processing (Volume 1: Long Papers), Beijing, China, 26–31 July 2015; Volume 1, pp. 250–259.
25. Faruqui, M.; Dodge, J.; Jauhar, S.K.; Dyer, C.; Hovy, E.; Smith, N.A. Retrofitting word vectors to semantic lexicons. *arXiv* **2014**, arXiv:1411.4166.
26. Jo, H. Expansional Retrofitting for Word Vector Enrichment. *arXiv* **2018**, arXiv:1808.07337.
27. Mohammad, S.; Dorr, B.; Hirst, G. Computing word-pair antonymy. In *Proceedings of the Conference on Empirical Methods in Natural Language Processing*; Association for Computational Linguistics: Stroudsburg, PA, USA, 2008; pp. 982–991.
28. Lobanova, A. *The Anatomy of Antonymy: A Corpus-Driven Approach*; University of Groningen: Groningen, The Netherlands, 2012.
29. Yih, W.t.; Zweig, G.; Platt, J.C. Polarity inducing latent semantic analysis. In *Proceedings of the 2012 Joint Conference on Empirical Methods in Natural Language Processing and Computational Natural Language Learning*; Association for Computational Linguistics: Stroudsburg, PA, USA, 2012; pp. 1212–1222.
30. Mohammad, S.M.; Dorr, B.J.; Hirst, G.; Turney, P.D. Computing lexical contrast. *Comput. Linguist.* **2013**, *39*, 555–590. [CrossRef]

31. Chang, K.W.; Yih, W.t.; Meek, C. Multi-relational latent semantic analysis. In Proceedings of the 2013 Conference on Empirical Methods in Natural Language Processing, Seattle, WA, USA, 18–21 October 2013; pp. 1602–1612.
32. Zhang, J.; Salwen, J.; Glass, M.; Gliozzo, A. Word semantic representations using bayesian probabilistic tensor factorization. In Proceedings of the 2014 Conference on Empirical Methods in Natural Language Processing (EMNLP), Doha, Qatar, 25–29 October 2014; pp. 1522–1531.
33. Santus, E.; Lu, Q.; Lenci, A.; Huang, C.R. Taking antonymy mask off in vector space. In Proceedings of the 28th Pacific Asia Conference on Language, Information and Computing, Phuket, Thailand, 12–14 December 2014; pp. 135–144.
34. Ono, M.; Miwa, M.; Sasaki, Y. Word embedding-based antonym detection using thesauri and distributional information. In Proceedings of the 2015 Conference of the North American Chapter of the Association for Computational Linguistics: Human Language Technologies, Denver, CO, USA, 31 May–5 June 2015; pp. 984–989.
35. Nguyen, K.A.; im Walde, S.S.; Vu, N.T. Integrating Distributional Lexical Contrast into Word Embeddings for Antonym-Synonym Distinction. In Proceedings of the 54th Annual Meeting of the Association for Computational Linguistics (Volume 2: Short Papers), Berlin, Germany, 7–12 August 2016.
36. Li, L.; Qin, B.; Liu, T. Contradiction detection with contradiction-specific word embedding. *Algorithms* **2017**, *10*, 59. [CrossRef]
37. Zahran, M.A.; Magooda, A.; Mahgoub, A.Y.; Raafat, H.; Rashwan, M.; Atyia, A. Word representations in vector space and their applications for arabic. In *International Conference on Intelligent Text Processing and Computational Linguistics*; Springer: New York, NY, USA, 2015; pp. 430–443.
38. Soliman, A.B.; Eissa, K.; El-Beltagy, S.R. Aravec: A set of arabic word embedding models for use in arabic nlp. *Procedia Comput. Sci.* **2017**, *117*, 256–265. [CrossRef]
39. Mihalcea, R.; Radev, D. *Graph-Based Natural Language Processing and Information Retrieval*; Cambridge University Press: Cambridge, UK, 2011.
40. Venkatesh, S.S. *The Theory of Probability: Explorations and Applications*; Cambridge University Press: Cambridge, UK, 2013.
41. NetworkX Developers. 2015. Available online: https://networkx.github.io/documentation/networkx-1.10/ (accessed on 4 July 2019).
42. Smart Words—A Handpicked Collection of Gems of the English Language. Available online: http://www.smart-words.org/list-of-synonyms/ (accessed on 4 July 2019).
43. Power Thesaurus. Available online: https://www.powerthesaurus.org (accessed on 4 July 2019).
44. Princeton University "About WordNet". 2010. Available online: https://wordnet.princeton.edu/ (accessed on 4 July 2019).
45. 100 Examples of Antonyms. Available online: https://www.powerthesaurus.org/100_examples_of_antonyms (accessed on 23 July 2018).
46. List 24-Synonyms. Available online: http://myenglishgrammar.com/list-24-synonyms.html (accessed on 23 July 2019).
47. Course Hero.docx-SYNONYMS. Available online: https://www.coursehero.com/file/38484777/course-herodocx/ (accessed on 23 July 2019).
48. Synonyms for the 96 Most Commonly Used Words in English. Available online: https://justenglish.me/2014/04/18/synonyms-for-the-96-most-commonly-used-words-in-english/ (accessed on 23 July 2019).
49. List 23-Antonyms. Available online: http://myenglishgrammar.com/list-23-antonyms.html (accessed on 23 July 2019).
50. Fry, E.B.; Kress, J.E. *The Reading Teacher's Book of Lists*; John Wiley & Sons: New York, NY, USA, 2012; Volume 55.
51. List of 30 Antonyms You Should Know. Available online: https://www.indiatoday.in/education-today/grammar-vocabulary/story/antonyms-264084-2015-09-21 (accessed on 23 July 2018).
52. Common Opposites-Antonyms Vocabulary Word List. Available online: https://www.enchantedlearning.com/wordlist/opposites.shtml (accessed on 23 July 2018).
53. Antonym Word List. Available online: http://slplessonplans.com/files/antonymlist.pdf (accessed on 23 July 2018).

54. Thesaurus.com. The World's Favorite Online Thesaurus! 2013. Available online: https://www.thesaurus.com/ (accessed on 4 July 2019).
55. Michael Fogleman: Random Phrases. Available online: https://www.michaelfogleman.com/phrases/ (accessed on 4 July 2019).
56. Miller, G.A.; Charles, W.G. Contextual correlates of semantic similarity. *Lang. Cogn. Process.* **1991**, *6*, 1–28. [CrossRef]
57. Rubenstein, H.; Goodenough, J.B. Contextual correlates of synonymy. *Commun. ACM* **1965**, *8*, 627–633. [CrossRef]
58. Finkelstein, L.; Gabrilovich, E.; Matias, Y.; Rivlin, E.; Solan, Z.; Wolfman, G.; Ruppin, E. Placing search in context: The concept revisited. *ACM Trans. Inf. Syst.* **2002**, *20*, 116–131.
59. Li, Q.; Li, S.; Zhang, S.; Hu, J.; Hu, J. A Review of Text Corpus-Based Tourism Big Data Mining. *Appl. Sci.* **2019**, *9*, 3300. [CrossRef]
60. Liu, J. [dataset] 515K Hotel Reviews Data in Europe. Available online: https://www.kaggle.com/jiashenliu/515k-hotel-reviews-data-in-europe (accessed on 12 October 2019).
61. Rizkallah, S.; Atiya, A.; Shaheen, S. Learning Spherical Word Vectors for Opinion Mining and Applying on Hotel Reviews. *Work. Pap.* **2020**.
62. Busygin, S. A new trust region technique for the maximum weight clique problem. *Discret. Appl. Math.* **2006**, *154*, 2080–2096. [CrossRef]
63. Busygin, S.; Butenko, S.; Pardalos, P.M. A heuristic for the maximum independent set problem based on optimization of a quadratic over a sphere. *J. Comb. Optim.* **2002**, *6*, 287–297. [CrossRef]
64. Hager, W.W. Minimizing a quadratic over a sphere. *Siam J. Optim.* **2001**, *12*, 188–208. [CrossRef]
65. Forsythe, G.E.; Golub, G.H. On the stationary values of a second-degree polynomial on the unit sphere. *J. Soc. Ind. Appl. Math.* **1965**, *13*, 1050–1068. [CrossRef]

© 2020 by the authors. Licensee MDPI, Basel, Switzerland. This article is an open access article distributed under the terms and conditions of the Creative Commons Attribution (CC BY) license (http://creativecommons.org/licenses/by/4.0/).

Article

Improving Sentence Retrieval Using Sequence Similarity

Ivan Boban [1,*], Alen Doko [2] and Sven Gotovac [3]

[1] Faculty of Mechanical Engineering, Computing and Electrical Engineering, University of Mostar, Mostar 88000, Bosnia and Herzegovina
[2] Institute for Software Technology, German Aerospace Center, 28199 Bremen, Germany; alen.doko@dlr.de
[3] Faculty of Electrical Engineering, Mechanical Engineering and Naval Architecture, University of Split, 21000 Split, Croatia; sven.gotovac@fesb.hr
* Correspondence: ivan.boban@hotmail.com or ivan.boban@student.fsre.ba; Tel.: +387-63-484-395

Received: 1 June 2020; Accepted: 19 June 2020; Published: 23 June 2020

Abstract: Sentence retrieval is an information retrieval technique that aims to find sentences corresponding to an information need. It is used for tasks like question answering (QA) or novelty detection. Since it is similar to document retrieval but with a smaller unit of retrieval, methods for document retrieval are also used for sentence retrieval like term frequency—inverse document frequency (TF-IDF), BM25, and language modeling-based methods. The effect of partial matching of words to sentence retrieval is an issue that has not been analyzed. We think that there is a substantial potential for the improvement of sentence retrieval methods if we consider this approach. We adapted TF-ISF, BM25, and language modeling-based methods to test the partial matching of terms through combining sentence retrieval with sequence similarity, which allows matching of words that are similar but not identical. All tests were conducted using data from the novelty tracks of the Text Retrieval Conference (TREC). The scope of this paper was to find out if such approach is generally beneficial to sentence retrieval. However, we did not examine in depth how partial matching helps or hinders the finding of relevant sentences.

Keywords: sentence retrieval; TF–ISF; BM25; language modeling; partial match; sequence similarity

1. Introduction

Information retrieval involves finding material (e.g., documents) of an unstructured nature (e.g., text), that satisfies an information need from within large collections [1]. Information retrieval systems generally consist of an index of documents and a query provided by the user [2]. Information retrieval systems should rank documents by their relevance after processing the documents. When the information retrieval system receives the query from the user, a system aims to provide documents from within the collection that are relevant to an arbitrary user information need [1].

Sentence retrieval is similar to document retrieval but with smaller unit of retrieval [3]. Sentence retrieval is defined as the task of acquiring relevant sentences as a response to a query, question, or reference sentence [2]. It can be used in various ways to simplify the end user task of finding the right information from document collections [4]. One of the first and most successful methods for sentence retrieval is the term frequency—inverse sentence frequency (TF-ISF) method, which is an adaptation of the term frequency—inverse document frequency (TF-IDF) method to sentence retrieval [3,5]. Also, BM25 and language modeling-based methods are used for sentence retrieval where the sentence is the unit of retrieval [6].

In this paper, we thoroughly tested the effect of partial matching of terms to sentence retrieval. Text matching was the basis for each natural language processing task [7,8].

We tested the TF-ISF, BM25, and language modeling-based method with sequence similarity presented as the partial matching of words.

For the testing and evaluation of new methods, data of the Text Retrieval Conference (TREC) novelty tracks [9–11] were used as a standard test collection for the sentence retrieval methods.

Many different information retrieval methods are used for sentence retrieval. These methods are always document retrieval methods which are adapted for sentences. Contrary to document retrieval, when implementing sentence retrieval, no processing is implemented that allows the non-exact or partial matching of words. We think that taking the partial matching of words into account has a great potential to improve sentence retrieval, especially when taking into account how little information a sentence contains and that every clue about the relevance of the sentence can be precious. The remainder of this paper is organized as follows. Previous work is shown in Section 2. The research objectives are presented in Section 3. New methods, experiments, and results are presented in Sections 4 and 5, respectively, and the conclusion is given in Section 6.

2. Previous Research

Sentence retrieval is similar to document retrieval, and sentence retrieval methods are usually simple adaptations of document retrieval methods where sentences are treated as documents [3,6]. The sentence retrieval task consists of finding relevant sentences from a document base which has been given a query [6].

Generally, when it comes to information retrieval, the TF-IDF method is still very much present today. For example, the authors of [12] presented a text document search system on distributed high-performance information systems, where initial document weighting was performed using the TF-IDF method. The weighting of text by the TF-IDF method, or the assignment of weight to each linguistic concept in comments from social networks, has also been described by the authors of [13].

The authors of [14] presented two different techniques (BM25 and TF-IDF) to extract the keywords from data collection using Twitter. TF-IDF has also been also used for novelty detection in news events [15]. TF-IDF is widely used for text pre-processing and feature engineering [13]. There have also been attempts to outperform TF-IDF. For example, the authors of [16] presented a Phrase-Based document similarity, which effectively outperformed term-based TF-IDF. The authors of [17] proposed a refined TF-IDF method, called TA TF-IDF, for calculating the weights of hot terms. The vector-space model is one of the most commonly used models for documents and sentence retrieval [2]. The authors of [18] proposed a method of analyzing patent texts based on the vector space model, with the features of patent texts being excluded. Using the proposed algorithm, the authors of [19] calculated the distance between document and topics, and then each document was represented as a vector.

When it comes to sentence retrieval, TF-ISF (the sentence retrieval variation of the TF-IDF method) is one of the first and most widely used methods for sentence retrieval [5]. TF-ISF has been shown to outperform other methods, like BM25-based methods and methods based on language modeling [5,20]. The sentences are represented as a collection of unique words with the weights of words that appear in the selected sentence [21]. The second method popularly used with sentence retrieval is query probability [2,6]. There have been multiple attempts to improve the standard TF-ISF method, which include analyzing the context in the form of a document and the previous, following, or current sentences [6]. The authors of [22] analyzed the effectiveness of contextual information for answer sentence selection.

In our research, we adapted tree standard retrieval models, TF-ISF, BM25 and the language modeling-based method, to improve sentence retrieval using the partial matching of words.

3. Research Objective

The aim of the research was to determine whether and to what extent the partial matching of words (terms between the query q and the sentence s) influences the performance of methods for sentence retrieval. The influence of partial matching of words were presented by experimental results on three ranking models: TF-ISF, BM25 and the language modeling-based method. Sequence similarity is a technique which allows matching of terms that are similar but not identical. By testing sequence similarity, we intend to add some weight to the question of whether or not it is generally profitable to use partial matching of terms for sentence retrieval.

In large, our research hypothesis was that the partial matching of words improves of sentence retrieval methods.

4. Partial Match of Terms Using Sequence Similarity

The bulk of sentence retrieval methods proposed in the literature are adaptations of standard retrieval models, such as TF-IDF, BM25, the language modeling-based method, where the sentence is the unit of retrieval [6].

In this work, we showed sentence retrieval using sequence similarity and presented the experimental results on three ranking models: TF-ISF (based on vector space model), BM25, and the language modeling-based methods. All three models were adapted in such a way to allow us to test the partial matching of terms.

4.1. TF-ISF Method with Sentence Retrieval

One of the first and most successful methods for sentence retrieval is the TF-ISF defined as [4,5,23]:

$$\text{TF-ISF}(s, q) = \sum_{t \in q} \log(tf_{t,q} + 1) \log(tf_{t,s} + 1) \log\left(\frac{n+1}{0.5 + sf_t}\right) \quad (1)$$

The TF-ISF method assess relevance of sentence s with regard to query q, where

- sf_t is the number of sentences in which the term t appears,
- n is the number of sentences in the collection,
- $tf_{t,q}$ is number of appearances of the term t in a query q, and
- $tf_{t,s}$ is number of appearances of the term t in a sentence s.

4.2. BM25 Model with Sentence Retrieval

The BM25 model uses document ranking, and this model can also be used for sentence retrieval. The ranking function of the BM25 method used to sentence retrieval is defined as [6]:

$$\text{BM25}(s, q) = \sum_{t \in q} \log \frac{N - sf(t) + 0.5}{sf(t) + 0.5} \cdot \frac{(k_1 + 1)c(t, s)}{k_1\left[(1-b) + b\frac{|s|}{avsl}\right] + c(t, s)} \cdot \frac{(k_3 + 1)c(t, q)}{k_3 + c(t, q)} \quad (2)$$

where

- N is the number of sentences in the collection,
- $sf(t)$ is the number of sentences in which the term t appears,
- $c(t, s)$ is the number of appearances of the term t in a sentence s,
- $c(t, q)$ is the number of appearances of the term t in a query q,
- $|s|$ is the sentence length,
- $avsl$ is the average sentence length, and
- k_1, k_3, and b are the adjustment parameters.

4.3. Sentence Retrieval with Language Model (LM)

The language modeling-based method (language mode) for document retrieval can be applied analogously to sentence retrieval. The probability of a query q given the sentence s can then be estimated using the standard LM approach [6]:

$$\text{LM}(q, s) = \prod_{t \in q} P(t|s)^{c(t,q)} \tag{3}$$

$$P(t|s) = \frac{c(t,s)}{|s|} \tag{4}$$

where

- $c(t,s)$ is number of appearances of the term t in a sentence s, and
- $|s|$ is the sentence length.

One of the most commonly used methods when it comes to sentence retrieval is Dirichlet smoothing, which, when applied to Method (3), gives:

$$\text{LM}(q, s) = \prod_{t \in q} \frac{c(t,s) + \mu P(t)}{|s| + \mu} \tag{5}$$

where

- $c(t,s)$ is the number of appearances of the term t in a sentence s,
- $|s|$ is the sentence length,
- μ is the parameter that control the amount of smoothing, and
- $P(t)$ can be calculated using the maximum likelihood estimator of the term in a large collection: $p(t, C)$ (where C is the collection) [6].

In the previous literature, previously presented ranking functions were combined with data pre-processing and stop word removal. Removing stop words is generally considered to be useful, since stop words do not contain any information [24].

There are several methods for removing stop words, which have been presented by the authors of [25]. Some papers [26] have also proposed time efficient methods. The method we used in this paper is based on a previously compiled list of words. The performance of functions was tested in its basic form with stop word removal.

4.4. Sentence Retrieval Using Sequence Similarity

When it comes to the effect of sequence similarity on sentence retrieval, we made use of the contextual similarity functions presented by the authors of [27]. This procedure enabled us to match of terms that were not identical but similar. Through analyzing the equation for the assessment of the common context by the authors of [27], we concluded that the same analogy could be used to find out if a certain term from query q and a certain term from sentence s share a common subsequence.

In Reference [27], the formula $\delta(N, M)$ determines the appearance of subsequence N in a sequence M. We can define the formula $\delta(q, s)$ analogous to the formula from Reference [27], with query q (instead of subsequence in [27]) and sentence s (instead of sequence M in [27]) as follows:

$$\delta(q, s) = \sum_{i=1}^{|q|} \sum_{j=i}^{|q|} |q_{ij} \cap s| \tag{6}$$

where

- q_{ij} presents subsequence of sequence s.

If sequence s does not contain the subsequence q_{ij}, there is no need to check for $qi(j+1)$ [27]. When the sequence q is a subsequence of s, the $\delta(q, s) = 1$.

Furthermore, we have to extend Formula (6) to include the normalization parameter T_σ that is given in work [27]. This solves the measurement problem that appears when larger sequences that have more subsequences are more similar than the sequences with shorter lengths, which is not correct [27]. In other words, T_σ is the coefficient which represents the total score that can be achieved under the assumption that the first sequence is a proper subsequence of the second, or $N \subseteq M$ [27]. After including the normalization parameter T_σ, we obtained:

$$\delta(q, s) = \frac{1}{T_\sigma} \sum_{i=1}^{|q|} \sum_{j=i}^{|q|} |q_{ij} \cap s| \tag{7}$$

where

- T_σ is the normalization parameter.

The importance of a word depends on its frequency inside its sentence [28] or the number of times a particular word occurs in the sentence [29]. However, the exact matching of terms was used, and the partial matching where words are similar but not identical was not considered. The assumption is that instead of the total matching, the existing methods for sentence retrieval can be improved through partial matching between subsequences and sequences, or in other words, between the term from the query and the term from the sentence.

In Equations (1), (2), and (5), $tf_{t,s}$ and $c(t,s)$ represent the number of appearances of term t in the sentence s. Here, too, the exact matching of terms was used.

If instead of using the parameter $tf_{t,s}$ in the method TF-ISF(s, q), and $c(t,s)$ in method BM25(s,q) and LM(q, s), we define the parameters $tf_{t,s \; (partial)}$ and $c(t,s)_{(partial)}$ which are also defined using the method $\delta(q, s)$, we can define $tf_{t,s \; (partial)}$ and $c(t,s)_{(partial)}$ parameters as follows:

$$sim(t,s)_{partial} = \frac{1}{T_\sigma} \sum_{i=1}^{|t|} \sum_{j=i}^{|s|} |t_{ij} \cap s| \tag{8}$$

where

- t_{ij} presents subsequence of sequence s (term t from the query as a subsequence of term from the sentence s as a sequence.

To include the partial matching of terms, we took all defined ranking functions and replaced $tf_{t,s}$ and $c(t,s)$ with $sim(t,s)_{partial}$, and defined a new ranking functions for all three ranking models.

We further optimized all of the formulas to only consider terms that already appeared in both the query and sentence or $t \in q \cap s$. The assumption is that if we have a minimum of one match between the query and the sentence, it is more probable that additional matches in other terms between the query and the sentence could be found using the sequence similarity.

New ranking functions have been defined in their final form, which assesses the relevancy of the sentences regarding the query q, and considers the partial match of the term t from the query in relation to the terms from the sentence (Equations (9)–(11)):

$$\text{TF-ISF}_{partial_{(t,s)}}(s,q) = \sum_{t \in q \cap s} \log(tf_{t,q} + 1) \log(sim(t,s)_{partial} + 1) \log\left(\frac{n+1}{0.5 + sf_t}\right) \tag{9}$$

$$\text{BM25}_{partial_{(t,s)}}(s,q) = \sum_{t \in q \cap s} \log \frac{N - sf(t) + 0,5}{sf(t) + 0,5} \cdot \frac{(k_1 + 1) \; sim(t,s)_{partial}}{k1\left[(1-b) + b\frac{|s|}{avsl}\right] + sim(t,s)_{partial}} \cdot \frac{(k_3 + 1)c(t,q)}{k_3 + c(t,q)} \tag{10}$$

$$LM_{partial_{(t,s)}}(q,s) = \prod_{t \in q \cap s} \frac{sim(t,s)_{partial} + \mu P(t)}{|s| + \mu} \qquad (11)$$

where

- $t \in q \cap s$ is the postulate that only terms that are in the query and in the sentence are considered. In this case, there was a minimum of at least one match of the terms from the query and from the sentence.

To repeat the point of the new ranking functions, it considers the total match of the query term and sentence term, as defined by the parameter $tf_{t,s}$ and $c(t,s)$ in the ranking functions TF-ISF (s, q), BM25(s, q), and LM(q, s).

The new ranking functions also consider additional appearances of terms from the query as the subsequence of terms from the sentence.

We denoted the new methods and their ranking function as shown in the Table 1.

Table 1. Overview of all sentence retrieval methods tested in this paper.

Method	Ranking Function
TF-ISF	TF-ISF(s, q)
TF-ISF$_{part}$	TF-ISF$_{partial_{(t,s)}}(s, q)$
BM25	BM25(s, q)
BM25$_{part}$	BM25$_{partial_{(t,s)}}(s, q)$
LM	LM(q, s)
LM$_{part}$	LM$_{partial_{(t,s)}}(q, s)$

5. Experiments and Results

The experiment was conducted using data from the novelty tracks of the Text Retrieval Conference (TREC). There were three TREC novelty tracks in the years from 2002 to 2004: TREC 2002, TREC 2003, and TREC 2004 [9–11]. The task was novelty detection, which consists of two subtasks: Finding relevant sentences and finding novel sentences. Our experiment was entirely focused on sentence retrieval, which represents the first task of novelty detection. Three data collections were used, each consisting of 50 topics (queries) and 25 documents per topic, with multiple sentences (Table 2) [30].

Table 2. Description of dataset characteristics.

Name of the Collection	Number of Topics (Queries)	Number of Documents per Topic	Number of Sentences
TREC 2002	50	25	57,792
TREC 2003	50	25	39,820
TREC 2004	50	25	52,447

When it comes to TREC topics, it must be emphasized that each one has a *title*, a *description*, and *narrative*. These three parts represent three versions of the same query but with different lengths. The *title* is the shortest query and *narrative* the longest. In our tests, we used the shortest version called "*title*." Figure 1 depicts the *title* of topic N1 from TREC 2003.

```
<top>
<num>Number: N1
<title>partial birth abortion ban
<toptype>opinion

<desc>Description:
Find opinions about the proposed ban on partial birth abortions.

<narr>Narrative: Relevant information includes opinions on partial
birth abortion and whether or not it should be legal.  Opinions that
also cover abortion in general are relevant.  Opinions on the
implications of proposed bans on partial birth abortions and the
positions of the courts are also relevant.
```

Figure 1. Example of query from Text Retrieval Conference (TREC) 2003 novelty track.

Every query was executed on 25 documents. Each of the documents consisted of multiple sentences as described in Table 2. Each sentence was marked with a beginning and ending tag. Each sentence had a number. Figure 2 shows an extract form document NYT19980629.0465 with sentence number 11.

```
<Sentence>
  <Name>NYT19980629.0465_11.txt</Name>
  <Content> Abortion-rights activists say the law is worded so vaguely that it
  could reasonably be interpreted to ban any number of abortion methods in even
  the first three months of a pregnancy, when a woman currently has an absolute
  right to seek an abortion.</Content>
</Sentence>
```

Figure 2. Example of the sentence part within the document from TREC 2003 novelty track.

Each TREC data collection also contains a list of relevant sentences. Figure 3 depicts an excerpt from the list of relevant sentences of TREC 2003.

```
N1 NYT19980629.0465:8
N1 NYT19980629.0465:11
N1 NYT19980629.0465:12
N1 NYT19980629.0465:13
N1 NYT19980629.0465:14
N1 NYT19980629.0465:15
N1 NYT19980629.0465:18
N1 NYT19980629.0465:24
N1 NYT19980629.0465:33
N1 NYT19980629.0465:34
N1 NYT19980629.0465:36
N1 NYT19980629.0465:37
N1 NYT19980629.0465:42
N1 NYT19980629.0465:43
```

Figure 3. An excerpt in the dataset that contains a list of relevant sentences.

The marked line in Figure 3 defines sentence 11 from the document NYT19980629.0465 as relevant to the topic (query) N1 ("partial birth abortion ban").

To test whether the new methods provide better sentence retrieval results than the existing methods, we compared the performances of the new methods in relation to the existing methods (baseline methods) using the following standard measures: P@10, the MAP, and the R-precision [1,6].

The precision at x or P@x can be defined as:

$$P@x(q_j) = \frac{\text{number of relevant sentences within top } x \text{ retrieved}}{x} \quad (12)$$

The P@10 values shown in this paper refer to average P@10 for 50 queries [30]. R-precision can be defined as [1]:

$$R - precision = \frac{r}{|Rel|} \quad (13)$$

where

- $|Rel|$ is the number of relevant sentences to the query, and
- R is the number of relevant sentences in top $|Rel|$ sentences of the result.

The R-precision values shown in this paper are (analogous to P@10) averages for 50 queries [30].

The Mean Average Precision and R-precision gave similar results and were used to test high recall. High recall means it is more important to find all of the relevant sentences, even if it means searching through many sentences including many that are nonrelevant. Meanwhile, P@10 is used for testing precision [30].

In terms of information retrieval, precision means it is more important to get only relevant sentences than finding all of the relevant sentence [30].

To compare the difference between methods, we used a two-tailed paired t-test with a significance level of $\alpha = 0.05$ [4]. The results of our tests are presented in tabular form.

Statistically significant differences in relation to the baseline methods are marked with a (*).

In each of the tested methods, we used stop word removal as pre-processing step.

Table 3 shows the results of our tests on two different versions of the TF-ISF method using TRECs 2002, 2003, and 2004.

Table 3. Test results of methods TF-ISF and TF-ISF$_{part}$.

Data Collection	Measures	TF-ISF	TF-ISF$_{part}$
TREC 2002	P@10	0.304	0.32
	MAP	0.196	* 0.204
	R-prec.	0.245	0.250
TREC 2003	P@10	0.692	0.714
	MAP	0.576	* 0.591
	R-prec.	0.547	* 0.560
TREC 2004	P@10	0.434	0.468
	MAP	0.324	* 0.335
	R-prec.	0.336	* 0.355

* Statistically significant differences in relation to the baseline methods.

Table 3 shows that the TF-ISF$_{part}$ methods provided better results and statistically significant differences in relation to the base TF-ISF method when the MAP measures was used in all three collections, and R-prec. in TREC 2003 and TREC 2004 collection. Better results were not achieved when using the P@10 measures.

Table 4 shows the results of our tests on two different versions of the BM25 model using TRECs 2002, 2003, and 2004.

Table 4. Test results of methods BM25 and BM25$_{part}$ ($k1 = 1.5$, $b = 0.75$, $k3 = 0$).

Data Collection	Measures	BM	BM$_{part}$
TREC 2002	P@10	0.142	* 0.33
	MAP	0.105	* 0.209
	R-prec.	0.097	* 0.255
TREC 2003	P@10	0.628	* 0.75
	MAP	0.464	* 0.601
	R-prec.	0.4281	* 0.565
TREC 2004	P@10	0.366	* 0.472
	MAP	0.242	* 0.342
	R-prec.	0.236	* 0.363

* Statistically significant differences in relation to the baseline methods.

The parameters settings for the BM25 model were $k1 = 1.5$, $b = 0.75$, $k3 = 0$.

Table 4 shows that the BM25$_{part}$ method (method using sequence similarity) provided better results and statistically significant differences in relation to the base method in all measures and collections.

Table 5 shows the results of our tests on two different version of the LM model using TREC collections from 2002, 2003, and 2004. The parameter settings for LM were $\mu = 100$.

Table 5. Test results of methods LM and LM$_{part}$ ($\mu = 100$).

Data Collection	Measures	LM	LM$_{part}$
TREC 2002	P@10	0.268	* 0.356
	MAP	0.170	* 0.207
	R-prec.	0.215	* 0.250
TREC 2003	P@10	0.71	0.7
	MAP	0.528	* 0.597
	R-prec.	0.501	* 0.567
TREC 2004	P@10	0.388	* 0.458
	MAP	0.287	* 0.334
	R-prec.	0.306	* 0.355

* Statistically significant differences in relation to the baseline methods.

Table 5 shows that the LM$_{part}$ method, as well the BM25$_{part}$ method, provided better results and statistically significant differences in relation to the base method in all measures and collections, except for the P@10 measures for TREC 2003 collection.

6. Conclusions

In this paper, we thoroughly tested sentence retrieval with sequence similarity, which allowed us to match words that were similar but not identical. We tested sentence retrieval methods with the partial matching of terms using TREC data. We adapted TF-ISF, BM25 and the language modeling-based method to test the partial matching of terms using sequence similarity.

We found out that the partial matching of terms using sequence similarity can benefit sentence retrieval in all three tested collection. We showed the benefits of partial matching using sequence similarity through statistically significant better results.

The reason for the better position of the sentence when we used adapted methods using sequence similarity is the additional matching of terms between the query q and the sentence s.

We conclude that partial matching of words is beneficial when combined with sentence retrieval. However, we did not analyze whether some nonrelevant sentences were falsely high ranked. Therefore, future research will include a thorough analyses of the effect of the partial matching of words on sentence retrieval. Future research will also include experiments using pre-processing methods, such as stemming and lemmatization or some other technique.

Author Contributions: Conceptualization, I.B. and A.D.; methodology, I.B. and A.D. and S.G.; software, I.B. and A.D.; validation, A.D. and S.G.; formal analysis, I.B.; investigation, I.B.; resources, I.B. and A.D.; data curation, I.B. and A.D.; writing—original draft preparation, I.B.; writing—review and editing, I.B. and A.D.; visualization, I.B.; supervision, S.G. All authors have read and agreed to the published version of the manuscript.

Funding: This research received no external funding.

Conflicts of Interest: The authors declare no conflict of interest.

References

1. Manning, C.D.; Raghavan, P.; Schutze, H. *Introduction to Information Retrieval*; Cambridge University Press: Cambridge, UK, 2008.
2. Murdock, V.G. Aspects of Sentence Retrieval. Ph.D. Thesis, University of Massachussetts, Amherst, MA, USA, 2006.
3. Doko, A.; Štula, M.; Seric, L. Using TF-ISF with Local Context to Generate an Owl Document Representation for Sentence Retrieval. *Comput. Sci. Eng. Int. J.* **2015**, *5*, 1–15. [CrossRef]
4. Doko, A.; Štula, M.; Seric, L. Improved sentence retrieval using local context and sentence length. *Inf. Process. Manag.* **2013**, *49*, 1301–1312. [CrossRef]
5. Allan, J.; Wade, C.; Bolivar, A. Retrieval and novelty detection at the sentence level. In Proceedings of the 26th Annual International ACM SIGIR Conference on Research and Development in Informaion Retrieval -SIGIR '03, Toronto, ON, Canada, 28 July–1 August 2003.
6. Fernández, R.T.; Losada, D.E.; Azzopardi, L. Extending the language modeling framework for sentence retrieval to include local context. *Inf. Retr.* **2010**, *14*, 355–389. [CrossRef]
7. Agarwal, B.; Ramampiaro, H.; Langseth, H.; Ruocco, M. A deep network model for paraphrase detection in short text messages. *Inf. Process. Manag.* **2018**, *54*, 922–937. [CrossRef]
8. Kenter, T.; de Rijke, M. Short Text Similarity with Word Embeddings. In Proceedings of the 24th ACM International on Conference on Information and Knowledge Management—CIKM '15, Melbourne, Australia, 19–23 October 2015.
9. Harman, D. Overview of the TREC 2002 novelty track. In Proceedings of the Eleventh Text Retrieval Conference (TREC), Gaithersburg, MD, USA, 19–22 November 2002.
10. Soboroff, I.; Harman, D. Overview of the TREC 2003 novelty track. In Proceedings of the Twelfth Text Retrieval Conference (TREC), Gaithersburg, MD, USA, 18–21 November 2003.
11. Soboroff, I. Overview of the TREC 2004 novelty track. In Proceedings of the Thirteenth Text Retrieval Conference (TREC), Gaithersburg, MD, USA, 16–19 November 2004.
12. Chiranjeevi, H.; Manjula, K.S. An Text Document Retrieval System for University Support Service on a High Performance Distributed Information System. In Proceedings of the 2019 IEEE 4th International Conference on Cloud Computing and Big Data Analysis (ICCCBDA), Chengdu, China, 12–15 April 2019.
13. Yahav, I.; Shehory, O.; Schwartz, D.G. Comments Mining With TF-IDF: The Inherent Bias and Its Removal. *IEEE Trans. Knowl. Data Eng.* **2018**, *31*, 437–450. [CrossRef]
14. Kadhim, A.I. Term Weighting for Feature Extraction on Twitter: A Comparison between BM25 and TF-IDF. In Proceedings of the 2019 International Conference on Advanced Science and Engineering (ICOASE), Zakho-Duhok, Iraq, 2–4 April 2019.
15. Fu, X.; Ch'Ng, E.; Aickelin, U.; Zhang, L. An Improved System for Sentence-level Novelty Detection in Textual Streams. *SSRN Electron. J.* **2015**. [CrossRef]
16. Niyigena, P.; Zuping, Z.; Khuhro, M.A.; Hanyurwimfura, D. Efficient Document Similarity Detection Using Weighted Phrase Indexing. *Int. J. Multimedia Ubiquitous Eng.* **2016**, *11*, 231–244. [CrossRef]
17. Zhu, Z.; Liang, J.; Li, D.; Yu, H.; Liu, G. Hot Topic Detection Based on a Refined TF-IDF Algorithm. *IEEE Access* **2019**, *7*, 26996–27007. [CrossRef]
18. Lei, L.; Qi, J.; Zheng, K. Patent Analytics Based on Feature Vector Space Model: A Case of IoT. *IEEE Access* **2019**, *7*, 45705–45715. [CrossRef]
19. Xue, M. A Text Retrieval Algorithm Based on the Hybrid LDA and Word2Vec Model. In Proceedings of the 2019 International Conference on Intelligent Transportation, Big Data & Smart City (ICITBS), Changsha, China, 12–13 January 2019.

20. Losada, D.E.; Fernández, R.T. Highly frequent terms and sentence retrieval. In *International Symposium on String Processing and Information Retrieval*; Springer: Berlin/Heidelberg, Germany, 2007; pp. 217–228.
21. Sharaff, A.; Shrawgi, H.; Arora, P.; Verma, A. Document Summarization by Agglomerative nested clustering approach. In Proceedings of the 2016 IEEE International Conference on Advances in Electronics, Communication and Computer Technology (ICAECCT), Pune, India, 2–3 December 2016.
22. Tan, C.; Wei, F.; Zhou, Q.; Yang, N.; Du, B.; Lv, W.; Zhou, M. Context-Aware Answer Sentence Selection with Hierarchical Gated Recurrent Neural Networks. *IEEE/ACM Trans. Audio Speech Lang. Process.* **2018**, *26*, 540–549. [CrossRef]
23. Losada, D.E. Statistical query expansion for sentence retrieval and its effects on weak and strong queries. *Inf. Retr.* **2010**, *13*, 485–506. [CrossRef]
24. Srividhya, V.; Anitha, R. Evaluating preprocessing techniques in text categorization. *J. Comput. Sci. Appl.* **2010**, *47*, 49–51.
25. Vijayarani, S.; Ilamathi, M.J.; Nithya, M. Preprocessing techniques for text mining-an overview. *Int. J. Comput. Sci. Commun. Netw.* **2015**, *5*, 7–16.
26. Behera, S. Implementation of a Finite State Automaton to Recognize and Remove Stop Words in English Text on its Retrieval. In Proceedings of the 2018 2nd International Conference on Trends in Electronics and Informatics (ICOEI), Tirunelveli, India, 11–12 May 2018.
27. Karic, I.; Vejzovic, Z. Contextual Similarity: Quasilinear-Time Search and Comparison for Sequential Data. In Proceedings of the 2017 International Conference on Control, Artificial Intelligence, Robotics & Optimization (ICCAIRO), Prague, Czech Republic, 20–22 May 2017.
28. Singh, J.; Singh, G.; Singh, R.; Singh, P. Morphological evaluation and sentiment analysis of Punjabi text using deep learning classification. *J. King Saud Univ.—Comput. Inf. Sci.* **2018**. [CrossRef]
29. Gupta, S.; Gupta, S.K. A Hybrid Approach to Single Document Extractive Summarization. *Int. J. Comput. Sci. Mob. Comput.* **2018**, *7*, 142–149.
30. Boban, I.; Doko, A.; Gotovac, S. Sentence Retrieval using Stemming and Lemmatization with Different Length of the Queries. *Adv. Sci. Technol. Eng. Syst. J.* **2020**, *5*, 349–354.

© 2020 by the authors. Licensee MDPI, Basel, Switzerland. This article is an open access article distributed under the terms and conditions of the Creative Commons Attribution (CC BY) license (http://creativecommons.org/licenses/by/4.0/).

Article

Paraphrase Identification with Lexical, Syntactic and Sentential Encodings

Sheng Xu [1,2], Xingfa Shen [1], Fumiyo Fukumoto [3,*], Jiyi Li [3], Yoshimi Suzuki [3] and Hiromitsu Nishizaki [3]

1. School of Computer Science and Technology, Hangzhou Dianzi University, HangZhou 310018, China ; 181050042@hdu.edu.cn (S.X.); shenxf@hdu.edu.cn (X.S.)
2. Integrated Graduate School of Medicine, Engineering, and Agricultural Sciences, Faculty of Engineering, University of Yamanashi, Kofu 400-8511, Japan
3. Graduate Faculty of Interdisciplinary Research, University of Yamanashi, Kofu 400-8511, Japan; jyli@yamanashi.ac.jp (J.L.); ysuzuki@yamanashi.ac.jp (Y.S.); hnishi@yamanashi.ac.jp (H.N.)
* Correspondence: fukumoto@yamanashi.ac.jp; Tel.: +81-55-220-8509

Received: 30 April 2020; Accepted: 9 June 2020; Published: 16 June 2020

Abstract: Paraphrase identification has been one of the major topics in Natural Language Processing (NLP). However, how to interpret a diversity of contexts such as lexical and semantic information within a sentence as relevant features is still an open problem. This paper addresses the problem and presents an approach for leveraging contextual features with a neural-based learning model. Our Lexical, Syntactic, and Sentential Encodings (LSSE) learning model incorporates Relational Graph Convolutional Networks (R-GCNs) to make use of different features from local contexts, i.e., word encoding, position encoding, and full dependency structures. By utilizing the hidden states obtained by the R-GCNs as well as lexical and sentential encodings by Bidirectional Encoder Representations from Transformers (BERT), our model learns the contextual similarity between sentences effectively. The experimental results by using the two benchmark datasets, Microsoft Research Paraphrase Corpus (MRPC) and Quora Question Pairs (QQP) show that the improvement compared with the baseline, BERT sentential encodings model, was 1.7% F1-score on MRPC and 1.0% F1-score on QQP. Moreover, we verified that the combination of position encoding and syntactic features contributes to performance improvement.

Keywords: paraphrase identification; encodings, R-GCNs; BERT; contextual features

1. Introduction

Paraphrase identification is the task to identify whether a pair of sentences is a paraphrase or not. It is highly related to the task of semantic textual similarity to measure the degree of semantic equivalence between two sentences and has been an interest as it is necessary to accomplish most NLP tasks such as question answering, information retrieval, textual entailment, and text summarization. With a recent surge of interest in neural networks, paraphrase identification based on deep learning techniques has been intensively studied. These attempts include Convolutional Neural Networks (CNNs) based model [1,2], Long Short-Term Memory (LSTM) [3], Bidirectional-LSTM (BiLSTM) [4], and gated recurrent averaging [5]. It enables us to utilize the contexts of the target sentences which are powerful for learning features from the training data. Despite some successes, the approaches explored so far rely on word sequence, not making use of different aspects of contexts simultaneously. Several efforts have been made to utilize different representations of the contexts. One attempt is pre-trained contextualized word/sentence representations [5–11]. They have been successfully applied to many NLP tasks, while they explicitly rely on not syntax but the sequential context of words by utilizing a large volume of data.

Motivated by the previous work mentioned in the above, we incorporate several contextual features into a unified framework, Relational Graph Convolutional Networks (R-GCNs) [12–14]. Consider the two sentences from the MRPC data shown in Figure 1. These two sentences are an example of non-paraphrase sentence pair. Adjacent words such as "Hong" "Kong" and "South" "Korea" marked with blue indicate compound nouns and those marked with red such as "0.2–0.4" "percent" and "0.3" "percent" show numeric modifiers. These sentences have different contents/meanings, while there exist many overlapping words such as "Australia", "Singapore", "flat" and "percent". The relative position information marked with blue and red is good indicators to discriminate whether these sentences are a paraphrase or not. Similarly, in the top sentence, "Korea" modifies "lost" with the *nsubj* (*nominal subject*) relation type, while in the second sentence, "Korea" modifies "added" with the *nsubj* relation type. This syntactic structure information also becomes clues that these sentences are not a paraphrase.

Our R-GCNs model integrates different features: (i) word encoding; (ii) position encoding; and (iii) full dependency structures as syntactic encoding from a sentence. We used word encoding obtained by Bidirectional Encoder Representations from Transformers (BERT) [11]. BERT models were pre-trained using a large corpus of sentences. The training is done by masking a few tokens in a sentence and the task is to predict the masked tokens. It learns to produce a powerful internal representation of words as word embedding. Position encoding is a technique to inject information about a token's position within a sentence into a deep learning model. We applied the Stanford parser [15,16] to the input sentences and obtained full dependency structures. Besides contexts with syntactic level, our Lexical, Syntactic, and Sentential Encodings (LSSE) learning model also makes use of contextual information with lexical and sentential levels obtained by the BERT model. Intuitively, by sharing rich contextual features, the model can produce a more meaningful representation to identify paraphrases.

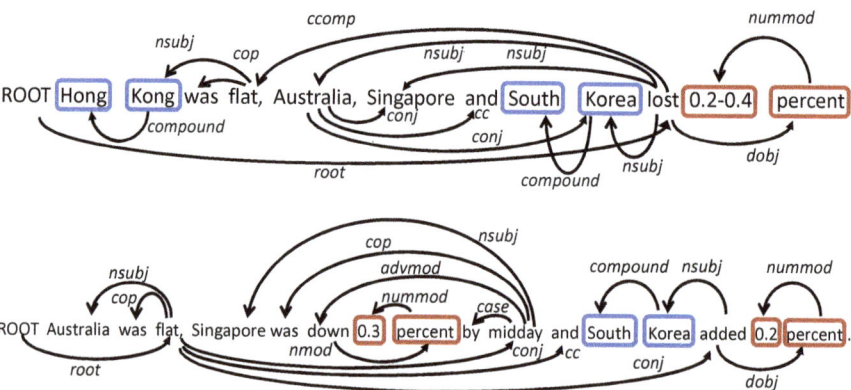

Figure 1. Non-paraphrase sentence pair from the MRPC corpus: Adjacent words such as "Hong" and "Kong" marked with blue indicate compound nouns and those such as "0.2–0.4" and "percent" marked with red show numeric modifiers.

The main contributions of our work can be summarized: (1) We propose a paraphrase identification method that makes use of contextual information with lexical, syntactic, and sentential levels; (2) We apply R-GCNs to utilize different features from local contexts; (3) The experimental results on the two benchmark datasets show that our model is comparable to the related work, and especially, the combination of syntactic features and position encoding contributes to performance improvement in our method.

2. Related Work

There is a large body of work on paragraph identification based on deep learning techniques. The early attempts include a recursive neural network (RNN) [17], CNNs [1,18], and a tree-based LSTM [19]. Despite some successes, techniques explored so far rely on word sequence, ignoring to make use of different aspects of contexts simultaneously.

Several efforts have been made to handle different representations for the same sentence in different contexts. One attempt is pre-trained contextualized language representations. Many authors have attempted to learn contextualized language representation by pre-training a language model with a large amount of unannotated data [7,9,20,21]. Melamud et al. proposed a method called context2vec which learns each sense annotation in the training data by using a bidirectional LSTM trained on an unlabeled corpus [7]. Peters et al. attempted to learn a model called Embeddings from Language Models (ELMo) by using two-layer bidirectional LSTM [9]. More recently, sentence or document encoders that produce contextual token representations have been processed by two steps: pre-trained from unlabeled text and fine-tuned for a supervised downstream task. These approaches can decrease the number of parameters to learn from scratch. One such attempt is Generative Pre-Training (GPT-2) which enhances the context-sensitive embedding [20]. It achieved previously state-of-the-art results in many sentence-level tasks including paraphrase identification from General Language Understanding Evaluation (GLUE) benchmark datasets [21]. However, the attempt is based on a left-to-right architecture. Therefore, every token can only attend to previous tokens, which may cause an issue when we apply it to token-level downstream tasks such as question answering and sentiment analysis.

Devlin et al. focused on the problem and presented a method, BERT, to pre-train deep bidirectional representations from an unlabeled text by jointly conditioning on both left and right context in all layers [11]. They adopted a Masked Language Model (MLM) by adding a next sentence prediction task into the pre-training to learn text-pair representations and can pre-train a deep bidirectional Transformer. Since then, BERT has realized a breakthrough in sentence representation learning which is broadly applied to various NLP tasks including the paraphrase identification task. Lample et al. extended the pre-training model to multiple languages and showed the effectiveness of cross-lingual pre-training. They attempted to integrate two approaches to learn cross-lingual language models (XLMs): the two unsupervised methods, i.e., Causal Language Modeling (CLM) and Masked Language Modeling (MLM), and a supervised method [22]. CLM consists of a Transformer Language model while MLM is based on the technique of Devlin et al. [11]. The supervised model, translation language modeling (TLM) is to improve cross-lingual pre-training which is based on MLM. The common framework related to pre-training mentioned in the above utilizes the Transformer that is the first full-attentional mechanism for learning long-term dependency [23]. Moreover, several approaches apply pre-trained language representation to a large variety of tasks such as named entity, semantic closeness including paraphrase identification and discourse relations through multi-task learning techniques [24–26].

Similar to the recent upsurge of pre-trained contextualized word/sentence representations, graph neural networks [27] such as GCNs [12–14], R-GCNs [28], and Densely Connected GCNs [29] have been successfully employed for many NLP tasks. Such attempts include neural machine translation (NMT) [30,31], pronoun resolution [32], relation extraction [33], semantic role labeling [34] and text classification [35–37]. Most of these attempts showed that the models have contributed to improving the performance on each task, while it has so far not been used for the paraphrase identification task. Moreover, most of them focus on one type of features, syntactic information, and integrate them into their graph model.

3. LSSE Learning Model

Our model leverages various contextual features obtained from the paraphrase-labeled data. Figure 2 illustrates our Lexical, Syntactic, and Sentential Encoding (LSSE) learning framework. The left-hand side of Figure 2 illustrates the overview of our LSSE and the right-hand side is its corresponding flow of the input/output.

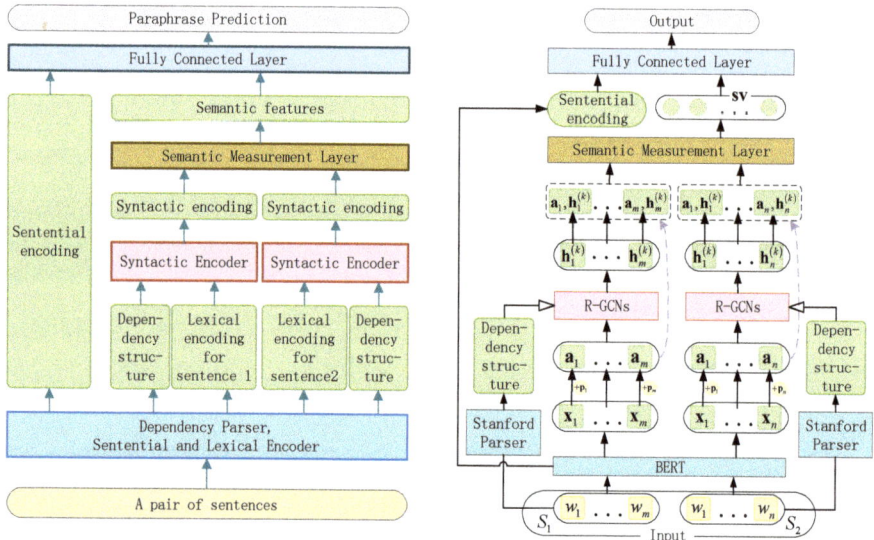

Figure 2. LSSE learning model: S_1 consisting a sequence of $w_1, w_2, \cdots, w_m$ and S_2 which consists of $w_1, w_2, \cdots, w_n$ are a pair of the input sentences. $\mathbf{x}_i$ refers to a word encoding and $\mathbf{p}_i$ indicates its position encoding. $\mathbf{a}_i \in \mathbb{R}^d$ refers to the encoded node feature, i.e., it is obtained by summing up word and position encodings. $\mathbf{h}_i^{(k)} \in \mathbb{R}^d$ is the hidden state of node v_i (w_i) in the $k+1$-th layer.

3.1. Lexical and Sentential Contexts Learning with BERT

The contextualized word representation that we use is BERT which is a Bidirectional Transformer model [11]. A transformer encoder computes the representation of each token through an attention mechanism concerning the surrounding tokens.

BERT architecture consists of two steps: pre-training and fine-tuning. The pre-training BERT model is trained on unlabeled data over different pre-training tasks. It can be easily fine-tuned for NLP tasks by just adding a fully-connected layer. It is pre-trained by using a combination of masked token prediction and next sentence prediction tasks. The input of the BERT is two sentences that are concatenated by a special token [SEP]. It consists of tokens that are segmented by BERT tokenizer using WordPiece embeddings vocabulary [38]. The representation of each token is the sum of the corresponding token, segment, and position embeddings. The first token of every input is the special token of [CLS], and the final hidden state corresponding to this [CLS] token is regarded as an aggregated representation of the input sentence pair. We used this aggregated representation as our sentential encoding of two sentences as well as each token embeddings.

3.2. Syntactic Context Learning with R-GCNs

We utilize R-GCNs to learn syntactic context. It can capture syntactic dependency structures naturally as well as word order because it allows the information to flow in the opposite direction of edges. For example, the sentence in the top of Figure 1, the word "0.2–0.4" modifies the word "percent".

Let S be a sentence and w_i be the i-th absolute position word within the sentence. Let also $G = (V, E)$ be a directed graph, where each node $v_i \in V$ indicates the information of word w_i, consisting of a word encoding x_i. BERT uses word pieces and not word embeddings. When w_i consists of several word pieces, we obtained the average value of all pieces corresponding to w_i and set it to the w_i embeddings. and its position encoding p_i shown in Figure 2. We can define a matrix $A \in \mathbb{R}^{d \times n}$ where each column $a_i \in \mathbb{R}^d$ refers to the encoded node feature of v_i, i.e., we sum up word and position encodings as lexical encoding, $a_i = x_i + p_i$. An edge from node v_i to v_j with a dependency relation type (label) $l \in L$ is denoted by $<v_i, v_j, l> \in E$, where L is a set of dependency relation types. Figure 3 illustrates dependency relations consisting of two information flows: from head to dependent and self-loop. Self-loop is to ensure that the representation of the encoded node feature at the $k + 1$-th hidden layer can also be informed by its corresponding representation at the k-th hidden layer [28].

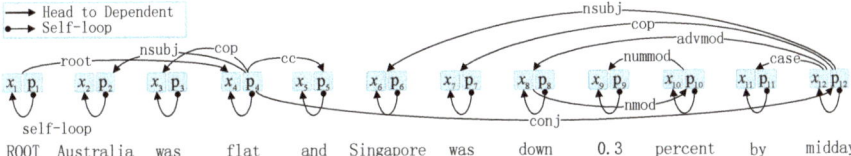

Figure 3. Dependency relations: "x_i" and "p_i" refer to the i-th word encoding and its position encoding, respectively. Arcs indicate two types of edges: (i) head to dependent with labeled syntactic relations such as *nsubj*(nominal subject) and *nummod* (numeric modifier); and (ii) self-loop.

The propagation model for calculating the forward-pass update of a node v_i in a local graph can be given by:

$$h_i^{(k+1)} = f\left[\sum_{l \in L} \sum_{j \in N_i^l} \left(\frac{1}{c_i^l} W_l^{(k)} h_j^{(k)} + b_l^{(k)}\right) + W_0^{(k)} h_i^{(k)}\right], \quad (1)$$

where $h_i^{(k)} \in \mathbb{R}^d$ is the hidden state of node v_i in the k-th layer of the neural network with d being the dimensionality of the hidden representations, especially the initial value of $h_i^{(0)}$ equals to a_i. N_i^l refers to the set of neighbor indices of node v_i under dependency label $l \in L$. c_i^l shows a normalization constant [28]. It can either be learned or chosen in advance. We empirically set c_i^l to 2 in the experiments. $W_l^{(k)} \in \mathbb{R}^{d \times d}$ stands for the weight matrix and $b_l^{(k)} \in \mathbb{R}^d$ refers to the bias vector under label $l \in L$ of the k-th hidden layer. We used 32 syntactic dependency relation types including *nsubj* and *dobj* provided by the Stanford parser for the first type of flows and their opposite direction types which would result in having 64 (32 × 2) dependency labels. $W_0^{(k)} \in \mathbb{R}^{d \times d}$ indicates self-loop convolution weights and f refers to an activation function. We use the ReLU function. Equation (1) shows that it accumulates transformed feature vectors of neighboring nodes which depend on the relation type and the flow of an edge through a normalized sum. Motivated by the method of Vashishth et al. [39], we also utilized a special gate mechanism. Our context learning model is given by:

$$h_i^{(k+1)} = f\left[\sum_{l \in L} \sum_{j \in N_i^l} g_{lj}^{(k)} \cdot \left(\frac{1}{c_i^l} W_l^{(k)} h_j^{(k)} + b_l^{(k)}\right) + W_0^{(k)} h_i^{(k)}\right], \quad (2)$$

where $g_{lj}^{(k)}$ is given by:

$$g_{lj}^{(k)} = \sigma\left(\hat{\mathbf{W}}_l^{(k)}\mathbf{h}_j^{(k)} + \hat{\mathbf{b}}_l^{(k)}\right). \quad (3)$$

$g_{lj}^{(k)}$ is the so-called gate mechanism [34,40] which is to reduce the effect of false dependency edges. The information from neighboring nodes may not be reliable as the dependency relations obtained by some NLP tools are not perfect. Therefore, it needs to be down-weighted. Similar to [32,34], we use the gate value obtained by Equation (3). σ refers to the sigmoid function so that the gate value ranging from 0 to 1. $\hat{\mathbf{W}}_l^{(k)} \in \mathbb{R}^{d \times d}$ and $\hat{\mathbf{b}}_l^{(k)} \in \mathbb{R}^d$ show weights and a bias for the gate under label $l \in L$ of the k-th hidden layer, respectively.

Figure 4 illustrates the R-GCNs model. The left-hand side of Figure 4 is the flow of the model and the right-hand side shows Graph Convolution in the R-GCNs. In the Graph Convolution part shown in the right-hand side of Figure 4, the update of a single node marked with red is computed. Activations from neighboring nodes marked with blue are collected and transformed for each dependency relation such as dep_1 and dep_N individually (for both "in" and "outgoing" edges). The results marked with green, each of which corresponds to $g_{lj}^{(k)} \cdot \left(\frac{1}{c_i}\mathbf{W}_l^{(k)}\mathbf{h}_j^{(k)} + \mathbf{b}_l^{(k)}\right)$ or $\mathbf{W}_0^{(k)}\mathbf{h}_i^{(k)}$ in Equation (2), are accumulated and passed through an activation function (ReLU). As shown in the left-hand side of Figure 4, in each hidden layer, the Graph Convolution is applied to update the state of each node of the graph. The output of the R-GCNs is the last hidden layer states. For each sentence, we applied R-GCNs.

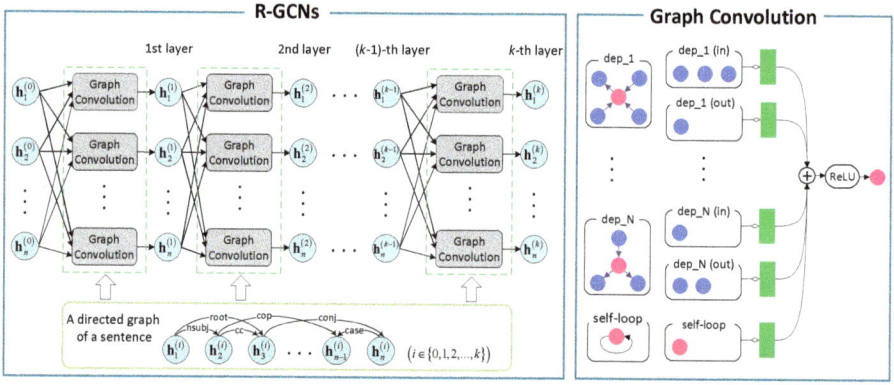

Figure 4. R-GCNs model [28]: The **left**-hand side is the flow of the model and the **right**-hand side shows Graph Convolution in the R-GCNs.

3.3. Paraphrase Identification

Because graph convolution of the R-GCNs model is a special form of Laplacian smoothing, it mixes the features of a node and its neighbors [41,42]. This smoothing operation makes the features of nodes less distinguishable [32]. Therefore, when the training data is small, it often the case that it does not work well. Adding more layers also does not work well as empirically it has been observed that the best performance is achieved with a 2-layer model [41]. Therefore, as illustrated in the right-hand side of Figure 2, after the hidden state $\mathbf{h}_i$ has been learned, we concatenate the hidden state $\mathbf{h}_i$ with the lexical encoding $\mathbf{a}_i$ to keep the original encoding. We obtain the syntactic encoding with the context information aggregated, i.e., $\mathbf{a}'_i = (\mathbf{a}_i, \mathbf{h}_i)$. The result by concatenation has a fixed length, i.e., $2 \times d$.

The two matrices $\mathbf{M}_{s_1} \in \mathbb{R}^{2d \times m}$ and $\mathbf{M}_{s_2} \in \mathbb{R}^{2d \times n}$ corresponding to each sentence $S_1 \in \mathbb{R}^{d \times m}$ and $S_2 \in \mathbb{R}^{d \times n}$ are obtained by R-GCNs and passed to the semantic measurement layer which is shown in Figure 5. For each of the two matrices $\mathbf{M}_{s_1}$ and $\mathbf{M}_{s_2}$, we applied the row-based average pooling over them and obtained two vectors, $\mathbf{u}_1$ and $\mathbf{u}_2 \in \mathbb{R}^{2d}$, respectively. We then calculate the similarity between these vectors, i.e., for each dimension, we applied L_1 distance, and obtain a similarity vector $\mathbf{sv} \in \mathbb{R}^{2d}$. The $\mathbf{sv}$ is further concatenated with sentential encoding obtained by BERT, and the result is passed to the fully connected layer **FC**. We set the size of the output layer of the **FC** to two. Finally, we apply the softmax function to obtain probabilities of two predicted labels, paraphrase or non-paraphrase, in the output layer. The network is trained with the objective that minimizes the binary cross-entropy loss of the predicted distributions and the actual distributions (one-hot vectors corresponding to the ground labels) by performing Adam optimization algorithm [43].

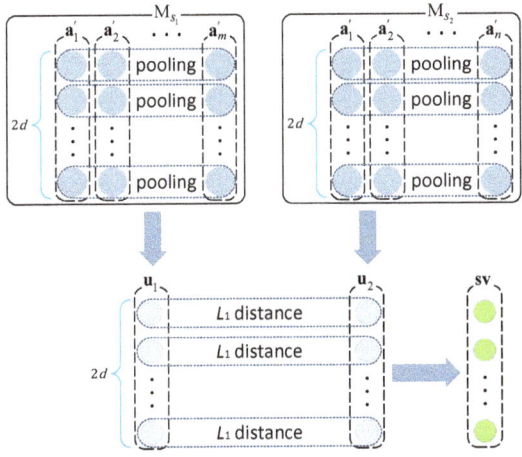

Figure 5. Semantic measurement: after the pooling operation, the similarity between sentences are calculated by using L_1 distance.

4. Experiments

4.1. Experimental Settings

We selected two benchmark datasets, Microsoft Research Paraphrase Corpus (MRPC) [44] and Quora Question Pairs (QQP) [45]. MRPC contains 5801 pairs of sentences extracted from news on the Internet and is annotated to capture the equivalence of paraphrase or semantic relationship between a pair of sentences.

The QQP dataset consists of three folds: 363,870 for training data, 40,431 for validation, and 390,965 for test data. Of these, training and validation data are annotated with a binary classification indicating whether these two questions are a paraphrase or not. We followed the method of Wang et al. [46]. More precisely, we merged training and validation data, and randomly selected 5000 paraphrases and 5000 non-paraphrases as the test set. Table 1 illustrates some sentence pairs from MRPC and QQP. Each data in Table 1 consists of the number of ID, two sentences and its ground labels that the sentences are a paraphrase (1) or non-paraphrase (0).

Table 1. Sentence pairs from MRPC and QQP datasets: Label indicates the ground-truth labels that the sentences are paraphrase (1) or non-paraphrase (0).

Data	#1 ID	#2 ID	#1 String	#2 String	Label
MRPC	2108705	2108831	Yucaipa owned Dominick's before selling the chain to Safeway in 1998 for USD 2.5 billion.	Yucaipa bought Dominick's in 1995 for USD 693 million and sold it Safeway for USD 1.8 billion in 1998.	0
	702876	702977	Amrozi accused his brother, whom he called "the witness", of deliberately distorting his evidence.	Referring to him as only "the witness", Amrozi accused his brother of deliberately distorting his evidence.	1
QQP	364011	490273	What causes stool color to change to yellow?	What can cause stool to come out as little balls?	0
	536040	536041	How do I control my horny emotions?	How do you control your horniness?	1

The paraphrase identification task is a binary classification. Given a pair of sentences, classify them as paraphrases or not paraphrases. All the datasets are parsed by using Stanford parser nlp.stanford.edu/software/lex-parser.shtml [16]. We utilized the BERT_base model as a pre-training model of the lexical and sentential encodings [11] due to the environment with the restricted computational resources. The experiments were conducted on Nvidia TITAN RTX (24GB memory). We used the same model settings as BERT, i.e., the number of training epochs was 3, the batch size was 8, and the number of dimensions of a word and position encoding vectors was 768. The learning rate was 2×10^{-5} by using Adam, learning rate warmup over the first 10,000 steps, and linear decay of the learning rate. We used a dropout probability of 0.1 on all layers in BERT. The number of hidden layers of R-GCNs was optimized by using Optuna https://github.com/pfnet/optuna where the range was [1, 2, 3, 4, 5, 6]. We used 10-fold cross-validation on training data as Phang et al. pointed out that BERT performances become unstable when a training dataset with fine-tuning is small [47]. As a result, we set the number of hidden layers to 2 in the experiments. Following by General Language Understanding Evaluation (GLUE) platform [21], gluebenchmark.com/tasks we used the Accuracy and/or F1-score for evaluation metrics. Throughout the experiments using two benchmark datasets, we choose BERT sentential encodings as a baseline model and implemented a fine-tuning approach in the same manner as with BERT [11].

4.2. Main Results

Table 2 shows the results by using MRPC data (Supplementary Materials). We can see from Table 2 that our model outperformed the baseline, BERT sentential encodings, by 2.0% accuracy and 1.8% F1 on the MRPC and 1.9% accuracy and 2.0% F1 on the QQP data. Why did our LSSE perform particularly strong on the dataset QQP? We notice that the volume of this dataset is larger than that of the MRPC dataset. This confirms our intuition that deep learning typically requires more training data to achieve high performance, and our model could successfully take this advantage on the QQP dataset.

Table 2. Main result by using test dataset: Baseline shows the result obtained by BERT sentential encodings [11]. Bold font shows the best result in each dataset.

Model	Baseline		LSSE	
	Acc	F1	Acc	F1
MRPC	84.3	88.1	**86.3**	**89.9**
QQP	88.7	88.4	**90.6**	**90.4**

Table 3 shows some examples obtained by both of the models. In Table 3, TP, FP, TN, and FN refer to an abbreviation of true positive, false positive, true negative, and false negative, respectively. "N" indicates the number of instances from the test data. For example "N = 70" in Table 3 shows that the number of "LSSE(TP) and BERT(FN)", i.e., the sentence pairs that were classified by LSSE as true positive and classified by BERT as false negative is 70. We can see that the number of "LSSE(TP) and BERT(FN)" is larger than that of "LSSE(FN) and BERT(TP)" in both datasets. However, the number of "LSSE(FP) and BERT(TN)" is larger than that of "LSSE(TN) and BERT(FP)". Most of the errors of FP in our model are in the case that two sentences share the same contents but one sentence has more detailed information of the other. For example in the MRPC dataset, one sentence (#1 String) includes additional information, "private creditors", while it is not mentioned in the second sentence (#2 String). BERT sentential encodings is a simple paraphrase identification compared to our model. But why such a relatively simple model leads to a better prediction for particular test data is not clear at this point. Answering this question requires future research.

Table 3. Example sentences obtained by our LSSE and BERT model: TP, FP, TN and FN refer to an abbreviation of true positive, false positive, true negative and false negative, respectively.

MRPC Dataset				
#1 String	#2 String	LSSE	BERT	N
Licensing revenue slid 21 percent, however, to USD 107.6 million.	License sales, a key measure of demand, fell 21 percent to USD 107.6 million.	TP	FN	70
For the entire season, the average five-day forecast track error was 259 miles, Franklin said.	The average track error for the five-day (forecast) is 323 nautical miles.	FN	TP	19
By Sunday night, the fires had blackened 277,000 acres, hundreds of miles apart.	Major fires had burned 264,000 acres by early last night.	TN	FP	36
Other countries and **private creditors** are owed at least USD 80 billion in addition.	Other countries are owed at least USD US80 billion (USD 108.52 billion).	FP	TN	53
QQP Dataset				
#1 String	#2 String	LSSE	BERT	N
What are the most intellectually stimulating movies you have ever seen?	What are the most intellectually stimulating films you have ever watched?	TP	FN	331
How do I get business ideas?	How can I think of a business idea?	FN	TP	212
How do I remove dry paint from my clothes?	How do I get acrylic paint out of my clothes?	TN	FP	201
How do Champcash make money from Chrome?	How do a Champcash customer make money from Chrome?	FP	TN	130

We also examined how the percentage of training data affects overall performance. Figure 6 shows an F1-score against the percentage of the MRPC training data. We run ten times for each volume of training data size except for 100% and obtained the average F1-score. Overall, the curves show that more training data helps the performance, while the curves obtained by LSSE drop slowly compared to the BERT sentential encodings. From the observation, we can conclude that our model works well compared to BERT sentential encodings.

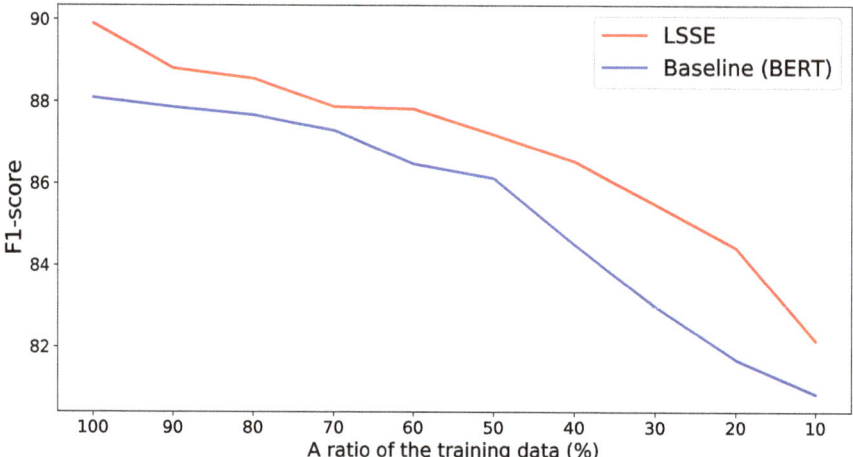

Figure 6. Performance against the percentage of the training data.

4.3. Comparison with Related Work

In MRPC dataset, we compared our model with eight related work, graph-based approach or approaches which utilize BERT_base model to make a fair comparison. These are classified into five types: (i) a relational graph-based approach, Str Align; (ii) BERT_base; (iii) Multi-task learning, GenSen and ERNIE 2.0; (iv) extending BERT pre-trained model, Trans FT, and StructBERT_base; and (v) an adversarial training algorithm, FreeLB-BERT, and its similar approach, ELECTRA.

1. **Str Align**

   Structural Alignment (Str Align) uses a hybrid representation, attributed relational graphs to encode lexical, syntactic and semantic information [48]. To create a relational graph, they used token, lemma, Part-of-Speech (POS) tag, Named Entity Recognition (NER) tag, and Word2Vec word embedding as an attribute of a node, and the dependency label by Stanford CoreNLP is attached to the edge as an attribute. Given two attributed relational graphs, the structural aligner generates an alignment. Then, the similarity score between the two graphs is applied to judge whether they are equivalent or not.

2. **BERT_base model**

   BERT is pre-train deep bidirectional representations from the unlabeled text by jointly conditioning on both left and right context in all layers [11]. We used BERT_base model which contains 12-layers, 12 self-attention heads and 768-dimensional of hidden size.

3. **GenSen**

   GenSen is multi-task learning for sentence representations where a single recurrent sentence encoder is shared across multiple tasks, i.e., multi-lingual NMT, natural language inference, constituency parsing, and skip-thought vectors [49]. The model for multi-task learning is a sequence-to-sequence model. We compared GenSen which utilizes BERT_base model.

4. **ERNIE 2.0**

   Enhanced Representation through kNowledge IntEgration (ERNIE) 2.0 is a multi-task learning model that learns pre-training tasks incrementally [25]. The architecture consists of pre-training and fine-tuning that is the same manner as BERT models. In the process of pre-training, ERNIE 2.0 continually construct unsupervised pre-training tasks with big data and prior knowledge involved, and then incrementally update the model through multi-task learning. In the fine-tuning with task-specific supervised data, the pre-trained model is applied to ten different NLP tasks in English and nine tasks in Chinese. We compared our model with ERNIE 2.0 using BERT_base model.

5. **Trans FT**

   Transfer Fine-Tuning (Trans FT) is an extended model of BERT to handle phrasal paraphrase relations. The model can generate suitable representations for semantic equivalence assessment instead of increasing the model size [50]. The authors inject semantic relations between a sentence pair into a pre-trained BERT model through the classification of phrasal and sentential paraphrases. After the training, the model can be fine-tuned in the same manner as BERT models. The model achieves improvement on downstream tasks that only have small amounts of training datasets for fine-tuning.

6. **StructBERT_base**

   StructBERT_base incorporates language structures into pre-training BERT_base model [51]. The architecture uses a multi-layer bidirectional Transformer network. It amplifies the ability of the masked language model task by shuffling a certain number of tokens after token masking and predicting the right order. To capture the relationship between sentences, StructBERT randomly swaps the sentence order and predicts the next sentence and the previous sentence as a new sentence prediction task. The model learns the inter-sentence structure in a bidirectional manner as well as to capture the fine-grained word structure in every sentence. In the fine-tuning process, the pre-trained model is applied to a wide range of downstream tasks including GLUE benchmark, Stanford Natural Language inferences (SNLI corpus) and extractive question answering (SQuADv1.1) with good performance.

7. **FreeLB-BERT**

   Free-Large-Batch aims to improve the generalization of pre-trained language models such as BERT, RoBERTAa [52], ALBERT [53] and T5 [54] by enhancing their robustness in the embedding space during finetuning on the downstream language understanding tasks [55]. The method adds norm-bounded adversarial perturbations to the embeddings on the input sentences by using a gradient-based method. Their technique on embedding-based adversaries can manipulate word embeddings which makes it produce powerful pre-trained language models. The results achieved new state-of-the-art on GLUE and AI2 Reasoning Challenge (ARC) benchmark datasets.

8. **ELECTRA-Base**

   "Efficiently Learning an Encoder that Classifies Token Replacements Accurately" (ELECTRA) pre-trains the network as a discriminator that predicts for every token whether it is an original or a replacement. The model trains two neural networks, a generator, and a discriminator. For a given position, the discriminator predicts whether the token of this position comes from the data rather than the generator distribution. The generator is trained to perform masked language modeling. After pre-training, the model fine-tune the discriminator on downstream tasks. ELECTRA-Base that we compared it with our LSSE model is pre-trained in the same manner as BERT_base model.

The results are shown in Table 4 (Supplementary Materials). We can see from Table 4 that LSSE showed a 1.5% accuracy and 1.0% F1-score improvement over BERT_base model. Moreover, our model is competitive for the best systems except for ELECTRA_Base, as ELECTRA_Base outperformed our LSSE by 0.3% in accuracy. This shows that our model can leverage contextual features obtained from the limited volume of the paraphrase-labeled data. We also compared our model with two approaches by using the QQP dataset.

Table 4. Comparative results with related work including state-of-the-art method: Str Align is based on attributed relational graphs. Bold font shows the best result.

MRPC Dataset		
Model	Acc	F1
Str Align [48]	78.3	84.9
BERT_base [11]	84.8	88.9
GenSen [49]	78.6	84.4
ERNIE 2.0 [25]	86.1	**89.9**
Trans FT [50]	-	89.2
StructBERT_base [51]	86.1	**89.9**
FreeLB-BERT [55]	83.5	88.1
ELECTRA-Base [56]	**86.7**	-
LSSE (Our model)	86.3	**89.9**

1. **BiMPM**

    A Bilateral Multi-Perspective Matching (BiMPM) model [46] encodes given two sentences with a BiLSTM encoder and the two encoded sentences are matched two directions. In each matching direction, each time step of one sentence is matched against all time-steps of another sentence from multiple perspectives. Then, another BiLSTM layer is utilized to aggregate the matching results into a fixed-length matching vector. Finally, a decision is made through a fully connected layer. The authors reported that the experimental results on standard benchmark datasets including QQP showed that the model achieved state-of-the-art performance on all the tasks.

2. **SSE**

    Shortcut-Stacked Sentence Encoder Model (SSE) is a model which enhances multi-layer BiLSTM with skip connection to avoid training error accumulation [57,58]. The input of the k-th BiLSTM layer which is the combination of outputs from all previous layers represents the hidden state of that layer in both directions. The final sentence embedding is the row-based max pooling over the output of the last BiLSTM layer. The experimental results by using eight benchmark datasets including QQP dataset shows that SSE improvs overall performance compared with the three baselines, InferSent [59], Pairwise word interaction model [60], and the decomposable attention model [61], especially it works well in the case that the number of training data is small.

Table 5 shows the results (Supplementary Materials). As we can be seen clearly from Table 5, LSSE outperforms two baseline models as the improvement is 2.4~2.8%. This indicates that our model works well compared with the sequence model and sentence encoding model based on BiLSTM.

Table 5. Comparative restuls in accuracy by using QQP: Bold font shows the best result.

QQP Dataset	
Model	Acc
BiMPM [46]	88.2
SSE [58]	87.8
LSSE (Our model)	**90.6**

4.4. Ablation Study

We recall that our model utilizes lexical and syntactic encodings including the baseline model. Moreover, the syntactic encoding integrates different features. We thus conducted ablation studies to empirically examine the impact of these features/encodings. The results are shown in Table 6.

Table 6. Ablation test: "PE" refers to position encoding and "SentE" indicates sentential encoding. "BERT tokenE" stands for lexical encoding by BERT. "–X" indicates the result by using LSSE without "X". Bold font shows the best result.

MRPC Dataset		
Model	Acc	F
LSSE (Our model)	**86.3**	**89.9**
–PE	85.3	89.0
–SentE	84.2	88.3
–SentE and –PE	83.5	88.1
–R-GCNs	85.7	89.5
–R-GCNs and –SentE	83.0	87.3
–R-GCNs and –BERT tokenE	84.3	88.1

Table 6 shows the results by using the MRPC dataset (Supplementary Materials). Overall, we can see that integrating different features from the contexts is effective as LSSE was the best performance. The results both without R-GCNs and BERT token encoding (–R-GCNs and –BERT TokenE) and without R-GCNs and sentential encoding (–R-GCNs and –SentE) are worse than those without R-GCNs (-R-GCNs). This shows that the combination of the sentential and lexical encoding is effective for paraphrase identification.

We note that the result by "–SentE" is better than that with "–SentE and –PE". This means that the combination of R-GCNs output, BERT token encoding and position encoding is better than that with only R-GCNs output and BERT token encoding. We can see a similar observation that the combination of sentential encoding, R-GCNs output, BERT token encoding, and position encoding more works well than that with sentential encoding, R-GCNs output, and BERT token encoding because our LSSE is better than the result by "–PE". From these observations, we can conclude that the combination of syntactic features and position encoding contributes to performance improvement.

4.5. Qualitative Analysis of Errors

We performed an error analysis by using the MRPC dataset to provide feedback for further improvement of our method. The number of false-positive and false-negative pairs of sentences was 61 and 38, respectively. These errors have occurred even though we used all the features or any combination of these features. We found that there are mainly three types of errors.

1. **Inclusion relation between sentences:** As we mentioned in Table 3, this error is that two sentences share the same contents but one sentence has more detailed information of the other.

    (1) "There's a Jeep in my parents' yard right now that's not theirs", said Perry, whose parents are vacationing in North Carolina.
    (2) "There's a Jeep in my parents' yard right now that's not theirs", she said.

    Sentence (1) and (2) are similar content and our model identified these sentences as paraphrases. However, according to the Microsoft Research definitions, https://www.microsoft.com/en-us/download/details.aspx?id=52398 these sentences should be identified as "non-paraphrase" because the sentence (1) includes the information marked with the underlined that "Perry's parents are vacationing in North Carolina" and it is a significantly larger superset of the sentence (2). We observed that 39 pairs were classified into this type.

2. **Dependency relation:** Dependency relation within a sentence is not correctly analyzed. For example, in the sentence (3), "<.DDJ>" is divided into four tokens("<", ".", "DDJ", and ">") by BERT tokenizer. As a result, the Stanford parser incorrectly analyzed that ">" modifies "added" with adverb modifier (advmod) relation. In total, 10 pairs of sentences were classified into this type.

(3) The Dow Jones industrial average <.DJI> added 28 points, or 0.27 percent, at 10,557, hitting its highest level in 21 months.

3. **Inter-sentential relations:** Two sentences which have inter-sentential relations are difficult to interpret correctly whether these sentences are paraphrase or not.

(4) British Airways' New York-to-London runs will end in October.
(5) British Airways plans to retire its seven Concordes at the end of October.

Sentences (4) and (5) have the same sense, while different expressions such as "New York-to-London" and "Concordes" are used and they are co-referred entities. To identify these sentences as "paraphrases" correctly, it requires not only local dependency, i.e., dependency structure within a sentence but also non-local dependency between sentences. There were nine pairs classified into this type.

Apart from these observations, we found that when the number of arcs from other nodes is small, the performance of R-GCNs has not improved because convolution mixes the features of a node and its neighbors. One solution is to incorporate more linguistics information such as tree-based structure [62,63], Named Entity Recognition, and Co-Reference Resolution into our framework to represent rich relations among nodes. This is a rich space for further exploration.

We recall that our model for lexical and sentential encodings are based on the BERT. The BERT pre-training model, an unsupervised manner is to learn general, domain-independent knowledge. However, most of the downstream tasks including paraphrase identification and even in the same task, there are several domain-specific data which are collected from different genres such as MRPC and QQP. It would be helpful to develop a good fine-tuning method in our future work.

5. Conclusions

We focused on the problem that how to interpret a diversity of context information as relevant features and proposed an approach by leveraging a variety of features with a neural-based learning model. For syntactic encodings, our LSSE model incorporates word encoding, position encoding, and full dependency structures into a unified framework, R-GCNs. By utilizing the hidden states obtained by the R-GCNs as well as lexical and sentential encodings by BERT, our model learns contextual similarity between sentences. The experimental results by using two datasets showed that our model attained at 86.3% accuracy and 89.9% F1-score in MRPC, and 90.6% accuracy in QQP data which are comparable to the related work on paraphrase identification methods. Moreover, throughout the ablation test, we found that the combination of position encoding and syntactic features contributes to performance improvement.

There are several interesting directions for future work. We should be able to obtain further advantages in efficacy in our syntactic embeddings obtained by the R-GCNs model. We empirically examined that the best performance is achieved with a two-layer model, while R-GCNs with more layers can be considered to capture richer neighborhood information of a graph. Guo et al. focused on this problem and proposed a densely connected graph convolutional network that introduces residual connections, dense connectivity, and graph attention techniques [29]. They reported that the model attained at the current state-of-the-art neural models in the English–German and English–Czech translation tasks. This is definitely worth trying with our LSSE learning model.

As we mentioned in Section 4.5, we found that more effective knowledge extraction improves the overall performance of paraphrase identification. Our model utilized BERT_base model for lexical and sentential encodings and applied it to two domain-specific data, MRPC and QQP. However, the BERT pre-training model is to learn general domain-independent knowledge. In the phase of fine-tuning, the model learns by using these domain-specific data which causes difficulty to estimate optimal parameters. Moreover, Phang et al. reported that BERT is unstable when a training dataset with fine-tuning is small [47]. One approach is to develop a knowledge transfer technique which is some empirical work along these lines in the deep learning field [64]. This is a rich space for further exploration.

Supplementary Materials: The following are available online at http://www.mdpi.com/2076-3417/10/12/4144/s1. Tables 2, 4, 5, 6.

Author Contributions: Conceptualization, F.F., and S.X.; methodology, S.X. and F.F.; software, S.X.; validation, S.X., F.F., X.S., and J.L.; investigation, S.X. and F.F.; writing—original draft preparation, S.X.; writing—review and editing, F.F., X.S., J.L., Y.S., and H.N.; supervision, F.F., and X.S.; funding acquisition, F.F. All authors have read and agreed to the published version of the manuscript.

Funding: This work was supported by the Grant-in-aid for JSPS, Grant Number 17K00299, and Support Center for Advanced Telecommunications Technology Research, Foundation.

Conflicts of Interest: The authors declare no conflict of interest.

References

1. He, H.; Gimpel, K.; Lin, J. Multi-perspective Sentence Similarity Modeling with Convolutional Neural Networks. In Proceedings of the 2015 Conference on Empirical Methods in Natural Language Processing, Lisbon, Portugal, 17–21 September 2015; pp. 1576–1586.
2. Yin, W.; Schütze, H.; Xiang, B.; Zhou, B. ABCNN: Attention-based Convolutional Neural Network for Modeling Sentence Pairs. *Trans. Assoc. Comput. Linguist.* **2016**, *4*, 259–272. [CrossRef]
3. Liu, P.; Qiu, X.; Huang, X. Modelling Interaction of Sentence Pair with Coupled-LSTMs. *arXiv* **2016**, arXiv:1605.05573.
4. Chen, Q.; Zhu, X.; Ling, Z.; Wei, S.; Jiang, H.; Inkpen, D. Enhanced LSTM for Natural Language Inference. In Proceedings of the 55th Annual Meeting of the Association for Computational Linguistics, Vancouver, BC, Canada, 30 July–4 August 2017; pp. 1657–1668.
5. Wieting, J.; Gimpel, K. Revisiting Recurrent Networks for Paraphrastic Sentence Embeddings. In Proceedings of the 55th Annual Meeting of the Association for Computational Linguistics, Vancouver, BC, Canada, 30 July–4 August 2017; pp. 2078–2088.
6. Wang, Y.; Huang, H.; Chong, F.; Zhou, Q.; Jiahui, G.; Xiong, G. CSE: Conceptual Sentence Embeddings based on Attention Model. In Proceedings of the 54th Annual Meeting of the Association for Computational Linguistics, Berlin, Germany, 7–12 August 2016; pp. 505–515.
7. Oren, M.; Jacob, G.; Ido, D. Context2vec: Learning Generic Context Embedding with Bidirectional LSTM. In Proceedings of the 20th SIGNLL Conference on Computational Natural Language Learning, Berlin, Germany, 11–12 August 2016; pp. 51–61.
8. Sanjeev, A.; Yingyu, L.; Tengyu, M. A Simple but Tough-to-Beat Baseline for Sentence Embeddings. In Proceedings of the 5th International Conference on Learning Representations, Toulon, France, 24–26 April 2017.
9. Mark, N.; Mohit, I.; Matt, G.; Christopher, C.; Kenton, L.; Luke, Z. Deep Contextualized Word Representations. In Proceedings of the 2018 Conference of the North American Chapter of the Association for Computational Linguistics: Human Language Technologies, New Orleans, LA, USA, 1–6 June 2018; pp. 2227–2237.
10. Cer, D.; Yang, Y.; Kong, S.; Hua, N.; Limtiaco, N.; St. John, R.; Constant, N.; Guajardo-Cespedes, M.; Yuan, S.; Tar, C.; et al. Univeral Sentence Encoder. *arXiv* **2018**, arXiv:1803.11175.
11. Jacob, D.; Ming-Wei, C.; Kenton, L.; Kristina, T. BERT: Pre-training on Deep Bidirectional Transfomers for Language Understanding. In Proceedings of the 2019 Conference of the North American Chapter of the Association for Computational Linguistics: Human Language Technologies, Minneapolis, MN, USA, 2–7 June 2019; pp. 24171–4186.
12. Michaël, D.; Xavier, B.; Pierre, V. Convolutiona Neural Networks on Graphs with Fast Localized Sectral Filtering. In Proceedings of the 30th Conference on Neural Information Processing Systems, Barcelona, Spain, 5–10 December 2016; pp. 3844–3852.
13. Thomas, K.; Max, W. SEMI-Supervised Classification with Graph Convolutional Networks. In Proceedings of the 5th International Conference on Learning Representations, Toulon, France, 24–26 April 2017.

14. Felix, W.; Tianyi, Z.; de, S.J.A.H.; Christopher, F.; Tao, Y.; Q, W.K. Simplifying Graph Convolutional Networks. In Proceedings of the 36th International Conference on Machine Learning, Long Beach, CA, USA, 9–15 June 2019; pp. 6861–6871.
15. Socher, R.; Bauer, J.; Manning, C.D.; Ng, A.Y. Parsing with Compositional Vector Grammars. In Proceedings of the 51st Annual Meeting of the Association for Computational Linguistics, Melbourne, Australia, 15–20 July 2018; pp. 455–465.
16. Danqi, C.; Manning, C.D. A Fast and Accurate Dependency Parser using Neural Networks. In Proceedings of the Conference on Empirical Methods in Natural Language Processing, Doha, Qatar, 25–29 October 2014; pp. 740–750.
17. Socher, R.; Huang, E.H.; Pennington, J.; Ng, A.Y.; Manning, C.D. Dynamic Pooling and Unfolding Recursive Autoencoders for Paraphrase Detection. In *Advances in Neural Information Processing Systems*; The MIT press: Cambridge, MA, USA, 2011; pp. 801–809.
18. Hu, B.; Lu, Z.; Li, H.; Chen, Q. Convolutional Neural Network Architectures for Matching Natural Language Sentences. In *Advances in Neural Information Processing Systems*; The MIT press: Cambridge, MA, USA, 2015; pp. 2042–2050.
19. Tai, K.S.; Socher, R.; Manning, C.D. Improved Semantic Representations from Tree-structured Long Short-term Memory Networks. In Proceedings of the 53rd Annual Meeting of the Association for Computational Linguistics, Beijing, China, 26–31 July 2015; pp. 1556–1566.
20. Radford, A.; Wu, J.; Child, R.; Luan, D.; Amodei, D.; Sutskever, I. Language models are unsupervised multitask learners. *OpenAI Blog* **2019**, *1*, 9.
21. Wang, A.; Singh, A.; Michael, J.; Hill, F.; Levy, O.; Bowman, S.R. GLUE: A Multi-task Benchmark and Analysis Platform for Natural Language Understanding. *arXiv* **2018**, arXiv:1804.07461.
22. Lample, G.; Conneau, A. Cross-lingual Language Model Pretraining. *arXiv* **2019**, arXiv:1901.07291.
23. Vaswani, A.; Shazeer, N.; Parmar, N.; Uszkoreit, J.; Jones, L.; Gomez, A.N.; Kaiser, L.; Polosukhin, I. Attention is All You Need. In *Advances in Neural Information Processing Systems*; The MIT press: Cambridge, MA, USA, 2017; pp. 5998–6008.
24. Subramanian, S.; Trischler, A.; Bengio, Y.; Pal, J.C. Learning General Purpose Distributed Sentence representations via Large Scale Multi-task Learning. In Proceedings of the 6th International Conference on Learning Representations, Vancouver, BC, Canada, 30 April–3 May 2018.
25. Sun, Y.; Wang, S.; Li, Y.; Feng, S.; Tian, H.; Wu, H.; Wang, H. ERNIE 2.0: A Continual Pre-training Framework for Language Understanding. *arXiv* **2019**, arXiv: 1907.12412.
26. Liu, X.; He, P.; Chen, W.; Gao, J. Multi-task Deep Neural Networks for Natural Language Understanding. *arXiv* **2019**, arXiv:1901.11504.
27. Wu, Z.; Pan, S.; chen, F.; Long, G.; Zhang, C.; Yu, P.S. A Comprehensive Survey on Graph Neural Networks. *arXiv* **2019**, arXiv:1901.00596.
28. Michael, S.; N, K.T.; Peter, B.; Rianne, V.D.B.; Ivan, T.; Max, W. Modeling Relational Data with Graph Convolutional Networks. In Proceedings of the European Semantic Web Conference, Crete, Greece, 3–7 June 2018; pp. 593–607.
29. Zhijiang, G.; Yan, Z.; Zhiyang, T.; Wei, L. Densely Connected Graph Convolutional Networks for Graph-to-Sequence Learning. *Trans. Assoc. Comput. Linguist.* **2019**, *7*, 297–312.
30. Joost, B.; Ivan, T.; Wilker, A.; Diego, M.; Khalil, S. Graph Convolutional Encoders for Syntax-aware Neural Machine Translation. In Proceedings of the 2017 Conference on Empirical Methods in Natural Language Processing, Copenhagen, Denmark, 7–11 September 2017; pp. 1957–1967.
31. Beck, D.; Haffari, G.; Cohn, T. Graph-to-Sequence Learning using Gated Graph Neural Networks. In Proceedings of the 56th Annual Meeting of the Association for Computational Linguistics, Melbourne, Australia, 15–20 July 2018; pp. 273–283.
32. Yinchuan, X.; Junlin, Y. Look Again at the Syntax: Relational Graph Convolutional Network for Gendered Ambiguous Pronoun Resolution. In Proceedings of the 1st Workshop on Gender Bias in Natural Language Processing, Florence, Italy, 2 August 2019; pp. 99–104.
33. Zhijiang, G.; Yan, Z.; Wei, L. Attention Guided Graph Convolutional Networks for Relation Extraction. In Proceedings of the 57th Annual Meeting of the Association for Computational Linguistics, Florence, Italy, 28 July–2 August 2019; pp. 241–251.

34. Diego, M.; Ivan, T. Encoding Sentences with Graph Convolutional Networks for Semantic Role Labeling. In Proceedings of the 2017 Conference on Empirical Methods in Natural Language Processing, Copenhagen, Denmark, 7–11 September 2017; pp. 1506–1515.
35. Hamilton, W.L.; Ying, R.; Leskovec, J. Inductive representation learning on large graphs. In Proceedings of the 31st Conference on Neural Information Processing Systems, Long Beach, CA, USA, 4–9 December 2017; pp. 1024–1034.
36. Peter, V.; Guillem, C.; Arantxa, C.; Adriana, R.; Pietro, L.; Yoshua, B. Graph Attention Networks. In Proceedings of the International Conference on Learning Representations, Vancouver, BC, Canada, 30 April–3 May 2018.
37. Liang, Y.; Chengsheng, M.; Yuan, L. Graph Convolutional Networks for Text Classification. In Proceedings of the 33rd AAAI Conference on Artificial Intelligence, Honolulu, HI, USA, 27 January–1 February 2019; pp. 7370–7377.
38. Wu, Y.; Schuster, M.; Chen, Z.; Le, Q.V.; Norouzi, M. Google's Neural Machine Translation System: Bridging the Gap between Human and Machine Translation. *arXiv* **2016**, arXiv:1609.08144.
39. Shikhar, V.; Manik, B.; Prateek, Y.; Piyush, R.; Chiranjib, B.; Partha, T. Incorporating Syntactic and Semantic Information in Word Embeddings using Graph Convolutional Networks. In Proceedings of the 57th Annual Meeting of the Association for Computational Linguistics, Florence, Italy, 28 July–2 August 2019; pp. 3308–3318.
40. Van den Oord, A.; Kalchbrenner, N.; Espeholt, L.; Vinyals, O.; Graves, A. Conditional Image Generation with PixelCNN Decoders. In Proceedings of the 30th Conference on Neural Information Processin System, Barcelona, Spain, 5–10 December 2016; pp. 4790–4798.
41. Li, Q.; Han, Z.; Wu, X.M. Deeper Insights into Graph Convolutional Networks for Semi-Supervised Learning. In Proceedings of the 32nd AAAI conference on Artificial Intelligence, New Orleans, LA, USA, 2–7 February 2018; pp. 3538–3545.
42. Yang, L.; Kang, Z.; Can, X.; Jin, D.; Yang, B.; Guo, Y. Topology Optimization based Graph Convolutional Network. In Proceedings of the 28th International Joint Conference on Artificial Intelligence, Macao, China, 10–16 August 2019; pp. 4054–4061.
43. Kingma, D.P.; Ba, J. ADAM: A Method for Stochastic Optimization. In Proceedings of the 3rd International Conference on Learning Representations, San Diego, CA, USA, 7–9 May 2015; pp. 1–15.
44. Dolan, W.B.; Brockett, C. Automatically Constructing a Corpus of Sentential Paraphrases. In Proceedings of the Third International Workshop on Paraphrasing, Jeju Island, Korea, 14 October 2005; pp. 9–16.
45. Shankar, I.; Nikhil, D.; Kornél, C. First Quora Dataset Release: Question Pairs. 2016. Available online: https://data.quora.com/First-Quora-Dataset-Releasee-Question-Pairs (accessed on 1 March 2020.)
46. Zhiguo, W.; Wael, H.; Radu, F. Bilateral Multi-Perspective Matching for Natural Language Sentences. In Proceedings of the Twenty-Sixth International Joint Conference on Artificial Intelligence, Melbourne, Australia, 19–25 August 2017; pp. 4144–4150.
47. Phang, J.; Fevry, T.; Bowman, S.R. Sentence Encoders on STILTs: Supplementary Training on Intermediate Labeled-data Tasks. *arXiv* **2019**, arXiv: 1811.01088.
48. Liang, C.; Paritosh, P.K.; Rajendran, V.; Forbus, K.D. Learning Paraphrase Identification with Structural Alignment. In Proceedings of the Twenty-Fifth International Joint Conference on Artificial Intelligence, New York, NY, USA, 9–15 July 2016; pp. 2859–2865.
49. Subramanian, S.; Trischler, A.; Bengio, Y.; Pal, C.J. Learning General Purpose Distributed Sentence Representations via Large Scale Multi-task Learning. *arXiv* **2018**, arXiv:1804.00079.
50. Yuki, A.; Junichi, T. Transfer Fine-Tuning: A BERT Case Study. In Proceedings of the 2019 Conference on Empirical Methods in Natural Language Processing and the 9th International Joint Conference on Natural Language Processing, Hong Kong, China, 3–7 November 2019; pp. 5393–5404.
51. Wei, W.; Bin, B.; Ming, Y.; Chen, W.; Zuyi, B.; Liwei, P.; Luo, S. StructBERT: Incorporating Language Structures into Pre-training for Deep Language Understanding. *arXiv* **2019**, arXiv:1908.04577.
52. Liu, Y.; Ott, M.; Goyal, N.; Du, J.; Joshi, M.; Chen, D.; Levy, O.; Lewis, M.; Zettlemoyer, L.; Stoyanov, V. RoBERTa: A Robustly Optimized BERT Pretraining Approach. *arXiv* **2019**, arXiv: 1907.11692.
53. Lan, Z.; Chen, M.; Goodman, S.; Gimpel, K.; Sharma, P.; Soricut, R. ALBERT: A Lite BERT for Self-supervised Learning of Language Representations. In Proceedings of the 8th International Conference on Learning Representations, Addis Ababa, Ethiopia, 26 April–1 May 2020.

54. Raffel, C.; Shazeer, N.; Roberts, A.; Lee, K.; Narang, S.; Matena, M.; Zhou, Y.; Li, W.; Liu, P.J. Exploring the Limits of Transfer Learning with a Unified Text-to-Text Transformer. *arXiv* **2019**, arXiv: 1910.10683.
55. Chen, Z.; Yu, C.; Zhe, G.; Siqi, S.; Thomas, G.; Jing, L. FreeLB: Enhanced Adversarial Training for Natural Language Understanding. *arXiv* **2019**, arXiv:1909.11764.
56. Clark, K.; Luong, M.T.; Le, Q.V.; Manning, C.D. ELECTRA: Pre-Training Text Encoders as Discriminators Rather than Generators. In Proceedings of the 8th International Conference on Learning Representations, Addis Ababa, Ethiopia, 26 April–1 May 2020.
57. Nie, Y.; Bansal, M. Shortcut-stacked Sentence Encoders for Multi-Domain Inference. In Proceedings of the 2nd Workshop on Evaluating Vector Space Representations for NLP, Copenhagen, Denmark, September 2017; pp. 41–45.
58. Wuwei, L.; Wei, X. Neural Network Models for Paraphrase Identification Semantic Textual Similarity Natural Language Inference and Question Answering. In Proceedings of the 27th International Conference on Computational Linguistics, Santa Fe, NM, USA, 20–26 August 2018; pp. 3890–3902.
59. Conneau, A.; Kiela, D.; Schwenk, H.; Barrault, L.; Bordes, A. Supervised Learning of Universal Sentence Representations from Natural Language Inference Data. In Proceedings of the 2017 Conference on Empirical Methods in Natural Language Processing, Copenhagen, Denmark, 7–11 September 2017; pp. 670–680.
60. He, H.; Lin, J. Pairwise Word Interaction Modeling with Deep Neural Networks for Semantic Similarity Measurement. In Proceedings of the 2016 Conference of the North American Chapter of the Association for Computational Linguistics: Human Language Technologies, San Diego, CA, USA, 12–17 June 2016; pp. 937–948.
61. Parikh, A.; Tom, O.; Das, D.; Uszkoreit, J. A Decomposable Attention Model for Natural Language Inference. In Proceedings of the 2016 Conference on Empirical Methods in Natural Language Processing, Austin, TX, USA, 1–5 November 2016; pp. 2249–2255.
62. Moschitti, A. Efficient Convolution Kernels for Dependency and Constituent Syntactic Trees. In Proceedings of the 17th European Conference on Machine Learning and the 10th European Conference on Principles and Practice of Knowledge Discovery in Databases, Berlin, Germany, 18–22 September 2006; pp. 318–329.
63. Moschitti, A.; Chu-Carroll, J.; Patwardhan, S.; Fan, J.; Riccardi, G. Using Syntactic and Semantic Structural Kernels for Classifying Definition Questions in Jeopardy! In Proceedings of the Conference on Empirical Methods in Natural Language Processing, Scotland, UK, 27–31 July 2011; pp. 712–724.
64. Papernot, N.; Abadi, M.; Úlfar, E.; Goodfellow, I.; Talwar, K. Semi-Supervised Knowledge Transfer for Deep Learning from Private Training Data. In Proceedings of the International Conference on Learning Representations, Toulon, France, 24–26 April 2017.

© 2020 by the authors. Licensee MDPI, Basel, Switzerland. This article is an open access article distributed under the terms and conditions of the Creative Commons Attribution (CC BY) license (http://creativecommons.org/licenses/by/4.0/).

Article

A Rule-Based Approach to Embedding Techniques for Text Document Classification

Asmaa M. Aubaid [1,2] and Alok Mishra [1,3,*]

1. Department MODES, Department of Software Engineering, Atilim University, Ankara 06830, Turkey; asmaamuhamed1971@yahoo.com
2. Ministry of Higher Education and Scientific Research, Directorates: Science and Technology, Directorate: Information Technology, Baghdad/Al-Jadria 10070, Iraq
3. Faculty of Logistics, Molde University College (Specialized University in Logistics), 6410 Molde, Norway
* Correspondence: alok.mishra@himolde.no or alok.mishra@atilim.edu.tr

Received: 11 April 2020; Accepted: 5 June 2020; Published: 10 June 2020

Abstract: With the growth of online information and sudden expansion in the number of electronic documents provided on websites and in electronic libraries, there is difficulty in categorizing text documents. Therefore, a rule-based approach is a solution to this problem; the purpose of this study is to classify documents by using a rule-based. This paper deals with the rule-based approach with the embedding technique for a document to vector (doc2vec) files. An experiment was performed on two data sets Reuters-21578 and the 20 Newsgroups to classify the top ten categories of these data sets by using a document to vector rule-based (D2vecRule). Finally, this method provided us a good classification result according to the F-measures and implementation time metrics. In conclusion, it was observed that our algorithm document to vector rule-based (D2vecRule) was good when compared with other algorithms such as JRip, One R, and ZeroR applied to the same Reuters-21578 dataset.

Keywords: text classification; rule-based; word embedding; Doc2vec

1. Introduction

There has been an urgency in terms of classifying the information available online in the past ten years, prompting researchers to focus on automatic text classification (ATC). A widely used research method for this problem depends on rule-based and embedding techniques. In the 1960s, rule-based approaches began to emerge; however, they became more common in the 1970s and 1980s [1]. The late 1980s witnessed the formation of same-time or concurrent operations and activation of rules within production systems, all of which carried on into the following decade. The rule-based system includes a set of rules that can be implemented for many purposes, including the support of decision-making or for a predictive decision in real implementations. It is possible to divide the methods of creating rules into the categories of 'conquer and separate' [2] and 'divide and conquer' [3]. This produces categorization rules in the intermediate form of a decision tree, such as C4.5, C5.0, and ID3 [2]. In the same manner, ID3 is a covering technique [4] with an approach in the form of 'if then' rules. The structure of the systems of rule-based methods depends on logic-specific types, such as deterministic logic, fuzzy logic, and probabilistic logic. It can also divide the system of rule-based into the following types: systems of fuzzy rule-based, deterministic rule-based and probabilistic rule-based and determine rule-based systems being in the context of bases of the rule, which includes bases of modular rules, single rules, and chained rules [5]. In practice, the task of ensemble learning may be performed in a parallel form, in a distributed manner or on mobile platforms according to given computing environments. Finally, rule-based systems are divided into three types, namely distributed, mobile and parallel [6]. The Reuters-21578 newswire benchmark and 20 Newsgroups are the most widely used benchmark corpora in the research community in the text categorization field. They can be found in comparative studies of different approaches using flat (i.e., non-hierarchical) category systems in this corpus [7]. Hierarchical text classifiers are among the first works in this field, experiments with two classifiers on the subset of the Reuters collection reported by Kollar and Sahami [8]. Our rule-based and embedding models contributed to classifying the categories of Reuter's dataset such as (Acq, Corn, Crude, Earn, Grain, and Ship) according to their contents. The objective of this manuscript is to provide deeper information about the performance of embedding to rule-based text classification. The main research question to explore is how varying rule-based affects the performance of text classification and we investigate the performance differences when combining our rules-based and one of the embedding models such as (doc2vec) in the task of text classification on the different datasets. We will implement many steps to acquire robust rules-based and embedding models using the Reuter 21578 and 20 Newsgroup corpora so as to make text categorization (TC) easier. Finally, Figure 1 summarizes the essential steps for a rule-based approach.

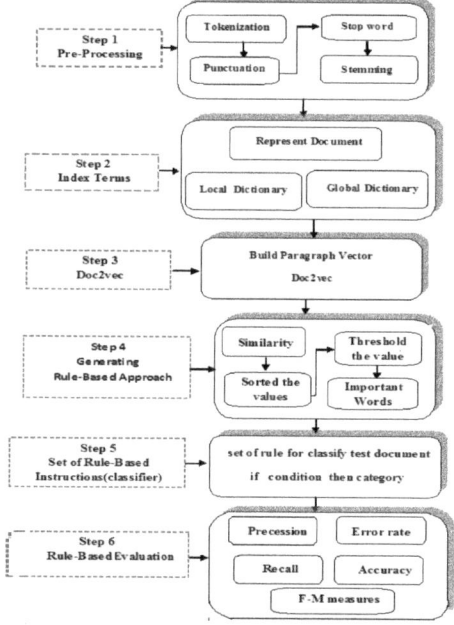

Figure 1. Steps of rule-based processing.

2. Related Work

Various studies relating to classification have been carried out taking a number of approaches. In classification systems, a rule-based learning approach to text categorization is utilized. Imaichi and Yanase suggested using rule-based methods selectively depending on the nature of the information to be extracted and make comparisons with the machine learning [9]. The model of rule-based learning consists of a set of rules learned from data [10]. Han Liu introduced an integrated framework for the design of systems of rule-based to implement missions of categorization, which included the process of rule representation, rule generation, and rule simplification. The study stressed the importance of the combination of different types of algorithms of rule learning techniques via ensemble learning [5]. Rule-based machine translation (RBMT) considers the unclear points pertaining to morphology and lexicon as serious challenges. A contribution by Rios and Göhring [11] describes an approach to resolving the forms of the morphologically ambiguous verb if a rule-based decision is not possible due to tagging errors or parsing. Cronin et al. developed an automated patient portal message classifiers with the rule-based approach using natural language processing (NLP) and the bag of words [12]. Ganglberger et al. discuss different automatic spike detection methods in order to improve detection performance and establish a user-adjustable sensitivity parameter mainly by examining the functioning of a rule-based system, artificial neural networks (ANNs) and random forests [13]. Accordingly, the rule-based system needed a feature selection to classify text documents. Feature selection can be performed by following one of three approaches, i.e., filter, wrapper or embedded approaches [14]. In this study, this depends on embedded methods to select a feature. The optimal parameters are learned by using the embedded method to perform the feature selection approach [15]. INRA (Institut national de la recherche agronomique) and Cnrs (Centre national de la recherche scientifique) at University Paris Saclay proposed a two-step method to normalize multi-word terms with concepts from a domain-specific ontology. In this method, they used vector representations of terms computed with word embedding information and hierarchical information from ontology concepts [16]. Le and Mikolov presented word2vec and later introduced the doc2vec algorithm based on adjusted techniques for learning how to embed texts identical to word2vec, thus turning doc2vec into a branch of word2vec [17]. In their work, doc2vec was applied to model embedding for text categorization. The motivation of this study was to classify text documents by taking a rule-based approach to embedding techniques and this work will assist us in determining the acceptable methods to follow for in-text categorization based upon measuring the related criteria. Finally, this manuscript comprises eight sections containing all the necessary information related to the rule-based approach using automatic text classification for the top ten categories of the Reuters-21578 and 20 Newsgroups data sets. Then, the paper is structured as follows: Section 1 introduces the rule-based and text classification approaches. Section 2 presents related work with the study. Section 3 explains in detail the research methodology. Section 4 presents the data analysis and results. Section 5 discusses the study results. Finally, Sections 6–8 provide a conclusion, future research directions and limitations

3. Materials and Methods

3.1. Embedding Methods

The presently applied rule-based with embedding technique comprises numerous factors and is used in many applications, one being text categorization. Embedding is one of the promising applications of unsupervised learning as well as transfer learning because embedding is induced by the large unlabeled corpus. Embedding is used two character-level embedding models (fast text and ELMo) and two document-level models (doc2vec and InferSent) to compare with word-level word2vec, all in accordance to the novel approach introduced by References [18]. The rule classification system uses the doc2vec model which is a type of the document embeddings of one of the embedding methods. There are three types of embedding: word2vec, character and doc2vec, as shown in the following.

3.1.1. Word Embedding

We can define "a word embedding" as content representation such that words of similar meaning also receive the same representation. This method deals with representing documents and words and it may be seen as one of the keys in the procedures ahead of deep learning when testing natural language processing (NLP) problems. Furthermore, it is a category of methodologies in which vectors that are real-valued are used in a predefined vector space to represent single words. Every word is determined to be a vector and the values of the vectors are discovered following a neural network method. Later, the technique is usually grouped into a profound learning field. The key to the approach is to use a densely dispersed representation for each word. A real-valued vector is utilized to represent each word, frequently tens of, or many, measurements. This is divided into hundreds and thousands or matched to larger numbers of dimensions required to represent a word, such as one-hot encoding [19].

3.1.2. Character Embedding

Word2vec is arranged based on the character n grams in a character embedding model. As character n grams is shared across words assuming a closed-world alphabet, these models can generate embedding for out of vocabulary (OOV) words as well as words that occur infrequently. The two character-level embedding patterns of fastText may be used as those appearing in References [20,21], which describe ELMo in the following manner:

- fastText: applies a 300 dimensional model pre -rained on Common Crawl and Wikipedia via the Continuous Bag of Words (CBOW). To generate a representation for joint multiword expressions (MWE), fastText considers every word as whitespace delimited, taking away every space and handling them in the form of a united compound. For instance, 'couch potato' becomes 'couchpotato.' In the case of paraphrases, it uses the same word averaging technique as word2vec.
- ELMo: utilizes the Elmo Embedder group of Python's allennlp library, being pre trained in SNLI and SQuAD, with a dimensionality of 1024. It is noted that the essential use case for ELMo is implemented by generating embedding in context. However, it does not provide any context in the input for compatibility with the other models. Thus, the benefits of the full potential of this model are unknown. Therefore, ELMo is not suitable since the relative compositionality of a compound is often predictable from its component words only [18], so the present study makes use of doc2vec.

3.1.3. Document Embedding

In this study, doc2vec is a proposal for paragraph-level embedding from the research team responsible for word2vec. It is possible to use the doc2vec approach to learn a model that can create an embedding technique in a specific document. In contrast to some of the known used methods (such as averaging word vectors, n gram models and bag of words (BOW)), doc2vec is public too and it can be utilized to create embedding from any length of text. From large corpora of raw text, it can train doc2vec in a totally unsupervised fashion. Doc2vec operates effectively once applied to represent extended texts [22]. In this paper, doc2vec (Distributed Memory Model) is used. Doc2vec is an offset to the present word embedding models and it is a popular method to learn word vectors. Moreover, it can be divided into two partitions.

3.1.3.1. A Distributed Memory Model

This part of doc2vec contributes to our study; our methodology for learning doc2vec is a model inspired by the techniques to learn the vectors of words. The inspiration is to provide a commitment to a forecast about words following in the sentence. Although the fact that a word vector is instated arbitrarily, as an indirect result, it can capture semantics from the forecasting task. Therefore, it will use this idea in our doc2vec and in the identical method. The doc2vec can also help in the estimating task of the following word since there are numerous settings that were inspected from the paragraph. In our doc2vec framework (see Figure 2), a unique vector is mapped to every paragraph and described by a column in matrix D for every word W. The two-word vectors and doc2vec are concatenated or averaged to estimate the next word in a context. In the experiments, the concatenation method was used to consolidate the vectors. The section token can be thought of as another word, and the paragraph works as memory recalling what is absent from the subject or the setting of the section itself. For the previous reason, the Distributed Memory Model of Paragraph Vectors (PV DM) is named doc2vec. The contexts are fixed-length and are inspected from a sliding window over a section. The paragraph of a vector is shared over all contexts produced from the same paragraph, but not over the paragraphs. In this model, predicting the fourth word is possible by using the chain or the average of the related vector along with a context of three words. The doc2vec is assumed to be the absent data from the present context and it can function as a memory of the paragraph subject. After being trained, the doc2vec can be utilized as vocabularies for the paragraph. In summary, the algorithm has two main stages:

1. Training stage to acquire word vectors W, soft max weights U; b and doc2vec D on as of now observed paragraphs.
2. The inference stage to acquire doc2vec D for new paragraphs by including more columns in D and a gradient descending on D while holding W, U, and b fixed. D is utilized to make a prediction about various specific labels utilizing a standard classifier [17].

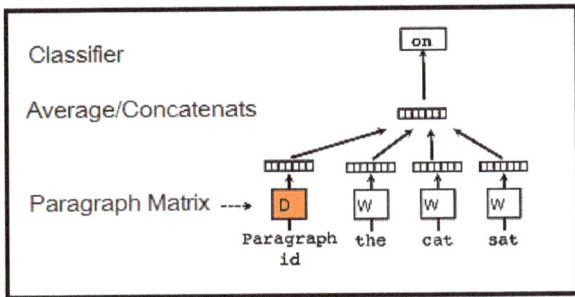

Figure 2. Learning model for doc2vec illustrating information absent in the present context and acting as a memory of the paragraph subject [17].

3.1.3.2. Distributed Bag of Words Model

The method described earlier involves forecasting the following words in a text window by using a concatenation of the doc2vec by vectors. Another approach is to eliminate the context words at the source by driving the model to estimate words sampled in any manner from the paragraph in the output. In reality, it means that for each round of stochastic gradient descent, a text window is examined, followed by sampling a random word from the text window and forming a classification task given the doc2vec, as shown in Figure 3 [17].

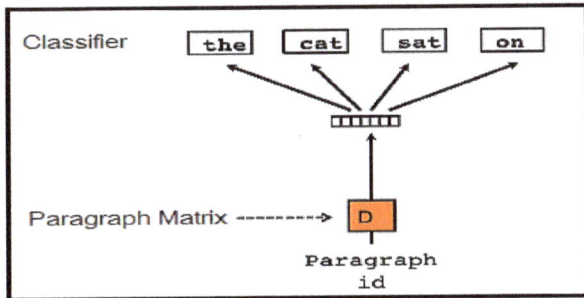

Figure 3. Version of doc2vec with Distributed Bag of Words. Here, the doc2vec was trained to predict the words in a small window [17].

To build the doc2vec model, the major stages of training need to be prepared and tested with a dataset, as shown in the following.

3.2. Data Sets

3.2.1. Data Sets Types

A dataset is defined as a collection of related, but separated, features of related data that can be accessed individually or in combination. It can be formed and arranged into a type of data structure. For example, a dataset may be contained in the collection of business data (identity, salaries, names, address, contact information, etc.). It is possible to transform a database and use it as a set of data and we can connect the data inside it with a particular type of information. We will evaluate the doc2vec model for our rule-based approach applied to the following two datasets.

3.2.1.1. Reuters-21578 Dataset

The Reuters Newswire in 1987 saw the emergence of documents of the Reuters-21578 collection and this is a publically available version of the well-known Reuters-21578 "ApteMod" corpus for text categorization. A Reuters Ltd. (S. Weinstein, S. Dobbins, and M. Topliss) and the Carnegie Group, Inc. (M. Cellio, P. Andersen, P. Hayes, Ir. Nirenburg, and L. Knecht) collected and indexed these documents according to certain categories. The Reuters-21578 collection is distributed in 22 files. Each of the first 21 files (reut2-000.sgm through reut2-020.sgm) contains 1000 documents, while the last (reut2-021.sgm) contains 578 documents. The files are in SGML format. Rather than going into the details of the SGML language, it is described how the SGML tags are used to divide each file, and each document, into sections. Each of the 22 files begins with a document type declaration line: <!DOCTYPE lewis SYSTEM "lewis.DTD">The documents of Reuters-21578 are divided into training and test sets. Each document has five-category tags, namely, TOPICS, PLACES, PEOPLE, ORGS, and EXCHANGES. Each category has the number of topics that are used for a document, but in this study focuses on the TOPIC category only.

3.2.1.2. 20 Newsgroups Dataset

About 20,000 newsgroup documents are collected in the 20 Newsgroups dataset and these documents are partitioned (almost) equally into 20 separate newsgroups. The data are organized into 20 different newsgroups, each corresponding to a different topic. Some of the newsgroups are very closely related to each other (including newsgroups such as comp.sys.mac.hardware and comp.sys.ibm.pc.hardware), while others are highly unrelated (including newsgroups such as misc.forsale and soc.religion.christian) [23].

3.2.2. Pre-Processing Data Sets

Pre-Processing is an important step for initializing the text, it takes an amount of processing time. Pre-Processing includes several steps such as tokenization, punctuation, stop and stop words.

3.2.2.1. Tokenizing

Tokenizing is a process of cutting the input text into pieces of words/tokens by remembering the sequence in the text that is in the tokenization and simultaneously discarding specific characters, such as punctuation [24]. Tokenizing is defined as the process of breaking down documents into words or terms called tokens. An entire text is lowercased when all the punctuation is removed and when applying the process of tokenization [25].

3.2.2.2. Punctuation

Defined as a set of marks, they are used to make sentences flow smoothly and express meaning accurately. These marks determine the place of pause or provide a signifying feeling to our words. Punctuation makes sentences pure by breaking ideas. Moreover, the punctuation points quotes, out titles and other main parts of the language. Finally, punctuation is vital in any text, necessitating their introduction. Examples include ",", "!", "?", "*".

3.2.2.3. Stop Word Removal

One important step in text classification is to eliminate stop words. A stop word is defined as a list of commonly used words that have an important function in a text but no meaning. A stop word in a text is removed to reduce noise terms, and as a result, the keyword remains [26]. Stop words are common words occurring in most documents, such as "the," "and," "from," "are," "to," etc. They are required to apply this processing because these stop words cannot decide the category of the document in the categorization system [25].

3.2.2.4. Stemming

When acquiring information, stemming changes a word form to its root by means of specific principles related to the target language [27]. This is vital due to the presence of affixes, which consist of prefixes, infixes, suffixes, and confixes (combinations of prefixes and suffixes) in derived words [28]. Stemming is a process of reducing the terms to their roots. For example, words such as "working," "worker" and "worked" are reduced to "work" and "crumbling" and "crumbled" are reduced to "crumb." This process is used to reduce the computing time and space as different forms of words are stemmed into a single word. In fact, this is the main advantage of this process [25].

3.3. Local Dictionary Creation

It is the role of the main dictionary to perform feature selection in text categorization with a different set of features being selected from each category. Several studies have been conducted which used this type of dictionary. In the local dictionary, a contrasting set of features is selected from each, independent of the other categories, and that dictionary works to increase the speed of the classification process for each category by selecting the most important features in that category. Table 1 introduces the local dictionary for a number of categories in the dataset.

Table 1. Local dictionary for some categories of the dataset.

Acq	Corn	Crude	Earn	Grain	Ship
dollar	govern	rise	second	govern	govern
unit	soybean	govern	unit	new	spokesman
relate	total	spokesman	rate	hectare	new
hold	office	new	bank	china	strike
place	report	study	project	credit	office
commissar	maize	total	bus	soybean	japan
share	ton	unit	result	total	report
result	union	end	figure	unit	iran
debt	earth	tanker	debt	end	boat

3.4. Rule-Based Approach

The rule based approach is considered to be one of the most flexible methods by which the black box of the process of the text classification technique can be shown. The details of a process of classification can be observed and it can add a number of tools or new instructions to obtain good results. The next subsections will explain the approach of rule-based in briefly.

3.4.1. Rules—Preliminary

A rule-based system is commonly comprised of a set of if then rules [29] expressed such that there are various approaches to information representation in the area of artificial intelligence. However, the most famous one may be in the form of if then rules defined as: "IF cause (antecedent) THEN effect (consequent)."

1. Rules: Data are used to derive the most known symbolic representations of knowledge:

    - A natural and smooth form of representation → possible search by humans and their interpretations;

2. A standard form of the rules;
3. If "condition" then "class";
4. Other forms: Class if conditions; conditions → class.

3.4.2. Rules—Formal Notations

Rule-based processes, also known as expert or generation systems represent a type of artificial intelligence. The rules in this system are used as the learning representation for the information that is coded into the system [30]. The expert system affects the implications of rule-based systems completely and it copies the reasoning of human experts in explaining an information-intensive issue. Instead of learning in a declarative, static manner as a course action of things that are valid, rule-based systems can be considered to be knowledge that can be represented as a set of rules determining what to do or what to conclude in various situations.

3.4.3. Structure of a Rule-Based Expert System

In the early 1970s, Simon and Newell from the University of Carnegie Mellon proposed a production system model which is the foundation of modern rule-based expert systems [31]. The idea of that production model was based on whenever humans applied knowledge (expressed as production rules); they can solve any problem represented by problem-specific information. The problem-specific information or facts in short-term memory and the production rules were stored in long-term memory. A rule-based expert system has five components: the database, the knowledge base, the explanation facilities, the inference engine, and the user interface [32].

3.5. Classification Methods

Classification is a data mining technique that assigns items in a set to the target class. The aim of classification is to visualize correctly the target categories for each case in the data [33]. Three rule-based classification methods are applied in addition to our rule-based (D2VRule) method that is taken as a benchmarking algorithm to be studied for the Reuters-21578 and 20 Newsgroups datasets.

3.5.1. JRip (RIPPER)

This algorithm is one of the essential and most well-known. A set of rules in growing the size is used to examine classes and a premier set of rules for each category is created using JRip (RIPPER) with gradually reduced errors by handling all the instances of a special decision in the training data as categories. It returns a set of rules that cover every member of that class. Therefore, it proceeds to the next categories and does the same, repeating these processes until every category covered [34].

3.5.2. One Rule (OneR)

Abbreviated to OneR, this method uses a simple algorithm in a text classification technique to create a decision tree with one level. From different instances, OneR can deduce simple but precise classification rules. In spite of its simplicity, OneR is able to treat lost values and lost numeric attributes more flexibly. The OneR algorithm generates one rule for each predictor (class) in the data. The rule with the minimum false rate is selected by depending on the principle of one rule for each attribute in the training data [35].

3.5.3. ZeroR

ZeroR is considered to be the simplest classification method based on the target and it disregards all other predictors. In spite of ZeroR lacking predictability power, it is helpful in determining the performance of a baseline as a metric for other classification methods. ZeroR constructs a hesitancy table for the feature and selects its highest hesitancy value [36].

3.6. Evaluation Measures

The performance evaluation feature selection approaches are computed using recall (R) and precision (P) [37].

3.6.1. Precision

Precision is defined as a percentage of relevant documents correctly retrieved by the system having a symbol (TP) with respect to every document relevant to humans (TP + FN) [37]:

$$Precision = \frac{TP}{TP+FP} = \frac{Retrieved\ Relevent}{Retrieved}, \qquad (1)$$

where

- TP (true positive) is defined as the correctly assigned number of documents to Class (i).
- FP (false positive) is defined as the incorrectly assigned number of documents to Class (i) by the classifier but which actually does not belong to that class.

3.6.2. Recall

The percentage of relevant documents correctly retrieved by the system (TP) with respect to every document relevant to humans is TP + FN. In other words, recall is equal to the ratio of the retrieved relevant documents to the relevant documents [37].

$$Recall(R) = \frac{TP}{TP+FN} = \frac{Retrieved\ Relevent}{Relevent}, \qquad (2)$$

where:

- TN (true negative) is defined as the classifier not assigning documents to Class (i); they actually do not belong to Class (i).
- FN (false negative) is defined as the classifier not assigning documents to Class (i); however, they actually do belong to Class (i).

3.6.3. F-Measure

This element is defined as a global estimation of the performance of an information retrieval (IR) system by combining measure precision (P) and recall (R) in a single measure called F-measure [37].

$$F-M = \frac{2(TP)}{FP+FN+2(TP)} = \frac{2(Retrieved\ Relevent)}{Relevent + Retrieved + 2(Retrieved\ Relevent)}. \qquad (3)$$

3.6.4. Error Rate Inverse of Accuracy

This element is defined as a global estimation of the performance of an information retrieval (IR) system by combining measure precision (P) and recall (R) in a single measure called F-measure [37].

$$Error\ Rate = \frac{FP+FN}{TP+TN+FP+FN}. \qquad (4)$$

3.6.5. Accuracy

Accuracy is defined as the percentage of documents correctly classified by the system [36]

$$Accuracy = \frac{TP+TN}{TP+TN+FP+FN}. \qquad (5)$$

4. Experiment Setup

In this section, we describe the experimental setup of a text classification system which includes the preprocessing, documents representation, rule-based induction in addition to evaluation metrics.

4.1. Preparing the Dataset

A collection of documents was used from the Reuters-21578 dataset (for the training dataset) and the top ten categories were selected for the 20 Newsgroups dataset. The first step of a prepared dataset was implemented using:

1. Tokenization
2. Punctuation
3. Stop word
4. Stemming

These approaches are explained in detail in the previous sections. Figure 4 explains the steps of preparing a dataset for a rule-based approach.

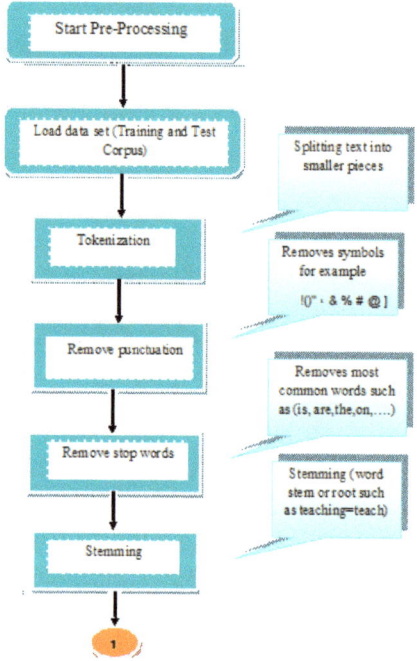

Figure 4. Dataset preparation for a rule-based approach.

4.2. Rule-Based Processing (Documents Representation)

The previous steps were necessary to begin the rule-based creation process; however, the following sections are more important to build our rule-based by using the doc2vec approach under a titled document to the vector rule based (D2VRule).

4.2.1. Terms Indexing

The term indexing was considered a necessary step to build the dictionary and had benefits fpr classification processes. This dictionary was named a local dictionary; it was considered the main dictionary to apply feature selection in text categorization. In this dictionary, a different set of features was selected from each category. Several studies have been performed using the local dictionary policy. In the local dictionary, a contrasting set of features was selected from each independently of the other categories, and this dictionary helped to increase the ability of the classification process for each category by selecting the most important terms in that category.

4.2.2. Doc2vec Creation

In this step, the doc2vec approach was taken (explained in detail in previous sections). A doc2vec model was built by using documents of the training dataset. This step was necessary in order to determine the similarity between vocabularies, which were sets of familiar words in the language of a document of a local dictionary as well as training documents to acquire important features selection (vocabularies). These were used to classify text documents of the test corpus.

4.2.3. Computing Similarity of Vocabularies

The vocabulary was extracted from documents by training the data set such that words that were similar or had a related meaning to other words were extracted. This can be of benefit when one wishes to avoid repeating the same word by concentrating on the value of similarity of vocabulary near to 1 and removing the vocabulary which has a value near to 0 (zero) by depending on a threshold value. The procedure of similarity was performed by building a doc2vec model to prepare documents and compute the similarity of vocabularies in a local dictionary with doc2vec itself using special instructions in Python (most similarity).

4.2.4. Sorting of Vocabularies

The values of similarities of vocabularies were arranged according to threshold values defined as points beyond which there was a change in the manner a program executes. In particular, the threshold value was represented as the value of the similarity of terms in documents and by which it determined the important words in these documents. Figure 5 presents the steps used to implement the rule.

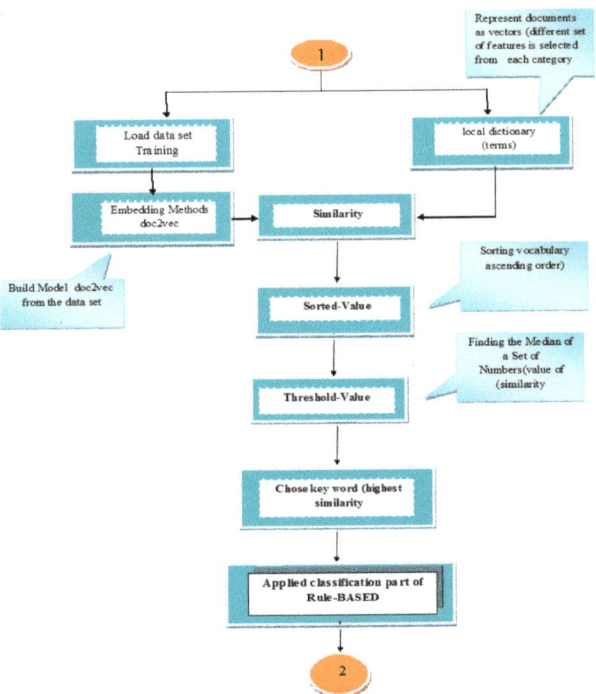

Figure 5. Steps for starting applied classification with rule-based (D2VRule).

4.3. Rule-Based Induction

Promising results can be obtained when applying our rule-based (D2VRule) to the number of standard problems in the text classification. Therefore, to classify the objects, it is necessary for most learning algorithms in the first step to transform these objects into a representation suitable for concept learning. The transformation process of electronic texts is discussed in the previous section of Part 1 and Part 2. In the D2VRule, as in other rule induction systems, it is defined as a decision rule that is a set of Boolean clauses linked by logical (AND, OR) operators which together imply membership in a particular class. A sequence of rules ending in a default rule with an empty set of clauses usually builds a hypothesis of a classification. When we apply the classification process, it can divide the core of the rules-base into two parts, with the left-hand sides of the rules being implemented sequentially until one of them evaluates to true, and the right-hand side of the rule being offered as the class prediction.

4.3.1. Set of Rule-Based Instructions

Text categorization was implemented by depending on a measurement metric called the feature selection metric. Its general idea was to determine the importance of words (vocabularies) using a measure that can remove non-informative words and retain informative words.

The following are some of the rule-based structures that will be generated for one of ten categories:

- if (("corn" € doc or "maiz" € doc)
- or ("wheat" € doc and "maiz" € doc)
- or ("tonn" € doc and "wheat" € doc
- and "corn" € doc))then
- category = "corn"

4.3.2. Rule-Based Evaluation

The rule-based categories were checked according to dataset categories and classification rules, followed by evaluation measurements being computed. The evaluation measurements include:

1. Precession measurements
2. Recall measurements
3. F-Measures
4. Error rate
5. Accuracy

Examples of an induction rule and the evaluation metrics are shown in Figure 6.

Finally, it can arrange the pre-processing of our rule-based approach according to the block diagrams in Figure 7 and build the block diagram of the rule-based technique. The following figure shows the processing of the rule-based approach for two partitions, which was used in the text classification technique.

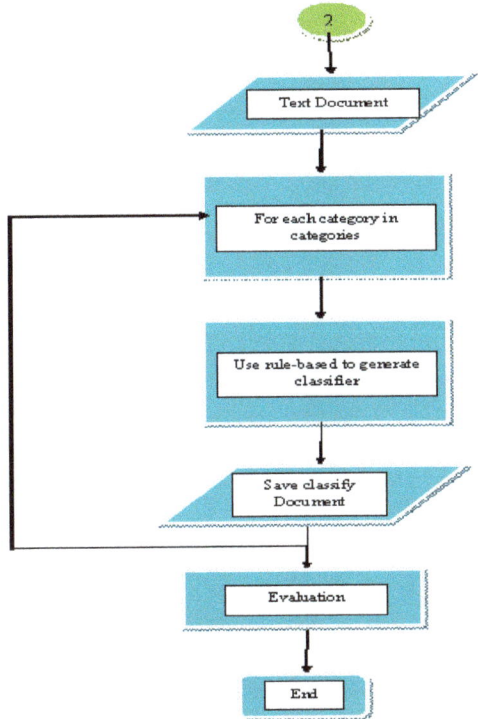

Figure 6. Steps of classification of rule-based and evaluation metrics.

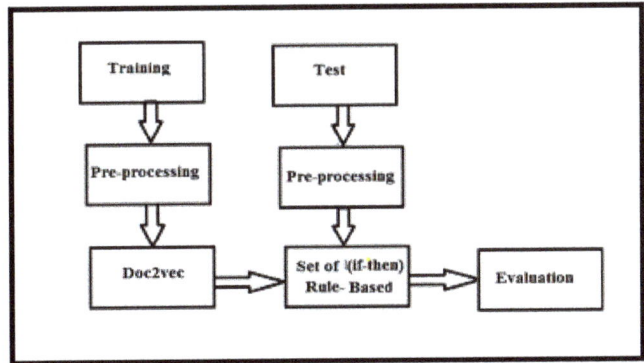

Figure 7. Rule-based approach.

5. Results

In this section, it is possible to encounter extensive investigations of precision, recall, F-measure, error rate, and accuracy criteria. Moreover, precision and recall formulations (Equations (1)–(4)) were used for the Reuters-21578 and 20 Newsgroups datasets to classify the top ten categories individually. The computations were compared in order to select the acceptable method to implement the text classification. In addition, our rule-based approach examined the acq, corn, crude, earn, grain, interest, money-fix, ship, trade, and wheat top ten categories for the Reuters-21578 dataset. For the 20 Newsgroups dataset, our rule-based approach examined the categories of data sets.

As seen in Figures 8–12, we explored the precision, recall, F-measures, error rates, and accuracy of a rule-based approach to classify the test documents when we selected the top ten categories of the Reuters-21578 and 20 Newsgroups datasets.

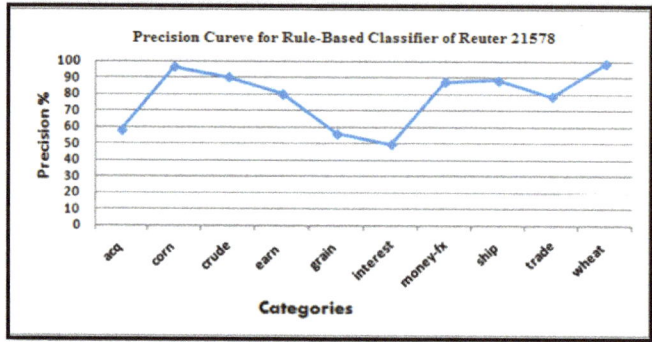

Figure 8. Variation in the precision of the rule-based text categorization technique for the Reuters-21578 dataset.

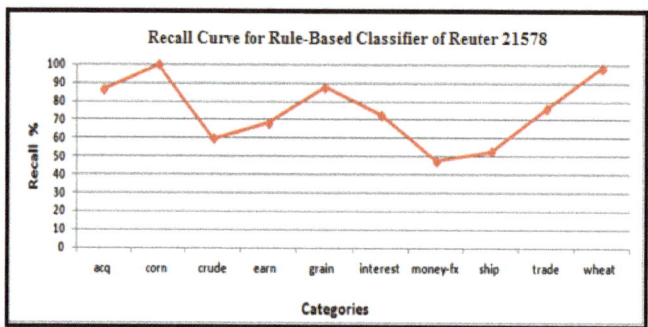

Figure 9. Variation in the recall of the rule-based text categorization technique for the Reuters 21587 dataset.

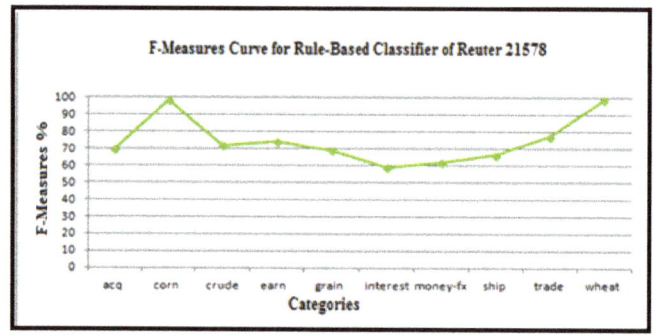

Figure 10. Variation in F-measures of the rule-based text categorization technique for the Reuters-21578.

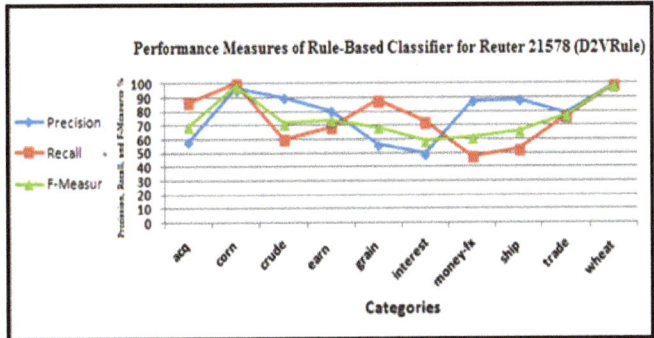

Figure 11. Performance measures of the rule-based classifier for the Reuters-21578 dataset.

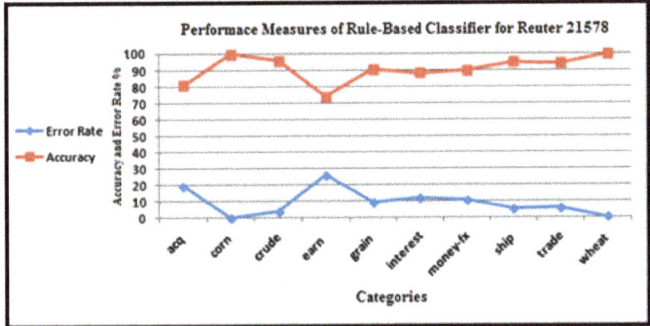

Figure 12. Performance of the rule-based text categorization technique for the Reuters-21578 dataset.

As shown in Figures 13–18, we explored the precision, recall, and accuracy of a rule-based approach to classify the test documents when we selected the top ten categories of the 20 Newsgroup dataset.

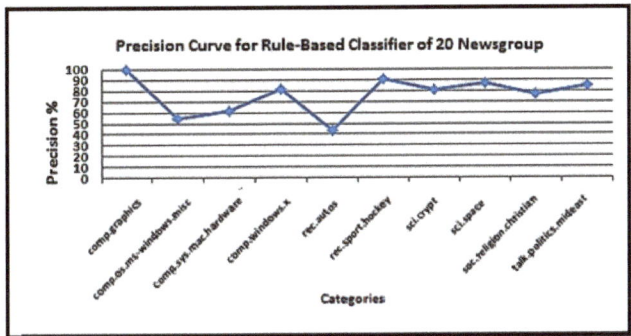

Figure 13. Variation in the precision of the rule-based text categorization technique for the 20 Newsgroups dataset.

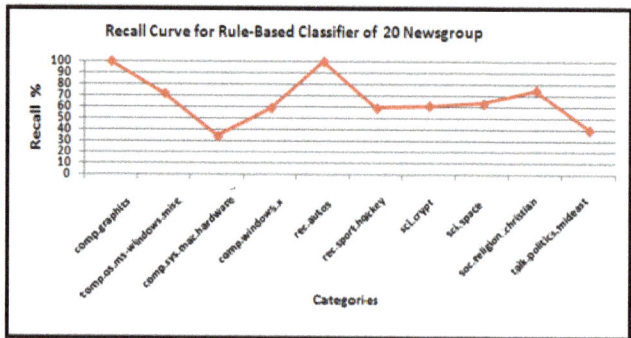

Figure 14. Variation in the recall of the rule-based text categorization technique for the 20 Newsgroups dataset.

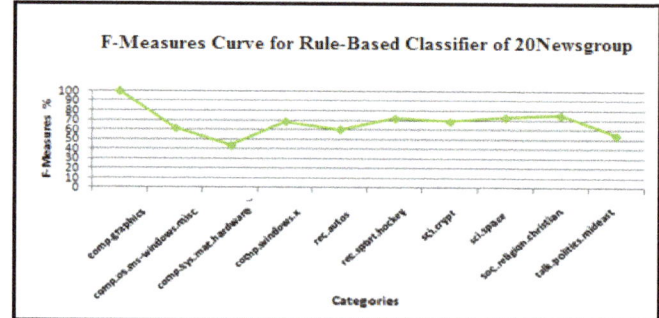

Figure 15. Variation in the F-measures of the rule-based text categorization technique for the 20 Newsgroups dataset.

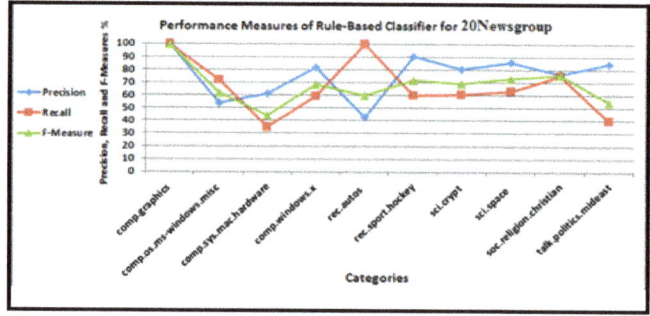

Figure 16. Performance measures of the rule-based classifier for the 20 Newsgroups dataset.

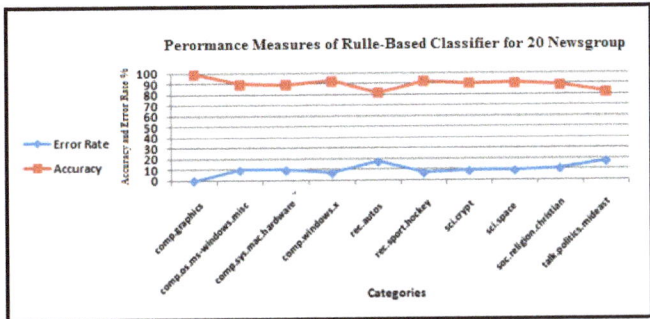

Figure 17. Performance of the text categorization system technique for the 20 Newsgroups dataset.

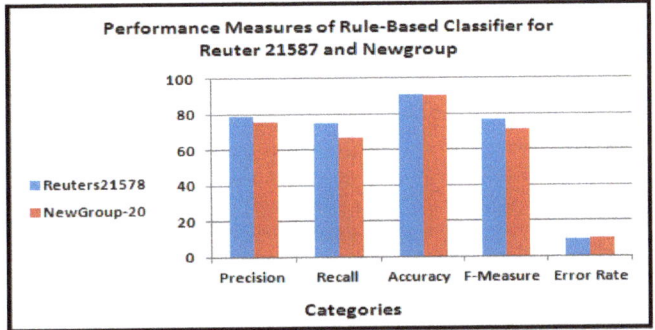

Figure 18. Comparison of performance results using the rule-based text categorization technique applied to different categories within the Reuters-21578 and 20 Newsgroups datasets.

Finally, when the rules for JRip, OneR and ZeroR were applied to the Reuters-21578 dataset, we obtained F-measures and accuracy metrics of 0.713–0.752, 0.506–0.598 and 0.219–0.39 for JRip, OneR and ZeroR, respectively. Table 2 introduces the comparison measurements among three rule-based classification methods, and the precision and recall of the system were averaged by using the micro-average method.

Table 2. Shows the comparison of the metrics among JRip, OneR, and ZeroR on the Reuters-21578 dataset.

It	Parameters	D2VRule	JRip	OneR	ZeroR
1	Precision	79	70.4	48.4	15.2
2	Recall	75	75.9	59.8	39.0
3	F-Measure	76.75	71.3	50.6	21.9
4	Accuracy	90.72	75.2	59.8	39

6. Discussion

The development of computer technologies, rule-based techniques, and automatic learning techniques can make information retrieval technology easier and more efficient. There exist many approaches to decision-making, such as rule-based and artificial neural networks. The rule-based approach is considered one of the most flexible methods by which the black box of the process of text classification techniques can be shown. The details of a process of classification can be seen and it can add some tools or new instructions to obtain good results. All preprocessing on two datasets (Reuters-21578 and 20 Newsgroups) is implemented using the Python programming language, an open-source tools framework, and a document-level embedding (doc2vec) technique to represent text documents being used, which appears to be more effective in the preparation of data. In addition, the rule-based approach would support the classification approach by improving the recall, precision and accuracy measurements of classification.

A suitable vocabulary (informative words) is selected according to the following criteria:

1. The highest value of similarity of the feature
2. The highest numbers of the term frequency (numbers of repetitions of important words in documents)
3. Highest numbers of document frequency (number of documents including the feature)

The recall, precision, F-measures, error rate and accuracy are obtained according to a suitable choice of vocabulary selection. It is clear that there are precision and other metrics evaluations in a rule-based approach to classify categories of test datasets affected by the above criteria. According to Ligęza [29], symbolic rules are some of the most popular knowledge representation and reasoning methods. Therefore, we have many reasons to view the rule-based approach as superior to other approaches. Firstly, for the naturalness of expression, expert knowledge can be used as guiding rules. Secondly, we have modularity, in which the rules-based approach can be considered an independent method. Thirdly, the restriction of syntax allows the construction of rules and checking of consistency using other programs [38]. Fourthly, it is a compact representation of general knowledge; it can easily form the representation of general knowledge about a problem. Fifthly, the provision of explanations is represented by the ability of the rule-based approach to provide explanations for any derived conclusions in a direct manner, which is considered to be a vital feature [39]. The information extraction techniques of the rule-based approach have been used effectively in commercial systems and are favored because they are easily understood and controlled [40]. The rule-based approach and temporal specificity score TSS based classification approaches are proposed, and the results show that the proposed rule-based classifier outperforms the other four algorithms by achieving 82% accuracy, whereas the TSS classification achieves 77% accuracy [41]. In 2019, Li et al. [42], they proposed a model where the performance for it was still good and mostly stable with respect to the F-measure, and from the curve of this measure, when the number of extracted keywords N was 7, the F-measure reached a maximum of 43.1% compared to Xia's work. [43], in which, the basic idea of TextRank used for keyword extraction was introduced. The process of constructing candidate keywords and the F-measure up to 37.28%, and all these previous results were less than our results, where F-measures reached 76.75%. Decision table, Ridor, OneR, DTNB and PART are five algorithms applied to the chess end game dataset and by using evaluation metrics to check the performance of these algorithms, it appears from the results that PART is the accept rule-based classification algorithm when compared with other studied rule based algorithms.

On the other hand, the OneR algorithm showed an overall low performance for every parameter, and when these results were matched with our results when applying the OneR rule to the Reuters-21578 dataset, it became clear that the OneR algorithm had low values of precision, recall, and F-Measures [44]. A single attribute-based classification (SAC) is needed to divide the original dataset into multiple one-dimensional datasets. The experimental results show that SACs performed better than the classical OneR algorithm. The performance of different classification methods was examined on the large dataset [45].

The algorithms tested were SMO, J48, Zero, OneR, RPart and the Naive Bayes algorithm. It was discovered that the highest error was found in the ZeroR classifier with an average score of approximately 0.5. The other algorithms ranged on average 0.1–0.2. Therefore, the ZeroR technique is not a good option for the classification of any dataset due to its many errors [46], these results are in agreement with our conclusion. The performance of three rule classifier algorithms, namely RIDOR, JRIP and Decision Table, using the Iris datasets, was calculated using the cross-validation parameter. Finally, it was observed that the JRIP technique is not a good option for classification [47], and when applying those algorithms to our dataset, it became apparent that our algorithm agrees with the results of other algorithms. In Reference [48], an improved hierarchical clustering algorithm has been developed based on association rules and these algorithms were tested on benchmark data set Reuters-21578, and the results (F-measures) produced by the association rule-based hierarchical clustering (ARBHC) method are better than the results of the traditional hierarchical algorithm, and these results (F-M equal to 29%) are so much less than our results. uRule is a new rule-based classification and prediction algorithm, it was proposed to classify a limited number of uncertain data, and the accuracy of the uRule classifier remains relatively stable like our rule-based, but our rule was applied on a huge of documents within Reuters and 20Newgroups datasets [49]. Reference [50] presents a new technique using state-of-art machine-learning methods, deep learning, and it is used to solve the problem of choosing the best structures and architectures of neural networks out of many possibilities, and it introduced the RMDL (random multimodel deep learning) for classification that combines multi deep learning models to produce better performance, they have evaluated this approach on datasets such as the Web of Science (WOS), Reuters, MNIST, CIFAR, IMDB, and 20NewsGroups dataset, Furthermore, the proposed approach shows improvement in classification accuracy for both text and image classification. Finally, this accuracy for Reuters-21578 and 20Newgroups datasets in the best case is equal to 90.69% and 87.91% respectively, but our result related to accuracy for the same datasets was 90.72%, 90.07% respectively.

This provides a better classification process according to evaluation metrics.

7. Conclusions

We selected our rule-based approach to classify text documents into ten categories for two datasets, which in our case were the Reuters-21578 and 20 Newsgroups datasets. Computer programming using Python was implemented. It was expected that these results would be beneficial for information retrieval systems and this work has assisted us in setting the acceptable methods for use in text classification by depending on precision, recall and accuracy approaches. In conclusion, the results were, in the case of Reuters-21578, 79% precision, 75% recall, and 76.75% F-measures, 9.28% error rate, and 90.72% accuracy measurement. For the 20 Newsgroups dataset, the results were 76% precision, 66.64% recall, 70.98% F-measures, 9.93% error rate, and 90.07% accuracy measurement. When we compared our algorithms with other algorithms (JRip, OneR, and ZeroR) for the Reuters-21578 dataset and by using the performance factors of precision, recall, F-measure, error rate, and classification accuracy, it was observed that our algorithm performed better than other algorithms and had a good classification process. Our intention is to make some improvements to the rule-based approach so as to be more active with the real-time dataset of the Reuters agency as well as selecting new types of machine learning.

8. Future Work

We intend to make further contributions, with some enhancements to the rule-based approach, which are more active with real-time datasets, such as newspaper datasets. Tagging content or products using categories as a way to improve browsing or to identify related content on your website. Platforms such as E-commerce, news agencies, content curators, blogs, directories, and likes can use automated technologies to classify and tag content and products.

9. The Limitations

Text classification is an important research problem in many fields. However, there are several challenges remaining in the processing of textual data [51].

1. Our results pertain to two specific datasets, namely Reuters-21578 and 20 Newsgroups.
2. We worked to improve the classification technique by taking a large number of documents in the training part of the dataset since the volume of the training data had an important role in learning a model. Training data must be labeled and be large enough to cover all upcoming classes.

3. The rules used were only for the English language and by adding a number of modifications; they can be suitable for a new language.
4. Information retrieval systems experience the diverse nature of texts with highly variable content, quality and length.

Author Contributions: Conceptualization, A.M.A. and A.M.; Data curation, A.M.A.; Formal analysis, A.M.A.; Investigation, A.M.; Methodology, A.M.A. and A.M.; Software, A.M.A. and A.M.; Supervision, A.M.; Validation, A.M.A.; Visualization, A.M.A.; Writing—original draft, A.M.A.; Writing—review and editing, A.M. All authors have read and agreed to the published version of the manuscript.

Funding: This research received no external funding.

Conflicts of Interest: The authors declare no conflict of interest.

References

1. Levy, O.; Goldberg, Y. Linguistic regularities in sparse and explicit word representations. In Proceedings of the Eighteenth Conference on Computational Language Learning, Baltimore, MD, USA, 26–27 June 2014; pp. 171–180.
2. Quinlan, R. *C4.5: Programs for Machine Learning*; Morgan Kaufmann Publishers Inc.: San Francisco, CA, USA, 1993; ISBN 1 55860 2380.
3. Partridge, D.; Hussain, K.M. *Knowledge Based Information Systems*; McGraw Hill, Inc.: New York, NY, USA, 1994; ISBN 0077076249.
4. Michalski, R.S. On the quasi-minimal solution of the general covering problem. In Proceedings of the Fifth International Symposium on Information Processing, Bled, Yugoslavia, 8–11 October 1969; Volume A3, pp. 125–128.
5. Han, L.; Alexander, G.; Cocea, M. *Rule Based Systems for Big Data: A Machine Learning Approach*; Springer: Cham, Switzerland, 2015; ISBN 10 3319236954.
6. Mendel, J.M. *Uncertain Rule Based Fuzzy Systems*; University of Southern California: Los Angeles, CA, USA, 2017; ISBN 978 3 319 51369 0.
7. Sebastiani, F. Machine learning in automated text categorization. *ACM Comput. Surv.* **2002**, *34*, 1–47. [CrossRef]
8. Koller, D.; Sahami, M. Hierarchically classifying documents using a very few words. In Proceedings of the International Conference on Machine Learning, San Mateo, CA, USA, August 1997; Morgan Kaufmann: San Mateo, CA, USA, 1997; Volume 14, pp. 170–178.
9. Imaichi, O.; Yanase, T.; Niwa, Y. A Comparison of Rule Based and Machine Learning Methods for Medical Information Extraction. In Proceedings of the International Joint Conference on Natural Language Processing Workshop on Natural Language Processing for Medical and Healthcare Fields, Nagoya, Japan, 14–18 October 2013; pp. 38–42.
10. Panthong, R.; Srivihok, A. Wrapper feature subset selection for dimension reduction based on ensemble learning algorithm. *Procedia Comput. Sci.* **2015**, *72*, 162–169. [CrossRef]
11. Rios, A.; Göhring, A. Machine Learning Applied to Rule Based Machine Translation. In *Hybrid Approaches to Machine Translation*; Costa Jussà, M., Rapp, R., Lambert, P., Eberle, K., Banchs, R., Babych, B., Eds.; Theory and Applications of Natural Language Processing; Springer: Cham, Switzerland, 2016.
12. Cronin, R.M.; Joshua, D.F.; Denny, J.C. A Comparison of Rule Based and Machine Learning Approaches for Classifying Patient Portal Messages. *Int. J. Med. Inform.* **2017**, *105*, 110–120. [CrossRef] [PubMed]
13. Ganglberger, W.; Gritsch, G.; Hartmann, M.M.; Fürbass, F.; Kluge, T. A Comparison of Rule Based and Machine Learning Methods for Classification of Spikes in EEG. *JCM* **2017**, *12*, 589–595. [CrossRef]
14. Suto, J.; Oniga, S.; Sitar, P.P. Comparison of wrapper and filter feature selection algorithms on human activity recognition. In Proceedings of the 2016 6th International Conference on Computers Communications and Control (ICCCC), Oradea, Romania, 10–14 May 2016; pp. 124–129.
15. Naseriparsa, M.; Bidgoli, A.M.; Varaee, T. A hybrid feature selection method to improve the performance of a group of classification algorithms. *Int. J. Comput. Appl.* **2013**, *69*, 28–35. [CrossRef]

16. Ferré, A.; Deléger, L.; Zweigenbaum, P.; Nédellec, C. Combining Rule Based and Embedding Based Approaches to Normalize Textual Entities with an Ontology. In Proceedings of the Eleventh International Conference on Language Resources and Evaluation (LREC 2018), Miyazaki, Japan, 7–12 May 2018; pp. 3443–3447.
17. Le, Q.; Mikolov, T. Distributed Representations of Sentences and Documents. In Proceedings of the 31st International Conference on MachineLearning, Beijing, China, 24 June 2014; Volume 32.
18. Nandakumar, N.; Salehi, B.; Baldwin, T. A Comparative Study of Embedding Models in Predicting the Compositionality of Multiword Expressions. In Proceedings of the Australasian Language Technology Association Workshop, Dunedin, New Zealand, 10–12 December 2018; pp. 71–76.
19. Stefanowski, J. Induction of Rules. Ph.D Thesis, Institute of Computing Sciences, Poznan University of Technology, Catania Troina, Italy, April 2008.
20. Bojanowski, P.; Grave, E.; Joulin, A.; Mikolov, T. Enriching word vectors with subword information. *Trans. Assoc. Comput. Linguist.* **2017**, *5*, 135–146. [CrossRef]
21. Peters, M.E.; Neumann, M.; Iyyer, M.; Gardner, M. Deep contextualized word representations. In Proceedings of the NAACL-HLT, New Orleans, LA, USA, 1–6 June 2018; pp. 2227–2237.
22. Lau, J.H.; Baldwin, T. An Empirical Evaluation of doc2vec with Practical Insights into Document Embedding Generation. In Proceedings of the 1st Workshop on Representation Learning for NLP. Association for Computational Linguistics, Berlin, Germany, 11 August 2016; pp. 78–86.
23. Rennie, J. 20 Newsgroup Data Set. Available online: http://qwone.com/~{}jason/20Newsgroups/ (accessed on 5 March 2019).
24. Deshmukh, P.R.; Ade, R. Classification of Students Using Psychometric Tests with the Help of Incremental Naive Bayes Algorithm. *Int. J. Comput. Appl.* **2014**, *89*, 27–31.
25. Karamcheti, A.C. A Comparative Study on Text Categorization. M.Sc. Thesis, University of Nevada Las Vegas, Las Vegas, NV, USA, 2010.
26. Arthana, R. Stop Word Indonesian (and Implementation on Apache LUCENE). Available online: http://www.rey1024.com/2012/06/stop-word-bahasa-indonesia-dan-implementasi-pada-apache-lucene/ (accessed on 10 June 2019).
27. Asian, J.; Williams, H.E.; Tahaghoghi, S.M.M. *Stemming Indonesian*; ACM: New York, NY, USA, 2003; Volume 6, pp. 1–33.
28. Adriani, M.; Asian, J.; Nazief, B.; Tahaghoghi, S.M.M.; Williams, H.E. Confix Stripping: Approach to Stemming Algorithm for Indonesian Language. *ACM Trans. Asian Lang. Inf. Process.* **2007**, *6*, 13.1–13.33. [CrossRef]
29. Ross, T.J. *Fuzzy Logic with Engineering Applications*; John Wiley & Sons Ltd.: West Sussex, UK, 2004.
30. Ligeza, A. Logical Foundations for Rule based Systems. In *Studies in Computational Intelligence*, 2nd ed.; Springer: Heidelberg, Germnay; AGH University of Science and Technology Press: Kraków, Poland, 2006; pp. XX, 309. ISBN1 10 3540291172. ISBN2 13 9783540291176.
31. Simon, A.; Newell, A. Human Problem Solving: The State of the Theory in 1970. *Am. Psychol. Assoc.* **1970**, *26*, 145–159. [CrossRef]
32. Negnevitsky, M. Rule based expert systems. In *Artificial Intelligence, a Guide to Intelligent Systems*, 2nd ed.; Pearson Education Limited: Harlow, UK, 2005; pp. 3–5.
33. Andreeva, P.; Dimitrova, M.; Radeva, P. Data Mining Learning Models and Algorithms for Medical Application. In Proceedings of the 18-th Conference on Systems for Automation of Engineering and Research SAER, Sofia, Bulgaria, April 2004; pp. 11–18.
34. Rajput, A.; Aharwal, R.P.; Dubey, M.; Saxena, S.P. J48 and JRIP Rules for E Governance Data. *IJCSS* **2011**, *5*, 201–207.
35. Buddhinath, G.; Derry, D. A Simple Enhancement to One Rule Classification. Ph.D. Thesis, Department of Computer Science & Software Engineering University of Melbourne, Melbourne, Australia, 2006.
36. Available online: https://www.saedsayad.com/zeror.htm (accessed on 23 March 2019).
37. Manning, C.D.; Prabhakar, R.; Hinrich, S. *Introduction to Information Retrieval*; Cambridge University Press: New York, NY, USA, May 2008; ISBN 13: 978 0521865715.
38. Available online: https://www.merospark.com/ (accessed on 13 April 2019).

39. Prentzas, J.; Hatzilygeroudisa, I. Categorizing Approaches Combining Rule Based and Case Based Reasoning. In *University of Patras and Technological Educational Institute of Lamia Greece*; Wiley online library; Blackwell Publishing Ltd.: Hoboken, NJ, USA, April 2007; Volume 24, Issue 2, pp. 97–122.
40. Khademi, S.; Haghighi, P.D.; Burstein, F.; Palmer, C. Enhancing rule based text classification of neurosurgical notes using filtered feature weight vectors. In *Australian Conference on Information Systems*; University of Wollongong, Computer Science: Wollongong, Australian, 2016; pp. 1–11.
41. Khan, S.U.R.; Islam, M.A.; Aleem, M.; Iqbal, M.A. Temporal specificity based text classification for information retrieval. *Turk. J. Electr. Eng. Comput. Sci.* **2018**, *26*, 2915–2926. [CrossRef]
42. Li, J.; Huang, G.; Fan, C.; Sun, Z.; Zhu, H. Key word extraction for short text via word2vec, doc2vec, and textrank. *Turk. J. Electr. Eng. Comput. Sci.* **2019**, *27*, 1794–1805. [CrossRef]
43. Wen, Y.; Yuan, H.; Zhang, P. Research on Keyword Extraction Based on Word2Vec Weighted TextRank. In Proceedings of the 2016 2nd IEEE International Conference on Computer and Communications (ICCC), Chengdu, China, 14–17 October 2016; pp. 2109–2113.
44. Mahajan, A.; Ganpati, A. Performance Evaluation of Rule Based Classification Algorithms. *Int. J. Adv. Res. Comput. Eng. Technol.* **2014**, *3*, 3546–3550.
45. Du, L.; Song, Q. A Simple Classifier based on a Single Attribute. In Proceedings of the 14th International Conference on High Performance Computing and Communications, Liverpool, UK, 25–27 June 2012; pp. 660–665.
46. Nasa, C. Evaluation of Different Classification Techniques for WEB Data. *Int. J. Comput. Appl.* **2012**, *52*, 34–40. [CrossRef]
47. Veeralakshmi, V.; Ramyachitra, D. Ripple down Rule learner (RIDOR) Classifier for IRIS Dataset. *Int. J. Comput. Sci. Eng.* **2015**, *4*, 79–85.
48. Rose, D.J. An Effect Association Rule-Based Hierarchical Algorithm for Text Clustting. *Int. J. Adv. Eng. Technol.* **2016**, *751*, 753.
49. Qin, B.; Xia, Y.; Prabhakar, S.; Tu, Y. A Rule-Based Classification Algorithm for Uncertain Data. In Proceedings of the IEEE 25th International Conference on Data Engineering, Shanghai, China, 29 March–2 April 2009; pp. 1633–1640. [CrossRef]
50. Heidarysafa, M.; Kowsari, K.; Brown, D.E.; Meimandi, K.J.; Barnes, L.E. An Improvement of Data Classification using Random Multimodel Deep Learning (RMDL). *Int. J. Mach. Learn. Comput.* **2018**, *8*, 298–310.
51. Losiewicz, P.; Oard, D.W.; Kostoff, R.N. Textual Data Mining to Support Science and Systems. *J. Intell. Inf. Syst.* **2000**, *15*, 99–119. [CrossRef]

© 2020 by the authors. Licensee MDPI, Basel, Switzerland. This article is an open access article distributed under the terms and conditions of the Creative Commons Attribution (CC BY) license (http://creativecommons.org/licenses/by/4.0/).

Article

Dual Pointer Network for Fast Extraction of Multiple Relations in a Sentence [†]

Seongsik Park [1] and Harksoo Kim [2,*]

[1] Computer and Communications Engineering, Kangwon National University, Chuncheon 24341, Korea; a163912@kangwon.ac.kr
[2] Computer Science and Engineering, Konkuk University, Seoul 05029, Korea
* Correspondence: nlpdrkim@konkuk.ac.kr; Tel.: +82-2-450-3499
[†] This paper is an extended version of paper published in The Second Workshop on Fact Extraction and VERification. (FEVER 2.0) at EMNLP-IJCNLP 2019, Hong Kong, China, 3–7 November 2019.

Received: 25 April 2020; Accepted: 30 May 2020; Published: 1 June 2020

Featured Application: Ontology construction module for AI applications.

Abstract: Relation extraction is a type of information extraction task that recognizes semantic relationships between entities in a sentence. Many previous studies have focused on extracting only one semantic relation between two entities in a single sentence. However, multiple entities in a sentence are associated through various relations. To address this issue, we proposed a relation extraction model based on a dual pointer network with a multi-head attention mechanism. The proposed model finds *n*-to-*1* subject–object relations using a forward object decoder. Then, it finds *1*-to-*n* subject–object relations using a backward subject decoder. Our experiments confirmed that the proposed model outperformed previous models, with an F1-score of 80.8% for the ACE (automatic content extraction) 2005 corpus and an F1-score of 78.3% for the NYT (New York Times) corpus.

Keywords: relation extraction; dual pointer network; context-to-entity attention

1. Introduction

Relation extraction is a task that involves recognizing semantic relations (i.e., tuple structures; {subject, relation, object triples}) among entities in a sentence [1]. Zeng et al. [2] divided sentences into three types according to the triplet overlap degree, i.e., normal, entity pair overlap (EPO), and single entity overlap (SEO). In the normal type, the triples do not have overlapped entities; in the EPO type, some triples have an overlapped entity pair; and in the SEO type, some triplets have an overlapped entity, but these triplets do not have overlapped entity pairs. In this study, we focus on promptly extracting both the normal and SEO types because most relations are included in these types, as shown in Figure 1.

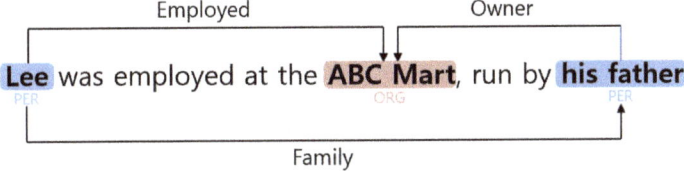

Figure 1. Subject-relation-object triples in a sentence. PER: person; ORG: organization.

In Figure 1, {Lee, employed, ABC Mart}, {Lee, Family, his Father} and {his Father, Owner, ABC Mart} are SEO types. To promptly extract these relations, we adopt the concept of dependency parsing in which dependent words point to the head words by scanning each word in a sentence. We propose a dual pointer network model to efficiently extract multiple relations from a sentence through forward scanning (i.e., scanning from the first word to the last) and backward scanning (i.e., scanning from the last word to the first). The proposed model discovers an object of the current subject during forward scanning. Through forward scanning, all normal type relations can be found. However, SEO type relations are only partially found because a subject should point to only one object in the pointer network architecture. To address this limitation, the proposed model performs backward scanning to identify the subject of the current object.

The remainder of this paper is organized as follows. In Section 2, we review previous studies on relation extraction. Section 3 describes the proposed dual pointer network model. In Section 4, we elaborate on the experimental setup and results. Finally, we conclude the study in Section 5.

2. Previous Works

With the significant success of deep neural networks in the field of natural language processing, many researchers have proposed various relation extraction models based on convolutional neural networks (CNNs). These include the CNN model based on max-pooling [3], the CNN model based on multiple sizes of kernels [4], the combined CNN model [5], and the contextualized graph convolutional network (C-GCN) model [6]. Relation extraction models based on recurrent neural network (RNNs) have also been proposed, including the long-short term memory (LSTM) model based on the dependency tree [7] and the LSTM model using the position-aware attention technique [8]. These models have focused on normal type extraction (i.e., extracting only one relation between two entities from a single sentence). However, many entities in a single sentence can form multiple relations. Some studies have proposed multiple relation extraction to resolve this problem. For example, Luan et al. [9] treated triples in sentences as a graph and proposed a multiple relations extraction model that iteratively extracts spans between triples in the graph. In the present study, we propose a relation extraction model to simultaneously find all possible relations among multiple entities in a sentence. The proposed model is based on the pointer network [10]. The pointer network is a sequence-to-sequence (Seq2Seq) model in which an attention mechanism [11] is modified to learn the conditional probability of an output, where the values correspond to positions in a given input sequence. We modify the pointer network to include dual decoders, an object decoder (a forward decoder) and a subject decoder (a backward decoder). The object decoder extracts n-to-1 relations as shown in the following example: {Lee, employed, ABC Mart} and {his Father, Owner, ABC Mart} are extracted from the sentence. The subject decoder extracts 1-to-n relations as shown in the following example: {Lee, employed, ABC Mart} and {Lee, Family, his Father} are extracted from the sentence.

3. Dual Pointer Network Model for Relation Extraction

Figure 2 illustrates the architecture of the proposed model. This consists of two parts, a context and entity encoder, and a dual pointer network decoder.

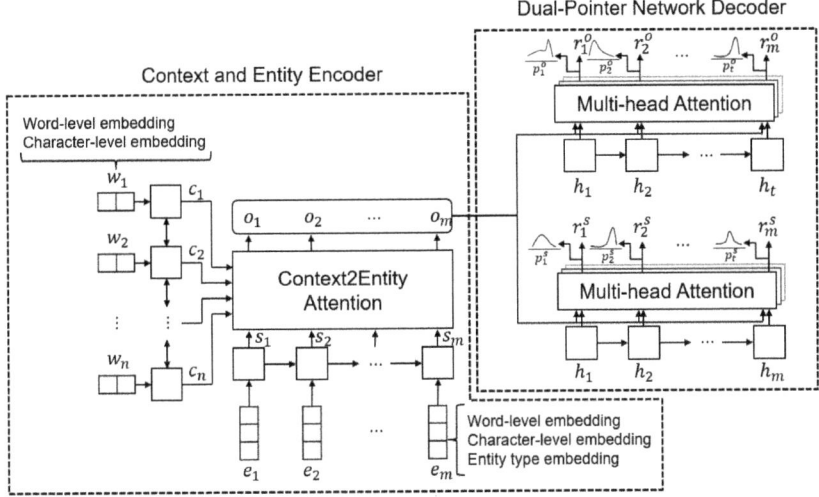

Figure 2. The overall architecture of dual pointer networks for relation extraction.

3.1. Context and Entity Encoder

The context and entity encoder computes the degree of association between words and entities in a given sentence. For example, $\{w_1, w_2, \ldots, w_i\}$ and $\{e_1, e_2, \ldots, e_m\}$ refer to word and entity embedding vectors, respectively. Figure 3 illustrates the process of word and entity embedding.

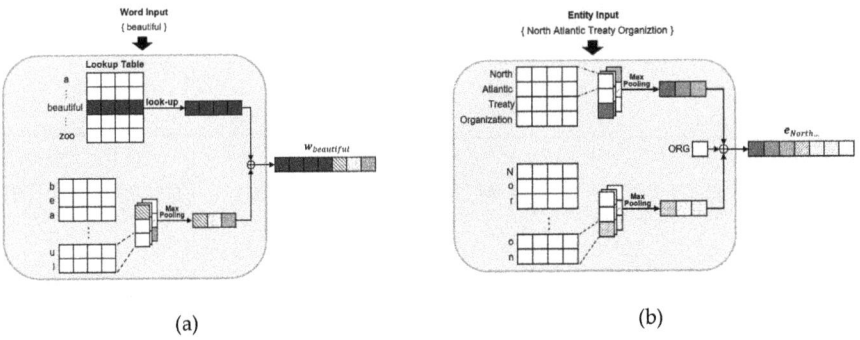

Figure 3. (**a**) Word embedding process, (**b**) Entity embedding process.

As shown in Figure 3, the word embedding vectors are concatenations of two types of embeddings: word-level GloVe [12] embeddings for representing the meaning of words and character-level CNN embeddings [13] for addressing out-of-vocabulary problems. The entity embedding vectors are concatenations of three types of embeddings: word-level CNN embedding for representing the meaning of entities composed of multiple words, character-level CNN embedding for addressing out-of-vocabulary problems, and entity type embedding for representing the categorical information of input entities. Word-level GloVe embeddings represent each word in the word-level CNN embedding.

The word embedding vectors are used as input for a bidirectional LSTM network to obtain contextual information as follows:

$$\begin{aligned} \overrightarrow{c}_i &= \text{LSTM}(w_i, \overrightarrow{c}_{i-1}), \\ \overleftarrow{c}_i &= \text{LSTM}(w_i, \overleftarrow{c}_{i-1}), \\ c_i &= [\overrightarrow{c}_i; \overleftarrow{c}_i], \end{aligned} \quad (1)$$

where w_i is an embedding vector of the i-th word in a sentence, and $[\overrightarrow{c}_i; \overleftarrow{c}_i]$ is a concatenation of $\overrightarrow{c}_i$ and $\overleftarrow{c}_i$ that represents the output vectors of a forward LSTM and a backward LSTM, respectively. The entity embedding vectors are used as input for a forward LSTM network because the entities are listed in the order that they appear in a sentence, as shown below.

$$s_t = \text{LSTM}(e_t, s_{t-1}), \quad (2)$$

where e_t is an embedding vector of the t-th one among all entities occurring in a sentence, and s_t is an output vector encoded by a forward LSTM. The output vectors of the bidirectional LSTM network $\{c_1, c_2, \ldots, c_i\}$ and the forward LSTM network $\{s_1, s_2, \ldots, s_t\}$ are used as input for the context-to-entity attention layer (as shown in Figure 2), to compute the relative degrees of association between words and entities. This is similar to the well-known multi-head attention mechanism [14], as shown below.

$$\begin{aligned} q_j &= w^a * split(q, n)_j, \\ a_j &= softmax(\tfrac{q_j k_j}{\sqrt{d}}), \\ head_j &= a_j v_j, \\ o_t &= relu(w^o[head_0; head_1; head_2; \ldots; head_n] + b^o), \end{aligned} \quad (3)$$

where the query q is set to s_t, the key k and the value v are set to C's. The query q is split into n vectors, where n is the number of heads. The attention score a_j is calculated by a scaled-dot product, where d is a normalization factor. The context-to-entity layer output o_t is determined through a fully-connected neural network (FNN) using a concatenation of n heads as input.

3.2. Dual Pointer Network Decoder

In a pointer network, attentions show the position distributions of an encoding layer. Since attention is highlighted at only one position, the pointer network has a structural limitation when one entity forms relations with several entities (for instance, "Lee" in Figure 1). The proposed model adopts a dual pointer network decoder (see Figure 2) to overcome this limitation. The first decoder called an object decoder, learns the position distribution from subjects to objects as follows:

$$\begin{aligned} h_t &= [e_t; s_t], \\ g_t &= \text{LSTM}(h_t, g_{t-1}), \\ score_t^{obj} &= v^{obj} \tanh(w^{obj}[O; g_t]), \\ a_t^{obj} &= softmax(score_t^{obj}), \\ \hat{p}_t^{obj} &= argmax(a_t^{obj}), \\ \hat{r}_t^{obj} &= argmax(u^{obj} \tanh(z^{obj}[a_t^{obj} O; g_t])), \end{aligned} \quad (4)$$

where h_t is a concatenation of the entity embedding vector e_t and the LSTM-encoded entity embedding vector s_t, and the decoding vector g_t (i.e., the t-th entity to determine its objects) is calculated by the forward LSTM. Then, a_t^{obj} is the position distribution based on the attention scores $score_t^{obj}$ between g_t and the other entities $o_1, \ldots, o_{t-1}, o_{t+1}, \ldots, o_m$ in the context-to-entity attention layer. $\hat{p}_t^{obj}$ and $\hat{r}_t^{obj}$ represent a position and a relation name of g_t's object, respectively. The weighting parameters $v, w, u,$ and z are set during the training phase. Conversely, the second decoder, called a subject decoder, learns the position distribution from objects to subjects in the same manner as the object decoder, as shown below.

$$\begin{aligned}
score_t^{sub} &= v^{sub}\tanh(w^{sub}[O; g_t]), \\
a_t^{sub} &= \text{softmax}(score_t^{sub}), \\
\hat{p}_t^{sub} &= \text{argmax}(a_t^{sub}), \\
\hat{r}_t^{sub} &= \text{argmax}(u^{sub}\tanh(z^{sub}[a_t^{sub}O; g_t])),
\end{aligned} \quad (5)$$

where $\hat{p}_t^{sub}$ and $\hat{r}_t^{sub}$ represent a position and a relation name of g_t's subject, respectively. In Figure 1, "Lee" should point to both "ABC mart" and "his father." This problem cannot be solved using the conventional forward decoder because it cannot point to multiple targets. However, the subject decoder (a backward decoder) resolves this problem, because "ABC mart" and "his father" can point to "Lee." Additionally, we adopt a multi-head attention mechanism to improve the performance of the dual pointer network; this is shown in the following equation.

$$\begin{aligned}
q_j &= w^l * split(q, n)_j, \\
a_j &= softmax(\tfrac{q_j k_j}{\sqrt{d}}), \\
head_j &= a_j v_j, \\
\hat{p}_t &= \text{argmax}(\tfrac{1}{n}\sum_{k=0}^{n} a_k), \\
\hat{r}_t &= \text{argmax}(relu(w^r[head_0; head_1; head_2; \ldots; head_n] + b^r)),
\end{aligned} \quad (6)$$

where the query q is set to g_t, the key k and the value v are set to O's. The position distribution $\hat{p}_t$ is calculated by an average of n multi-head attention vectors, and the relation name $\hat{r}_t$ is determined through an FNN using a concatenation of n heads as the input.

3.3. Implementation detail

The context and entity encoder comprised 256 hidden units in each layer, and the dual pointer network decoder comprised 512 hidden units. We adopted a 0.1 drop-out probability for all the LSTM cells. We used 8 heads, with 32 units per head, for the multi-head attention. The vocabulary size and word-embedding size was set to 16,925 and 300, respectively. The filter size of the CNNs for character and word embeddings were 3, 4, and 5. The total number of filters was 100. 50-dimensional random initialized vectors were used for the character and entity embeddings. A cross-entropy function was used as a cost function to maximize the log-probability as follows:

$$\begin{aligned}
CE(y, \widetilde{y}) &= -\sum_i^C y_i \log(\widetilde{y}_i), \\
Loss &= \tfrac{\alpha}{2}\left(CE(p^{sub}, \widetilde{p}^{sub}) + CE(p^{obj}, \widetilde{p}^{obj})\right) + \tfrac{(1-\alpha)}{2}\left(CE(r^{sub}, \widetilde{r}^{sub}) + CE(r^{obj}, \widetilde{r}^{obj})\right),
\end{aligned} \quad (7)$$

where y is the target answer, $\widetilde{y}$ is the score distribution of the model prediction, and C is the number of target classes. The loss is calculated by the cross-entropy combination of all targets and predictions. The weighting factor α was experimentally set to 0.6 as a scalar value.

4. Evaluation

4.1. Datasets and Experimental Setting

We evaluated the proposed model using the following benchmark datasets.

ACE-2005 corpus [15]: The automatic content extraction (ACE) dataset included seven major entity types and six major relation types. The ACE-2005 corpus does not properly evaluate models that extract multiple triples from a sentence. Therefore, if some triples in the ACE-2005 corpus share a sentence (i.e., some triples occur in the same sentence), the triples were merged, as shown in Figure 4.

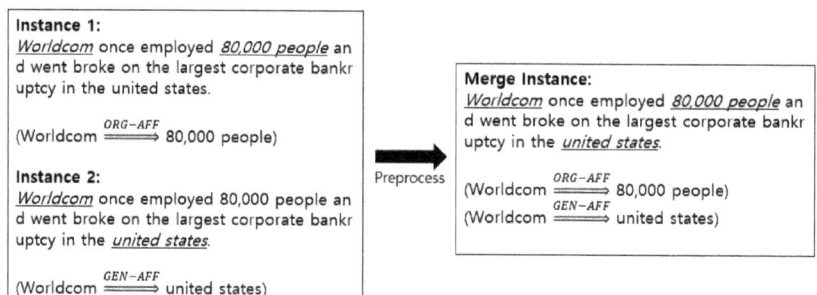

Figure 4. ACE-2005 data preprocess. ORG-AFF: organization-affiliation; GEN-AFF: general entity-affiliation.

As a result, we obtained a dataset annotated with multiple triples. We divided the new dataset into a training set (5023 sentences), a development set (629 sentences), and a test set (627 sentences) by a ratio of 8:1:1. Table 1 shows the composition of the preprocessed ACE-2005 corpus in detail.

Table 1. Composition of the preprocessed ACE-2005 corpus.

# of entities per sentence (avg/max)	3.5/22
# of triples per sentence (avg/max)	1.5/11
# of entity types	7
# of relation types	7

NYT corpus [16]: This is a news corpus sampled from news articles published in the New York Times (NYT). The training data is automatically labeled using distant supervision. The NYT corpus was manually converted to a relation extraction dataset by Zheng et al. [17]. We excluded sentences without relation facts from Zheng's corpus. Finally, we obtained 66,202 sentences in total. We used 59,581 sentences for training and 6621 for testing. Table 2 shows the composition of the NYT corpus in detail.

Table 2. Composition of the NYT corpus.

# of entities per sentence (avg/max)	3.2/20
# of triples per sentence (avg/max)	1.7/26
# of entity types	3
# of relation types	25

Table 3 shows sample sentences and their tripe relations in the ACE-2005 corpus and the NYT corpus.

Table 3. Sample of the ACE-2005 corpus and the NYT corpus. PER-SOC: person-social.

Dataset	Sentence	Triple
ACE-2005	Do you travel to meet up with family or friends during the holidays?	{you, PER-SOC, family}, {you, PER-SOC, friends}
NYT	Clarence Charles Newcomer was born on Jan. 18, 1923, in the Lancaster County town of Mount Joy, Pa.	{Lancaster County,/location/location/contains, Mount Joy}, {Clarence Charles Newcomer,/people/person/place_of_birth, Mount Joy}

To evaluate the experimental results, we adopted the standard micro precision, recall, and F1 score:

$$\text{Recall} = \frac{\text{\# of correct predict}}{\text{\# of all triple in the dataset}}$$
$$\text{Precision} = \frac{\text{\# of correct predict}}{\text{\# of all triple in the model predict}} \quad (8)$$
$$F1 - \text{score} = \frac{2 \cdot Precision \cdot Recall}{Precision + Recall}$$

4.2. Experimental Results

In the first experiment, we evaluated the effectiveness of the multi-head attention in the dual pointer network decoder; the results are summarized in Table 4. The evaluation was performed using the ACE-2005 corpus.

Table 4. Performance for different attention mechanisms in the dual pointer network decoder.

Model	Recall	Precision	F1-Score
Single-head	0.800	0.759	0.779
Multi-head	0.832	0.787	0.808

In Table 4, single-head refers to a conventional attention mechanism proposed by Bahdanau et al. [11]. As shown in Table 4, the multi-head attention mechanism used in the proposed model demonstrated better performance than the single-head one. Then, using the ACE-2005 corpus, we evaluated the effectiveness of multi-head attention in the context and entity encoder; the results are summarized in Table 5.

Table 5. Performance for different attention mechanisms in the context and entity encoder.

Model	Recall	Precision	F1-Score
BIDAF-C2Q	0.819	0.766	0.792
BIDAF-C2Q&Q2C	0.821	0.792	0.806
Multi-head	0.832	0.787	0.808

In Table 5, BIDAF [18] refers to a machine-reading and comprehension (MRC) model based on a co-attention mechanism between a query and a context. C2Q and Q2C are referring to mean context-to-query attention and query-to-context attention used in the BIDAF model, respectively. As shown in Table 5, the multi-head attention mechanism used in the proposed model showed the best F1-score. The p-values of F1-scores between multi-head and the comparison models were from 5.0E-4 to 0.0039. This implies that the performance differences are statistically significant at the 0.05 level.

In the second experiment, we compared the proposed model with previous state-of-the-art models. Table 6 compares the performance of the proposed model and with other models for the ACE-2005 corpus.

Table 6. Performance comparison on the ACE-2005 corpus.

Model	Recall	Precision	F1-Score
SPTree [6]	0.54	0.57	0.56
FCM [19]	0.49	0.72	0.58
DYGIE [9]	0.57	0.64	0.60
Span-Level [20]	0.58	0.68	0.63
HRCNN [21]	-	-	0.74
Walk-Based [22]	0.60	0.70	0.64
Our model	0.83	0.79	0.81

In Table 6, SPTree [6] is a model that applies the dependency information between the entities. In FCM [19], handcrafted features are combined with word embeddings. DYGIE [9] dynamically generates spans between entities and spans' representations. Span-Level [20] jointly performs entity mention detection and relation extraction. HRCNN [21] is a hybrid model of CNN, RNN, and FNN. Walk-Based [22] is a graph-based neural network model. As shown in Table 6, the proposed model outperformed all models across all metrics. The p-values of F1-scores between the proposed model and the comparison models were from 5.81E-8 to 1.37E-5. This implies that the performance differences are statistically significant at the 0.001 level. Table 7 compares the performance of the proposed model with existing models for the NYT corpus.

Table 7. Performance comparisons on the NYT corpus.

Model	Recall	Precision	F1-Score
NovelTag [17]	0.414	0.615	0.495
MultiDecoder [2]	0.566	0.610	0.587
GraphRE [23]	0.600	0.639	0.619
Our model	0.820	0.749	0.783

In Table 7, NovelTag [17] is an end-to-end model that extracts entities and their relations based on a novel tagging scheme designed for relation extraction. MultiDecoder [2] is a Seq2Seq-based model that combines the entity and relation extraction using a decoder with a copy mechanism. GraphRE [23] is a joint model that extracts entities and their relationships using graph convolutional networks (GCN) [24]. As shown in Table 7, the proposed model outperformed all models. It is not reasonable to directly compare the proposed model with these models because it requires gold-labeled entities, while the other models automatically extract entities from sentences. Although direct comparison is unfair, the proposed model exhibited considerably better performance. If we adopt a state-of-the-art named entity tagger based on BERT [25] with F1-scores of 0.9 or more, the proposed model is expected to show F1-scores of 0.662 or more based on simple multiplication. Figure 5 describes the performances according to relation types.

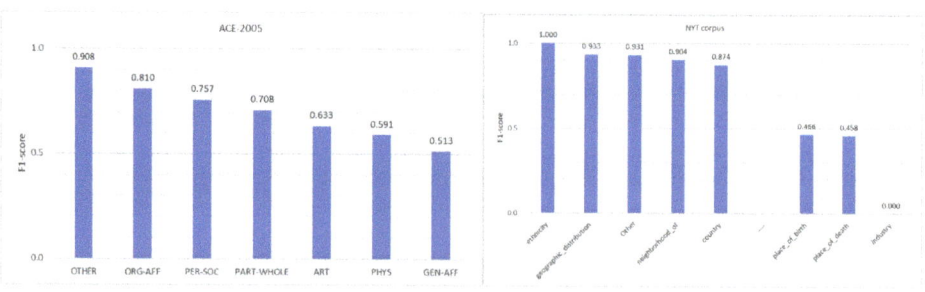

Figure 5. Performances per relation type.

As shown in the right graph of Figure 5, the proposed model obtained the F1-score of 1.0 for the relation type "ethnicity", but it obtained the F1-score of 0.0 for the relation type "industry". The imbalance of training data caused these performance differences. For example, the "industry" relation did not occur in the NYT training data at all.

The cases where the proposed model incorrectly extracted relations were also grouped in Table 8.

Table 8. Main reasons for errors in the ACE-2005 corpus (underline denotes incorrect results). ART: artifact; GEN-AFF: general entity-affiliation; PHYS: physical; PART-WHOLE: part of whole.

Input Sentence	Correct Relation	Predicted Relation
Iraqi forces responded with artillery fire	{Iraqi forces, ART, artillery} {Iraqi forces, GEN-AFF, Iraqi}	{Iraqi forces, PART-WHOLE, Iraqi} {Iraqi forces, GEN-AFF, Iraqi}
It is the first time they have had freedom of movement with cars and weapons since the start of the intifada	{they, ART, cars} {they, ART, weapons}	{they, ART, cars}
It was in northern Iraq today that an eight artillery round hit the site occupied by Kurdish fighters near Chamchamal	{Kurdish fighters, PHYS, the site} {the site, PHYS, Chamchamal} {Kurdish, GEN-AFF, Kurdish fighters} {the site, PART-WHOLE, northern Iraq}	{Kurdish fighters, PHYS, the site} {the site, PHYS, Chamchamal} {the site, PART-WHOLE, northern Iraq} {Kurdish fighters, ART, artillery}

Most incorrect predictions included cases where the decoders incorrectly pointed out subjects or objects, and these incorrect entities lead to incorrect relation names, as shown in the first and third sentences in Table 8. In some cases, the decoder did not point out subjects or objects. As a result, any triples in a sentence were not omitted, as shown in the second sentence.

5. Conclusions

We proposed a relation extraction model to find all possible relations among multiple entities in a sentence simultaneously. The proposed model is based on pointer networks with multi-head attention mechanisms. To extract all possible relations from a sentence, we modified a single decoder into a dual decoder. In the dual decoder, the object decoder extracts n-to-1 subject–object relations, and the subject decoder extracts 1-to-n subject–object relations. The results from the experiments with the ACE-2005 corpus and the NYT corpus confirmed that the proposed model shows an improvement in performance. Our future work will focus on an end-to-end model that directly extracts entities and their relations. In addition, we will focus on a method for improving performance using a large-scale language model like BERT [25].

Author Contributions: Conceptualization, H.K.; methodology, H.K.; software, S.P.; validation, S.P.; formal analysis, H.K.; investigation, H.K.; resources, S.P.; data curation, S.P.; writing—original draft preparation, S.P.; writing—review and editing, H.K.; visualization, H.K.; supervision, H.K.; project administration, H.K.; funding acquisition, H.K. All authors have read and agreed to the published version of the manuscript.

Funding: This work was supported by the Institute for Information & Communications Technology Planning & Evaluation (IITP) grant funded by the Korean government (MSIT) (No. 2013-0-00131, Development of Knowledge Evolutionary WiseQA Platform Technology for Human Knowledge Augmented Services). This work was also supported by the Institute for Information & Communications Technology Planning & Evaluation (IITP) grant funded by the Korean government (MSIT) (No.2020-0-00368, A Neural-Symbolic Model for Knowledge Acquisition and Inference Techniques).

Acknowledgments: We especially thank the members of the NLP laboratory at Kangwon National University and Konkuk University for their technical support.

Conflicts of Interest: The authors declare no conflict of interest.

References

1. Choi, M.; Kim, H. Extraction of Instances with Social Relations for Automatic Construction of a Social Network. *J. KIISE Comput. Pract. Lett.* **2011**, *17*, 548–552. (In Korean)
2. Zeng, X.; Zeng, D.; He, S.; Liu, K.; Zhao, J. Extracting Relational Facts by an End-to-End Neural Model with Copy Mechanism. In Proceedings of the 56th Annual Meeting of the Association for Computational Linguistics, Melbourne, Australia, 15–20 July 2018; pp. 506–514.
3. Zeng, D.; Liu, K.; Lai, S.; Zhou, G.; Zhao, J. Relation Classification via Convolutional Deep Neural Network. In Proceedings of the 24th International Conference on Computational Linguistics, Dublin, Ireland, 23–29 August 2014; pp. 2335–2344.
4. Nguyen, T.H.; Grishman, R. Relation extraction: Perspective from convolutional neural networks. In Proceedings of the North American Chapter of the Association for Computational Linguistics on Human Language Technology, Denver, CO, USA, 31 May–5 June 2015; pp. 39–48.
5. Yu, J.; Jiang, J. Pairwise Relation Classification with Mirror Instances and a Combined Convolutional Neural Network. In Proceedings of the 26th International Conference on Computational Linguistics, Osaka, Japan, 11–16 December 2016; pp. 2366–2377.
6. Zhang, Y.; Qi, P.; Manning, C.D. Graph Convolution over Pruned Dependency Trees Improves Relation Extraction. In Proceedings of the 2018 Conference on Empirical Methods in Natural Language Processing, Brussels, Belgium, 31 October–4 November 2018; pp. 2205–2215.
7. Miwa, M.; Bansal, N. End-to-End Relation Extraction using LSTMs on Sequences and Tree Structures. In Proceedings of the 54th Annual Meeting of the Association for Computational Linguistics, Berlin, Germany, 7–12 August 2016; pp. 1105–1116.
8. Zhang, Y.; Zhong, V.; Chen, D.; Angeli, G.; Manning, C.D. Positionaware Attention and Supervised Data Improve Slot Filling. In Proceedings of the Conference on Empirical Methods in Natural Language Processing, Copenhagen, Denmark, 9–11 September 2017; pp. 35–45.
9. Luan, Y.; Wadden, D.; He, L.; Shah, A.; Ostendorf, M.; Hajishirzi, H. A General Framework for Information Extraction using Dynamic Span Graphs. In Proceedings of the North American Chapter of the Association for Computational Linguistics on Human Language Technology, Minneapolis, MN, USA, 2–7 June 2019; pp. 3036–3046.
10. Vinyals, O.; Fortunato, M.; Jaitly, N. Pointer Networks. In Proceedings of the Advances in Neural Information Processing Systems, Montreal, QC, Canada, 7–12 December 2015; pp. 2692–2700.
11. Bahdanau, D.; Cho, K.; Bengio, Y. Neural Machine Translation by Jointly Learning to Align and Translate. In Proceedings of the International Conference on Learning Representations 2015 (ICLR 2015), San Diego, CA, USA, 7–9 May 2015.
12. Pennington, J.; Socher, R.; Manning, C.D. GloVe: Global Vectors for Word Representation. In Proceedings of the Conference on Empirical Methods in Natural Language Processing, Doha, Qatar, 25–29 October 2014; pp. 1532–1543.
13. Park, S.; Jang, Y.; Park, K.; Kim, H. Named Entity Recognizer Using Gloval Vector and Convolutional Neural Network Embedding. *J. KITI Telecommun. Inf.* **2018**, *22*, 30–32. (In Korean)
14. Vaswani, A.; Shazeer, N.; Parmar, N.; Uszkoreit, J.; Jones, L.; Gomez, A.N.; Kaiser, L.; Polosukhin, I. Attention All You Need. In Proceedings of the Advances in Neural Information Processing Systems, Long Beach, CA, USA, 4–9 December 2017; pp. 5998–6008.
15. ACE 2005 Multilingual Training Corpus. Available online: https://catalog.ldc.upenn.edu/LDC2006T06 (accessed on 31 May 2020).
16. Ren, X.; Wu, Z.; He, W.; Qu, M.; Voss, C.R.; Ji, H.; Abdelzaher, T.F.; Han, J. Cotype: Joint Extraction of Typed Entities and Relations with Knowledge Bases. In Proceedings of the International World Wide Web Conference, Perth, Australia, 3–7 April 2017; pp. 1015–1024.
17. Zheng, S.; Wang, F.; Bao, H.; Hao, Y.; Zhou, P.; Xu, B. Joint Extraction of Entities and Relations Based on a Novel Tagging Scheme. In Proceedings of the 55th Annual Meeting of the Association for Computational Linguistics, Vancouver, BC, Canada, 30 July–4 August 2017; pp. 1227–1236.
18. Seo, M.; Kembhavi, A.; Farhadi, A.; Hajishirz, H. Bi-Directional Attention Flow for Machine Comprehension. In Proceedings of the International Conference on Learning Representations 2017 (ICLR 2017), Toulon, France, 24–26 April 2017.

19. Gormley, M.R.; Yu, M.; Dredze, M. Improved Relation Extraction with Feature-Rich Compositional Embedding Models. In Proceedings of the Conference on Empirical Methods in Natural Language Processing, Lisbon, Portugal, 17–21 September 2015; pp. 1774–1784.
20. Dixit, K.; Onaizan, Y.A. Span-Level Model for Relation Extraction. In Proceedings of the 57th Annual Meeting of the Association for Computational Linguistics, Florence, Italy, 28 July–2 August 2019; pp. 5308–5314.
21. Kim, S.; Choi, S. Relation Extraction using Hybrid Convolutional and Recurrent Networks. In Proceedings of the Korea Computer Congress 2018 (KCC 2018), Jeju, Korea, 20–22 June 2018; pp. 619–621. (In Korean).
22. Christopoulou, F.; Miwa, M.; Ananiadou1, S. A Walk-based Model on Entity Graphs for Relation Extraction. In Proceedings of the 56th Annual Meeting of the Association for Computational Linguistics, Melbourne, Australia, 15–20 July 2018; pp. 81–88.
23. Fu, T.J.; Li, P.H.; Ma, W.Y. GraphRel: Modeling Text as Relational Graphs for Joint Entity and Relation Extraction. In Proceedings of the 57th Annual Meeting of the Association for Computational Linguistics, Florence, Italy, 28 July–2 August 2019; pp. 1409–1418.
24. Kipf, T.; Welling, M. Semisupervised Classification with Graph Convolutional Networks. In Proceedings of the International Conference on Learning Representations 2017 (ICLR 2017), Toulon, France, 24–26 April 2017.
25. Devlin, J.; Chang, M.W.; Lee, K.; Toutanova, K. BERT: Pre-training of Deep Bidirectional Transformers for Language Understanding. In Proceedings of the North American Chapter of the Association for Computational Linguistics on Human Language Technologies, Minneapolis, MN, USA, 2–7 June 2019; pp. 4171–4186.

© 2020 by the authors. Licensee MDPI, Basel, Switzerland. This article is an open access article distributed under the terms and conditions of the Creative Commons Attribution (CC BY) license (http://creativecommons.org/licenses/by/4.0/).

Letter

Evolutionary Neural Architecture Search (NAS) Using Chromosome Non-Disjunction for Korean Grammaticality Tasks

Kang-moon Park [1], Donghoon Shin [2,*] and Yongsuk Yoo [3,*]

[1] Department of Computer Science, College of Natural Science, Republic of Korea Naval Academy, Changwon-si 51704, Korea; kmun422@naver.com
[2] Department of Mechanical Systems Engineering, Sookmyung Women's University, Seoul 04310, Korea
[3] Department of Foreign Languages, College of Humanities, Republic of Korea Naval Academy, Changwon-si 51704, Korea
* Correspondence: dhshin@sookmyung.ac.kr (D.S.); yong.yoo@uconn.edu (Y.Y.); Tel.: +82-2-710-9154 (D.S.); +82-55-907-5268 (Y.Y.)

Received: 19 April 2020; Accepted: 14 May 2020; Published: 17 May 2020

Featured Application: Neural Architecture Search (NAS) on linguistic tasks.

Abstract: In this paper, we apply the neural architecture search (NAS) method to Korean grammaticality judgment tasks. Since the word order of a language is the final result of complex syntactic operations, a successful neural architecture search in linguistic data suggests that NAS can automate language model designing. Although NAS application to language has been suggested in the literature, we add a novel dataset that contains Korean-specific linguistic operations, which adds great complexity in the patterns. The result of the experiment suggests that NAS provides an architecture for the language. Interestingly, NAS has suggested an unprecedented structure that would not be designed manually. Research on the final topology of the architecture is the topic of our future research.

Keywords: deep learning; neural architecture search; word ordering; Korean syntax

---

1. Introduction

In this paper, we apply a modified neural architecture search (NAS) proposed in [1–6] to a grammaticality task for Korean linguistic phenomena. To our knowledge, it is a novel approach to language modeling of Korean linguistic phenomena in terms of automatic neural architecture design. The successful application of deep learning in various fields is due to its automation of pattern finding and powerful performance on difficult problems [7,8]. The fields include image recognition [9,10], natural language processing (NLP) [11,12], game artificial intelligence (AI) [13], self-driving system [14,15], and agriculture [16], among many others. In particular, the deep learning methods have been applied to the fields of psycholinguistics, which attempt to identify the cognitive processing of human languages [17]. This success requires a need for architecture engineering, where more complex neural architectures are designed manually for different tasks. Although open-source toolkits for deep learning have become more various and easy to use [18], the diversity of tasks raises the need for the automation of architecture engineering. NAS, which aims to automate architecture engineering, focuses on automation of engineering architectures, and NAS methods have shown successful results in various tasks including image classification [19,20], object detection [21], or semantic segmentation [22].

NAS can be treated as a subfield of autoML [1] and significantly overlaps with hyper-parameter optimization [23]. Hyper-parameter optimization (HPO) mainly uses Bayesian optimization; however, it cannot generate the topology of neural architecture. The purpose of Baysian optimization is not on the generation of a topology. By its design, this focuses on parameter optimization of a neural architecture. The optimized neural architecture by the HPO would not change the final topology of the original neural network. The autoML thus contains two steps: the first step is to generate topology by using NAS; the second step is to optimize the hyperparameter of the neural network created by NAS. To generate topology, we need to adopt an evolutionary algorithm. While there are many different kinds of evolutionary algorithms available, the algorithms in question are required to begin from the minimum structure. Here we adopt the variable chromosome genetic algorithm [6], which does not require the minimum structure. This translates into a more efficient tuning method for existing deep learning models to achieve a higher rate of accuracy, as we can start directly from the previous status into a higher accuracy model.

In line with this growing interest in automated architecture engineering, we apply the NAS method to word order patterns found in Korean. Linearization is a process of generating grammatical word orders for a given set of words. Syntactic linearization systems refer to the process of making the grammatical word orders with their syntactic trees. Various word order patterns have been accounted for under syntactic linearization [24,25]. Recently, various language models have been widely tested with various types of word ordering tasks including sentence corrections and word predictions using sequence-to-sequence approaches. They have been compared in terms of their accuracy, and the literature has proven successful on the tasks even without any explicit syntactic information [26]. The Korean language poses an interesting challenge in word order patterns due to two linguistic phenomena: (i) scrambling [4], which permits different ordering of elements, as shown in (1); and (ii) argument ellipsis [5], which permits the missing argument as shown in (2) (the missing argument is crossed in the example). These two properties add complexity into word order patterns, which only exhibit a resulting linear word order that contains underlying linguistic operations.

(1) a. John-i   Mary-lul   coahanta.
       John-subject   Mary-object   like
       'John likes Mary.'
    b. Mary-lul   Johin-i   coahanta.
       Mary-object   John-subject   like
       'John likes Mary.'

(2) a. (John-i)   Mary-lul   coahanta.
    b. John-i   (Mary-lul)   coahanta.
    c. (John-i)   (Mary-lul)   coahanta.

Our application of the NAS model to identify word order patterns in Korean yields interesting findings. We show that the patterns in Korean shown above do not require recurrent neural network language models [27] for the desired result. To our knowledge, the application of NAS with a genetic algorithm to language modeling sheds new light on the automated architecture engineering of language models.

This paper is organized as follows: Section 2 introduces NAS with a genetic algorithm suggested in previous research [6]. Section 3 expresses methodology of NAS, Section 4 conducts an experiment on Korean word order patterns. Subsequently, Section 5 contains a discussion and conclusion.

2. Background

2.1. Automated Machine Learning (AutoML)

AutoML is a state-of-the-art deep learning technique that automates the designing of neural network architecture for deep learning. Designing architecture is the most important stage in deep learning, since several types of performance are determined by the design. The majority of the current architecture is developed manually, which is both a time-consuming and error-prone process [1]. However, as problems for deep learning tasks have scaled up to more challenging and complex tasks, a manual design has become more difficult [28].

The goal of autoML is to find the best performing learning algorithm without human intervention [29]. There are several approaches to autoML: hyper-parameter optimization (HPO), metalearning, and NAS.

HPO aims to find an optimal hyperparameter in a specific neural network. A hyperparameter is a parameter that is necessary for a deep learning process [30]. The optimization of a hyperparameter is very difficult because each deep learning process has different hyperparameters [2,3]. HPO finds these hyperparameters automatically using various methods. Bayesian optimization (BO) is the most famous method for this.

Metalearning can improve the performance of neural networks by using metadata. The challenge for the meta-learning methods is that it must learn from the prior experience in a systematic, data-driven way [2]. However, the final performance of the meta-learning methods is generally lower than the HPO or NAS.

NAS techniques provide an auto-design process for the topology of deep neural network architecture. Recent deep neural networks have been more complex due to their several layers and nodes with links. However, most of the neural network architectures are designed by human experts [2]. Instead, NAS can generate the topology of a neural network architecture automatically. While NAS has similarities with HPO, the difference is that NAS does not focus on parameter tuning.

2.2. Neural Architecture Search (NAS)

NAS has three stages: search space, search strategy, and performance estimation strategy [1,31]. In the search space, we have to define which architectures can be represented. To simplify the size of the search space, it is necessary to incorporate prior knowledge. This stage is highly dependent on human experts. The search strategy is the most important process in NAS; it determines how to explore the search space. The performance estimation strategy evaluates the performance of neural networks to achieve the goal of NAS, which is to find the architecture with the highest performance.

There are many different search strategies to explore the search space of the artificial neural network, such as Bayesian optimization (BO), reinforcement learning (RL), and an evolutionary algorithm (EA). HPO methods employ BO successfully; however, it is not appropriate to generate topology of the neural network due to its goal being within HPO [32,33]. In order to design the topology of the neural network, RL can be considered [34]. RL rewards the agents for their actions distributed by their efficiency. EAs have been adopted by researchers to provide evolving artificial neural networks. The characteristics of the EA methodology is that it generates the topology of neural network architecture with its evolving processes. Since CoDeepNEAT has employed EA for image recognition successfully [28], EA has been a focus of attention in the field. However, EA employs a constructive algorithm which requires a minimum architecture for initialization. In order to overcome this limitation, we will use the variable chromosome genetic algorithm (VCGA) with chromosome non-disjunction [6]. It does not need minimum architecture since it uses a new genetic operation to make the destructive method as well as a constructive method. Since the linguistic dataset we are dealing with has not been tested previously, it does not have any sample of a minimum architecture as well as a middle architecture. VCGA does not care for this issue as it does not require the minimum architecture. It enables us to search the optimal architecture for the dataset. In particular, for this reason, VCGA is used for the current language task since the final result of the experiment can show the topology of the architecture.

3. Methodology

We used the modified NAS that is originally proposed in [6] in this experiment. It uses genetic algorithms, where several genetic operators make different offsprings from their parents. The proposed method adopts a special genetic operation, called the chromosome non-disjunction, in order to allow the destructive searching not possible in conventional auto-design artificial neural networks (ANN) architectures [6]. The chromosome non-disjunction operation provides the variability for designing an ANN architecture. Consequently, our approach does not need to start from the minimum architecture. Instead, the designer should define the initial ANN architecture.

Figure 1 shows the system configuration of a modified NAS. It consists of a genetic algorithm (GA) generator and a group of neural networks (NN) generators. The genetic operator has three operations: (i) a cross-over operation that blends information of parents to make various but parent-like offspring; (ii) a mutation operation that changes a random gene to make it different from parents; and (iii) a non-disjunction operation [6] that makes two offspring where one has less information and the other one has more information.

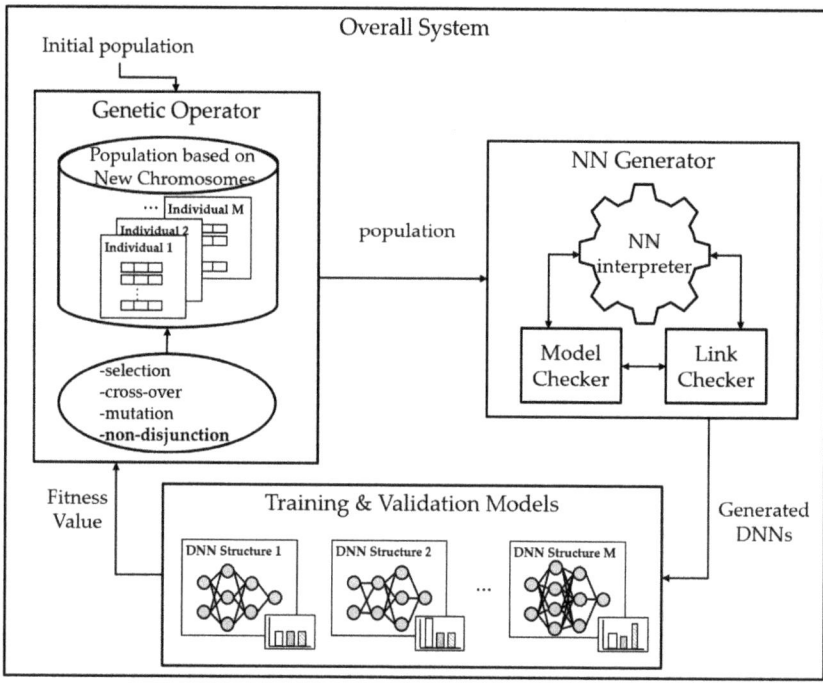

Figure 1. Overall methodology.

The GA operator has a role in controlling the population. It makes new generations of individuals which present ANN architectures. The genetic operator consists of selection, cross-over, mutation, and non-disjunction. The selection operator selects the appropriate individuals which survive from the application of the fitness function as defined in Equation (1). The cross-over operator mixes the chromosomes between the two parents. The mutation operator mutates a part of the information of the parents. The non-disjunction can add or discard the layers or the connections.

The chromosomes are organized with two types: neuron type and connection type. The neuron type of chromosome contains the information of the neuron or layer. It presents the unique number of layers, the numbers of inputs, activation function, stride, etc. The connection type of chromosome contains the information of the connection between two layers with the unique number of them. We refer readers to Park et al [6] for further details on the algorithm of generating NN using chromosomes.

The NN generator designs neural architectures from chromosomes in individuals and evaluates them. The deep neural architecture generator interprets chromosomes with a node checker and link checker. Every individual has several chromosomes, which means layers and links. However, not all individuals are runnable and learnable. Some have broken connections, and some have unmatched input/output. The model checker and link checker classify these inappropriate neural architectures. The NN architecture evaluator implements training and testing with deep learning. Users must prepare preprocessed training data and testing data. Then, fitness values, which are calculated by NN generators, are sent to the GA operator.

The accuracy of the experiment is calculated by fitness function. Fitness function (Equation (1)) is defined as follows:

$$fitness = (1 - loss) - R * \frac{num_{layer}}{num_{avg}} * (2 * (1 - loss) - 1) \tag{1}$$

where R means the coefficient of dependency rate of the number of layers between 0 to 1. Num_{layer} means the number of layers and num_{avg} means the average of the number of layers.

4. Experiment

4.1. Distribution of Grammatical Sentences in Four-Word Level Sentences in Korean

We have created four-word level sentences in Korean that contain seven syntactic categories: noun phrase, verb phrase, prepositional phrase, adjective phrase, adverbs, complementizer phrase, and auxiliary phrases, which result in 2401 combinations. To confirm the grammaticality of each combination, we have consulted the Sejong Corpus and two linguists, and the distribution of grammaticality is given below. To our knowledge, the data used in this experiment present a novel approach since we have added two syntactic operations that are not visible in the Sejong Corpus. In Table 1, one example of sentences containing scrambling and ellipsis is presented. Although the input slots are counted as four, the underlying sentence may contain more than four words, as shown in the table. This is because few of them can be elided (deleted words), and the orders can be changed. One of the example sentences is given in Table 1. To our knowledge, the data used in this experiment present a novel approach since we have added two syntactic operations that are not visible in the Sejong Corpus.

Figure 2 shows the grammaticality of the dataset; it consists of 113 sentences (circles) that are grammatical. Figure 1 consists of five dimensions, including colors. The X-axis refers to the first slot of four words, and Y and Z refer to the second and the third slot, respectively. The color spectrum refers to the fourth-word slot. The O/X represents grammaticality, which is presented as an output value of the artificial neural network.

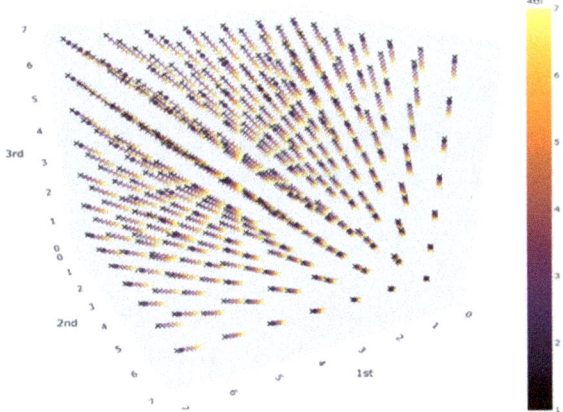

Figure 2. Distribution of input data.

Although our experiment is limited to the four-word level, the Korean language adds a great deal of complexity into patterns due to its underlying syntactic operations. For example, the sentence in Table 1 counts as grammatical even though more than four words are present underlyingly.

Table 1. An example of input data.

Jane-i	Yepputako	John	Maryekey	Cipeysey	Malhassta
Jane	pretty	John	Mary	home	said
1st input	2nd input			3rd input	4th input
"At home, John said to Mary that Jane is pretty."					

4.2. Experiment Setups

We ran the experiment of NAS on Korean grammaticality judgment data. The initial neural network of our NAS model is shown in Figure 3. This neural network consists of one input layer, one hidden layer, and one output layer. This hidden layer has five nodes and Rectified Linear Unit (ReLU) as an activation function. The loss of the initial neural architecture model is about 0.270816. Parameters of these experiments are shown in Table 2.

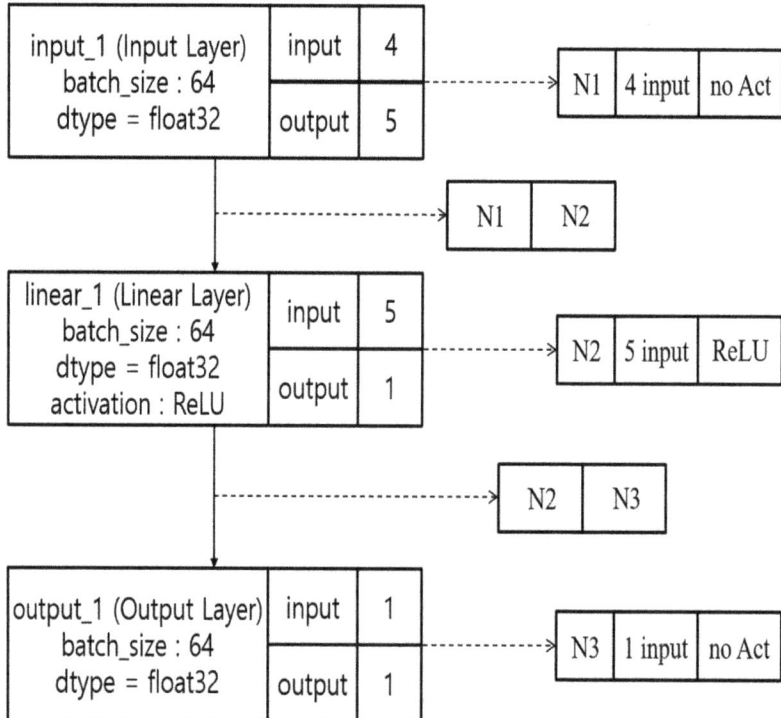

Figure 3. Initial architecture.

Table 2. Parameters of experiment.

Parameter	Value
Population	50
Generations	30
Mutant rate	0.05
Cross-over rate	0.05
Non-disjunction rate	0.1
Learning rate	0.01
Criterion	MSELoss

4.3. Experiment Results

Figure 4 shows the entire evolution process of the experiment. The number of chromosomes means the complexity of the neural architecture. It starts with five chromosomes within three layers and grows to nine chromosomes. The loss of an auto-designed neural architecture starts from 0.270816 to 0.000096. The final architecture has a linear layer with five nodes and five links to the output layer from a linear layer, as shown in Figure 5. It added a connection to the output layer from the hidden layer every evolution step and converged after generation 6. The resulting topology we have in Figure 5 is rather interesting. While there has to be one-to-one correlation between the input and output, the five outputs of the hidden layer are added into the one input of the output layer. In other words, the five outputs are identical.

The final result of the experiment shows that the initial neural architecture with the loss of 0.270816 is successfully evolved into the converged neural architecture with a loss that is close to 0. In each evolution stage, we have noticed the addition of links into the output layer by one. While the mechanism behind the addition needs to be explored, the final result with the loss that is close to 0 means the NAS can successfully find a neural architecture for the Korean language data.

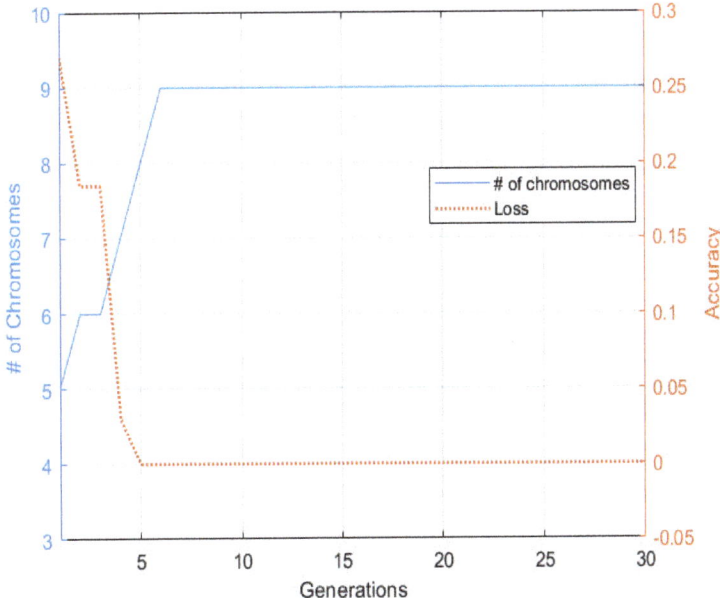

Figure 4. Evolution process of experiment.

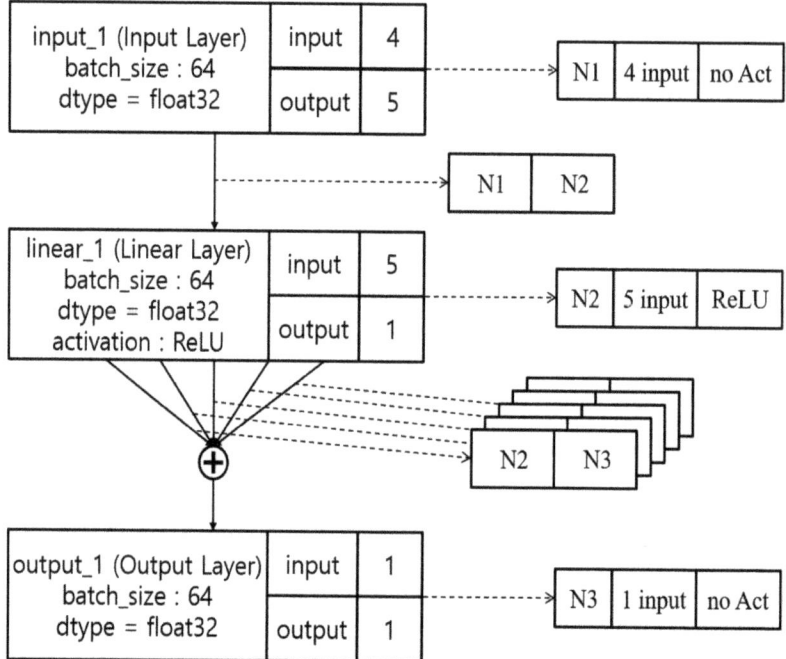

Figure 5. Final architecture of experiment.

5. Discussion and Conclusions

The results of this experiment show that it is plausible to apply the NAS method to linguistic data. In spite of the complexity of the data we have used, the NAS method has been successful in the automation of architecture designing. The experiment sheds new light on language modeling that is generally focused on replicating word order patterns under recurrent neural networks. Furthermore, this work contributes to the field of computational psycholinguistics, since the resulting model could be associated to the block box problem of the generated language models. The result above shows that a simple linear layer can learn the complex patterns in the linguistic data. However, the result of the paper is somewhat limited due to the small amount of the dataset. In further researches, the expanded dataset will be employed, and this will enable the direct comparison between the current NAS and RNN. Furthermore, a modified NAS that can generate RNN will be also researched.

However, we need to improve the data with more inputs. We predict the number of inputs would not affect the topology of the final architecture. In addition to this, cross-linguistic studies that involve more than one language are in order for future research.

Furthermore, the final topology is rather intriguing in that it is not suggested anywhere but only found in the automation of architecture designing. We speculate this structure to be language specific, yet we need to expand our dataset as well as the methodology. This fork-like structure in Figure 4 needs to be investigated in various aspects; this will be done in future research.

Author Contributions: Conceptualization, K.-m.P. and Y.Y.; methodology, K.-m.P.; software, K.-m.P.; validation, Y.Y. and D.S.; formal analysis, K.-m.P.; investigation, Y.Y.; resources, Y.Y.; data curation, Y.Y.; writing—original draft preparation, K.-m.P. and Y.Y.; writing—review and editing, Y.Y. and D.S.; visualization, K.-m.P.; supervision, Y.Y.; project administration, K.-m.P.; funding acquisition, D.S. All authors have read and agreed to the published version of the manuscript.

Funding: This research was supported by the 2020 National Research Projects of Naval Research Center, Republic of Korea Naval Academy, and by the Sookmyung Women's University Research Grants (1-2003-2008).

Conflicts of Interest: The authors declare no conflict of interest.

References

1. Elsken, T.; Metzen, J.H.; Hutter, F. Neural architecture search: A survey. *arXiv* **2018**, arXiv:1808.05377.
2. Hutter, F.; Kotthoff, L.; Vanschoren, J. *Automated Machine Learning*; Springer: Berlin/Heidelberg, Germany, 2019.
3. Adam, G.; Lorraine, J. Understanding neural architecture search techniques. *arXiv* **2019**, arXiv:1904.00438.
4. Saito, M. Some Asymmetries in Japanese and Their Theoretical Implications. Ph.D. Thesis, NA Cambridge, Cambridge, UK, 1985.
5. Kim, S. Sloppy/strict identity, empty objects, and NP ellipsis. *J. East Asian Linguist.* **1999**, *8*, 255–284. [CrossRef]
6. Park, K.; Shin, D.; Chi, S. Variable chromosome genetic algorithm for structure learning in neural networks to imitate human brain. *Appl. Sci.* **2019**, *9*, 3176. [CrossRef]
7. Wang, T.; Wen, C.-K.; Jin, S.; Li, G.Y. Deep learning-based CSI feedback approach for time-varying massive MIMO channels. *IEEE Wirel. Commun. Lett.* **2018**, *8*, 416–419. [CrossRef]
8. Hohman, F.; Kahng, M.; Pienta, R.; Chau, D.H. Visual analytics in deep learning: An interrogative survey for the next frontiers. *IEEE Trans. Vis. Comput. Graph.* **2018**, *25*, 2674–2693. [CrossRef] [PubMed]
9. Li, A.A.; Trappey, A.J.; Trappey, C.V.; Fan, C.Y. E-discover state-of-the-art research trends of deep learning for computer vision. In Proceedings of the 2019 IEEE International Conference on Systems, Man and Cybernetics (SMC), Bari, Italy, 6–9 October 2019; pp. 1360–1365.
10. Han, X.; Laga, H.; Bennamoun, M. Image-based 3D object reconstruction: State-of-the-art and trends in the deep learning era. *IEEE Trans. Pattern Anal. Mach. Intell.* **2019**, *1*, 1. [CrossRef] [PubMed]
11. Lopez, M.M.; Kalita, J. Deep learning applied to NLP. *arXiv* **2017**, arXiv:1703.03091.
12. Young, T.; Hazarika, D.; Poria, S.; Cambria, E. Recent trends in deep learning based natural language processing. *IEEE Comput. Intell. Mag.* **2018**, *13*, 55–75. [CrossRef]
13. Justesen, N.; Bontrager, P.; Togelius, J.; Risi, S. Deep learning for video game playing. *IEEE Trans. Games* **2019**, *12*, 1. [CrossRef]
14. Hatcher, W.G.; Yu, W. A survey of deep learning: Platforms, applications and emerging research trends. *IEEE Access* **2018**, *6*, 24411–24432. [CrossRef]
15. Simhambhatla, R.; Okiah, K.; Kuchkula, S.; Slater, R. Self-driving cars: Evaluation of deep learning techniques for object detection in different driving conditions. *SMU Data Sci. Rev.* **2019**, *2*, 23.
16. Kamilaris, A.; Prenafeta-Boldú, F.X. Deep learning in agriculture: A survey. *Comput. Electron. Agric.* **2018**, *147*, 70–90. [CrossRef]
17. Linzen, T.; Dupoux, E.; Goldberg, Y. Assessing the ability of LSTMs to learn syntax-sensitive dependencies. *Trans. Assoc. Comput. Linguist.* **2016**, *4*, 521–535. [CrossRef]
18. Rebortera, M.A.; Fajardo, A.C. An enhanced deep learning approach in forecasting banana harvest yields. *Int. J. Adv. Comput. Sci. Appl.* **2019**, *10*, 275–280. [CrossRef]
19. Zoph, B.; Vasudevan, V.; Shlens, J.; Le, Q.V. Learning transferable architectures for scalable image recognition. In Proceedings of the IEEE Conference on Computer Vision and Pattern Recognition, Salt Lake City, UT, USA, 18–22 June 2018; pp. 8697–8710.
20. Real, E.; Aggarwal, A.; Huang, Y.; Le, Q.V. Regularized evolution for image classifier architecture search. In Proceedings of the AAAI Conference on Artificial Intelligence, Honolulu, HI, USA, 27 January–1 February 2019; Volume 33, pp. 4780–4789.
21. Zoph, B.; Cubuk, E.D.; Ghiasi, G.; Lin, T.-Y.; Shlens, J.; Le, Q.V. Learning data augmentation strategies for object detection. *arXiv* **2019**, arXiv:1906.11172.
22. Chen, L.-C.; Zhu, Y.; Papandreou, G.; Schroff, F.; Adam, H. Encoder-decoder with atrous separable convolution for semantic image segmentation. In Proceedings of the European Conference on Computer Vision (ECCV), Munich, Germany, 8–14 September 2018; pp. 801–818.
23. Feurer, M.; Hutter, F. Hyperparameter optimization. In *Automated Machine Learning*; Springer: Berlin/Heidelberg, Germany, 2019; pp. 3–33.
24. Zhang, Y.; Clark, S. Syntax-based grammaticality improvement using CCG and guided search. In Proceedings of the Conference on Empirical Methods in Natural Language Processing, Association for Computational Linguistics, Edinburgh, UK, 27–29 July 2011; pp. 1147–1157.

25. Liu, Y.; Zhang, Y.; Che, W.; Qin, B. Transition-based syntactic linearization. In Proceedings of the 2015 Conference of the North American Chapter of the Association for Computational Linguistics: Human Language Technologies, Denver, CO, USA, 31 May–5 June 2015; pp. 113–122.
26. Schmaltz, A.; Kim, Y.; Rush, A.M.; Shieber, S.M. Adapting sequence models for sentence correction. *arXiv* **2017**, arXiv:1707.09067.
27. Mikolov, T.; Sutskever, I.; Chen, K.; Corrado, G.S.; Dean, J. Distributed representations of words and phrases and their compositionality. In Proceedings of the Advances in Neural Information Processing Systems, Lake Tahoe, CA, USA, 5–10 December 2013; pp. 3111–3119.
28. Miikkulainen, R.; Liang, J.; Meyerson, E.; Rawal, A.; Fink, D.; Francon, O.; Raju, B.; Shahrzad, H.; Navruzyan, A.; Duffy, N. Evolving deep neural networks. In *Artificial Intelligence in the Age of Neural Networks and Brain Computing*; Elsevier: Amsterdam, The Netherlands, 2019; pp. 293–312.
29. Wong, C.; Houlsby, N.; Lu, Y.; Gesmundo, A. Transfer learning with neural automl. In Proceedings of the Advances in Neural Information Processing Systems, Montreal, QC, Canada, 3–8 December 2018; pp. 8356–8365.
30. Wicaksono, A.S.; Supianto, A.A. Hyper parameter optimization using genetic algorithm on machine learning methods for online news popularity prediction. *Int. J. Adv. Comput. Sci. Appl.* **2018**, *9*, 263–267. [CrossRef]
31. Weng, Y.; Zhou, T.; Li, Y.; Qiu, X. NAS-Unet: Neural architecture search for medical image segmentation. *IEEE Access* **2019**, *7*, 44247–44257. [CrossRef]
32. Kandasamy, K.; Neiswanger, W.; Schneider, J.; Poczos, B.; Xing, E.P. Neural architecture search with bayesian optimisation and optimal transport. In Proceedings of the Advances in Neural Information Processing Systems, Montreal, QC, Canada, 3–8 December 2018; pp. 2016–2025.
33. Ma, L.; Cui, J.; Yang, B. Deep neural architecture search with deep graph bayesian optimization. In Proceedings of the 2019 IEEE/WIC/ACM International Conference on Web Intelligence (WI), Thessaloniki, Greece, 14–17 October 2019; pp. 500–507.
34. Zoph, B.; Le, Q.V. Neural architecture search with reinforcement learning. *arXiv* **2016**, arXiv:1611.01578.

© 2020 by the authors. Licensee MDPI, Basel, Switzerland. This article is an open access article distributed under the terms and conditions of the Creative Commons Attribution (CC BY) license (http://creativecommons.org/licenses/by/4.0/).

Article

Source Code Assessment and Classification Based on Estimated Error Probability Using Attentive LSTM Language Model and Its Application in Programming Education

Md. Mostafizer Rahman *, Yutaka Watanobe * and Keita Nakamura

School of Computer Science and Engineering, Graduate Department of Computer and Information Systems, The University of Aizu, Aizu-Wakamatsu, Fukushima 965-8580, Japan; keita-n@u-aizu.ac.jp
* Correspondence: mostafiz26@gmail.com (M.M.R.); yutaka@u-aizu.ac.jp (Y.W.)

Received: 23 March 2020; Accepted: 21 April 2020; Published: 24 April 2020

Abstract: The rate of software development has increased dramatically. Conventional compilers cannot assess and detect all source code errors. Software may thus contain errors, negatively affecting end-users. It is also difficult to assess and detect source code logic errors using traditional compilers, resulting in software that contains errors. A method that utilizes artificial intelligence for assessing and detecting errors and classifying source code as correct (error-free) or incorrect is thus required. Here, we propose a sequential language model that uses an attention-mechanism-based long short-term memory (LSTM) neural network to assess and classify source code based on the estimated error probability. The attentive mechanism enhances the accuracy of the proposed language model for error assessment and classification. We trained the proposed model using correct source code and then evaluated its performance. The experimental results show that the proposed model has logic and syntax error detection accuracies of 92.2% and 94.8%, respectively, outperforming state-of-the-art models. We also applied the proposed model to the classification of source code with logic and syntax errors. The average precision, recall, and F-measure values for such classification are much better than those of benchmark models. To strengthen the proposed model, we combined the attention mechanism with LSTM to enhance the results of error assessment and detection as well as source code classification. Finally, our proposed model can be effective in programming education and software engineering by improving code writing, debugging, error-correction, and reasoning.

Keywords: language modeling; classification; error probability; error assessment; logic error; neural network; LSTM; attention mechanism; programming education

1. Introduction

A huge amount of software is written in educational institutions and industry, making software reliability increasingly important. Source code usually contains multiple types of error, including syntax, semantic, communication, calculation, and logic errors. A single error is often enough to cause software failure. It is sometimes difficult for student or professional programmers to identify logic errors in source code, even with the help of traditional compilers. Helping programmers, especially novice programmers, properly assess and classify source code errors has become an important research topic in software engineering and programming education [1,2]. In general, software is debugged before it is released. Each software package must pass several testing phases. A crucial testing phase is error debugging. Student and professional programmers spend a huge amount of time trying to find source code errors. The entire source code must be searched to find even a single error, which is a tedious, cumbersome, and time-consuming task. Student and professional programmers often make some common errors, such as missing semicolons, delimiters, or braces, and logic errors. These errors may be caused by a lack of experience or attention to detail. Both novice and experienced programmers make such errors, as reported in a study of programmers who build errors (Google) [3].

Machine learning (ML)-based classifiers can predict source code errors after being trained on a correct source code corpus [4–6]. Source code classifiers can assist programmers in fixing potential errors, thereby increasing source code correctness and reliability. Traditional source code error prediction methods consist of two steps, namely the extraction of features from training datasets and the development of an ML model (supervised or unsupervised) for classification. Previous research has concentrated on the design of preferential metrics to obtain higher accuracy. Features can be divided into Halstead [7] features depending on operators and operands, McCabe [8] features, and CK [9] features extracted from object-oriented programs. Most supervised and unsupervised classifiers are unable to properly classify source code using extracted features, inside the features logic, syntax, and semantic errors may exist. Feature-based traditional classifiers consider only the current features instead of checking all source code sequences.

Due to the sensitivity of source code, error assessment, detection, and classification is a challenging task. Traditional compilers cannot accurately assess source code errors. Therefore, a method based on artificial intelligence (AI) is required to assist programmers in the assessment and detection of such errors. Artificial neural networks (ANNs) are attractive for this task.

Natural language processing (NLP) has recently produced a lot of remarkable results in applications such as language processing, speech recognition, and machine translation. An n-gram model is an example of a stochastic language model for predicting the next item or word based on a large text corpus. N-gram models such as bi-gram, tri-gram, skip-gram [10], and GloVe [11] are statistical language models that can be applied to language modeling. The availability of large text corpuses has made NLP techniques effective. A language model is useful and intuitive for short repeated source code sequences. However, for complex software engineering, the NLP language model is less useful. Many researchers have focused on source code error assessment and classification using language modeling. An ANN-based language model could be a replacement for error assessment and detection as well as source code classification. Recurrent neural network (RNN)-based models have recently achieved some success in language modeling. An RNN can hold a larger source code sequence context compared with that for traditional n-gram and other language models [12]. RNNs have limitations in terms of representing such large contexts due to gradient vanishing or exploding [13], making it difficult to train RNN-based models using long source code sequences. RNNs are thus effective for only short source code sequences. RNNs have been extended to long short-term memory (LSTM) networks to avoid gradient vanishing or exploding. LSTM can remember both short and long source code sequences using an internal gate structure.

In this paper, we present a language model for assessing and detecting various source code errors (logic, syntax, semantic, runtime, etc.) as well as classifying the source code as correct (error-free) or incorrect based on the estimated error probability. We developed the language model using LSTM combined with the attention mechanism (hereafter referred to as LSTM-AttM). LSTM-AttM is more powerful and effective than a basic RNN, standard LSTM, and other traditional baseline models. We trained RNN, LSTM, and LSTM-AttM models with various numbers of hidden layers (50, 100, 200, 300, and 400) using a large correct source code corpus collected from an online judge system. For the evaluation process, source code with and without errors were used as the input to the model. The model then assessed and detected syntax and logic errors with locations in code and classified the source code as either correct or incorrect based on the estimated error probability. The LSTM-AttM model can detect many common errors in source code, including logic errors. The LSTM-AttM network can use long source code sequences as the input to generate the optimal output. The proposed model was tuned with various numbers of hyperparameters and hidden layers to optimize it in terms of perplexity, accuracy, training time, and other performance measurement metrics. The output of the proposed model will be helpful for student and professional programmers as well as programming education and software engineering. The contributions of our research are as follows:

- Our proposed model can provide a thorough evaluation of source code which includes error detection, correct word prediction with line numbers, as well as classification. Thus, for learning programming, the model can act as an intelligent compiler.
- The logic and syntax error detection accuracies are 92.2% and 94.8%, respectively, which are much better than those for state-of-the-art models.
- The proposed model can classify source code as being either correct or incorrect based on the estimated error probability. The average precision, recall, and F-measure values for source code classification based on syntax and logic errors are much higher than those of reference benchmark models.
- We combined the attention mechanism with the proposed neural network model to strengthen the language model. Generally, in source codes, a single line can have a long dependency on the previous line, in which case the attention mechanism uses all the hidden states of the past to make accurate predictions.
- The proposed model can help novice and experienced programmers quickly fix their source code, thus saving valuable time.

The rest of this paper is organized as follows. Section 2 presents the background and literature review. Section 3 describes LSTM neural networks. Section 4 presents the proposed approach. Section 5 presents the data collection and normalization processes. Section 6 presents the experimental results and evaluations. Section 7 discusses the results. Finally, Section 8 concludes this research and provides suggestions for future work.

2. Background and Literature Review

In the source code, a single line may have reliance on the preceding lines, making it difficult to evaluate complex source code by any conventional language model. The LSTM based language model is a promising method for source code error assessment and classification.

Information and communication technology has become an influential economic catalyst. A huge amount of source code is written and compiled globally. AI can be applied to assess source code errors. AI-based language models are often used for source code assessment and classification to obtain human-like responses. Many researchers have used AI-based models to detect source code errors in software engineering and programming education.

Pu et al. [10] proposed a source code correction method based on LSTM using code segment similarities. The study leveraged the sequence-to-sequence (seq2seq) neural network model with natural language processing tasks for the code correction process. Another study [12] proposed a deep software language model based on RNNs. The experimental results showed that the model outperforms traditional language models such as n-gram and cache-based n-gram in a Java corpus. The software language model shows great promise in the field of software engineering. Terada et al. [14] proposed an LSTM-based model for programming education where the model predicts the next word by analyzing incomplete source code. Novice programmers often struggle to write a complete program from scratch. To help them, the model predicts the next word to complete a program. The LSTM-based model achieved a high degree of prediction accuracy. Fault detection in source code has become an important research topic [1]. In one study [15], source code defect prediction was performed based on churn metrics combined with source code dependencies. In another [16], an extensive analysis of metrics and static code attributes was conducted for error prediction. Arar et al. [17] selected suitable features by employing a naive Bayes classifier. Jing et al. [18] introduced a vocabulary learning model that calculates the incorrect classification cost for the prediction of source code defects. Various ML approaches [19–21] have been proposed for classification, recommendation, and estimation problems. Alreshedy et al. [22] presented an ML-based language model for classifying source code snippets based on the programming language. In their work, a multinomial naive Bayes classifier was applied and code snippets from the website Stack Overflow were used as experimental data. Ram and Nagappan [23] proposed a hierarchical model that uses convolutional neural networks (CNNs) and LSTM for sentiment analysis in software engineering. This analysis model outperforms reference state-of-the-art models. Reyes et al. [24] classified archived source code by type of programming language using an LSTM network. Empirical results showed that the LSTM network outperformed the naive Bayes classifier and linguist classifier.

Terada and Watanobe [25] presented a method for the automatic generation of fill-in-the-blank problems for novice programmers using k-means clustering and the bidirectional LSTM model. The k-means clustering method is used to select ideal source code from an online judge system and the code to be made blank (to be filled with appropriate words using the bidirectional LSTM model). Tai et al. [26] presented a model called Tree-LSTM where an LSTM network works like a tree. The model evaluates the tasks of prediction of semantic relatedness based on sentence pairs and sentiment classification. Pedroni and Meyer [27] presented a survey-based analysis that focused on what type of compiler message helps novice programmers identify errors and what actions should be taken regarding source code errors. They experimentally showed which type of message helps most. Saito and Watanobe [28] proposed a learning path recommendation system for novice students based on their desired learning ability chart. The students were clustered and an excellent student from each cluster was selected. The model extracted features from the selected excellent students. Finally, the model used the features as training input to the neural network. An LSTM network was used to predict the learning path of the students. In another study [29], a source code bug detection technique that uses LSTM was proposed. The hyperparameters of LSTM were adjusted to determine the optimal perplexity and training time. The LSTM network produces a plausible outcome for source code bug detection. Fan et al. [30] presented an attention-based RNN for source code defect prediction. F-measure score and the area under the curve (AUC) were used as model evaluation metrics. The proposed model improved the source code classification process. The F-measure score and AUC had 14% and 7% better accuracy than those of state-of-the-art models, respectively. Ohashi et al. [31] proposed a source code classification model that uses a CNN. The model classifies source code based on the type of algorithm in the code. During CNN model training, all source code is converted into a simple structure of code without any variables, functions, keywords, etc. The obtained classification accuracy of the CNN model is very high.

In summary, many promising methods have proposed. Most researchers utilized traditional supervised and unsupervised classifiers, RNNs, LSTM, or CNNs as language models for source code classification and other applications. RNNs are much better than traditional language models such as n-gram, but have limitations in terms of handling long input sequences. LSTM is a variant of RNNs that overcomes the shortcomings of RNNs. The model proposed in the present study combines the attention mechanism with LSTM (LSTM-AttM). The LSTM-AttM network is used as a language model for source code assessment and classification based on the estimated error probability. The LSTM-AttM network outperforms LSTM because the latter uses only the last hidden state outcome for prediction. In contrast, LSTM-AttM considers all previous hidden state outcomes for prediction. Most of the studies used different models for source code classification based on errors, programming language detection, archive code classification, and simple error detection. On the other hand, our proposed model specifically identifies logic, syntax and other errors in the source code. Furthermore, the model can predict the correct words in place of the error location. Overall our proposed LSTM-ATM model differs from other models in achieving unique goals.

3. Long Short-Term Memory Network

An LSTM network is a type of RNN. The LSTM network has been effectively used in the field of deep learning. The main advantage of an LSTM network is ease of training because it does not face problems such as gradient vanishing or exploding. LSTM can process entire input (source code, video, speech, image) sequences. An LSTM network memory unit consists of four attributes, namely a forget gate, a cell state, an input gate, and an output gate. The cell state remembers the information of the entire sequence and the three gates control the input and output of the cell, as shown in Figure 1.

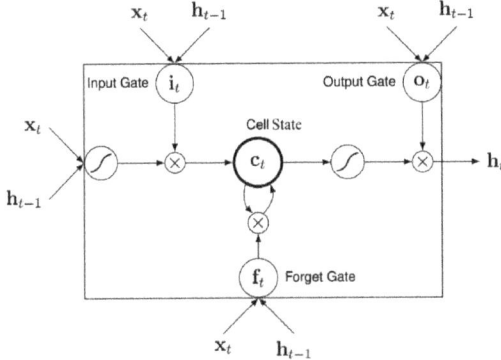

Figure 1. Internal structure of a simple long short-term memory (LSTM) unit.

At the start of the process, the forget gate checks which information to throw away and which information to keep in the cell state. Equation (1) is used for the forget gate. It is calculated at cell state c_{t-1} using hidden state h_{t-1} and input x_t. The output of the forget gate, between 0 and 1, is produced by the sigmoid function. An output value of 1 (0) means keep (remove) all information in (from) the cell state.

$$f_t = \sigma\left(W_f[h_{t-1}, x_t] + b_f\right) \tag{1}$$

To store a new piece of information in the cell state, the input gate decides which value will be updated using the sigmoid function. The tanh function creates a new candidate value $\widetilde{c}_t$ for the cell state.

$$i_t = \sigma(w_i \cdot [h_{t-1}, x_t] + b_i) \tag{2}$$

$$\widetilde{c}_t = \tanh(w_c \cdot [h_{t-1}, x_t] + b_c) \tag{3}$$

Then, the old cell state c_{t-1} is used to update c_t.

$$c_t = f_t * c_{t-1} + i_t * \widetilde{c}_t \tag{4}$$

We can now calculate the output of LSTM, which is based on a filtered version of the cell state. The sigmoid function decides which part of the cell state is going to the output and then updates the weight accordingly.

$$o_t = \sigma(w_o \cdot [h_{t-1}, x_t] + b_o) \tag{5}$$

$$h_t = o_t * \tanh(c_t) \tag{6}$$

The combination of the attention mechanism with LSTM improves model performance for fault assessment and detection and the classification of source code.

4. Proposed Approach

In the proposed model, an LSTM-AttM network is used as a seq2seq language model for error assessment and detection as well as source code classification. We trained the proposed model using correct source code. The model then generated the error probability through the softmax layer for each error candidate word based on the context vector c_t of all previous hidden states and the current state output h_t. The estimated error probability is also used to classify the source code as either correct (error-free) or incorrect. The proposed LSTM-AttM model can identify many kinds of error (logic, syntax, semantic, etc.) in source code to increase source code reliability. The workflow of the proposed model is shown in Figure 2.

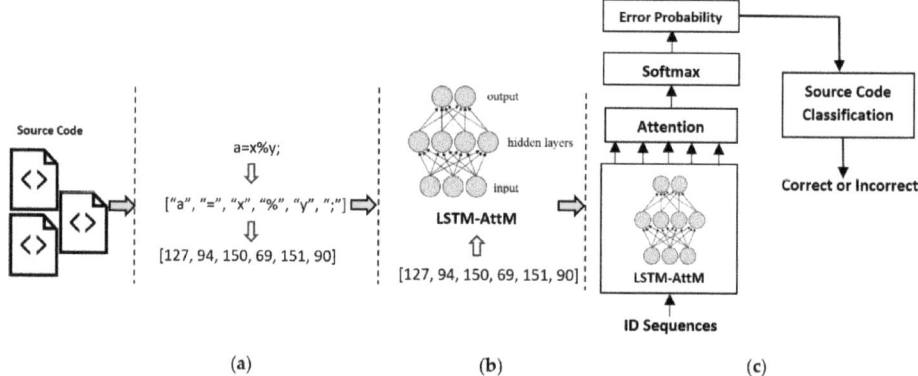

Figure 2. Workflow of proposed model: (**a**) word embedding and encoding process, (**b**) training of LSTM combined with the attention mechanism (LSTM-AttM) network using IDs, and (**c**) error probability prediction followed by the softmax layer and source code classification.

Proposed LSTM-AttM Model Architecture

The attention mechanism has been adapted for performing various tasks [32–35]. It is most commonly used in seq2seq modeling. A neural network that utilizes the attention mechanism is called an attentive neural network. The conventional seq2seq model cannot properly process a long sequence of input because only the last hidden state of the input is used as a context vector for output [36]. The attention mechanism maps the most relevant words from the input sequence and then assigns a higher weight to these words to enhance the output accuracy. We incorporated the attention mechanism with LSTM, as shown in Figure 3, to better predict short and long sequences of source code. The proposed LSTM-AttM model creates a potential application domain in programming education arena.

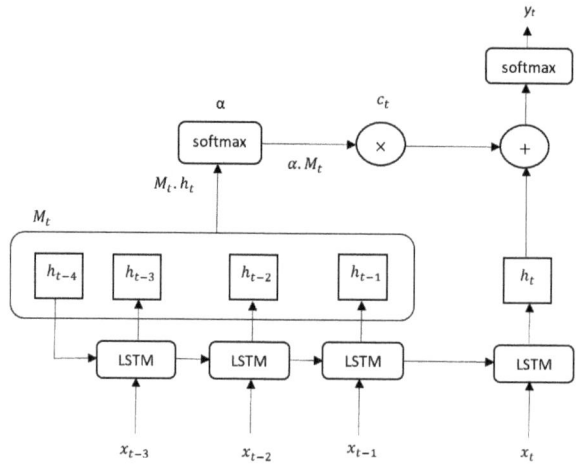

Figure 3. Architecture of proposed LSTM-AttM network model.

Attention is a vector or dense output layer with a softmax function. It is used to enhance the performance of machine translators and seq2seq models. Recently, the attention mechanism has achieved great success in machine translation tasks. A machine translator sometimes compresses long sequenced sentences into a fixed-length vector. Therefore, information may be lost. The attention mechanism mitigates this problem. Although LSTM has outstanding performance in terms of capturing long-range dependencies, a hidden state carries all the information into a fixed-length vector [36]. The attention mechanism has been applied to neural language models such as LSTM to overcome this problem [37]. The attention mechanism allows a neural language model to retrieve and make use of pertinent information in all previous hidden states, improving network retention. The mathematical details of the attention mechanism are described in previous work [38]. For attention, we use external memory M for previous hidden states, which is denoted as $M_t = [h_{t-M} \ldots \ldots \ldots h_{t-1}] \in \mathbb{R}^{k*M}$. At time step t, the context vector c_t and attention weight α_t. Now, the model uses the attention layer between h_t and the hidden states in M_t. We defined our attention-based LSTM model by the following equations.

$$A_t = M_t.h_t \tag{7}$$

$$\alpha_t = softmax(A_t) \tag{8}$$

$$c_t = M_t \alpha_t^T \tag{9}$$

For predicting the next word at time step t, the calculation is based on current hidden states h_t and context vector c_t. The vocabulary spaces are obtained using the softmax function to produce the final probability $y_t \in \mathbb{R}^v$. G_t is an output vector.

$$G_t = \tanh(w^g[w^h(h_t) + w^m(c_t)]) \tag{10}$$

$$y_t = softmax(w^v G_t + b^v) \tag{11}$$

where $w^g \in \mathbb{R}^{k*2k}$ and $w^v \in \mathbb{R}^{v*k}$ are trainable projection matrices, $b^v \in \mathbb{R}^v$ is a trainable bias vector, and v is the vocabulary size.

The attention mechanism facilitates the extraction of more accurate features from input sequences, and thus the LSTM-AttM network increases the performance of the proposed model.

5. Data Collection and Normalization

In the present research, we collected all the datasets from the Aizu Online Judge (AOJ) system [39,40]. The AOJ system has more than 2000 problems and 65,000 users as of February 2020. The problems and algorithms are divided into categories [28]. The AOJ system has more than 4 million source code samples for various problems. A total of 18 programming languages, including C++, C, Ruby, and Python, are supported by the AOJ system. The system keeps all statistical information on programming and the submission logs of individual users. These resources can be used to conduct research in programming education and software engineering. To train the proposed model, we took correct solutions for Insertion Sort (IS), Greatest Common Divisor (GCD), Prime Numbers (PN), Bubble Sort (BS), and Selection Sort (SS) problems from the AOJ system. All the source code was written in the C language. The selected source code was archived on the AOJ system from August 2018 to September 2019. The total numbers of correct source code submissions for IS, GCD, PN, BS, and SS are 2285, 1821, 1538, 2425, and 2294, respectively. The overall solution success rates for IS, GCD, PN, BS, and SS are 35.16%, 49.86%, 30.8%, 47.74%, and 59.79%, respectively. A total of 10,362 correct and incorrect source codes were used for model training where the number of correct and incorrect codes was equal. Of the total source codes, we used 90% of the code for model training and 10% for testing. To evaluate the error in the source code, we randomly selected 100 new source codes from each category. A total of 500 source codes were examined by the model for logical, syntax, and others error evaluation. For classification, we selected approximately 1300 erroneous source codes from all categories to evaluate the effectiveness of the classification.

Before model training, we refined all source code by removing unnecessary elements. We adopted the source code conversion procedure applied in a previous study [29]. Initially, we removed all comments, line breaks (\n), and tabs (\t) from the source code because they are not relevant for error assessment and classification. The source code was converted to word sequences and then functions, keywords, variables, and characters were considered as normal words. Each word was encoded with an ID. The IDs for functions, variables, keywords, and characters are shown in Table 1. Any user-defined functions and variables in the source code not defined in Table 1 were assigned unique IDs from a defined range in the encoding process. The entire process, called word embedding and encoding, is shown in Figure 4.

Table 1. Partial list of defined IDs for keywords, characters, and numbers.

ID	Word	ID	Word	ID	Word	ID	Word
30	auto	46	int	62		78	.
31	break	47	long	63	!	79	/
32	case	48	register	64	?	80	0
33	char	49	return	65	_	81	1
34	const	50	short	66	"	82	2
35	continue	51	signed	67	#	83	3
36	default	52	sizeof	68	$	84	4
37	do	53	static	69	%	85	5
38	double	54	struct	70	&	86	6
39	else	55	switch	71	'	87	7
40	enum	56	typedef	72	(	88	8
41	exturn	57	union	73	)	89	9
42	float	58	unsigned	74	*	90	;
43	for	59	void	75	+	91	:
44	goto	60	volatile	76	,	92	<
45	if	61	while	77	~	93	>
94	=	110	O	126	'	142	p
95	@	111	P	127	a	143	q
96	A	112	Q	128	b	144	r
97	B	113	R	129	c	145	s
98	C	114	S	130	d	146	t
99	D	115	T	131	e	147	u
100	E	116	U	132	f	148	v
101	F	117	V	133	g	149	w
102	G	118	W	134	h	150	x
103	H	119	X	135	i	151	y
104	I	120	Y	136	j	152	z
105	J	121	Z	137	k	153	{
106	K	122	[	138	l	154		
107	L	123	\	139	m	155	}
108	M	124	]	140	n		
109	N	125	^	141	o		

After the training process, the performance of the model was evaluated in terms of source code assessment and classification accuracy. To predict the next ID sequence, the model uses the prefix of all ID sequences using the attention mechanism. The ID sequences are transformed in several phases followed by a softmax layer to generate the probability for the next ID sequence or candidate word. In the proposed model, a word is considered as an error candidate whose probability is less than 0.1 [29]. The difference between the predicted and actual results is called perplexity. The perplexity is calculated at the softmax layer at each time step to observe the loss function.

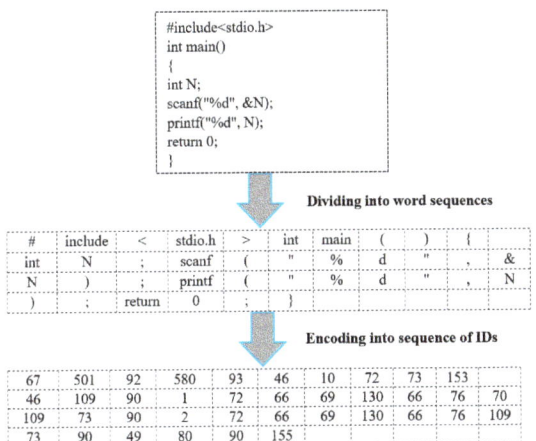

Figure 4. Word embedding and encoding process for source code.

The softmax layer receives the vector $x = [x_1, x_2, \ldots, x_n]$ and returns the probability vector $p = [p_1, p_2, p_3, \ldots, p_n]$, expressed as follows:

$$P_i = \frac{\exp(x_i)}{\sum_{j=1}^{k} \exp(x_j)} \tag{12}$$

where $i = 1, 2, 3, 4, \ldots, k$.

Perplexity, expressed below, is a standard performance measurement. It indicates how well a probability model predicts a sample. A lower value indicates a better model.

$$H_p \approx -\frac{1}{N} \sum_{i}^{m} log_2 p\ (W_i | W_{i-n+1}^{i-1}) \tag{13}$$

where $|N|$ is the length of the sample, w_i is an ID in a sample, and $P(w_i)$ is the probability of w_i.

6. Experimental Results and Evaluations

We developed a general model that can be trained on any type of problem set. In the present research, we selected the source code for IS, PN, GCD, BS, and SS for the experiments. We trained an RNN, LSTM, and the LSTM-AttM network with various numbers of hidden layers (50, 100, 150, and 200). We recorded the epoch-wise perplexity and training times during the training period. The perplexity determines the efficacy of a language model. The evaluation and training processes were performed on a computer with an Intel Core i7-5600U CPU (2.60 GHz) with 8 GB of RAM running 64-bit Windows 10.

6.1. Experimental Setup

In our study, we use Python's chainer framework to create deep learning model architecture. Also, we considered the large number, length, and complexity of the source code to develop our proposed model. Before the start of training, we defined several hyperparameters for the experiment to obtain better results. First, we determine the number of hidden layers and epochs. Then the number of neurons was determined based on the number of hidden layers. Thus, the neurons were equal to the defined number of hidden layers. For example, If hidden layers $h_l = 100, 200, 300, 400$, and so on. Thus, the neurons at each hidden layer will be equal to the number of hidden layers, such as $n\_units = h_l$

where n_units = neurons at each layer and h_l = number of hidden layers. Dropout was used to regularize the LSTM network performance to avoid overfitting. To obtain better training accuracy dropout ratio was set to 0.5 [41]. We optimized the LSTM network using the Adam optimization algorithm [42]. Particularly, optimizer smoothing the model learning by binding together loss function and model parameters in order to produce better training accuracy. The learning rate or step size of our network was $l = 0.001$. The network weights were updated based on the value of l during training. A higher (lower) value of l makes initial learning faster (slower). The values of β_1 and β_2, the exponential decay rates for the first- and second-moment estimates, were set to 0.001 and 0.999, respectively. It is often effective to reduce the learning rate when training is running. Without exponential decay, the loss function cannot start again to diverge after decreased a certain point. The value of ε ($= 1e^{-8}$) was used to prevent division by zero in the implementation. We trained our network with various numbers of hidden layers (50, 100, 150, 200, 250, 300, and 400). The corresponding models are called the 50-layer model, 100-layer model, and so on. We evaluated the performance of all models to determine the optimal number of hidden layers.

6.2. Perplexity, Training, and Hidden Layer Selection

The performance of a language model strongly depends on training time and perplexity. Perplexity also determines how good a model training process as well as calculates the model loss function. During training with various numbers of hidden layers, we calculated the epoch-wise perplexity to determine the optimal number of hidden layers. Correct source code samples were selected from the AOJ system for training. The perplexity at the last epoch (30th) of training for each type of program is shown in Figure 5.

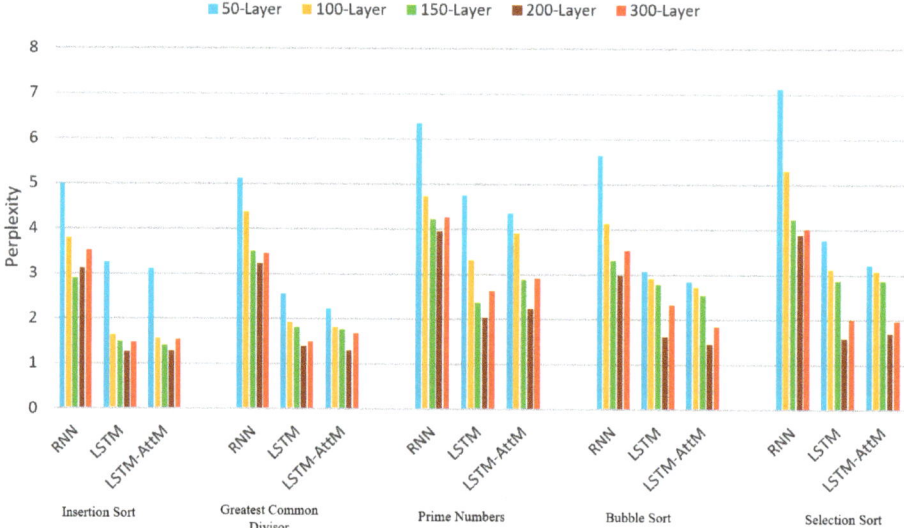

Figure 5. Perplexity values at last epoch of proposed and other state-of-the-art models during the training period for various problem sets.

The figure shows that the 200-layer model had the lowest perplexity during the training period. The epoch-wise perplexity for the 200-layer model for various problem sets is shown in Figure 6.

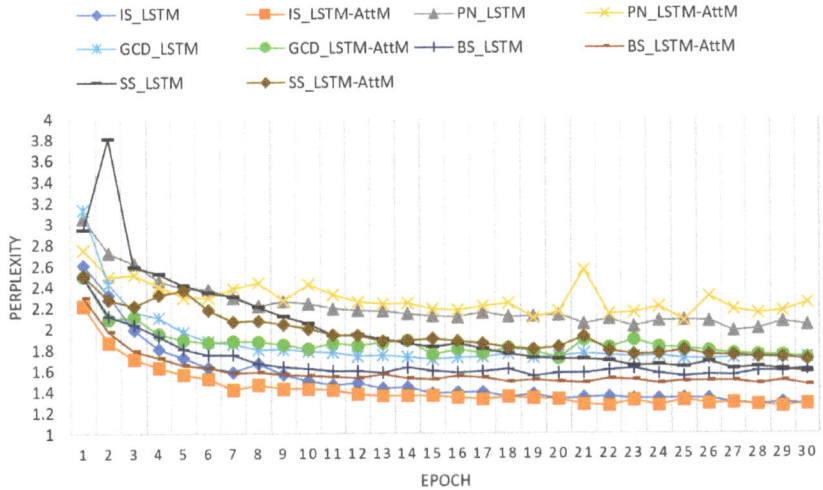

Figure 6. Epoch-wise perplexity for LSTM and LSTM-AttM models with 200 hidden layers for various problems.

Based on these results, we selected 200 hidden layers for LSTM-AttM and the other state-of-the-art models for all subsequent experiments. The training accuracies for the RNN, LSTM, and LSTM-AttM models are listed in Table 2.

Table 2. Average training accuracy of models for various problem sets.

Problem	Training Accuracy (%)					
	Correct Source Codes			Incorrect Source Codes		
	RNN	LSTM	LSTM-AttM	RNN	LSTM	LSTM-AttM
Insertion Sort	70	81	94	68.3	82.4	93.6
Greatest Common Divisor	68	80	92	71.5	81	92.3
Prime Numbers	75	83	90	73.5	84.5	90
Bubble Sort	72	79	89	73.2	81.7	90
Selection Sort	65	78	87	66	80	89.6

After model training, we evaluated the performance of the proposed model in terms of the detection of syntax, logic, and other errors as well as source code classification (correct or incorrect). We selected source code with errors for model validation and testing. Our goal was to evaluate the performance of the proposed model in terms of how accurately it assesses and detects errors in source code. To evaluate model performance, we adopted three evaluation indices, namely error detection accuracy (EDA), error prediction accuracy (EPA), and model accuracy (MA), respectively defined below.

$$EDA = \frac{Actual\ Error\ Word\ (AEW)}{Total\ Detected\ Errors\ (TDE)} \times 100\% \qquad (14)$$

$$EPA = \frac{Actual\ Correct\ Word\ (ACW)}{Total\ Predicted\ Words\ (TPW)} \times 100\% \qquad (15)$$

$$MA = \frac{EDA + EPA}{2} \qquad (16)$$

The proposed model detects errors in source code by utilizing the trained correct source code corpus. Of the detected errors, there are some true errors, which are called actual error words (AEWs). Of the predicted words, there are some true correct words, which are called actual correct words

(ACWs). It is noted that the estimated probabilities of AEW and ACW should be more than 0.90. We used the above-mentioned evaluation indices to measure the performance of the models in terms of syntax and logic error assessment and detection.

6.3. Syntax Error Assessment and Detection

A syntax error is an error where the program violates a structural rule of a certain programming language. To compile, source code must follow the structural rules of a programming language, if it does not, the compiler will output syntax errors. Common examples of syntax error include misspelled keywords, missing single or double quotes, missing matching brackets, and a missing semicolon at the end of a statement. To assess and detect syntax errors in source code, the proposed LSTM-AttM language model calculates the error probability of each error candidate word. The error probability determines the possibility of syntax errors in source code. The proposed model assesses the source code thoroughly and detects syntax error candidates, as shown in Figure 7.

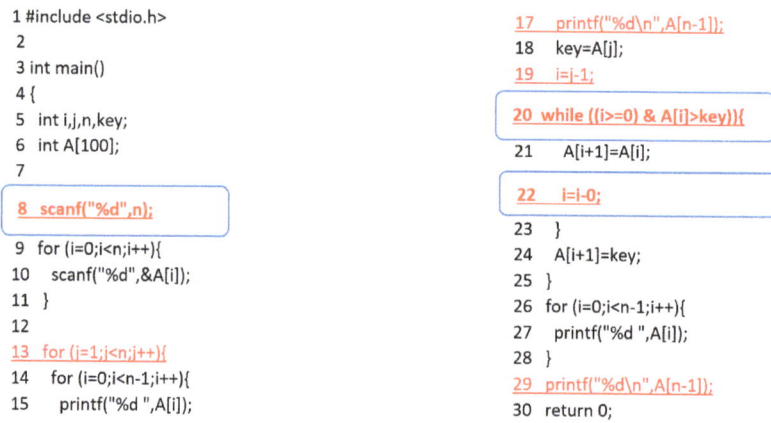

Figure 7. Syntax error assessment and detection for source code evaluated using LSTM-AttM.

In the figure, the proposed LSTM-AttM model assesses the source code and estimates the error probability for each error candidate word. The corresponding location (line number) of each detected word is listed in Table 3. The error probability determines the syntax error possibility for a particular candidate word and location in the source code. Although the model detected all the potential locations of syntax error, the detected error candidates might not have all been accurately identified. Words with an error probability of more than 0.98 are outlined in blue in Figure 7. We considered these errors to be confirmed syntax errors.

Table 3. Estimated error probability for source code in Figure 7.

Line Number	Error Candidate (Probability < 0.1)	Suggested Word	Estimated Error Probability
8	n	&	0.9999918
13	1	0	0.60096426
17	n	key	0.7747942
19	i	n	0.4699676
20	(	&	0.98158526
22	0	1	0.9885606

To compare our model with baseline models, in addition to the above-mentioned example (Figure 7) a large number of erroneous source code samples were used for the evaluation process.

The obtained results are listed in Table 4. The syntax error assessment and detection accuracy results for the proposed model for all problem sets are better than those for the state-of-the-art models.

Table 4. Assessment results of syntax error detection for erroneous source code.

Problem	Accuracy (%)		
	RNN	LSTM	LSTM-AttM
Insertion Sort	83	88	98
Greatest Common Divisor	81	90	95
Prime Numbers	74	85	93
Bubble Sort	80	80	96
Selection Sort	69	78	92
Average	77.4	84.2	94.8

6.4. Logic Error Assessment and Detection

A logic error in source code generates unexpected program output. The cause of logic error is typically the incorrect application of mathematical logic in source code. Conventional compilers cannot detect or assess logic error, and thus student and professional programmers must check the entire source code line by line. This is a major problem, especially for novice programmers. A simple program with logic error is shown in Figure 8. The program takes in an array of numbers and then outputs it. In the example, four numbers are given for an array but because of incorrect logic, only three of them are output.

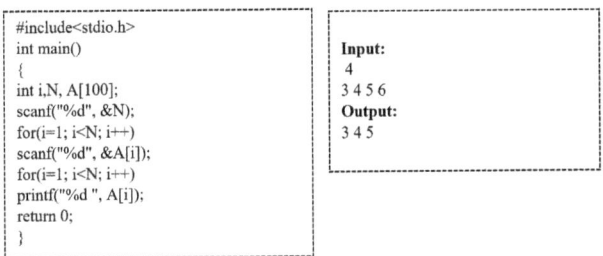

Figure 8. Example of source code with logic error and its input and output.

Logic error assessment and detection is a challenging task for traditional compilers. The proposed attention-based language model identifies logic error candidate words in source code to reduce the time required to check for such errors. To identify logic errors, the model should be able to calculate long dependent sequences of source code. We thus designed the seq2seq language model by combining the attention mechanism with LSTM. We compared its performance with other state-of-the-art models. Source code with logic error (an example for BS) was evaluated by the LSTM-AttM model. The results are shown in Figure 9. The source code assessment and detection results are listed in Table 5. The results reveal the effectiveness of the proposed LSTM-AttM model. The proposed model assessed and identified logic errors and their locations in source code. The estimated error probability ensures the logic error possibility on a particular line (blue outline) of source code. The model detected two logic errors on line 6 and generated the corresponding error probabilities (see Table 5). The estimated error probabilities are both more than 0.90, indicating possible logic errors on line 6 of the source code.

```
 1  #include<stdio.h>              13      b[j]=b[j-1];
 2  int main()                     14      b[j-1]=m;
 3  {                              15      n++;
 4      int a,b[100],i,j,n=0,m;    16      }
 5      scanf("%d",&a);            17      }
                                   18  }
 6      for(i=1;i<a;i++){          19  for(i=0;i<a-1;i++){
 7      scanf("%d",&b[i]);         20      printf("%d ",b[i]);
 8      }                          21  }
 9      for(i=0;i<a-1;i++){        22  printf("%d\n",b[i]);
10          for(j=a-1;j>i;j--){    23  printf("%d\n",n);
11              if(b[j]<b[j-1]){   24  return 0;
12                  m=b[j];        25  }
```

Figure 9. Logic error assessment and detection for source code evaluated using LSTM-AttM.

Table 5. Estimated error probability for erroneous source code in Figure 9.

Line Number	Error Candidates (Probability < 0.1)	Suggested Word	Estimated Error Probability
6	1	0	0.9727551
6	a	=	0.92732173

To assess logic errors, we selected source code from the AOJ system that generated a runtime error (i.e., failure during execution) judge verdict. Runtime errors can be caused by invalid pointer references (segmentation fault), overflow, division by zero, memory access violations, and uninitialized memory access. In the experiment, in addition to the above-mentioned example (Figure 9) a large number of source code samples with logic errors were used. The evaluation results are listed in Table 6. As shown, the proposed language model outperformed the reference benchmark models.

Table 6. Assessment results of logic error detection for erroneous source code.

Problem	Accuracy (%)		
	RNN	LSTM	LSTM-AttM
Insertion Sort	60	75	95
Greatest Common Divisor	57	81	96
Prime Numbers	63	77	90
Bubble Sort	65	80	91
Selection Sort	56	78	89
Average	60.2	78.2	92.2

6.5. Source Code Classification

In this section, we present the source code classification performance of the proposed LSTM-AttM and existing state-of-the-art models. We considered various kinds of error in source code, including semantic, syntax, logic, and communication errors. We evaluated the source code classification performance of the proposed model and state-of-the-art models by considering error occurrences in the source code. The proposed model calculated the error probability of each error candidate word to classify the source code.

In our model, each variable, keyword, operator, operand, class, function, etc. in the source code was considered as a normal word. The model generated the error probability for each error candidate word followed by the softmax layer. In general, our model detects error candidate words and estimates the corresponding error probability for each one. If the estimated error probability for any word is greater than 0.90, the source code is classified as incorrect. To evaluate the classification performance, we compared our model with some baseline methods, namely standard LSTM, RNN, and the random forest (RF) method with a deep belief network (DBN) [43].

The performance of classification was evaluated in terms of precision, recall, and F-measure indices, respectively expressed as follows:

$$Precision\ (P_i) = \frac{TP_i}{TP_i + FP_i} \tag{17}$$

$$Recall\ (R_i) = \frac{TP_i}{TP_i + FN_i} \tag{18}$$

$$F-measure = \frac{2 * P_i * R_i}{P_i + R_i} \tag{19}$$

where TP_i is the true positive rate (erroneous source code classified as erroneous), FP_i is the false positive rate (correct source code classified as erroneous), and FN_i is the false negative rate (erroneous source code classified as correct). F-measure is the harmonic mean between precision and recall. Usually, it is difficult to always obtain excellent precision and recall. If all samples are classified as erroneous, the recall will be high but precision will be low. F-measure is a balance between precision and recall. The F-measure value is between 0 and 1, where a higher value indicates better classification.

We evaluated the model performance in terms of classification accuracy using source code samples with logic and syntax errors. Figure 10 shows the classification results for source code with syntax errors. The results show that the precision and recall values for the proposed model are better than those for the other models.

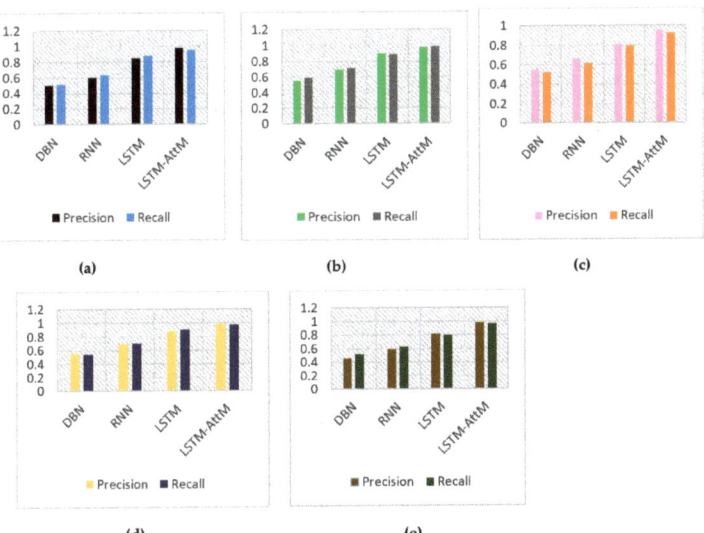

Figure 10. Comparison of precision and recall values for classification of source code with syntax errors for (**a**) Insertion Sort (IS), (**b**) Greatest Common Divisor (GCD), (**c**) Prime Numbers (PN), (**d**) Bubble Sort (BS), and (**e**) Selection Sort (SS).

We calculated the precision and recall values of each type of problem set. The proposed model had better values than those of the other models. The average precision, recall, and F-measure values are listed in Table 7.

Table 7. Average precision, recall, and F-measure values for classification of source code with syntax errors.

Model	Precision	Recall	F-Measure
DBN	0.50	0.50	0.50
RNN	0.54	0.58	0.56
LSTM	0.85	0.85	0.85
LSTM-AttM	0.97	0.96	**0.96**

Figure 11 shows the classification results for source code with logic errors. The average precision, recall, and F-measure values are listed in Table 8. The F-measure value indicates the excellent performance of the proposed LSTM-AttM model.

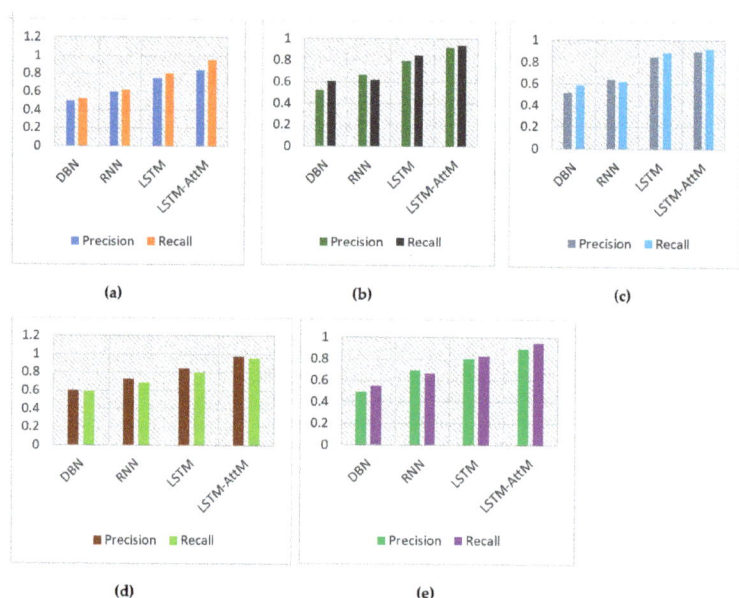

Figure 11. Comparison of precision and recall values for classification of source code with logic errors for (**a**) IS, (**b**) GCD, (**c**) PN, (**d**) BS, and (**e**) SS.

Table 8. Average precision, recall, and F-measure values for classification of source code with logic errors.

Model	Precision	Recall	F-Measure
DBN	0.53	0.50	0.51
RNN	0.55	0.56	0.55
LSTM	0.81	0.84	0.82
LSTM-AttM	0.91	0.95	**0.93**

6.6. Classification Result Comparison with Benchmark Models

We compared our experimental classification results with those for some baseline models. All the researches have a unique goal to achieve by respective research methodology. Nevertheless, we compared our proposed research with the most similar works. The results are presented in Table 9.

Table 9. Comparison with baseline models for defective source code classification.

Model	Description	F-Measure
RF+DBN [43]	RF is used for classification based on hidden features extracted using DBN.	0.50
RNN	A basic RNN is used to develop a language model for source code fault detection and prediction.	0.55
LSTM	A standard LSTM network is adapted to develop a language model for source code error detection, prediction, and classification.	0.79
DP-ARNN [30]	DP-ARNN is a defect prediction model that uses attention-based RNNs.	0.56
LSTM [29]	A source code error detection and prediction model based on a deep LSTM-based language model.	0.83
LSTM-AttM (Proposed)	A deep seq2seq language model that uses an attention mechanism + LSTM [29] network with customized hyperparameters for source code error assessment and detection and source code classification based on estimated error probability.	0.94

7. Discussion

The present research focused on source code fault assessment and classification. In software engineering and programming education, logic error assessment in source code is challenging for both student and professional programmers. We conducted experiments to assess and detect logic, semantic, and syntax errors in source code and classify source code as correct or incorrect using various models. The experimental results were compared with those for traditional unsupervised and other neural-network-based unsupervised models. The proposed model had the best performance.

The performance of a seq2seq language model strongly depends on the selection of the optimal number of hidden layers. This selection is based on the perplexity value. We calculated the perplexity during the training period. Figure 5 shows the perplexity of the RNN, LSTM, and LSTM-AttM models with various numbers of hidden layers at last epoch for various problems. The perplexity of 100, 150, and 300 layers are much higher than the 200 layers. Figure 6 shows the epoch-wise perplexity of models with 200 hidden layers for various problems. The perplexity was lowest for the 200-layer models that is why we selected 200-layer models for all experiments. We measured the training accuracy of the proposed language model and other models. The proposed LSTM-AttM model had the highest training accuracy (see Table 2).

In software engineering and programming education, the assessment and detection of logic errors in source code is a challenge. To address this problem, we used an attention-based language model using a deep LSTM neural network. After slight modification in source code pre-processing phase, the proposed model can be useful for any type of source code (Python, C++, Java, etc.). While a software system may be large, it has several functions (routines) that each have a limited number of lines. Some source codes are similar to such a routine. The difficulty level of each source code is not one, some source code uses complex mathematical logic and functions and some use simple. To evaluate our model, we used mixed (easy, medium, and hard) source code for error detection. The syntax error assessment and detection accuracy (see Table 4) for the proposed LSTM-AttM model was better than those for the LSTM and RNN models. The average accuracy of the proposed LSTM-AttM model was 94.8%, whereas those of LSTM and RNN models were 84.2% and 77.4%, respectively. The logic error assessment and detection accuracy is shown in Table 6. For logic error detection, the proposed model

(92.2%) outperformed LSTM (78.2%) and RNN (60.2%). To assess and detect logic errors in source code, the attention mechanism considers all input sequences because logic error detection is more complex than other error detection. The proposed model will especially help novice programmers most.

One of our main goals was to classify source code as either correct or incorrect. For this task, we used the estimated error probability of source code. The proposed LSTM-AttM model detects error candidates in source code and estimates the corresponding error probability for each error candidate word. The weight of the estimated error probability might vary because the language model generates the error probability for each error candidate word based on the training corpus. When the estimated error probability of any error candidate word is more than 0.90, the source code is treated as incorrect. The syntax error classification results are shown in Figure 10 and the average precision, recall, and F-measure values are listed in Table 7. The obtained precision, recall, and F-measure values of the proposed model are 0.97, 0.96, and 0.96, respectively, and those of the LSTM model are 0.85, 0.85, and 0.85, respectively. The precision and recall values for the classification of source code with logic errors for various problem sets are shown in Figure 11. The proposed model outperformed the LSTM and RNN models. The average precision, recall, and F-measure values for the classification of source code with logic errors are listed in Table 8. The average precision, recall, and F-measure values for the proposed model are 0.91, 0.95, and 0.93, respectively, better than those for the LSTM and RNN models. These classification comparison results verify the superiority of the proposed LSTM-AttM model over existing state-of-the-art models.

Source code classification results were also compared with those for some baseline models in Table 9. The F-measure value for the proposed model is 0.94, which is far better than those for the baseline models.

Finally, the experimental evaluation results demonstrate the superiority of the proposed model. Learners may get stuck when looking for logic errors and may thus spend a huge amount of time trying to fix them. In such cases, the proposed model can assist learners to accelerate the learning process. The model identifies errors and predicts the correct words, it also gives the line number for errors. The model can thus help students and programmers improve their programming skills and effectively create programs.

8. Conclusion and Future Work

In this study, we proposed an attention-based LSTM language model for assessing and classifying source code. In both programming education and software engineering, the proposed model can effectively help programmers. Conventional compilers cannot assess and detect logic errors in source code, and thus unexpected program output is generated. To avoid this adverse circumstance, the neural network-based language model achieves great success. The experimental results show that the accuracies of syntax and logic error detection using the LSTM-AttM model are approximately 94.8% and 92.2%, respectively. The proposed model calculates the error probability of all error candidate words in the source code and uses it to classify the source code as either correct or incorrect. The average precision, recall, and F-measure values of the proposed model are 0.97, 0.96, and 0.96, respectively, for the classification of source code with syntax errors and 0.91, 0.95, and 0.93, respectively, for the classification of source code with logic errors; these values are better than those for existing state-of-the-art models. The proposed model shows better performance for long sequences of source code compared to that for LSTM and RNN. Our model contributes to source code error assessment, detection, and classification, especially logic error detection and classification, for which conventional compiler fail. Furthermore, our model predicts the correct words in place of the error in the source code, making these predicted words helpful for students and programmers to quickly fix the incorrect code. In particular, newborn programmers will benefit more from the proposed model in learning programming. The proposed model has some limitations. Error assessment and detection accuracy are sometimes below the expected values. When the estimated error probability of an error candidate word is below 0.9, the proposed model does not consider this word as an error candidate even though it might be an error. The experimental results obtained from the source code based on the C programming language do not ensure that the model's performance will be the same as using other programming languages. In the future, we will work to resolve these issues using bidirectional LSTM and other deep neural networks. The proposed model can be integrated with an online-based judge system to evaluate source code.

Author Contributions: Conceptualization, M.M.R., Y.W. and K.N.; Data curation, M.M.R; Formal analysis, M.M.R; Funding acquisition, Y.W.; Methodology, M.M.R and Y.W.; Resources, M.M.R; Software, M.M.R; Supervision, Y.W.; Validation, M.M.R; Visualization, M.M.R; Writing – original draft, M.M.R; Writing – review & editing, M.M.R, Y.W. and K.N. All authors have read and agreed to the published version of the manuscript.

Funding: This work was supported by the Japan Society for the Promotion of Science (JSPS) under KAKENHI grant number 19K12252.

Conflicts of Interest: The authors declare no conflicts of interest.

Data Availability: We collected all the training and test datasets from the Aizu Online Judge (AOJ) system. The resources were accessed through the APIs for the websites https://onlinejudge.u-aizu.ac.jp/ and http://developers.u-aizu.ac.jp/index.

References

1. Minku, L.L.; Mendes, E.; Turhan, B. Data mining for software engineering and humans in the loop. *Prog. Artif. Intell.* **2016**, *5*, 307–314. [CrossRef]
2. Monperrus, M. Automatic software repair: A bibliography. *ACM Comput. Surv. (Csur)* **2018**, *51*, 1–24. [CrossRef]
3. Seo, H.; Sadowski, C.; Elbaum, S.; Aftandilian, E.; Bowdidge, R. Programmers' build errors: A case study (at google). In Proceedings of the 36th International Conference on Software Engineering (ICSE '14), Hyderabad, India, 31 May–7 June 2014; pp. 724–734.
4. Li, Z.; Jing, X.-Y.; Zhu, X. Progress on approaches to software defect prediction. *IET Softw.* **2018**, *12*, 161–175. [CrossRef]
5. Ozakıncı, R.; Tarhan, A. Early software defect prediction: A systematic map and review. *J. Syst. Softw.* **2018**, *144*, 216–239. [CrossRef]
6. Catal, C.; Diri, B. A systematic review of software fault prediction studies. *Expert Syst. Appl.* **2009**, *36*, 7346–7354. [CrossRef]
7. Halstead, M.H. *Elements of Software Science (Operating and Programming Systems Series)*, 2nd ed.; Elsevier: Amsterdam, The Netherlands, 1977.
8. McCabe, T.J. A complexity measure. *IEEE Trans. Softw. Eng.* **1976**, *SE-2*, 308–320. [CrossRef]
9. Jureczko, M.; Spinellis, D.D. Using object-oriented design metrics to predict software defects. In *Models and Methods of System Dependability*; Oficyna Wydawnicza Politechniki Wrocławskiej: Wrocław, Poland, 2010; pp. 69–81.
10. Pu, Y.; Narasimhan, K.; Solar-Lezama, A.; Barzilay, R. Sk_p: A neural program corrector for mooc. In Proceedings of the 2016 ACM SIGPLAN International Conference on Systems, Programming, Languages and Applications: Software for Humanity, Amsterdam, The Netherlands, 30 October–4 November 2016; pp. 39–40.
11. Pennington, J.; Socher, R.; Manning, C.D. Glove: Global vectors for word representation. In Proceedings of the 2014 Conference on Empirical Methods in Natural Language Processing (EMNLP), Doha, Qatar, 25–29 October 2014; pp. 1532–1543.
12. White, M.; Vendome, C.; Linares-Vásquez, M.; Poshyvanyk, D. Toward deep learning software repositories. In Proceedings of the 12th Working Conference on Mining Software Repositories (MSR '15), Florence, Italy, 16–17 May 2015; pp. 334–345.
13. Bengio, Y.; Boulanger-Lewandowski, N.; Pascanu, R. Advances in optimizing recurrent networks. In Proceedings of the 2013 IEEE International Conference on Acoustics, Speech and Signal Processing, Vancouver, BC, Canada, 26–31 May 2013; pp. 8624–8628.
14. Terada, K.; Watanobe, Y. Code Completion for Programming Education based on Recurrent Neural Network. In Proceedings of the 2019 IEEE 11th International Workshop on Computational Intelligence and Applications (IWCIA), Hiroshima, Japan, 9–10 November 2019; pp. 109–114.

15. Nagappan, N.; Ball, T. Using software dependencies and churn metrics to predict field failures: An empirical case study. In Proceedings of the First International Symposium on Empirical Software Engineering and Measurement (ESEM 2007), Madrid, Spain, 20–21 September 2007; pp. 364–373.
16. Moser, R.; Pedrycz, W.; Succi, G. A comparative analysis of the efficiency of change metrics and static code attributes for defect prediction. In Proceedings of the 30th International Conference on Software Engineering, Leipzig, Germany, 10–18 May 2008; pp. 181–190.
17. Arar, O.F.; Ayan, K. A feature dependent naive Bayes approach and its application to the software defect prediction problem. *Appl. Soft Comput.* **2017**, *59*, 197–209. [CrossRef]
18. Jing, X.-Y.; Ying, S.; Zhang, Z.-W.; Wu, S.-S.; Liu, J. Dictionary learning based software defect prediction. In Proceedings of the 36th International Conference on Software Engineering, Hyderabad, India, 31 May–7 June 2014; pp. 414–423.
19. Rahman, M.M.; Watanobe, Y. An efficient approach for selecting initial centroid and outlier detection of data clustering. In *Advancing Technology Industrialization Through Intelligent Software Methodologies, Tools and Techniques*; IOS Press: Amsterdam, The Netherlands, 2019; Volume 318, pp. 616–628.
20. Intisar, C.M.; Watanobe, Y. Classification of Online Judge Programmers based on Rule Extraction from Self Organizing Feature. In Proceedings of the 9th International Conference on Awareness Science and Technology (iCAST), Fukuoka, Japan, 19–21 September 2018; pp. 313–318.
21. Intisar, C.M.; Watanobe, Y. Cluster Analysis to Estimate the Difficulty of Programming Problems. In Proceedings of the 3rd International Conference on Applications in Information Technology (ICAIT '18), Aizu-Wakamatsu, Japan, 1–3 November 2018; pp. 23–28.
22. Alreshedy, K.; Dharmaretnam, D.; Germán, D.M.; Srinivasan, V.; Gulliver, T.A. SCC: Automatic Classification of Code Snippets. In Proceedings of the 2018 IEEE 18th International Working Conference on Source Code Analysis and Manipulation (SCAM), Madrid, Spain, 23–24 September 2018; pp. 203–208.
23. Ram, A.; Nagappan, M. Supervised Sentiment Classification with CNNs for Diverse SE Datasets. *arXiv* **2018**, arXiv:1812.09653.
24. Reyes, J.; Ramírez, D.; Paciello, J. Automatic classification of source code archives by programming language: A deep learning approach. In Proceedings of the 2016 International Conference on Computational Science and Computational Intelligence (CSCI), Las Vegas, NV, USA, 15–17 December 2016; pp. 514–519.
25. Terada, K.; Watanobe, Y. Automatic Generation of Fill-in-the-Blank Programming Problems. In Proceedings of the 2019 IEEE 13th International Symposium on Embedded Multicore/Many-core Systems-on-Chip (MCSoC), Singapore, 1–4 October 2019; pp. 187–193.
26. Tai, K.S.; Socher, R.; Manning, C.D. Improved semantic representations from tree-structured long short-term memory networks. In Proceedings of the 53rd Annual Meeting of the Association for Computational Linguistics and the 7th International Joint Conference on Natural Language Processing, Beijing, China, 26–31 July 2015; pp. 1556–1566.
27. Pedroni, M.; Meyer, B. Compiler error messages: What can help novices? In Proceedings of the 39th SIGCSE Technical Symposium on Computer Science Education, Portland, OR, USA, 12–15 March 2008; pp. 168–172.
28. Saito, T.; Watanobe, Y. Learning Path Recommendation System for Programming Education based on Neural Networks. *Int. J. Distance Educ. Technol. (Ijdet)* **2019**, *18*, 36–64. [CrossRef]
29. Teshima, Y.; Watanobe, Y. Bug detection based on LSTM networks and solution codes. In Proceedings of the 2018 IEEE International Conference on Systems, Man, and Cybernetics (SMC), Miyazaki, Japan, 7–10 October 2018; pp. 3541–3546.
30. Fan, G.; Diao, X.; Yu, H.; Yang, K.; Chen, L. Software Defect Prediction via Attention-Based Recurrent Neural Network. *Sci. Program.* **2019**, *2019*, 6230953. [CrossRef]
31. Ohashi, H.; Watanobe, Y. Convolutional Neural Network for Classification of Source Codes. In Proceedings of the 2019 IEEE 13th International Symposium on Embedded Multicore/Many-core Systems-on-Chip (MCSoC), Singapore, Singapore, 1–4 October 2019; pp. 194–200.
32. Graves, A. Generating Sequences with Recurrent Neural Networks. *arXiv* **2014**, arXiv:1308.0850.
33. Mnih, V.; Heess, N.; Graves, A.; Kavukcuoglu, K. Recurrent models of visual attention. In Proceedings of the 27th International Conference on Neural Information Processing Systems (NIPS), Montreal, QC, Canada, 8–13 December 2014; pp. 2204–2212.

34. Luong, T.; Pham, H.; Manning, C.D. Effective approaches to attention-based neural machine translation. In Proceedings of the 2015 Conference on Empirical Methods in Natural Language Processing (EMNLP), Lisbon, Portugal, 17–21 September 2015; pp. 1412–1421.
35. Chen, J.; Zhang, H.; He, X.; Nie, L.; Liu, W.; Chua, T.-S. Attentive collaborative filtering: Multimedia recommendation with item- and component-level attention. In Proceedings of the 40th International ACM SIGIR Conference on Research and Development in Information Retrieval (SIGIR '17), Shinjuku, Tokyo, Japan, 7–11 August 2017; pp. 335–344.
36. Cheng, J.; Dong, L.; Lapata, M. Long short-term memory-networks for machine reading. In Proceedings of the 2016 Conference on Empirical Methods in Natural Language Processing (EMNLP), Austin, TX, USA, 1–5 November 2016; pp. 551–561.
37. Bahdanau, D.; Cho, K.; Bengio, Y. Neural machine translation by jointly learning to align and translate. In Proceedings of the 3rd International Conference on Learning Representations (ICLR), San Diego, CA, USA, 7–9 May 2015; pp. 1–15.
38. Li, J.; Wang, Y.; Lyu, M.R.; King, I. Code completion with neural attention and pointer networks. In Proceedings of the 27th International Joint Conference on Artificial Intelligence (IJCAI'18), Stockholm, Sweden, 13–19 July 2018; pp. 4159–4165.
39. Watanobe, Y. Aizu Online Judge. 2017. Available online: https://onlinejudge.u-aizu.ac.jp/ (accessed on 10 October 2019).
40. Aizu Online Judge. Developers Site (api). 2004. Available online: http://developers.u-aizu.ac.jp/index (accessed on 10 October 2019).
41. Srivastava, N.; Hinton, G.; Krizhevsky, A.; Sutskever, I.; Salakhutdinov, R. Dropout: A simple way to prevent neural networks from overfitting. *J. Mach. Learn. Res.* **2014**, *15*, 1929–1958.
42. Kingma, D.P.; Ba, J. Adam: A Method for Stochastic Optimization. In Proceedings of the 3rd International Conference for Learning Representations (ICLR), San Diego, CA, USA, 7–9 May 2015; pp. 1–13.
43. Hinton, G. Deep belief networks. *Scholarpedia* **2009**, *4*, 2009. [CrossRef]

© 2020 by the authors. Licensee MDPI, Basel, Switzerland. This article is an open access article distributed under the terms and conditions of the Creative Commons Attribution (CC BY) license (http://creativecommons.org/licenses/by/4.0/).

Article

Cooperative Multi-Agent Reinforcement Learning with Conversation Knowledge for Dialogue Management

Shuyu Lei *[ORCID], Xiaojie Wang and Caixia Yuan

Center for Intelligence of Science and Technology (CIST), Beijing University of Posts and Telecommunications, Beijing 100876, China; xjwang@bupt.edu.cn (X.W.); yuancx@bupt.edu.cn (C.Y.)
* Correspondence: leishuyu@bupt.edu.cn

Received: 25 March 2020; Accepted: 9 April 2020; Published: 15 April 2020

Abstract: Dialogue management plays a vital role in task-oriented dialogue systems, which has become an active area of research in recent years. Despite the promising results brought from deep reinforcement learning, most of the studies need to develop a manual user simulator additionally. To address the time-consuming development of simulator policy, we propose a multi-agent dialogue model where an end-to-end dialogue manager and a user simulator are optimized simultaneously. Different from prior work, we optimize the two-agents from scratch and apply the reward shaping technology based on adjacency pairs constraints in conversational analysis to speed up learning and to avoid the derivation from normal human-human conversation. In addition, we generalize the one-to-one learning strategy to one-to-many learning strategy, where a dialogue manager can be concurrently optimized with various user simulators, to improve the performance of trained dialogue manager. The experimental results show that one-to-one agents trained with adjacency pairs constraints can converge faster and avoid derivation. In cross-model evaluation with human users involved, the dialogue manager trained in one-to-many strategy achieves the best performance.

Keywords: dialogue management; user simulation; reward shaping; conversation knowledge; multi-agent reinforcement learning

---

1. Introduction

A task-oriented dialogue system can help people accomplish specific goals, such as booking a hotel, seeking a restaurant information. A typical text-based task-oriented dialogue system mainly comprises three parts—Natural Language Understanding (NLU), Dialogue Management (DM), and Natural Language Generation (NLG). DM plays a vital role which infers dialogue state from NLU and provides appropriate action for NLG, and it has attracted much attention in recent years.

Recently, reinforcement learning has been widely studied as a data-driven approach for modeling DM [1–9], where a state tracker maintains dialogue states and a policy model chooses a proper action according to the current dialogue state. In most recent studies [4–9] on task-oriented dialogue tasks, Deep Reinforcement Learning (DRL) was utilized to train the policy model in order to achieve maximum long-term reward through interacting with a manual user simulator. To this end, most of the studies need the additional development of a user simulator in task-oriented dialogue system.

To address the time-consuming development of simulator policy issue, we propose a Multi-Agent Dialogue Model (MADM) where an end-to-end dialogue manager cooperates with a user simulator to fulfill the dialogue task. Since user simulator is treated as one agent in multi-agent, the simulator policy can be optimized in an automatic manner rather than laboring development. Different from prior work [10], we optimize the cooperative policies concurrently via multi-agent reinforcement learning from scratch without supervised initializing process. For user simulator reward function, we use the reward shaping technique [11] based on the adjacency pairs in conversational analysis [12] to make the simulator learn real user behaviors quickly. In addition, we generalize the one-to-one learning strategy to one-to-many learning strategy where a dialogue manager cooperates with various user simulators to improve the performance of trained dialogue manager. We obtain these various user simulators through changing the adjacency pairs settings, and then we mixture them with a dialogue manager to optimize the cooperative policies via multi-agent reinforcement learning.

Compared with MADM without the constraints, MADM trained with adjacency pairs constraints can converge faster and avoid derivation from normal human-human conversation. The experimental results also show that the dialogue manager trained with one-to-many strategy achieves the best performance in cross-model evaluation with human users involved. To summary, our main contributions in this work are three-fold:

1. We propose an MADM to optimize the cooperative policies between an end-to-end dialogue manager and a user simulator concurrently from scratch.
2. We apply reward shaping technique based on adjacency pairs to user simulator to speed learning and to help the MADM generate normal human-human conversation.
3. We further generalize the one-to-one learning strategy to one-to-many learning strategy to improve the performance for trained dialogue manager.

The rest of the paper is organized as follows—Section 2 gives an overview of related work. Section 3 describes the MADM model in detail. Section 4 discusses the experimental results and evaluations. Section 5 gives the conclusive discussions and the description of future work.

2. Related Work

Data-driven DM has become an active research area in the field of task-oriented dialogue system. In recent years, a lot of promising studies [1,2,4,7–9] worked on the policy model in dialogue system pipeline. Meanwhile, some studies [13–15] built the DM and NLU into an end-to-end model. In the above studies, the dialogue policy was optimized with a user simulator as a trial-and-error manner in reinforcement learning. However, the development of a user simulator was complex and it took considerable time to built an appropriate user policy. Additionally, some studies [4,5,14,16] relied on considerable supervised data. Reference [16] proposed an end-to-end model by jointly training NLU and DM with supervised learning. References [4,5,14] applied the demonstration data to speed up the convergence in a supervised manner. Preparing such supervised data is also laborious. Although some studies [3,17] could optimize the policy model via on-line human interaction, these methods required considerable human interaction. Meanwhile, the initial performance was still relatively poor, which could impact negatively on the user experience. Different from the above studies, the dialogue management in our framework is optimized from scratch without any laborious preparation for supervised data and development of user policy.

As the user simulator plays a vital role in reinforcement learning for optimizing dialogue policy, the studies on the user simulator also received a lot of attention. References [18–24] utilized the data-driven approach to develop the user simulator. However, such statistic-based methods required a lot of corpus. Once the training data were not sufficient, the data-driven simulator could only produce a simplex response. Dialogue management trained with such simplex simulator might converge to a solution with poor generalization performance. In addition, the obtained policy was uncontrollable with statistic-based methods. Thus, an alternative approach was based on agenda rules. Reference [25] proposed an agenda-based approach that does not necessarily need training data but can be trained in case such data are available. This agenda-based simulator was realistic enough to successfully test many DRL algorithms [6] and train a dialogue policy. However, the developer must maintain the rules operating on agenda, working as simulation policy, with domain expertise. Different from above studies, user simulator in our framework is optimized from scratch without the need of pre-defined rules or dialogue corpus.

To address the time-consuming development for simulator policy, recent studies [10,26,27] proposed a one-to-one dialogue model where a dialogue manager and a user simulator were optimized concurrently. Different from the above studies, our proposed MADM applies the reward shaping technique [11] based on the adjacency pairs in conversational analysis [12], which can help the cooperative policies learn from scratch quickly. By the method of reward shaping, our proposed MADM avoids running a learning algorithm multiple times in a study [26] and collects the corpora in studies [10,27].

Recently, multi-agent reinforcement learning has been applied in many interesting research areas. References [28,29] proposed a cooperative 'image guessing' game between two agents – Q-BOT and A-BOT– who communicate in natural language dialog so that Q-BOT can select an unseen image from a lineup of images. References [30,31] showed it was possible to train a multi-agent model for negotiation where agents with different goals attempt to agree on common decisions. Reference [32] pointed out that a competitive multi-agent environment trained with self-play could produce behaviors that were far more complex than the environment itself. Different from the above studies, we use the multi-agent reinforcement learning to model the cooperation between dialogue manager and user simulator.

3. Model

3.1. Notation

We consider a cooperative multi-agent reinforcement learning as a Decentralized Partially Observable Markov Decision Processes (Dec-POMDP) [33] defined with a tuple $(\alpha, \mathcal{S}, \{\mathcal{A}_i\}_{i \in \alpha}, \mathcal{T}, \{\mathcal{O}_i\}_{i \in \alpha}, \mathcal{Z}, \{\mathcal{R}_i\}_{i \in \alpha})$, where α is a set of n agents, $\mathcal{S}$ is a set of states of the world and the possible joint configuration of all the agents, $\mathcal{A}_i$ is a set of actions for agent i, the joint action space are defined as $\mathcal{A} = \mathcal{A}_1 \times ... \times \mathcal{A}_n$, $\mathcal{T} : \mathcal{S} \times \mathcal{A} \times \mathcal{S} \rightarrow [0,1]$ is a state transition function, $\mathcal{O}_i$ is a set of observations for agent i, the joint observation space are denoted as $\mathcal{O} = \mathcal{O}_1 \times ... \times \mathcal{O}_n$, $\mathcal{Z} : \mathcal{S} \times \mathcal{A} \times \mathcal{O} \rightarrow [0,1]$ is an observation function, $\mathcal{S}_i : \mathcal{S} \times \mathcal{A} \times \mathcal{S} \rightarrow \mathbb{R}$ is a reward function for agent i. For the cooperative multi-agent reinforcement learning, each agent i has the equal reward in every time step t. Each agent i chooses its own actions according to the policy function $\pi_i : \mathcal{O}_i \times \mathcal{A}_i \rightarrow [0,1]$. Each agent i aims to maximize its own long-term discounted reward $R_i = \sum_{t=0}^{T} \gamma^t r_{i,t}$, where γ is a discount factor and T is the time horizon.

3.2. Multi-Agent Dialogue Model (MADM)

We propose an MADM where a dialogue manager cooperates with a user simulator to fulfill the dialogue task based on cooperative multi-agent reinforcement learning. The entire architecture is illustrated in Figure 1. The basic MADM has two agents: a dialogue manager and a user simulator. This basic MADM can be generalized to MADM with multiple agents—a dialogue manager and various user simulators. The dialogue manager takes the historical dialogue sequence as input and then produces the selected action. The user simulator takes the action from the dialogue manager and then produces a user utterance back to dialogue manager. The dialogue manager and the user simulator are described in detail, respectively, as follows.

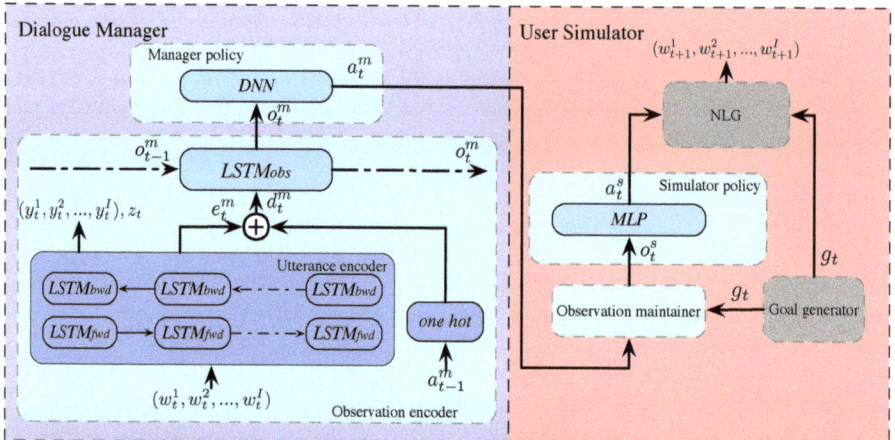

Figure 1. The cooperative multi-agent dialogue model between dialogue manager and user simulator.

3.2.1. Dialogue Manager

Dialogue manager consists of two parts: an observation encoder and a manager policy as shown in Figure 1. The observation encoder is employed to map historical dialogue sequence to observation representation. As some slot dependent actions (e.g., *confirm*()) need to combine with slot values from user utterances to make up an integral action, observation encoder also produces the slot values from user utterance through slot filling and intent recognition. The manager policy is applied to map the observation representation to a selected action for responding to user simulator. Observation encoder and manager policy are described in detail, respectively, as follows.

Observation encoder: the historical dialogue sequence $h_t = [a_0^m, u_1, ..., a_{t-1}^m, u_t]$ is encoded to an observation representation o_t^m, meanwhile, the slot values information y^t and the intent recognition information z^t are output, where a_{t-1}^m denotes the selected action from manager in time step $t-1$, $u_t = [w_t^1, w_t^2, ..., w_t^I]$ denotes the user utterance in time step t, w_t^i denotes the i-th word (or i-th character in Chinese) in the user utterance u_t, and $\hat{y}_t = [\hat{y}_t^1, \hat{y}_t^2, ..., \hat{y}_t^I]$ denotes the slot label information on user utterance u_t. To this end, a hierarchical recurrent neural network (HRNN) is applied to model observation encoder. In the bottom layer of HRNN, a bidirectional LSTM [34] with attention pooling is employed to obtain the sentence representation e_t^m for user utterance u_t, which is computed as follows:

$$\overrightarrow{c}_t^i = LSTM_{fwd}(\overrightarrow{c}_t^{i-1}, e(w_t^i)) \quad (1)$$

$$\overleftarrow{c}_t^i = LSTM_{bwd}(\overleftarrow{c}_t^{i+1}, e(w_t^i)) \quad (2)$$

$$e_t^i = \sum_{i=1}^{I} \alpha_i [\overrightarrow{c}_t^i \oplus \overleftarrow{c}_t^i] \quad (3)$$

$$\alpha_i = \frac{\exp q_t^i}{\sum_{i=1}^{I} \exp q_t^i} \quad (4)$$

$$q_t^i = g([\overrightarrow{c}_t^i \oplus \overleftarrow{c}_t^i]), \quad (5)$$

where $\overrightarrow{c}_t^i$ and $\overleftarrow{c}_t^i$ are the outputs of forward and backward LSTM in bottom layer of HRNN, respectively, e_t^i denotes the embedding of word w_t^i, $\oplus$ is the concatenation operator, α_i is the attention weights, and g is a feed-forward neural network. The bidirectional LSTM also outputs the slot values information $\hat{y}_t$ and the intent recognition information $\hat{z}^t$, which is computed as follows:

$$\hat{y}_t^i = \arg\max_{l}(softmax(\overrightarrow{c}_t^i \oplus \overleftarrow{c}_t^i)) \tag{6}$$

$$\hat{z}_t = \arg\max_{k}(softmax(\overrightarrow{c}_t^I \oplus \overleftarrow{c}_t^0)), \tag{7}$$

where l denotes the set of slot labels and k denotes the set of intent labels. In top layer of HRNN, a forward LSTM is applied to integrate the last observation representation o_{t-1}^m, last manager action a_{t-1}^m and current sentence representation e_t^m into current observation representation o_t^m, which is computed as follows:

$$d_t^m = e_t^m \oplus o(a_{t-1}^m) \tag{8}$$

$$o_t^m = LSTM_{obs}(o_{t-1}^m, d_t^m), \tag{9}$$

where d_t^m is the concatenation of sentence representation e_t^m and last action representation $o(a_{t-1}^m)$, and $o(a_{t-1}^m)$ is a one-hot vector with the corresponding action position set to 1.

Manager policy: the observation representation o_t^m is projected to the selected action a_t^m. To this end, a deep neural network (DNN) is applied to model manager policy, which is computed as follows:

$$\pi^m(a_t^m|o_t^m) = softmax(DNN(o_t^m)), \tag{10}$$

where policy function $\pi^m(a_t^m|o_t^m)$ is a probability distribution on the action space. The selected action a_t^m is drawn from the distribution $\pi^m(a_t^m|o_t^m)$. For convenience, $\pi^m(a_t^m|o_t^m;\theta^m)$ is denoted as the policy function of dialogue manager, where θ^m are the parameters of the manager policy.

3.2.2. User Simulator

User simulator is composed of four parts: a simulator observation maintainer, a goal generator, a simulator policy, and an NLG as shown in Figure 1. The observation maintainer is applied to obtain the observation representation for user simulator. The goal generator is used to produce the user goal (e.g., slot value) and simulate the goal change during a dialogue. The simulator policy is applied to map the observation representation to a selected action for generating a user utterance. The NLG is applied to generate the next user utterance to dialogue manager. The four parts of user simulator are described in detail, respectively, as follows.

Observation maintainer: the observation representation o_t^s is a concatenated vector composed of three parts: an embedding $o(a_t^m)$ for manager action a_t^m, a binary variable b_t that indicates whether the slot value in manager action a_t^m is null, and an indicative vector v_t that denotes which type of slot value in confirm-action received from manager is different from user goal g_t in time step t.

Goal generator: the user goal is generated at the start of the dialogue by sampling the candidate slot values uniformly. As the initial goal may change in a real user dialogue, the variation of user goals are also simulated during the interaction. For each session, the user goals are sampled from the candidate slot values randomly at the beginning of the dialogue, meanwhile, an indicative vector c_c, which counts the number of variations for each slot, is set to be a zeroes vector. This indicative vector c_c is used to limit the number of variations for each slot to avoid overly complex conversations. In each turn, a variation probability p_v is sampled from $[0,1]$ randomly, if this variation probability p_v is bigger than threshold probability p_{th}, then a random slot is selected to change the corresponding value to another one from candidate slot values. Once a slot value is changed, the corresponding value of variation slot in indicative vector c_c is added 1. If the number of variations for some slots exceed the limitation number, those slots will not be changed, even though the variation probability p_v is bigger than threshold probability p_{th}.

Simulator policy: the observation representation o_t^s is mapped to the selected action a_t^s. To this end, a multi-layer perceptron (MLP) is applied to model simulator policy, which is computed as follows:

$$\pi^s(a_t^s|o_t^s) = softmax(MLP(o_t^s)), \tag{11}$$

where policy function $\pi^s(a_t^s|o_t^s)$ is a probability distribution on the action space. The selected action a_t^s is drawn from the distribution $\pi^s(a_t^s|o_t^s)$. For convenience, $\pi^s(a_t^s|o_t^s;\theta^s)$ is denoted as policy function of user simulator, where θ^s are the parameters of the simulator policy.

NLG: the selected action a_t^s is projected to next user utterance u_{t+1} for replying to dialogue manager. A template-based NLG is used to produce such user utterances. The responding template is drawn from a set of pre-defined templates according to the selected action a_t^s. To assure the generalization and expressiveness, the templates are delexicalized by replacing concrete slot values with their slot names. For some slot dependent actions (e.g., inform()), the drawn template is lexicalized with the goal slot values to generate the final user utterance. An example of user utterance generation is shown in Figure 2, where B-loc, I-loc and O denote the slot labels of the beginning character of a location, inter character of a location and other characters, respectively.

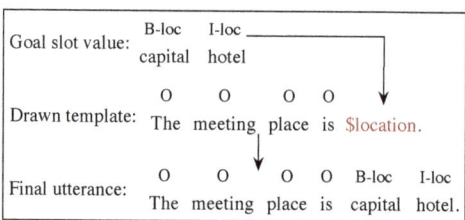

Figure 2. An example of user utterance generation.

3.3. Cooperative Training

Policy gradient: the policy gradient is applied to compute an estimate of the gradient of policy parameters in order to maximize the long-term discounted reward. In a cooperative dialogue, the gradient of manager policy and simulator policy are denoted as follows:

$$\nabla_{\theta^m} J(\theta^m) = \mathbb{E}_{\pi^m,\pi^s}[A^m(a^m,o^m)\nabla_{\theta^m}\log \pi^m(a^m|o^m)] \tag{12}$$

$$\nabla_{\theta^s} J(\theta^s) = \mathbb{E}_{\pi^m,\pi^s}[A^s(a^s,o^s)\nabla_{\theta^s}\log \pi^s(a^s|o^s)], \tag{13}$$

where $A^m(a^m,o^m)$ is the advantage function of manager, and $A^s(a^s,o^s)$ is the advantage function of simulator. REINFORCE with a baseline algorithm [35] is applied to estimate the advantage functions. Thus, the advantage function $A^m(a^m,o^m)$ and the advantage function $A^m(a^m,o^m)$ are computed as follows:

$$A^m(a_t^m,o_t^m) = \sum_{j=0}^{J}\gamma^j r_{t+j} - V^{\pi^m}(o_t^m;\phi^m) \tag{14}$$

$$A^s(a_t^s,o_t^s) = \sum_{j=0}^{J}\gamma^j r_{t+j} - V^{\pi^s}(o_t^s;\phi^s), \tag{15}$$

where $V^{\pi^m}(o_t^m;\phi^m)$ is the value function of manager with parameters ϕ^m to estimate the return on observation o_t^m, and $V^{\pi^s}(o_t^s;\phi^s)$ is the value function of simulator with parameters ϕ^s to estimate the return on observation o_t^s. The loss functions of $V^{\pi^m}(o_t^m;\phi^m)$ and $V^{\pi^s}(o_t^s;\phi^s)$ are computed as follows:

$$J(\phi^m) = \frac{1}{2}[A^m(a_t^m,o_t^m)]^2 \tag{16}$$

$$J(\phi^s) = \frac{1}{2}[A^s(a_t^s,o_t^s)]^2. \tag{17}$$

The value function $V^{\pi^m}(o_t^m;\phi^m)$ and policy function $\pi^m(a_t^m|o_t^m;\theta^m)$ share the same parameters, meanwhile, the slot filling and intent recognition are optimized in a supervised manner jointly. To this end, the total loss function of dialogue manager is computed as follows:

$$J_r(\theta^m) = -A^m(a^m,o^m)\nabla_{\theta^m}\log \pi^m(a^m|o^m) + \frac{1}{2}[A^m(a^m,o^m)]^2 \tag{18}$$

$$J_s(\theta^m) = \sum_{t=1}^{T}\sum_{i=1}^{I}\hat{y}_t^i\log y_t^i + \sum_{t=1}^{T}\hat{z}_t\log z_t \tag{19}$$

$$J_w(\theta^m) = (1-\lambda)J_r(\theta^m) + \lambda J_s(\theta^m), \tag{20}$$

where $\lambda \in (0,1]$ is a balance coefficient. Similar to dialogue manager, the value function $V^{\pi^s}(o_t^s;\phi^s)$ and policy function $\pi^s(a_t^s|o_t^s;\theta^s)$ share the same parameters in user simulator. The total loss function of user simulator is computed as follows:

$$J_w(\theta^s) = -A^s(a^s,o^s)\nabla_{\theta^s}\log \pi^s(a^s|o^s) + \frac{1}{2}[A^s(a^s,o^s)]^2. \tag{21}$$

The two total-loss functions are optimized cooperatively after a complete dialogue. In this way, the dialogue manager and the user simulator are optimized cooperatively and simultaneously. The alternate training method was tried to optimize dialogue manager and user simulator, and empirical results show that alternate training method (every 10 training steps alternately) has slower convergence than joint training method and achieves the same performance with training jointly.

Above all, the dialogue manager and the user simulator are optimized cooperatively in a one-to-one manner. To improve the dialogue manager generalization performance, this one-to-one cooperation is generalized to one-to-many cooperation where a dialogue manager cooperates with various user simulators. These various user simulators are obtained through changing the settings of adjacency pairs as described in the next paragraph. For one training step, dialogue manager interacts with one user simulator to fulfill a complete dialogue, then the dialogue manager and the current simulator are optimized via one-to-one training. For next training step, dialogue manger changes to anther simulator to learn the cooperative policies. In this way, the dialogue management and the various user simulators are optimized in a one-to-many manner alternately. We tried to use multi one-to-one parallelly then share the gradient of dialogue manager, and empirically observed that sharing gradient optimization is slower than learning one-by-one.

Reward shaping based on adjacency pairs: In cooperative multi-agent reinforcement learning, each agent has the same reward for every time step. The naive reward function is assigned as follows:

- Manager reward $r(s_{t-1},a_{t-1}^m,s_t)$ and simulator reward $r(s_{t-1},a_{t-1}^s,s_t)$ are both +1, if s_t is a successful completed state.
- Manager reward $r(s_{t-1},a_{t-1}^m,s_t)$ and simulator reward $r(s_{t-1},a_{t-1}^s,s_t)$ are both −1, if s_t is not a successful completed state until the maximum length T in a dialogue.
- Manager reward $r(s_{t-1},a_{t-1}^m,s_t)$ and simulator reward $r(s_{t-1},a_{t-1}^s,s_t)$ are both −0.01 in otherwise.

This credit-assignment approach is sparse and delayed when a successful cooperative dialogue between dialogue manager and user simulator has a long trajectory. In cold start situation, as the initial cooperative polices are nearly random, the successful dialogue with a long trajectory is easier to be generated than one with a short trajectory. This credit-assignment approach leads to a slow convergence. To alleviate this problem, we use the reward shaping technique [11] based on the adjacency pairs in conversational analysis [12] to substitute the reward in user simulator. The reward based on the adjacency pairs is assigned as follows:

- Simulator reward $r(s_{t-1}, a^s_{t-1}, s_t)$ is -0.01, if s_t is a non-terminal state and the action pair $[a^m_{t-1}, a^s_{t-1}]$ does not belong to the set of adjacency pairs.
- Simulator reward $r(s_{t-1}, a^s_{t-1}, s_t)$ is r_s, if s_t is a non-terminal state and the action pair $[a^m_{t-1}, a^s_{t-1}]$ does not belong to the set of adjacency pairs, where r_s is the shaping reward greater than -0.01.
- Manager reward $r(s_{t-1}, a^m_{t-1}, s_t)$ and simulator reward $r(s_{t-1}, a^s_{t-1}, s_t)$ are both $+1$, if s_t is a successful completed state.
- Manager reward $r(s_{t-1}, a^m_{t-1}, s_t)$ and simulator reward $r(s_{t-1}, a^s_{t-1}, s_t)$ are both -1, if s_t is not a successful completed state until the dialogue reaches maximum length T in a dialogue.
- Manager reward $r(s_{t-1}, a^m_{t-1}, s_t)$ is -0.01, if s_t is a non-terminal state.

Through changing the set of adjacency pairs, various user simulators can be obtained. For non-shaped reward setting, each agent has the equal reward every time step. For shaped reward setting, each agent aims to maximize its own long-term discounted reward.

4. Experiment

To assess the performance, cross-model evaluation [36] is applied that is, training on one simulator and testing on the other. In our cross-model evaluation, human users also take part in the test for different dialogue managers. The evaluation is happened on Chinese meeting room booking tasks. It is worth nothing that our proposed framework can be directly utilized on English tasks by substituting Chinese characters to English words as inputs.

4.1. Dataset

The dataset was collected from 300 human-human dialogues on booking Chinese meeting room task. The average length of collected dialogues is approximately 16 turns. For the NLG in user simulator, 255 pre-defined templates and 240 slot values are extracted from collected dialogues. The dialogue manager consists of 7 dialogue acts and 3 slots and the user simulator consists of 10 dialogue acts, as shown in Table 1.

Table 1. lists all dialogue acts in details.

	Dialogue Acts
Dialogue manager	ask_date,ask_location,ask_attendance, confirm_date,confirm_location,confirm_attendance,bye
User simulator	inform_date,inform_location,inform_attendance,update_date, update_location,update_attendance,affirm,deny,error,hello

4.2. Cross-Model Evaluation with Human Users Involved

4.2.1. Users for Cross-Model Evaluation

To access the performance on different dialogue managers, simulated users and human users take part in the cross-model evaluation.

A group of user simulators (Group-S): This group of user simulators is obtained through changing the settings of adjacency pairs and is optimized with the dialogue manager in MADM as one-to-many strategy via multi-agent reinforcement learning. The Group-S is composed of five different simulators: all-simulator where all the types of adjacency pairs is applied to reward shaping, ask-simulator where only ask-action adjacency pairs (e.g., ask_loc() to inform_loc()) is applied to reward shaping, confirm-simulator where only confirm-action adjacency pairs (e.g., confirm_loc() to affirm()) is applied to reward shaping, bye-simulator where only bye-action adjacency pairs (e.g., bye() to bye()) is applied to reward shaping and naive-simulator where no adjacency pairs is applied. The shaping reward r_s is set to +0.01. The probability of simulating goal change is set to 0.5. Each slot is limited to change once to avoid overly complex conversations. For the NLG, the collected pre-defined templates are used to generate the user utterance through lexicalization as described in Section 3.2.2. Different dialogue managers are tested with each simulator in Group-S through interacting 200 episodes.

A rule-based user simulator (Rule-S): This simulator is developed according to the mode proposed in Reference [25,37]. The naive reward function is used in Section 3.3. The same settings in Group-S is used for goal generator and NLG. Different dialogue managers are tested with this Rule-S through interacting 200 episodes.

Human Users: 25 graduate volunteers are recruited to conduct human users test. Comparing different model subjectively on human users always suffers from unfairness and human user may fit in the system gradually. Thus, human users test is conducted in a paralleled manner and is evaluated in objective assessment whether the system can help users accomplish tasks or not. Before testing, the specific user goals are allocated to each users. In the guide of the same allocated goal, the human users use the same natural language to interact with different dialogue managers. Each of the volunteers conducts two parallel tests on different dialogue managers.

4.2.2. Dialogue Managers for Cross-Model Evaluation

To benchmark the dialogue manager from MADM trained as one-to-many strategy, five dialogue managers take part in the cross-model evaluation.

A dialogue manager from MADM trained as one-to-many strategy (M-MADM-OM): This end-to-end dialogue manager is built based on the dialogue manager as described in MADM and optimized with the Group-S concurrently via multi-agent reinforcement learning. The character is used as the model inputs, the size of character embedding is set to 8, the hidden sizes of the LSTM in bottom layer of HRNN and LSTM in bottom layer of HRNN are both set to 16, the sizes of two hidden layers in DNN are both set to 16 and the balance coefficient λ is 0.5.

A dialogue manager trained with Rule-S (Rule-M): This end-to-end dialogue manager is implemented with the same inputs and structures as dialogue manager in MADM and is optimized with the Rule-S through REINFORCE with baseline algorithm.

Yang 2017 [16]: A end-to-end dialogue manager is implemented as those in Reference [16]. The hidden size of the LSTM for NLU and system action prediction are both set to 16. This model is optimized with standard supervised learning.

Zhao 2016 [13]: A end-to-end dialogue manager is implemented with the same inputs and structure as those in Reference [13]. The hidden size of the LSTM is set to 256. The size of hidden layer which maps LSTM output to action is 128. As the model in Reference [13] can only parse a Yes/No answer, we connect this model with additional NLU. This NLU is modeled with a bi-directional LSTM separately. The hidden size of separate bi-directional LSTM is set to 32. This model optimized with REINFORCE with baseline outperforms the one optimized with deep Q-learning after repeated experiments in our dialogue tasks. Thus, REINFORCE with baseline algorithm is used to optimize this model with the Rule-S.

Peng 2018 [9]: A dialogue manager implements a model with the same inputs and structures as dialogue manager in MADM. This dialogue manager is optimized with deep dyna-Q with a world model and a user simulator. The world model is implemented with the same structure as in Reference [9], where the input is the concatenation of an observation representation o_t^m and an embedding of dialogue manager action a_t^m, where the size of hidden layer is set to 16. The user simulator uses the same setting in Rule-S.

4.2.3. Results

The results of the cross-model evaluation on success rate and average turns are shown in Table 2. In Group-S test, M-MADM-OM achieves the best performance. In Rule-S test, although M-MADM-OM does not achieve the best performance, it is only 0.2% lower than Rule-M and Peng 2018 [9]. In human users test, M-MADM-OM achieves the best performance. Above all, our proposed M-MADM-OM achieves the best performance in cross-model evaluation.

Table 2. Cross-model evaluation on Success Rate (SR) and Average Turns (AT).

	Group-S		Rule-S		Human Users	
	SR	AT	SR	AT	SR	AT
M-MADM-OM	**0.902**	**18.86**	0.925	17.28	**0.84**	**18.04**
Rule-M	0.582	24.94	**0.945**	**17.04**	0.76	19.56
Yang2017	0.577	25.03	0.860	21.56	0.68	21.08
Zhao2016	0.433	27.77	0.890	20.99	0.68	20.02
Peng2018	0.428	27.86	**0.945**	18.44	0.72	20.32

For the simulators performance, comparing Group-S test with Rule-S test, dialogue managers trained with Rule-S show the bad performance while interacting with Group-S. This phenomenon shows that Group-S may generate some user behaviors that Rule-S are unable to simulate. Comparing Group-S test with human users test, the results of human users are better than Group-S, which means that Group-S generate some user behaviors that human users may not produce. Even so, to our surprise, the Group-S can improve the concurrent dialogue manager performance on human users test.

Since our method applies a dynamic adjusted simulator without extensive involving of human laboring, the built model is more time efficient in a long run, even though it is slower in learning an optimal dialogue manager compared with the one-to-one methods with rule-based user simulator (including the work in Reference [9]). As empirical analysis, we observed that dialogue manager with dynamic adjusted simulator is four hours slower than deep dyna-Q method in Reference [9] as the same experimental settings, finally we obtained the optimized simulator with better generalization ability and without involving any more human efforts.

4.2.4. Good Case Study

Considering the improvement on M-MADM-OM in real scenario, two examples compared between M-MADM-OM and Rule-M are shown in Table 3. The Rule-M may fail in the case that the user always gives irrelevant answer (e.g., system request the number of people and user inform the date of the meeting). On the other hand, the M-MADM-OM can tackle such irrelevant answer and guide the user to inform the rest of slots. This is because the Group-S may generate more user behaviors than Rule-S, and M-MADM-OM can learn more robust policy for real scenario than Rule-M.

Table 3. Two sample dialogue sessions on human users comparing M-MADM-OM with Rule-M dialogue manager (SYS: system, USR: human user).

M-MADM-OM	Rule-M
1 SYS: Hello, where is the meeting?	1 SYS: Hello, where is the meeting?
2 USR:The location is in bupt technology building.	2 USR:The location is in bupt technology building.
3 SYS: Please confirm, the meeting place is in bupt technology building?	3 SYS: Please confirm, the meeting place is in bupt technology building?
4 USR:Yes.	4 USR:Yes.
5 SYS: How many people are there?	5 SYS: How many people are there?
6 USR:The meeting will be held at 10 a.m. on 5 April 2019.	6 USR:The meeting will be held at 10 a.m. on 5 April 2019.
7 SYS: Will the meeting be held at 10 a.m. on 5 April 2019?	7 SYS: How many people are there?
8 USR:Sorry, please change 2 p.m. on 5 April 2019.	8 USR:The meeting will be held at 10 a.m. on 5 April 2019.
9 SYS: Please confirm. the meeting be held at 2 p.m. on 5 April 2019?	9 SYS: How many people are there?
10 USR:Pefect.	.
11 SYS: How many people are there?	.
12 USR:Eight.	.
13 SYS: Is there eight people to participate?	32 SYS: How many people are there?
14 USR:For sure.	
15 SYS: Booked at 14:00 on 5 April 2019 Sixth meeting room at bupt technology building for you, if there are any questions, please call 010-52810888, good bye.	
Success	**Failure:** System does not book the right meeting room within the max turn

4.3. Ablation

The ablation experiments are conducted to evaluate efficiency of the different settings on adjacency pairs for reward shaping and the generalization performance on M-MADM-OM.

4.3.1. Adjacency Pair Performance

Considering reward shaping influence on convergence, the different adjacency pairs settings for reward shaping are compared. There are five settings: all the types of adjacency pairs, only ask-action adjacency pairs, only confirm-action adjacency pairs, only bye-action adjacency pairs and naive reward function. The training curves are shown in Figure 3. These success rate curves are obtained through testing dialogue managers with their respective learning simulator after every 300 training steps. Two settings (i.e., all the types of adjacency pairs and only ask-action adjacency pairs) achieve the best performance on speed up learning.

As the learning from scratch may cause that learned policy deviate from normal human-human conversation, these final dialogue managers are also tested with human users to check whether they deviate from normal human-human conversation or not. The same paralleled test strategy as described in Section 4.2.1 is conducted in human users test. The success rate and average turns are shown in Table 4. Results show that only all the types of adjacency pairs outperform the Rule-M. Other settings show bad performance on human users test. There are two reason for this: slow convergence and derivation from normal human-human conversation. Above results demonstrate that all the types of adjacency pairs for reward shaping can speed learning and avoid derivation from normal human-human conversation.

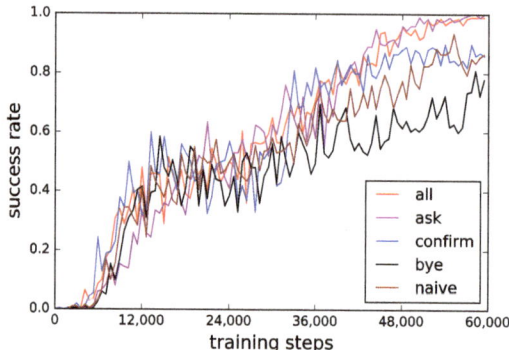

Figure 3. Training curves for different adjacency pairs settings.

Table 4. Human users evaluation on Success Rate (SR) and Average Turns (AT).

	Human Users	
	SR	AT
All	0.80	19.80
Ask	0.62	23.22
Confirm	0.30	27.30
Bye	0.22	20.00
Naive	0.32	21.30
Rule-M	0.76	19.56

4.3.2. Comparison of Various Simualtors Settings in One-to-Many Learning

Considering the various simualtors settings in one-to-many learning, we compare the combination of multiple simulators. Since we change the adjacency pairs settings to obtain the different user simulators, we can get 31 combinations based on five seed simulators (i.e., all, ask, confirm, bye and naive). We compare M-MADM-OM with the dialogue managers trained with all combinations containing two simulators, and then show the success rate and average turns in Table 5. We observe that dialogue managers trained with the conbinations containing an all-simulator outperform those dialogue managers trained without the all-simulator on the Group-S and the Rule-S, meanwhile, we observe that all the dialogue managers can achieve the roughly same performance on corresponding trained simulators. We obtain the same results in one-to-three and one-to-four learning. Through the aforementioned results, we think user behaviors generated by the all-simulator can cover user behaviors generated by the Rule-S and the other simulators can generate some user behaviors that the Rule-S can not generate. Thus, we use the combination of five seed simulators to train the M-MADM-OM jointly to improve the robustness and generalization.

Table 5. The different combinations of seed simulators in one-to-two learning on Success Rate (SR) and Average Turns (AT) (Corresponding-S denotes the corresponding training simulators).

	Group-S		Rule-S		Corresponding-S	
	SR	AT	SR	AT	SR	B
M-MADM-OM	0.902	18.86	0.925	17.28	0.902	18.86
all&ask	0.875	19.42	0.895	19.01	0.905	18.93
all&confirm	0.860	19.64	0.895	18.95	0.910	18.92
all&bye	0.825	20.34	0.905	18.65	0.905	18.85
all&naive	0.835	20.07	0.880	19.27	0.900	18.94
ask&confirm	0.825	24.94	0.645	23.73	0.895	18.91
ask&bye	0.760	21.43	0.645	25.52	0.900	18.89
ask&naive	0.815	20.02	0.550	24.73	0.895	18.93
confirm&bye	0.730	22.08	0.590	18.95	0.895	18.91
confirm&naive	0.725	22.23	0.505	17.04	0.905	18.89

4.3.3. One-to-One Learning vs. One-to-Many Learning

Considering the difference between one-to-one learning strategy and one-to-many learning strategy. The cross-model evaluation is conducted on two dialogue managers: M-MADM-OM and M-MADM-OO, where the M-MADM-OO is optimized via one-to-one learning strategy with all the types of adjacency pairs for reward shaping. For the users in cross-model evaluation, a simulator (MADM-S) trained with M-MADM-OO, Group-S, Rule-S and human users are employed. The results of cross-evaluation on comparing M-MADM-OM with M-MADM-OO is shown in Table 6. Results show that M-MADM-OM outperforms M-MADM-OO in cross-model evaluation, which demonstrates that one-to-many learning strategy can improve the generalization performance of dialogue manager.

Table 6. Cross-model evaluation on Success Rate (SR) and Average Turns (AT).

	MADM-S		Group-S		Rule-S		Human Users	
	SR	AT	SR	AT	SR	AT	SR	AT
M-MADM-OM	0.980	17.38	0.902	18.86	0.925	17.28	0.84	18.04
M-MADM-OO	0.975	17.47	0.775	21.27	0.935	18.23	0.78	19.80

5. Conclusions

We introduce a MADM, where an end-to-end dialogue manager cooperates with a user simulator to fulfill a dialogue task. For user simulator reward function, we use the reward shaping technique based on the adjacency pairs to make the simulator learn real user behaviors quickly while learning from scratch. The experimental results show that reward shaping technique speeds up learning and avoids derivation from normal human-human conversation. In addition, we generalize the one-to-one learning strategy to one-to-many learning strategy where a dialogue manager cooperates with various user simulators, which are obtained by changing the adjacency pairs settings. The experimental results also show that the dialogue manager from MADM-OM achieves the best performance on human users involving cross-model evaluation.

In our proposed MADM, there are several models that can be applied to get utterance embedding in dialogue manager, such as TextCNN [38], BERT [39] and XLnet [40]. But these contextualized model is orthogonal to MADM. In the future, we are planning to substitute these models to the bottom bidirectional LSTM in dialogue manager. In addition, we will collect more dataset to enrich the templates expressiveness for NLG and train the models iteratively.

Author Contributions: Methodology, S.L.; formal analysis, X.W.; data curation, S.L.; writing–original draft preparation, S.L.; writing–review and editing, C.Y.; funding acquisition, X.W. All authors have read and agreed to the published version of the manuscript.

Funding: This research was funded by NSFC (No.61273365).

Acknowledgments: This paper is supported by 111Project (No. B08004), Beijing Advanced Innovation Center for Imaging Technology, Engineering Research Center of Information Networks of MOE, China. The authors would like to thank the reviewers for their comments and suggestions.

Conflicts of Interest: The authors declare no conflict of interest.

Abbreviations

The following abbreviations are used in this manuscript:

NLU	Natural Language Understanding
DM	Dialogue Management
NLG	Natural Language Generation
DRL	Deep Reinforcement Learning
MADM	Multi-Agent Dialogue Model
HRNN	Hierarchical Recurrent Neural Network
LSTM	Long Short-Term Memory
DNN	Deep Neural Network
MLP	Multi-Layer Perceptron
ST	Success Rate
AT	Average Turns

References

1. Williams, J.D.; Young, S. Scaling POMDPs for spoken dialog management. *TASLP* **2007**, *15*, 2116–2129. [CrossRef]
2. Young, S.; Gasic, M.; Thomson, B.; Williams, J.D. POMDP-Based Statistical Spoken Dialog Systems: A Review. *Proc. IEEE* **2013**, *5*, 1160–1179. [CrossRef]
3. Gašić, M.; Breslin, C.; Henderson, M.; Kim, D.; Szummer, M.; Thomson, B.; Tsiakoulis, P.; Young, S. On-line policy optimisation of bayesian spoken dialogue systems via human interaction. In Proceedings of the 2013 IEEE International Conference on Acoustics, Speech and Signal Processing, Vancouver, BC, Canada, 26–31 May 2013; pp. 8367–8371.
4. Fatemi, M.; Asri, L.E.; Schulz, H.; He, J.; Suleman, K. Policy networks with two-stage training for dialogue systems. *arXiv* **2016**, arXiv:1606.03152.
5. Su, P.H.; Budzianowski, P.; Ultes, S.; Gasic, M.; Young, S. Sample-efficient Actor-Critic Reinforcement Learning with Supervised Data for Dialogue Management. *arXiv* **2017**, arXiv:1707.00130.
6. Casanueva, I.; Budzianowski, P.; Su, P.H.; Mrkšić, N.; Wen, T.H.; Ultes, S.; Rojas-Barahona, L.; Young, S.; Gašić, M. A benchmarking environment for reinforcement learning based task oriented dialogue management. *arXiv* **2017**, arXiv:1711.11023.
7. Weisz, G.; Budzianowski, P.; Su, P.H.; Gasic, M. Sample Efficient Deep Reinforcement Learning for Dialogue Systems With Large Action Spaces. *IEEE/ACM Trans. Audio Speech Lang. Process.* **2018**, 2083–2097. [CrossRef]
8. Peng, B.; Li, X.; Gao, J.; Liu, J.; Chen, Y.N.; Wong, K.F. Adversarial advantage actor-critic model for task-completion dialogue policy learning. In Proceedings of the 2018 IEEE International Conference on Acoustics, Speech and Signal Processing (ICASSP), Calgary, AB, Canada, 15–20 April 2018; pp. 6149–6153.
9. Peng, B.; Li, X.; Gao, J.; Liu, J.; Wong, K.F. Deep Dyna-Q: Integrating Planning for Task-Completion Dialogue Policy Learning. *arXiv* **2018**, arXiv:1801.06176.
10. Liu, B.; Lane, I. Iterative policy learning in end-to-end trainable task-oriented neural dialog models. In Proceedings of the 2017 IEEE Automatic Speech Recognition and Understanding Workshop (ASRU), Okinawa, Japan, 16–20 December 2017; pp. 482–489.
11. Ng, A.Y.; Harada, D.; Russell, S. Policy invariance under reward transformations: Theory and application to reward shaping. In Proceedings of the Sixteenth International Conference on Machine Learning (ICML), Bled, Slovenia, 27–30 June 1999; pp. 278–287.
12. Liddicoat, A.J. Adjacency pairs. In *An Introduction to Conversation Analysis*; Bloomsbury Publishing: London, UK, 2011; pp. 143–145.
13. Zhao, T.; Eskenazi, M. Towards End-to-End Learning for Dialog State Tracking and Management using Deep Reinforcement Learning. *arXiv* **2016**, arXiv:1606.02560.

14. Williams, J.D.; Atui, K.A.; Zweig, G. Hybrid Code Networks: practical and efficient end-to-end dialog control with supervised and reinforcement learning. *arXiv* **2017**, arXiv:1702.03274.
15. Dhingra, B.; Li, L.; Li, X.; Gao, J.; Chen, Y.N.; Ahmad, F.; Deng, L. Towards End-to-End Reinforcement Learning of Dialogue Agents for Information Access. *arXiv* **2017**, arXiv:1609.00777.
16. Yang, X.; Chen, Y.N.; Hakkani-Tür, D.; Crook, P.; Li, X.; Gao, J.; Deng, L. End-to-end joint learning of natural language understanding and dialogue manager. In Proceedings of the 2017 IEEE International Conference on Acoustics, Speech and Signal Processing (ICASSP), New Orleans, LA, USA, 5–9 March 2017; pp. 5690–5694.
17. Pietquin, O.; Geist, M.; Chandramohan, S. Sample efficient on-line learning of optimal dialogue policies with kalman temporal differences. In Proceedings of the Twenty-Second International Joint Conference on Artificial Intelligence, Barcelona, Spain, 16–22 July 2011; pp. 1878–1883.
18. Scheffler, K.; Young, S. Automatic learning of dialogue strategy using dialogue simulation and reinforcement learning. In Proceedings of the Second International Conference on Human Language Technology Research, San Diego, CA, USA, 24–27 March 2002; pp. 12–19.
19. Cuayáhuitl, H.; Renals, S.; Lemon, O.; Shimodaira, H. Human-computer dialogue simulation using hidden markov models. In Proceedings of the IEEE Workshop on Automatic Speech Recognition and Understanding, San Juan, Puerto Rico, 27 November–1 December 2005; pp. 290–295.
20. Pietquin, O.; Dutoit, T. A probabilistic framework for dialog simulation and optimal strategy learning. *IEEE Trans. Audio Speech Lang. Process.* **2006**, *14*, 589–599. [CrossRef]
21. Keizer, S.; Gasic, M.; Mairesse, F.; Thomson, B.; Yu, K.; Young, S. Modelling user behaviour in the HIS-POMDP dialogue manager. In Proceedings of the 2008 IEEE Spoken Language Technology Workshop, Goa, India, 15–19 December 2008; pp. 121–124.
22. Chandramohan, S.; Geis, M.; Lefèvre, F.; Pietquin, O. User Simulation in Dialogue Systems Using Inverse Reinforcement Learning. In Proceedings of the 12th Annual Conference of the International Speech Communication Association, Florence, Italy, 27–31 August, 2011; pp.1025–1028.
23. El Asri, L.; Hem, J.; Suleman, K. A Sequence-to-Sequence Model for User Simulation in Spoken Dialogue Systems. *Interspeech* **2016**, 1151–1155. [CrossRef]
24. Kreyssig, F.; Casanueva, I.; Budzianowski, P.; Gasic, M. Neural User Simulation for Corpus-based Policy Optimisation of Spoken Dialogue Systems. *arXiv* **2018**, arXiv:1805.06966.
25. Schatzmann, J.; Thomson, B.; Weilhammer, K.; Ye, H.; Young, S. Agenda-based user simulation for bootstrapping a POMDP dialogue system. *NAACL-HLT* **2007**, 149–152. [CrossRef]
26. English, M.S.; Heeman, P.A. Learning mixed initiative dialog strategies by using reinforcement learning on both conversants. *EMNLP* **2005**, 1011–1018. [CrossRef]
27. Chandramohan, S.; Geist, M.; Lefèvre, F.; Pietquin, O. Co-adaptation in spoken dialogue systems. In *Natural Interaction with Robots, Knowbots and Smartphones*; Springer: New York, NY, USA, 2014; pp. 343–353.
28. Das, A.; Kottur, S.; Moura, J.M.; Lee, S.; Batra, D. Learning cooperative visual dialog agents with deep reinforcement learning. In Proceedings of the IEEE International Conference on computer Vision, Venice, Italy, 22–29 October 2017; pp. 2951–2960.
29. Kottur, S.; Moura, J.; Lee, S.; Batra, D. Natural language does not emerge 'naturally' in multi-agent dialog. *arXiv* **2017**, arXiv:1706.08502.
30. Georgila, K.; Nelson, C.; Traum, D. Single-agent vs. multi-agent techniques for concurrent reinforcement learning of negotiation dialogue policies. In Proceedings of the 52nd Annual Meeting of the Association for Computational Linguistics, Baltimore, MD, USA, 22–27 June 2014; pp. 500–510.
31. Lewis, M.; Yarats, D.; Dauphin, Y.; Parikh, D.; Batra, D. Deal or No Deal? End-to-End Learning of Negotiation Dialogues. *arXiv* **2017**, arXiv:1706.05125.
32. Bansal, T.; Pachocki, J.; Sidor, S.; Sutskever, I.; Mordatch, I. Emergent complexity via multi-agent competition. *arXiv* **2018**, arXiv:1710.03748.
33. Bernstein, D.S.; Givan, R.; Immerman, N.; Zilberstein, S. The complexity of decentralized control of Markov decision processes. *Math. Oper. Res.* **2002**, *27*, 819–840. [CrossRef]
34. Hochreiter, S.; Schmidhuber, J. Long short-term memory. *Neural Comput.* **1997**, *9*, 1735-1780. [CrossRef]
35. Sutton, R.S.; Barto, A.G. Policy gradient methods. In *Reinforcement Learning: An Introduction*; MIT Press: Cambridge, MA, USA, 1998; pp. 329–331.

36. Schatztnann, J.; Stuttle, M.N.; Weilhammer, K.; Young, S. Effects of the user model on simulation-based learning of dialogue strategies. In Proceedings of the IEEE Workshop on Automatic Speech Recognition and Understanding, San Juan, Puerto Rico, 27 November–1 December 2005; pp. 220–225.
37. Li, X.; Lipton, Z.C.; Dhingra, B.; Li, L.; Gao, J.; Chen, Y.N. A user simulator for task-completion dialogues. *arXiv* **2016**, arXiv:1612.05688.
38. Kim, Y. Convolutional neural networks for sentence classification. *arXiv* **2014**, arXiv:1408.5882.
39. Devlin, J.; Chang, M.W.; Lee, K. Toutanova K. Bert: Pre-training of deep bidirectional transformers for language understanding. *arXiv* **2019**, arXiv:1810.04805.
40. Yang, Z.; Dai, Z.; Yang, Y.; Carbonell, J.; Salakhutdinov, R.R.; Le, Q.V. Xlnet: Generalized autoregressive pretraining for language understanding. In Proceedings of the 2019 Conference on Neural Information Processing Systems, Vancouver Convention Centre, Vancouver, BC, Canada, 8–14 December 2019; pp. 5754–5764.

© 2020 by the authors. Licensee MDPI, Basel, Switzerland. This article is an open access article distributed under the terms and conditions of the Creative Commons Attribution (CC BY) license (http://creativecommons.org/licenses/by/4.0/).

Article

A Hybrid Deep Learning Model for Protein–Protein Interactions Extraction from Biomedical Literature

Changqin Quan [1,*], Zhiwei Luo [1] and Song Wang [2]

1. Graduate School of System Informatics, Kobe University, 1-1, Rokkodai-cho, Nada-ku, Kobe 657-8501, Japan; luo@gold.kobe-u.ac.jp
2. School of Elec Eng, Comp and Math Sci; Curtin University, Kent St, Bentley WA 6102, Australia; Song.Wang@curtin.edu.au
* Correspondence: quanchqin@gold.kobe-u.ac.jp

Received: 11 March 2020; Accepted: 9 April 2020; Published: 13 April 2020

Abstract: The exponentially increasing size of biomedical literature and the limited ability of manual curators to discover protein–protein interactions (PPIs) in text has led to delays in keeping PPI databases updated with the current findings. The state-of-the-art text mining methods for PPI extraction are primarily based on deep learning (DL) models, and the performance of a DL-based method is mainly affected by the architecture of DL models and the feature embedding methods. In this study, we compared different architectures of DL models, including convolutional neural networks (CNN), long short-term memory (LSTM), and hybrid models, and proposed a hybrid architecture of a bidirectional LSTM+CNN model for PPI extraction. Pretrained word embedding and shortest dependency path (SDP) embedding are fed into a two-embedding channel model, such that the model is able to model long-distance contextual information and can capture the local features and structure information effectively. The experimental results showed that the proposed model is superior to the non-hybrid DL models, and the hybrid CNN+Bidirectional LSTM model works well for PPI extraction. The visualization and comparison of the hidden features learned by different DL models further confirmed the effectiveness of the proposed model.

Keywords: protein–protein interactions; deep learning (DL); convolutional neural networks (CNN); bidirectional long short-term memory (bidirectional LSTM)

1. Introduction

Protein–protein interactions (PPIs) play important roles in various biological processes and are of pivotal importance in the regulation of biological systems, and are consequently implicated in the development of disease states [1]. The exponentially increasing size of biomedical literature and the limited ability of manual curators to discover PPIs in text has led to delays in keeping PPI databases, such as BIND (The Biomolecular Interaction Network Database) [2], MINT (The Molecular INTeraction Database) [3], and The IntAct molecular interaction database [4], updated with the current findings. Consequently, this causes a bottleneck when leveraging the valuable information that is currently available in order to develop personalized health care solutions.

Previous studies have explored different methods for PPI extraction. The dominant techniques generally fall under the following three broad categories: co-occurrence-based methods [5], rule-and-pattern-based methods [6,7], and statistical machine learning (ML)-based methods [8–12]. Co-occurrence- based methods measure the correlation between each pair of entities by co-occurrence. A major weakness of these methods is their tendency for having a high recall, but a low precision. This is mainly because when entities do not appear in pairs in the training set, no co-occurrence with correlation can be recorded. Rule-and-pattern-based methods employ predefined patterns and rules to match the labelled sequence.

Although traditional rule-and-pattern-based methods have achieved high accuracy, their sophistication in pattern design and attenuated recall performance make them unsuitable for practical usage. Compared with co-occurrence- and rule–pattern-based methods, ML-based methods show a much better performance and generalization. In particular, the recent surge of interest in deep learning (DL) methods is due to the fact that they have been shown to outperform previous state-of-the-art techniques for PPI extraction tasks.

Generally, ML based approaches cast the problem of PPIs extraction into a classification problem. Suppose to extract the binary PPIs between entity e_1 and entity e_2 in a given sentence $= w_1 w_2 \ldots e_1 \ldots e_2 \ldots w_n$, where w_i is a word in S. The classification model is constructed to output 1 when e_1 and e_2 are related, otherwise it is 0. The inputs of the classification model are the features extracted from S. A key difference between traditional ML and DL is in how features are extracted and represented. Traditional ML-based methods usually collect words around target entities as features, such as unigram, bigram, and some semantic and syntactic features, and then these features are put into a bag-of-words model and encoded into one-hot type representations. However, such representations are unable to capture semantic relations among words or phrases and fail in generalizing the long context dependency [13]. The former issue is rendered as "vocabulary gap" (e.g., the words "depend" and "rely" are different in one-hot representations, albeit their similar linguistic functions). The latter one is introduced because of the n-order Markov restriction that attempts to alleviate the issue of "curse of dimensionality." Moreover, the inability to extract features automatically leads to laborious manual efforts in designing features.

Different from one-hot encoding representation, word distribution representation is proposed to solve the "vocabulary gap" problem by mapping words to dense vectors of real numbers in a low-dimensional space [14,15]. In addition to using words as features, some semantic and syntactic features, such as part-of-speech (POS), word position, and dependency path between two entities, can also be embedded in their distribution representations for feature learning.

Recent studies have proposed several feature embedding methods combining DL models for PPI extraction. Most of these studies focused on finding effective linguistic features for embedding or on tuning model hyperparameters for a certain framework of DL (e.g., convolutional neural networks (CNN) and long short-term memory (LSTM)). Different from previous work, this study focuses on exploring hybrid deep learning architecture for PPI extraction tasks. Our contributions can be summarized as follows:

(1) we propose a hybrid architecture of a bidirectional LSTM+CNN model for PPI extraction. The proposed model is able to solve the main issue of the inability to model long-distance contextual information with CNN for PPI extraction in a long sentence. Furthermore, CNN is applied to encode the important information contained in the bidirectional LSTM networks, and to extract the local features and structure information effectively.

(2) two embeddings (word-embeddings and shortest dependency path (SDP) embedding) are novelty applied as the inputs of for the bidirectional LSTM networks, which are able to capture semantical and syntactical features effectively.

(3) we investigate the hidden features learned by different DL models by reducing the feature dimensions and visualizing these features, which can help to compare the classification performance of these hidden features trained by different DL models in an approximate way.

The outline of the paper is as follows: Section 2 discusses related works. The framework of the model is introduced in Section 3. The experimental study is shown in Section 4. Section 5 is the discussion and Section 6 is the conclusion.

2. Related Work

Recent natural language processing (NLP) research is now increasingly focusing on the use of new DL architectures and algorithms to solve difficult NLP tasks, including PPI extraction from biomedical literature. This section reviews significant DL-related models and methods that have been employed for PPI extraction tasks.

The convolutional neural network (CNN) was originally developed for image recognition tasks [16–18] and has been successfully applied to the NLP domain by exploiting distributed representations for words (word embeddings). Collobert and Weston [19] made the first work to show the utility of pre-trained word embeddings. They proposed a neural network architecture that forms the foundation of many current approaches. The work also established word embeddings as a useful tool for PPI extraction tasks.

Like many other natural language tasks, using CNN along with word embeddings has been shown to be effective in PPI extraction tasks [20], as they have the ability to extract salient n-gram features from the input sentence in order to create an informative latent semantic representation of the sentence for downstream tasks [21–23]. Hua and Quan [24] proposed a CNN with pre-trained word vectors of the shortest dependency path between entity pairs for PPI extraction. In the literature [25], Quan extended their work to propose a multichannel convolutional neural network (MCCNN) that enables the fusion of multiple pre-trained word embeddings from various data sources (PubMed, PMC (PubMed Central), MedLine, and Wikipedia), and consequently expands the coverage of input vocabulary. A similar work includes the multichannel dependency-based convolutional neural network model (McDepCNN) [26], which combines CNN along with more syntactic features (e.g., part-of-speech, chunk, named entity, dependency, and position feature) for input embedding. CNN has been shown to outperform previous state-of-the-art techniques for PPI extraction. However, the main issue with CNNs is their inability to model long-distance contextual information and to preserve sequential order in their representations [22,27].

Comparatively, the recurrent neural network (RNN) model [28] is able to model long-distance contextual information by memorizing over previous computations and utilizing this information in current processing. However, simple RNN-based methods suffer from the vanishing gradient problem, which makes it hard to learn and tune the parameters of the earlier layers in the network. This limitation was overcome by various networks, such as long short-term memory (LSTM) [29]. In addition, Lai et al. [30] proposed the bidirectional recurrent neural network (bidirectional RNN) to capture the semantic information in different directions for sentence modeling. LSTM has also recently been applied for PPI extraction [31,32]. These studies yield a comparable performance, but much more attention has been paid to selecting the classification features or tuning model hyperparameters.

Hybrid models that combine CNN with RNN have aroused some interest in the DL domain, and several different combinations of architecture have been proposed for different subjects [33]. In the NLP domain, Zhou et al. [34] proposed C-LSTM, which combines CNN with LSTM for text classification. It takes advantage of CNN to extract a sequence of higher-level phrase representations and feeds them into LSTM to represent sentences. In the literature [35], a CNN–bidirectional gated recurrent unit (BiGRU) model, integrating CNN and bidirectional gated recurrent unit (BiGRU), is proposed for sentence semantic classification. This model utilizes CNN to obtain intermediate representations, and utilizes BiGRU to obtain contextual representations and semantic distribution. Inspired by these works, this study explores hybrid deep learning architecture for PPI extraction tasks.

3. The Model Description

The architecture of the proposed hybrid deep learning model is shown in Figure 1. By employing bidirectional LSTM to extract the semantic information in both the preceding and succeeding contexts, the proposed model is able to solve the main issue of the inability to model long-distance contextual information with CNN for PPI extraction in a long sentence. Furthermore, CNN is applied to encode the important information contained in the bidirectional LSTM networks, and to capture the local features and structure information effectively. As shown in Figure 1, two embeddings (word-embeddings and SDP embedding) are novelty applied as the input of bidirectional LSTM networks, which is able to capture semantical and syntactical features effectively.

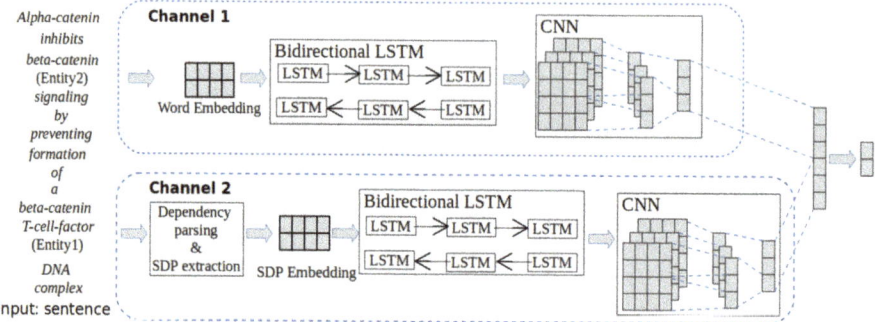

Figure 1. Architecture of the hybrid deep learning model. The input of the model is a sentence which is through two embeddings (word-embeddings and shortest dependency path (SDP) embedding). The two embeddings are separately fed to a bidirectional long short-term memory (LSTM) network followed by a convolutional neural networks (CNN) network, as two separate channels. The outputs of the CNN networks of the two channels are concatenated together for classification.

3.1. Model Input

In the expression of PPIs, most of the interaction words are verbs and nouns, and thus dependency parsing is particularly well-suited for relation extraction because the dependency grammar (DG) views the verb as the structural center of all of the clause structure. Dependency parsing has been well used for PPI extraction in previous studies [25,26,33]. Given an input sentence, we extract the SDP (shortest dependency path) by dependency parsing. Figure 2 shows the dependency parsing graph (Stanford parser [36] and a visualization tool [37] are utilized).

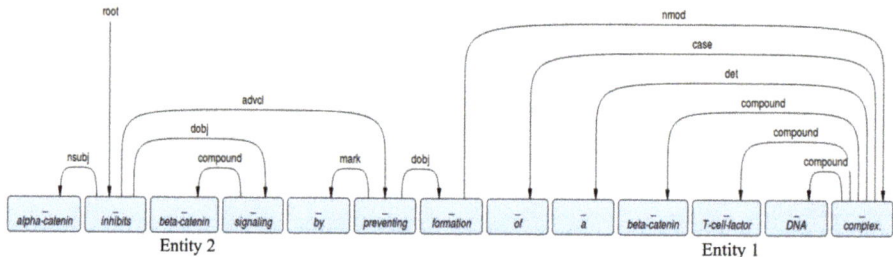

Figure 2. The dependency parsing graph for the sentence "alpha-catenin inhibits beta-catenin (Entity 2) signaling by preventing the formation of a beta-catenin T-cell-factor (Entity 1) DNA complex" (dependency relations are shown by the arrow lines). The shortest dependency path extracted between the target entity pairs is "T-cell-factor (Entity 1) compound complex nmod formation dobj preventing advcl inhibits dobj signaling compound beta-catenin (Entity 2)".

The extracted SDPs are treated as texts for the embedding. Embedding is a feature learning process where words from the vocabulary are mapped to vectors of real numbers in a low-dimensional space relative to the vocabulary size. For notation, we use $D \in R^{|V| \times d}$ to represent the pretrained embedding, where V is the vocabulary and d is the embedding dimension. Specifically, for word-embedding, V is composed of the words from the input sentences and for SDP embedding, V is composed by the symbols from the input SDPs.

When we assign each word (or symbol) in an input sentence (or SDP) with a corresponding row vector from D, we would get a matrix representation $P \in R^{N \times d}$ for an input sentence (or SDP). The word-embedding and SDP embedding are two $c \times N \times d$ tensors, where c is the input size of the channel, N is the max length of input sentences, and d is the embedding dimension.

The input of the model is a sentence that goes through two embedding channels, namely: (1) pretrained word embedding trained on the PubMed abstract corpus [38] and (2) SDP embedding trained on the shortest dependency paths extracted between target entity pairs.

3.2. Intermediate Structure

As shown in Figure 1, the two channel embeddings each separately pass through a bidirectional LSTM network consequent with a CNN network. bidirectional LSTM enables learning long-term dependencies for both the preceding and succeeding contexts. After that, CNN encodes the important information contained in the bidirectional LSTM networks.

The bidirectional LSTM network is a combination of Bidirectional RNNs with LSTM, using an input word embedding sequence $(e_1, e_2, \ldots, e_N)$, where N denotes the max length of input sequences. As illustrated in Figure 3, bidirectional RNNs compute the forward hidden sequence $\overrightarrow{h}$, the backward hidden sequence $\overleftarrow{h}$, and the output sequence y by iterating the forward layer from $t = (1, \ldots, N)$, the backward layer from $t = (N, \ldots, 1)$ and then updating the output layer as follows:

$$\overrightarrow{h}_t = S\left(W_{e\overrightarrow{h}} e_t + W_{\overrightarrow{h}\overrightarrow{h}} \overrightarrow{h}_{t-1} e_t + b_{\overrightarrow{h}}\right) \quad (1)$$

$$\overleftarrow{h}_t = S\left(W_{e\overleftarrow{h}} e_t + W_{\overleftarrow{h}\overleftarrow{h}} \overleftarrow{h}_{t+1} e_t + b_{\overleftarrow{h}}\right) \quad (2)$$

$$y_t = W_{\overrightarrow{h} y} \overrightarrow{h}_t + W_{\overleftarrow{h} y} \overleftarrow{h}_t + b_y \quad (3)$$

where W denotes weight matrices, b denotes bias vectors, and S is the hidden layer function on each element of a vector.

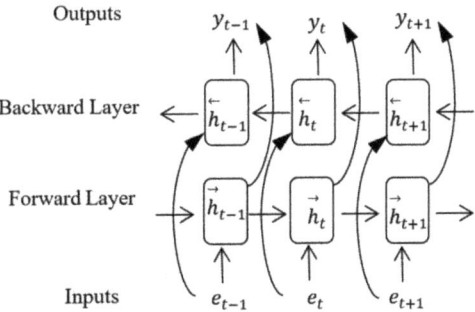

Figure 3. Illustration of the bidirectional recurrent neural network.

In the bidirectional LSTM network, each unit of RNN is an LSTM (Figure 4):

$$f_t = \sigma\left(W_{ef} e_t + W_{hf} h_{t-1} + W_{cf} c_{t-1} + b_f\right) \quad (4)$$

$$i_t = \sigma(W_{ei} e_t + W_{hi} h_{t-1} + W_{ci} c_{t-1} + b_i) \quad (5)$$

$$o_t = \sigma(W_{eo} e_t + W_{ho} h_{t-1} + W_{co} c_t + b_o) \quad (6)$$

$$c_t = f_t c_{t-1} + i_t \tanh(W_{ec} e_t + W_{hc} h_{t-1} + b_c) \quad (7)$$

$$h_t = o_t \tanh(c_t) \quad (8)$$

where σ is the logistic sigmoid function, and f_t, i_t, o_t, c_t are the forget gate, input gate, output gate, and cell state, respectively at the time step t.

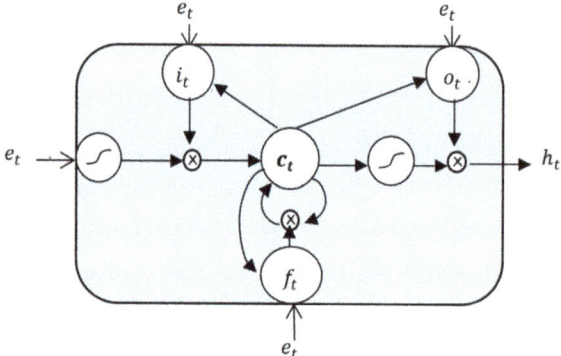

Figure 4. Illustration of the long short-term memory (LSTM) cell.

The bidirectional LSTM network outputs for both channels are each separately fed to CNN networks. Given an output sequence y_i of the bidirectional LSTM network, it is input into the convolutional layer. The convolutional layer contains a set of filters for different window sizes g, and computes the output feature map C as follows:

$$C = [m_1, m_2, \ldots, m_{N-g+1}] \qquad (9)$$

$$m_i = f(W_i y_{i:i+g-1} + b_i) \qquad (10)$$

where f is an activation function, b is a bias term, and is element-wise multiplication.

Then the concatenation operation is applied to join multiple outputs from the Max-Pooling layer into a single tensor for each channel. Finally, the CNN network outputs for both channels are concatenated to a unique vector and fed to a fully connected layer.

4. Datasets and Experimental Setup

4.1. Datasets and Preprocessing

Two benchmarking corpora, Aimed [39] and BioInfer [40], were used for the experiments and evaluation. The Aimed dataset was manually tagged, which includes 1955 sentences, and was considered as the standard dataset for the PPI extraction tasks. BioInfer was developed by the Turku BioNLP group [41], and contains 1100 sentences.

To ensure the generalization of features, we use a similar data preprocessing method to the authors of [9], by replacing two target entities with special symbols "Entity 1" and "Entity 2", separately, and entities that are not target entities are all represented as "Entity". Text preprocessing includes dependency parsing and shortest dependency paths (SDPs) extraction. If there is an interaction between the two entities, we consider this instance as a positive one; otherwise, we consider it as a negative one. Table 1 shows the statistics for the PPIs corpora.

Table 1. Statistics for protein–protein interactions (PPIs) corpora.

	Sentence Num.	Positive Num.	Negative Num.
BioInfer	1100	2534	7132
AIMed	1955	1000	4834

4.2. The Experiments

4.2.1. Pretrained Embeddings

There are two pretrained embeddings used in our model, namely: word embedding and SDP embedding. The pretrained word embedding is trained on PMC and PubMed (Pyysalo et al. [38]), with a vocabulary size of 4,087,446 words. The SDP embedding is trained on the shortest dependency paths extracted between the target entity pairs from PPIs corpora by Gensim Word2Vec tool (CBOW training algorithm, Radim Řehůřek and Petr Sojka, Brno, Czech Republic) [42]. The vocabulary size of the SDP embedding on the BioInfer corpus and Aimed corpus is 1840 words and 1349 words, respectively. Corresponding to the word and SDP embeddings, two types of input, sentences and the shortest dependency paths (SDPs) between target entity pairs, are fed into the model as inputs, separately.

4.2.2. Parameter Setting

The parameter setting is summarized in Table 2.

Table 2. Parameter setting.

Parameter	Aimed	BioInfer
Max length of sentences	133	95
Max length of SDPs	31	35
Optimization algorithm	Adam	
Learning rate	1×10^{-4}	
Number of epochs	100	
Training batch size	128	
Bidirectional LSTM network		
Number of LSTM units	100	
Dropout rate	0.2	
Recurrent dropout rate	0.2	
CNN network		
Window sizes	(3, 4, and 5)	
Num. of filters on each window size	100	
Dropout rate after each max pooling layer	0.5	
Activation function in convolution layer	Relu	

4.2.3. Implementation and Evaluation Metrics

Keras 2.2.4 (https://keras.io/) is applied to implement the models. The configurations of the machine are as follows: GPU—Quadro M1200/PCIe/SSE2, Nvidia, Santa Clara, CA, USA; CPU—Intel®Core™ i7-7820HQ CPU @ 2.90GHz × 8 Intel, Colorado Springs, CO, USA; System—Ubuntu 18.04.2 LTS 64-bit Memory, 16 GiB, Canonical Ltd., London, UK.

We use the average F1 macro score to evaluate the performances of the DL models using the 10-cross-validation (10-fold CV) method. In the calculation of each fold, we calculate the F1 macro score on the entire testing data by creating a Callback function at the end of each epoch, instead of a batch-wise average value.

4.3. Performance Comparison

The performance of the proposed DL model is compared with the state-of-the-art non-hybrid models and hybrid models. Table 3 shows the comparison results.

CNN-based models [24–26] and LSTM-based models [31,32] have been applied for PPI extraction recently. However, there are many differences in the text preprocessing strategies (e.g., protein entities are generalized with special symbols or protein IDs, utilizing different tokenization and parsing tools, and utilizing filtering rules or not) and other experimental setups (e.g., hyperparameter settings and evaluation metrics). These make it difficult to compare the performance of the DL models directly.

In our experiments, we compare the non-hybrid models (1–5 in Table 3) and hybrid models (6–7 in Table 3) with the same experimental settings, except for the models and the inputs of the models.

Table 3. Comparison of the F1 macro score for deep learning (DL) models on benchmark datasets.

	Approach	BioInfer	Aimed
	Non-hybrid		
(1)	CNN+word embedding	70.4	68.8
(2)	CNN+word embedding+SDPs embedding	71.7	69.3
(3)	LSTM+word embedding	72.2	71.6
(4)	LSTM+word embedding+SDPs embedding	73.0	71.9
(5)	Bidirectional LSTM+word embedding+ SDPs embedding	73.4	72.4
	Hybrid		
(6)	CNN+Bidirectional LSTM+word embedding+ SDPs embedding	73.3	70.0
(7)	Bidirectional LSTM+CNN+word embedding+ SDPs embedding (the proposed)	74.4	73.7

By comparing CNN-based models 1 with 2, and LSTM-based models 3 with 4 in Table 3, it can be found that the two embeddings (word-embedding and SDP embedding) input is able to improve the performance for both CNN- and LSTM-based models. This result demonstrates the effectiveness of integrating word embedding and SDP embedding for PPI extraction. The interaction verbs (e.g., "affect" and "bind") and dependency relation symbols (e.g., "nsubj" and "dobj") in the SDPs could provide useful information for classifying target protein pairs and extracting the relations.

It is also observed that the LSTM model outperforms the CNN model in the two datasets. The bidirectional LSTM achieved the best performance among the non-hybrid models.

As a hybrid model, we compare the proposed bidirectional LSTM+CNN model (7 in Table 3) with the hybrid CNN+bidirectional LSTM model (6 in Table 3), which is a variant of C-LSTM proposed by the authors of [34]. C-LSTM learns the sentence representation by combining CNN and LSTM, and has been shown to be superior to CNN and LSTM for some text classification tasks. The results show that the proposed bidirectional LSTM+CNN model outperforms the CNN+bidirectional LSTM model greatly for PPI extraction in both of the datasets.

4.4. Hidden Features Visualization and Comparison

We further investigate the hidden features learned by different DL models by reducing the feature dimensions and visualizing these features. We choose four DL models (2, 4, 6, and 7 in Table 3, represent CNN, LSTM, and the two hybrid-based DL models, respectively) for the visualization.

We first split the dataset into two parts randomly, as follows: training set 90% and testing set 10%. Using the same training set, we train the DL models separately. Then, we create a truncated model for each DL model. The truncated model keep the same network layers until the last hidden feature layer. Then, we set the weights for it from the trained model. The truncated model is used to predict the features for the testing data. After that, we apply principal component analysis (PCA) [43] to reduce the features predicted by the truncated model to a lower dimension. The PCA variance is 1.00, which implies that the reduced dimensions do represent the hidden features well (scale 0 to 1). Then, t-Distributed Stochastic Neighbor Embedding (t-SNE) [44] is applied for the visualization.

Figure 5 illustrates the scatter plots of the hidden features on the last layer of the DL models (CNN, LSTM, CNN+bidirectional LSTM, and Bidirectional LSTM+CNN) after dimensionality reduction.

In Figure 5, the comparison of the four DL models (CNN, LSTM, CNN+bidirectional LSTM, and bidirectional LSTM+CNN) on both datasets shows that bidirectional LSTM+CNN has a much better classification performance than the other models.

Figure 6 illustrates the F1-score increasing trends of the four DL models as the number of epochs increase. The datasets are split into two parts randomly, as follows: training set 90% and testing set 10%.

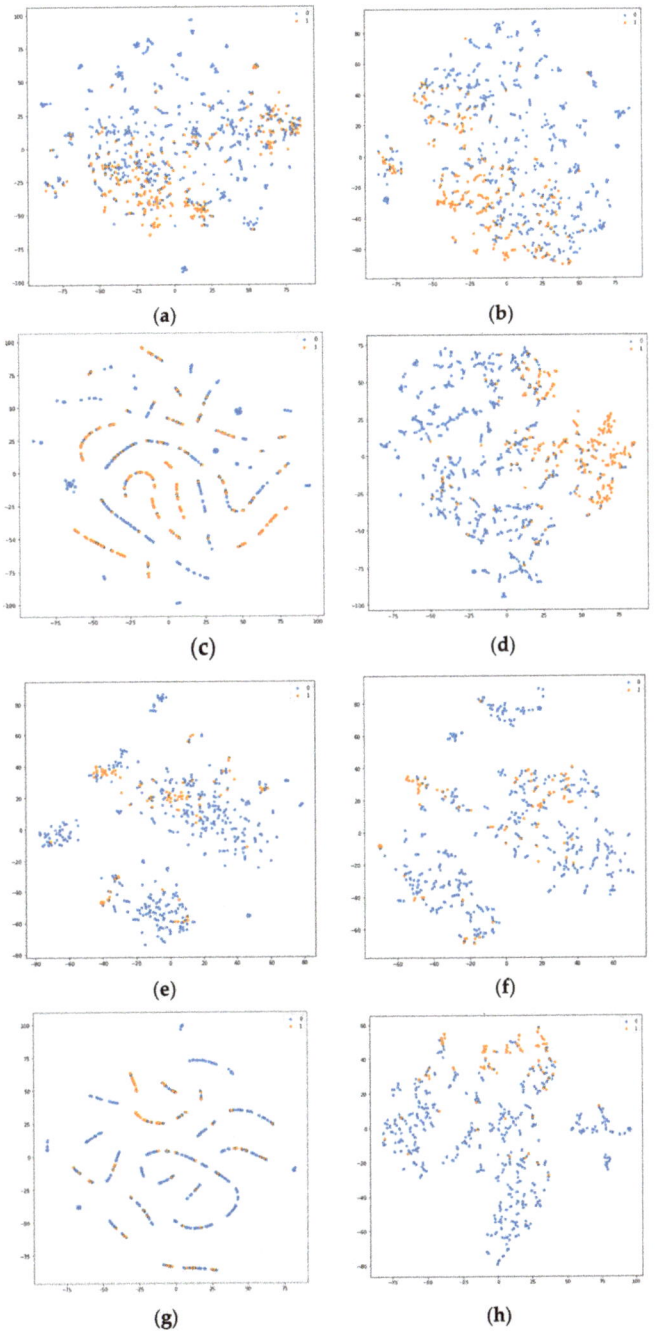

Figure 5. The scatter plots of the hidden features in the last layer of DL models (CNN, LSTM, CNN+bidirectional LSTM, and bidirectional LSTM+CNN) after dimensionality reduction in the Bioinfer and Aimed datasets. (**a**) CNN on Bioinfer; (**b**) LSTM on Bioinfer; (**c**) CNN+bidirectional LSTM on Bioinfer; (**d**) Bidirectional LSTM+CNN on Bioinfer; (**e**) CNN on Aimed; (**f**) LSTM on Aimed; (**g**) CNN+bidirectional LSTM on Aimed; (**h**) Bidirectional LSTM+CNN on Aimed

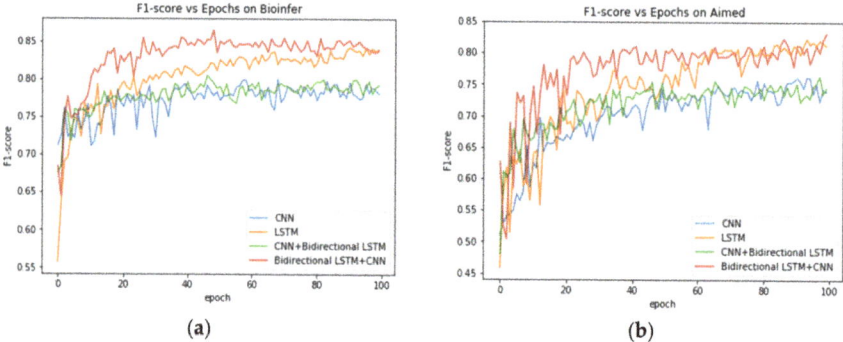

Figure 6. The F1-score increasing trends of the DL models as the number of epochs increase, (**a**) F1-score vs Epochs on Bioinfer; (**b**) F1-score vs Epochs on Aimed

As can be seen from Figure 6, bidirectional LSTM+CNN produces a high F1-score with less epochs than the other models. It also keeps a high classification performance as the number of epochs increases. We also found that LSTM also could obtain a high F1-score on some points, but it needs more training than the proposed bidirectional LSTM+CNN model.

5. Discussion

Recently, DL models have been shown to be superior to traditional ML models in many NLP tasks. In PPI extraction tasks, the performance of a DL-based method is mainly affected by the architecture of the DL models and the feature embedding methods. In this study, we compared different architectures of DL models, including CNN, LSTM, and hybrid models, and found that the proposed bidirectional LSTM+CNN model is superior to the other DL models for PPI extraction. As more complex network architectures (e.g., a deep hybrid model with more layers or a deep reinforcement learning model) have not been considered in this study, there is still space for further improvement of the DL model architecture.

In addition to the DL model architecture, the feature embedding methods also have an effect on the classification performance. In DL models, the input semantic and syntactic features are embedded in their distribution representations for feature learning. Previous studies have experimented with some different feature embeddings (such as ngram, part-of-speech (POS), word position, and dependency path). In this study, the stacked pretrained word embedding and SDP embedding are fed into a two embedding channel (word embedding and SDP embedding) architecture, such that the model can extract the feature information more accurately. With more feature channels, an improved performance can be expected.

The difference in the text preprocessing strategies (e.g., protein entities are generalized with special symbols or protein IDs, utilizing different tokenization and parsing tools, and utilizing filtering rules or not) and other experimental settings (e.g., hyperparameter settings and evaluation metrics) make it difficult to compare the performance of the DL models directly. This study did not directly compare the results with other related studies. Instead, under the same experimental environment, our experiments covered all of the DL models that have been applied in previous studies [24–26,31,32]. It would be more objective to compare the performance of different DL models directly. The experiments of this study used two standard PPI datasets, and a more robust DL model can be expected when using large-scale training data.

DL models are generally opaque, meaning that although they can produce accurate predictions, it is not clear how or why a given prediction is made. This study investigated the hidden features learned by different DL models by reducing feature dimensions and visualizing these features. This would help us to compare the classification performance of these hidden features trained by different

DL models in an approximate way. However, how to connect an input with the hidden features and how to control them during training stage are still challenging problems.

6. Conclusions

In this paper, a hybrid DL model is proposed for PPI extraction tasks. The model innovatively integrates bidirectional LSTM with CNN in a two-embedding channel (word embedding and SDP embedding) architecture.

CNN with word embeddings has been shown to be effective in PPI extraction tasks, as it has the ability to extract salient n-gram features from the input sentence to create an informative latent semantic representation of the sentence. However, a main issue with CNNs is their inability to model long-distance contextual information for PPI extraction in a long sentence. To solve this problem, we employ bidirectional LSTM to extract the semantic information in both the preceding and succeeding contexts, because the architecture of LSTM is able to model long-distance contextual information by memorizing over previous computations and utilizing this information in current processing. Furthermore, CNN is applied to encode the important information contained in the bidirectional LSTM networks, and to capture the local features and structure information effectively.

Under the same experimental environment, the results show that the proposed model is superior to the non-hybrid DL models, including CNN-based and LSTM-based models. In addition, the proposed bidirectional LSTM+CNN model outperformed another hybrid model (CNN+bidirectional LSTM model) greatly for PPI extraction. The visualization and comparison of the hidden features learned by different DL models further confirmed the effectiveness of the proposed model.

For future work, we will apply the proposed hybrid DL model to other NLP tasks in order to explore its applicability, and will consider more complex network architectures (e.g., a deep hybrid model with more layers or a deep reinforcement learning model) to improve the performance.

Author Contributions: C.Q. and Z.L. conceived and designed the model; C.Q. performed the experiment and analyzed the results; C.Q. wrote the preliminary version of this manuscript; Z.W.L. and S.W. revised the manuscript. All authors have read and agreed to the published version of the manuscript.

Funding: This study was partially supported by the National Natural Foundation of China under grant no. 61472117.

Conflicts of Interest: The authors declare no conflict of interest.

References

1. Scott, D.E.; Bayly, A.R.; Abell, C.; Skidmore, J. Small molecules, big targets: Drug discovery faces the protein–protein interaction challenge. *Nat. Rev. Drug Discov.* **2016**, *15*, 533–550. [CrossRef] [PubMed]
2. Bader, G.D.; Betel, D.; Hogue, C.W.V. BIND: The biomolecular interaction network database. *Nucleic Acids Res.* **2003**, *31*, 248–250. [CrossRef] [PubMed]
3. Zanzoni, A.; Montecchi-Palazzi, L.; Quondam, M.; Ausiello, G.; Helmer-Citterich, M.; Cesareni, G. MINT: A molecular interaction database. *FEBS Lett.* **2002**, *513*, 135–140. [CrossRef]
4. Kerrien, S.; Aranda, B.; Breuza, L.; Bridge, A. The intact molecular interaction database in 2012. *Nucleic Acids Res.* **2012**, *38*, D525. [CrossRef] [PubMed]
5. Bunescu, R.; Mooney, R.; Ramani, A.; Marcotte, E. Integrating co-occurrence statistics with information extraction for robust retrieval of protein interactions from medline. In Proceedings of the HLT-NAACL Workshop on Linking Natural Language Processing and Biology (BioNLP '06), New York, NY, USA, 8 June 2006; pp. 49–56.
6. Fundel, K.; Küffner, R.; Zimmer, R. RelEx—Relation extraction using dependency parse trees. *Bioinformatics* **2007**, *23*, 365–371. [CrossRef]
7. Segura-Bedmar, I.; Martínez, P.; De Pablo-Sánchez, C. A linguistic rule-based approach to extract drug-drug interactions from pharmacological documents. *BMC Bioinform.* **2011**, *12* (Suppl. 2). [CrossRef]

8. Cui, B.; Lin, H.; Yang, Z. SVM-based protein-protein interaction extraction from medline abstracts. In Proceedings of the 2nd International Conference on Bio-Inspired Computing: Theories and Applications (BIC-TA '07), IEEE, Zhengzhou, China, 14–17 September 2007; pp. 182–185.
9. Erkan, G.; Özgür, A.; Radev, D.R. Semi-supervised classification for extracting protein interaction sentences using dependency parsing. In Proceedings of the Joint Conference on Empirical Methods in Natural Language Processing and Computational Natural Language Learning (EMNLP-CoNLL '07), Prague, Czech Republic, 28–30 June 2007; Volume 7, pp. 228–237.
10. Sun, C.; Lin, L.; Wang, X. Using maximum entropy model to extract protein-protein interaction information from biomedical literature. In Proceedings of the Third International Conference on Intelligent Computing, ICIC 2007, Qingdao, China, 21–24 August 2007; pp. 730–737.
11. Segura-Bedmar, I.; Martínez, P.; de Pablo-Sánchez, C. Using a shallow linguistic kernel for drug-drug interaction extraction. *J. Biomed. Inform.* **2011**, *44*, 789–804. [CrossRef]
12. Quan, C.; Wang, M.; Ren, F. An unsupervised text mining method for relation extraction from biomedical literature. *PLoS ONE* **2014**, *9*, e102039. [CrossRef]
13. Arora, K.; Rangarajan, A. A Compositional Approach to Language Modeling. *arXiv* **2016**, arXiv:1604.00100.
14. Bengio, Y.; Schwenk, H.; Senécal, J.-S.; Morin, F.; Gauvain, J.L. Neural probabilistic language models. In *Innovations in Machine Learning, Studies in Fuzziness and Soft Computing*; Springer: Berlin, Germany, 2006; pp. 137–186.
15. Mikolov, T.; Chen, K.; Corrado, G.; Dean, J. Efficient estimation of word representations in vector space. In Proceedings of the ICLR, Scottsdale, AZ, USA, 2–4 May 2013.
16. Krizhevsky, A.; Ilya, S.; Hinton, G.E. ImageNet classification with deep convolutional neural networks. *Adv. Neural Inf. Process. Syst.* **2012**, 1097–1105. [CrossRef]
17. Khawaldeh, S.; Pervaiz, U.; Rafiq, A.; Alkhawaldeh, R. Noninvasive Grading of Glioma Tumor Using Magnetic Resonance Imaging with Convolutional Neural Networks. *Appl. Sci.* **2018**, *8*, 27. [CrossRef]
18. Dong, J.; Gao, Y.; Lee, H.; Zhou, H. Action Recognition Based on the Fusion of Graph Convolutional Networks with High Order Features. *Appl. Sci.* **2020**, *10*, 1482. [CrossRef]
19. Collobert, R.; Weston, J. A unified architecture for natural language processing: Deep neural networks with multitask learning. In Proceedings of the 25th International Conference on Machine Learning, Helsinki, Finland, 5–9 July 200; ACM: New York, NY, USA; pp. 160–167.
20. Rios, A.; Kavuluru, R. Convolutional neural networks for biomedical text classification: Application in indexing biomedical articles. In Proceedings of the 6th ACM Conference on Bioinformatics, Computational Biology and Health Informatics, Atlanta, GA, USA, 30 August–2 September 2015; ACM: New York, NY, USA; pp. 258–267.
21. Collobert, R.; Weston, J.; Bottou, L.; Karlen, M.; Kavukcuoglu, K.; Kuksa, P. Natural language processing (almost) from scratch. *J. Mach. Learn. Res.* **2011**, *12*, 2493–2537.
22. Kalchbrenner, N.; Grefenstette, E.; Blunsom, P. A convolutional neural network for modelling sentences. In Proceedings of the 52nd Annual Meeting of the Association for Computational Linguistics, Baltimore, MD, USA, 22 June 2014; pp. 655–665.
23. Kim, Y. Convolutional neural networks for sentence classification. In Proceedings of the 2014 Conference on Empirical Methods in Natural Language Processing (EMNLP), Doha, Qatar, 25–29 October 2014; Association for Computational Linguistics: Stroudsburg, PA, USA; pp. 1746–1751.
24. Hua, L.; Quan, C. A shortest dependency path based convolutional neural network for protein-protein relation extraction. *BioMed Res. Int.* **2016**. [CrossRef] [PubMed]
25. Quan, C.; Hua, L.; Sun, X.; Bai, W. Multichannel convolutional neural network for biological relation extraction. *BioMed Res. Int.* **2016**, 1–10. [CrossRef]
26. Peng, Y.; Lu, Z. Deep learning for extracting protein-protein interactions from biomedical literature. In Proceedings of the BioNLP, Vancouver, Canada, 4 August 2017; pp. 29–38.
27. Tu, Z.; Hu, B.; Lu, Z.; Li, H. Context-dependent translation selection using convolutional neural network. In Proceedings of the 53rd Annual Meeting of the Association for Computational Linguistics and the 7th International Joint Conference on Natural Language Processing, Beijing, China, 26–31 July 2015; pp. 536–541.
28. Funahashi, K.-I.; Nakamura, Y. Approximation of dynamical systems by continuous time recurrent neural networks. *Neural Netw.* **1993**, *6*, 801–806. [CrossRef]
29. Hochreiter, S.; Schmidhuber, J. Long short-term memory. *Neural Comput.* **1997**, *9*, 1735–1780. [CrossRef]

30. Lai, S.; Xu, L.; Liu, K.; Zhao, J. Recurrent convolutional neural networks for text classification. In Proceedings of the AAAI, Austin, TX, USA, 25–30 January 2015; Volume 333, pp. 2267–2273.
31. Hsieh, Y.L.; Chang, Y.-C.; Chang, N.W.; Hsu, W.L. Identifying Protein-protein Interactions in Biomedical Literature using Recurrent Neural Networks with Long Short-Term Memory. In Proceedings of the Eighth International Joint Conference on Natural Language Processing, Taipei, Taiwan, 27 November–1 December 2017; pp. 240–245.
32. Yadav, S.; Ekbal, A.; Saha, S.; Kumar, A.; Bhattacharyya, P. Feature Assisted bi-directional LSTM Model for Protein-Protein Interaction Identification from Biomedical Texts. *Knowl. Based Syst.* **2019**, *166*, 18–29. [CrossRef]
33. Chen, X.; Xie, H.; Cheng, G. Trends and Features of the Applications of Natural Language Processing Techniques for Clinical Trials Text Analysis. *Appl. Sci.* **2020**, *10*, 2157. [CrossRef]
34. Zhou, C.; Sun, C.; Liu, Z.; Lau, F.C.M. A C-LSTM Neural Network for Text Classification. *arXiv* **2015**, arXiv:1511.08630.
35. Zhang, D.; Tian, L.; Chen, Y. Combining Convolution Neural Network and Bidirectional Gated Recurrent Unit for Sentence Semantic Classification. *IEEE Access* **2018**, *6*, 73750–73759. [CrossRef]
36. Stanford Parser. Available online: https://nlp.stanford.edu/software/lex-parser.shtml (accessed on 27 December 2019).
37. CoNLL-U Viewer. Available online: http://www.let.rug.nl/kleiweg/conllu/ (accessed on 27 December 2019).
38. Pyysalo, S.; Ginter, F.; Moen, F.; Salakoski, T. Distributional semantics resources for biomedical text processing. In Proceedings of the Languages in Biology and Medicine (LBM '13), Tokyo, Japan, 12–13 December 2013; pp. 39–44.
39. Razvan, C.B.; Ruifang, G.; Rohit, J.K.; Edward, M.M.; Raymond, J.M.; Arun, K.R.; Yuk, W.W. Comparative experiments on learning information extractors for proteins and their interactions. *Artif. Intell. Med.* **2005**, *33*, 139–155.
40. Pyysalo, S.; Ginter, F.; Heimonen, J.; Björne, J.; Boberg, J.; Järvinen, J.; Salakoski, T. BioInfer: A corpus for information extraction in the biomedical domain. *BMC Bioinform.* **2007**, *8*, 1–24. [CrossRef] [PubMed]
41. Turku BioNLP group. Available online: http://bionlp.utu.fi/ (accessed on 27 December 2019).
42. Gensim–Deep Learning with Word2vec. Available online: https://radimrehurek.com/gensim/models/word2vec.html (accessed on 5 October 2019).
43. Jolliffe, I.T. *Principal Component Analysis*, 2nd ed.; Springer-Verlag: New York, NY, USA, 2002.
44. Maaten, L.V.D.; Hinton, G.E. Visualizing High-Dimensional Data Using t-SNE. *J. Mach. Learn. Res.* **2008**, *9*, 2579–2605.

© 2020 by the authors. Licensee MDPI, Basel, Switzerland. This article is an open access article distributed under the terms and conditions of the Creative Commons Attribution (CC BY) license (http://creativecommons.org/licenses/by/4.0/).

Article

Medical Instructed Real-Time Assistant for Patient with Glaucoma and Diabetic Conditions

Ubaid Ur Rehman [1,2], Dong Jin Chang [3], Younhea Jung [3], Usman Akhtar [1], Muhammad Asif Razzaq [1] and Sungyoung Lee [1,*]

[1] Department of Computer Science and Engineering, Kyung Hee University (Global Campus), 1732 Deogyeong-daero, Giheung-gu, Yongin-si, Gyeonggi-do 17104, Korea; ubaid.rehman@khu.ac.kr (U.U.R.); usman@oslab.khu.ac.kr (U.A.); asif.razzaq@oslab.khu.ac.kr (M.A.R.)
[2] School of Electrical Engineering and Computer Science, National University of Sciences and Technology, Islamabad 44000, Pakistan
[3] Department of Ophthalmology, Catholic University of Korea Yeouido Saint Mary's Hospital, Seoul 07345, Korea; hpalways@catholic.ac.kr (D.J.C.); younhea@hotmail.com (Y.J.)
* Correspondence: sylee@oslab.khu.ac.kr (S.L.); Tel.: +82-31-201-2514

Received: 21 February 2020; Accepted: 22 March 2020; Published: 25 March 2020

Abstract: Virtual assistants are involved in the daily activities of humans such as managing calendars, making appointments, and providing wake-up calls. They provide a conversational service to customers around-the-clock and make their daily life manageable. With this emerging trend, many well-known companies launched their own virtual assistants that manage the daily routine activities of customers. In the healthcare sector, virtual medical assistants also provide a list of relevant diseases linked to a specific symptom. Due to low accuracy and uncertainty, these generated recommendations are untrusted and may lead to hypochondriasis. In this study, we proposed a Medical Instructed Real-time Assistant (MIRA) that listens to the user's chief complaint and predicts a specific disease. Instead of informing about the medical condition, the user is referred to a nearby appropriate medical specialist. We designed an architecture for MIRA that considers the limitations of existing virtual medical assistants such as weak authentication, lack of understanding multiple intent statements about a specific medical condition, and uncertain diagnosis recommendations. To implement the designed architecture, we collected the chief complaints along with the dialogue corpora of real patients. Then, we manually validated these data under the supervision of medical specialists. We then used these data for natural language understanding, disease identification, and appropriate response generation. For the prototype version of MIRA, we considered the cases of glaucoma (eye disease) and diabetes (an autoimmune disease) only. The performance measure of MIRA was evaluated in terms of accuracy (89%), precision (90%), sensitivity (89.8%), specificity (94.9%), and F-measure (89.8%). The task completion was calculated using Cohen's Kappa ($k = 0.848$) that categorizes MIRA as 'Almost Perfect'. Furthermore, the voice-based authentication identifies the user effectively and prevent against masquerading attack. Simultaneously, the user experience shows relatively good results in all aspects based on the User Experience Questionnaire (UEQ) benchmark data. The experimental results show that MIRA efficiently predicts a disease based on chief complaints and supports the user in decision making.

Keywords: primary healthcare; chief complaint; virtual medical assistant; spoken natural language; disease diagnosis; medical specialist

1. Introduction

With the emerging trends of technology, virtual assistants help users complete their daily routine tasks efficiently. Most of the virtual assistants use artificial intelligence and provide personalized assistance to the users in the form of managing calendars, controlling smart environments, navigation, making an appointment, providing wake-up calls, and many more things [1]. Many applications from different domains currently have their own built-in virtual assistants such as televisions [2], mobile devices [3], vehicles [4], and the Internet of things [5,6]. The virtual assistant is also known as a chatbot, dialogue manager, virtual agent, interactive assistant, or conversational agent. Many well-known companies including Apple (Siri), Google (Assistant), Samsung (Bixby) and Amazon (Alexa) introduced their own virtual assistants. These virtual assistants provide an interactive user interface (text, speech, or both) that have the ability to understand requests, handle complex tasks, and generate an appropriate response using the machine learning model [7].

In the healthcare sector, the adoption of machine learning facilitated diagnosis [8,9], treatment [10,11], and streamlining of administrative tasks [12]. With the popularity of virtual assistants, healthcare is also moving toward this technology. It prevents unnecessary visits to the doctor, which reduces the administrative burden, increases efficiency, and support clinical decisions. According to a survey conducted in [13], primary care physicians spent more time managing electronic medical records (EMRs) than engaging with patients. Therefore, several virtual medical assistants were introduced, such as Nuance [14], Suki [15], and Robin Healthcare [16], which automate the process of documenting clinical information using artificial intelligence and provide services to the healthcare provider [17–19]. Moreover, several virtual medical assistants provide trusted information based on an analysis of medical symptoms, which include MedWhat [20], Your.MD [21], and Sensely [22]. These provide personal healthcare assistance using medical knowledge on the web, and EMR. These virtual medical assistants show a list of relevant diseases that match the input symptoms.

Suppose, a statement 'I have abdominal pain' is linked with a list of conditions, which include bowel cancer, constipation, Crohn's disease, and gluten intolerance. The recommendation is predicted based on one symptom and requires approval from the medical specialist [23]. Due to the low accuracy and uncertainty of the existing virtual medical assistants, the resulting list of conditions may lead to depression, anxiety, and hypochondriasis [24]. To the best of our knowledge, none of the existing virtual medical assistants in the natural language processing domain considered real-time disease diagnosis based on the user's chief complaint, which has the utmost priority, stated in the patient's own words, and is the main reason for the patient's visit. It may be possible that more than one disease has the same kind of chief complaint, making it hard to identify a specific disease. Furthermore, every person has their own accent and way of explaining the chief complaint, so understanding this type of conversation is a challenge for the virtual medical assistant as well.

In this study, we considered the challenges faced by the existing virtual medical assistant and proposed a solution in terms of the Medical Instructed Real-time Assistant (MIRA). MIRA supports primary healthcare services and uses spoken natural language for interactive communication to achieve a high success rate on task completion [25]. Moreover, MIRA analyzes the user's chief complaint and predicts a specific disease. Then, the users are referred to a nearby appropriate medical specialist based on the predicted disease. For the prototype version of MIRA, we used the chief complaint of glaucoma and diabetes based on the availability of collaborative medical specialists from the Yeouido Saint Mary's Hospital, Republic of Korea.

The main contributions provided by this study are summarized as follows:

- We introduced the MIRA that identifies a disease based on user's chief complaint, understands single and multiple intent statements about a specific medical condition, and generates an appropriate response.
- We added an identity and access manager, a session manager, and security event logging and monitoring to the MIRA architecture. These provide strong authentication, manage the conversational state, and monitor the system for anomalies, respectively.
- We created a dataset of 816 patient chief complaints that were manually validated under the supervision of medical specialists, and were classified into glaucoma, diabetes, and other labels under the broad category of diseases.

- We designed stock phrases from the recorded 816 dialogue corpora that contain 11,532 utterances. Each utterance was manually annotated for intent and context identification.
- We evaluated MIRA based on a performance measure (including accuracy, precision, sensitivity, specificity, and f-measure), task completion, security, and user experience.

The rest of this paper is organized as follows. The overview of literature related to virtual medical assistants is described in Section 2. Then, Section 3 provides a comprehensive description of the MIRA methodology including system architecture, digital brain, and a case study. Subsequently, the evaluation of MIRA is presented in Section 4. Finally, Section 5 summarizes the work proposed in this study.

2. Related Work

We performed a systematic search of existing literature from the well-known digital libraries such as IEEE, ScienceDirect, ACM, Springer, PubMed, and Scopus. Based on this study, we focused on a spoken dialogue-based system that supports healthcare services. Therefore, we excluded the literature that does not focus on healthcare services and uses text, click, or touch as an interactive medium. Moreover, the studies that considered the Wizard-of-Oz concept were also filtered out. Based on these criteria, we found 14 studies and classified them into Finite State Assistants (10 studies) and Frame-based Assistants (4 studies). A comprehensive description of each category is provided in the subsequent sections.

2.1. Finite State Assistants

The finite state assistant asks a series of relevant questions to make a decision. This type of assistant does not support personalized recommendations because it follows the same sequential steps for each user. Philip et al. designed an Embodied Conversational Agent (ECA) for sleep disorder patients that ask questions using the Epworth Sleepiness Scale and identify the somnolence patients [26]. Similarly, the mental disorder diagnostic system conducts an interview based on DSM-5 criteria and identifies patients with major depressive disorders [27]. Moreover, an ECA was proposed for autism spectrum disorder patients that use audiovisual features for teaching social communication skills [28]. The proposed system is also effective for those experiencing social complications. To reduce hospitalization of suicidal patients, an e-caring avatar was proposed in [29], which involves patients in self-care conversations and recommends relevant videos. To monitor chronic pain patients, Levin et al., proposed a Pain Monitoring Voice Diary that asks a sequence of questions and identifies the severity of pain accordingly [30]. Moreover, the virtual agent for monitoring diabetic patients was proposed in [31], which makes a phone call once a week to collect vitals. Similarly, the spoken dialogue-based diabetic monitoring system collects patient vitals and helps physicians provide recommendations remotely based on the recorded information [32]. Virtual human interviewers are becoming popular due to anonymity and rapport building that supports posttraumatic stress disorder patients. Lucus et al., proposed a virtual human interviewer, which conducts an interview with military service members involved in an intense situation and identifies the symptoms associated with their mental state [33]. A similar kind of virtual agent was proposed in [34], which interacts with the users and identifies their mental symptoms using mixed methods for triangulation of data. Moreover, a rule-based patient-centric application was proposed in [35], which provides medical coaching services.

2.2. Frame-Based Assistants

The frame-based assistant analyzes and extracts the content from the user's conversation, then fills in the existing template to generate an appropriate response. The generated response may be personalized depending upon the business logic and training model of the corresponding virtual assistant. Ireland et al., proposed 'Harlie', which converses with the user on a variety of topics and helps in the neurological conditions of Parkinson's patients [36]. Similarly, a virtual nurse was proposed in [37] to support maternal healthcare and provide guidance to expectant mothers during pregnancy. A few smartphone applications are also available that provide medical information after the analysis of symptoms such as MedWhat [20], Your.MD [21], and Sensely [22]. Giorgino et al., proposed a virtual medical assistant that interacts with hypertensive patients and collects relevant data, which help the physician to evaluate the risk of cardiovascular disease [38]. In [39], the virtual medical assistant supports general practitioners by analyzing patient health conditions (using a breast cancer ontological model) and recommending an oncologist.

2.3. Limitations of Existing Studies

According to our survey analysis, we identified three limitations in the existing studies that focused on spoken dialogue-based virtual medical assistants.

- None of the existing studies considered security as a primary factor except [30], which uses the traditional PIN-based authentication mechanism [40], and it is vulnerable to brute-force attack [41]. The virtual medical assistant interacts with users and gathers health-related information. The leakage of such information may lead to different attacks such as masquerading, and ransomware [42,43]. Moreover, commercially available applications such as Your.MD [21], and Sensely [22] only comply with the security standards.
- Most of the existing studies along with commercially available virtual medical assistants analyze the input symptoms, and either provide a list of specific diseases or relevant information [44]. None of the existing spoken dialogue-based system considered patient chief complaint corpora for disease prediction or medical advice.
- Limited studies focused on frame-based assistants due to various challenges such as intent identification, context awareness, and appropriate response generation. However, it provides interactions in a natural way (i.e., similar to humans) and keeps the user motivated to continue the conversation [45].

2.4. Medical Awareness Survey

We conducted a survey to assess medical awareness among university students and determine the need for MIRA. For this purpose, we designed a questionnaire and obtained approval from the Kyung Hee University Ethics Assessment Committee (KHU-EAC) after rigorous analysis of privacy aspects. The questionnaire was distributed via email among different departments including Computer Science and Engineering, Electrical and Electronic Engineering, Biomedical Engineering, Life Sciences, and Foreign Languages. The survey form was active for five consecutive working days. We received 119 responses from the age group (18 to 36 years) across 11 countries (International Students). Figure 1 presents the country-based distribution of participants along with gender ratio of male (50.8%) and female (49.2%). The participants responded to five polar questions as shown in Table 1. The survey result showed that 25% of the respondents had an awareness of medication and take medicine without doctor consultation (such as aspirin for pain and fever, amoxicillin for infection, and many more). These participants are also able to identify appropriate medical specialists based on their symptoms. The remaining 75% discuss with friends, family or general physicians. Healthcare services are expensive in most countries. Therefore, the majority of respondents preferred to discuss their symptoms with friends or family, which helps them to determine whether to seek an appropriate medical specialist. However, a small number of participants are not open to these discussions due to personal reasons. Overall, the majority of participants were excited about an application that understands speech-based natural language, determines specific disease based on chief complaints, and recommends a nearby appropriate medical specialist.

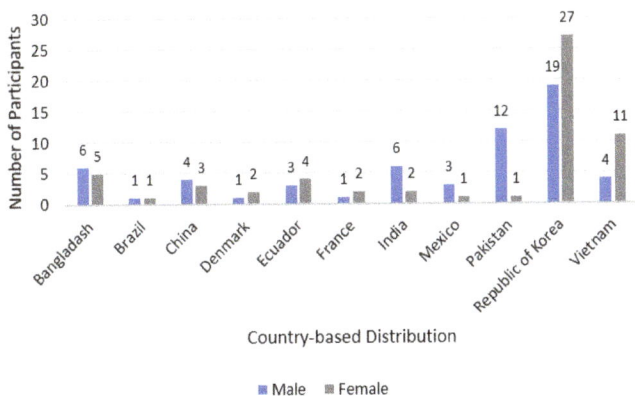

Figure 1. Medical awareness survey: Country-based distribution of participants along with gender ratio.

Table 1. Medical awareness survey questionnaire results.

Serial No.		Questions	Responses	
1		Do you have awareness of medication?	Yes (25%)	No (75%)
2		Are healthcare services expensive in your country?	Yes (83.3%)	No (16.7%)
3	3a	Based on your chief complaint, can you make a decision about an appropriate medical specialist?	Yes (25%)	No (75%)
	3b	If you selected 'No' in 3a, then with whom will you discuss the situation?	Friends or Family (61.1%)	General Physician (38.9%)
	3c	In the case of 'Friends or Family' in 3b, does the discussion help you to decide about the appropriate medical specialist?	Yes (63.6%)	No (36.4%)
4		Are you interested in a smartphone application that listens to your chief complaint and recommends a nearby appropriate medical specialist?	Yes (91.7%)	No (8.3%)
5		What type of interactive communication medium would you prefer for the smartphone application?	Speech-based (70.8%)	Text-based (29.2%)

3. Methodology

In this section, we deliver a comprehensive description of our designed state-of-the-art virtual medical assistant (MIRA), which provides efficient and reliable service to the user. First, we describe the overall system architecture of MIRA as shown in Figure 2, where the three modules (such as identity and access manager, session manager, and security event logging and monitoring) are introduced and integrated with the basic architecture (i.e., voice user interface, speech recognition, natural language understanding, and dialogue manager). Then, the next sub-section provides details about the composition of the MIRA's digital brain, which includes the knowledge source and stock phrases that support natural language understanding and appropriate response generation. Finally, we provide a case study at the end of this section that gives a better understanding of the MIRA.

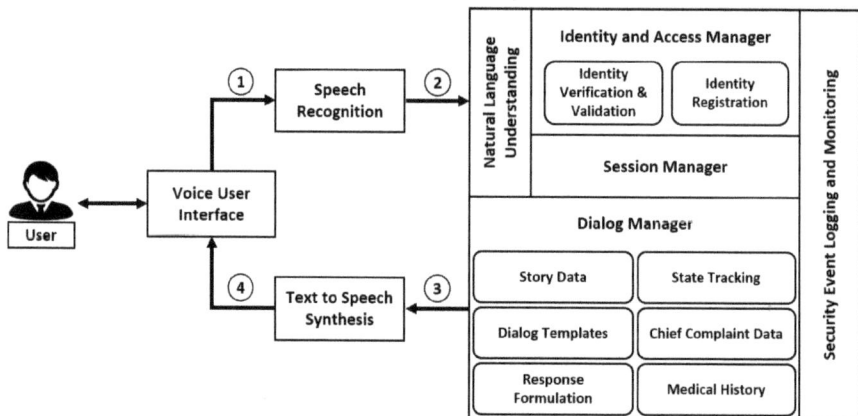

Figure 2. MIRA system architecture.

3.1. MIRA System Architecture

As illustrated in Figure 2, we added the identity and access manager, session manager, and security event logging and monitoring to the existing architecture of the virtual assistant [46,47], which overcomes the identified limitation of existing literature and virtual medical assistants. Here, the voice user interface provides an interactive communication medium between the MIRA and the user. We developed the prototype version of MIRA for Android due to wider compatibility with devices. Therefore, any smart devices (including smartwatches, smartphones, tablets, laptops, and some vendor-specific devices) that contain a microphone, speaker, and support Android can use the MIRA application. The speech recognition module recognizes human speech, then breaks it into voice samples, and transcribes each voice sample into text using the neural network algorithm for signal processing [48]. The MIRA speech recognition module automatically transcribes the voice sample in a context-specific format. Then the Natural Language Understanding (NLU) module determines the intent of user's input based on the trained model. We used the Rasa framework for machine learning-based NLU and dialogue management [49]. For tokenization and part of speech annotation, we extracted the semantic concepts from the Unified Medical Language System (UMLS) [50]. The NLU also analyzes the nature of intent and forwards a request to a specific module (such as identity and access manager, session manager, or dialogue manager).

To the best of our knowledge, MIRA is the only virtual medical assistant that uses the concept of identity and access management [51]. We used our designed voice-based authentication protocol that identifies the user based on their voice samples [52]. Instead of random text, we matched the Mel-Frequency Cestrum Coefficients (MFCC) of each natural language input to provide a strong authentication mechanism. Moreover, the identity and access management consists of two sub-modules such as identity registration, and identity verification and validation. To use MIRA services, the user has to complete the registration process using the identity registration sub-module. For this purpose, MIRA collects a smart device identifier along with personal information such as name, address, gender, age, medical history, and voice samples. Among the collected information, the smart device identifier along with voice samples support authentication. The medical history, gender, and age help in the personalized recommendation. Moreover, this module also analyzes the collected information to avoid duplication and assigns a unique identifier of 7 digits, which can be used in a crisis such as authentication failure, identity verification, or permanent data removal. The identity verification and validation sub-module verifies and validates the identity of a registered user. First, the smart device identifier links a user to the information that they provided during the registration phase. To authenticate the user, the smart device identifier helps to retrieve the provided voice sample MFCC; it is then compared with the calculated MFCC of natural language input to calculate the similarity index (SI). If the SI greater than 70%, then the user gets authenticated and MIRA generates an appropriate response.

The session manager assigns a session identifier to the authenticated users, which binds with the user identity and is valid for a specific session only. We used the keyword spotting technique, which detects 'Hello MIRA' and 'Bye MIRA' keywords in the spoken utterances. 'Hello MIRA' is used to initiate a session, and all the communication during this period is bound with the issued session identifier. The 'Bye MIRA' is used to terminate the ongoing session. We used two types of templates 'Hello [Given Name], How may I help you?' and 'Hello [Given Name], How may I help you today?' for greeting a new user with no medical history, and an established user with a medical history, respectively. Moreover, MIRA checks the validity of a corresponding session upon receiving an input request. In the case of timeout (idle for 60 minutes), the renewal request is forwarded to the session manager.

The dialogue manager is responsible for scenario understanding, state tracking and managing the flow of the conversation. This module identifies the conversational context from the natural language input and generates an appropriate response. It may be possible that the user starts another conversation without terminating or concluding the previous one. This type of conversation handling is not in the scope of this study. Moreover, the dialogue manager consists of six sub-modules. (i) The story data are used to train the dialogue management model. A story is the representation of a complete dialogue between the user and virtual assistant. We designed the story data manually from the recorded dialogue corpora that facilitate MIRA to make the conversation real and natural. (ii) The state tracking is the core module of MIRA that predicts the user goal (represented by slot-value pairs) at every dialogue turn. It maintains the conversation state, performs an action based on policy, and generates a relevant response after analyzing the natural language input. (iii) The dialogue templates consist of predefined statements that can be used by filling in the keyword. Although we trained a model to understand conversation and response generation, some statements are similar and common except for the keyword. Consider the statements 'Do you feel hungry?' and 'Do you feel tired?'. Both sentences are similar except for the keywords 'hungry' and 'tired'. To improve the performance and response generation of MIRA, we used templates for these kinds of statements that have similar semantics. (iv) The chief complaint data is the knowledge source that helps identify the conversation context. Based on the identified context, MIRA analyzes the dialogue corpora and asks a follow-up question. (v) The medical history consists of the health record that a user provided during registration. It also stores each recommendation along with the key attributes (sign and symptom) that results from the conversation between MIRA and the user. Keeping these health records helps the MIRA to generate a personalized decision for future conversations. (vi) The response formulation has a challenging role in the interaction because it generates a relevant response based on the input query. Therefore, this module takes the necessary information from different sub-modules of the dialogue manager and generates an appropriate text-based statement.

The text to speech synthesis analyzes and processes the text-based statement using natural language processing. Then, it converts the processed text into synthesized speech using digital signal processing and conveys it to the end-user in a polite female voice. MIRA deals with healthcare data and directs the user to a nearby appropriate medical specialist based on the chief complaints. This kind of dialogue contains sensitive information and its leakage may lead to serious consequences such as a masquerading and ransomware attacks. The security event logging and monitoring module continuously monitors the communication channels for anomalies. Also, it collects the information, which can be used as an audit trail for intrusion prevention and event management. With the proposed system architecture, MIRA understands single and multiple intent statements, supports adaptability, and provides data control.

3.2. Understanding the MIRA Digital Brain

According to [53], a virtual assistant consists of a digital brain, which is divided into a knowledge source, stock phrases, and conversation memory. Our state-of-the-art MIRA's digital brain is divided into a knowledge source, and stock phrases. We incorporated the conversation memory inside the stock phrases for efficient response generation. The knowledge source is an important part of a virtual assistant that helps in understanding the context of a conversation. Our proposed MIRA focused on the identification of a disease based on the user's chief complaint. In this regard, the first challenge that we faced was the selection of an appropriate dataset. We analyzed the publicly available datasets on the Internet, but to the best of our knowledge, none of the available datasets in English considered the patient chief complaint. Most of the datasets considered medical terminologies that are hard to understand for non-medical professionals. Therefore, we decided to create a dataset considering the patient chief complaints. For this purpose, we selected two well-known diseases, glaucoma and diabetes, due to the availability of collaborative medical specialists from the Yeouido Saint Mary's Hospital in the Republic of Korea. Under the hospital's legal policy (Institutional Review Board approval) and HIPAA (Health Insurance Portability and Accountability Act), we briefed the participants before their medical examinations, and a written consent form was signed by each participant. This form explained that the data would be collected anonymously and strictly used for research purposes (considered the privacy aspects) only. We collected 816 patient chief complaints and, based on the medical specialist's recommendation, classified them into glaucoma (48.5%), diabetes (46.2%), and other (5.3%). These labels were assigned based on the broad category of diseases. The glaucoma label consists of all patients, which includes angle-closure suspect, glaucoma suspect, and pure glaucoma patients. Similarly, the diabetes label consists of all types of diabetic patients, which include type 1, type 2, and gestational. The other label consists of those patients that have diseases except glaucoma and diabetes, including normal conditions. We represented the data in tabular form that consist of 816 rows and 32 columns. Each row represents one patient with potential symptoms, while the columns represent observed features for that patient, including the class of diagnosis label (glaucoma, diabetes, or other). Table 2 describes 31 features of the MIRA dataset. Collecting such data helps us to identify specific patients based on their chief complaints since the categorization of these patients is based on different laboratory test results and medical specialist opinion.

After the creation of the knowledge source, the next challenge was to identify the most appropriate predictive model. For this purpose, we used MOD [54], which filters out seven applicable machine learning models (including decision trees, naive Bayes, K-nearest neighbors, random forest, random tree, decision stump, and deep learning) based on the provided dataset features. To determine the accuracy of each predictive model for MIRA's dataset, we used RapidMiner with 10-fold cross-validation and evaluated the predictive model accuracy as shown in Figure 3. The result shows higher accuracy for the deep learning model (99.14%) because it learns from data incrementally and identifies the hidden relationships. Therefore, we selected deep learning as the best suitable predictive model for MIRA. The predictive model along with knowledge source helps in context identification of a dialogue corpus, which determines the category of the disease such as glaucoma, diabetes, or other. The stock phrases help MIRA to understand the user intent (what the user is trying to say) and support response generation. We searched online for publicly available patient-doctor dialogue corpora in the English language, but none of the relevant datasets were found. Therefore, we decided to design the dialogue corpus from the recorded patient-doctor conversation, which includes 816 dialogue corpora (11,532 utterances). We manually annotated each utterance for NLU and the dialogue manager to make the interactive environment of MIRA as real and natural as possible.

Table 2. MIRA Dataset features with ranges, measurement units, and meaning of each feature.

Feature Name	Value Range	Measurement Unit	Meaning
Age	[17, 73]	Years	Age of the patients
Gender	0, 1	Category	Male or Female
Urinating often	0, 1	Boolean	Frequent urination can be a symptom of many diseases such as diabetes
Feeling thirsty	0, 1	Boolean	Urge to drink too much may indicate diseases such as diabetes
Feeling hungry	0, 1	Boolean	Patient may feel strong hunger due to low blood sugar; it may indicate diabetes because of an abnormal glucose level
Extreme fatigue	0, 1	Boolean	Uncontrolled blood glucose may leads to tiredness
Blurry vision	0, 1	Boolean	In diabetes, a high blood glucose level may lead to temporary blurring of eyesight; moreover, damaged optic nerves increase the intraocular pressure that may leads to haziness or blurry vision
Slow-healing wounds	0, 1	Boolean	High blood glucose level may affect the blood circulation, which may leads to the slow-healing of wounds.
Weight loss	0, 1	Boolean	The body starts burning fat and muscle for energy with insufficient insulin
Has tingling sensation	0, 1	Boolean	Diabetic neuropathy may lead to tingling sensations in fingers, toes, hands, and feet, and burning may occur as well
Pain	0, 1	Boolean	Diabetic neuropathy may leads to pain in different body parts such as arms, legs or sometimes the whole body
Numbness of hands	0, 1	Boolean	Diabetic neuropathy may lead to numbness of hands
Numbness of foot	0, 1	Boolean	Diabetic neuropathy may lead to numbness of feet
Burning sensation in eye	0, 1	Boolean	Stinging or irritating sensation in the eyes
Color vision impairment	0, 1	Boolean	Color vision impairment is the initial symptom of glaucoma
Difficulty walking	0, 1	Boolean	Glaucoma patients frequently complain of difficulty walking
Difficulty in stair climbing	0, 1	Boolean	Glaucoma patients frequently complain of difficulty climbing stairs
Difficulty in face recognition	0, 1	Boolean	Glaucoma patients frequently complain of difficulty recognizing faces
Difficulty driving	0, 1	Boolean	Glaucoma patients frequently complain of difficulty driving
Double vision	0, 1	Boolean	Diplopia is considered to be a warning for glaucoma
Dryness of eyes	0, 1	Boolean	Dryness of eyes is due to the lack of proper tear production
Swelling of eyelids	0, 1	Boolean	Occurs due to inflammation or excess of fluid
Tear in eyes with a strong glare	0, 1	Boolean	Unusual squinting or blinking due to a strong glare or light
Image quality decrease	0, 1	Boolean	Peripheral vision loss may be an early symptom of glaucoma
Itchiness	0, 1	Boolean	Itchiness caused due to the low quantity of eye fluid or low interocular pressure
Nausea and vomiting	0, 1	Boolean	Severe eye pain may cause nausea and vomiting
Headache	0, 1	Boolean	Severe eye pain may cause headache
Night blindness	0, 1	Boolean	Nyctalopia is a condition where the eye is unable to adapt to the surrounding conditions such as low-light, or nighttime
Redness of eyes	0, 1	Boolean	Caused due to swollen or dilated blood vessels
Severe eye pain	0, 1	Boolean	The rapid eye pressure increase causes severe eye pain
Sudden onset of visual disturbances usually in low light	0, 1	Boolean	The basic signs and symptoms of acute angle closure glaucoma

3.3. Case Study

To understand the working scenario of MIRA, consider John Doe, a registered user, who wants to discuss his medical condition with MIRA and is looking for an appropriate medical specialist nearby. John started the conversation by saying 'Hello MIRA'. The speech recognition recognizes the natural language input as received from the voice user interface, transcribes it into text, and sends

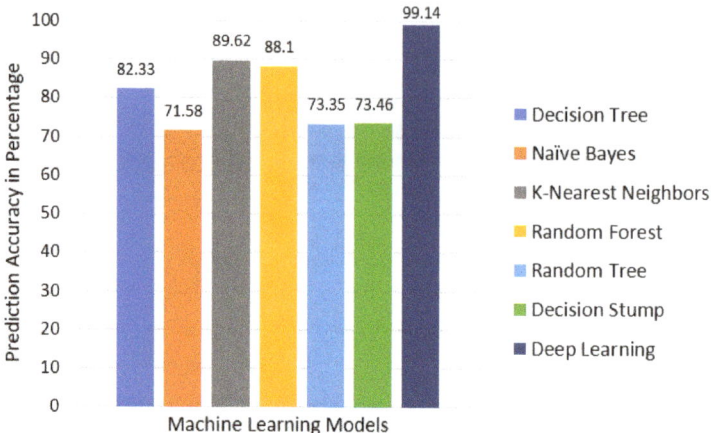

Figure 3. MIRA prediction accuracy with machine learning models.

it to the NLU to identify the intent of the utterance, which is a greeting in this case. The intent-text pair (intent: greeting, Text: Hello MIRA) along with voice-print is sent to the identity and access manager, which verifies and validates John's identity using the MFCC matching technique. Upon approval, the request is forwarded to the session manager, which determines whether John has an ongoing session or the phrase is to initiate a new conversational session. According to the session manager, John does not have an ongoing session. Therefore, the session manager generates a new session identifier linked with John's identity and forwards the request to the dialogue manager for generating a relevant response. At first, the dialogue manager analyzes the state for an ongoing conversation using state tracking, then infers the intent of the request based on the chief complaint data and medical history. In this case, John did not provide any medical history during the registration phase and initiated the conversation with a greeting utterance, which does not link to any of the chief complaints. Therefore, the inferred request is forwarded to the story data for selecting an appropriate story. Then, a new user greeting template is selected using the dialogue templates and is forwarded to the response formulation, which customizes the template based on the user identifier to generate a text statement. The text to speech synthesis receives this text, transcribes it into a spoken response, and plays it on a smart device speaker. A similar procedure will be followed for handling each dialogue corpus. At any point of the conversation, the user can say 'Bye MIRA' to terminate the session. Figure 4 illustrates the MIRA implementation model for handling a complex conversation. The different colored lines present the workflow and inter-connectivity between the basic modules.

Figure 5 presents the MIRA smartphone application screenshots. The user interface shows a circularly shaped gray button on the main screen, which can be used to activate MIRA by pressing the button. Upon activation, MIRA starts listening, and the color of the button changes to bright green. We set the listening duration to 5 seconds, but it can be changed to 1 minute from the application setting. When the time is up, MIRA starts analyzing the spoken natural language and changes the button color to orange. We used the color change technique because warm colors have a positive impact on the user's emotions and behavior as per psychology [55]. Furthermore, MIRA displays the input and output natural language on the smartphone screen in the form of a chat bubble for better understanding along with the spoken response. MIRA switches to an idle state (gray color), if the user does not speak for 5 seconds, which requires reactivation by pressing the gray button. However, the session identifier will be valid until the user terminates by saying 'Bye MIRA' or the conversation is idle for 60 consecutive minutes. As a final recommendation, a frame of Google maps shows the nearby appropriate medical specialist. By clicking the map frame, the query will open in Google maps.

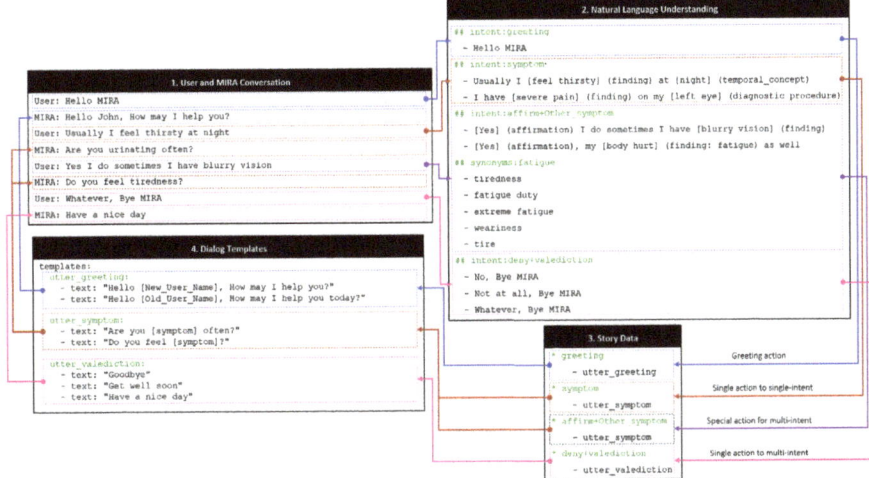

Figure 4. MIRA implementation model for conversational handling.

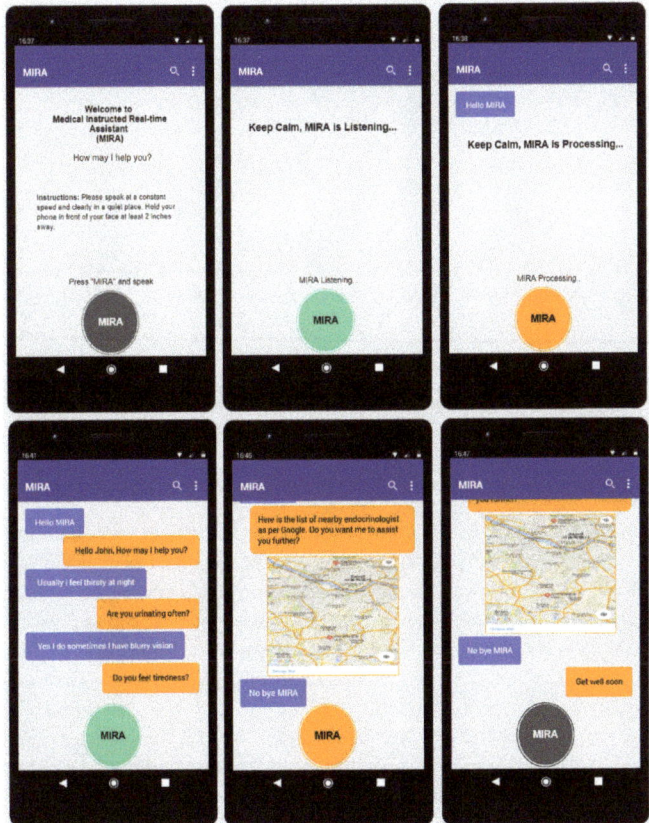

Figure 5. MIRA smartphone application screenshot on android pie.

4. Evaluation

MIRA provides efficient and reliable healthcare services to the users. To ensure productivity, we evaluated MIRA based on performance measures, task completion, security, and user experience. For this purpose, we circulated a call for participants on the university's mailing list and social media. A total of 33 participants belonging to seven countries registered, including 20 males and 13 females within the age group of 18 to 43 years as shown in Figure 6. The participants were affiliated with different departments such as Healthcare Subject Matter Experts (5), Medical Practitioners (4), and students belonging to Medical (7), Computer Science (9), Bioinformatics (3), Life Science (3), and International Relations (2) disciplines. Each participant was given a set of procedural documents, which contained a checklist of tasks, consent form, hints for acting as a particular patient type, and a user experience questionnaire. The consent form clearly describes the data collection procedure, including audio and video recording of interactions with MIRA, data storage, data usage, and disposal details. Moreover, participants were shortly briefed about the goal of the activity, and we instruct them to sign the consent form after reading it carefully. Upon agreement, the voice sample along with demographic information (name, address, gender, age, and medical history) was collected to complete the MIRA registration process.

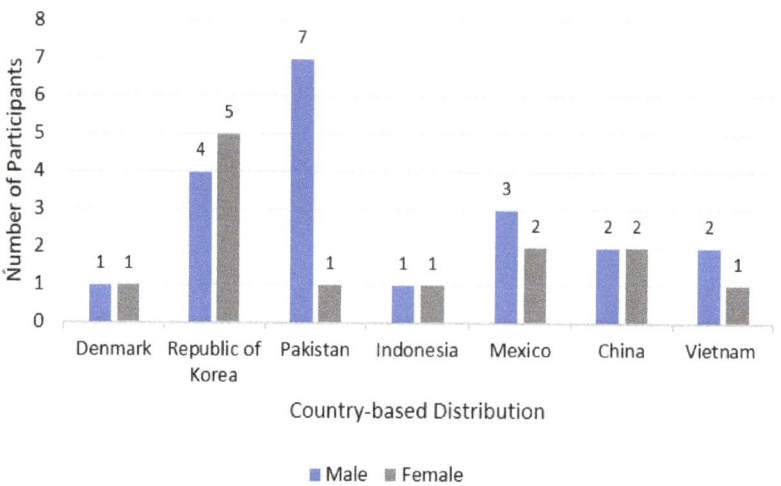

Figure 6. Country-based distribution of MIRA evaluation participants.

As per the scope of this study, MIRA predicts glaucoma and diabetes based on the trained model. The remaining diseases including normal conditions are out of scope and are considered under the other label. Therefore, MIRA analyzed user interactions, identified chief complaints, and categorized these as glaucoma, diabetes, or other. Among the 33 registered participants, 17 did not belong to the medical profession. For this reason, we provided a list of chief complaints as described in Table 3, which guide the participants to act as a patient for three health conditions. In the case of other label, we selected cardiovascular and orthopedic chief complaints that are similar to glaucoma and diabetes. If MIRA did not generate a final recommendation for some reason, then it politely responded 'I am sorry, I am not able to diagnose your disease based on the provided knowledge. Do you want me to assist you further?'. Moreover, the participants were allowed to use synonyms, ask questions in a random sequence, and interact in a natural way of communication.

Table 3. Sample of hints for acting as glaucoma, diabetes, and other, patient types.

Chief Complaints of Different Diseases (Feel Free to Use Any Synonyms Related to These Chief Complaints)		
Glaucoma	Diabetes	Other
Blurry vision	Blurry vision	Sweating
Burning sensation or dryness or itchiness in eye(s)	Extreme fatigue	Pain
Color vision impairment	Feeling very hungry	Nausea and vomiting
Difficulty in driving, face recognition, stair climbing, and walking	Feeling very thirsty	Shortness of breath
Double vision or decrease in image quality or sudden onset of visual disturbance usually in low light	Numbness of feet	Discomfort in body parts such as neck, jaw, shoulder, upper back, or abdominal
Nausea and vomiting with headache	Numbness of hands	Unusual fatigue
Night blindness	Pain	Lightheadedness or dizziness
Red eyes	Slow healing of cuts and bruises	Stiffness
Severe eye pain	Tingling sensation	Swelling
Swelling in eyelid	Urinating often	Instability
Tears in eyes with a strong glare	Weight loss	Deformity

4.1. Experimental Setup

We set up an interactive environment based on the availability of resources, which includes three android smartphones (Samsung Galaxy S7), three iPhones (6s), three cell phone holders, and three tripod mounts. The MIRA application was installed on three android smartphones, and these were attached to classroom desks with the help of cell phone holders, which can be adjusted. The three iPhones attached to tripod mounts were used for audio and video recording of each user's interaction with MIRA. Complete sets of equipment were placed at three corners of the classroom, which include an android smartphone, cell phone holder, iPhone, tripod mount, classroom desk, and chair. Only three participants can interact with MIRA simultaneously in the design experimental setup. Therefore, we divided the participants into 11 groups (three members per group) based on their availability and feasibility. Each member of the group can interact with MIRA independently for an allocated time of 60 minutes while acting like a patient using the provided hints.

4.2. Performance Evaluation

To assess the effectiveness of MIRA, we used the common performance evaluation measure based on an independently distributed confusion matrix, as described in Table 4. The values were assigned based on the final recommendation label. The diagonal and off-diagonal values of the confusion matrix present correctly classified and incorrectly classified results, respectively. Similarly, the rows and columns of the confusion matrix show actual values per label and predicted value per label, respectively. Furthermore, the characteristics of performance evaluation measurement are reflected in terms of accuracy, precision, sensitivity, specificity, and F-measure. The corresponding description along with formulas for these measures are described as follows. Each participant completed the interaction for three health conditions that included glaucoma, diabetes, and other. Figure 7 illustrates the value of each label. We recorded a total of 99 dialogue corpus based on the interactions of 33 participants.

Table 4. MIRA confusion matrix.

	Glaucoma	Diabetes	Other
Glaucoma	30	1	2
Diabetes	3	28	2
Other	1	1	31

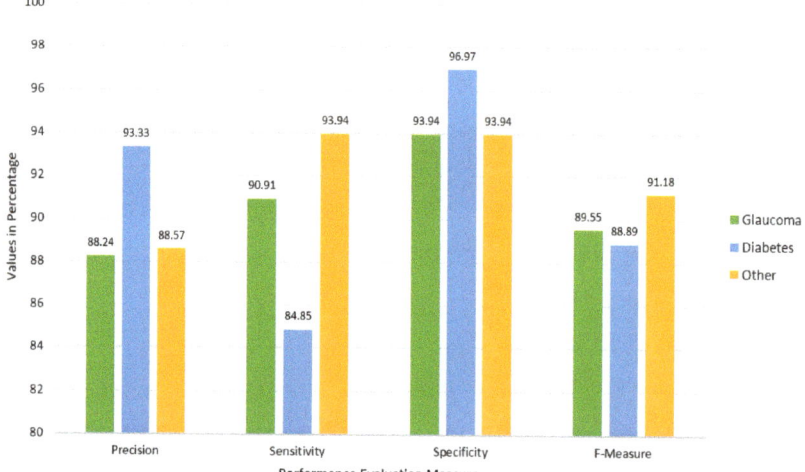

Figure 7. Performance evaluation measure of interactive scenarios.

- Accuracy identifies the effectiveness of an algorithm based on the probability of true values as stated in Equation (1). MIRA gets an overall accuracy of 89.8% because it correctly identified 90.9% glaucoma (30), 84.8% diabetes (28), and 93.9% other (31) labels among the recorded dialogue corpus (99).

$$Accuracy = \frac{Sum of Correctly Classified}{Total Number of Classification} \quad (1)$$

- Precision or confidence presents the positive predictive value of a label that can be derived using Equation (2). We obtained the precision for each label including glaucoma (88.24%), diabetes (93.33%), and other (88.57%), with an average precision of 90%.

$$Precision = \frac{True Positive}{True Positive + False Positive} \quad (2)$$

- Sensitivity (also known as recall) corresponds to the true positive rate of a specific label and can be computed with Equation (3) for glaucoma (90.91%), diabetes (84.85%), and other (93.94%), with an average value of 89.8%.

$$Sensitivity = \frac{True Positive}{True Positive + False Negative} \quad (3)$$

- Specificity corresponds to the true negative rate and can be computed using Equation (4) for a specific label for glaucoma (93.94%), diabetes (96.97%), and other (93.94%), with an average value of 94.9%.

$$Specificity = \frac{True Negative}{False Positive + True Negative} \quad (4)$$

- The F-measure, also known as F-score or F1-score, is the weighted harmonic mean of precision and sensitivity (recall) as stated in Equation (5). The F-Measures for each label in MIRA were as follows: glaucoma (89.55%), diabetes (88.89%), and other (91.18%), with an average value of 89.8%. We used $\beta = 1$ that evenly balances the F-score based on precision and sensitivity.

$$F - Measure = \frac{(\beta^2 + 1) * Precision * Sensitivity}{\beta^2 * Precision + Sensitivity} \quad (5)$$

4.3. Task Completion

Task completion is an important factor in the virtual assistant. It measures the task success probability of dialogue corpora. To assess MIRA's task completion, we used the PARADISE (PARAdigm for DIalogue System Evaluation) framework that uses the Kappa coefficient to operationalize the measure of task-based success [56]. The Kappa coefficient k measures the success rate of task completion and is computed with Equation (6).

$$k = \frac{P(A) - P(E)}{1 - P(E)} \quad (6)$$

$P(A)$ is the proportion of times that agreement occurs between the actual and scenario attribute value. $P(E)$ is the proportion of times when the agreement between the actual and scenario attribute value is expected. The value of k considers task complexity and assesses the virtual assistant by correcting for the expected agreement and performing different tasks. If agreement is only expected by chance, then $k = 1$ and $k = 0$ for total agreement and no agreement, respectively. Moreover, if the expected chance of agreement ($P(E)$) is unknown, then it can be calculated from the confusion matrix using Equation (7).

$$P(E) = \sum_{i=1}^{n} \left(\frac{t_i}{T}\right)^2 \quad (7)$$

Here, t_i is the sum of the ith column frequency of the confusion matrix. T is the sum of frequency $t_1 + t_2 + ... + t_n$ in the confusion matrix. Similarly, P(A) can be calculated from the confusion matrix with Equation (8), if unknown.

$$P(A) = \frac{\sum_{i=1}^{n} M(i,i)}{T} \quad (8)$$

MIRA task completion based on the PARADISE framework gives Expected Agreement $P(E) = 0.334$, Actual Agreement $P(A) = 0.898$, and Kappa Coefficient $k = 0.848$. The interpretation of Kappa categorized MIRA as 'Almost Perfect' in term of task completion [57].

4.4. Security

Healthcare applications deal with sensitive data such as medical records, health conditions, and quality of life. The illegal usage of these data may lead to several attacks. For this purpose, we launched a masquerading attack based on the scope of this study. The prevention of masquerading attack also minimizes the risk of ransomware.

The masquerading attack uses a fake identity to gain unauthorized access [58]. To launch this attack on MIRA, we asked the members of each group to shift their positions. Suppose the participants on positions C, B, and A will shift to A, C, and B respectively. Then, the adjacent member gets access to the authenticated user account of MIRA and starts an interaction. During the analysis of natural language input, MIRA verifies the device identifier, but is unable to validate the MFCC value.

Therefore, MIRA holds the ongoing session and asks the participant for identity verification as 'Sorry for the interruption, malicious activity was detected. To proceed with the ongoing session, please enter your seven digit identity verification key'. At this stage, the user has to enter the identity verification key to interact with MIRA. Moreover, if an unauthorized user wants to interact after session time out (60 minutes), then MIRA will respond as 'I am sorry, but I am not able to verify your identity. Do you want me to assist you through the registration process?'. Furthermore, one smart device identifier can bind with multiple user identities, which means that more than one user can use the same device, but registration is mandatory for each user. The results show that MIRA prevents against masquerading attacks because none of the participants were able to interact with other user applications due to voice-based authentication.

4.5. User Experience

After interacting with MIRA, the participants were asked to fill out the User Experience Questionnaire (UEQ) [59], which covers all the aspect of user experience in a comprehensive way. The UEQ is widely used as a subjective measurement of user experience and provides a data analysis tool for assessing user responses. Therefore, we used it to evaluate the MIRA user experience. It consists of 26 items using a 7 point Likert scale for rating. The results of these 26 items are mapped with 6-dimensional scales such as attractiveness (6 items), perspicuity (4 items), efficiency (4 items), dependability (4 items), stimulation (4 items), and novelty (4 items) as shown in Figure 8. The x-axis and y-axis present the list of items and rating scales (extremely good(+3), neutral (0), horribly bad (-3)), respectively. Furthermore, the 6-dimensional scales are grouped into pragmatic quality (perspicuity, efficiency, and dependability), and hedonic quality (stimulation, originality). The pragmatic deals with task-related quality aspects, while the hedonic describes non-task related quality aspects.

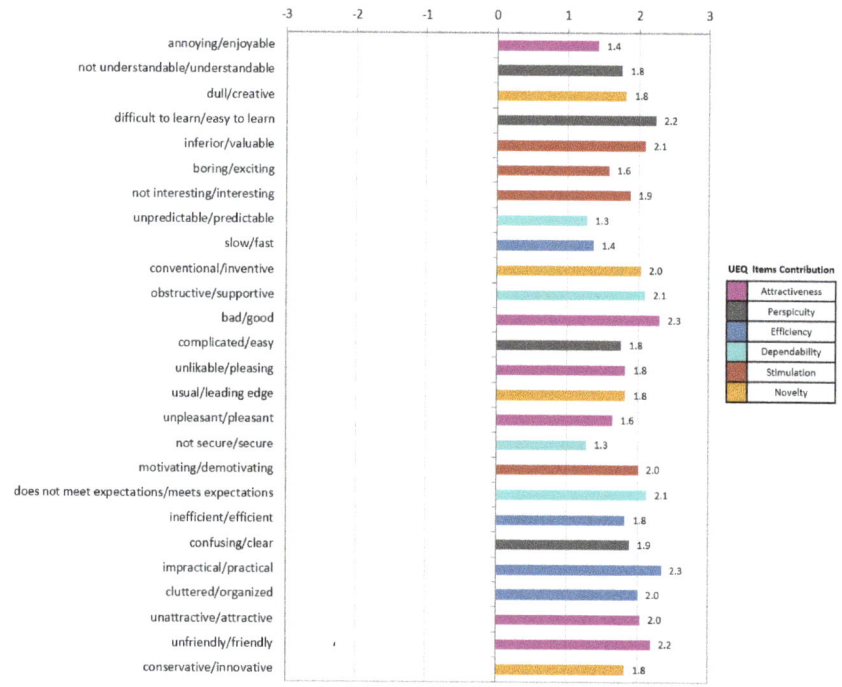

Figure 8. MIRA user experience questionnaire mean value per item.

Figure 9 illustrates the result of MIRA based on 6-dimensional scales, which exhibit accurate measurements because the values are greater than 1.6. Moreover, Figure 10 presents MIRA's attractiveness and pragmatic quality along with hedonic quality, where the value is greater than 1.80, reflecting a positive evaluation based on UEQ criteria. To identify the correlation of items per scale, UEQ uses Cronbach's alpha-coefficient, which measures the consistency of a scale as shown in Table 5. The value of attractiveness is higher than 0.7, which means that all users enjoyed the interactions with MIRA. Most of the participants recommend an avatar instead of a simple user interface for MIRA. Therefore, the alpha-coefficient value of novelty was less than 0.5. Furthermore, Figure 11 presents a comparative analysis of MIRA based on the UEQ benchmark dataset, which consists of 401 product evaluations collected from 18483 participants. The results show that MIRA is relatively good in all aspects based on the benchmark data.

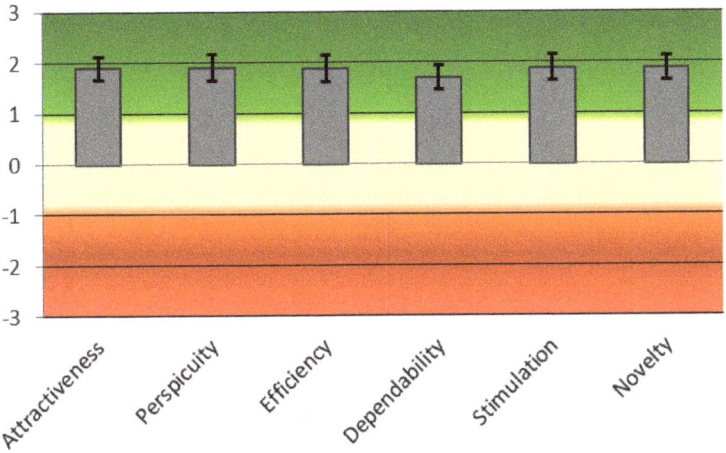

Figure 9. MIRA user experience questionnaire resulting scores on six dimensional scale.

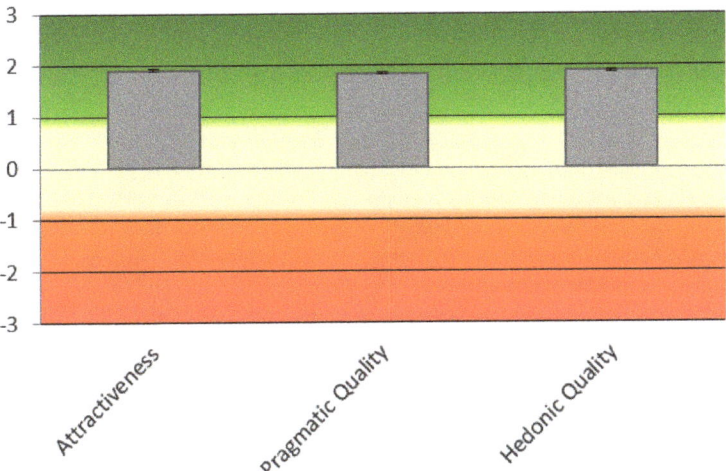

Figure 10. MIRA user experience questionnaire aggregated score of pragmatic and hedonic qualities.

Table 5. Correlation of items per scale using Cronbach's Alpha Coefficient.

Scale	Alpha-Coefficient
Attractiveness	0.74
Perspicuity	0.67
Efficiency	0.77
Dependability	0.60
Stimulation	0.67
Novelty	0.48

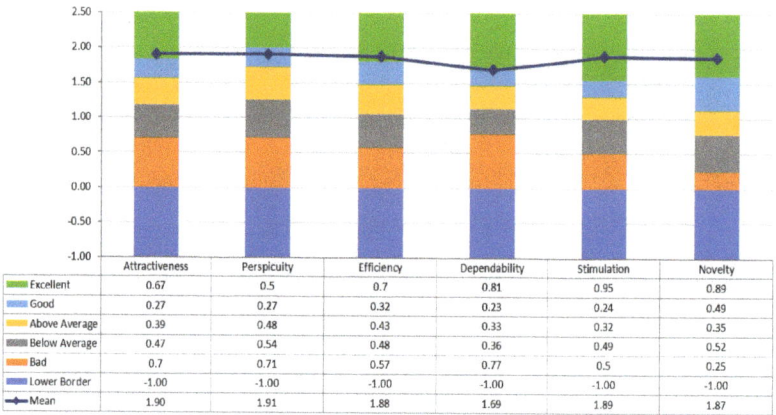

Figure 11. MIRA user experience questionnaire scores on six dimensions scales along with benchmark data.

4.6. Discussion

MIRA was evaluated by 33 participants belonging to different domains, age groups, genders, and diverse nationalities. The participants were given 60 minutes to complete a list of tasks during the interaction with MIRA. Among the 33 participants, 27 completed their tasks at an average time of 40 minutes because their interaction was smooth with little or no misinterpretation. However, 6 participants took an average of 55 minutes due to several misinterpretations such as 'thirsty' as 'thirty', 'tired' as 'tire', 'driving' as 'diving', and 'tear' as 'tire'. Based on these interactions, MIRA gets an overall accuracy of 89% because it used the deep learning predictive model, which learns from the data incrementally and manages complex dialogues efficiently. We considered the macro-average instead of micro-average for calculating precision (90%), sensitivity (89.8%), specificity (94.9%), and F-measure (89.8%) of the complete system. Please note that the macro-average gives equal weight to each class label, while the micro-average results are biased towards the larger class label. Therefore, we showed impressive results for MIRA in terms of efficiency and effectiveness. Moreover, the PARADISE framework was used to evaluate the task completion of MIRA, where the actual agreement $(P(A) = 0.898)$ is better than agreement-by-chance $(P(E) = 0.334)$. Because the stock phrases were designed from real conversations that facilitated MIRA for a better understanding of natural language input. The Cohen's Kappa value $(k = 0.848)$ was interpreted as 'Almost Perfect' because MIRA generated the response in a real and natural way using a female voice that keeps the user motivated to continue the interaction.

MIRA also keeps a record of the conversational dialogue corpus along with final recommendation about the appropriate medical specialist that supports personalized interactions with the established user. For the prototype version of MIRA, we considered authentication instead of confidentiality, integrity, and availability. A strong authentication mechanism minimizes the risk of exploiting security vulnerabilities but will affect the performance and efficiency of the system. Therefore, we used the lightweight version of our designed voice-based authentication protocol, which identifies the user based on the extracted MFCC value of natural language utterances; this method was evaluated for masquerading attack. The results showed that MIRA successfully identified the user in real time based on their voice samples and strongly resisted a masquerading attack.

We used UEQ for evaluating the user experience because it provides ease of data analysis and calculates the necessary statistics accordingly. Due to reliability, different organizations used UEQ for evaluating their products and consider it to be a good measure. According to UEQ, MIRA was evaluated in terms of attractiveness, pragmatic quality, and hedonic quality, where the value of pragmatic is smaller than the other two qualities (attractiveness and hedonic). This is due to the low value of secure and predictable items under the category of pragmatic quality because some participants considered secure in terms of security, but it evaluates the user's feelings regarding the interaction control. Moreover, MIRA uses synonyms of specific words for generating a relevant response, which may be unpredictable for a conversational scenario in some situations. Suppose in one interaction MIRA asked a user, 'How about your empty-bellied?' instead of 'Do you feel extremely hungry?'. The value of pragmatic quality is affected by these two factors. However, the overall results of UEQ present positive feedback, and users were satisfied with MIRA's interactive communication.

After the completion of tasks, the participants were awarded a shopping coupon worth 30,000 KRW as an incentive. The participants belonged to diverse nationalities that helped assess how MIRA deals with a variety of accents as well. According to our analysis, some participants do not realize the voice-based authentication mechanism due to the lightweight protocol until they were asked to switch their positions for performing a masquerading attack. In the future we plan to evaluate MIRA with real glaucoma and diabetic patients, then compare the results of both assessments. Furthermore, we will evaluate MIRA for relevant emerging cyber-attacks.

5. Conclusions

In this study, we introduced a state-of-the-art virtual medical assistant, MIRA, that interacts with the user in a spoken natural language, diagnoses a disease based on a user's chief complaint, and refers the user to a nearby appropriate medical specialist. The key contribution of MIRA includes disease identification based on chief complaint, understanding single and multiple intents, a voice-based authentication mechanism, conversational state tracking, and continuous monitoring of the system for detecting anomalies. Moreover, we designed a chief complaint dataset and stock phrases from the recorded dialogue corpora. MIRA is the first assistant of its kind that considers security aspects (such as authentication), which requires improvements in terms of transmission security and audit control to become HIPAA compliant. The designed knowledge source of MIRA considered glaucoma and diabetes chief complaints only, which can be extended to other medical conditions in the future.

There are many challenges in developing these kinds of interactive systems such as privacy concerns, accuracy constraints, correct decision making, precise response generation, and gaining user trust. The compliance with standards may help in risk minimization. Besides these challenges, it is beneficial for society, especially in underdeveloped countries, where people are suffering from many diseases due to the lack of healthcare facilities. These kinds of virtual medical assistants help the patient identify an appropriate medical specialist and reduce healthcare cost. Also, it supports medical practitioners and students in clinical decision making.

Author Contributions: U.U.R. is the principal researcher, who proposed the idea, designed and developed the prototype version, conducted the experiments based on the designed scenarios, and wrote the paper. D.J.C. and Y.J. provided the medical related information, supported in data acquisition and analysis. U.A. and M.A.R. contributed to participant management, English proofreading and finalized content flow in the manuscript. S.L. supervised the whole process, provided advisory feedback, and reviewed the manuscript. All authors have read and agreed to the published version of the manuscript.

Funding: This research was supported by the MSIT (Ministry of Science and ICT), Korea, under the ITRC (Information Technology Research Center) support program (IITP-2017-0-01629) supervised by the IITP (Institute for Information & communications Technology Promotion). This work was supported by the Institute for Information & communications Technology Promotion (IITP) grant funded by the Korea government (MSIT) (No. 2017-0-00655). This work was also supported by the National Research Foundation (NRF) under the NRF-2016K1A3A7A03951968 and NRF-2019R1A2C2090504.

Conflicts of Interest: The authors declare no conflict of interest.

References

1. Canbek, N.G.; Mutlu, M.E. On the track of artificial intelligence: Learning with intelligent personal assistants. *J. Hum. Sci.* **2016**, *13*, 592–601.
2. Van Os, M.; Saddler, H.J.; Napolitano, L.T.; Russell, J.H.; Lister, P.M.; Dasari, R. Intelligent Automated Assistant for TV User Interactions. US Patent 9,338,493, 2016.
3. Bartie, P.; Mackaness, W.; Lemon, O.; Dalmas, T.; Janarthanam, S.; Hill, R.L.; Dickinson, A.; Liu, X. A dialogue based mobile virtual assistant for tourists: The SpaceBook Project. *Comput. Environ. Urban Syst.* **2018**, *67*, 110–123.
4. Page, L.C.; Gehlbach, H. How an artificially intelligent virtual assistant helps students navigate the road to college. *AERA Open* **2017**, *3*, 2332858417749220.
5. Lam, M.S. Keeping the Internet Open with an Open-Source Virtual Assistant. In *Proceedings of the 24th Annual International Conference on Mobile Computing and Networking*; ACM: New York, NY, USA, 2018; pp. 145–146.
6. Austerjost, J.; Porr, M.; Riedel, N.; Geier, D.; Becker, T.; Scheper, T.; Marquard, D.; Lindner, P.; Beutel, S. Introducing a Virtual Assistant to the Lab: A Voice User Interface for the Intuitive Control of Laboratory Instruments. *SLAS TECHNOL. Transl. Life Sci. Innov.* **2018**, *23*, 476–482.
7. Yan, R.; Song, Y.; Wu, H. Learning to respond with deep neural networks for retrieval-based human-computer conversation system. In *Proceedings of the 39th International ACM SIGIR Conference on Research and Development in Information Retrieval*; ACM: New York, NY, USA, 2016; pp. 55–64.
8. Hwang, E.J.; Jung, J.Y.; Lee, S.K.; Lee, S.E.; Jee, W.H. Machine Learning for Diagnosis of Hematologic Diseases in Magnetic Resonance Imaging of Lumbar Spines. *Sci. Rep.* **2019**, *9*, 6046.
9. Omondiagbe, D.A.; Veeramani, S.; Sidhu, A.S. Machine Learning Classification Techniques for Breast Cancer Diagnosis. In *IOP Conference Series: Materials Science and Engineering*; IOP Publishing: Bristol, UK, 2019; Volume 495, p. 012033.
10. Pigoni, A.; Delvecchio, G.; Madonna, D.; Bressi, C.; Soares, J.; Brambilla, P. Can Machine Learning help us in dealing with treatment resistant depression? A review. *J. Affect. Disord.* **2019**, *259*, 21–26.
11. Künzel, S.R.; Sekhon, J.S.; Bickel, P.J.; Yu, B. Metalearners for estimating heterogeneous treatment effects using machine learning. *Proc. Natl. Acad. Sci. USA* **2019**, *116*, 4156–4165.
12. Callahan, A.; Shah, N.H. Machine learning in healthcare. In *Key Advances in Clinical Informatics*; Elsevier: Amsterdam, The Netherlands, 2017; pp. 279–291.
13. Sinsky, C.; Colligan, L.; Li, L.; Prgomet, M.; Reynolds, S.; Goeders, L.; Westbrook, J.; Tutty, M.; Blike, G. Allocation of physician time in ambulatory practice: a time and motion study in 4 specialties. *Ann. Intern. Med.* **2016**, *165*, 753–760.
14. Nuance AI-Powered Virtual Assistants for Healthcare. Available online: https://www.nuance.com/healthcare/ambient-clinical-intelligence/virtual-assistants.html (Accessed on March 13, 2019).
15. Suki Let Doctors Focus on What Matters. Available online: https://www.suki.ai/about-us (Accessed on March 23, 2019).
16. Robin Healthcare. Available online: https://www.robinhealthcare.com (Accessed on March 24, 2019).
17. UHS Drives Quality through Cloud Speech and CDI Workflow. Available online: https://www.nuance.com/content/dam/nuance/en_us/collateral/healthcare/case-study/cs-uhs-en-us.pdf (Accessed on March 15, 2019).

18. Plastic Surgery Specialist Reduces Time Per Patient Note. Available online: https://resources.suki.ai/home/case-study-dr-ereso-plastic-surgeon (Accessed on March 24, 2019).
19. Plastic Surgery Specialist Reduces Time Per Patient Note. Available online: https://www.mobihealthnews.com/news/north-america/voice-enabled-clinician-workflow-tool-robin-healthcare-raises-115m (Accessed on October 02, 2019).
20. Medwhat Virtual Medical Assistant. Available online: https://medwhat.com/ (Accessed on April 02, 2019).
21. Your.MD Symptom Checker. Available online: https://www.your.md/ (Accessed on April 02, 2019).
22. Sensely Engage Your Members. Reduce Your Costs. Available online: https://www.sensely.com/ (Accessed on April 02, 2019).
23. Bickmore, T.W.; Trinh, H.; Olafsson, S.; O'Leary, T.K.; Asadi, R.; Rickles, N.M.; Cruz, R. Patient and consumer safety risks when using conversational assistants for medical information: An observational study of Siri, Alexa, and Google Assistant. *J. Med. Internet Res.* **2018**, *20*, e11510.
24. Semigran, H.L.; Linder, J.A.; Gidengil, C.; Mehrotra, A. Evaluation of symptom checkers for self diagnosis and triage: Audit study. *BMJ* **2015**, *351*, h3480.
25. Crestani, F.; Du, H. Written versus spoken queries: A qualitative and quantitative comparative analysis. *J. Am. Soc. Inf. Sci. Technol.* **2006**, *57*, 881–890.
26. Philip, P.; Bioulac, S.; Sauteraud, A.; Chaufton, C.; Olive, J. Could a virtual human be used to explore excessive daytime sleepiness in patients? *Presence Teleop. Vir. Environ.* **2014**, *23*, 369–376.
27. Philip, P.; Micoulaud-Franchi, J.A.; Sagaspe, P.; De Sevin, E.; Olive, J.; Bioulac, S.; Sauteraud, A. Virtual human as a new diagnostic tool, a proof of concept study in the field of major depressive disorders. *Sci. Rep.* **2017**, *7*, 42656.
28. Tanaka, H.; Negoro, H.; Iwasaka, H.; Nakamura, S. Embodied conversational agents for multimodal automated social skills training in people with autism spectrum disorders. *PloS ONE* **2017**, *12*, e0182151.
29. Dimeff, L.A.; Jobes, D.A.; Chalker, S.A.; Piehl, B.M.; Duvivier, L.L.; Lok, B.C.; Zalake, M.S.; Chung, J.; Koerner, K. A novel engagement of suicidality in the emergency department: Virtual Collaborative Assessment and Management of Suicidality. In *General Hospital Psychiatry*; Elsevier: Amsterdam, The Netherlands, 2018.
30. Levin, E.; Levin, A. Spoken dialog system for real-time data capture. In Proceedings of the Ninth European Conference on Speech Communication and Technology, Lisbon, Portugal, 4–8 September 2005.
31. Black, L.A.; McTear, M.; Black, N.; Harper, R.; Lemon, M. Appraisal of a conversational artefact and its utility in remote patient monitoring. In Proceedings of the 18th IEEE Symposium on Computer-Based Medical Systems, Dublin, Ireland, 23–24 June 2005; pp. 506–508.
32. Harper, R.; Nicholl, P.; McTear, M.; Wallace, J.; Black, L.A.; Kearney, P. Automated phone capture of diabetes patients readings with consultant monitoring via the web. In Proceedings of the 15th Annual IEEE International Conference and Workshop on the Engineering of Computer Based Systems, ECBS, Belfast, UK, 31 March–4 April 2008; pp. 219–226.
33. Lucas, G.M.; Rizzo, A.; Gratch, J.; Scherer, S.; Stratou, G.; Boberg, J.; Morency, L.P. Reporting mental health symptoms: breaking down barriers to care with virtual human interviewers. *Front. Robot. AI* **2017**, *4*, 51.
34. Yokotani, K.; Takagi, G.; Wakashima, K. Advantages of virtual agents over clinical psychologists during comprehensive mental health interviews using a mixed methods design. *Comput. Hum. Behav.* **2018**, *85*, 135–145.
35. Ali, T.; Hussain, J.; Amin, M.B.; Hussain, M.; Akhtar, U.; Khan, W.A.; Lee, S.; Kang, B.H.; Hussain, M.; Afzal, M.; et al. The Intelligent Medical Platform: A Novel Dialogue-Based Platform for Health-Care Services. *Computer* **2020**, *53*, 35–45.
36. Ireland, D.; Atay, C.; Liddle, J.; Bradford, D.; Lee, H.; Rushin, O.; Mullins, T.; Angus, D.; Wiles, J.; McBride, S.; et al. Hello Harlie: Enabling Speech Monitoring Through Chat-Bot Conversations. *Studi. Health Technol. Inf.* **2016**, *227*, 55–60.
37. Mugoye, K.; Okoyo, H.; Mcoyowo, S. Smart-bot Technology: Conversational Agents Role in Maternal Healthcare Support. In Proceedings of the IEEE 2019 IST-Africa Week Conference (IST-Africa), Nairobi, Kenya, 8–10 May 2019; pp. 1–7.
38. Giorgino, T.; Azzini, I.; Rognoni, C.; Quaglini, S.; Stefanelli, M.; Gretter, R.; Falavigna, D. Automated spoken dialogue system for hypertensive patient home management. *Int. J. Med. Inf.* **2005**, *74*, 159–167.
39. Beveridge, M.; Fox, J. Automatic generation of spoken dialogue from medical plans and ontologies. *J. Biom. Inf.* **2006**, *39*, 482–499.

40. Clarke, N.L.; Furnell, S.M.; Rodwell, P.M.; Reynolds, P.L. Acceptance of subscriber authentication methods for mobile telephony devices. *Comput. Secur.* **2002**, *21*, 220–228.
41. Raza, M.; Iqbal, M.; Sharif, M.; Haider, W. A survey of password attacks and comparative analysis on methods for secure authentication. *World Appl. Sci. J.* **2012**, *19*, 439–444.
42. McDermott, D.S.; Kamerer, J.L.; Birk, A.T. Electronic Health Records: A Literature Review of Cyber Threats and Security Measures. *Int. J. Cyber Res. Educ. (IJCRE)* **2019**, *1*, 42–49.
43. Frumento, E. Cybersecurity and the Evolutions of Healthcare: Challenges and Threats Behind Its Evolution. In *m_Health Current and Future Applications*; Springer: Berlin, Germany, 2019; pp. 35–69.
44. Kao, H.C.; Tang, K.F.; Chang, E.Y. Context-aware symptom checking for disease diagnosis using hierarchical reinforcement learning. In Proceedings of the Thirty-Second AAAI Conference on Artificial Intelligence, New Orleans, LO, USA, 2–7 February 2018.
45. Morreale, S.P.; Spitzberg, B.H.; Barge, J.K. *Human Communication: Motivation, Knowledge, and Skills*; Cengage Learning: Boston, MA, USA, 2007.
46. Glass, J. Challenges for spoken dialogue systems. In *Proceedings of the 1999 IEEE ASRU Workshop*; MIT Laboratory fot Computer Science: Cambridge, MA, USA, 1999.
47. Kang, S.; Ko, Y.; Seo, J. A dialogue management system using a corpus-based framework and a dynamic dialogue transition model. *AI Commun.* **2013**, *26*, 145–159.
48. Li, Y.; Feng, Z.; Xiao, Y.; Huang, J. A neural network algorithm for signal processing of LFMCW or IFSCW system. In Proceedings of the 1999 Asia Pacific Microwave Conference—APMC'99—Microwaves Enter the 21st Century, Conference Proceedings (Cat. No.99TH8473), Singapore, 30 November–3 December 1999; Volume 3, pp. 900–903.
49. Rasa Documentation. Available online: https://rasa.com/docs/rasa/ (Accessed on March 19, 2020).
50. Unified Medical Language System Documentation. Available online: https://www.nlm.nih.gov/research/umls/index.html (Accessed on March 19, 2020).
51. Hummer, M.; Groll, S.; Kunz, M.; Fuchs, L.; Pernul, G. Measuring Identity and Access Management Performance-An Expert Survey on Possible Performance Indicators. In Proceedings of the 4th International Conference on Information Systems Security and Privacy, Funchal - Madeira, Portugal, 22–24 January, 2018. Available online: https://www.scitepress.org/Papers/2018/65577/65577.pdf (Accessed on 23 July 2019)
52. Rehman, U.U.; Lee, S. Natural Language Voice based Authentication Mechanism for Smartphones. In *Proceedings of the 17th Annual International Conference on Mobile Systems, Applications, and Services*; ACM: New York, NY, USA, 2019; pp. 600–601.
53. Biswas, M. AI and Bot Basics. In *Beginning AI Bot Frameworks*; Springer: Berlin, Germany, 2018; pp. 1–23.
54. Find Machine Learning Algorithms for Your Data. Available online: https://mod.rapidminer.com/ (Accessed on April 22, 2020).
55. Elliot, A.J.; Maier, M.A. Color psychology: Effects of perceiving color on psychological functioning in humans. *Ann. Rev. Psychol.* **2014**, *65*, 95–120.
56. Walker, M.A.; Litman, D.J.; Kamm, C.A.; Abella, A. PARADISE: A framework for evaluating spoken dialogue agents. *arXiv preprint* **1997**, cmp-lg/9704004.
57. Landis, J.R.; Koch, G.G. The measurement of observer agreement for categorical data. *Biometrics* **1977**, 159–174. Available online: https://www.jstor.org/stable/pdf/2529310.pdf (Accessed on 23 March 2019)
58. Pejovic, V.; Bojanic, S.; Carreras, C.; Nieto-Taladriz, O. Detecting masquerading attack in software and in hardware. In Proceedings of the MELECON 2006—2006 IEEE Mediterranean Electrotechnical Conference, Malaga, Spain, 16–19 May 2006; pp. 836–838.
59. Schrepp, M. User Experience Questionnaire Handbook. In *All you Need to Know to Apply the UEQ Successfully in Your Project*; 2015. Available online: https://www.ueq-online.org/Material/Handbook.pdf (Accessed on 12 May 2019)

© 2020 by the authors. Licensee MDPI, Basel, Switzerland. This article is an open access article distributed under the terms and conditions of the Creative Commons Attribution (CC BY) license (http://creativecommons.org/licenses/by/4.0/).

Article

Assessment of Word-Level Neural Language Models for Sentence Completion [†]

Heewoong Park and Jonghun Park *

Department of Industrial Engineering & Center for Superintelligence, Seoul National University, Seoul 08826, Korea; hee188@snu.ac.kr
* Correspondence: jonghun@snu.ac.kr; Tel.: +82-2-880-7174
† This paper is an extended version of our paper published in the proceedings of 2018 IEEE International Congress on Information Science and Technology (CiSt).

Received: 24 January 2020; Accepted: 12 February 2020; Published: 16 February 2020

Abstract: The task of sentence completion, which aims to infer the missing text of a given sentence, was carried out to assess the reading comprehension level of machines as well as humans. In this work, we conducted a comprehensive study of various approaches for the sentence completion based on neural language models, which have been advanced in recent years. First, we revisited the recurrent neural network language model (RNN LM), achieving highly competitive results with an appropriate network structure and hyper-parameters. This paper presents a bidirectional version of RNN LM, which surpassed the previous best results on Microsoft Research (MSR) Sentence Completion Challenge and the Scholastic Aptitude Test (SAT) sentence completion questions. In parallel with directly applying RNN LM to sentence completion, we also employed a supervised learning framework that fine-tunes a large pre-trained transformer-based LM with a few sentence-completion examples. By fine-tuning a pre-trained BERT model, this work established state-of-the-art results on the MSR and SAT sets. Furthermore, we performed similar experimentation on newly collected cloze-style questions in the Korean language. The experimental results reveal that simply applying the multilingual BERT models for the Korean dataset was not satisfactory, which leaves room for further research.

Keywords: BERT; bidirectional RNN; cloze test; Korean dataset; machine comprehension; neural language model; sentence completion

---

1. Introduction

In the research domain of machine reading comprehension (MRC), a cloze-style task whose objective is to restore the removed portion of text has been widely used to evaluate a machine's level of understanding [1–3]. Sentence completion is a specific type of cloze-style task whose goal is to choose a correct word or phrase from the provided list of candidates to fill in the blank in a question sentence. Despite its simplicity, this class of questions can assess diverse abilities including linguistic proficiency, common knowledge, and logical reasoning at different levels.

To date, several publications have evaluated reading comprehension models through sentence completion tests. As an earlier comparative study, Zweig et al. [4] tested various methods based on different language models (LMs) and topic models against the Microsoft Research (MSR) Sentence Completion Challenge [5] and the Scholastic Aptitude Test (SAT) sentence completion questions, while these two datasets have become standard benchmark test sets for subsequent studies. Mikolov et al. [6] achieved an improved accuracy on the MSR by using the combination of skip-gram and recurrent neural network (RNN) LMs for sentence completion. Subsequently, deep neural models have received continuous attention for sentence completion, while Tang [7] and Woods [8] attained comparable results with classical non-neural feature based methods. In [9], the authors introduced a neural model named context2vec, which embeds a target word by considering the surrounding sentential context, demonstrating its usefulness in sentence completion in addition to word sense disambiguation and lexical substitution. Tran et al. [10] established the state-of-the-art results on the MSR set with Recurrent Memory Network (RMN), which stacked memory network blocks on RNN for language modeling.

Recently, Park et al. [11] revisited the word-level RNN LM based approach for sentence completion. Motivated by the empirical fact that the performance of the RNN LM highly depends on the number of nodes and optimization parameters [12,13], Park et al. demonstrated that their implementation of RNN LM surpassed the state-of-the-art models on the MSR set despite its simple architecture. Furthermore, they proposed a bidirectional version, which delivered additional performance gains by exploiting future context information. The authors also validated the RNN LMs against the SAT dataset, and they achieved higher accuracy than the other previously published results.

This work extends the study of Park et al. [11] with extensive experiments on various sentence completion methods based on neural LMs. To clarify which modification of the RNN LM mainly brings the performance gain, we added more experimental results for different choices of the network. Furthermore, this paper introduces and compares three criteria for selecting the answer based on a trained LM for sentence completion.

This study also includes a supervised learning approach that directly receives supervision from sentence completion questions. Specifically, we employed a task transfer framework that pre-trains an LM with a large text corpus and adapts it for sentence completion by modifying the network structure slightly and learning from a few questions. This framework has been emerging as a new paradigm in natural language understanding owing to its great success on many datasets [14–17]. In this work, we mainly follow the approach of Devlin et al. [16], while comparing pre-trained networks of BERT [16] and GPT2 [18], both of which are based on transformer architecture [19].

Another contribution of this paper is that we collected cloze-style questions written in Korean and evaluated the methods mentioned above with this dataset. There are few non-English datasets in MRC [20,21], which hinders the verification of the effectiveness of models in cases of other languages. The new dataset consists of 1823 multiple-choice questions from the Test of Proficiency in Korean (TOPIK). We conducted the performance analysis of our RNN LM and multilingual BERT models on this dataset.

In summary, our contributions are following:

- We demonstrate that, when properly trained, simple RNN LMs are highly competitive for the sentence completion. Our word RNNs achieved results beyond the previous best reported on the MSR and SAT datasets.
- We verify that the transfer learning approach that pre-trains a transformer-based LM from large data and fine-tunes the model for the target task is also viable for the sentence completion. Our experiments compared various pre-trained networks along with different settings for fine-tuning, showing that the performance varied significantly with different networks, and we were able to obtain state-of-the-art results for both datasets under certain configurations.
- The new cloze-style dataset written in Korean was collected from the government's official examinations. Experimental results show that the models that were effective for the English datasets underperformed on the Korean dataset, leaving space for further investigation.
- The PyTorch implementation code (https://github.com/heevery/sentence-completion) for experimentation is made available to encourage subsequent studies on neural approaches in machine comprehension.

The remainder of this paper is organized as follows. In the next section, we begin with discussions on related work. In Section 3, we delineate word-level RNN LMs, formalize how to apply these LMs to sentence completion, and describe a fine-tuning approach that employs transformer-based models. Sections 4 and 5 show the results of experiments on the MSR and SAT sets, respectively. Then, we present the new dataset and performance analysis on this set in Section 6. Finally, the paper is concluded in the last section.

2. Related Work

The machine comprehension of text or MRC, in which a machine is expected to answer a question in the form of natural language given a relevant source text, has become a major research topic in both academia and industry [22]. A natural language question that requests information such as WH-questions can be converted to the cloze-style counterpart in most cases by a simple algorithm that constructs a declarative sentence with the answer and masks it. Owing to its wide coverage and ease of generation, cloze-style datasets have been curated for different text domains and applications, including children's book test [3], CNN and daily mail reading comprehension [1], summary cloze [23], and story cloze [24]. For this class of task, LM-based approaches have often served as solid baselines when the masked answers are from the daily vocabulary such as verbs and prepositions in children's book test [3] or everyday life narratives [24,25]. Moreover, thanks to the gradual development of training techniques for neural LM, its performance has been improved [12,13]. Establishing a simple but effective baseline provides one of the key foundations for this kind of research, and this work attempts to make contributions along this line for the sentence completion task with state-of-the-art LMs.

Meanwhile, building a general-purpose feature extractor for text data has been a long-standing goal, as ImageNet-pretrained classifiers often play such a role for image data [26]. Among the notable breakthroughs were ELMo [27] and ULMFit [14] that learn an LSTM-based LM from large-scale plain text data and use the hidden representations as contextualized word embeddings of an input word sequence. Subsequently, a transformer-based LM equipped with a self-attention mechanism significantly reduced the LM perplexity and the error metrics of downstream tasks [15], while a bidirectional transformer-based model called BERT showed impressive results [16]. Numerous studies are still ongoing to further improve this transfer learning approach, including adding translation task objectives to provide high-quality supervision in pre-training [28], permutation-based language modeling to reduce the pretrain–finetune discrepancy [17], and robustly optimized pre-training [29]. However, the transfer learning approach has not been tested against the sentence completion datasets, and we aim to provide a variety of experimental results based on it.

Another interesting observation on transformer-based LMs is that multilingual models which were pre-trained from multiple monolingual corpora were able to generalize information across different languages [30]. Wu and Dredze [31] confirmed that a multilingual BERT model performed well uniformly across languages in document classification, named entity recognition, and part-of-speech tagging, when fine-tuned with a small amount of target language supervision for the downstream task. The more surprising finding of their work is that, even in a zero-shot cross-lingual setting, where the multilingual model is fine-tuned with task-specific data from one language and tested in another language, the multilingual BERT achieved comparable performance with the other models that require some cross-lingual supervision. A recent study further suggested that shared subword embeddings were not necessary, and monolingual models were also able to learn some universal linguistic abstractions [32]. Motivated by the above empirical evidence, we conjecture that multilingual BERT models might also perform well on the Korean cloze questions and accordingly considered them in our experiments.

3. Methods

3.1. Word-Level RNN LM

RNN based word-level LMs [33] that exploit the advantage of RNN in modeling sequential data have been widely applied in natural language processing [22]. The goal of word-level language modeling is to estimate the probability of the next word based on a previous text. Let $w_1, w_2, ..., w_n$ denote a word sequence. Then, a typical word-level RNN LM approximates the conditional probability of the tth position, $p(w_t|w_1, w_2, ..., w_{t-1})$, by encoding the context words with RNN layers and decoding the output to the probability vector. In the following, we describe in turn a word-level RNN LM used in this work (referred to as word RNN henceforth), its bidirectional version, and another variant that adopts a training strategy called masked LM [16].

The unidirectional word RNN transforms each input word to a learnable embedding vector of size d_{emb}. Then, recurrent layers take the word embedding and the previous hidden states where the past text has been encoded. We choose Long Short-Term Memory (LSTM) for the recurrent cell type and set the number of recurrent layers, l to 2, following the authors of [12,34]. A fully-connected layer reduces the dimension of the output hidden vector of the topmost recurrent layer from d_{hid} to d_{out}. After the linearly projected vector is multiplied by an output embedding matrix, the softmax operation produces the likelihood of the next word, $P_{LM}(w_i|w_1, w_2, ..., w_{i-1})$. The training objective for the network is to minimize the negative log-likelihood of target words, also known as categorical cross-entropy loss. Dropout is applied between recurrent layers [34].

For the bidirectional version, we design it to infer a target word based on not only the previous words but also the subsequent words, which means the output of the network estimates $p(w_i|w_1, w_2, ..., w_{i-1}, w_{i+1}, ..., w_n)$. Although this formulation cannot be applied for the language modeling in which a model is required to generate one word at a time from scratch, it fits in the sentence completion, which determines the missing word based on both sides. Some probabilistic interpretation of bidirectional modeling for sequences was suggested by Berglund et al. [35], who showed the effectiveness of bidirectional reconstruction on inferring omitted symbolic tokens such as characters in text and notes in midi-encoded music. It is noteworthy that our bidirectional model fuses forward and backward hidden layers before the softmax operation rather than just ensembles the output distributions of forward and backward LMs as in [14,27].

To be specific, our bidirectional word RNN (Figure 1) has separate word embedding lookup tables for forward and backward directions, similar to context2vec [9]. Each word embedding is connected to either forward or backward directional LSTM layers. The network then aggregates the output of the bidirectional hidden layers into a final output vector. The aggregation consists of conducting a separate linear projection for each hidden layer vector and then adding the two projected vectors. This way of aggregation was slightly better than concatenation followed by a single linear projection in our preliminary experiments. The main difference between our bidirectional word RNN and context2vec is that our model computes the negative likelihood loss rather than an approximation of pointwise mutual information between the target word and the context during training.

Lastly, we present a variant based on masked LM training, which is a crucial strategy to pre-train bidirectional Transformers for language understanding [16]. We apply this to our bidirectional word RNN to see if the training strategy has a synergy with RNN-based architecture in place of the transformer-based one. Instead of aggregating the one-step-ahead hidden state from the forward layer and the one-step-behind hidden state from the backward layer, the masked LM version aggregates the current step hidden states from both directions. As an illustrative example, the bidirectional word RNN aggregates the forward hidden representation of '*was*' and the backward hidden representation of '*his*' for predicting '*she*' in Figure 1, while the masked LM fuses the both directional hidden states at the position of '*she*' to reconstruct it. For the masked LM training, 15% of the input tokens were replaced with noise data, and the network learned to reconstruct these tokens with the cross-entropy loss. Among the 15%, 80% of them were masked with [MASK] tokens, 10% of them were substituted with random words, and the others were kept unchanged, as suggested in [16].

3.2. LM-Based Scoring

This subsection describes three scoring strategies with respect to how to apply a trained word RNN to sentence completion. Suppose the tth position is blank, $w_1, w_2, ..., w_{t-1}, w_{t+1}, ..., w_n$ are context words, and $c^1, c^2, ..., c^m$ are candidate choices for the blank. Blank scoring strategy selects the choice word that maximizes the conditional likelihood, $P_{LM}(c|w_1, w_2, ..., w_{t-1})$ for a typical unidirectional LM or

$P_{biLM}(c|w_1, w_2, ..., w_{t-1}, w_{t+1}, ..., w_n)$ for our bidirectional model, where $c \in \{c^1, c^2, ..., c^m\}$. This strategy is equivalent to picking the choice that minimizes the cross-entropy loss on the blank. In the case that a choice text spans more than a word, the strategy computes the score by summing the loss over the blank span and multiplying by -1.

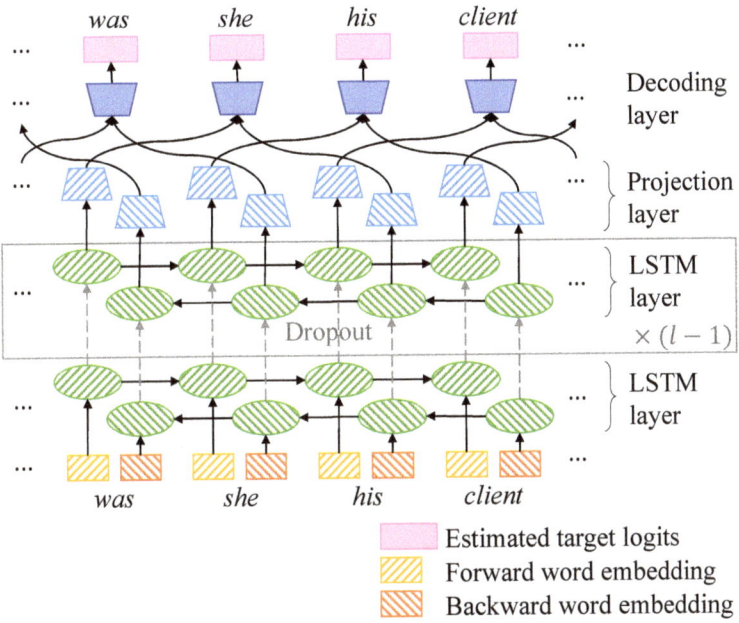

Figure 1. Bidirectional word RNN (modified from Figure 1 in [11]).

In the unidirectional case, however, the blank scoring strategy does not reflect any contextual information from future words following the blank. To compensate for this defect, we adopt the full scoring strategy that minimizes the cross-entropy loss on the entire sentence instead of the blank. Let $w_1^j, w_2^j, ..., w_{n_j}^j$ be the word sequence obtained by replacing the blank with a choice word c^j, or phrase composed of multiple words $c_1^j, c_2^j, ..., c_{r_j}^j$ where $n_j = n - 1 + r_j$. Then, the strategy computes the score as $\sum_{i=2}^{n_j} \log P_{LM}(w_i^j | w_1^j, w_2^j, ..., w_{i-1}^j)$ for the unidirectional LM or $\sum_{i=2}^{n_j-1} \log P_{bi}(w_i^j | w_1^j, w_2^j, ..., w_{i-1}^j, w_{i+1}^j, ..., w_{n_j}^j)$ for the bidirectional one, where $j = 1, 2, ..., m$. Even in the bidirectional case, we observed that the full scoring strategy performed better than the former, although the blank scoring strategy also considers the future context.

The third strategy, referred to as partial scoring strategy [36], computes the score as the likelihood of the subsequent text conditioned on the choice word and its preceding text. For a unidirectional LM, the score of c is defined as $\sum_{i=t+1}^{n} \log P_{LM}(w_i | w_1, ..., w_{t-1}, c, ..., w_{i-1})$, where the tth position is blank. Since $P_{LM}(w_i | w_1, w_2, ..., w_{i-1})$ for $i = 1, ..., t-1$ does not depend on c, the strategy is equivalent to picking the choice that minimizes $\sum_{i \neq t} \log P_{LM}(w_i | w_1, ..., w_{t-1}, c, ..., w_{i-1})$, which equals the full score minus the blank score. From this formulation, the partial score of c for the bidirectional model can be naturally derived as $\sum_{i<t} \log P_{biLM}(w_i | w_1, ..., w_{i-1}, w_{i+1}, ..., w_{t-1}, c, ..., w_n) + \sum_{i>t} \log P_{biLM}(w_i | w_1, ..., w_{t-1}, c, ..., w_{i-1}, w_{i+1}, ..., w_n)$. While Trinh and Le [36] reported that the partial scoring strategy outperformed the full scoring strategy for pronoun disambiguation problems, we observed that it did not hold for the sentence completion.

For networks based on masked LM training, we can apply the blank scoring strategy by defining the score of choice c as $P_{mask}(c|w_1, w_2, ..., w_{t-1}, \texttt{[MASK]}, w_{t+1}, ..., w_n)$, where [MASK] is inserted in the blank. If a choice text consists of multiple words, the corresponding number of [MASK] tokens are inserted. Since it is not straightforward to apply either the partial or full scoring strategy to masked LM based networks, we did not take them into account.

3.3. Fine-Tuning Pre-Trained LM for Sentence Completion

We introduce a supervised learning approach for the case in which a few sentence-completion examples are available for model training. To mitigate this data insufficiency, which often occurs in fully-supervised settings due to the difficulty in collecting high-quality MRC data, recently researchers have proposed a task transfer framework that pre-trains an LM with a large amount of plain text, slightly modifies the network structure, and then fine-tunes it with a small dataset of the target task. For multiple-choice classification, the authors of [15,16] introduced a transferring method that adds a new simple linear regression layer to a pre-trained LM at the first [15] or the last [16] time step of the topmost hidden layers; obtains the scalar output values of input sequences corresponding to choices; and performs the softmax operation to those values to produce a probability vector for answers. We employ it for multi-choice questions for the sentence completion in a straightforward manner.

For construction of model input, we fill the blank with a choice word as in the full scoring strategy and insert a special [CLS] token at the first time step at which the output vector of the topmost hidden layer is fed into the simple linear regression layer. In contrast to Radford et al. [15] and Devlin et al. [16], the delimiter tokens are not inserted between question and choice texts, since the text filled with the correct answer forms a syntactically and semantically correct sentence. For a similar reason, while BERT LM also takes as input segment identifiers, which indicate if the corresponding token belongs to the question or the choice text, we feed the same segment identifier for the entire sequence into the model. An experiment in the following section shows that this simple method was sufficient for the sentence completion.

4. MSR Sentence Completion

First, we considered the MSR Challenge dataset [5] to evaluate the aforementioned methods. The MSR sentence completion set includes 1040 questions whose source sentences are from five Sherlock Holmes novels. Human workers were engaged in constructing the question sentences with five candidate choices for each question to ensure that the questions require semantic knowledge as well as logical inference [5]. We trained the neural LMs with the official training corpus for the challenge to compare with previous work, and then further investigated how much the performance can be improved with a larger model that was pre-trained with external data.

4.1. Results with the Official Training Data

For experiments in this subsection, we used 522 novels from Project Gutenberg written in the nineteenth-century, which is the specified standard training corpus of the MSR Challenge. We preprocessed the data through sentence splitting, followed by word tokenization and lower-casing to feed word sequences into the word RNNs. Sentences consisting of more than eighty or less than ten words were filtered out. As a result, the vocabulary was composed of 64K words after converting any word with fewer than six occurrences in the corpus to [UNK] token.

To be specific about the implementation, d_{emb}, d_{hid}, and d_{out} were set to 200, 600, and 400, respectively. We set the forward and backward embedding sizes of the bidirectional word RNN to be equal. We trained all networks for ten epochs with stochastic gradient descent while applying 10% dropout. Twenty sentences of the same length comprised a mini-batch. Gradients were clipped at the maximum norm of 5.0 and normalized by the mini-batch size [34]. The learning rate was started at 0.5 and decreased by half at the beginning of each epoch after the fifth epoch. We determined these settings by inspecting the performance on the first 520 questions of the MSR set, referred to as development set, following prior work [9,37]. Accordingly, we refer to the remaining MSR questions as test set.

First, we investigated the performance of different language modeling and scoring strategies (Table 1). We optimized the networks repeatedly with five different random seeds and considered the average accuracy of those networks as a model accuracy. As expected, the full scoring was far more beneficial than the blank scoring in the unidirectional cases. Likewise, the accuracy of the bidirectional LM increased when using the full scoring compared to the blank scoring. In contrast to Trinh and Le [36], the partial scoring strategy was inferior to the full scoring strategy. This can be explained by the fact that a special word related to the answer appears in the following text of the blank in all questions of Levesque et al. [38], whereas the presence of a special word is not ensured in the MSR questions. In addition, the masked LM was inferior to the others, which differs from Devlin et al. [16]. It would seem that the masked LM requires more training data and prefers the transformer architecture rather than RNN layers. The performance gaps are visualized in Figure 2, where the error bars signify the minimum and maximum accuracies obtained by five networks with different random seeds.

Table 1. Performance comparison of word RNNs for different scoring strategies on the MSR set. We trained each model five times with different random seeds and report the average accuracy with the standard deviation in parentheses.

LM Formulation	Accuracy [%]		
	Blank	Full	Partial
Unidirectional LM	50.5 (0.4)	69.4 (0.8)	56.4 (0.9)
Bidirectional LM	69.8 (0.5)	72.3 (1.1)	63.7 (1.4)
Masked LM	N/A	58.2 (1.6)	N/A

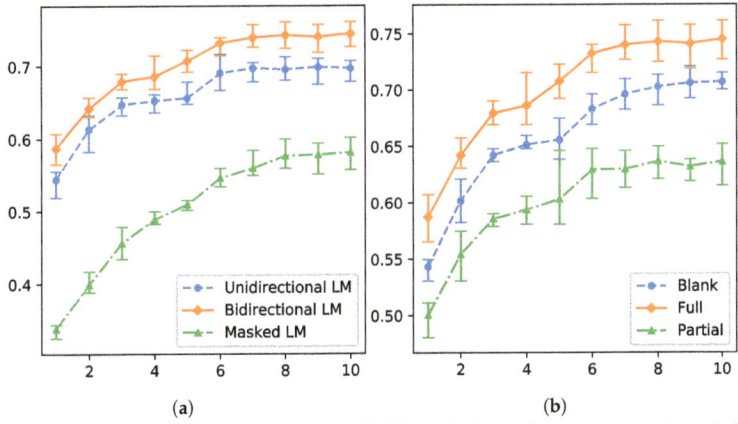

Figure 2. Performance comparison for different LM formulation and scoring strategies: (**a**) the full scoring was applied except for the masked LM; and (**b**) the bidirectional model was used. The x-axis represents the number of epochs and the y-axis represents the validation accuracy for the MSR dataset.

To justify the choice of the network size, we plot the validation results for the different numbers of nodes in Figure 3. The unidirectional word RNN was evaluated on the MSR validation set with different d_{emb}, d_{hid}, and d_{out} values. Figure 3 verifies that the choice of d_{hid} greatly affected the performance, while smaller embedding sizes than d_{hid} led to better results possibly due to a regularization effect. We further experimented with more numbers of nodes, but the accuracy increase was negligible.

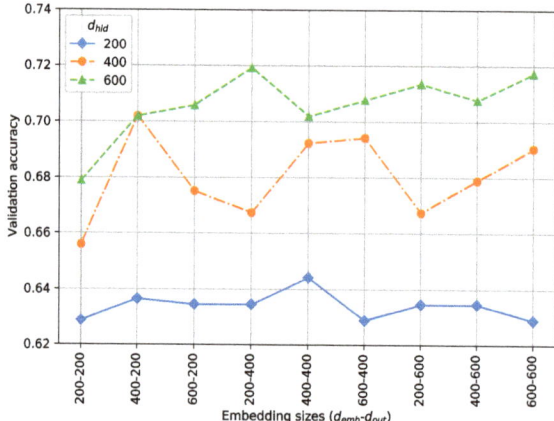

Figure 3. Performance comparison for different numbers of nodes.

Table 2 compares the accuracy results of previous work with ours. An ensemble of differently initialized RNNs having the same dimensions was defined by selecting the option that minimizes the average loss obtained from the RNNs. All of our results in Table 2 were obtained by using the full scoring strategy. To present the approximate network sizes, we specify the dimensions in the first column as (d_{emb}-d_{hid}-d_{out}).

Table 2. Accuracy results (%) for the MSR Challenge dataset. The accuracies in italic were from their corresponding publications. We present the accuracy results of the development and test sets using a slash if they were measured separately. We report the average accuracy with the standard deviation if a model was optimized repeatedly.

Model (d_{emb}-d_{hid}-d_{out})	Accuracy
RNNLMs [39]	*55.4*
Skip-gram [6]	*48.0*
Skip-gram + RNNLMs [6]	*59.2/58.7*
NPMI + Co-occ. Freq. + LSA + CBOW + CSKIP [7]	*48*
PMI using Unigrams + Bigrams + Trigrams [8]	*61.44*
Context2vec (300-600-600) [9]	*66.2/64.0*
LSTM (256-256-256) [10]	*56.0*
Unidirectional-RM (512-512-512) [10]	*69.2*
Bidirectional-RM (512-512-512) [10]	*67.0*
Unidirectional word RNN (200-600-400)	69.1 (0.9)/69.6 (0.8)
Bidirectional word RNN (200-600-400)	72.5 (1.4)/72.0 (2.0)
Unidirectional word RNN ensemble	72.0/71.5
Bidirectional word RNN ensemble	**74.1/74.6**

Interestingly, even the performance of our unidirectional word RNN was on par with or slightly above the previous best accuracy results on the MSR dataset. As examined in Figure 3, most accuracy gains compared to the LSTM of Tran et al. [10] were attributed to the appropriate embedding and hidden sizes, and miscellaneous training settings contributed to additional gains. When compared to the RMN [10], which contains a memory block consisting of two lookup tables for additional word embeddings and calculates an attention distribution over context words at every timestep, our RNN is simple and computationally inexpensive. In addition, our bidirectional version achieved the best result among the individual models while the ensemble of those five networks further improved the performance by leveraging the stochastic nature of deep learning. As mentioned above, adding more nodes to the unidirectional word RNN (200-600-400) was not helpful. This implies that the benefit of bidirectional modeling did not come from mere increase of the number of learnable weights but from incorporation of future context information. These results disagree with Tran et al. [10], whose bidirectional model compared unfavorably with the unidirectional model.

4.2. Results with External Data

While the official training corpus is highly similar and relevant to the question sentences in terms of linguistic styles and time periods of writing, the limited data may hinder the learning of a deep neural network. We applied various pre-trained models that learn from large external data for the MSR questions (Table 3). LM1B represents the best single model of Józefowicz et al. [12], who experimented variants of LSTM-based LMs on the 1B word benchmark [40], which consists of news text of about one billion words. We also include variants of BERT and GPT2 models which have shown compelling results on many language understanding tasks with fine-tuning on small data or zero-shot task transfer. We obtained the pre-trained weights of LM1B and the others from their publicly available repositories (https://github.com/tensorflow/models/tree/master/research/lm_1b, https://huggingface.co/transformers/pretrained_models.html). According to the results of the scoring strategies (see Table 1), we applied the full scoring except for the BERT family for which we deployed the blank scoring strategy since BERT adopts masked language modeling. We adhere to this policy for further experiments unless noted otherwise.

Table 3. Accuracy results (%) of pre-trained models without fine-tuning for the MSR questions. The best model trained with the official dataset is presented at the first row for comparison.

Model	Dev.	Test
Bidirectional word RNN ensemble	74.1	74.6
LM1B	70.2	67.7
BERT-base-uncased	55.38	58.46
BERT-base-cased	60.58	60.19
BERT-base-multilingual-uncased	22.50	20.58
BERT-base-multilingual-cased	41.54	41.92
BERT-large-uncased	54.23	55.00
BERT-large-cased	52.69	49.23
BERT-large-uncased-wwm	**77.69**	**77.12**
BERT-large-cased-wwm	75.19	77.12
GPT2	46.73	44.04
GPT2-medium	54.62	52.69

Although LM1B yielded better accuracy than the models of previous publications, its accuracy could not reach those of our word RNNs, and even its size was substantially larger than ours. Among BERT models, the performance differences between the case-sensitive ones (indicated as '-cased') and the corresponding case-insensitive ones (indicated as '-uncased') were inconsistent across different training settings. The multilingual BERTs that were trained from Wikipedia dumps of about one hundred languages were inferior to the monolingual ones, without fine-tuning to the target language. The authors of BERT have warned that lower-casing non-Latin alphabets could result in somewhat unwanted outcomes (https://github.com/google-research/bert), which might be the reason for the poor accuracy of BERT-base-multilingual-uncased. Despite having three times more learnable parameters, BERT-large models performed worse than BERT-base models without whole-word-masking. The whole-word-masking technique masks all-at-once the group of tokenized wordpieces [41] corresponding to a word during masked LM training (see details in https://github.com/google-research/bert). With this modification, whole-word-masking BERTs (indicated as '-wwm') outperformed the BERT-large models without whole-word-masking and even surpassed the best ensemble model that was trained from the official training data. On the other hand,

GPT2 models, designed to be used with minimal adaptation, were less effective than BERT-base for the MSR set.

Next, we applied the fine-tuning methods described in Section 3.3 to the transformer-based models for the MSR set. The last one hundred questions of the development set were assigned to the holdout set for tuning optimization parameters and model selection, while the others were used for gradient updates. Among various design variables for optimization, we presumed that the learning rate and the decision on which layers to either freeze or fine-tune were the most important ones throughout preliminary experiments. Thus, a grid search for them was conducted with BERT-large-uncased-wwm, which achieved the best performance in the above experiment. We constructed each batch to contain only a single question and ran five epochs of gradient updates while using the slanted triangular learning rate schedule of warm-up for the first epoch. Unless noted otherwise, the optimizer was kept the same as the implementation employed (https://github.com/huggingface/transformers) [42].

Figure 4 displays holdout accuracies for different learning rates and subsets of weights to freeze during fine-tuning. The results show that the maximum accuracy that can be obtained by an appropriate learning rate did not differ much across different choices of updatable layers unless only a few top layers were updated. It indicates that we can achieve a satisfactory accuracy by only tuning learning rates while spending less effort on determining which layers to freeze. This simplification is more practically convenient than gradual unfreezing [14], which increases the number of trainable weights as iterations progress. Consequently, we took the approach that updates all layers for the remaining experiments.

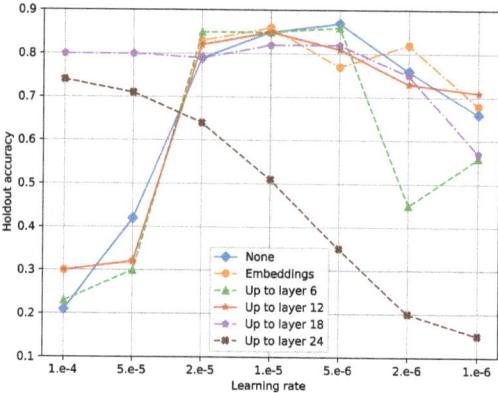

Figure 4. Holdout accuracies for different learning rates and subsets of weights to freeze during fine-tuning. Up to layer l in the legend indicates the setting that fixes the weights of the first l self-attention layers as well as the embeddings. Note that, since the experimented BERT contains 24 self-attention layers in total, the bottommost setting updates the regression layer only.

Next, we conducted an experiment to validate the proposed method for the construction of input sequences. Table 4 indicates that our simplified approach was comparable or superior to the others, and, accordingly, we used it for the following experiments.

Finally, we present the MSR test accuracies of the fine-tuned models in Table 5. To see the effect of fine-tuning, we also display side by side the corresponding results without fine-tuning, which were copied from Table 3. The learning rate was chosen from $\{1 \times 10^{-4}, 5 \times 10^{-5}, 2 \times 10^{-5}, 1 \times 10^{-5}, 5 \times 10^{-6}, 2 \times 10^{-6}, 1 \times 10^{-6}\}$ for each pre-trained model by comparing the best holdout accuracy results of five individual runs of fine-tuning with different random seeds. As shown in Table 5, the accuracies increased after fine-tuning for most pre-trained models, among which BERT-large models without the whole-word-masking strategy gained the most substantial amount of increase.

Nonetheless, the whole-word-masking models were still at the top through improving the accuracy by a healthy margin compared to the models that learned from the official training data.

Table 4. Accuracy results (%) on the holdout set for different input construction methods. For each method, we performed five runs of fine-tuning with different random seeds, and the average accuracy is reported with the standard deviation in parentheses.

Input Construction	Accuracy
Proposed method	84.2 (2.3)
with [SEP]	84.2 (1.3)
with segment identifiers	84.6 (2.9)
with [SEP] and segment identifiers	74.6 (1.8)

Table 5. Accuracy results (%) of transformer-based models for the MSR test set with and without fine-tuning, which are presented in w/o FT and w/FT columns, respectively.

Model	w/o FT	w/FT
BERT-base-uncased	58.46	68.65
BERT-base-cased	60.19	73.27
BERT-base-multilingual-uncased	20.58	21.92
BERT-base-multilingual-cased	41.92	47.88
BERT-large-uncased	55.00	79.23
BERT-large-cased	49.23	79.42
BERT-large-uncased-wwm	**77.12**	**86.15**
BERT-large-cased-wwm	77.12	85.77
GPT2	44.04	38.27
GPT2-medium	52.69	59.23

5. SAT Sentence Completion

To further verify our findings, we gathered 152 sentence completion questions from the eight SAT practice exams provided by College Board (https://www.collegeboard.org) between 2003 and 2014. The reading part of the collected practice set includes sentence completion questions, each of which has one or two blanks in a sentence and provides five candidate choices. The collected SAT set contains that of Tang [7] but is covered by that of Woods [8].

Since any standard training corpus is not specified for the SAT set, previous researchers used different training corpora such as GloWbe [43], English Gigaword (LDC2009T13), and Wikipedia dumps. We used 1B word benchmark [40] to train the word RNNs, whose d_{emb}, d_{hid}, and d_{out} were set to 500, 2000, and 500, respectively. The learning rate was initialized to 1.0 and then multiplied by 0.8 after every epoch. We applied importance sampling to the output embedding matrix with sample size of 8192 [12] to deal with the large vocabulary size, which was 409K even after lower-casing. Other training details were kept identical to those for the MSR set, described in Section 4.1.

Table 6 shows the SAT evaluation results, including the previous best results. We also evaluated the word RNNs that had been trained on the MSR official training corpus (denoted by 19C novels). With more training data and larger network sizes, the SAT accuracies of the word RNNs increased considerably, exceeding the previously published results while being comparable to that of LM1B. Note that, besides its large size, LM1B utilized character level CNN layers to acquire intermediate representations for 793K word types [12], requiring more computing resources than our RNNs. In addition, bidirectional modeling was beneficial, as observed in Table 2.

Similar to the experimentation in Section 4.2, we also evaluated the transformer-based models with and without fine-tuning (Table 7). Since the SAT set is not large enough for splitting, we treated the entire MSR set as the training set while assigning the last hundred questions to the held-out validation set. With the learning rate that had been selected for each pre-trained model in the previous section, we obtained the best model by re-running the fine-tuning five times on the new training set with different random seeds.

Table 6. Accuracy results (%) for the SAT set. The accuracies in italic were copied from their corresponding publications. We report the average accuracy with the standard deviation if a model was optimized repeatedly.

Model (d_{emb}-d_{hid}-d_{out})	Training Corpus	Accuracy
NPMI + Co-occ. Freq. + LSA + CBOW + CSKIP [7]	GloWbe	*59*
PMI using Unigrams + Bigrams + Trigrams [8]	English Gigaword	*58.95*
Unidirectional word RNN (200-600-400)	19C novels	29.6 (1.5)
Bidirectional word RNN (200-600-400)		33.3 (2.0)
Unidirectional word RNN (500-2000-500)	1B word benchmark	66.5
Bidirectional word RNN (500-2000-500)		69.1
LM1B (1024-8196-1024)	1B word benchmark	71.0

Table 7. Accuracy results (%) of transformer-based models for the SAT set with and without fine-tuning, which are presented in w/o FT and w/FT columns, respectively.

Model	w/o FT	w/FT
BERT-base-uncased	30.92	42.11
BERT-base-cased	30.92	52.63
BERT-base-multilingual-uncased	17.11	22.37
BERT-base-multilingual-cased	23.03	36.84
BERT-large-uncased	25.66	73.03
BERT-large-cased	27.63	73.03
BERT-large-uncased-wwm	**63.82**	80.26
BERT-large-cased-wwm	59.87	**80.92**
GPT2	38.16	32.24
GPT2-medium	53.29	53.29

Among the networks without fine-tuning, the whole-word-masking models were outstanding, while being outperformed by the word RNNs. Fine-tuning with the MSR questions was quite beneficial to the BERT models for the SAT questions, which indicated that the model learned a common solving strategy that worked across questions from different source texts. In addition, the BERT-large models outperformed the BERT-base models after fine-tuning, possibly due to the fact that the sentences and choice texts of the SAT questions were written using a difficult vocabulary compared to the MSR questions. As a result, the fine-tuned whole-word-masking models achieved state-of-the-art performance on the SAT questions.

6. TOPIK Cloze Questions

In this section, we attempt to confirm how effective the aforementioned methods are for a dataset other than in English. To do this, we newly collected 1823 cloze-style questions from Test of Proficiency in Korean (TOPIK) (https://www.topik.go.kr), provided by the website (https://studytopik.go.kr). TOPIK aims to assess the linguistic ability and guide the learning of the Korean language for non-native Korean speakers, and its results may be a prerequisite for entrance into universities or employment in companies and public institutions.

Tables 8 and 9 show the statistics of the collected TOPIK dataset. According to the level of difficulties, TOPIK test types have been divided into Levels 1–6 (lower is easier) until 2004, novice/intermediate/advanced from 2004 to 2014, and Level I/II (I is easier than II) since 2014. Most of the multiple-choice cloze-style questions appear in the easier test types except that 78 questions are from Level II. TOPIK is composed of sections including vocabulary, reading, and writing. Each section contains a different number of cloze-style questions, while the lengths of questions in the writing section are larger than those of the others. Each question was tagged with 'long' or 'short' for its passage length and 'single' or 'multi' for the number of speakers. We counted for each tag type the number of words after splitting with whitespace and punctuation. While the passage lengths of the collected questions are not restricted to a single sentence, more than 70% are questions tagged as 'short', whose passages contain fewer than 10 words on average. Some instances from the TOPIK dataset are shown in Table 10.

Table 8. Statistics of the cloze-style questions collected from previous TOPIK tests.

Section	Type	The Number of Questions					
		Level 1	Level 2	Novice	Level I	Level II	Total
Vocabulary	Short-single	30	28	175			233
	Short-multi	78	91	303			472
	Long-single	6	14	48			68
	Long-multi	32	12	102			146
	Subtotal	146	145	628			919
Reading	Short-single	26	19	100	36	12	193
	Short-multi	4					4
	Long-single	19	13	65	49	66	212
	Subtotal	49	32	165	85	78	409
Writing	Short-single	25	22				47
	Short-multi	109	94	129			332
	Long-single		32	21			53
	Long-multi	41	22				63
	Subtotal	175	170	150			495
Total		370	347	943	85	78	1823

Table 9. Lengths of the cloze-style questions collected from previous TOPIK tests.

Section	Type	Passage Length		Choice Length	
		Words	Chars	Words	Chars
Vocabulary	Short-single	5.9	14.7	1.0	2.0
	Short-multi	11.2	25.0	1.3	3.5
	Long-single	42.4	107.7	1.7	4.2
	Long-multi	30.5	69.7	1.4	3.9
	Subtotal	15.2	35.6	1.3	3.3
Reading	Short-single	9.7	25.3	1.0	3.3
	Short-multi	10.2	26.0	1.2	5.0
	Long-single	52.4	139.1	2.3	6.6
	Subtotal	31.8	84.3	1.7	5.0
Writing	Short-single	14.0	35.9	3.7	10.1
	Short-multi	10.9	24.5	3.4	8.7
	Long-single	45.3	117.0	4.0	11.1
	Long-multi	41.4	93.1	3.4	8.5
	Subtotal	18.8	44.2	3.5	9.1
Total		19.9	48.9	5.0	5.2

Table 10. Samples from the TOPIK dataset.

Type	Question	Translation
Short-single	돈을 찾으러 _____ 에 갑니다. 1. 은행 2. 운동장 3. 경찰서 4. 백화점	I'm going to the _____ to find the money. 1. **bank** 2. playground 3. police office 4. department store
Short-multi	아침에 다 같이 식사하세요? 우리는 _____ 시간이 다 다르니까 같이 못 먹어요. 1. 쉬는 2. 끝나는 3. **일어나는** 4. 내는	Do you eat together in the morning? No, we can't eat together because the times we _____ are different. 1. rest 2. finish 3. **wake up** 4. pay
Long-single	친절은 다른 사람을 위한 따뜻한 마음과 행동입니다. 친절한 사람은 다른 사람에게 _____ 행동을 하지 않습니다. 그리고 남이 어려울 때 적극적으로 도와 줍니다. 친절한 말과 행동은 이 세상을 더 아름답게 만듭니다. 1. 좋은 2. 기쁜 3. **나쁜** 4. 착한	Kindness is a warm heart and action for others. Kind people do not act _____ others. They actively help when others are in trouble. Kind words and actions make this world more beautiful. 1. well with 2. happy with 3. **bad to** 4. nicely to
Long-multi	경찰관: 어디에서 잃어 버리셨어요? 아주머니: 택시 안에 놓고 내렸어요. 경찰관: 가방이 _____ 아주머니: 까만 색 큰 가방이에요. 경찰관: 뭐가 들어 있습니까? 아주머니: 지갑이요. 꼭 찾아야 하는데요. 경찰관: 알아보겠습니다. 아주머니: 아저씨, 꼭 좀 부탁드립니다. 경찰관: 너무 걱정하지 마십시오. 댁에 가서 기다리세요.. 1. **어떻게 생겼어요?** 2. 어떤 가게에서 샀어요? 3. 어떻게 만들었어요? 4. 어디에서 샀어요?	Officer: Where did you lose it? Ma'am: I left it in the cab. Officer: Your bag, _____ Ma'am: It's a big black bag. Officer: What do you have in it? Ma'am: My wallet, I must find it. Officer: I'll see what I can do. Ma'am: Please, officer. Officer: Don't worry too much, go home and wait. 1. **what does it look like?** 2. what store did you buy it from? 3. how did you make it? 4. where did you buy it?

We evaluated our word RNNs and the transformer-based models against the TOPIK dataset, which was split in half for development and test. We trained the word RNNs with the Sejong corpus (downloaded through https://ithub.korean.go.kr/user/total/database/corpusManager.do), applying the wordpiece tokenizer that was used for the BERT-base-multilingual-cased model. The network size and the training details were identical to those for the MSR experiment. The pre-trained BERT multilingual models were evaluated with or without fine-tuned in the same manner as the previous sections.

As shown in Table 11, with or without fine-tuning, the BERT models were inferior to our word RNNs. Moreover, the uncased BERT without fine-tuning was on par with a random classifier, whose expected accuracy is 25% for the TOPIK questions, each of which contains four choices. BERT-base-multilingual-cased was also not satisfactory on the Korean dataset as well as on the English datasets (see Sections 4.2 and 5), which requires further inspection and analysis to utilize multilingual models properly. Meanwhile, bidirectional modeling was not effective, which is likely due to the inadequate size of the training corpus having fewer than 20M words.

For further analysis, we visualize the mean accuracies of the models on the TOPIK development set for different difficulty levels and question types for each section in Figure 5. The fine-tuned models received supervision directly from the development set, thus being excluded from the analysis. Since we trained the word RNNs repeatedly with different random seeds, their mean accuracies are presented. As can be seen, the vocabulary part was relatively easy, while the writing section was difficult for the models, whose accuracy correlated with the length of the choice text. The word RNNs yielded low accuracy when there were multiple speakers in the question compared to the single-speaker case since the training corpus does not contain many articles in the form of conversations. Meanwhile, the accuracies dropped as the difficulty levels increased (from Level 1 to 2, and from Level I to II) for the word RNNs. Lastly, the accuracy patterns over the subsets of the two BERT models were similar, which implies that the uncased model did not operate just randomly although its average performance was on par with a random classifier.

Appl. Sci. **2020**, *10*, 1340

Table 11. Accuracy results (%) for the TOPIK set. We report the average accuracy with the standard deviation if a model was optimized repeatedly. For the fine-tuned (FT) models, the held-out accuracies are presented in Dev. column.

Model	Dev.	Test
Unidirectional word RNN	43.4 (0.5)	42.3 (0.6)
Bidirectional word RNN	43.3 (0.5)	40.8 (1.1)
BERT-base-multilingual-uncased	25.8	24.9
BERT-base-multilingual-cased	29.9	32.6
FT BERT-base-multilingual-uncased	30.0	27.3
FT BERT-base-multilingual-cased	38.0	33.7

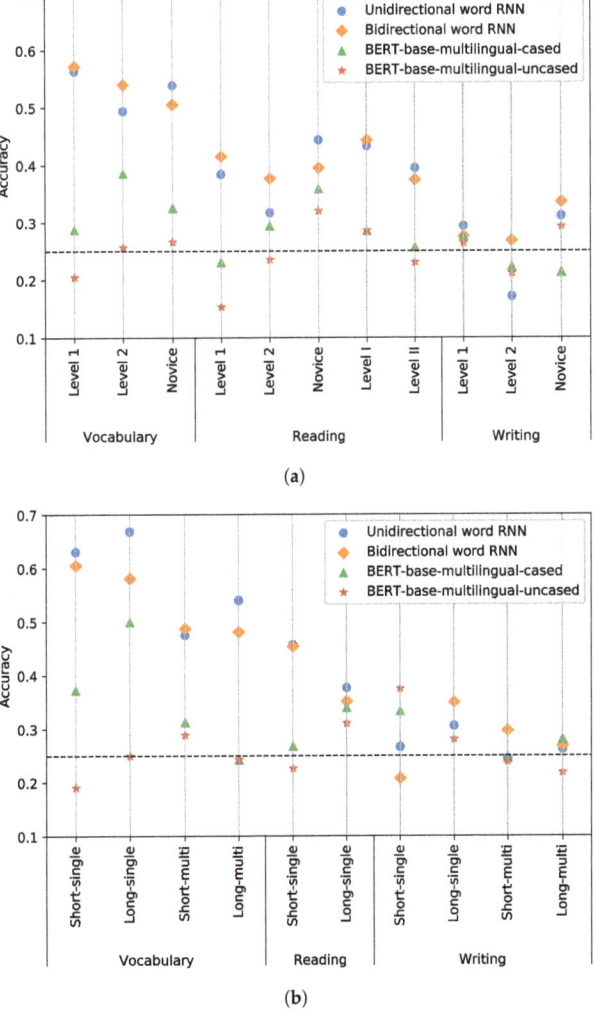

Figure 5. Performance analysis on the TOPIK set. The mean accuracies for each difficulty level and question type are shown in (**a**,**b**), respectively. The black dotted line signifies the accuracy of a random classifier, which equals 0.25.

One possible direction to improve pre-trained multilingual LMs for MRC questions in a target language is to apply unsupervised domain adaptation [44]. Hundreds of questions would not be enough for a multilingual LM to fully adapt to both the target language and the downstream task. Accordingly, additional training of a pre-trained LM with unlabeled text data in a target language will be useful. Part-of-speech tags and dependency edges and labels can be augmented as supervision [45] to provide more explicit syntactic information in the target language. Inserting adapter modules [46] to the multilingual LM can be an efficient solution to capture language-specific properties with the modules while retaining universal linguistic abstractions learned by the pre-trained model. In addition, starting from a multilingual model optimized with translation-based objectives [28,47] and adapting it with available cross-lingual supervision for the target language and the downstream task is another interesting research direction. Since research on multilingual transfer learning is still active, we are currently investigating how to effectively apply those newly proposed methods to the TOPIK dataset.

7. Conclusions

In this study, we explored various methods based on neural LMs for sentence completion. With well-tuned network sizes and optimization parameters, we were able to enhance the performance of word RNNs, which reached beyond the previous state-of-the-art results on the MSR and SAT datasets. Furthermore, by fine-tuning the pre-trained transformer-based LMs with a few sentence-completion examples, we improved the accuracies significantly for both datasets. In addition, this paper presents the experiments on the newly collected cloze-style questions in the Korean language. The experimental results reveal that applying the multilingual BERT models for the Korean dataset led to unsatisfactory results, which necessitates further investigation. We hope our reproducible benchmarks help subsequent research to develop and validate diverse neural approaches in language understanding.

Author Contributions: Conceptualization, data curation, methodology, software, and writing—original draft, H.P.; and project administration, writing—review and editing, funding acquisition, methodology, and supervision, J.P. All authors have read and agreed to the published version of the manuscript.

Funding: Kakao Corp., Kakao Brain Corp., and National Research Foundation of Korea

Acknowledgments: This work was supported by Kakao and Kakao Brain corporations, and in part by the National Research Foundation of Korea (NRF) grant funded by the Korea government (MSIT) (No. NRF-2019R1F1A1053366). The authors thank the administrative support from the Institute for Industrial Systems Innovation of Seoul National University.

Conflicts of Interest: The authors declare no conflict of interest.

References

1. Hermann, K.M.; Kociský, T.; Grefenstette, E.; Espeholt, L.; Kay, W.; Suleyman, M.; Blunsom, P. Teaching Machines to Read and Comprehend. In Proceedings of the NIPS, Vancouver, BC, Canada, 7–12 December 2015; pp. 1693–1701.
2. Chen, D.; Bolton, J.; Manning, C.D. *A Thorough Examination of the CNN/Daily Mail Reading Comprehension Task*; ACL (1); The Association for Computer Linguistics: Stroudsburg, PA, USA, 2016.
3. Hill, F.; Bordes, A.; Chopra, S.; Weston, J. The Goldilocks Principle: Reading Children's Books with Explicit Memory Representations. *arXiv* **2016**, arXiv:1511.02301.
4. Zweig, G.; Platt, J.C.; Meek, C.; Burges, C.J.C.; Yessenalina, A.; Liu, Q. *Computational Approaches to Sentence Completion*; ACL (1); The Association for Computer Linguistics: Stroudsburg, PA, USA, 2012; pp. 601–610.
5. Zweig, G.; Burges, C.J.C. *A Challenge Set for Advancing Language Modeling*; WLM@NAACL-HLT; Association for Computational Linguistics: Stroudsburg, PA, USA, 2012; pp. 29–36.
6. Mikolov, T.; Chen, K.; Corrado, G.; Dean, J. Efficient Estimation of Word Representations in Vector Space. *arXiv* **2013**, arXiv:1301.3781.
7. Tang, E. Assessing the Effectiveness of Corpus-Based Methods in Solving SAT Sentence Completion Questions. *JCP* **2016**, *11*, 266–279. [CrossRef]

8. Woods, A. *Exploiting Linguistic Features for Sentence Completion*; ACL (2); The Association for Computer Linguistics: Stroudsburg, PA, USA, 2016.
9. Melamud, O.; Goldberger, J.; Dagan, I. Context2vec: Learning Generic Context Embedding with Bidirectional LSTM. In Proceedings of The 20th SIGNLL Conference on Computational Natural Language Learning, Berlin, Germany, 11–12 August 2016; pp. 51–61.
10. Tran, K.M.; Bisazza, A.; Monz, C. *Recurrent Memory Networks for Language Modeling*; HLT-NAACL; The Association for Computational Linguistics: Stroudsburg, PA, USA, 2016; pp. 321–331.
11. Park, H.; Cho, S.; Park, J. Word RNN as a Baseline for Sentence Completion. In Proceedings of the 2018 IEEE 5th International Congress on Information Science and Technology (CiSt), Marrakech, Morocco, 21–27 October 2018; pp. 183–187.
12. Józefowicz, R.; Vinyals, O.; Schuster, M.; Shazeer, N.; Wu, Y. Exploring the Limits of Language Modeling. *arXiv* **2016**, arXiv:1602.02410.
13. Melis, G.; Dyer, C.; Blunsom, P. On the State of the Art of Evaluation in Neural Language Models. *arXiv* **2018**, arXiv:1707.05589.
14. Howard, J.; Ruder, S. *Universal Language Model Fine-tuning for Text Classification*; ACL (1); Association for Computational Linguistics: Stroudsburg, PA, USA, 2018; pp. 328–339.
15. Radford, A.; Narasimhan, K.; Salimans, T.; Sutskever, I. *Improving Language Understanding by Generative Pre-Training*; Technical Report; OpenAI: San Francisco, CA, USA 2018.
16. Devlin, J.; Chang, M.; Lee, K.; Toutanova, K. *BERT: Pre-training of Deep Bidirectional Transformers for Language Understanding*; NAACL-HLT (1); Association for Computational Linguistics: Stroudsburg, PA, USA, 2019; pp. 4171–4186.
17. Yang, Z.; Dai, Z.; Yang, Y.; Carbonell, J.G.; Salakhutdinov, R.; Le, Q.V. XLNet: Generalized Autoregressive Pretraining for Language Understanding. *arXiv* **2019**, arXiv:1906.08237.
18. Radford, A.; Wu, J.; Child, R.; Luan, D.; Amodei, D.; Sutskever, I. Language models are unsupervised multitask learners. *OpenAI Blog* **2019**, *1*, 9.
19. Vaswani, A.; Shazeer, N.; Parmar, N.; Uszkoreit, J.; Jones, L.; Gomez, A.N.; Kaiser, L.; Polosukhin, I. Attention is All you Need. In Proceedings of the Advances in neural information processing systems, Long Beach, CA, USA, 4–9 December 2017; pp. 5998–6008.
20. Hardalov, M.; Koychev, I.; Nakov, P. Beyond English-only Reading Comprehension: Experiments in Zero-Shot Multilingual Transfer for Bulgarian. *arXiv* **2019**, arXiv:1908.01519.
21. Cui, Y.; Liu, T.; Chen, Z.; Wang, S.; Hu, G. Consensus Attention-based Neural Networks for Chinese Reading Comprehension. *arXiv* **2016**, arXiv:1607.02250.
22. Liu, S.; Zhang, X.; Zhang, S.; Wang, H.; Zhang, W. Neural Machine Reading Comprehension: Methods and Trends. *Appl. Sci.* **2019**, *9*, 3698. [CrossRef]
23. Deutsch, D.; Roth, D. *Summary Cloze: A New Task for Content Selection in Topic-Focused Summarization*; EMNLP/IJCNLP (1); Association for Computational Linguistics: Stroudsburg, PA, USA, 2019; pp. 3718–3727.
24. Schwartz, R.; Sap, M.; Konstas, I.; Zilles, L.; Choi, Y.; Smith, N.A. *Story Cloze Task: UW NLP System*; LSDSem@EACL; Association for Computational Linguistics: Stroudsburg, PA, USA, 2017; pp. 52–55.
25. Xie, Q.; Lai, G.; Dai, Z.; Hovy, E.H. Large-scale Cloze Test Dataset Designed by Teachers. *arXiv* **2017**, arXiv:1711.03225.
26. Huh, M.; Agrawal, P.; Efros, A.A. What makes ImageNet good for transfer learning? *arXiv* **2016**, arXiv:1608.08614.
27. Peters, M.E.; Neumann, M.; Iyyer, M.; Gardner, M.; Clark, C.; Lee, K.; Zettlemoyer, L. *Deep Contextualized Word Representations*; NAACL-HLT; Association for Computational Linguistics: Stroudsburg, PA, USA, 2018; pp. 2227–2237.
28. Conneau, A.; Lample, G. Cross-lingual Language Model Pretraining. In Proceedings of the Advances in Neural Information Processing Systems, Vancouver, BC, Canada, 8–14 December 2019; pp. 7057–7067.
29. Liu, Y.; Ott, M.; Goyal, N.; Du, J.; Joshi, M.; Chen, D.; Levy, O.; Lewis, M.; Zettlemoyer, L.; Stoyanov, V. RoBERTa: A Robustly Optimized BERT Pretraining Approach. *arXiv* **2019**, arXiv:1907.11692.
30. Pires, T.; Schlinger, E.; Garrette, D. *How Multilingual is Multilingual BERT?* ACL (1); Association for Computational Linguistics: Stroudsburg, PA, USA, 2019; pp. 4996–5001.
31. Wu, S.; Dredze, M. *Beto, Bentz, Becas: The Surprising Cross-Lingual Effectiveness of BERT*; EMNLP/IJCNLP (1); Association for Computational Linguistics: Stroudsburg, PA, USA, 2019; pp. 833–844.

32. Artetxe, M.; Ruder, S.; Yogatama, D. On the Cross-lingual Transferability of Monolingual Representations. *arXiv* **2019**, arXiv:1910.11856.
33. Mikolov, T.; Karafiát, M.; Burget, L.; Cernocký, J.; Khudanpur, S. Recurrent neural network based language model. In Proceedings of the Eleventh Annual Conference of the International Speech Communication Association, Chiba, Japan, 26–30 September 2010; pp. 1045–1048.
34. Zaremba, W.; Sutskever, I.; Vinyals, O. Recurrent Neural Network Regularization. *arXiv* **2014**, arXiv:1409.2329.
35. Berglund, M.; Raiko, T.; Honkala, M.; Kärkkäinen, L.; Vetek, A.; Karhunen, J. Bidirectional Recurrent Neural Networks as Generative Models. In Proceedings of the NIPS, Vancouver, BC, Canada, 7–12 December 2015; pp. 856–864.
36. Trinh, T.H.; Le, Q.V. A Simple Method for Commonsense Reasoning. *arXiv* **2018**, arXiv:1806.02847.
37. Mirowski, P.; Vlachos, A. *Dependency Recurrent Neural Language Models for Sentence Completion*; ACL (2); The Association for Computer Linguistics: Stroudsburg, PA, USA, 2015; pp. 511–517.
38. Levesque, H.J.; Davis, E.; Morgenstern, L. The Winograd Schema Challenge. In Proceedings of the Thirteenth International Conference on the Principles of Knowledge Representation and Reasoning, Rome, Italy, 10–14 June 2012.
39. Mikolov, T. Statistical language models based on neural networks. In Proceedings of the Google, Mountain View, CA, USA, 2 April 2012.
40. Chelba, C.; Mikolov, T.; Schuster, M.; Ge, Q.; Brants, T.; Koehn, P.; Robinson, T. One billion word benchmark for measuring progress in statistical language modeling. *arXiv* **2014**, arXiv:1312.3005.
41. Wu, Y.; Schuster, M.; Chen, Z.; Le, Q.V.; Norouzi, M.; Macherey, W.; Krikun, M.; Cao, Y.; Gao, Q.; Macherey, K.; et al. Google's Neural Machine Translation System: Bridging the Gap between Human and Machine Translation. *arXiv* **2016**, arXiv:1609.08144.
42. Wolf, T.; Debut, L.; Sanh, V.; Chaumond, J.; Delangue, C.; Moi, A.; Cistac, P.; Rault, T.; Louf, R.; Funtowicz, M.; et al. HuggingFace's Transformers: State-of-the-art Natural Language Processing. *arXiv* **2019**, arXiv:1910.03771.
43. Davies, M.; Fuchs, R. Expanding horizons in the study of World Englishes with the 1.9 billion word Global Web-based English Corpus (GloWbE). *English World-Wide* **2015**, *36*, 1–28. [CrossRef]
44. Han, X.; Eisenstein, J. *Unsupervised Domain Adaptation of Contextualized Embeddings for Sequence Labeling*; EMNLP/IJCNLP (1); Association for Computational Linguistics: Stroudsburg, PA, USA, 2019; pp. 4237–4247.
45. Kondratyuk, D.; Straka, M. *75 Languages, 1 Model: Parsing Universal Dependencies Universally*; EMNLP/IJCNLP (1); Association for Computational Linguistics: Stroudsburg, PA, USA, 2019; pp. 2779–2795.
46. Houlsby, N.; Giurgiu, A.; Jastrzkebski, S.; Morrone, B.; de Laroussilhe, Q.; Gesmundo, A.; Attariyan, M.; Gelly, S. Parameter-Efficient Transfer Learning for NLP. *Proc. Mach. Learn. Res.* **2019**, *97*, 2790–2799.
47. Conneau, A.; Khandelwal, K.; Goyal, N.; Chaudhary, V.; Wenzek, G.; Guzmán, F.; Grave, E.; Ott, M.; Zettlemoyer, L.; Stoyanov, V. Unsupervised Cross-lingual Representation Learning at Scale. *arXiv* **2019**, arXiv:1911.02116.

© 2020 by the authors. Licensee MDPI, Basel, Switzerland. This article is an open access article distributed under the terms and conditions of the Creative Commons Attribution (CC BY) license (http://creativecommons.org/licenses/by/4.0/).

Article

Reliable Classification of FAQs with Spelling Errors Using an Encoder-Decoder Neural Network in Korean

Youngjin Jang and Harksoo Kim *

Program of Computer and Communications Engineering, Kangwon National University, Chuncheon 24341, Korea; dan_yon@kangwon.ac.kr
* Correspondence: nlpdrkim@kangwon.ac.kr; Tel.: +82-33-250-6388

Received: 7 October 2019; Accepted: 3 November 2019; Published: 7 November 2019

Abstract: To resolve lexical disagreement problems between queries and frequently asked questions (FAQs), we propose a reliable sentence classification model based on an encoder-decoder neural network. The proposed model uses three types of word embeddings; fixed word embeddings for representing domain-independent meanings of words, fined-tuned word embeddings for representing domain-specific meanings of words, and character-level word embeddings for bridging lexical gaps caused by spelling errors. It also uses class embeddings to represent domain knowledge associated with each category. In the experiments with an FAQ dataset about online banking, the proposed embedding methods contributed to an improved performance of the sentence classification. In addition, the proposed model showed better performance (with an accuracy of 0.810 in the classification of 411 categories) than that of the comparison model.

Keywords: FAQ classification; encoder-decoder neural network; multi-level word embeddings

1. Introduction

Frequently asked questions (FAQs) in commercial services based on social media (e.g., chatbot for online banking) accommodate both customer needs and business requirements. As a useful tool for information access, most commercial services provide customers with a keyword search. However, sometimes the keyword search does not perform well in FAQ retrieval because of lexical disagreements between users' queries and the predefined questions in an FAQ set, as shown in Figure 1.

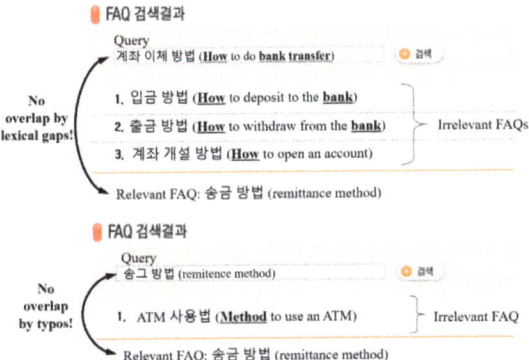

Figure 1. Motivational example.

In Figure 1, the lexical disagreements are caused by using different words with the same meanings (e.g., remittance vs. bank transfer), and by using incorrect words with spelling errors (e.g., remittance vs. remitence). To resolve these lexical disagreement problems, most FAQ retrieval systems expand keywords by looking up synonym dictionaries and bridge lexical gaps between different words with the same meanings. However, they cannot cope with the lexical agreement problem caused by spelling errors because it is impossible to pre-construct a synonym dictionary containing all misspelled keywords. Recently, FAQ classification models based on deep learning have been proposed because they have the ability to cluster semantically or lexically similar words through various distributed representation schemes like word embeddings and character embeddings. In this paper, we propose an FAQ classification model based on an encoder-decoder neural network with multiple word embedding vectors instead of keyword search methods. To increase FAQ classification performance, the proposed model adopts class embeddings, including domain knowledge of each FAQ category.

2. Previous Works

Initial sentence classification models based on deep learning were n-gram models using convolutional neural networks (CNNs) [1–5]. The authors of [3] proposed a CNN architecture using diverse versions of pre-trained static word vectors and variable size convolution filters. It was shown in [2] that simple convolutions of word n-grams could contribute to improving the performance of sentence classification by fine-tuning pre-trained static word vectors like Word2Vec [6]. These n-gram models were effective in exploring the regional syntax of words, but they could not account for order-sensitive situations where the order of words was critical to the meaning of a sentence. To overcome this problem, [7] proposed a classification model combined with a recurrent neural network (RNN) and a CNN. Then, some studies demonstrated that sub-word units like character n-grams could contribute to improving the performance of downstream natural language processing (NLP) tasks [8–13]. The authors of [12] proposed a part-of-speech tagging model based on an RNN in which each word is represented by a combination of Korean alphabet embeddings for making the model robust to typing errors. The authors of [13] proposed a character-level CNN model for text classification which showed that the character-level CNN model could achieve state-of-the-art or competitive results. In addition, [14] demonstrated that domain embeddings (i.e., embeddings of predefined categories) could contribute to improving the performance of large-scale domain classification. Recently, bidirectional encoder representations from transformers (BERT) was proposed [15], which is deeply bidirectional, unsupervised language representation that is pre-trained using a large amount of plain text corpus. BERT has shown state-of-the-art performance in many downstream NLP tasks such as classification, sequence labeling, and span prediction by learning task-specific vectors through fine-tuning. In sentence classification tasks such as sentiment analysis and semantic textual similarity analysis, BERT also outperformed the previous state-of-the-art models.

3. FAQ Classification Using an Encoder-Decoder Neural Network

Figure 2 shows the overall architecture of the proposed FAQ classification model. As shown in Figure 2, the proposed model consists of an embedding layer, a transformer encoder with attentions, and an RNN decoder.

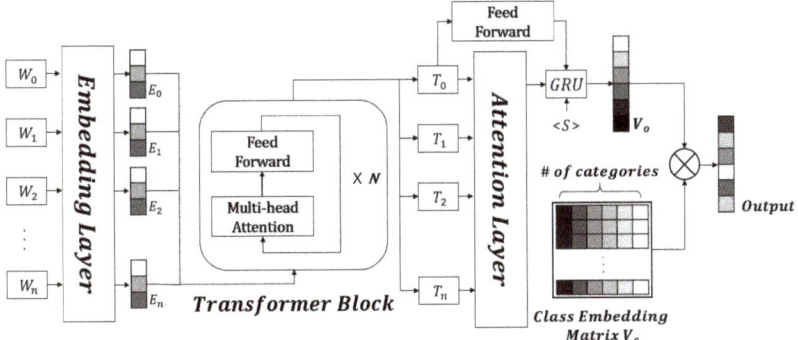

Figure 2. Overall architecture of the proposed model.

To make the proposed model robust to lexical disagreements, the embedding layer consists of three types of embedding vectors: Fixed word embedding vectors, fine-tuned word embedding vectors, and character-level word embedding vectors using a CNN. We expect that the fixed word embedding vectors represent domain-independent meanings of each word, and the fine-tuned word embedding vectors represent domain-specific meanings of each word. For example, we hope that "transfer" has the domain-independent meaning "move something" and the domain-specific meaning "send money" in a banking domain. We also expect that the character-based word embedding vectors alleviate lexical disagreement problems that are raised by spelling errors. For example, we hope that the misspelled word "remitence" has a similar vector representation with "remittance." In Figure 2, W_0 and E_0 are [CLS] (a special symbol added in front of every input example) and an embedding of [CLS], respectively. W_i except W_0 and E_i except E_0 are the i-th word in a sentence, and its embedding vector concatenated with three types of word embedding vectors, respectively. Figure 3 exemplifies three types of word embedding vectors.

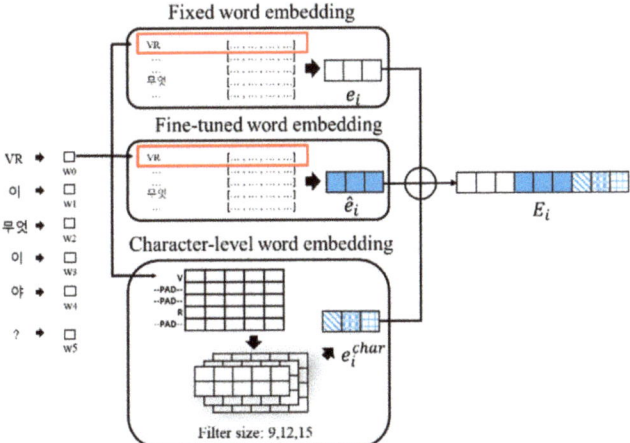

Figure 3. Embedding layer of the proposed model. The Korean sentence "VR 이 무엇이야?" means "What is VR?" in English.

In Figure 3, e_i, $\hat{e}_i$, and e_i^{char} are a fixed word embedding vector, a fine-tuned word embedding vector, and a character-level word embedding vector of the i-th one among n words in an input sentence

S (i.e., an input query or a predefined question in a FAQ set), respectively. e_i^{char} is generated by a CNN, as shown in the following equation.

$$e_i^{char} = CNN(c_1, c_2, \ldots, c_j, \ldots, c_l), \qquad (1)$$

where c_j is the j-th one among l characters in a word w_i. In this paper, a character refers to the Korean characters called *jamo*. A final word embedding vector E_i is represented by the concatenation of e_i, $\hat{e}_i$, and e_i^{char}, as shown in the following equation:

$$E_i = \left[e_i; \hat{e}_i; e_i^{char}\right]. \qquad (2)$$

To supplement word embedding vectors with contextual information, we adopt an encoder-decoder neural network in which word embedding vectors are encoded by a transformer's encoder [16]. The output T_i of the transformer's encoder is represented by a multi-head scaled dot-product self-attention mechanism, as shown in the following equations.

$$Q = K = V = E \qquad (3)$$

$$Attention(Q, K, V) = softmax\left(\frac{QK^T}{\sqrt{d_k}}\right)V, \qquad (4)$$

where E is one among n word embedding vectors, and Q, K, and V are a query, a key, and a value for calculating attentions, respectively. Then, d_k is the size of E for scaling dot-products. In Equation (4), the query, key, and value are the same vectors according to Equation (3). This case is called self-attention, relating different positions of a single sequence $E_1, E_2, \ldots, E_n$, to compute a representation of the sequence. Self-attention has been successfully used in various NLP tasks, such as machine translation, machine reading comprehension, abstractive document summarization, etc. The query, key, and value are first linearly transformed into N heads. Then, each head is entered into Equation (4). Therefore, the self-attention is calculated N times, making it so-called multi-headed.

The first output T_0 (the final output vector of the special [CLS] token) of the transformer's encoder is input as an initial value of the RNN decoder, implemented by a gated recurrent unit (GRU) [17] with Luong's encoder-decoder attention mechanism [18], after passing through a fully connected neural network (FNN). Figure 4 shows the RNN decoder with Luong's encoder-decoder attention mechanism in detail.

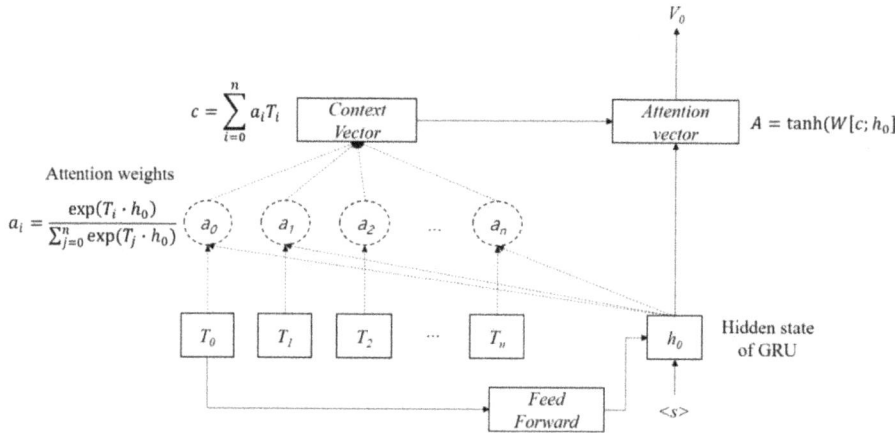

Figure 4. Recurrent neural network (RNN) decoder with Luong's encoder-decoder attention mechanism.

As shown in Figure 4, each attention weight a_i is induced by inner products between each output T_i of the transformer's encoder and the first hidden state h_o of the RNN decoder. The attention weights mean how much each output T_i is associated with the hidden state h_o. Then, the context vector c is constructed by the weighted sum of a_i and T_i. Finally, the RNN decoder generates an output vector V_o using the FNN-encoded input sentence $FNN(T_0)$, the start symbol <S>, and the context vector c, as shown in the following equation:

$$V_o = Dec(FNN(T_0), <s>, c). \tag{5}$$

To supplement the output vector V_o with domain-specific knowledge, we adopt a domain embedding scheme proposed by [14]. We define one class embedding vector per FAQ category, as shown in the following equation.

$$V_{C_t} = mean(\sum_k e_k), \tag{6}$$

where V_{C_t} is a class embedding vector that is calculated as an average of the word embedding vectors, e_k's, in sentences belonging to the t-th FAQ category. Finally, to classify input sentences into FAQ categories, we use an FNN. The vector of inner products between the output vector V_o of the RNN decoder and the class embedding matrix V_C is used as an input vector of the FNN.

4. Evaluation

4.1. Data Sets and Experimental Settings

We collected an FAQ dataset (10,495 pairs of FAQs about online banking). The FAQ dataset is a set of users' queries manually annotated with FAQ categories. The queries had many spacing errors and spelling errors because they were collected from a real mobile app service. An FAQ in the dataset consists of, on average, 23.3 *eumjeols* (Korean syllables) and contains, on average, 0.7 typo-like spelling errors and spacing errors. The number of FAQ categories was 411. Table 1 shows a sample of the FAQ dataset.

Table 1. Sample of the FAQ dataset.

Sentence (Korean)	Sentence (English)	ID of FAQ Category
간편 이체	Easy bank transfer	3
쉽게 송금하는 방법	How to easily send money	3
비밀 번호 변경	How to change the password	7
비번 바꾸는 법	How to change PW	7

Figure 5 shows a full histogram of the data distribution over the full 411 categories. Figure 6 shows the distribution of FAQ categories according to the number of queries included in each FAQ category.

As shown in Figures 5 and 6, 63% of FAQ categories included less than six queries. To evaluate the proposed model, we divided the FAQ dataset into a training set, a validation set, and a test set by a ratio of 8:1:1 according to a random sampling scheme. As an evaluation measure, we used an accuracy calculation.

To implement the proposed model, we pre-trained GloVe [19] by using 20 GB of Korean news articles. Then, we used the GloVe as the word embedding vectors in Equation (2). The vocabulary size of the GloVe was 210,867. We initialized the character-level embedding vectors with random values. The vocabulary size of the character-level embedding vectors was 132. We set the sizes of embedding vectors (i.e., e_i, $ê_i$, and e_i^{char}) to 100, 100, and 300, respectively. We set the sizes of the class embedding matrix (i.e., V_C) to 100 × 411. We set the hidden size, the attention head size, and the number of layers in the transformer's encoder to 500, 12, and 6, respectively. We set the hidden size of the GRU neural network to 100. The model optimization was done with Adam [20] at a learning rate of 0.00005, and the learning rate was halved if the performance of the validation set did not improve. The dropout rate was set to 0.2, and the mini-batch size was set to 64 sentences, respectively. We empirically set the learning rate, the dropout rate, and the mini-batch size in order to obtain the best performances.

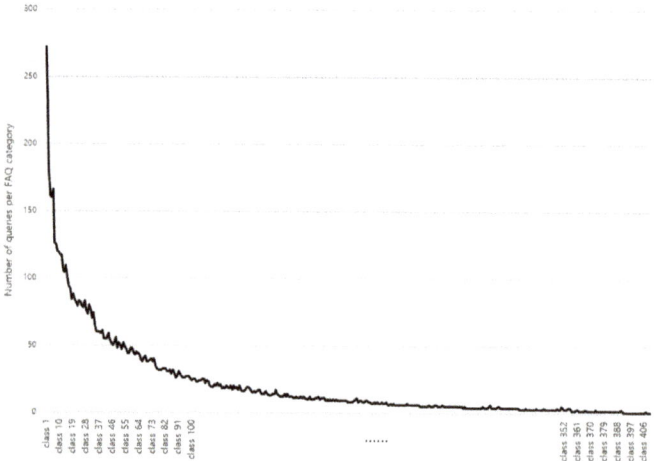

Figure 5. Distribution of the number of queries over the full FAQ categories.

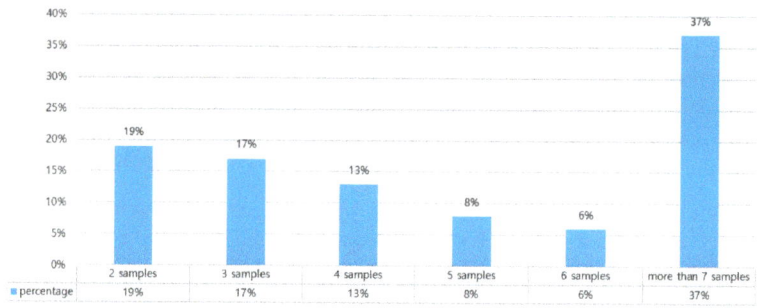

Figure 6. Distribution of FAQ categories according to the number of queries.

4.2. Experimental Results

The first experiment was to evaluate the effectiveness of the proposed embedding methods by comparing the performance changes, as shown in Table 2.

Table 2. Performance changes according to the use of embedding methods.

Model	Accuracy
WordEmbed (baseline)	0.705
WordEmbed + CharEmbed	0.756
WordEmbed + Char & TunedEmbed	0.784
WordEmbed + Char & TunedEmbed + ClassEmbed	0.810

In Table 2, the baseline model (WordEmbed) uses fixed GloVe embeddings as input vectors. CharEmbed, TunedEmbed, and ClassEmbed refer to the character-level word embeddings, the fine-tuned word embeddings, and the class embeddings that are proposed in this paper, respectively. As shown in Table 2, the proposed embedding methods contributed to increasing the performance of FAQ classification.

The second experiment was to compare the proposed model with the previous models, as shown in Table 3.

Table 3. Performance comparison.

Model	Accuracy
CNN	0.638
OKAPI	0.705
BERT-Multilingual	0.779
Proposed Model	0.810

In Table 3, CNN is the sentence classification model based on a CNN [2] in which pretrained word vectors are converted into feature maps by convolution operations based on multiple filters. OKAPI is the Okapi BM25 retrieval model [21] which is a state-of-the-art ranking function used in document retrieval. BERT-Multilingual is a multilingual version of BERT [15] that is pretrained using a large multilingual text corpus, including Korean. In our experiments, BERT-Multilingual was fine-tuned for 15 epochs by using the FAQ dataset. As shown in Table 3, the proposed model outperformed both the well-known sentence classification model and the keyword search model.

The last experiment was to compare the performance changes of the proposed model according to the size of training data, as shown in Figure 7.

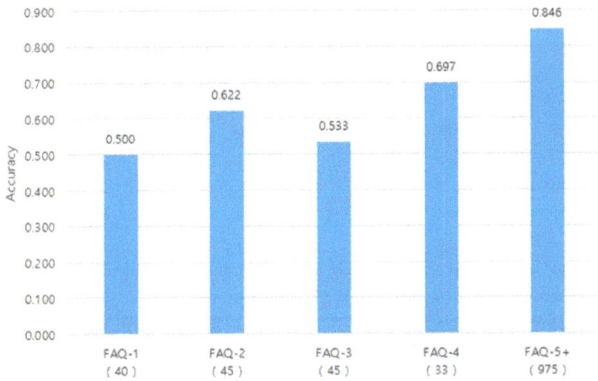

Figure 7. Performance changes according to the size of training data. "5+" means five or more.

In Figure 7, FAQ-n indicates FAQ categories in which n queries (i.e., n training data) are contained. The parenthesized values indicate the number of FAQ categories associated with each FAQ-n in the test data. It can be seen from the figure that the proposed model needed at least five training data per FAQ category in order to obtain an accuracy of more than 0.8.

5. Conclusions

We proposed a high-performance sentence classification model based on an encoder-decoder model with an attention mechanism. For bridging the lexical gaps between users' queries and FAQs, we used three types of word embeddings (fixed word embeddings, fine-tuned word embeddings, and character-level word embeddings) as inputs to the transformer's encoder. For supplementing domain knowledge associated with categories, we added class embeddings to the outputs of the RNN decoder. In the experiments with the FAQ dataset, the proposed model outperformed the comparison models. We found that the proposed embedding methods contributed to improving the performance of sentence classification. The proposed model showed low performances in FAQ categories containing a small number of training data. To reduce this problem, we need to adopt pre-trained language models like BERT and XLNet [22] as encoders. In the future, we will try to combine the proposed model with a chatbot model for assisting online banking customers. Therefore, we will study a method to return a nil category to make the chatbot model generate proper responses when users' queries are not associated with any one of the predefined FAQ categories.

Author Contributions: Conceptualization, H.K. and Y.J.; methodology, H.K. and Y.J.; software, Y.J.; validation Y.J.; formal analysis, Y.J.; investigation, Y.J.; data curation, Y.J.; writing—original draft preparation, Y.J.; writing—review and editing, H.K.; visualization, H.K.; supervision, H.K.; project administration, H.K.; funding acquisition, H.K.

Funding: This work was supported by Shinhan Bank. It was also supported by the National Research Foundation of Korea (NRF) and grant funded by the Korea government (MSIP) (No.2016R1A2B4007732).

Acknowledgments: The authors would like to thank the members of the NLP laboratory in Kangwon National University for their technical support. We would specially like to thank Sebin Kim, Dongho Kang, and Hyunki Jang at Shinhan Bank for their financial and technical support.

Conflicts of Interest: The authors declare no conflicts of interest.

References

1. Kalchbrenner, N.; Grefenstette, E.; Blunsom, P. A Convolutional Neural Network for Modelling Sentences. In Proceedings of the 52nd Annual Meeting of the Association for Computational Linguistics (Volume 1: Long Papers), Baltimore, MD, USA, 22–27 June 2014; pp. 655–665.
2. Kim, Y. Convolutional Neural Networks for Sentence Classification. In Proceedings of the 2014 Conference on Empirical Methods in Natural Language Processing, Doha, Qatar, 25–29 October 2014; pp. 1746–1751.
3. Yin, W.; Schütze, H. Multichannel Variable-size Convolution for Sentence Classification. In Proceedings of the Nineteenth Conference on Computational Natural Language Learning, Beijing, China, 30–31 July 2015; pp. 204–214.
4. Yu, L.; Hermann, K.; Blunsom, K.; Pulman, S. Deep Learning for Answer Sentence Selection. In Proceedings of the NIPS Deep Learning and Representation Learning Workshop, Montreal, QC, Canada, 12 December 2014.
5. Zhang, Y.; Roller, S.; Byron, C. Mgnc-cnn: A Simple Approach to Exploiting Multiple Word Embeddings for Sentence Classification. In Proceedings of the 2016 Conference of the North American Chapter of the Association for Computational Linguistics: Human Language Technologies, San Diego, CA, USA, 12–17 June 2016; pp. 1522–1527.
6. Mikolov, T.; Sutskever, H.; Chen, K.; Corrado, G.; Dean, J. Distributed Representations of Words and Phrases and their Compositionality. In Proceedings of the 26th International Conference on Neural Information Processing Systems (Volume 2), Lake Tahoe, NE, USA, 5–10 December 2013; pp. 3111–3119.
7. Hsu, S.; Moon, C.; Jones, P.; Nagiza, F. A Hybrid CNN-RNN Alignment Model for Phrase-Aware Sentence Classification. In Proceedings of the 15th Conference of the European Chapter of the Association for Computational Linguistics: Volume 2, Short Papers, Valencia, Spain, 3–7 April 2017; pp. 443–449.
8. Kim, Y.; Jernite, Y.; Sontag, D.; Rush, A. Character-Aware Neural Language Models. In Proceedings of the AAAI 2016, Phoenix, AZ, USA, 12–17 February 2016; pp. 2741–2749.
9. Lee, J.; Cho, K.; Hofmann, T. Fully Character-Level Neural Machine Translation without Explicit Segmentation. *Trans. Assoc. Comput. Linguist.* **2017**, *5*, 365–378. [CrossRef]
10. Ling, W.; Trancoso, I.; Dyer, C.; Black, A. Character-based Neural Machine Translation. In Proceedings of the 54th Annual Meeting of the Association for Computational Linguistics, Berlin, Germany, 7–12 August 2016; pp. 357–361.
11. Park, S.; Byun, J.; Beak, S.; Cho, Y.; Oh, A. Subword-level Word Vector Representations for Korean. In Proceedings of the Association for Computational Linguistics, Melbourne, Australia, 15–20 July 2018; pp. 2429–2438.
12. Seo, D.; Chung, Y.; Kang, I. A typing error-robust Korean POS tagging using Hangul Jamo combination-based embedding. In Proceedings of the of the HCLT, Daegu, Korea, 13–14 October 2017; pp. 203–208. (In Korean).
13. Zhang, X.; Zhao, J.; LeCun, Y. Character-level Convolutional Networks for Text Classification. In *Advances in Neural Information Processing Systems 28(NIPS 2015)*; Courant Institute of Mathematical Sciences: New York, NY, USA, 2015.

14. Kim, Y.; Kim, D.; Kumar, A.; Sarikaya, R. Efficient Large-Scale Domain Classification with Personalized Attention. In Proceedings of the Association for Computational Linguistics, Melbourne, Australia, 15–20 July 2018; pp. 2214–2224.
15. Devlin, J.; Chang, M.; Lee, K.; Toutanova, K. BERT: Pre-training of Deep Bidirectional Transformers for Language Understanding. *arXiv* **2019**, arXiv:1810.04805v2.
16. Vaswabu, A.; Shazeer, N.; Parmar, N.; Uszkoreit, J.; Jones, L.; Gomez, A.N.; Kaiser, L.; Polosukhin, I. Attention Is All You Need. In Proceedings of the 31st International Conference on Neural Information Processing Systems, Long Beach, CA, USA, 4–9 December 2017; pp. 6000–6010.
17. Chung, J.; Gulcehre, C.; Cho, K.; Bngio, Y. Empirical Evaluation of Gated Recurrent Neural Networks on Sequence Modeling. *arXiv* **2014**, arXiv:1412.3555v1.
18. Luong, M.; Pham, H.; Manning, C. Effective Approaches to Attention-based Neural Machine Translation. In Proceedings of the Association for Computational Linguistics, Lisbon, Portugal, 17–21 September 2015; pp. 1412–1421.
19. Pennington, J.; Socher, R.; Manning, C. Glove: Global Vectors for Word Representation. In Proceedings of the Empirical Methods in Natural Language Processing, Doha, Qatar, 25–29 October 2014; pp. 1532–1543.
20. Kingma, D.; Ba, L. Adam: A Method for Stochastic Optimization. *arXiv* **2017**, arXiv:1412.6980v9.
21. Robertson, S.; Walker, S.; Jones, S.; Beaulieu, M.; Gatford, M. Okapi at TREC-3. In Proceedings of the TREC-3, Gaithersburg, MD, USA, 2–4 November 1994; pp. 109–126.
22. Yang, Z.; Dai, Z.; Yang, Y.; Carbonell, J.; Salakhutdinov, R.; Le, Q.V. XLNet: Generalized Autoregressive Pretraining for Language Understanding. *arXiv* **2019**, arXiv:1906.08237.

© 2019 by the authors. Licensee MDPI, Basel, Switzerland. This article is an open access article distributed under the terms and conditions of the Creative Commons Attribution (CC BY) license (http://creativecommons.org/licenses/by/4.0/).

Article

A Text Abstraction Summary Model Based on BERT Word Embedding and Reinforcement Learning

Qicai Wang [1], Peiyu Liu [1,*], Zhenfang Zhu [2,*], Hongxia Yin [1], Qiuyue Zhang [1] and Lindong Zhang [1]

1. School of Information Science and Engineering, Shandong Normal University, Jinan 250358, China; 2018020907@stu.sdnu.edu.cn (Q.W.); 2018020908@stu.sdnu.edu.cn (H.Y.); 2018309063@stu.sdnu.edu.cn (Q.Z.); 2018020898@stu.sdnu.edu.cn (L.Z.)
2. School of Information Science and Electrical Engineering, Shandong Jiaotong University, Jinan 250357, China
* Correspondence: liupy@sdnu.com.cn (P.L.); zhuzf@sdjtu.edu.cn (Z.Z.); Tel.: +86-131-8889-9297 (P.L.); +86-137-9310-0702 (Z.Z.)

Received: 9 October 2019; Accepted: 29 October 2019; Published: 4 November 2019

Abstract: As a core task of natural language processing and information retrieval, automatic text summarization is widely applied in many fields. There are two existing methods for text summarization task at present: abstractive and extractive. On this basis we propose a novel hybrid model of extractive-abstractive to combine BERT (Bidirectional Encoder Representations from Transformers) word embedding with reinforcement learning. Firstly, we convert the human-written abstractive summaries to the ground truth labels. Secondly, we use BERT word embedding as text representation and pre-train two sub-models respectively. Finally, the extraction network and the abstraction network are bridged by reinforcement learning. To verify the performance of the model, we compare it with the current popular automatic text summary model on the CNN/Daily Mail dataset, and use the ROUGE (Recall-Oriented Understudy for Gisting Evaluation) metrics as the evaluation method. Extensive experimental results show that the accuracy of the model is improved obviously.

Keywords: BERT word embedding; text summary; reinforce learning

1. Introduction

Text summarization is a task of compressing long text into short one meanwhile keeping up the central idea. Automatic text summarization is one of the core tasks in natural language processing (NLP) and information retrieval. As information techniques develop and change rapidly, especially for Mobile Internet, there is a huge amount of data will inevitably be produced day to day. Nowadays, the traditional manual summarization method is difficult to suit the needs of information retrieval in people's daily life. Therefore, automatic summarization is becoming more and more important in the wave of mass information.

The text summary method can be classified into two paradigms: extractive and abstractive. The extractive method extracts the important sentences or a section of text from the original text and combines them to form a summary [1–4], while the abstractive method will generate novel words which do not exist in the source text and while retaining the original meaning [5–8]. Compared with the difference between them, the extraction paradigm is relatively simple and ensures grammatical correctness, but the semantics are inconsistent; while the abstraction paradigm is more concise, but redundant. When summarizing a very long text, the extractive approach is too simple and the readability is poor, and the abstract method of compressing a long input sequence with a single fixed-length vector may cause the information loss, neither of them could perform the long text summary better. At present, some neural network models [9,10] combine the advantages of extractive and abstractive approaches. Firstly, selecting key sentences from the source text by the extractive method, then generating a summary of these sentences by the abstractive method. Reference [11] proposed a new model for the long text summary, which abstracts the summary by using a deep communication agent, first of all, dividing the long input text into multiple agents encoders, and then generating the summary through a unified decoder. Although these methods have achieved good results, due to the limitation of specific data sets and the small amount of data, their word embedding effect is not obvious and the semantic features of a text cannot be fully obtained.

In view of the above problems, we utilize the advantages of the pre-trained language model, BERT (Bidirectional Encoder Representations from Transformers) [12], which is successfully applied in many NLP tasks, and we use the pre-trained representation of BERT as the text representation of all our models. BERT has been pre-trained on a large amount of unlabeled corpus to generate better word embedding. Inspired by [9], we proposed a new method that integrates the extractive network and abstractive network by using reinforcement learning. CNN/Daily Mail was used as the experimental dataset in this paper. Firstly, we convert the human written abstractive summaries to the ground truth labels. Secondly, we pre-train two sub-models respectively, the extractive model is trained according to the generated pseudo-document summary data pairs, namely, the article and the ground truth labels are paired; the abstractive model is trained on the basis of the ground truth labels and the abstractive summaries labels. Finally, in order to train a complete end-to-end model, we use the strategy gradient of reinforcement learning to bridge two well-trained networks.

In addition, in order to obtain better sentence and document vectors in the extractive sub-model, we use the hierarchical self-attention mechanism. As we all know, each word contributes differently to sentence semantics, and so does each sentence to document semantics.

Empirically, on CNN/Daily Mail dataset, we used the ROUGE (Recall-Oriented Understudy for Gisting Evaluation) metrics to evaluate the performance of our method. Our approach was the new state-of-the-art. On the DUC2002 dataset, we only used it as a test dataset due to the small scale. The experimental results show that our model has better generalization ability.

Our major contributions can be summarized as follows:

(1) In this paper, we applied BERT word embedding to the text summarization task, and improved the performance of the task by taking advantage of the rich semantic features of BERT word embedding.
(2) We train a single unified model, which combines the advantages of universal language model BERT, extraction method, and abstraction method.
(3) Our approach is based on the strategy gradient of reinforcement learning and bridges the abstractive model and the extractive model. We have carried experiments on a large dataset to find that our approach achieves state-of-the-art ROUGE scores.

The rest of our paper is organized as follows. In Section 2, the related work is described. In Section 3, the proposed approach is presented in detail. Section 4 describes the related content of the experiments. We show the result and analysis of the result in Section 5. Section 6 presents conclusions and future work.

2. Related Works

Text summarization has been widely studied in recent years. We first introduce the related works of extractive and abstractive summarization and then introduce the related works of reinforcement learning and self-attention. Finally, we introduce a few related works with BERT (Bidirectional Encoder Representations from Transformers) and word embedding.

The previous works [1–4] mainly focused on extractive methods. References [1–3] select sentences using RNN (Recurrent Neural Network) to get the vector representations of sentences and articles. Reference [4] uses RNN and graph convolutional networks to compute the importance of sentences. Although the extractive method can easily achieve a relatively high score, the consistency is usually poor. The sequence-to-sequence (seq2seq) model [13,14] has been successfully applied in various NLP tasks such as NMT (Neural Machine Translate), QA (Question Answering), and Image Captioning. The sequence model can freely read or generate text content that makes abstraction practical. Reference [5] is the first to apply the attention mechanism model based on seq2seq to abstractive text summarization. Compared with traditional methods, this method shows an obvious performance improvement. The network [6] copies words from the source article by pointing or generate new words from the vocabulary. References [7,15] also integrate pointer network [16] into their model to handle the problem of OOV(Out-Of-Vocabulary) words. Other new methods (e.g., [8]) based on the seq2seq framework are proposed, and all of them have achieved effectively result. Although abstractive models are relatively concise by generating new words, due to the input text being too large, they cause the problems of loss of information and high computational cost. The models [9,10] combined the advantages of the extractive method and abstractive method and proposed a hybrid extractive-abstractive architecture. The extractive network is used to extract the sentences with obvious semantics from the input sequence, and then the abstractive network summarizes the selected sentences and generates the final text summary.

There is a common problem of exposure bias in these models which are built on seq2seq framework, namely, the reference abstract and the words generated by the previous time step are used as the input of decoder in the training stage, and only the words generated by the previous time step are used in the test stage; and the cross-entropy loss function was used in the training, but the metrics were used in the test such as ROUGE, BLEU, etc. Previous works [3,7–9,11] used reinforcement learning [17] to mitigate these existing problems. Reference [3] used reinforcement learning for ranking sentences in pure extraction-based summarization. Reference [7] used reinforcement learning policy gradient methods for abstractive summarization. Reference [8] used actor-critic policy methods for abstractive summarization. Reference [11] combined a few independent and cooperative agents to form an end-to-end training model by reinforcement learning. However, none of these methods used reinforcement learning to bridge the non-differentiable computation of two neural networks. Following the previous work [9], we also used reinforcement learning in the model to bridge the pre-trained extractive network and abstractive network.

The attention mechanism has been successfully used in a variety of NLP tasks such as machine translation [18] and text summarization [5,6]. We all know that each element in a sequence contributes differently to the sequence. So self-attention is widely used in language modeling [19], sentiment analysis [20], and other tasks. The hierarchical self-attention is also used to encode sentences and documents for the extractive model in [21]. Inspired by [21], we use self-attention for document representation.

Word embedding representations of the aforementioned model usually exist in two ways: direct learning and pre-trained. Direct learning is the way that gets the word representation in the process of model training, while pre-trained is the way that gets the word embedding initialization by training word2vec on the dataset. For example, direct learning is used in the models [6,9], while models [10,22] used word2vec as word embedding in their models. Although the aforementioned work makes a beneficial exploration in the direction of model structure combination, it does not consider the role of the pre-training universal language model, but applies it to the text summary model. The pre-trained model was trained from large amounts of unlabeled text and has got more complete word representation. The embedded vectors from pre-trained models are richer and more precise, whether in spatial dimensions or semantic features.

BERT is the latest representation of the pre-trained language model, which has recently succeeded in many NLP tasks. BERT is pre-trained for large scale text data, combining word representations and sentence representations in a large transformer [23]. The strategies of applying pre-trained BERT are mainly divided into feature-based and fine-tuning methods. Our method does not follow the tasks of the literature [12], but uses a feature-based strategy, because BERT can generate better contextualized token embeddings, thus our model based on top of them can get better performance.

From the above analysis, the word vectors of the pre-trained models (BERT) are used as task input respectively in this paper, reinforcement learning is used to integrate the extraction network and generation network into a unified model. From a human-written manual summary, first of all, we need to fully understand the main meaning of the article, then select key sentences according to the context information of the article, and then rewrite the selected sentences. The model in this paper adopts the same idea, and the corresponding relationship between them is shown in Figure 1.

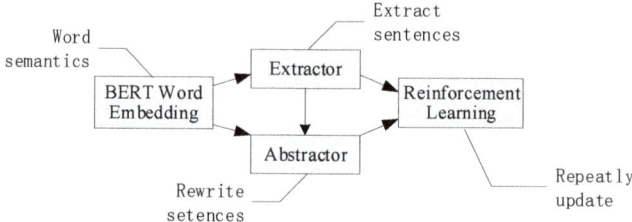

Figure 1. Automatic summary vs. manual summary.

3. Methods

3.1. Problems

The text summarization task can be seen as: in the case of fully understanding the information of the input text, we select the important sentences from the input sequence, and then these sentences are rewritten to the shorter version that do not change the main meaning. Our whole model is consists of two sub-models: the extraction agent and abstraction agent. Formally, the input article is regarded as a sequence of sentences. $s = [s_1, s_2 \cdots s_m]$, m is the index of input sentence sequence, each sentence is a sequence of words. $s_i = [w_1, w_2, \cdots, w_n]$, n is the index of the word sequence. We select the important sentences from the sequence s to make a new sequence: $s' = [s'_1, s'_2, \cdots, s'_k]$, $K < M$, and then generate the summary s″ by rewriting the sequence s′. In the case of mentioned above, namely, by fitting the training data, firstly find the extraction function: $f_1 : s' = f_1(s)$, then find the abstraction function: $f_1 : s' = f_1(s)$, so the final objective function that will be obtained $f : s'' = f_2(f_1(s))$. The overall flowchart of this model can be seen in Figure 2.

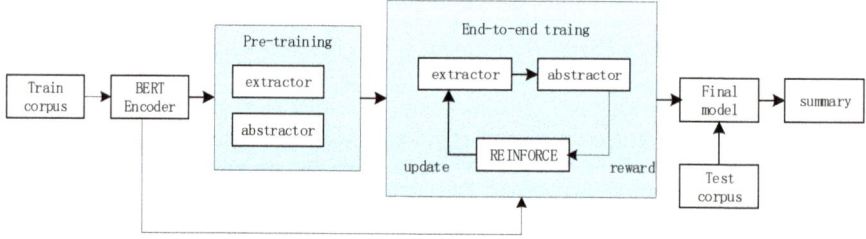

Figure 2. Automatic summary vs. manual summary.

In our works, we used BERT as our encoder for word tokens and sentences. Our main processes include: firstly, we pre-trained our sub-models: abstractor and extractor; secondly, we trained the full end-to-end model with REINFORCE LEARNING, which can bridge the sub-models. The three training processes are mapped to the fitting processes of the aforementioned functions, respectively.

3.2. Word Embedding

Word embedding is based on the distributed hypothesis of word representation. Word embedding represents natural language words as low-dimensional vector representations that computers could understand. The semantic relevance of words can be measured by the similarity between vectors. Word embedding now commonly used in NLP tasks include Word2Vec, Glove, BERT, etc.

There are two existing strategies to apply pre-trained language representations to downstream tasks: feature-based and fine-tuning [12]. Although BERT is mainly used in a fine-tuning mode in most NLP tasks, we use it as a feature-based mode and only use it as our encoder for text representation. As the same as BERT, the WordPiece tokenizer is used for input text sequence. Experiments show that the WordPiece [24] tokenizer is more effective than the natural tokenizer (here, 'natural tokenizer' refers to the method of word segmentation based on space, comma and other punctuation, and CoreNLP toolkits (https://stanfordnlp.github.io/CoreNLP/) are generally used in the experiment.). BERT can express tokenized words as corresponding word embeddings, as well as the sentences in the article are input into the BERT model, and the sentence vector representation of each sentence is obtained. The above process is expressed as Formula (1)

$$r_m = BERT(s_m) \ \ s_m \in S, m \in [0, M] \tag{1}$$

where M is the number of sentences, m is the index of a sentence, s_m denotes the text of the mth sentence, S is the set of sentences, r_m is the sentence vector. Next, word embeddings or sentence vectors are used as input in both extractor and abstractor.

3.3. Extraction Model

Our extraction model is motivated by [21,22]. The main difference is that our extractor uses BERT as a sentence encoder and the document encoder adopts the self-attention mechanism. We take a similar computation method and make some changes by adding a unidirectional GRU. Each sentence of the document is visited sequentially to obtain a shortlist of remarkable sentences with high recall to further facilitate the abstractor is our objectives.

The model consists of three components: a sentence encoder, a document encoder, and a sentence extractor. The sentence encoder adopts BERT as the encoder, a bidirectional GRU with self-attention is used to encode document, a unidirectional GRU is used to compute the summary representation. Then, the representation, the document vector and the hidden state of bi-GRU are involved in the computation of the sentence score. The architecture of the model is shown in Figure 3.

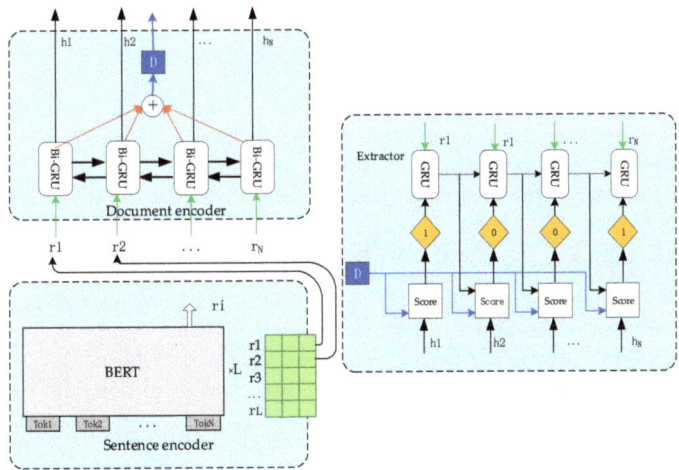

Figure 3. Extraction network model illustration.

After getting the vector representation of sentences by BERT encoder, we can summarize information of documents from both directions. It includes the forward GRU $\overrightarrow{h_t}$ and a backward GRU $\overleftarrow{h_t}$

$$\overrightarrow{h_t} = \overrightarrow{GRU}\left(r_t, \overrightarrow{h_{t-1}}\right) \tag{2}$$

$$\overleftarrow{h_t} = \overleftarrow{GRU}\left(r_t, \overleftarrow{h_{t+1}}\right) \tag{3}$$

where r_t is the sentence vector of tth sentence in the time step t.

Both GRU and LSTM are based on RNN (Recurrent Neural Network), there is no evidence to show which one is the best [25,26]. However, GRU is simpler, more efficient, fewer parameters and easier to implement. Therefore, we use a bidirectional GRU to encode the sentences in the documents and a unidirectional GRU to obtain the summary representation which taking account of decisions made previously. A GRU is a recurrent network with two gates, u_g called the update gate and r_g the reset gate, it can be described by the following equations

$$u_{gj} = \sigma\left(W_{ux}x_j + W_{uh}h_{j-1} + b_u\right) \tag{4}$$

$$r_{gj} = \sigma\left(W_{rx}x_j + W_{rh}h_{j-1} + b_r\right) \tag{5}$$

$$h'_j = tanh\left(W_{hx}x_j + W_{hh}\left(r_{gj} \odot h_{j-1}\right) + b_h\right) \tag{6}$$

$$h_j = \left(1 - u_{gj}\right) \odot h'_j + u_j \odot h_{j-1} \tag{7}$$

where the W's and b's are learnable parameters and h_j is the real valued hidden vector at time step j and x_j is the corresponding input vector namely aforementioned r_i and $\odot$ denotes the Hadamard product.

We concatenated the forward and the backward GRU hidden states to get the vector h_t, which summarizes the information of the sentence s_t and its context, as in Equation (8),

$$h_t = \left[\overrightarrow{h_t}, \overleftarrow{h_t}\right] \tag{8}$$

where d_h denotes the size of hidden vector, M is the number of sentences in the document, so the $h_D \in R^{M*2d_h}$ denotes the whole GRU hidden states, as in Equation (9),

$$H_D = (h_1, h_2, \ldots, h_M) \tag{9}$$

We all know that we pay more or less attention to each sentence according to its contribution to the article. The representation of the whole document is modeled as a weighted sum of the concatenated hidden states of the bidirectional GRU by a self-attention mechanism [26]. We take the concatenated hidden states H_D as input and yield a vector of weights, a_D, as output, calculated as shown in Equation (10),

$$a_D = softmax\left(W_{s_2} tanh\left(W_{s_1} H_D^T\right)\right) \tag{10}$$

where W_{s_2} and W_{s_1} are learnable parameters, $W_{s_2} \in R^{k*2d_h}$, $W_{s_2} \in R^k$, k is a hyper-parameter can be set arbitrarily. The softmax() is the normalized function used to normalize the attention weights, which sum up to 1. After getting the attention vector a_D, the document vector is obtained as a weighted sum of the GRU hidden states weighted by a_D, as shown in Figure 4, and Equation (11),

$$d = a_D H_D \tag{11}$$

where $a_D \in R^{1*M}$, $d \in R^{1*2d_h}$, so the document representation is a vector whose dimension is d.

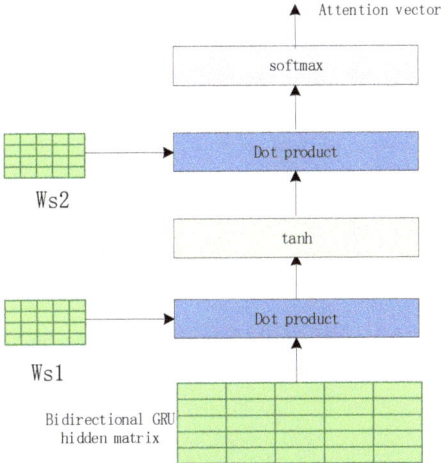

Figure 4. The self-attention unit.

For extractor, each sentence is viewed sequentially again, where a logistic layer makes a binary decision as to whether that sentence belongs to the summary, as shown in Equation (12)

$$P(y_j = 1|h_j, O_j, d) = \sigma\left(W_c h_j + h_j^T W_{sal} d - h_j^T W_{red}\tanh(O_{j-1}) + W_p p_j + b\right) \quad (12)$$

where y_j is a binary variable indicating whether the jth sentence is included in the summary, h_j is the hidden state of bi-GRU at the jth time step, O_{j-1} is the dynamic representation of the summary before the jth time step, d is the document vector, W_c, W_{sal}, W_{red}, W_p, and b are all learnable parameters. The expression $W_c h_j$ denotes the information content of the jth sentence, $h_j^T W_{sal} d$ represents the salience of the sentence with respect to the article, $h_j^T W_{red}\tanh(O_{j-1})$ obtains the redundancy of the sentence with respect to the current representation of the summary, $W_p p_j$ is the position of the sentence with respect to the article. O_{j-1} is calculated using Equation (13)

$$O_{j-1} = GRU\left(Sel_{j-1} r_{j-1}, O_{j-2}\right) \quad j \geq 2 \quad (13)$$

where $Sel_{j-1} \in \{0, 1\}$, O_0 a zero vector.

We do not follow the loss function of the literature [21,22], where they used the negative log-likelihood. We use cross entropy loss as the loss function, as shown in Equation (14)

$$L_{ext} = -\frac{1}{M}\sum_{j=1}^{M}\left(g_j \log \beta_j + (1 - g_j) \log(1 - \beta_j)\right) \quad (14)$$

where $g_j \in \{0, 1\}$ is the ground-truth label for the sentence and M is the number of sentences. When $g_j = 1$, it suggests that the jth sentence should be attended to help abstractive summarization. β_j is the normalize attention weights using softmax(), as shown in Equation (15)

$$\beta_j = \frac{\exp\left(P(y_j = 1|h_j, O_j, d)\right)}{\sum_{j=1}^{M} \exp\left(P(y_j = 1|h_j, O_{j-1}, d)\right)} \quad (15)$$

In the end-to-end training phrase, β_j as the sentence-level attention will be focused on abstract summaries.

Essentially, our extraction model is a binary classifier, which classifies whether the sentences in the input text sequence are important or not.

3.4. Abstraction Model

Another part of our method is an abstraction model that rewrites the previously selected key sentences and then generates a concise and readable summary. We use the pointer-generator network proposed by [6]. The pointer-generator network facilitates copying words from the source text via pointing [16], which improves accuracy and processing ability of OOV words, while retaining the ability to generate new words [6]. The network contains an encoder and a decoder and can be seen as a balance between extractive and abstractive methods. Many similar studies [6,7,11] show that such a model can effectively improve the performance of text summary. More details of the network can be found in the literature [6].

Although we used the pointer-generator network, we made some changes to improve the performance and accuracy of the model. Compared with the vanilla network [6], there are some differences: first, inspired by [10], the new network introduces the updated word attention combined with sentence-level and word-level attentions as same as [10]; second, we replace the LSTM in the network with the GRU, since the GRU is simpler and requires fewer parameters; third, the two models input different amounts of data, when the article reaches 400 tokens the input of the vanilla network is truncated, which causes loss of information, the input of the new network is the key sentences from aforementioned extraction model; fourth, the word embedding of two models are different, the word2vec is used for the vanilla pointer-generator network, the BERT is used in our abstractive network. In addition, the WordPiece tokenizer can help to process the OOV words. The architecture of the updated pointer-generator network is shown in Figure 5.

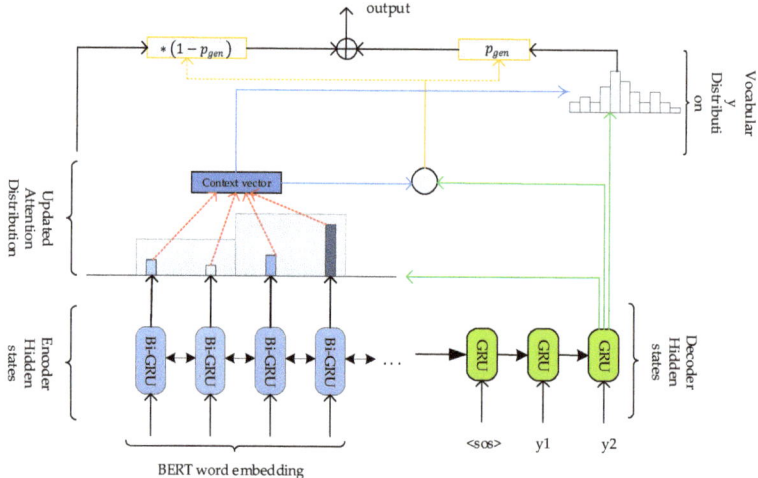

Figure 5. Model of pointer-generator network [10].

There is a lot of evidence that attention mechanism is very important for NLP tasks (e.g., [5,19,23]). We use the sentence-level modulate the word-level attention such that words in less attended sentences are less likely to be generated [10]. Take the simple scalar multiplication of the aforementioned sentence attention β_m in sec 3.3 and the word attention α_n^t of the mth sentence, and then renormalize the result into the new attention. The updated word attention μ_n^t,

$$\mu_n^t = \frac{\alpha_n^t \times \beta_m}{\sum_n \alpha_n^t \times \beta_m}. \tag{16}$$

The final probability distribution of word w is related to the updated word attention μ^t as follows

$$P_{final}(w) = p_{gen}(h^*)P_{vocab}(h^*, w) + \left(1 - p_{gen}(h^*)\right) \sum_{n:w_n=w} \mu_n^t \tag{17}$$

$$h_n^* = \sum_n \mu_n^t h_n \tag{18}$$

where $p_{gen}(h^*) \in [0, 1]$ is the generating probability (see Equation (8) in [6]), $P_{vocab}(h^*, w)$ is the probability distribution over word w being decoded, h^* is the context vector, a function of the updated word attention μ^t, h_n is the encoder hidden state for the nth word.

During pre-training, the loss is the negative log likelihood, we minimize the loss as

$$L_{abs} = -\frac{1}{T}\sum_{t=1}^{T} \log P_{final}(w_t^*, \mu^t) \tag{19}$$

where w_t^* is the target word in the reference abstractive summary at the time step t. The coverage mechanism [6] is also used to prevent the abstractor from repeatedly putting the focus on the same point. In each decoder step t, the coverage vector c^t is calculated as follows, which is the sum of attention over all previous timesteps

$$c^t = \sum_{t'=1}^{t-1} \mu^{t'} \tag{20}$$

Moreover, coverage loss L_{cov} is calculated as

$$L_{cov} = \frac{1}{T}\sum_{t=1}^{T}\sum_{n=1}^{N} \min(\mu^t, c_n^t) \tag{21}$$

We also apply the inconsistency loss as same as [10], the inconsistency loss is calculated by Equation (22)

$$L_{inc} = \sum_{t=1}^{T} \log\left(\frac{1}{|\kappa|}\sum_{n\in\kappa} \alpha_n^t \times \beta_m\right) \tag{22}$$

where κ is the set of top K attended words and T is the number of words in the summary. In conclusion, the final loss of abstraction model is

$$L_{final\_abs} = L_{abs} + \lambda_1 L_{cov} + \lambda_2 L_{inc}. \tag{23}$$

where λ_1, λ_2 are hyper-parameters.

3.5. Training Procedure

The training process of our method is divided into two phases: (1) pre-training phase, (2) full training phase. Without well-trained extractor, the extractor would often select irrelevant sentences, and without well-trained abstractor, the extractor would get noisy reward. We first pre-train the extractor by minimizing L_{ext} in Equation (14) and the abstractor by minimizing L_{final_abs} in Equation (23), respectively, and then, we apply standard policy gradient methods of reinforcement learning to bridge together these two networks and to train the whole model in an end-to-end fashion.

3.5.1. Pre-Training

The sentences with high informativity are our goal of the extractor, the extracted sentences should contain as much information as possible to generate an abstract summary. In order to train the extractive model, we need ground truth labels for each document, but our train corpus only contains human written abstractive summaries, so we need to convert the abstractive summaries to extractive labels. Similar to the extractive model of [22], we compute the ROUGE-L recall score [27] between sentence and the reference abstractive summary, and measure the informativity of each sentence in the document by score. We sort and select the sentences in order from high to low. We add one sentence at a time if the new sentence can increase the score of all the selected. The selected sentences should be the ones that maximize the ROUGE score with respect to gold summaries. Finally, we obtain the ground truth labels and train our extraction model by minimizing Equation 14. We use the ROUGE scores of the selected sentences as sentence-level attention of the corresponding sentences, respectively.

When pre-training, the abstractor takes ground truth sentences of the previously extracted as input. The sentence-level attention of these input sentences is viewed as hard attention, which involves the calculation of attention consistency. In the pre-training stage, we finally get these two well-trained extractor and abstractor.

3.5.2. End-to-End Training

During full training stage, we employ a hybrid extractive-abstractive architecture, with policy gradient of reinforcement learning to bridge together the aforementioned two pre-trained networks. We first use an extractor agent to select important sentences and then employ an abstractor to paraphrase each of these extracted sentences. In this stage, RL training work is as follows: if a good sentence is selected by the extractor, the ROUGE match would be high after the abstractor paraphrase and thus the action is encouraged. If a bad sentence is selected, the generated sentence would not match the reference summary after rewrites and if the ROUGE score is low, the action is discouraged.

3.6. Reinforcement Learning

The abstraction model is the seq2seq model with copy mechanism, which can compress extracted sentences into short text. We use reinforcement learning to connect the two models to form a unified model for optimal training. We regard the existing training data as the environment, and the extractive and abstractive models as agents of reinforcement learning. The agent observes the state from the environment and then performs the extraction and abstraction. The abstraction summary is more similar to the reference summary in the environment, we will get the higher score of the reward. If the final summary does not match the reference summary, will get a lower score. Our reward function is shown in Formula (24).

$$f_{reward} = ROUGEL_{F1}(s_{gold}, f_2(s')) \quad (24)$$

The corresponding relationship between the agent part and the environment part in reinforcement learning is shown in Figure 6.

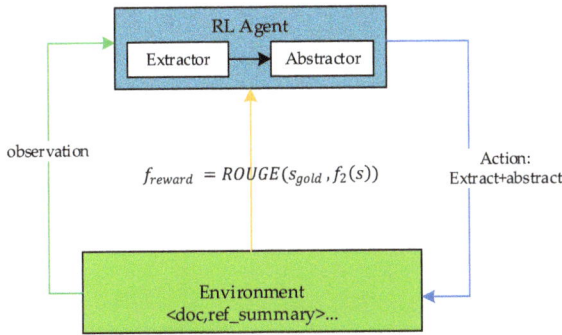

Figure 6. Illustration of reinforcement learning for summary model.

3.7. Redundancy Issue

In our work, we first perform the extraction operation to obtain the extracted sentences semantically independent of each other, which greatly reduces the frequency of common redundancy problems in the abstraction model. As the extracted sentences inescapable have semantic crossover, there is still a little redundancy. For simplicity, we did not use the same coverage mechanism as in the previous work [6] to define a coverage vector, sum up the previous time step's attention, and then use the coverage loss function to avoid repeatedly paying attention to the same position. We employ the same reranking strategy as [7,9]. When conducting beam-search, the same triples are not allowed, and then all combinations of the generated summary sentence bundles are reranked, and the smallest and shortest combination are selected as the final summary.

4. Experiments

4.1. Datasets

The proposed method uses two well-known datasets as our experimental dataset: CNN/Daily Mail and DUC2002. The first dataset proposed by [28] for reading comprehension tasks and then reused for extractive [22] and abstractive text summarization tasks [6]. In recent years, the dataset has been widely used in automatic text summary tasks due to its large data volume and long text content. In this dataset, there are 287,113 data for training, 13,368 for validation, and 11,490 for testing. On average, there are about 28 sentences per document in the training set [22]. The basic statistics of the dataset are shown in Table 1. This dataset includes the anonymous version and the non-anonymous version. The former is that all entity names of the data are replaced by special tag words, while the latter is the original data. We adopt the non-anonymous version. The CNN/Daily Mail data consists of several document summary pairs, each of which corresponds to a few highlighted sentences in manual annotated documents.

Table 1. Basic statistics of the CNN/Daily Mail dataset.

	Train	Validation	Test
Pairs of data	287,113	13,368	11,490
Article length	749	769	778
Summary length	55	61	58

The second dataset is DUC2002 (http://www-nlpir.nist.gov/projects/duc/guidelines/2002.html), which is only used as a test-only test set since the size of the dataset is small. It contains 567 news articles and the corresponding single-document summarization, or the multi-document summarization generated for the same topics. In our work, we used the single-document summarization task. To verify the generalization ability of models, we use the DUC article as the test input of our trained model. We evaluate the results using the official ROUGE F1 script.

4.2. Detail

We use PyTorch (https://pytorch.org) as our deep learning framework, and then we use the python package PyTorch-Transformers (https://github.com/huggingface/pytorch-transformers) as our BERT encoder, formerly known as pytorch-pretrained-bert. It should be noted that we do not need special tokens (e.g., CLS, SEP) when encoding sentences.

Instead of extracting the list of words from the dataset as previous work ([6,9], etc.), we directly use the vocabulary of the pre-trained BERT model as our vocabulary. The BERT model has two types of vocabulary: the case-sensitive and the case-insensitive, we chose the case-insensitive vocabulary with a total of 30,522 words for the experiment. For comparison, in our experiments, we use the word embedding with 768 dimensions and 1024 dimensions as the word vector representation respectively.

We use the Adam optimizer [29] and apply early stopping based on the validation set. We apply gradient clipping using 2-norm of 2.0. The batch size is 32 for all the training. For all GRU-RNNs, the hidden layer number is set to 1, the hidden state size is set to 256, so the concatenated hidden state size is 512, and the sentence attention context vector also has a dimension of 512. The learning rate of ML (Machine Learning) is set to 3×10^{-4}. The maximum length of the input text sequence sentences is set to 100, the maximum number of sentences is set to 60.

When pre-training the extractor, k is a hyper-parameter of Equation (10), k is set to 256. When pre-training the abstractor, the maximum length of the sentence of the summary is set to 30, λ_1, λ_2 are all set to 1 in Equation (23). When full training end-to-end model, the discount factor of reinforcement learning is set to 0.95, and the early stop factor is set to 3.

4.3. Metrics

Pyrouge package was used to write evaluation scripts for evaluation, and the ROUGE (Recall-Oriented Understudy for Gisting Evaluation) was used as the standard for experimental evaluation. The ROUGE standard was first used in reference [27] and subsequently became the metric for evaluating the generated summary model. The 'similarity' between the generated summary and the reference summary is evaluated by calculating the same number of units. Among them, rouge-1 (unigram), rouge-2 (bi-gram) and rouge-L (the longest common subsequences) are the most widely used in single document abstract.

For all datasets, according to previous works [6,9,10], we use ROUGE-1, ROUGE-2, and ROUGE-L on full-length F1 as evaluation metrics in the reported experimental results.

4.4. Baselines

To further illustrate the superiority of the proposed model over two datasets, we compare it with several baseline models. Note that, most models serve as baselines on the CNN/Daily Mail dataset. All comparison models are described in detail as follows:

- Leading sentences (Lead-3): It directly extracts the first three sentences of the article as a summary. This model as extractive baseline.
- Refresh: The model proposed by [3], takes the reinforcement learning objective as the extraction baseline and optimizes the rouge evaluation index globally.
- SummaRuNNer: It is proposed by [22] to generate the summary by extracting some key subset of the content for the article, as an extractive baseline.
- HSSAS: It is proposed by [21] to employ the self-attention mechanism to create a good sentence and document embeddings, as an extractive baseline.
- NeuSum: It is proposed by [30] to extract the document summarization by jointly learning to score and select sentences, as an extractive baseline.

- Pointer-generator+coverage: It is proposed by [6] to copy words from the source article and retain the ability to generate new words, as an abstractive baseline.
- Inconsistency loss: The method proposed by [10], which uses sentence-level attention to modulate the word-level attention, introduces inconsistency loss function to penalize the inconsistency between two attentions, as an abstractive baseline.
- DCA: The method proposed by [11], which encodes long text with the deep communication agents and then connects to a single decoder to generate a focused and coherent summary through reinforcement learning, is the best abstract model in 2018 and serve as an abstractive baseline.
- RNN-ext+abs+rl+rerank: It is proposed by [9], which first selects salient sentences and then rewrites them abstractly to generate a concise overall summary, as an abstractive baseline.

5. Result and Analysis

Due to our model employing a hybrid approach of extractive and abstractive, we can not only generate the final abstract summaries, but also the extract summaries. So three groups of experiments were conducted on CNN/Daily Mail dataset: the extraction experimental group, the complete experimental group, and the comparison experimental group. In the comparison of the experimental group, we compared the effects of the base one and the large model of BERT, the effects of the tokenizers, and the effects of reinforcement learning. The results of extractive experiments are shown in Table 2, and full experiments are shown in Table 3.

Table 2. Performance comparison of models with respect to the extractive baselines on CNN/Daily Mail.

Model	R-1	R-2	R-L	R-AVG
Lead-3 [6]	40.34	17.70	36.57	31.54
Refresh [3]	40.00	18.20	36.60	31.60
SummaRuNNer [22]	39.9	16.3	35.1	30.43
HSSAS [21]	42.3	17.8	37.6	32.57
NeuSUM [30]	41.59	19.01	**37.98**	32.86
(m1) BEAR (ext+base)	42.43	**20.36**	37.23	33.34
(m2) BEAR (ext +large)	**42.54**	20.35	37.24	**33.38**

Table 3. Performance comparison of models with respect to the abstractive baselines on CNN/Daily Mail.

Model	R-1	R-2	R-L	R-AVG
Pointer Generator + Coverage [6]	39.53	17.28	36.38	31.06
Inconsistency loss [10]	40.68	17.97	37.13	31.93
DCA [11]	41.69	19.47	37.92	33.11
Rnn-ext + abs + RL + rerank [9]	40.88	17.80	38.54	32.41
(m3) BEAR (ext + abs + base)	39.84	18.83	37.35	32.01
(m4) BEAR (ext + abs + RL + base)	40.91	19.88	38.45	33.08
(m5) BEAR (base + nature)	40.95	17.89	38.55	32.80
(m6) BEAR (base + WordPiece)	41.76	20.20	39.39	33.78
(m7) BEAR (large + WordPiece)	**41.95**	**20.26**	**39.49**	**33.9**

5.1. Result

In the extraction experimental group, only sentences are selected without rewriting, in other words, the abstraction fitting function is f2 (s′) = s′, and the rest are the same as the full experiment. As shown in Table 2, the experimental results of m1, m2 have many advantages in the ROUGE-1 standard compare with extractive baselines [3,6,22,30], and are slightly higher than the method in the literature [21]. In the ROUGE-2 standard, our method has an obvious effect. In the ROUGE-L standard, our model is superior to the models Refresh [3] and Lead-3 [6], but lower than the model NeuSUM [30].

In the complete experimental group, the experimental results of our model are significantly improved compared with the earlier work and baseline model. As we all know, we obtain the highest ROUGE score for the current abstraction summary in the CNN/Daily Mail dataset. As shown in Table 3, compared with the baseline model [9], the scores of ROUGE-1, ROUGE-2, ROUGE-L, and R-AVG are respectively improved 1.07%, 2.46%, 0.95%, and 1.46%.Compared with the highest scoring model [11] in 2018, the score of Rouge-1 is only slightly improved, but these two metrics of Rouge-2 and Rouge-L are significantly improved, and these two models we have fully trained are also significantly better than the abstraction methods [6,10].

We also compared our best model with the best extractive baseline model and the best abstractive baseline model. The comparison bar chart is shown in Figure 7.

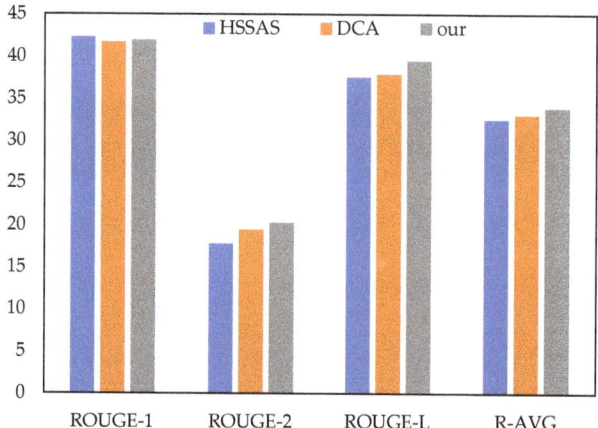

Figure 7. Performance comparison with respect to the best baselines on CNN/Daily Mail.

5.2. Ablation Study

In the comparison group, three comparison experiments are analyzed as follows:

Pre-trained BERT model with multiple versions, we used two versions in experiments: the base-uncased and the large-uncased. In terms of pre-training complexity and the dimension of word embeddings, the large-uncased version should be more powerful than the base-uncased. As shown in Figure 8, in our extraction experiment (m1, m2) and the full experiment (m6, m7), the experimental results are very comparable, and the large results are slightly better than the base version results, and the difference in the performance of these two versions was not as much as we expected.

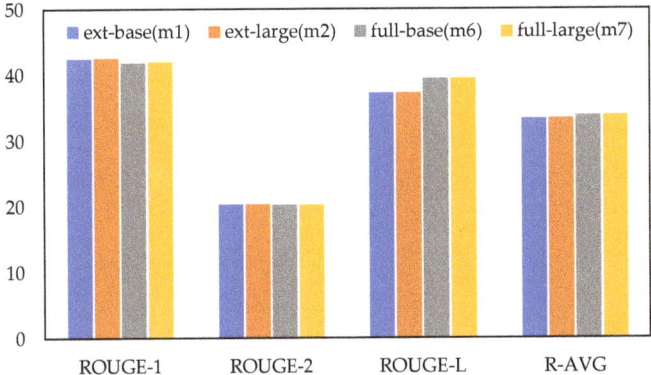

Figure 8. Performance comparison of the BERT$_{base}$ mode with respect to the BERT$_{large}$ model of BERT.

When comparing the effect of WordPiece (m6) and natural (m5) tokenizer, the improvement of WordPiece tokenizer is more obvious than that of the traditional tokenizer, with an average increase of nearly 1 percentage point. There are two main reasons for this. Firstly, BERT adopts the WordPiece tokenizer in their training process, and the word embedding obtained is more suitable for the tokenizer. Secondly, it shows that the WordPiece tokenizer is more effective than natural tokenizer, and the new tokenizer can capture richer semantic features. The comparison between two tokenizers is shown in Figure 9.

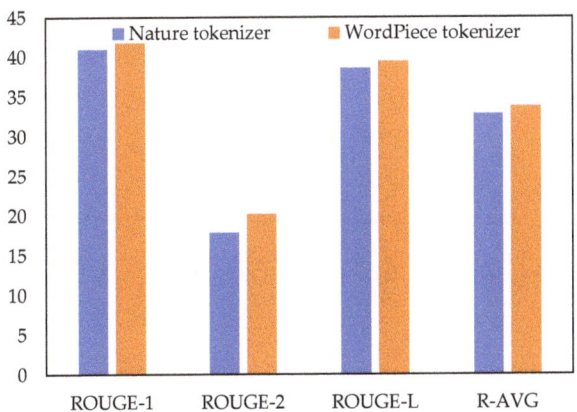

Figure 9. Performance comparison of tokenizer mode.

The reinforcement learning method was adopted in the experiment except model m3. Since many previous works [7,10,11] have proved the effectiveness of reinforcement learning, this paper only used the combination of the base model and WordPiece tokenizer for comparison and did not use other combinations of the experiment for cross-comparison. By comparing the experimental model (m3) with the model (m4), the scores of the model (m4) using reinforcement learning are more than 1 percentage point higher than that of the model (m3), which proves that the effect of reinforcement learning is quite significant in our experiment. The effect of reinforcement learning is shown in Figure 10.

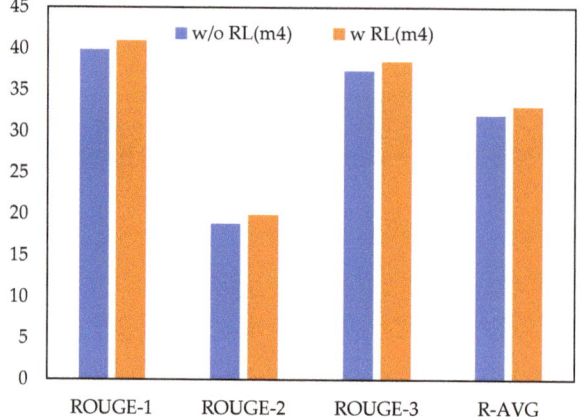

Figure 10. Performance comparison of the effect of reinforcement learning.

Also, by comparing model (m3) with the rnn-ext+abs model in paper [9], all the scores of the model (m3) are more than 1 percentage point higher, which further proves that the word embedding vector of BERT has the same result as reinforcement learning in our experiment and has the same significant effect.

5.3. Generalization

Because the DUC2002 dataset is too small to train such a complex model, we only use it as our test dataset. To test the generalization of our model, we directly use the trained model to summarize the DUC article. Table 4 shows the generalization of our method to the DUC2002 dataset. The results show that our model has better generalization ability than the other two models. The results of pointer-generator model and rnn-ext+abs+RL model are obtained from [9].

Table 4. Generalization to DUC-2002(F1).

Models	R-1	R-2	R-L	R-AVG
Pointer-generator	37.22	15.78	33.90	28.97
Rnn-ext + abs + RL	39.46	17.34	36.72	31.17
BEAR (m7)	40.53	19.85	38.37	32.92

5.4. Redundancy Issue

Extracted sentences can effectively reduce the redundancy in the abstract model from the source. For there may be some semantic cross, we use the rerank strategy mentioned earlier. As shown in Table 3, our model evaluation score is higher than these two models in [6,10]. As shown in Table 5, the sample sentences are concise and clear. Experiments show that our strategy can effectively reduce redundancy and improve the accuracy of the evaluation.

Table 5. Speed comparison between BEAR, rnn-ext+abs+RL, and pointer-generator.

	Pre-Traing	Training	Total Training	Test	GPU
BEAR	19 h	6 h	22 h	0.67 h	K80
Rnn-ext + abs + RL	4.15 h	15.56 h	19.71 h		K40
Pointer-generator			76 h		K40

5.5. Training Speed

In the experiment, we train on a single Tesla K80 GPU, the extracted pre-training time is about 6 h, the abstracted pre-training time is about 19 h, the mixed training time is about 3 h, and the test time is about 40 min. Since extraction training and abstraction training can be carried out in parallel, the total experimental time is about 23 h. When training the summary model, we use the extracted statement training model instead of the whole document, and we can draw a conclusion that training with a few sentences is faster than training with the whole document. The experiment shows that this paper is faster than the pointer-generator [6] in the calculation, but the speed is not as fast as that of [9], because the high dimension of BERT word embedding increases the computational complexity. The speed comparison results are shown in Table 5.

In addition, the resource consumption of deep learning is increasingly a concern for researchers, and we also estimate the carbon footprint of one training. According to the search result, the power of Tesla K80 GPU is 0.3 kw/h, and the average carbon emission is 0.433 kg/kwh (data from the U.S. EIA). It can be estimated that our carbon footprint is about 3 kg.

5.6. Case Study

We present two examples in Table 6 for comparison. As we can intuitively see from the sample of the final summary, it is more concise, as shown in Table 6. The strategy of eliminating repetition can effectively reduce semantic crossover and make the content of the summary more compact, which not only maintains semantic relevance, but also takes into account the readability and fluency of language.

Table 6. Examples of generated summaries on CNN/Daily Mail dataset.

Reference:
"17 americans were exposed to the ebola virus while in sierra leone in march", "another person was diagnosed with the disease and taken to hospital in maryland", "national institutes of health says the patient is in fair condition after weeks of treatment."
Model (m4):
five americans were monitored for three weeks at an omaha hospital. one of the five had a heart—related issue on saturday and has been discharged but hasn't left the area, taylor wilson wrote. they were exposed to ebola in sierra leone in march but none developed the virus. the others have already gone home.
Model (m7):
five americans were monitored for three weeks at an omaha, nebraska. they all had contact with a colleague who was diagnosed with the disease. the last of 17 patients who were being monitored are expected to be released by thursday. more than 10,000 people have died in a west african epidemic of ebola.

Also, we can find that the first sentence of model m4 and model m7 is basically the same, while the latter three sentences are quite different. Semantically, model m7 is more relevant to the reference than model m4, and the second and fourth sentences of model m4 are somewhat off topic, which is the main reason for the low score. The final summary of model m7, although different from the reference, talks about the same thing.

6. Conclusions and Future Work

At present, BERT has achieved the most advanced performance in many NLP tasks, but few works combine it with the extract model and abstract model for text summarization by the strategy gradient of reinforcement learning. We propose a new method to combine these methods into a unified model that has been validated in summary tasks or other tasks. Experiments show that the model proposed in this paper achieves the best results in the CNN/Daily Mail dataset. In the future, we will select another pre-training model that is more suitable for the generative task and combine the fine-tuning pre-training model with the abstractive summary task.

Author Contributions: Conceptualization, Q.W. and P.L.; Funding acquisition, P.L.; Methodology, Q.W.; Project administration, Z.Z.; Resources, P.L. and Z.Z.; Software, Q.W.; Validation, Q.W.; Visualization, Q.W.; Writing—original draft, Q.W.; Writing—review and editing, H.Y., Q.Z., and L.Z.

Funding: This work was supported by the National Social Science Fund(19BYY076), the Science Foundation of the Ministry of Education of China (no. 14YJC860042), and the Shandong Provincial Social Science Planning Project (no. 19BJCJ51/18CXWJ01/18BJYJ04/16CFXJ18).

Acknowledgments: Thanks to all commenters for their valuable and constructive comments.

Conflicts of Interest: The authors declare no conflict of interest.

References

1. Cheng, J.; Lapata, M. Neural summarization by extracting sentences and words. In Proceedings of the 54th Annual Meeting of the Association for Computational Linguistics, Berlin, Germany, 7–12 August 2016; Volume 1, pp. 484–494.
2. Nallapati, R.; Zhou, B.; Santos, C.N.D.; Gulcehre, C.; Xiang, B. Abstractive text summarization using sequence-to-sequence rnns and beyond. In Proceedings of the SIGNLL Conference on Computational Natural Language Learning, Berlin, Germany, 11–12 August 2016; p. 280.
3. Narayan, S.; Cohen, S.B.; Lapata, M. Ranking sentences for extractive summarization with reinforcement learning. In Proceedings of the 2018 Conference of the North American Chapter of the Association for Computational Linguistics: Human Language Technologies, New Orleans, LA, USA, 2–4 June 2018; pp. 1747–1759.
4. Yasunaga, M.; Zhang, R.; Meelu, K.; Pareek, A.; Srinivasan, K.; Radev, D. Graph-based neural multi-document summarization. In Proceedings of the 21st Conference on Computational Natural Language Learning, Vancouver, BC, Canada, 3–4 August 2017; pp. 452–462.
5. Rush, A.M.; Chopra, S.; Weston, J. A neural attention model for abstractive sentence summarization. In Proceedings of the 2015 Conference on Empirical Methods in Natural Language Processing, Lisbon, Portugal, 17–21 September 2015; pp. 379–389.
6. See, A.; Liu, P.J.; Manning, C.D. Get to the point: Summarization with pointer-generator networks. In Proceedings of the 55th Annual Meeting of the Association for Computational Linguistics, Vancouver, BC, Canada, 30 July–4 August 2017; pp. 1073–1083.
7. Paulus, R.; Xiong, C.; Socher, R. A deep reinforced model for abstractive summarization. In Proceedings of the Sixth International Conference on Learning Representations, Vancouver, BC, Canada, 30 April–3 May 2018.
8. Li, P.; Bing, L.; Lam, W. Actor-critic based training framework for abstractive summarization. *arXiv* **2018**, arXiv:1803.11070V2.
9. Chen, Y.C.; Bansal, M. Fast abstractive summarization with reinforce-selected sentence rewriting. In Proceedings of the 56th Annual Meeting of the Association for Computational Linguistics, Melbourne, Australia, 15–20 July 2018; pp. 675–686.
10. Hsu, W.T.; Lin, C.K.; Lee, M.Y.; Min, K.; Tang, J.; Sun, M. A unified model for extractive and abstractive summarization using inconsistency loss. In Proceedings of the 56th Annual Meeting of the Association for Computational Linguistics, Melbourne, Australia, 15–20 July 2018; pp. 132–141.
11. Celikyilmaz, A.; Bosselut, A.; He, X.; Choi, Y. Deep communicating agents for abstractive summarization. In Proceedings of the 2018 Conference of the North American Chapter of the Association for Computational Linguistics: Human Language Technologies, New Orleans, LA, USA, 2–4 June 2018; pp. 1662–1675.
12. Devlin, J.; Chang, M.W.; Lee, K.; Toutanova, K. Bert: Pre-training of deep bidirectional transformers for language understanding. In Proceedings of the 2019 Conference of the North American Chapter of the Association for Computational Linguistics: Human Language Technologies, Minneapolis, MN, USA, 2–7 June 2019; pp. 4171–4186.

13. Sutskever, I.; Vinyals, O.; Le, Q.V. Sequence to sequence learning with neural networks. In Proceedings of the 27th International Conference on Neural Information Processing Systems, Montreal, QC, Canada, 8–13 December 2014; pp. 3104–3112.
14. Cho, K.; Van, M.B.; Gulcehre, C.; Bahdanau, D.; Bougares, F.; Schwenk, H.; Bengio, Y. Learning phrase representations using RNN encoder-decoder for statistical machine translation. In Proceedings of the 2014 Conference on Empirical Methods in Natural Language Processing, Doha, Qatar, 25–29 October 2014; pp. 1724–1734.
15. Gu, J.; Lu, Z.; Li, H.; Li, V.O.K. Incorporating copying mechanism in sequence-to-sequence learning. In Proceedings of the 54th Annual Meeting of the Association for Computational Linguistics, Berlin, Germany, 7–12 August 2016; pp. 1631–1640.
16. Vinyals, O.; Fortunato, M.; Jaitly, N. Pointer networks. In Proceedings of the International Conference on Neural Information Processing Systems, Montreal, QC, Canada, 7–10 December 2015.
17. Sutton, R.S.; Barto, A.G. *Introduction to Reinforcement Learning Cambridge*; MIT Press: Cambridge, MA, USA, 1998; Volume 2.
18. Bahdanau, D.; Cho, K.; Bengio, Y. Neural machine translation by jointly learning to align and translate. *Comput. Sci.* **2014**.
19. Lin, Z.; Feng, M.; Santos, C.N.D.; Yu, M.; Xiang, B.; Zhou, B. A Structured Self-Attentive Sentence Embedding. *arXiv* **2017**, arXiv:1703.03130.
20. Li, Z.; Wei, Y.; Zhang, Y.; Yang, Q. Hierarchical attention transfer network for cross-domain sentiment classification. In Proceedings of the Thirty-Second AAAI Conference on Artificial Intelligence, New Orleans, LA, USA, 2–7 February 2018.
21. Al-Sabahi, K.; Zuping, Z.; Nadher, M. A hierarchical structured self-attentive model for extractive document summarization (hssas). *IEEE Access* **2018**. [CrossRef]
22. Nallapati, R.; Zhai, F.; Zhou, B. Summarunner: A recurrent neural network based sequence model for extractive summarization of documents. In Proceedings of the Thirty-First AAAI Conference on Artificial Intelligence, San Francisco, CA, USA, 4–9 February 2017; pp. 3075–3081.
23. Vaswani, A.; Shazeer, N.; Parmar, N.; Uszkoreit, J.; Jones, L.; Gomez, A.N. Attention is all you need. *Adv. Neural Inf. Process. Syst.* **2017**, 5998–6008.
24. Wu, Y.; Schuster, M.; Chen, Z.; Le, Q.V.; Norouzi, M.; Macherey, W. Google's neural machine translation system: Bridging the gap between human and machine translation. *arXiv* **2016**, arXiv:1609.08144V2.
25. Chung, J.; Gulcehre, C.; Cho, K.; Bengio, Y. Empirical evaluation of gated recurrent neural networks on sequence modeling. *arXiv* **2014**, arXiv:1412.3555.
26. Greff, K.; Srivastava, R.K.; Koutník, J.; Steunebrink, B.R.; Schmidhuber, J. Lstm: A search space odyssey. *IEEE Trans. Neural Netw. Learn. Syst.* **2015**, *28*, 2222–2232. [CrossRef] [PubMed]
27. Lin, C.Y. ROUGE: A Package for Automatic Evaluation of summaries. In Proceedings of the Workshop on Text Summarization Branches Out, Barcelona, Spain, 25–26 July 2004; pp. 74–81.
28. Hermann, K.M.; Kocisky, T.; Grefenstette, E.; Espeholt, L.; Kay, W.; Suleyman, M.; Blunsom, P. Teaching Machines to Read and Comprehend. In Proceedings of the 28th International Conference on Neural Information Processing Systems, Montreal, QC, Canada, 7–12 December 2015; pp. 1693–1701.
29. Kingma, D.P.; Ba, J. Adam: A method for stochastic optimization. *Comput. Sci.* **2014**.
30. Zhou, Q.; Yang, N.; Wei, F.; Huang, S.; Zhou, M.; Zhao, T. Neural document summarization by jointly learning to score and select sentences. In Proceedings of the 56th Annual Meeting of the Association for Computational Linguistics, Melbourne, Australia, 15–20 July 2018; Volume 1, pp. 654–663.

© 2019 by the authors. Licensee MDPI, Basel, Switzerland. This article is an open access article distributed under the terms and conditions of the Creative Commons Attribution (CC BY) license (http://creativecommons.org/licenses/by/4.0/).

Article

Multi-Turn Chatbot Based on Query-Context Attentions and Dual Wasserstein Generative Adversarial Networks

Jintae Kim [1], Shinhyeok Oh [1], Oh-Woog Kwon [2] and Harksoo Kim [1,*]

[1] Program of Computer and Communications Engineering, Kangwon National University, Chuncheon 24341, Korea; wlsxo1119@kangwon.ac.kr (J.K.); osh7605@kangwon.ac.kr (S.O.)
[2] Electronics and Telecommunications Research Institute, Daejeon 34129, Korea; ohwoog@etri.re.kr
* Correspondence: nlpdrkim@kangwon.ac.kr; Tel.: +82-33-250-6388

Received: 20 August 2019; Accepted: 16 September 2019; Published: 18 September 2019

Abstract: To generate proper responses to user queries, multi-turn chatbot models should selectively consider dialogue histories. However, previous chatbot models have simply concatenated or averaged vector representations of all previous utterances without considering contextual importance. To mitigate this problem, we propose a multi-turn chatbot model in which previous utterances participate in response generation using different weights. The proposed model calculates the contextual importance of previous utterances by using an attention mechanism. In addition, we propose a training method that uses two types of Wasserstein generative adversarial networks to improve the quality of responses. In experiments with the DailyDialog dataset, the proposed model outperformed the previous state-of-the-art models based on various performance measures.

Keywords: multi-turn chatbot; dialogue context encoding; WGAN-based response generation

1. Introduction

Chatbots are computer systems that feature natural conversation with people. Recently, generative chatbots that generate responses directly by the models have been developed with advances in deep learning. Based on the number of dialogue contexts that chatbots should consider to generate responses, chatbot models are divided into two categories: single-turn and multi-turn. Single-turn chatbots generate a response based on an immediately preceding utterance called a user's query (i.e., a user's utterance just before the response). Multi-turn chatbots generate a response based on multiple previous utterances, called a dialogue context, as well as a user's query. Table 1 shows the differences between the responses of single- and multi-turn chatbots.

Table 1. Examples of chitchat.

ID	Speaker	Utterance
(1)	User	I like pork.
(2)	Chatbot	Me too.
(3)	User	So I like Chinese food.
(4)	Chatbot	I prefer Korean foods to Chinese food.
(5)	User	Why?
(6-1)	Chatbot-*SING*	No reason.
(6-2)	Chatbot-*MULT*	Korean food is healthier.

In Table 1, Chatbot-*SING* and Chatbot-*MULT* are single- and multi-turn chatbots, respectively. As shown, Chatbot-*SING* generates the short and safe response, "No reason" because it cannot look up any other previous utterances except the immediately preceding one, "Why?". Compared with Chatbot-*SING*, Chatbot-*MULT* generates the more context-aware response, "Korean foods are healthier.", because it can look up the full dialogue history. Although multi-turn chatbots are more natural and informative, implementing multi-turn chatbots is not easy because they must determine the previous utterances that are associated with a response and also the degree to which those previous utterances affect the generation of a response. To overcome this problem, we propose a multi-turn chatbot model in which previous utterances are effectively and differently considered to generate responses using an attention mechanism. In addition, the proposed model uses two types of generative adversarial network (GAN) architectures [1–4]: One maps a vector representation of a dialogue history to a vector representation of a response, and the other maps a vector representation of a generated response (i.e., a decoded response) to a vector representation of an original response (i.e., an encoded response). The first GAN plays the role of generating a response vector associated with a dialogue history, and the second GAN plays the role of generating a surface sentence (i.e., a sequence of words) to realize a response vector.

The remainder of this paper is organized as follows: In Section 2, we review the previous studies on generative chatbots, and in Section 3, we describe the proposed multi-turn chatbot model. In Section 4, we explain the experimental setup and report some of our experimental results. We provide a conclusion to our study in Section 5.

2. Previous Works

Most of the recent approaches on generative chatbots are primarily based on sequence-to-sequence (Seq2Seq) learning. Seq2Seq is a supervised learning algorithm in which the input and the generated output are each a sequence of words [5,6]. In general, Seq2Seq models consist of two recurrent neural networks (RNNs): An RNN for encoding inputs and an RNN for generating outputs. Previous studies have demonstrated that chatbots based on Seq2Seq models often respond with either a safe response problem (i.e., the problem returning short and general responses such as "Okay" and "I see") or a semantically erroneous response [7,8]. A variational auto-encoder (VAE) is a continuous latent variable model intended to learn a latent space using a given set of samples. The model consists of an encoder and decoder: The encoder maps inputs into latent variables, and the decoder generates outputs that are similar to the inputs based on the latent variables. As a result, VAEs represent high-level semantics of the responses and help chatbots to generate various responses [9,10]. However, VAE models tend to suffer from collapse problems, where the decoder learns to ignore the latent variable and simplifies the latent variable to a standard normal distribution [11,12]. This problem has been partially solved by learning latent variable space through adversarial learning [12]. In addition, various studies using GAN architecture have been conducted [1–4]. However, adversarial learning for discrete tokens is difficult because of non-differentiability [2,4]. To solve these problems, various studies have been conducted, including those on a hybrid model of a GAN and reinforcement learning [4,13]. These studies have problems when considering non-differentiability. Moreover, they must calculate the word probability distribution of each step of the decoder to learn a discriminant model. In this study, we propose a learning method that does not consider non-differentiability when learning using a GAN because it uses the response vector generated by the decoder. To generate natural responses in multi-turn dialogues, we propose an attention method between a query and its previous utterances that helps chatbots selectively consider the given context.

3. Multi-Turn Chatbot Model Based on Dual Wasserstein Generative Adversarial Networks

The proposed model consists of three sub-modules: a query encoder, a query-to-response (QR) mapper, and a response-to-response (RR) mapper, as shown in Figure 1.

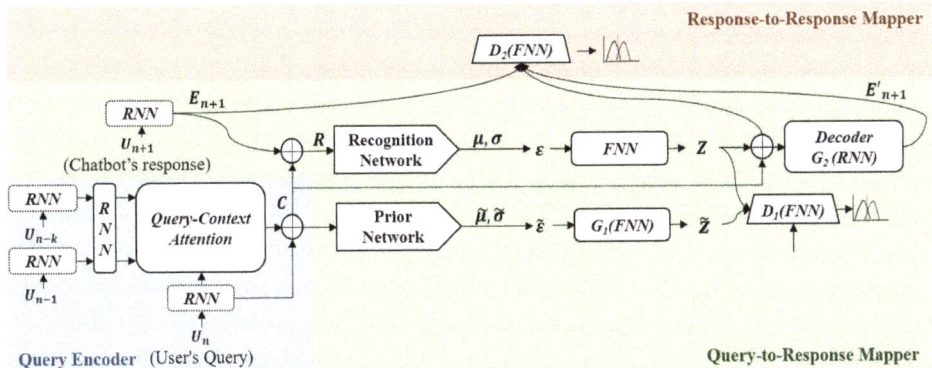

Figure 1. Overall architecture of the proposed chatbot. RNN: recurrent neural network; FNN: fully-connected neural network.

The query encoder returns a query vector embedding a current utterance U_n (i.e., user query) and a dialogue context composed of k previous utterances U_{n-1}, U_{n-2}, ..., U_{n-k}, by using RNNs and a scaled dot product attention mechanism [14]. At training time, the QR mapper makes a query vector similar to an RNN-encoded response vector (i.e., a vector of a next utterance U_{n+1}; a vector of a chatbot's response) through an adversarial learning scheme. Then, it decodes an encoded response vector through an auto-encoder learning scheme. At the inference time, a query vector is input to a response decoder based on an RNN. The RR mapper makes an encoded response vector similar to a response vector decoded by the RNN through an adversarial learning scheme.

3.1. Query Encoder

Given a current utterance U_n (user query) and its dialogue context composed of k utterances, U_{n-k}, ..., U_{n-1}, the query encoder encodes each utterance by using gated recurrent unit (GRU) networks [15], as shown in the following equation:

$$E_i = GRU(U_i) \quad (1)$$

where E_i is an utterance vector encoded by a GRU network (i.e., the last output vector of a GRU network). Then, the query encoder reflects contextual information to each encoded utterance by using GRU networks, as shown in the following equation:

$$\widetilde{E}_i = GRU(E_i) \quad (2)$$

where $\widetilde{E}_i$ is an output vector of the ith step in a GRU network. To strongly reflect the contextual associations between the current and previous utterances, the query encoder computes attention scores through the well-known scaled dot products [14] between the encoded current utterance E_n and the encoded previous utterances $\widetilde{E}_{n-k}$, ..., $\widetilde{E}_{n-1}$ as shown in the following equation:

$$a_i = \frac{1}{Z} exp(\frac{\widetilde{E}_i \circ E_n}{\sqrt{d}}), \text{ where } i \neq n \quad (3)$$

where Z and d are a normalization factor and the size of an encoded vector, respectively. Then, the query encoder computes an attention vector A known as a query-to-context (QC) attention, which represents a dialogue context that should be considered to generate a response, as shown in the following equation:

$$A = \sum_{i=1}^{k} a_i \widetilde{E}_i \tag{4}$$

Finally, the query encoder returns a query vector in which the encoded current utterance E_n and the QC attention A are concatenated, as shown in the following equation:

$$Q = E_n \oplus A. \tag{5}$$

3.2. Query-to-Response Mapper

The QR mapper plays the role of mapping a query vector into a response vector. To enhance the mapping performance, we adopt the wasserstein auto-encoder (WAE) model [12], in which a Wasserstein GAN (WGAN) [16] is used to optimize a generator. The reason we choose the WGAN is that it has been shown to produce good results in text generation [16]. Given a dialogue history $U_{n-k}, \ldots, U_{n-1}, U_n$ and a next utterance U_{n+1} (chatbot response), the QR mapper encodes the next utterance by using gated recurrent unit (GRU) networks [15] and generates a gold response vector R by concatenating the query vector Q that embeds the dialogue history and the encoded next utterance E_{n+1}, as shown in the following equation:

$$R = Q \oplus E_{n+1}. \tag{6}$$

Then, the QR mapper adds two Gaussian noises ε and $\widetilde{\varepsilon}$ to the gold response vector R and the query vector Q by using prior networks that are fully-connected neural networks (FNNs) resulting in means and co-variances, respectively. The Gaussian noises are transformed into two latent variables, namely Z, representing a gold response, and $\widetilde{Z}$ representing a query, through FNNs. The training process of the QR mapper consists of two steps. In the first stage of training, the FNN-based discriminator D_1 (i.e., a classifier based on a FNN), as given in Figure 1, tries to distinguish the fake vector $\widetilde{Z}$ from the real vector Z. Through this training process, the QR mapper makes the query vector Q similar to the gold response vector R. In the second stage of training, the RNN-based response decoder G_2 (i.e., a language model based on an RNN), as given in Figure 1, tries to properly reconstruct a sequence of words in a gold response. At the inference time, the query vector Q is transformed into the latent variable $\widetilde{Z}$. Then, the latent variable $\widetilde{Z}$ is input to the response decoder G_2.

3.3. Response-to-Response Mapper

The RR mapper plays the role of mapping a generated response vector into an encoded response vector in an auto-encoder model. To enhance the mapping performance, we adopt the WAE model [12] again. Through the WAE process based on WGAN, we expect that the qualities of generated responses will be enhanced because the response decoder refers outputs of the response encoder once again. Given an RNN-encoded next utterance E_{n+1} (i.e., a last output vector of the response encoder; an encoded response of a chatbot) and an RNN-decoded next utterance E'_{n+1} (i.e., a last output vector of the response decode; a decoded response of a chatbot), the RR mapper makes E'_{n+1} similar to E_{n+1} through adversarial learning. When training begins, an encoded gold response E_{n+1}, a gold latent variable Z, and a decoded gold response E'_{n+1} are input to the FNN-based discriminator D_2 as given in Figure 1. The discriminator tries to distinguish E'_{n+1} from E_{n+1}.

3.4. Implementation and Training

The proposed model was implemented using TensorFlow 1.4 [17]. The RNNs in the query encoder were bidirectional GRU networks [18] with 300 hidden units in each direction. The RNNs in the QR mapper were GRU networks with 1421 hidden units. The dimensions of QC attentions were 600. The discriminators (i.e., D_1 in the QR mapper and D_2 in the RR mapper) were three-layer FNNs with rectified linear unit activation [19]. The vocabulary size was set to 16,925, and all the out-of-vocabulary words were defined to the special token "UNK" meaning an unknown word. The word-embedding size was 200, and word-embedding vectors were initialized using pre-trained Glove vectors [20]. The size of the dialogue context was set to 10 with a maximum utterance length of 41. The response decoder used a greedy decoding algorithm. In the training step, the mini-batch size was set to 32. The training process of the entire model consisted of three steps. First, the WGAN in the QR mapper was trained through adversarial learning. Then, the entire model, except the RR mapper, was trained through multi-task learning to maximize the log probability for the response decoder to generate correct words. Finally, the WGAN in the RR mapper was trained through adversarial learning. All adversarial learning that was employed reduced the Wasserstein distance [16]. In addition, the gradient penalty was used when training the discriminant models [21], and its hyper-parameter λ was set to 10. To maximize the log-probability, a cross-entropy function was used. In the inference step, $\widetilde{Z}$ was used instead of Z as a latent variable.

4. Evaluation

4.1. Data Sets and Experimental Settings

We evaluated our model on a DailyDialog dataset [22], which has been widely used in recent studies. DailyDialog has 13,118 daily conversations for English learners. The datasets are separated into training, validation, and testing as 8:1:1. Bilingual evaluation understudy (BLEU) [23,24], bag-of-words (BOW) embedding [25], and Distinct [7] were used as performance measures. BLEU measures the number of generated responses that contain word n-gram overlaps with gold responses, as shown in the following equation:

$$\text{BLEU} = \min(1, \frac{\text{length of a generated sentence}}{\text{length of a gold sentence}})(\prod_{i=1}^{n} \text{precison}_i)^{\frac{1}{n}} \qquad (7)$$

where n is the maximum number length of n-grams considered and is commonly set to 4, and $precison_i$ is a word i-gram precision (i.e., the number of correct word i-grams divided by the number of word i-grams in a generated sentence). Precision of BLEU is an average score of BLEUs of 10 generated sentences per query, and Recall of BLEU is a maximum score among BLEUs of 10 generated sentences per query. The BOW embedding metric is the cosine similarity of BOW embedding between generated and gold responses. The BOW embedding metric consists of three metrics: Greedy [26], Average [27], and Extrema [28]. In our test, the maximum BOW embedding score among the 10 sampled responses was reported. The distinct score, such as Intra-dist or Inter-dist, computes the diversity of the generated responses. Dist-n is defined as the ratio of unique word n-grams over all word n-grams in the generated responses. Intra-dist is defined as the average of distinct values within each sampled response, and Inter-dist as the distinct value among all sampled responses.

4.2. Experimental Results

Our first experiment involved evaluating the effectiveness of the proposed model at the architecture level, as shown in Table 2.

In Table 2, WAE is a conditional WAE model [12] that is the baseline model because it has similar architecture to that of the proposed model. WAE + query encoder (QE) is a modified WAE in which the encoding module of a dialog context is changed into the proposed query encoder. WAE + QE +

RR is a modified WAE + QE to which the RR mapper (i.e., WGAN for response generation) is added. As shown in Table 1, WAE + QE showed better BLEU-R and BLEU-F1 than did WAE. This means that the proposed query encoder can provide some assistance in generating words in gold responses by selectively looking up dialogue contexts. The final model, WAE + QE + RR, showed better performance than did WAE + QE at all measures except Intra-dist. This means that WGAN for response generation improves the overall quality of responses.

Table 2. Performance comparison based on change in architecture.

Model	BLEU			BOW Embedding			Intra-dist		Inter-dist	
	R	P	F1	A	E	G	Dist-1	Dist-2	Dist-1	Dist-2
WAE	0.341	0.278	0.306	0.948	0.578	0.846	0.830	0.940	0.327	0.583
WAE + QE	0.442	0.268	0.334	0.947	0.680	0.845	**0.913**	**0.995**	0.322	0.475
WAE + QE + RR	**0.463**	**0.283**	**0.351**	**0.949**	**0.688**	**0.851**	0.902	0.993	**0.371**	**0.585**

P: Precision, R: Recall, F1: F1 score, A: Average, E: Extrema, G: Greedy. BLEU: bilingual evaluation understudy; BOW: bag-of-words; WAE: wasserstein auto-encoder; QE: query encoder; RR: response-to-response. The bolds indicate the highest scores in each evaluation measure.

In the second experiment, we compared the performance of the proposed model with those of the previous state-of-the-art models, as shown in Table 3.

Table 3. Performance comparison between proposed and previous models.

Model	BLEU			BOW Embedding			Intra-dist		Inter-dist	
	R	P	F1	A	E	G	Dist-1	Dist-2	Dist-1	Dist-2
HRED	0.232	0.232	0.232	0.915	0.511	0.798	0.935	0.969	0.093	0.097
CVAE	0.265	0.222	0.242	0.923	0.543	0.811	0.938	0.973	0.177	0.222
CVAE-BOW	0.256	0.224	0.239	0.923	0.540	0.812	**0.947**	0.976	0.165	0.206
CVAE-CO	0.259	0.244	0.251	0.914	0.530	0.818	0.821	0.911	0.106	0.126
WAE	0.341	0.278	0.306	0.948	0.578	0.846	0.830	0.940	0.327	0.583
WAE + QE + RR	**0.463**	**0.283**	**0.351**	**0.949**	**0.688**	**0.851**	0.902	**0.993**	**0.371**	**0.585**

The bolds indicate the highest scores in each evaluation measure.

In Table 3, HRED is a generalized Seq2Seq model with a hierarchical RNN encoder [29]. CVAE is a conditional VAE model with KL-annealing [9]. CVAE-BOW is a conditional VAE model with a BOW loss [9]. CVAE-CO is a collaborative conditional VAE model [10]. WAE is a conditional WAE model [12]. As shown in Table 3, the proposed model, WAE + QE + RR, outperformed the comparison models at all measures except Dist-1.

5. Conclusions

We proposed a generative, multi-turn chatbot model. To generate responses that consider dialogue histories, the proposed model used the query-context attention mechanism in the query encoding step. Furthermore, to improve the quality of responses, the proposed model used two types of WGAN: A WGAN for dialogue modeling and a WGAN for response generation. In experiments with DailyDialog datasets, the proposed model outperformed the previous state-of-the-art models and generated responses with higher quality. The proposed chatbot model has the lack of a consistent personality because it is typically trained using many dialogues from different speakers. To alleviate this problem, we will study how to have a chatbot that maintains a consistent persona. In addition, we will study how a chatbot can search and use outer knowledge for open-domain dialogue.

Author Contributions: Conceptualization, H.K. and J.K.; methodology, J.K.; software, J.K.; validation, J.K. and S.O.; formal analysis, J.K.; investigation, J.K.; resources, S.O.; data curation, S.O.; writing—original draft preparation, J.K.; writing—review and editing, H.K.; visualization, H.K.; supervision, H.K. and O.-W.K.; project administration, H.K. and O.-W.K.; funding acquisition, H.K. and O.-W.K.

Funding: This work was supported by the Institute of Information and Communications Technology Planning and Evaluation (IITP), grant funded by the Korean government (MSIT) (2019-0-0004, Development of semi-supervised learning language intelligence technology and Korean tutoring service for foreigners), and was partially supported by the National Research Foundation of Korea (NRF), grant funded by the Korean government (MSIP) (No.2016R1A2B4007732). This work was also partially supported by the Hyundai motor group.

Acknowledgments: We would especially like to thank the members of NLP laboratory in Kangwon National University for their technical support.

Conflicts of Interest: The authors declare no conflict of interest.

References

1. Goodfellow, I.; Pouget-Abadie, J.; Mirza, M.; Xu, B.; Warde-Farley, D.; Ozair, S.; Courville, A.; Bengio, Y. Generative Adversarial Nets. In *Advances in Neural Information Processing Systems*; Guyon, I., Luxburg, U.V., Bengio, S., Wallach, H., Fergus, R., Vishwanathan, S., Garnett, R., Eds.; Curran Associates, Inc.: Red Hook, NY, USA, 2014; pp. 2672–2680.
2. Li, J.; Monroe, W.; Shi, T.; Jean, S.; Ritter, A.; Jurafsky, D. Adversarial Learning for Neural Dialogue Generation. *arXiv* **2017**, arXiv:1701.06547.
3. Xu, Z.; Liu, B.; Wang, B.; Chengjie, S.U.; Wang, X.; Wang, Z.; Qi, C. Neural Response Generation via GAN with an Approximate Embedding Layer. In Proceedings of the 2017 Conference on Empirical Methods in Natural Language Processing, Copenhagen, Denmark, 9 September 2017; pp. 617–626.
4. Yu, L.; Zhang, W.; Wang, J.; Yu, Y. Seqgan: Sequence Generative Adversarial Nets with Policy Gradient. In Proceedings of the Thirty-First AAAI Conference on Artificial Intelligence, San Francisco, CA, USA, 13 February 2017.
5. Vinyals, O.; Le, Q. A neural conversational model. *arXiv* **2015**, arXiv:1506.05869.
6. Shang, L.; Lu, Z.; Li, H. Neural Responding Machine for Short-Text Conversation. In Proceedings of the 53rd Annual Meeting of the Association for Computational Linguistics and the 7th International Joint Conference on Natural Language Processing, Beijing, China, 26–31 July 2015; Volume 1, pp. 1577–1586.
7. Li, J.; Galley, M.; Brockett, C.; Gao, J.; Dolan, B. A Diversity-Promoting Objective Function for Neural Conversation Models. In Proceedings of the NAACL-HLT, San Diego, CA, USA, 1–26 July 2016; pp. 110–119.
8. Sato, S.; Yoshinaga, N.; Toyoda, M.; Kitsuregawa, M. Modeling Situations in Neural Chatbots. In Proceedings of the ACL 2017, Student Research Workshop, Vancouver, BC, Canada, 30 July–4 August 2017; pp. 120–127.
9. Zhao, T.; Zhao, R.; Eskenazi, M. Learning Discourse-level Diversity for Neural Dialog Models using Conditional Variational Autoencoders. In Proceedings of the 55th Annual Meeting of the Association for Computational Linguistics, Vancouver, BC, Canada, 30 July–4 August 2017; Volume 1, pp. 654–664.
10. Shen, X.; Su, H.; Niu, S.; Demberg, V. Improving Variational Encoder-Decoders in Dialogue Generation. In Proceedings of the Thirty-Second AAAI Conference on Artificial Intelligence, Lyon, France, 23–27 April 2018.
11. Goyal, P.; Hu, Z.; Liang, X.; Wang, C.; Xing, E.P. Nonparametric Variational Auto-Encoders for Hierarchical Representation Learning. In Proceedings of the IEEE International Conference on Computer Vision, Sinaia, Romania, 19–21 October 2017; pp. 5094–5102.
12. Gu, X.; Cho, K.; Ha, J.W.; Kim, S. DialogWAE: Multimodal Response Generation with Conditional Wasserstein Auto-Encoder. *arXiv* **2018**, arXiv:1805.12352.
13. Shen, T.; Lei, T.; Barzilay, R.; Jaakkola, T. Style Transfer from Non-Parallel Text by Cross-Alignment. In *Advances in Neural Information Processing Systems*; Guyon, I., Luxburg, U.V., Bengio, S., Wallach, H., Fergus, R., Vishwanathan, S., Garnett, R., Eds.; Curran Associates, Inc.: Red Hook, NY, USA, 2017; pp. 6830–6841.
14. Vaswani, A.; Shazeer, N.; Parmar, N.; Uszkoreit, J.; Jones, L.; Gomez, A.N.; Kaiser, Ł.; Polosukhin, I. Attention is All You Need. In *Advances in Neural Information Processing Systems*; Guyon, I., Luxburg, U.V., Bengio, S., Wallach, H., Fergus, R., Vishwanathan, S., Garnett, R., Eds.; Curran Associates, Inc.: Red Hook, NY, USA, 2017; pp. 5998–6008.
15. Cho, K.; Van Merriënboer, B.; Bahdanau, D.; Bengio, Y. On the properties of neural machine translation: Encoder-decoder approaches. *arXiv* **2014**, arXiv:1409.1259.

16. Arjovsky, M.; Chintala, S.; Bottou, L. Wasserstein GAN. *arXiv* **2017**, arXiv:1701.07875.
17. Abadi, M.; Barham, P.; Chen, J.; Chen, Z.; Davis, A.; Dean, J.; Devin, M.; Ghemawat, S.; Irving, G.; Isard, M.; et al. Tensorflow: A System for Large-Scale Machine Learning. In Proceedings of the 12th {USENIX} Symposium on Operating Systems Design and Implementation ({OSDI} 16), Savannah, GA, USA, 2–4 November 2016; pp. 265–283.
18. Cho, K.; van Merrienboer, B.; Gulcehre, C.; Bahdanau, D.; Bougares, F.; Schwenk, H.; Bengio, Y. Learning Phrase Representations using RNN Encoder–Decoder for Statistical Machine Translation. In Proceedings of the 2014 Conference on Empirical Methods in Natural Language Processing (EMNLP), Doha, Qatar, 25–29 October 2014; pp. 1724–1734.
19. Nair, V.; Hinton, G.E. Rectified Linear Units Improve Restricted Boltzmann machines. In Proceedings of the 27th International Conference on Machine Learning (ICML-10), Haifa, Israel, 21–24 July 2010; pp. 807–814.
20. Pennington, J.; Socher, R.; Manning, C. Glove: Global Vectors for Word Representation. In Proceedings of the 2014 Conference on Empirical Methods in Natural Language Processing (EMNLP), Doha, Qatar, 25–29 October 2014; pp. 1532–1543.
21. Gulrajani, I.; Ahmed, F.; Arjovsky, M.; Dumoulin, V.; Courville, A.C. Improved Training of Wasserstein GANs. In *Advances in Neural Information Processing Systems*; Guyon, I., Luxburg, U.V., Bengio, S., Wallach, H., Fergus, R., Vishwanathan, S., Garnett, R., Eds.; Curran Associates, Inc.: Red Hook, NY, USA, 2017; pp. 5767–5777.
22. Li, Y.; Su, H.; Shen, X.; Li, W.; Cao, Z.; Niu, S. DailyDialog: A Manually Labelled Multi-turn Dialogue Dataset. In Proceedings of the Eighth International Joint Conference on Natural Language Processing, Taipei, Taiwan, 27 November–1 December 2017; Volume 1, pp. 986–995.
23. Papineni, K.; Roukos, S.; Ward, T.; Zhu, W.J. BLEU: A Method for Automatic Evaluation of Machine Translation. In Proceedings of the 40th Annual Meeting on Association for Computational Linguistics, Philadelphia, PA, USA, 6 July 2002; Association for Computational Linguistics: Stroudsburg, PA, USA, 2002; pp. 311–318.
24. Chen, B.; Cherry, C. A Systematic Comparison of Smoothing Techniques for Sentence-Level Bleu. In Proceedings of the Ninth Workshop on Statistical Machine Translation, Baltimore, MD, USA, 26–27 June 2014; pp. 362–367.
25. Liu, C.W.; Lowe, R.; Serban, I.; Noseworthy, M.; Charlin, L.; Pineau, J. How not to Evaluate Your Dialogue System: An Empirical Study of Unsupervised Evaluation Metrics for Dialogue Response Generation. In Proceedings of the 2016 Conference on Empirical Methods in Natural Language Processing, Austin, TX, USA, 1–4 November 2016; pp. 2122–2132.
26. Rus, V.; Lintean, M. A Comparison of Greedy and Optimal Assessment of Natural Language Student Input using Word-to-Word Similarity Metrics. In Proceedings of the Seventh Workshop on Building Educational Applications Using NLP, Montréal, QC, Canada, 7 June 2012; Association for Computational Linguistics: Stroudsburg, PA, USA, 2012; pp. 157–162.
27. Mitchell, J.; Lapata, M. Vector-Based Models of Semantic Composition. In Proceedings of the ACL-08: HLT, Columbus, OH, USA, 15–20 June 2008; pp. 236–244.
28. Forgues, G.; Pineau, J.; Larchevêque, J.M.; Tremblay, R. Bootstrapping Dialog Systems with Word Embeddings. In Proceedings of the Nips, Modern Machine Learning and Natural Language Processing Workshop, Geneva, Switzerland, 12 December 2014.
29. Serban, I.V.; Sordoni, A.; Bengio, Y.; Courville, A.; Pineau, J. Building End-to-End Dialogue Systems Using Generative Hierarchical Neural Network Models. In Proceedings of the Thirtieth AAAI Conference on Artificial Intelligence, Phoenix, AZ, USA, 12–17 February 2016; pp. 3776–3783.

© 2019 by the authors. Licensee MDPI, Basel, Switzerland. This article is an open access article distributed under the terms and conditions of the Creative Commons Attribution (CC BY) license (http://creativecommons.org/licenses/by/4.0/).

Article

A Text-Generated Method to Joint Extraction of Entities and Relations

Haihong E *, Siqi Xiao and Meina Song

School of Computer Science, Beijing University of Posts and Telecommunications, Beijing 100876, China
* Correspondence: ehaihong@bupt.edu.cn; Tel.: +86-156-0010-5933

Received: 26 July 2019; Accepted: 2 September 2019; Published: 10 September 2019

Abstract: Entity-relation extraction is a basic task in natural language processing, and recently, the use of deep-learning methods, especially the Long Short-Term Memory (LSTM) network, has achieved remarkable performance. However, most of the existing entity-relation extraction methods cannot solve the overlapped multi-relation extraction problem, which means one or two entities are shared among multiple relational triples contained in a sentence. In this paper, we propose a text-generated method to solve the overlapped problem of entity-relation extraction. Based on this, (1) the entities and their corresponding relations are jointly generated as target texts without any additional feature engineering; (2) the model directly generates the relational triples using a unified decoding process, and entities can be repeatedly presented in multiple triples to solve the overlapped-relation problem. We conduct experiments on two public datasets—NYT10 and NYT11. The experimental results show that our proposed method outperforms the existing work, and achieves the best results.

Keywords: relation extraction; entity recognition; information extraction; long short-term memory network

1. Introduction

Entity-relation extraction is the core task and important segment in the fields of information extraction, knowledge graph, natural language understanding, etc. In recent years, knowledge graph [1] has been widely applied. Many achievements have also been made in the downstream tasks such as question answering and retrieval based on knowledge graph. The basis for constructing the knowledge graph is to build a knowledge base. In the knowledge base, the structured relational triples are preserved in formats such as <*entity 1*, *rel*, *entity 2*>, which means that there is a relation *rel* between *entity 1* and *entity 2*. The goal of entity-relation extraction task is to extract the semantic relations between entity pairs from unstructured text. With the application of deep learning in joint learning and distant supervision, the relation extraction task has obtained rich research results.

The supervised entity-relation extraction methods can be divided into pipeline and joint learning. The pipeline methods take the named entity recognition (NER) and relation classification (RC) as two separate subtasks, and extract the relations between entities based on the completion of entity recognition [2–4]. However, this kind of methods ignores the relevance between these two subtasks. Recent work using joint learning [5–8] can make use of the tight interaction information between entities and relations and use a single model to extract entities and classify the relations between entities simultaneously, which solves the problems of the pipeline method well. However, most of the existing work often requires complex feature engineering or relies heavily on the NLP tools to extract features.

Moreover, most existing relation extraction models focus on scenarios dealing with a single relation within one sentence, but there are usually multiple relations between entity mentions in one sentence. Sentences can be divided into three classes based on the degree of entity overlap [9], as shown in Table 1: (1) Normal: a sentence belongs to Normal class if none of its triplets have overlapped entities; (2) Entity Pair Overlap: some of its triplets have overlapped entity pair; (3) Single Entity Overlap: some of its triplets have an overlapped entity and these triplets do not have overlapped entity pair. Even though there are already several works to address the triplet overlap issue [9–11], their effects are far from good enough, cannot solve the problems of relation extraction in complex situations very well. As a result, the triplet overlap issue is not actually addressed.

Table 1. Examples of three classes: Normal, Entity Pair Overlap, and Single Entity Overlap. S1 belongs to Normal class because there are no overlaps in its triplets; S2 belongs to Entity Pair Overlap class since the entity pair (Sudan, Khartoum) are overlapped; S3 belongs to Single Entity Overlap class because the entity *Los Angeles* is overlapped and its two triplets have no overlapped entity pairs.

Class	Sentence	Relation Triples
Normal	S1: Chicago is in the United States.	<The United States, **contains**, Chicago>
Entity Pair Overlap	S2: News of the list's existence unnerved officials in Khartoum, Sudan's capital.	<Sudan, **contains**, Khartoum> <Sudan, **capital**, Khartoum>
Single Entity Overlap	S3: John, 23, who lives in Los Angeles, California.	<John, **placelived**, Los Angeles> <California, **contains**, Los Angeles>

In reality, natural language texts, such as news and blogs, usually express multiple relations and it is also common that one or more entity mentions appear among multiple relations. Therefore, it is necessary to extract overlapping relations from the perspective of practical application scenarios. The overlapping multi-relation extraction problem is more complex than single-relation extraction because the single-relation extraction scenario can be basically divided into the following two types: (1) for sentences with the given entity pairs, relation classification can be modeled as a text classification problem; (2) for sentences with non-annotated target entity pairs, the model assumes that sentence contains only one pair of entities and relation classification is performed after entity recognition; these two cases usually use the *softmax* function in the relation classification phrase, so only one relation can be extracted. In the multi-relation extraction situation, we need to find every complete relational triple. The model needs to simultaneously extract the relation and the corresponding entity pairs. Reference [8] provided an idea to integrate entity mention and relation type information into each label, this two information can be obtained simultaneously when tagging each word. Zeng's [9] work is similar to ours, which is based on a sequence-to-sequence learning framework, but it cannot extract multi-word entities because of the model design.

To tackle this problem, we completely convert entity-relation extraction task into text generation task. We generate entity pairs and relational representation words according to source texts, without any additional feature engineering. The task of generating target texts from source texts, including text summarization [12,13], machine translation [14,15]. In the text summarization task, target texts are keywords or key sentences that are copied from source texts or generated from vocabulary through the semantic understanding of source text contents. For the relation extraction task, our target texts are the entity pairs contained in the source texts and their corresponding relations, i.e., relational triplets.

In this paper, we adopt a sequence-to-sequence framework with the pointer, where using the encoder to obtain the semantic encoding vector and the decoder with pointer is used to generate entities or relations. Inspired by the text summarization paper [16], we also use a generation probability p_{gen} as a soft switch to select whether the current decoding time is more likely to copy words from the original input or to generate words from the vocabulary. According to the specific situation of the original input, one or more groups of relational triplets are generated, thereby implementing the joint extraction of entities and relations. Entities can be repeated in multiple triplets, which can solve the problem of overlapped multiple relational triplet extraction.

The main contributions of our work are concluded as follows:

(1) We completely convert the entity-relation extraction to the text generation task, and use a unified decoding method to generate entities and relational expressions as target text to realize the joint extraction of entities and relations.
(2) Based on the text generation framework, the model is designed to generate multiple groups of relational triplets. Entities can be repeated in multiple triplets to solve the problem of overlapped multiple relational tuples.
(3) We conduct experiments on NYT10 and NYT11 public datasets, and the experimental results show that we proposed method outperforms state-of-the-art with 4.7% and 11.4% improvements in F1 score, respectively.

The remainder of the paper is organized as follows: Section 2 reviews the related works. Section 3 describes the proposed method in detail. In Section 4, datasets and settings used in the experiment are presented and Section 5 shows the results. Section 6 discusses the performance comparison between our model and the baseline methods. Section 7 concludes the paper.

2. Related Work

Entity and relation extraction methods can be divided into pipeline and joint learning.

Pipeline method regards entity recognition and relation extraction as two separate tasks, and extracts relations based on entity recognition. Some pipeline methods based on RNN and CNN models have been proposed. Ref. [17] first used RNN for relation extraction. Ref. [4] first introduced CNN to this task. Refs. [2,18–20], improved on the previous work and enhanced the effect of relation extraction. The pipeline method has the disadvantages of error propagation, ignoring the relevance between these two subtasks and generating redundant information, while joint learning method proposed in recent years which uses a single model to extract entities and relations simultaneously and can use the close interaction information between entities and relations.

The joint learning method is further divided into feature-based structured systems [21] and neural network models. Ref. [7] first used neural network methods with the dependency tree to jointly extract entities and relations. Ref. [22] proposed a hybrid neural network which has two channels after the encoding layer, one links to the NER module, the other feeds into the relation extraction module. Ref. [5] first introduced the attention mechanism in combination with bidirectional LSTMs for joint extraction of entities and relations. Ref. [8] proposed an entity-relation extraction method based on a novel tagging scheme. This method completely transforms the joint learning model into sequence labeling problem, it can extract multiple relations, but cannot deal with entity overlap because the model can only assign a label to each word. Ref. [11] based on Zheng's work [8], further transformed the joint task into a graph problem and proposed a transition-based method, can model underlying dependencies between relations and identify overlapped relational triples.

Ref. [9] first proposed a solution for overlapping relation extraction, and divided the sentences into three classes according to the degree of entity overlap: Normal, Entity Pair Overlap, and Single Entity Overlap. They proposed an end-to-end model based on sequence-to-sequence learning with copy mechanism, copying entity pairs from the original input, and classifying the relation types in the predefined relational table. Unlike [9], our model uses a unified way to generate token at any time in the decoding process, instead of judging whether to copy entities or predict relations at different steps. By calculating a generate probability distribution, the model can automatically learn whether entities or relations should be generated at each moment. At the same time, because [9] presupposes that a relational triple is generated every three steps, they can only recognize the last word of a multi-word entity. While our model does not limit the number of words contained in each relational triple, it can recognize multi-word entities and can copy entity words from the original text.

3. Materials and Methods

In this section, we first formalize the description of the entity-relation problem. Then, we introduce the sequence-to-sequence model with the pointer we use in detail.

3.1. Problem Formulation

Giving the training data [x, y], x represents the input text of the model and y represents the target output. In the target sentence, we use '.' to divide multiple triples, and within the triple, we use ',' to divide relational words, the first entity, and the second entity.

The goal of the model is to generate one or more groups of relational triplets according to the specific situation in the source text, while allowing entities to be repeatedly presented. The model can copy words from the source text by the pointer or generate words from the predefined vocabulary. The overall structure of our model is shown in Figure 1.

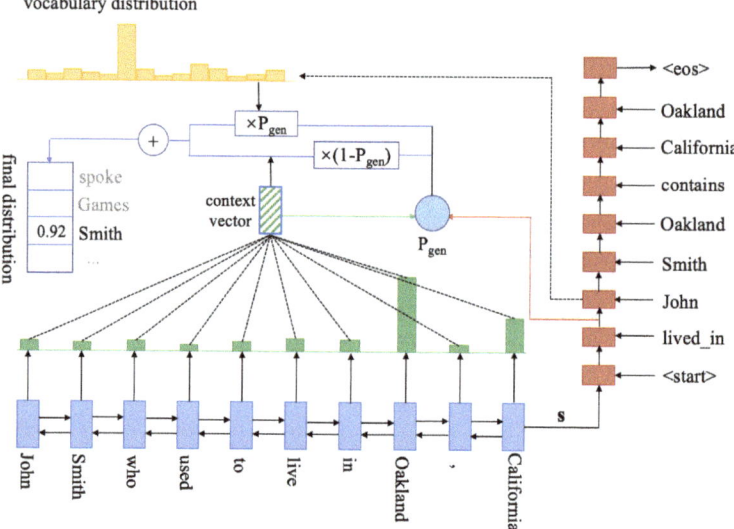

Figure 1. The overall structure of our model. The blue block represents the bidirectional LSTMs in the encoder, the red block represents the unidirectional LSTM in the decoder, the green block represents the attention weight distribution, and the yellow block represents the final generation probability distribution. All these above descriptions will be introduced in Section 3.

3.2. Model Description

3.2.1. Encoder

Giving a sentence $s = [w_1, w_2, ..., w_n]$, where w_t represent the t-th word in the sentence of length n, we first convert the word with one hot encoding into the embedding matrix through the word embedding layer, and get $e = [x_1, x_2, ..., x_n]$, where $x_t \in R^d$ represents the embedding vector of t-th word. The embedding layer randomly initializes the embedding matrix and updates the weight parameters with the training of the model.

Then, we use LSTM to further encode the sequence. Long Short-Term Memory (LSTM) is a variant of Recurrent Neural Network (RNN) which is widely used in various NLP tasks because it has ability to capture long-term dependencies and solve the problem of gradient vanish in RNN. Specifically, we use bidirectional LSTMs (Bi-LSTMS) which consists of two separate LSTM layers. The forward LSTM layer $\overrightarrow{h}$ encodes the input sequence from x_1 to x_n. Similarly, the backward LSTM layer $\overleftarrow{h}$ will encode the input sequence from x_n to x_1. We then concatenate $\overrightarrow{h_t}$ and $\overleftarrow{h_t}$ to represent final encoder information of t-th word, denoted as $h_t = [\overrightarrow{h_t}, \overleftarrow{h_t}]$, in this way, the encoder vector of each step can obtain the semantic information of its context.

$$\begin{aligned}
f_t &= \sigma(W_f \cdot [h_{t-1}, x_t] + b_f) \\
i_t &= \sigma(W_i \cdot [h_{t-1}, x_t] + b_i) \\
\tilde{C}_t &= \tanh(W_c \cdot [h_{t-1}, x_t] + b_c) \\
C_t &= f_t * C_{t-1} + i_t * \tilde{C}_t \\
o_t &= \sigma(W_o \cdot [h_{t-1}, x_t] + b_o) \\
h_t &= o_t * \tanh(C_t)
\end{aligned} \quad (1)$$

In LSTM, as shown in Equation (1), x_t represents the word vector of the t-th word, and h_t represents the hidden state vector at the time t. W and b represent the weight matrices and bias vectors that can be learned, respectively.

3.2.2. Decoder

The decoder is aimed to generate tokens consisting of a layer of unidirectional LSTM.

$$o_t, s_t = cell([x_{t-1}, h_t^*], s_{t-1}) \quad (2)$$

In Equation (2), *cell* is an LSTM unit, during training x_{t-1} represents the embedding of the previous word in the target output sequence; in the test phase, it represents the embedding of the word generated by the model at the previous step, and s_{t-1} represents the decoding state at time $t-1$. At the same time, we use the attention mechanism to calculate the weight of the hidden vectors in the encoder at the current decoding time, the attention distribution can be viewed as a probability distribution over the source words. The greater the attention weight, the greater the influence on the word generated at the current decoding time. In addition, h_t^* represents the weighted sum of the encoder hidden states based on attention weight, i.e., context vector. We use the attention calculation method of [14] to obtain the context vector:

$$\begin{aligned}
e_i^t &= v^T \tanh(W_h h_i + W_s s_t + b_{attn}) \\
a^t &= softmax(e^t) \\
h_t^* &= \sum_i a_i^t h_i
\end{aligned} \quad (3)$$

where v, W_h, W_s, and b_{attn} in Equation (3) are learnable parameters, h_i represents the hidden state vector of the encoder at time i.

a^t is the influence weight in attention which is also a probability distribution. When the model wants to 'copy' a word from the original text, the word with the largest weight value will be selected as the predicted word. Therefore, we also call a^t 'pointer'.

Then the context vector is concatenated with the decoder state s_t and fed through linear layers to produce the vocabulary distribution P_{vocab}:

$$P_{vocab} = softmax(W_v[s_t, h_t^*] + b_v) \quad (4)$$

where W_v and b_v are learnable parameters, P_{vocab} is a probability distribution over all words in the predefined vocabulary.

To make the model have the ability to copy words from the source text, and to retain the ability to select words through the predefined vocabulary, we calculate a generation probability $p_{gen} \in [0, 1]$ at each decoding step, refer to [16]:

$$p_{gen} = \sigma(w_h^T * h_t^* + w_s^T s_t + w_x^T x_t + b_{gen}) \quad (5)$$

where w_h, w_s, w_x and b_{gen} are learnable parameters and σ is the sigmoid function, p_{gen} is calculated by context vector h_t^*, decoder state s_t, and decoder input x_t. p_{gen} is aimed to select the word output at the current decoding time, with a greater probability of copying from the source text or more likely to be generated from the predefined vocabulary.

And now we get the final probability distribution:

$$P(w) = p_{gen} P_{vocab}(w) + (1 - p_{gen}) \sum_i a_i^t \quad (6)$$

where a^t represents the attention weight on the hidden states of the encoder. We select the word with the greatest probability as the predicted word of the current step. In the test phase, the embedding of this word will be sent to the next decoding step.

For entities, the model will tend to copy from the source text, so that for entities that do not appear in the predefined vocabulary (unseen entities), the model also has the ability to correctly identify; for relational expressions, the model is more tend to generate from the vocabulary.

3.2.3. Training and Decoding

During training, given a batch of data with B sentences $S = \{s_1, s_2, ..., s_B\}$ with their corresponding target sequences $Y = \{y_1, y_2, ..., y_B\}$, where $y_i = \{w_i^1, w_i^2, ..., w_i^T\}$ is the reference of i-th sentence. The loss function is defined as follows:

$$loss = \frac{1}{B \times T} \sum_{i=1}^{B} \sum_{t=1}^{T} -\log(P(w)) \quad (7)$$

where T is the maximum time step of decoder.

While decoding, the model adopts beam search to increase the accuracy of the output. The advantage of beam search is that we have multiple choices at each step, instead of selecting the word with the highest probability at each time, in case that the optimal local prediction is incorrect. The candidate predictions are ranked by global scores; thus, error propagation can be alleviated.

4. Experimental Setup

In this section, we present our experimental results on two different public datasets NYT10 and NYT11, and compare them with the baseline methods to demonstrate the effectiveness of our model from multiple perspectives.

4.1. Dataset

We conduct experiments on two public datasets NYT10 and NYT11. NYT (New York Times) dataset is developed by distant supervision method. The original corpus in this dataset is extracted from sentences in New York Times articles. NYT10 and NYT11 are two versions of NYT dataset. Specifically, NYT10 dataset contains 29 valid relations, including 74,345 sentences, which is originally released by [23]. NYT11 is relatively small, including 24 valid relations, which is provided by [24]. We filtered the sentences that do not contain valid triples in the dataset, leaving 66,336 sentences. The training set, valid set, and test set are split by random sampling. Some statistical data of the two datasets are shown in Table 2.

Table 2. Statistics of NYT10 and NYT11 datasets.

	NYT10	NYT11
Relation types	29	24
Training set	66,828	58,356
Training tuples	84,166	98,393
Test set	4000	4998
Test tuples	5010	8226

4.2. Settings

We set 256 as the hidden state dimension of LSTM, 128 as the word embedding dimension, and the batch size is 16. We set the maximum number of decoding steps to 60, so the model can generate up to 10 groups of relational triples. We use Adam to optimize parameters and learning rate is set to 0.001 during training. We set beam size is 4, which means that the top 4 optimal generated sequences are preserved during the decoding phase, and finally the one with the highest probability is selected as the final output.

4.3. Baseline and Evaluation Metrics

We select four models as our baselines, CoType is a joint extraction model based on feature system. SPTree uses neural network model with abundant linguistic resources. Noveltagging and MultiDecoder both use neural network to jointly extract entities and relations without additional features. These models all achieved the best results at that time.

- CoType [24]: a domain-independent framework by jointly embedding entity mentions, relation mentions, text features, and type labels into representations, which formulates extraction as a global embedding problem.
- SPTree [7]: an end-to-end relation extraction model that represents both word sequence and dependency tree structures using bidirectional sequential and tree-structured LSTM-RNNs.
- Noveltagging [8]: an approach that treats joint extraction as a sequential labeling problem using a tagging schema where each tag encodes entity mentions and relation types at the same time to achieve joint extraction of entities and relations.
- MultiDecoder [9]: a sequence-to-sequence learning framework with a copy mechanism for joint extraction, where multiple decoders are applied to generate triples to handle overlapping relations, completing the extraction of a relational triple every three steps. This method is the first time to solve the overlapping problem of multi-relational extraction.

We compare our method with the above four baselines on NYT10 and NYT11 dataset respectively. In addition, we evaluate the performance of each model with micro Precision, Recall, and F1 score. Only when the relation and entity pair are all correct, we think this relational triplet is correctly predicted, where an entity is considered correct if the head and tail offsets are both correct. We used the source code provided by above baselines to reproduce their performance on NYT10 and NYT11 dataset, respectively.

5. Results

In this section, we will show the experimental results of our proposed method and baseline methods on NYT10 and NYT11, we reproduce the results of the baseline methods.

Model Performance

In which Table 3 shows the comparison of extraction effects on test sets of NYT10 and NYT11, respectively. It can be found that our proposed method is better than baseline methods both on NYT10 and NYT11 datasets, and outperforms [9] with 4.7% and 11.4% improvements in F1 score, respectively. At the same time, to prove the ability of our model to extract overlapped multi-relations, we respectively divide two subsets from the NYT10 and NYT11 test sets. All sentences in one subset have entity pair overlap, and all sentences in the other subset have single entity overlap. Please note that some sentences may exist in both cases, in this experiment, this kind of sentence will exist in both subsets. We compare our model with Noveltagging and MultiDecoder. Figures 2 and 3 show the precision, recall, and F1 score of entity pair overlap and single entity overlap on NYT10 and NYT11 datasets, respectively. In the figure, blue, yellow, and green blocks represent the experimental results of Noveltagging, MultiDecoder, and our model, respectively. As we can see, our model can handle overlapped multi-relation extraction better than the baseline methods on both datasets.

Table 3. Comparison of results of our model and baselines in NYT10 and NYT11 datasets.

Model	NYT10			NYT11		
	Precision	Recall	F1	Precision	Recall	F1
CoType	-	-	-	0.417	0.320	0.362
SPTree	0.464	0.591	0.519	0.493	0.634	0.555
Noveltagging	0.563	0.334	0.419	0.622	0.341	0.440
MultiDecoder	0.543	0.530	0.536	0.586	0.574	0.580
Our Method	**0.592**	**0.533**	**0.561**	**0.702**	**0.598**	**0.646**

Bold numbers represent the results of proposed method and are also the highest scores of the three evaluation metrics (precision, recall and F1 score) in the comparative experiment.

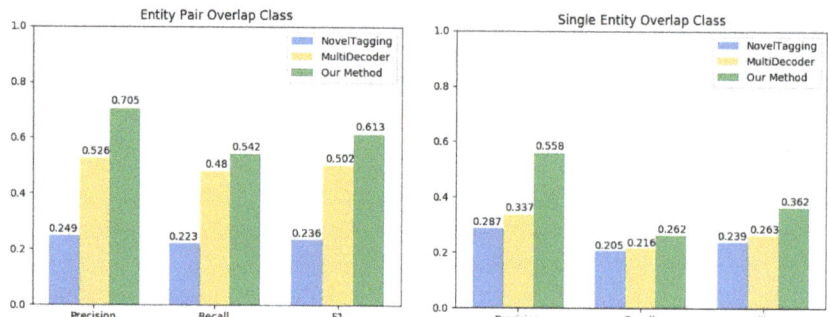

Figure 2. Results of our model and baseline models in Entity Pair Overlap class and Single Entity Overlap class in NYT10 dataset.

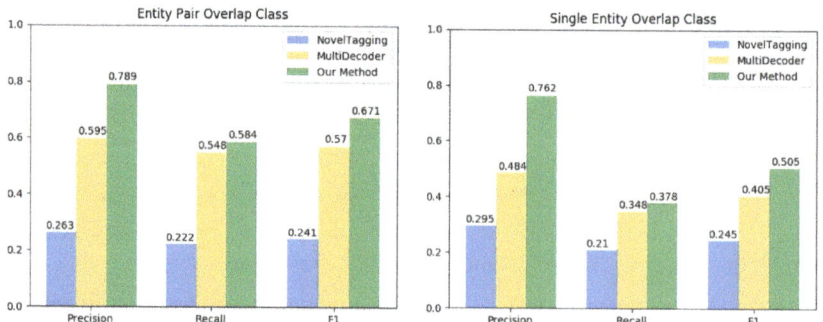

Figure 3. Results of our model and baseline models in Entity Pair Overlap class and Single Entity Overlap class in NYT11 dataset.

6. Discussion

In this section, we focus on the advantages of our model over other baselines, and explain and analyze the experimental results in detail.

6.1. Comparison of Overall Performance

Table 3 shows the Precision, Recall, and F1 scores of the baseline models and our proposed method. CoType is a feature-based system whose performance is not as good as neural network models. SPTree uses more linguistic resources (e.g., POS tags, chunks, syntactic parsing trees) to obtain better results Noveltagging method [8] cannot solve the problem of overlapping multi-relations because it can only assign a tag to each word in the sequence, which leads to a decrease in accuracy. Ref. [9] decides to copy entities or predict relations according to different decoding steps. The copy mechanism is used to calculate the probability distribution to select entities on the source texts at the time of entity recognition, and at the steps of relation prediction, the probability distribution is calculated on the relational table. While, during decoding, we do not distinguish the generation time of entities or relations, and relational words are also distributed in the predefined vocabulary, rather than having a separate relational table. We adopt a more unified decoding method, the predicted word at any time is generated by calculating the mixed probability distribution $P(w)$ over the vocabulary at each decoding step. We hope that the model can learn whether to generate entities or relational words at each step in the process of training.

Meanwhile, we set a maximum decoding step of 60 to generate up to 10 relational triples, while [9] can generate up to 5 relational triples. At the same time, Zeng's model can extract multiple triples, but it is limited to the $3t + 1$, $3t + 2$ ($5 > t > = 0$) to generate the first entity and the second entity of the current triple. According to its presupposition, multi-word entity cannot be extracted completely, which is a disadvantage in its model design. Our method can extract the whole part of each entity completely, so when we judge whether the model extracts a triple correctly, Zeng's model is more relaxed than our model, because it is equivalent to just extracting the last word in the entity as if the entity was correctly extracted.

6.2. Comparison of Overlapped Multi-Relations Extraction Performance

To further contrast with baselines, we experiment with sentences of different entity overlap degrees, respectively. Figures 2 and 3 show the experimental results of our proposed method and two of our baseline methods (Noveltagging and MultiDecoder), respectively. As we can see in Entity Pair Overlap class and Single Entity Overlap class, our method performs much better than others. We think that our method generates entities and their relations as target texts, if there are multiple relations between the entity pairs or an entity belongs to multiple triplets, then it can be understood that this entity or entity pair has more abundant semantic information, and these entities will get more attention at the moment of decoding. Therefore, there are greater probabilities for the model to select them from the source texts. Thus, our method is more suitable for processing the relation extraction in entity overlap case than [9]. Again, Noveltagging [8] cannot assign multiple tags to a single word, which makes it impossible to extract overlapped relational triples.

6.3. Comparison of the Multiple Relational Triples Extraction Performance

We further divide the NYT11 test set and classify test set into 7 subclasses according to the relation number of the entity pairs in each sentence. We test the extraction capability of our model and MultiDecoder on each class which contains 1, 2, 3, 4, 5, 6 and >= 7 relational triples, respectively. The results are shown in Figure 4, we can see that as the number of relations contained in a sentence increases, the performance of MultiDecoder decreases. However, when the sentence has one to four relational triples, the effect of our model is gradually increasing, and achieves the best performance when the number of relations is 4. When the number of relations between the same entity pair is greater than 4, the extraction effects will gradually decrease.

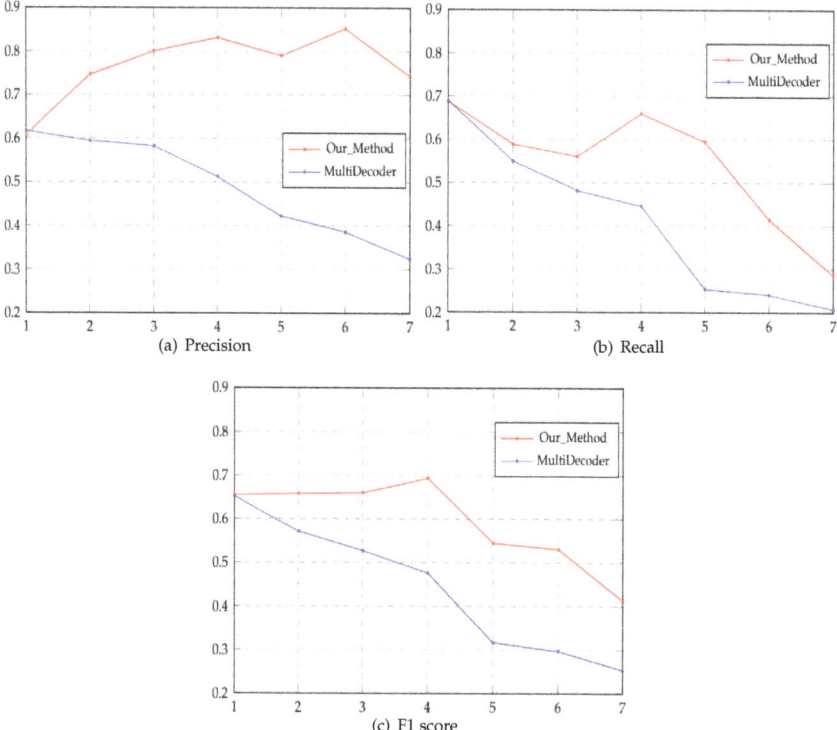

Figure 4. Results of Precision, Recall and F1 score of sentences that contains different number of triplets of our model and MultiDecoder on NYT11 dataset.

As the number of relations increases, extraction becomes more difficult, so the performance of MultiDecoder decreases gradually. For our model, as mentioned earlier, if there are multiple relations between entities, it will be more likely to be noticed when decoding and thus extracted, but this is within a certain threshold range (<=4), when the number of relations continues to increase, our model will also have a performance degradation.

We will analyze why F1 score is the highest when there are 4 relational triples in a sentence from the perspective of the proportion of entity pair overlap in each subclass. From Figures 2 and 3, we can see that our model is more suitable for dealing with entity pair overlap class than single entity overlap class. If there are more than two relations in the sentence, there will usually be one of two types of overlapping situations. Therefore, we analyze the proportion of entity pair overlap situation in these sentences which contain more than two relations. We count the number of relations that an entity pair contains when there are 2, 3, and 4 relations in the sentence respectively, if the entity pair contains 2 or more relations, it means there is entity pair overlap.

Table 4 shows the statistical results. From the table, we can see that in the subclass containing 4 triples in the sentence, has the largest proportion of entity overlap, reaching 80%, which is beyond the other subclasses, so we think this is the reason makes the model perform best on this subclass. The more relations are contained in sentences, the more complex the extraction is. When sentences contain more relations (>4), we consider the following two reasons leading to the performance degradation of the model. First, since our model generates relatively independent words rather than sentences with contextual contexts, it is relatively weak for LSTM to generate such a long sequence without coherent semantics. Secondly, because the training set contains less than 3% of the sentences with more than 4 relations, the model is not sufficient to learn this situation.

Table 4. Statistics Results.

	1	2	3	>=4	Percentage
sentences containing **2** relation triples	514	943	-	-	0.647
sentences containing **3** relation triples	210	72	182	-	0.547
sentences containing **4** relation triples	70	71	12	194	**0.800**

Bold numbers represent the largest proportion of entity pair overlap in the three cases.

6.4. Case Study

Table 5 shows three examples of our model extracted from the NYT11 dataset, corresponding to three categories: normal, single entity overlap, and entity pair overlap. The first sentence belongs to the normal class and does not have multiple relations. 'contains' means the relation of entity *America* and entity *Houston*. Our model generate 'contains' from predefined vocabulary and copy *America*, *Houston* from input text. The second sentence contains two relations in which there is overlap of a single entity, *Italy*. The third sentence contains two relations where entity pairs overlapped, <*Microsoft, Bill Gates*>. The entity pair in the last sentence is <*Somerset County, Quecreek*>, but the model only copies the last word 'County' in *Somerset County* from the original text, and does not extract entity completely. In this case, we think that the triple predicted by the model is wrong.

Table 5. Extraction examples of our models. The first column in the table is the input of the model, and the second column is the corresponding sentences of the output of the model. As described in Section 3.1 above, multiple relational triples in the model output are separated by '.' and ',' separates relational words and two entities within each triple.

Input	Output of Our Model
Kevin Steurer is helping complete arrangements for a family trip to **Houston** , **America** .	contains , America , Houston .
You can take the train from many cities in **Italy** to **Lecce** , which is about 45 min from **Otranto** by car.	contains , Italy , Lecce . contains , Italy , Otranto .
The real power at **Microsoft** resides with its longtime leaders—**Bill Gates**, the co-founder and chairman.	work_in , Bill Gates , Microsoft . founder , Microsoft , Bill Gates .
Somerset County has experienced disaster , with the crash of flight and nine coal miners trapped at **Quecreek**.	contains, County, Quecreek

7. Conclusions

In this paper, we propose to completely transform the entity-relation extraction task into the text generation task to solve the entity overlap problem in relation extraction. We use a pointer-based sequence-to-sequence framework to enable the model to copy words from the source text or to select words from the predefined vocabulary. We further analyze the extraction ability of our model on different degrees of entity overlap, and classify the sentences according to the different number of relations between two entities, and test the extraction effects of our model on these subclasses. We conduct experiments on the public datasets NYT10 and NYT11. The experimental results show that our method outperforms the baselines.

Author Contributions: Conceptualization, H.E. and S.X.; Data curation, H.E.; Formal analysis, H.E.; Funding acquisition, H.E.; Investigation, S.X.; Methodology, S.X.; Project administration, H.E.; Resources, H.E.; Software, H.E.; Supervision, H.E.; Validation, H.E., S.X. and M.S.; Visualization, H.E.; Writing—original draft, S.X.; Writing—review & editing, H.E., S.X. and M.S.

Funding: This work was supported in part by the National Key R&D Program of China under Grant SQ2018YFB140079.

Conflicts of Interest: The authors declare no conflict of interest.

Abbreviations

The following abbreviations are used in this manuscript:

RC   Relation Classification
NER   Named Entity Recognition
LSTM Long Short-Term Memory
RNN   Recurrent Neural Network
CNN   Convolutional Neural Network

References

1. Zhao, M.; Wang, H.; Guo, J.; Liu, D.; Xie, C.; Liu, Q.; Cheng, Z. Construction of an Industrial Knowledge Graph for Unstructured Chinese Text Learning. *Appl. Sci.* **2019**, *9*, 2720.
2. Cai, R.; Zhang, X.; Wang, H. Bidirectional recurrent convolutional neural network for relation classification. In Proceedings of the 54th Annual Meeting of the Association for Computational Linguistics (Volume 1: Long Papers), Berlin, Germany, 7–12 August 2016; Volume 1, pp. 756–765.
3. Hashimoto, K.; Miwa, M.; Tsuruoka, Y.; Chikayama, T. Simple customization of recursive neural networks for semantic relation classification. In Proceedings of the 2013 Conference on Empirical Methods in Natural Language Processing, Seattle, WA, USA, 18–21 October 2013; pp. 1372–1376.
4. Zeng, D.; Liu, K.; Lai, S.; Zhou, G.; Zhao, J. Relation classification via convolutional deep neural network. In Proceedings of the COLING 2014, the 25th International Conference on Computational Linguistics: Technical Papers, Dublin, Ireland, 23–29 August 2014; pp. 2335–2344.
5. Katiyar, A.; Cardie, C. Investigating lstms for joint extraction of opinion entities and relations. In Proceedings of the 54th Annual Meeting of the Association for Computational Linguistics (Volume 1: Long Papers), Berlin, Germany, 7–12 August 2016; Volume 1, pp. 919–929.
6. Katiyar, A.; Cardie, C. Going out on a limb: Joint extraction of entity mentions and relations without dependency trees. In Proceedings of the 55th Annual Meeting of the Association for Computational Linguistics (Volume 1: Long Papers), Vancouver, BC, Canada, 30 July–4 August 2017; Volume 1, pp. 917–928.
7. Miwa, M.; Bansal, M. End-to-end relation extraction using lstms on sequences and tree structures. *arXiv* **2016**, arXiv:1601.00770.
8. Zheng, S.; Wang, F.; Bao, H.; Hao, Y.; Zhou, P.; Xu, B. Joint extraction of entities and relations based on a novel tagging scheme. *arXiv* **2017**, arXiv:1706.05075.
9. Zeng, X.; Zeng, D.; He, S.; Liu, K.; Zhao, J. Extracting Relational Facts by an End-to-End Neural Model with Copy Mechanism. In Proceedings of the 56th Annual Meeting of the Association for Computational Linguistics (Volume 1: Long Papers), Melbourne, Australia, 15–20 July 2018; Volume 1, pp. 506–514.
10. Christopoulou, F.; Miwa, M.; Ananiadou, S. A Walk-based Model on Entity Graphs for Relation Extraction. In Proceedings of the 56th Annual Meeting of the Association for Computational Linguistics (Volume 2: Short Papers), Melbourne, Australia, 15–20 July 2018; Volume 2, pp. 81–88.
11. Wang, S.; Zhang, Y.; Che, W.; Liu, T. Joint Extraction of Entities and Relations Based on a Novel Graph Scheme. In Proceedings of the IJCAI, Stockholm, Sweden, 13–19 July 2018; pp. 4461–4467.
12. Nallapati, R.; Zhai, F.; Zhou, B. Summarunner: A recurrent neural network based sequence model for extractive summarization of documents. In Proceedings of the Thirty-First AAAI Conference on Artificial Intelligence, San Francisco, CA, USA, 4–9 February 2017.
13. Zhang, Y.; Li, D.; Wang, Y.; Fang, Y.; Xiao, W. Abstract Text Summarization with a Convolutional Seq2seq Model. *Appl. Sci.* **2019**, *9*, 1665.
14. Bahdanau, D.; Cho, K.; Bengio, Y. Neural machine translation by jointly learning to align and translate. *arXiv* **2014**, arXiv:1409.0473.
15. Cheng, Y.; Yang, Q.; Liu, Y.; Sun, M.; Xu, W. Joint training for pivot-based neural machine translation. In Proceedings of the IJCAI, Melbourne, Australia, 19–25 August 2017.

16. See, A.; Liu, P.J.; Manning, C.D. Get to the point: Summarization with pointer-generator networks. *arXiv* **2017**, arXiv:1704.04368.
17. Socher, R.; Huval, B.; Manning, C.D.; Ng, A.Y. Semantic compositionality through recursive matrix-vector spaces. In Proceedings of the 2012 Joint Conference on Empirical Methods in Natural Language Processing and Computational Natural Language Learning, Jeju Island, Korea, 12–14 July 2012; pp. 1201–1211.
18. Xu, K.; Feng, Y.; Huang, S.; Zhao, D. Semantic relation classification via convolutional neural networks with simple negative sampling. *arXiv* **2015**, arXiv:1506.07650.
19. Santos, C.N.D.; Xiang, B.; Zhou, B. Classifying relations by ranking with convolutional neural networks. *arXiv* **2015**, arXiv:1504.06580.
20. Xu, Y.; Mou, L.; Li, G.; Chen, Y.; Peng, H.; Jin, Z. Classifying relations via long short term memory networks along shortest dependency paths. In Proceedings of the 2015 Conference on Empirical Methods in Natural Language Processing, Lisbon, Portugal, 17–21 September 2015; pp. 1785–1794.
21. Yu, X.; Lam, W. Jointly Identifying Entities and Extracting Relations in Encyclopedia Text via A Graphical Model Approach. In Proceedings of the International Conference on Coling, Beijing, China, 23–27 August 2010.
22. Zheng, S.; Hao, Y.; Lu, D.; Bao, H.; Xu, J.; Hao, H.; Xu, B. Joint entity and relation extraction based on a hybrid neural network. *Neurocomputing* **2017**, *257*, 59–66.
23. Riedel, S.; Yao, L.; McCallum, A. Modeling relations and their mentions without labeled text. In *Joint European Conference on Machine Learning and Knowledge Discovery in Databases*; Springer: Berlin/Heidelberg, Germany, 2010; pp. 148–163.
24. Ren, X.; Wu, Z.; He, W.; Qu, M.; Voss, C.R.; Ji, H.; Abdelzaher, T.F.; Han, J. Cotype: Joint extraction of typed entities and relations with knowledge bases. In Proceedings of the 26th International Conference on World Wide Web, Perth, Australia, 3–7 April 2017; pp. 1015–1024.

© 2019 by the authors. Licensee MDPI, Basel, Switzerland. This article is an open access article distributed under the terms and conditions of the Creative Commons Attribution (CC BY) license (http://creativecommons.org/licenses/by/4.0/).

Article

Information Extraction from Electronic Medical Records Using Multitask Recurrent Neural Network with Contextual Word Embedding

Jianliang Yang [1], Yuenan Liu [1], Minghui Qian [1,*], Chenghua Guan [2] and Xiangfei Yuan [2]

1. School of Information Resource Management, Renmin University of China, 59 Zhongguancun Avenue, Beijing 100872, China
2. School of Economics and Resource Management, Beijing Normal University, 19 Xinjiekou Outer Street, Beijing 100875, China
* Correspondence: qmh@ruc.edu.cn; Tel.: +86-139-1031-3638

Received: 13 August 2019; Accepted: 26 August 2019; Published: 4 September 2019

Abstract: Clinical named entity recognition is an essential task for humans to analyze large-scale electronic medical records efficiently. Traditional rule-based solutions need considerable human effort to build rules and dictionaries; machine learning-based solutions need laborious feature engineering. For the moment, deep learning solutions like Long Short-term Memory with Conditional Random Field (LSTM–CRF) achieved considerable performance in many datasets. In this paper, we developed a multitask attention-based bidirectional LSTM–CRF (Att-biLSTM–CRF) model with pretrained Embeddings from Language Models (ELMo) in order to achieve better performance. In the multitask system, an additional task named entity discovery was designed to enhance the model's perception of unknown entities. Experiments were conducted on the 2010 Informatics for Integrating Biology & the Bedside/Veterans Affairs (I2B2/VA) dataset. Experimental results show that our model outperforms the state-of-the-art solution both on the single model and ensemble model. Our work proposes an approach to improve the recall in the clinical named entity recognition task based on the multitask mechanism.

Keywords: clinical named entity recognition; information extraction; multitask model; long short-term memory; conditional random field

1. Introduction

Along with the popularization of medical information systems, more and more electronic medical records (EMR) are produced. As most of the content in EMRs involves unstructured texts, interpretation from specialists is needed to acquire relevant information in EMRs. However, in the face of large-scale EMRs, automated solutions are indispensable. Clinical named entity recognition (CNER) is a particular case in natural language processing (NLP) information extraction tasks, and it aims to extract specific conceptions from unstructured texts, such as problems, medical tests, and treatments [1], which is an essential process for transforming unstructured EMR texts into structured medical data. A highly effective CNER solution will help improve the efficiency of analyzing large-scale EMRs, thus supporting extensive medical research and the development of medical information systems.

Traditional clinical named entity solutions are rule-based, for example, Medical Language Extraction and Encoding System (MedLEE) [2], MetaMap [3], clinical Text Analysis and Knowledge Extraction System (cTAKES) [4], and KnowledgeMap [5]. Rule-based systems need considerable human effort to build basic rules and sometimes a specialized sub-field dictionary, which is specific to the existing entities, with a weak ability to recognize new entities and misspellings [6]. Rule-based systems have a high precision score; however, due to the limited rules, they have a low recall in general [7]. Given the disadvantages of rule-based systems, systems based on machine learning were proposed for implementing clinical information extraction to reduce the reliance on human-built rules and dictionaries. Furthermore, an increasing number of public medical sequence labeling datasets such as the Center for Informatics for Integrating Biology and the Bedside (I2B2) 2010 [8] and Semantic Evaluation (SemEval) 2014 [9] offer data fundamentals for training machine learning models. Machine learning models like support vector machine (SVM), conditional random field (CRF), and hidden Markov model (HMM) achieved superior results [10–12]. Among these models, linear chain CRF [13] could be one of the most widely used algorithms on account of its strong ability to model the state transition in the token sequence and tag sequence. Compared to rule-based systems, systems based on machine learning let the system learn rules based on the clinical records instead of prior defined rules, which enhances the system's ability to identify unknown entities.

Solutions based on machine learning usually contain two main processes: feature engineering and classification [7]. However, the feature engineering process is a weak link in machine learning systems. Researchers need to manually select possible features and design feature combinations, which is time-consuming, and the features selected could be exclusive to the given task. Being limited by the cognitive differences and deficiencies of humans, manually identified features are incomplete [14]. With the development of deep learning, more researchers focused on deep learning models to implement named entity recognition. Compared to machine learning-based solutions, the advantage of deep learning can free the feature engineering part by changing it to an automated process in the training process. Among deep NLP studies, one branch of recurrent neural networks, the long short-term memory network (LSTM), is a prevalent model for feature extraction due to its ability to keep memories of preceding contents of each token [15]. Recent works used bi-directional LSTM (biLSTM) to extract features and a CRF model to infer sequence labels, called the biLSTM–CRF hybrid model. Compared to machine learning algorithms, the biLSTM–CRF model achieved considerable performance compared to previous machine learning models [16–19]. Furthermore, biLSTM–CRF models use unsupervised pretrained word embeddings as features instead of manually engineered features, which reduces human factors in the system.

Recently, contextual word embeddings such as Embeddings from Language Models (ELMo) [20] and Bidirectional Encoder Representations from Transformers (BERT) [21] brought new improvements to the named entity recognition (NER) task. Embedding algorithms like Word2vec [22] and GloVe [23] are based on the meanings of words (the meaning is speculated by word co-occurrences), and they map each word to a vector using a language model. However, in different contexts, the same word may have different meanings. For instance, the meaning of the word "bank" in "go to the riverbank" and "go to the bank to deposit" is different. Contextual word embedding algorithms solve this problem by giving various embedding vectors of the same word in various contexts [20,21]. In CNER studies, models with pretrained contextual word embeddings in medical corpora outperformed those with Word2vec and GloVe [24].

With the proposal of contextual word embedding, methods like character combined embeddings and attention mechanism are yet to be tested, and prior studies based on deep learning did not pay enough attention to the system's perception of unknown entities, as the recall of those systems is relatively low. Our study hypothesizes that, through combining contextual word embedding, multitask, and attention mechanisms, the system can achieve better performance than previous works and recognize more unknown entities. Thus, we propose a multitask biLSTM–CRF model with pretrained ELMo contextual word embeddings to extract clinical named entities. The multitask mechanism separates the NER task into two parts: named entity discovery and named entity classification, in which the classification task is the primary task, and the discovery task is the secondary task. Usually, the secondary task in a multitask model can be seen as a regularizer [25]; this mechanism was implemented to reduce noise in the social media named entity recognition task [26]. We constructed the multitask mechanism to enhance the model's perception of unknown entities to improve recall.

In addition, we drew a self-attention mechanism into the model. Experiments were done on the I2B2 2010/VA [8] dataset. The results show that our model outperforms the typical LSTM–CRF models with ELMo contextual word embeddings. Our work provides an approach to improve the system's performance and perception of unknown entities based on multitask mechanism.

The paper is organized as follows: Section 2 summarizes previous studies on methods of clinical named entity recognition and describes the multitask recurrent neural network model and the ELMo pretrained contextual word embedding. Section 3 presents the experimental setting and results. Section 4 discusses the experimental results. At last, Section 5 concludes the findings of this study and describes some possible future directions based on this work.

2. Materials and Methods

In this section, we describe related work on clinical named entity recognition and how our model was designed. Section 2.1 describes related work on clinical named entity recognition. Section 2.2 describes the algorithm of ELMo contextual word embedding and its pretraining corpus. Section 2.3 describes the structure of the bi-directional LSTM with attention layers. Section 2.4 describes the multitask mechanism, which consists of the sequential inference task and the entity discovery task.

2.1. Related Work on Clinical Named Entity Recognition

The development of clinical named entity recognition systems approximately goes through three stages, which are rule-based systems (also known as knowledge-based or lexicon-based), feature engineered machine learning systems, and deep learning systems. Rule-based systems mainly rely on search patterns in the form of characters and symbols which contain the content information of some specific entity. Once the search patterns are built, the rule-based system searches records based on these pre-defined patterns. Prior works commonly built regular expressions to express the recognizing rules for named entities, and those regular expressions contained names or part of the names of target entities. Savova et al. extracted peripheral arterial disease (PAD) if the phrase in medical notes matched the pre-defined regular expressions. [27]; Bedmar et al. used similar methods to extract drug entities [28]. The rule-based system works like a retrieval system, and it compares every phrase to its regular expressions to check if the phrase is a named entity. However, the system can recognize an entity only if it fits some regular expressions; in other words, if the system has more regular expressions, it would recognize more entities. A well-performed rule-based system needs abundant lexicon resources to pre-define search patterns [6,29]. Knowledge bases like Unified Medical Language System (UMLS) [30] and DrugBank [31] are commonly used for the pre-definition work. Furthermore, a rule-based system can accurately identify a named entity that appears in its lexicon but becomes helpless for named entities not in its lexicon. Hence, the rule-based system usually has high precision but low recall [7]. Also, building and maintaining a domain-specific lexicon with regular expressions needs many resources. In the face of those shortcomings, machine learning-based systems were put forward.

Machine learning-based systems allow the system itself to learn rules and patterns from clinical records, which decreases the manual work in constructing them. SVM, logistic regression (LR), and CRF are the most commonly implemented algorithms in these systems [29]. These systems achieved relatively excellent performance [32–35]. For implementing algorithms like SVM, LR, and CRF, pivotal content and structural information should be provided and converted into particular forms to allow the learning model to understand sequences and learn patterns. Therefore, feature engineering becomes essential in machine learning-based systems [14]. For example, Roberts et al. implemented SVM to recognize anatomic locations from medical reports, and nine features including lemmas of words, grammatical dependency structure information, and path along the syntactic parse tree were engineered [32]. Sarker et al. implemented three classification approaches including SVM, naïve Bayes, and maximum entropy to extract adverse drug reaction entities; n-grams features, UMLS semantic types, sentiment scores, and topic-based features were engineered [33]. Rochefort et al.

identified geriatric competency exposures from students' clinical notes with LR; features including the number of notes, bag of words features, concept code features, Term Frequency–Inverse Document Frequency (TF-IDF) features, and semantic type features were engineered [34]. Deleger et al. recognized pediatric appendicitis score (PAS) from clinical records with CRF, and more than 20 features were engineered [35]. Manual feature selection is time-consuming, and, as there is no general standard, the manually identified features are usually incomplete [14]. Moreover, some of the features are also based on the medical knowledge base [33,34], which indicates that feature engineering processes also need abundant knowledge resources. Feature engineered machine learning systems can learn rules and patterns through a training process, which dramatically improves efficiency, and studies showed that these systems achieve considerable performance [32–35]. However, the system's performance highly relies on the features that humans selected, which decreases the robustness of the system.

Along with the development of deep learning in NLP, systems based on deep learning methods were proposed. Compared to systems based on machine learning algorithms, one of the best advantages of deep learning systems is the avoidance of manual work. It benefits from unsupervised pretrained embeddings like Word2vec [22] and GloVe [23]. Actually, the first neural network architecture proposed by Collobert et al. for NER tasks constructed features by orthographic information and lexicons which also contained manual work [25], whereas Collobert et al. improved his model by replacing those manually built features with word embedding, which converts a word into an N-dimension vector through an unsupervised training process [36]. Studies on CNER based on deep learning methods mainly follow two directions. One is to optimize the learning model, and the other is to construct or pre-train better embeddings, which can provide more information for the learning model.

For the studies on learning models, Collobert et al. firstly proposed a model with convolution layers to capture local information in the sequence [36]. Models based on Recurrent Neural Network (RNN) were proposed due to its superior ability in sequence learning. Huang et al. proposed a bi-directional LSTM model for sequence labeling and showed that assembling a CRF layer on top of an LSTM could improve performance [37]. Lample et al. proposed the biLSTM–CRF model for NER [38]. The biLSTM with CRF-based model showed its success in many CNER studies. Chalapathy et al. extracted clinical concepts with a biLSTM–CRF architecture, and achieved 83.88% F1 score, 84.36% precision score, and 83.41% recall score on the 2010 I2B2/VA dataset (the version with 170 training notes), which was better than all prior work [7]. Xu et al. extracted disease named entities with the same architecture, and achieved 80.22% F1, which was also better than prior work [39]. Wu et al. compared CRFs, Structured Support Vector Machines (SSVMs), semi-Markov, Convolutional Neural Network (CNN), and biLSTM–CRF on the 2010 I2B2/VA dataset (the version with 349 training notes) and found that biLSTM–CRF achieved the best performance among all learning models with 85.94% F1 score [14]. Xu et al. combined biLSTM–CRF with a global attention mechanism, and conducted experiments on the 2010 I2B2/VA dataset (the version with 170 training notes). They achieved 85.71% F1 score, 86.27% precision score, and 85.15% recall score, which performed the best compared to prior work [19]. At present, biLSTM–CRF is the most approved learning architecture for CNER tasks.

For studies on embeddings, word embedding was widely used in NER tasks. Chalapathy et al. compared random embedding, Word2vec, and GloVe in biLSTM–CRF, and found that the system with GloVe outperformed others [7]. Habibi et al. showed that the pre-training process of word embedding is crucial for NER systems, and, for domain-specific NER tasks, domain-specific embeddings could improve the system's performance [40]. Liu et al. used pretrained Word2vec embeddings on (Medical Literature Analysis and Retrieval System Online) MEDLINE and Wikipedia corpus and achieved considerable performance compared to other studies [41]. As a word can be seen as a sequence of characters, and characters in a word contain parts of a word's meaning and orthographic information, character-level embedding is quite useful for NER tasks. Normally, character-level embeddings are not pretrained; they are initialized randomly and trained by a sub-CNN or sub-RNN in the whole architecture. Liu et al. combined Word2vec embedding and an LSTM-trained character-level embedding as features of a word, which performed much better than only word embeddings [41].

Zeng et al. combined a Word2vec embedding, and a CNN-trained character-level embedding as features of a word, which performed better for some indicators [18]. Along with the development of contextual word embeddings, studies [20,21] showed that contextual embeddings achieved better performance than previous work [7,14,19]. Just like Word2vec embedding, a domain-specific pretrained contextual embedding model performs better in the domain-specific NER task. Zhu et al. compared general pretrained ELMo and clinical pretrained ELMo, and found that clinical ELMo performed much better than general ELMo. They achieved 88.60% F1 score, 89.34% precision score, and 87.87% recall score on the 2010 I2B2/VA dataset (the version with 170 training notes) [24]. Si et al. compared Word2vec, GloVe, fastText, ELMo, BERT-base, BERT-large, and Bio-BERT, and found that BERT-large achieved the best performance [42].

In general, systems with biLSTM–CRF architecture and contextual word embedding set the new state-of-the-art record in many CNER datasets at present [24,42]. However, methods that combine character-level embedding and attention mechanisms, such as in References [41] and [19], with contextual word embeddings are yet to be tested. Moreover, among the existing studies [7,14,19,40–42], the systems all had a relatively low recall, which indicates that those systems were not sensitive enough to unknown entities. Aguilar et al. proposed a multitask system for NER in social media in order to reduce noise, and their system achieved the highest F1 score and decent precision score compared to other systems [26]. Aguilar et al.'s work indicates that we can try to introduce the multitask mechanism in CNER tasks to make the system more sensitive to emerging clinical concepts.

In our work, we design a multitask attention-based biLSTM–CRF model (Att-biLSTM–CRF) to test the effect of the multitask mechanism in the CNER task. Compared with rule-based systems and machine learning-based systems, our work is based on deep learning, whereby we do not rely on human-designed rules and manually engineered features, which significantly improves our system's robustness and usability. Compared to prior work based on deep learning, we combine the biLSTM–CRF architecture, clinical pretrained context embedding, attention mechanism, and multitask mechanism in order to achieve better performance than prior work. Specifically, we test whether the multitask mechanism can improve the system's recall.

2.2. ELMo Contextual Word Embedding

ELMo is a pretrained contextual word embedding model. It is a bidirectional *LSTM* (biLSTM) language model which can generate context-dependent word embeddings [20]. The prediction process of the biLSTM language model is to maximize the log-likelihood of the probability of token *i* from both directions.

$$\sum_{i=1}^{N} (\log p(t_i \mid t_1, t_2 \ldots, t_{i-1}; \Theta_x, \overrightarrow{\Theta}_{LSTM}, \Theta_s) + \log p(t_i \mid t_{i+1}, t_{i+2} \ldots, t_N; \Theta_x, \overleftarrow{\Theta}_{LSTM}, \Theta_s)), \quad (1)$$

where t_i is token *i*, $(t_1, t_2 \ldots t_{i-1})$ is the forward context of token *i*, $(t_{i+1}, t_{i+2} \ldots, t_N)$ is the backward context of token *i*, Θ_x represents the parameters of the token's representations, $\overrightarrow{\Theta}_{LSTM}$ represents the *LSTM* parameters in the forward direction, $\overleftarrow{\Theta}_{LSTM}$ represents the *LSTM* parameters in the backward direction, and Θ_s represents the parameters of the Softmax layer. Then, ELMo combines the representation from each layer of token *i* as follows:

$$R_i = \left\{ h_{i,j}^{LSTM} \middle| j = 0, 1, \ldots, L \right\}, \quad (2)$$

where R_i is the representation of token i, and $h_{i,j}^{LSTM}$ is the hidden layer which is equal to $[\overrightarrow{h}_{i,j}^{LSTM} ; \overleftarrow{h}_{i,j}^{LSTM}]$. ELMo collapses the representations from all layers into one single vector. For a specific task, the ELMo representation of token i is calculated by

$$ELMo_i^{task} = \gamma^{task} \sum_{j=0}^{L} s_j^{task} h_{k,j}^{LSTM}, \qquad (3)$$

where γ^{task} is the scalar factor to adjust the scale of vector based on the feature of a specific task, and s_j^{task} is the normalized weight of each layer.

ELMo showed better performance in several NLP tasks compared to other context-independent embedding models like Word2vec and GloVe [20]. For some specific domains, a domain-pretrained ELMo model had better performance than generalized ELMo [43,44]. In the clinical NER task, the LSTM–CRF model with ELMo pretrained on the medical corpus Multiparameter Intelligent Monitoring in Intensive Care III (MIMIC III) [45] significantly outperformed the same model with generalized ELMo [24]. In our work, we use the MIMIC III medical corpus pretrained ELMo to produce word embeddings as input variables. Thus, the main comparison is between our work and previous work with clinical ELMo embeddings.

2.3. The Att-biLSTM Model

A recurrent neural network (RNN) is a type of neural network designed to handle sequential data. For sequential data such as stock price data within a period and every token in one sentence, the data in step t typically have some relationships with the previous step. In a language model, the RNN can "remember" the information before the current step, which makes it suitable for sequence prediction [46]. Particularly, for a sequential data series $x_{task} = \{x_0, x_1, x_2, \ldots, x_t, \ldots, x_n\}$ where x_t is the t step of x_{task}, the model calculates the hidden cell output h_t by x_t and h_{t-1} for each step at first; then, computing hidden state outputs of all the steps, the model computes its output o_{task}, and each o_t is calculated by h_t. The mathematical expression of the forward propagation process is as follows:

$$i_t = \tanh(Ux_t), \qquad (4)$$

$$h_t = Wh_{t-1} + i_t + bias_h, \qquad (5)$$

$$o_t = Vh_t + bias_o, \qquad (6)$$

where U is the weight of the input layer, W is the weight in the hidden cell, and V is the weight of the output layer. U, W, and V are shared for all steps. Commonly, after computing the outputs, another layer is added based on the task. For a classification task, a softmax function is usually used to normalize the probability of each class.

Theoretically, a naïve RNN model can handle the previous information for each step. However, in practice, the problems of vanishing gradient and exploding gradient in backpropagation through time (BPTT) result in it failing to learn enough information from previous steps and handle long-term dependencies [47]. Facing this dilemma, the LSTM model was implemented. The LSTM model combats the vanishing gradient and exploding gradient problem by its gating and cell state mechanism [15]. The mechanism includes a forget gate f, an input gate I, and a cell state C. The forward propagation process in an LSTM cell is as follows:

$$f_t = \sigma(W_{fh}h_{t-1} + W_{fx}x_t + bias_f), \qquad (7)$$

$$I_t = \sigma(W_{ih}h_{t-1} + W_{ix}x_t + bias_i), \qquad (8)$$

$$C_t = f_tC_{t-1} + i_t\tanh(W_{Ch}h_{t-1} + W_{cx}x_t + bias_C), \qquad (9)$$

$$z_t = \sigma(W_{zh}h_{t-1} + W_{zx}x_t + bias_o), \tag{10}$$

$$h_t = z_t \tanh(C_t), \tag{11}$$

where f_t is the forget weight, and σ is the sigmoid function which restricts f_t between [0, 1]. In the range, 0 means to completely forget previous information, and 1 means to completely remember the previous information. I_t is the input weight of cell t, and it decides how much information should enter the cell. C_t is the value of the current cell t. It consists of previous information adjusted by the forget gate and current information by the input gate. At last, the output of the LSTM cell h_t is the cell state value normalized by a tanh function and then adjusted by z_t, in which z_t decides how much information should be added to the output.

In our work, the model needs to decide a token's label not only by the previous tokens but also by the tokens behind it; thus, we use a two-layer biLSTM to gather information on each token from both directions (shown in Figure 1). As described above, a single bidirectional LSTM generates an output $\overrightarrow{h_t}$ and, for a biLSTM, it uses two independent single LSTM layers to generate an output $[\overrightarrow{h_t}, \overleftarrow{h_t}]$. $[\overrightarrow{h_t}, \overleftarrow{h_t}]$ is the final representation of token t in our model.

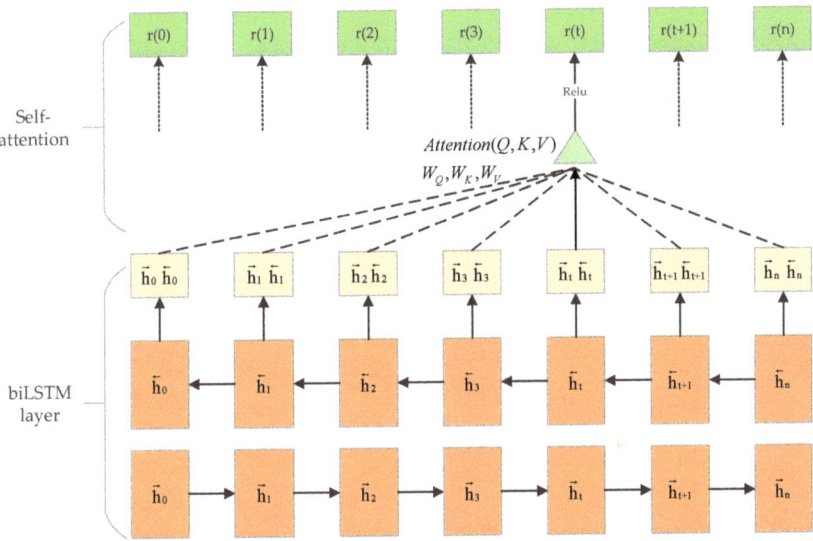

Figure 1. The architecture of attention-based bidirectional Long Short-term Memory (Att-biLSTM). The biLSTM layer captures input data and generates embeddings from two directions. The embedding of each token from two directions is concatenated into one vector as the output of the biLSTM layer. Then, the vectors go through a multi-head self-attention layer. A relu function activates the outputs of the attention layer. Dropout is applied in the biLSTM layer. This part is a part of the encoder in our model.

Considering that, when human beings classify a token into some kind of entity, they may rely on some similar representations around it, we add a multi-head self-attention layer [48] after the biLSTM layer. In this layer, we compute the attention score by a query vector (Q), a key vector (K), and a value vector (V).

$$\text{Attention}(Q, K, V) = \text{softmax}\left(\frac{QK^T}{\sqrt{d_k}}\right)V, \tag{12}$$

where d_k is the number of dimensions in K to scale the dot product of Q and K. Based on the self-attention mechanism, Q, K, and V are computed from the same input, which is the biLSTM representation in our model. Specifically, $Q = [\overrightarrow{h}_t, \overleftarrow{h}_t]W_Q$, $K = [\overrightarrow{h}_t, \overleftarrow{h}_t]W_K$, and $V = [\overrightarrow{h}_t, \overleftarrow{h}_t]W_V$. We use two heads to capture information from different perspectives; then, we concatenate the attention matrices and send them into a dense layer to obtain the final representation. The architecture of the Att-biLSTM part in our work is shown in Figure 1.

2.4. Multitask Mechanism

After the model obtains the representations from the Att-biLSTM, it separates the NER task into a primary task and a secondary task. The primary task is a sequential inference task, and the secondary task is an entity discovery task. The two tasks are conducted simultaneously.

In the sequential inference task, the representation vectors are sent to a CRF model to decide which label should be assigned on each token. The reason that we do not use a dense layer and softmax function to estimate the class of each token is that the label of each token has sequential dependence, and the softmax function can capture the dependence information. For instance, it is impossible that a label representing the beginning of an entity follows another beginning label in one entity in the real data, but it may happen in the prediction if we use a dense layer and a softmax function. The CRF model can infer the dependence of token t with token $t-1$ and token $t+1$ in a sequence by its state transition algorithm [13]. Thus, a CRF layer is used to infer the sequence in our model. Specifically, giving a sequence $x = \{x_0, \ldots, x_t, \ldots, x_n\}$ and its label sequence $y_{task} = \{y_0, \ldots, y_t, \ldots, y_n\}$, it complies with the following Markov property:

$$P(y_t|x, y_0, \ldots y_{t-1}, y_{t+1}, \ldots, y_n) = P(y_t|x, y_{t-1}, y_{t+1}). \tag{13}$$

Then, $P(y_{task}|x)$ is a chain conditional random field, and the conditional probability of y_{task} is

$$P(y_{task1}|x) = \frac{exp\left(\sum_{i,k}^{n,K_1} \lambda_k t_k(y_{i-1}, y_i, x, i) + \sum_{i,l}^{n,K_2} \mu_l s_l(y_i, x, i)\right)}{Z(x)}, \tag{14}$$

where t_k is a transition eigenfunction, s_l is a state feature function, λ_k and μ_l are weight parameters, K_1 is the number of transition features, and K_2 is the number of state features. $Z(x)$ is a normalization function to normalize the probability. t_k and λ_k can be united into one feature function: $f_k(y, x) = \sum_{i=1}^{n} f_k(y_{i-1}, y_i, x, i)$. Then, the probability of given sequence x with label sequences y_{task1} is expressed by the following equation:

$$P(y_{task1}|x; w) = \frac{exp\left(\sum_{k=1}^{m} \sum_{i=1}^{n} w_k f_k(y_{i-1}, y_i, x, i)\right)}{\sum_{y'=0}^{z} exp\left(\sum_{k=1}^{m} \sum_{i=1}^{n} w_k f_k(y'_{i-1}, y'_i, x, i)\right)}, \tag{15}$$

where w is the weight matrix of f_k, and z is the set of labels in the label sequence. To maximize $P(y_{task1}|x; w)$, we optimize w by the log-likelihood estimation algorithm. To obtain the label sequence y_{task1}, we use the Viterbi algorithm to decode the label sequence solved by the CRF layer. Before the representations enter the CRF layer, they go through a dense layer first, and this dense layer has 13 output neural cells which represent all 13 labels.

In the entity discovery task, the representations generated from the Att-biLSTM are sent into a binary classifier; this classifier classifies a token as being an entity or not. A dense layer with two output neural cells is used to represent the two classes, and a softmax function is used to normalize the probability. The following equation expresses the probability of given sequence x with label sequences y_{task2}:

$$P(y_{task2}|x; w) = \frac{\sum_{i=1}^{n} exp(x^T w_i)}{\sum_{k}^{K} \sum_{i=1}^{n} exp(x^T w_i^k)}. \tag{16}$$

In the backpropagation process, the loss values of two tasks are combined by a linear process, which is

$$loss_{total} = \gamma_1 loss_{t1} + \gamma_2 loss_{t2}, \tag{17}$$

where γ_1 and γ_2 are factors of two loss values, and they represent the priority of the two tasks. In every backpropagation process, the model computes the total loss and conducts gradient descent. The entire architecture of our model is shown in Figure 2. The source code of our model was published online in the Supplementary Materials.

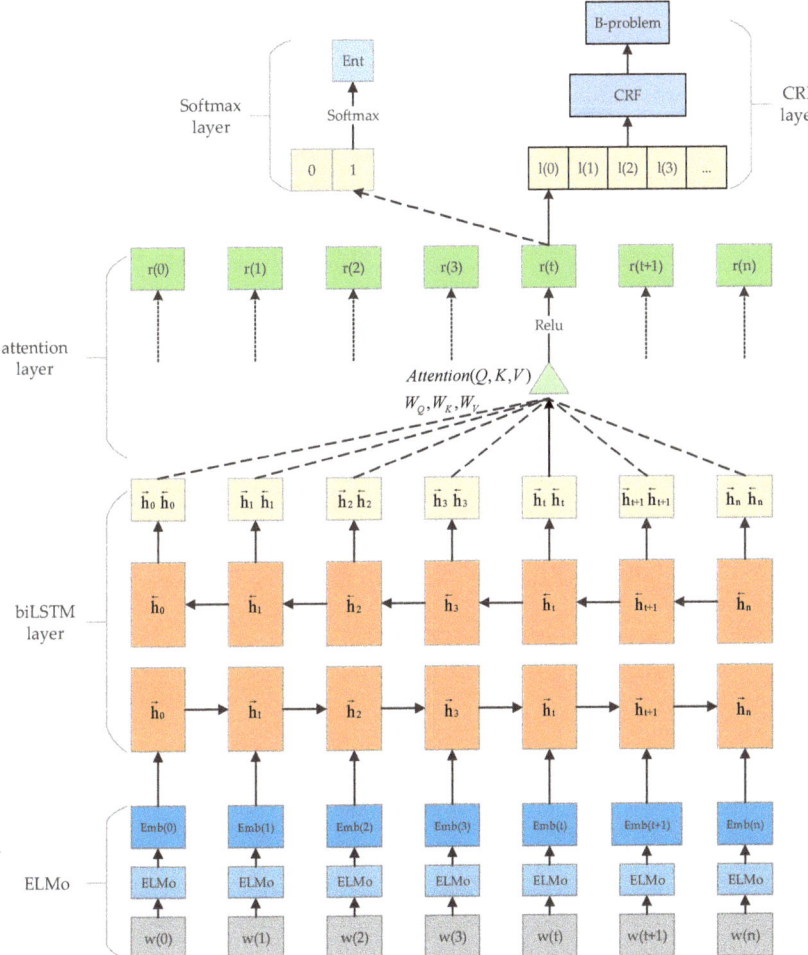

Figure 2. The architecture of our model. Firstly, the tokens in a sequence enter the pretrained Embeddings from Language Models (ELMo) model, and ELMo outputs the contextual embeddings of each token. Then, the Att-biLSTM layer receives the contextual embeddings and outputs the encoded vector of each token. At last, the encoded vectors are sent to the softmax layer to conduct the entity discovery task and to the Conditional Random Field (CRF) layer to decode the sequential labels synchronously.

3. Results

To test the model's performance, in this section, we describe the process of experiments and the experimental results. Section 3.1 describes the dataset we use. The dataset 2010 I2B2/VA is a public dataset for the CNER task, and several studies conducted experiments on this dataset [7,19,24]. Section 3.2 describes the experimental setting such as hyperparameters and the learning optimizer. Section 3.3 describes the evaluation metrics, for which exact precision, recall, and F1 are used. Section 3.4 describes the results of our experiments.

3.1. Dataset

To examine our model, we used the 2010 I2B2/VA dataset from the 2010 I2B2 challenge. This dataset is a set of medical records contributed by Partners Healthcare, Beth Israel Deaconess Medical Center, and the University of Pittsburgh Medical Center [8]. The records in the dataset are in text format, and the dataset is already separated into a training set and testing set. There are three different entities in the dataset: problem, test, and treatment. The descriptions of records, sentences, and tokens are shown in Table 1. In the training set, there are 7073 problem entities, 4844 test entities, and 4606 entities. In the testing set, there are 12,592 problem entities, 9225 test entities, and 9344 treatment entities.

Table 1. Descriptions of training set and testing set in the 2010 Informatics for Integrating Biology & the Bedside/ Veterans Affairs (i2b2/VA) dataset.

Dataset	Records	Sentences	Tokens	Tokens Per Sentence
Training set	170	16,315	149,666	9.17
Testing set	256	27,626	267,758	9.69

3.2. Experimental Setting

In our experiment, we labeled the data with BIEOS format (label prefix B is the token in the beginning of an entity, label prefix I is the token inside an entity, label prefix E is the token at the end of an entity, label prefix O is the token outside any entity, and label prefix S is a single entity). For the training progress, we used the Adam optimizer [49] to train the model and tune the hyperparameters by random search [50]. The early stopping strategy was used to prevent overfitting. The final hyperparameters are shown in Table 2. We implemented our model on the pytorch library on Python 3.7.

Table 2. Hyperparameters chosen in our work.

Hyperparameters	Value
Dimension of Embeddings from Language Models (ELMo)	1024
Bidirectional Long Short-term Memory (biLSTM) hidden size	256
Number of biLSTM layers	2
Number of attention heads	2
Dropout rate	0.5
Learning rate	0.001
Batch size	64
Epochs	100

3.3. Evaluation Metrics

The evaluation metric followed the regulation "Evaluation Methods and Procedures for 2010 I2B2/VA Challenge" [51]. We used the exact F1, exact precision, and exact recall score to evaluate the performance of our model as most works using this dataset did. "Exact" means that the concept entities extracted must match the ground-truth entities exactly both in terms of boundaries and concept type. The definitions of precision, recall, and F1 are shown below.

$$Precision_c = \frac{TP_c}{TP_c + FP_c},\tag{18}$$

$$Recall_c = \frac{TP_c}{TP_c + FN_c},\tag{19}$$

$$F1_c = \frac{2*(Recall_c * Precision_c)}{Recall_c + Precision_c},\tag{20}$$

where c is the tag of an entity; TP_c stands for the true positives of entity c, which means that the actual tag of this entity is c, and the predicted tag is also c; FP_c stands for the false positives, which means that the actual tag of this entity is not c, but the predicted tag is c; and FN_c stands for false negatives, which means that the actual tag of this entity is c, but the predicted tag is not c. Specifically, as we used the exact metrics, we treated a predicted entity as a true positive only if it matched both the boundary and tag type of the corresponding actual entity. Micro F1 was used to integrate all $F1_c$.

3.4. Results

We trained the model with different ransom seeds 10 times, and the mean and standard deviations of metrics are reported. Table 3 shows the performance of our model, and the performances from other models which experimented on the same dataset. Our solution in single-model mode achieved an exact F1 score of 87.53 ± 0.11%, exact precision of 87.75 ± 0.18%, and exact recall of 87.32 ± 0.26%. Before our work, the best performing single model was the "ELMo (clinical) + BiLSTM–CRF (single) model" [24], which also used clinical pretrained ELMo word embeddings. We obtained an improvement of 0.69% in mean F1, an improvement of 0.31% in mean precision, and an improvement of 1.06% in mean recall compared with the best performing model.

Table 3. Results of experiments on the 2010 i2b2/VA dataset.

Solutions	F1	Precision	Recall
GloVe-biLSTM–CRF [7]	83.88	84.36	83.41
Clinical Named Entity Recognition system (CliNER) 2.0 [52]	83.8	84.0	83.6
Att-biLSTM–CRF + Transfer [19]	85.71	86.27	85.15
ELMo (General) + BiLSTM–CRF (Single) [24]	82.54 ± 0.14	83.26 ± 0.25	81.84 ± 0.22
Word2vec + multitask-Att-biLSTM–CRF	78.70	79.98	77.47
ELMo (General) + multitask-Att-biLSTM–CRF	83.00	82.91	83.09
ELMo (Clinical) + BiLSTM–CRF (Single) [24]	86.84 ± 0.16	87.44 ± 0.27	86.25 ± 0.26
Our model (Single)	87.53 ± 0.11	87.75± 0.18	87.32 ± 0.26
ELMo (Clinical) + BiLSTM–CRF (Ensemble) [24]	88.60	89.34	87.87
Our model (Ensemble)	88.78	89.11	88.46

Additionally, we build an ensemble model based on 10 single models trained on different random seeds [53]. The ensemble model classified tokens based on a voter mechanism that chose the most voted label by the 10 single models. The results of our ensemble model are also shown in Table 3. We can see that our ensemble model achieved an F1 score of 88.78, precision of 89.11, and recall of 88.46. Compared to the previous best solution "ELMo (clinical) + BiLSTM–CRF (ensemble)", our model improved by 0.18% in F1 and 0.59% in recall, but had a lower performance for precision (−0.23%). The F1 and precision had a slight variation between our model and the previous best solution, but we can see a noticeable improvement in recall, just like the comparison between the single models. The improvement in recall agrees with the aim of the multi-task mechanism in our model, which was to enhance the model's sensibility to unknown tokens. To see how the multitask mechanism performed if different embedding methods were implemented, we changed the embedding part of our system to general pretrained Word2vec and general pretrained ELMo, and the results are shown in Table 3. The result shows that the system with Word2vec embeddings performs not as good as we expected. The reason may be that the hyperparameters and label format of our system were adjusted for the contextual word embedding. However, the system with general ELMo performed better compared to the result in Reference [24]. The result indicates that the multitask mechanism may have better performance with contextual word embeddings.

The evaluation of the prediction for each type of medical entities is shown in Table 4. We can see that the performance of our system on predicting problem entities was better than the other two kinds of entities in all three indicators, and the prediction of medical test was a little worse than problem and treatment entities. The reason for this difference may be the imbalance of the training dataset, in which there were 7073 problem entities, 4844 test entities, and 4606 entities. However, the prediction results of the three entities were quite close with tiny standard deviations (0.21 F1 score, 0.25 precision, and 0.16 recall), which indicates that our system is stable when predicting the different types of entities.

Table 4. Evaluation of each type of entity.

Entity Type	F1	Precision	Recall
Medical Test	88.37	88.61	88.13
Problem	89.03	89.40	88.66
Treatment	88.96	89.34	88.58
SD	0.21	0.25	0.16

Some works using the 2010 I2B2/VA original dataset are not reported in Table 3, because those works used the original larger dataset of 2010 I2B2/VA which contained 349 records in its training set and 477 records in its testing set [41,42]. For some reason, I2B2 now only provides a smaller dataset with 170 records in the training set and 256 records in the testing set. Theoretically, the same model trained on the larger dataset should perform better than on the smaller dataset. However, our model performed even better than most models trained on the original larger dataset [12,41]. For the works conducted on the smaller dataset, the solution "ELMo (clinical) + BiLSTM–CRF (ensemble)" [24] was the previous state-of-the-art model, and the result shows that our model significantly outperformed the state-of-the-art model in recall and slightly outperformed it in F1 score.

4. Discussion

The experimental results both on the single model and ensemble model showed the ability to improve the system's recall using an additional entity discovery task. According to the results from previous CNER models [7,12,19,24,41,42], those models with a single task always had a relatively lower recall compared to their precision; however, it could be used to discover more entities in practice. In our model, the multitask mechanism was used to balance discovering more entities and correctly identifying entities, and the use of the additional task can be seen as a process to add extra weights to discovering clinical entities. For the models with a single task, the model optimizes parameters only by the loss of the ground-truth tags and estimated tags by cross-entropy. Compared to the models with a single task, the multitask model tends to optimize parameters based primarily on if a token is an entity, and correspondingly reduces the reliability on a token being assigned the right tag. In the backpropagation process, gradients are independent of each other in the softmax and CRF parts. Then, by backpropagating to the encoder parts, the gradients from the two parts are merged; thus, the multitask mechanism mainly changes the way of encoding.

5. Conclusions

In this paper, we firstly discussed recent work on clinical named entity recognition and highlighted the new improvements brought by contextual embeddings. Then, we proposed the multitask

Att-biLSTM–CRF model with contextual embeddings. The multitask mechanism separates the entity recognition task into two simultaneous sub-tasks, entity discovery and sequential inference. Our experiment conducted on the 2010 I2B2/VA dataset showed that our model achieved better performance than the previous state-of-the-art solution. Notably, our model improved the recall significantly, which agrees with what we expected.

Our algorithm improved the perception of unknown entities just as we hypothesized, which means that the system should have a better capability to deal with emerging medical concepts without extra training resources. This idea could not only be applied in medical concept extraction, but also other medical named entity recognition applications such as drug names and adverse drug reactions, as well as named entity recognition tasks in other fields. For future studies, we want to put forward two ideas. One is a transfer learning idea. We can already see the improvements brought by the multitask mechanism in this paper, and the multitask mechanism can be seen as a task-oriented regularizer. Therefore, it could be meaningful to train the model for the entity discovery task so as to regularize the model first, and then implement transfer learning to train the same model for the sequential inference task. Another idea is that, in previous work, character-level embedding was very useful for improving the system's performance; thus, it would be worthwhile to build a model with combined character-level embedding and contextual word embedding.

Supplementary Materials: The source code is available at https://github.com/jeffy129/multi_cner.

Author Contributions: Conceptualization, J.Y. and Y.L.; data curation, J.Y. and C.G.; methodology, J.Y. and M.Q.; resources, J.Y.; software, J.Y. and X.Y.; investigation, J.Y. and Y.L.; supervision, M.Q.; validation, J.Y. and M.Q.; visualization, J.Y. and Y.L.

Funding: This research was supported by the China Scholarship Council (CSC) (grant number: 201806360227), also was partially supported the Major Project for the Research and Application of Generic Technologies of National Quality Infrastructure (NQI) (grant number:2018YFF0215803-3) and the Ministry of Education in China (MOE) Project of Humanities and Social Sciences (grant number:18YJA630087).

Conflicts of Interest: The authors declare no conflicts of interest.

References

1. Meystre, S.M.; Savova, G.K.; Kipper-Schuler, K.C.; Hurdle, J.F. Extracting information from textual documents in the electronic health record: A review of recent research. *Yearb. Med. Inform.* **2008**, *17*, 128–144.
2. Friedman, C.; Alderson, P.O.; Austin, J.H.; Cimino, J.J.; Johnson, S.B. A general natural-language text processor for clinical radiology. *J. Am. Med. Inform. Assoc.* **1994**, *1*, 161–174. [CrossRef] [PubMed]
3. Aronson, A.R.; Lang, F.-M. An overview of MetaMap: Historical perspective and recent advances. *J. Am. Med. Inform. Assoc.* **2010**, *17*, 229–236. [CrossRef] [PubMed]
4. Savova, G.K.; Masanz, J.J.; Ogren, P.V.; Zheng, J.; Sohn, S.; Kipper-Schuler, K.C.; Chute, C.G. Mayo clinical Text Analysis and Knowledge Extraction System (cTAKES): Architecture, component evaluation and applications. *J. Am. Med. Inform. Assoc.* **2010**, *17*, 507–513. [CrossRef] [PubMed]
5. Denny, J.C.; Irani, P.R.; Wehbe, F.H.; Smithers, J.D.; Spickard, A., III. The KnowledgeMap project: Development of a concept-based medical school curriculum database. In Proceedings of the AMIA Annual Symposium Proceedings, Washington, DC, USA, 8–12 November 2003; pp. 195–199.
6. Liu, S.; Tang, B.; Chen, Q.; Wang, X. Drug name recognition: Approaches and resources. *Information* **2015**, *6*, 790–810. [CrossRef]
7. Chalapathy, R.; Borzeshi, E.Z.; Piccardi, M. Bidirectional LSTM–CRF for clinical concept extraction. *arXiv* **2016**, arXiv:1611.08373.
8. Uzuner, Ö.; South, B.R.; Shen, S.; DuVall, S.L. 2010 i2b2/VA challenge on concepts, assertions, and relations in clinical text. *J. Am. Med. Inform. Assoc.* **2011**, *18*, 552–556. [CrossRef] [PubMed]
9. Pradhan, S.; Elhadad, N.; Chapman, W.; Manandhar, S.; Savova, G. Semeval-2014 task 7: Analysis of clinical text. In Proceedings of the 8th International Workshop on Semantic Evaluation (SemEval 2014), Dublin, Ireland, 23–24 August 2014; pp. 54–62.

10. Boag, W.; Wacome, K.; Naumann, T.; Rumshisky, A. CliNER: A lightweight tool for clinical named entity recognition. In Proceedings of the AMIA Joint Summits on Clinical Research Informatics, San Francisco, CA, USA, 23–25 March 2015.
11. Wang, Y.; Patrick, J. Cascading classifiers for named entity recognition in clinical notes. In Proceedings of the Workshop on Biomedical Information Extraction, Association for Computational Linguistics, Borovets, Bulgaria, 14–16 September 2009; pp. 42–49.
12. DeBruijn, B.; Cherry, C.; Kiritchenko, S.; Martin, J.; Zhu, X. Machine-learned solutions for three stages of clinical information extraction: The state of the art at i2b2 2010. *J. Am. Med. Inform. Assoc.* **2011**, *18*, 557–562. [CrossRef]
13. Lafferty, J.; McCallum, A.; Pereira, F.C. Conditional random fields: Probabilistic models for segmenting and labeling sequence data. In Proceedings of the 18th International Conference on Machine Learning (ICML 2001), Williamstown, MA, USA, 28 June–July 1 2001; pp. 282–289.
14. Wu, Y.; Jiang, M.; Xu, J.; Zhi, D.; Xu, H. Clinical named entity recognition using deep learning models. In Proceedings of the AMIA Annual Symposium Proceedings, Washington, DC, USA, 4–8 November 2017; pp. 1812–1819.
15. Hochreiter, S.; Schmidhuber, J. Long short-term memory. *Neural Comput.* **1997**, *9*, 1735–1780. [CrossRef]
16. Unanue, I.J.; Borzeshi, E.Z.; Piccardi, M. Recurrent neural networks with specialized word embeddings for health-domain named-entity recognition. *J. Biomed. Inform.* **2017**, *76*, 102–109. [CrossRef]
17. Luo, L.; Yang, Z.; Yang, P.; Zhang, Y.; Wang, L.; Lin, H.; Wang, J. An attention-based BiLSTM–CRF approach to document-level chemical named entity recognition. *Bioinformatics* **2017**, *34*, 1381–1388. [CrossRef] [PubMed]
18. Zeng, D.; Sun, C.; Lin, L.; Liu, B. LSTM–CRF for drug-named entity recognition. *Entropy* **2017**, *19*, 283. [CrossRef]
19. Xu, G.; Wang, C.; He, X. Improving clinical named entity recognition with global neural attention. In Proceedings of the Asia-Pacific Web (APWeb) and Web-Age Information Management (WAIM) Joint International Conference on Web and Big Data, Macau, China, 23–25 July 2018; pp. 264–279.
20. Peters, M.E.; Neumann, M.; Iyyer, M.; Gardner, M.; Clark, C.; Lee, K.; Zettlemoyer, L. Deep contextualized word representations. *arXiv* **2018**, arXiv:1802.05365.
21. Devlin, J.; Chang, M.-W.; Lee, K.; Toutanova, K. Bert: Pre-training of deep bidirectional transformers for language understanding. *arXiv* **2018**, arXiv:1810.04805.
22. Mikolov, T.; Chen, K.; Corrado, G.; Dean, J. Efficient estimation of word representations in vector space. *arXiv* **2013**, arXiv:1301.3781.
23. Pennington, J.; Socher, R.; Manning, C. Glove: Global vectors for word representation. In Proceedings of the 2014 Conference on Empirical Methods in Natural Language Processing (EMNLP), Doha, Qatar, 25–29 October 2014; pp. 1532–1543.
24. Zhu, H.; Paschalidis, I.C.; Tahmasebi, A. Clinical Concept Extraction with Contextual Word Embedding. *arXiv* **2018**, arXiv:1810.10566.
25. Collobert, R.; Weston, J. A unified architecture for natural language processing: Deep neural networks with multitask learning. In Proceedings of the 25th International Conference on Machine Learning (ICML 2008), Helsinki, Finland, 5–9 July 2008; pp. 160–167.
26. Aguilar, G.; Maharjan, S.; López-Monroy, A.P.; Solorio, T. A Multi-task Approach for Named Entity Recognition in Social Media Data. In Proceedings of the Third Workshop on Noisy User-generated Text of Association for Computational Linguistics, Copenhagen, Denmark, 7 September 2017; pp. 148–153.
27. Savova, G.K.; Fan, J.; Ye, Z.; Murphy, S.P.; Zheng, J.; Chute, C.G.; Kullo, I.J. Discovering peripheral arterial disease cases from radiology notes using natural language processing. In Proceedings of the AMIA Annual Symposium Proceedings, Washington, DC, USA, 13–17 November 2010; pp. 722–726.
28. Bedmar, I.S.; Martínez, P.; Herrero Zazo, M. Semeval-2013 task 9: Extraction of drug-drug interactions from biomedical texts (ddiextraction 2013). In Proceedings of the Second Joint Conference on Lexical and Computational Semantics (*SEM), Volume 2: Seventh International Workshop on Semantic Evaluation (SemEval 2013), Atlanta, GA, USA, 13–14 June 2013; pp. 341–350.
29. Wang, Y.; Wang, L.; Rastegar-Mojarad, M.; Moon, S.; Shen, F.; Afzal, N.; Liu, S.; Zeng, Y.; Mehrabi, S.; Sohn, S. Clinical information extraction applications: A literature review. *J. Biomed. Inform.* **2018**, *77*, 34–49. [CrossRef]
30. Hebbring, S.J. The challenges, advantages and future of phenome—Wide association studies. *Immunology* **2014**, *141*, 157–165. [CrossRef]

31. Law, V.; Knox, C.; Djoumbou, Y.; Jewison, T.; Guo, A.C.; Liu, Y.; Maciejewski, A.; Arndt, D.; Wilson, M.; Neveu, V. DrugBank 4.0: Shedding new light on drug metabolism. *Nucleic Acids Res.* **2013**, *42*, D1091–D1097. [CrossRef]
32. Roberts, K.; Rink, B.; Harabagiu, S.M.; Scheuermann, R.H.; Toomay, S.; Browning, T.; Bosler, T.; Peshock, R. A machine learning approach for identifying anatomical locations of actionable findings in radiology reports. In Proceedings of the AMIA Annual Symposium Proceedings, Chicago, IL, USA, 3–7 November 2012; pp. 779–788.
33. Sarker, A.; Gonzalez, G. Portable automatic text classification for adverse drug reaction detection via multi-corpus training. *J. Biomed. Inform.* **2015**, *53*, 196–207. [CrossRef]
34. Rochefort, C.M.; Buckeridge, D.L.; Forster, A.J. Accuracy of using automated methods for detecting adverse events from electronic health record data: A research protocol. *Implement. Sci.* **2015**, *10*, 5. [CrossRef]
35. Deleger, L.; Brodzinski, H.; Zhai, H.; Li, Q.; Lingren, T.; Kirkendall, E.S.; Alessandrini, E.; Solti, I. Developing and evaluating an automated appendicitis risk stratification algorithm for pediatric patients in the emergency department. *J. Am. Med. Inform. Assoc.* **2013**, *20*, e212–e220. [CrossRef]
36. Collobert, R.; Weston, J.; Bottou, L.; Karlen, M.; Kavukcuoglu, K.; Kuksa, P. Natural language processing (almost) from scratch. *J. Mach. Learn. Res.* **2011**, *12*, 2493–2537.
37. Huang, Z.; Xu, W.; Yu, K. Bidirectional LSTM–CRF models for sequence tagging. *arXiv* **2015**, arXiv:1508.01991.
38. Lample, G.; Ballesteros, M.; Subramanian, S.; Kawakami, K.; Dyer, C. Neural architectures for named entity recognition. *arXiv* **2016**, arXiv:1603.01360.
39. Xu, K.; Zhou, Z.; Hao, T.; Liu, W. A bidirectional LSTM and conditional random fields approach to medical named entity recognition. In Proceedings of the International Conference on Advanced Intelligent Systems and Informatics 2015 (AISI 2015), Beni Suef, Egypt, 28–30 November 2015; pp. 355–365.
40. Habibi, M.; Weber, L.; Neves, M.; Wiegandt, D.L.; Leser, U. Deep learning with word embeddings improves biomedical named entity recognition. *Bioinformatics* **2017**, *33*, i37–i48. [CrossRef] [PubMed]
41. Liu, Z.; Yang, M.; Wang, X.; Chen, Q.; Tang, B.; Wang, Z.; Xu, H. Entity recognition from clinical texts via recurrent neural network. *BMC Med. Inform. Decis. Mak.* **2017**, *17*, 67. [CrossRef]
42. Si, Y.; Wang, J.; Xu, H.; Roberts, K. Enhancing Clinical Concept Extraction with Contextual Embedding. *arXiv* **2019**, arXiv:1902.08691. [CrossRef] [PubMed]
43. Jin, Q.; Liu, J.; Lu, X. Deep Contextualized Biomedical Abbreviation Expansion. *arXiv* **2019**, arXiv:1906.03360.
44. Jin, Q.; Dhingra, B.; Cohen, W.W.; Lu, X. Probing biomedical embeddings from language models. *arXiv* **2019**, arXiv:1904.02181.
45. Johnson, A.E.; Pollard, T.J.; Shen, L.; Li-wei, H.L.; Feng, M.; Ghassemi, M.; Moody, B.; Szolovits, P.; Celi, L.A.; Mark, R.G. MIMIC-III, a freely accessible critical care database. *Sci. Data* **2016**, *3*, 160035. [CrossRef] [PubMed]
46. Mikolov, T.; Karafiát, M.; Burget, L.; Černocký, J.; Khudanpur, S. Recurrent neural network based language model. In Proceedings of the 17th Annual Conference of the International Speech Communication Association, Makuhari, Chiba, Japan, 26–30 September 2010; pp. 1045–1048.
47. Pascanu, R.; Mikolov, T.; Bengio, Y. On the difficulty of training recurrent neural networks. In Proceedings of the 30th International Conference on Machine Learning (ICML 2013), Atlanta, GA, USA, 16–21 June 2013; pp. 1310–1318.
48. Vaswani, A.; Shazeer, N.; Parmar, N.; Uszkoreit, J.; Jones, L.; Gomez, A.N.; Kaiser, Ł.; Polosukhin, I. Attention is all you need. In Proceedings of the Advances in Neural Information Processing Systems, Long Beach, CA, USA, 4–9 December 2017; pp. 5998–6008.
49. Kingma, D.P.; Ba, J. Adam: A method for stochastic optimization. *arXiv* **2014**, arXiv:1412.6980.
50. Bergstra, J.; Bengio, Y. Random search for hyper-parameter optimization. *J. Mach. Learn. Res.* **2012**, *13*, 281–305.
51. I2B2. Evaluation Methods and Procedures for 2010 i2b2/VA Challenge. Available online: https://www.i2b2.org/NLP/Relations/assets/Evaluation%20methods%20for%202010%20Challenge.pdf (accessed on 25 May 2019).
52. Boag, W.; Sergeeva, E.; Kulshreshtha, S.; Szolovits, P.; Rumshisky, A.; Naumann, T. CliNER 2.0: Accessible and Accurate Clinical Concept Extraction. *arXiv* **2018**, arXiv:1803.02245.
53. Kohavi, R. A study of cross-validation and bootstrap for accuracy estimation and model selection. In Proceedings of the 1995 International Joint Conference on AI, Montreal, QC, Canada, 20–25 August 1995; pp. 1137–1145.

 © 2019 by the authors. Licensee MDPI, Basel, Switzerland. This article is an open access article distributed under the terms and conditions of the Creative Commons Attribution (CC BY) license (http://creativecommons.org/licenses/by/4.0/).

Review

A Review of Text Corpus-Based Tourism Big Data Mining

Qin Li [1,2], Shaobo Li [3,4,*], Sen Zhang [1,2], Jie Hu [5] and Jianjun Hu [3,6,*]

1. Chengdu Institute of Computer Application, Chinese Academy of Sciences, Chengdu 610041, China
2. University of Chinese Academy of Sciences, Beijing 100049, China
3. School of Mechanical Engineering, Guizhou University, Guiyang 550025, China
4. Guizhou Provincial Key Laboratory of Public Big Data (Guizhou University), Guiyang, Guizhou 550025, China
5. College of Big Data Statistics, GuiZhou University of Finance and Economics, Guiyang, Guizhou 550025, China
6. Department of Computer Science and Engineering, University of South Carolina, Columbia, SC 29208, USA
* Correspondence: lishaobo@gzu.edu.cn (S.L.); jianjunh@cse.sc.edu (J.H.); Tel.: +01-803-777-7304 (J.H.)

Received: 25 June 2019; Accepted: 6 August 2019; Published: 12 August 2019

Abstract: With the massive growth of the Internet, text data has become one of the main formats of tourism big data. As an effective expression means of tourists' opinions, text mining of such data has big potential to inspire innovations for tourism practitioners. In the past decade, a variety of text mining techniques have been proposed and applied to tourism analysis to develop tourism value analysis models, build tourism recommendation systems, create tourist profiles, and make policies for supervising tourism markets. The successes of these techniques have been further boosted by the progress of natural language processing (NLP), machine learning, and deep learning. With the understanding of the complexity due to this diverse set of techniques and tourism text data sources, this work attempts to provide a detailed and up-to-date review of text mining techniques that have been, or have the potential to be, applied to modern tourism big data analysis. We summarize and discuss different text representation strategies, text-based NLP techniques for topic extraction, text classification, sentiment analysis, and text clustering in the context of tourism text mining, and their applications in tourist profiling, destination image analysis, market demand, etc. Our work also provides guidelines for constructing new tourism big data applications and outlines promising research areas in this field for incoming years.

Keywords: tourism big data; text mining; NLP; deep learning

---

1. Introduction

Text is an effective and widely existing form of opinion expression and evaluation by users, as shown by the large number of online review comments over tourism sites, hotels, and services. As a direct expression of users' needs and emotions, text-based tourism data mining has the potential to transform the tourism industry. Indeed, tourists' decision-making is dramatically influenced by the travel experience of other individuals [1] in forms of tourism reviews or blogs, etc. These texts can give valuable insight for potential tourists, and assist them in optimizing destination choices and exploring travel routes, or for tourism practitioners to improve their services. Tourism platforms such as TripAdvisor and Ctrip now routinely provide an explosive amount of text data, which makes it possible to use deep learning [2], NLP [3], and other machine learning [4,5] and data mining techniques for tourism analysis. Studies [6,7] have shown that the competitiveness of the tourism industry dramatically relies on tourists' sentiment and opinions about the events occurring during the travel. In order to utilize this user-generated content properly and further to meet the needs of tourists and promote the tourism industry, we need to analyze and exploit tourists' needs and opinions, and then identify the problems of tourism services or destinations, which has become a new path for tourism development. Besides, as tourism needs become increasingly personalized, visitors begin to pursue self-likeness, self-worth, and diversified travel experiences, and they are no longer willing to endure delays or waits. How to recognize and respond to visitors' behaviors and needs quickly and identify potential customers have become essential factors for the success of tourism stakeholders. By exploiting the subjective information contained in tourism text data, we can assist tourism stakeholders to provide better services for tourists.

A large number of text mining techniques have been proposed and applied to tourism text data analysis for creating tourist profiles [8–15] and making effective market supervision [16–25]. These approaches exploit a variety of text representation strategies [26–32] and use different NLP techniques for topic extraction [33], text classification [34], sentiment analysis [35], and text clustering [36]. Moreover, while aiming to make computers understand human language, NLP has become the essential tool for text data analysis and is undergoing fast-pace growing based on the applications of deep learning in word embedding, syntax analysis, machine translation, and text understanding. Machine learning-based NLP techniques have been widely used in tourism text analysis, with superior results [19,25]. In addition, due to its high capability for extracting selective and invariant features from texts, and its independency of prior knowledge and linguistic resources, deep learning has been reported to achieve higher performance than other approaches on many NLP tasks [32]. A range of deep learning algorithms such as deep neural networks (DNNs), recurrent neural networks (RNNs), and convolutional neural networks (CNNs), along with special DNN techniques such as memory strategies and attention mechanisms [37], have been successfully applied to NLP tasks.

Due to the significance of tourism text data mining and the emergence of a large number of recent applied text mining techniques with diverse design strategies and methodologies, this paper aims to give a systematic review of these tourism text data mining techniques and applications. This paper divides NLP techniques into two types, in which NLP based on language scenes requires knowledge rather than text, such as knowledge of the domains and common sense, while text corpus-based big data analysis requires only an amount of text data for macro analysis. Figure 1 shows the basic process of applying text corpus-based NLP techniques to tourism analysis.

The structure of the paper is as follows: Section 2 introduces the recent text representation strategies and summarizes the basic applications of text corpus-based NLP techniques and their applications to tourism text data analysis in recent years. Section 3 provides a global analysis of the special tourism application techniques from the perspective of tourists and market. Section 4 also provides guidelines to be followed in the design of tourism value analysis or tourism recommendation systems, and outlines the most promising areas in the future of text corpus-based tourism big data mining. Section 5 summarizes our work from the exploration of the existing techniques.

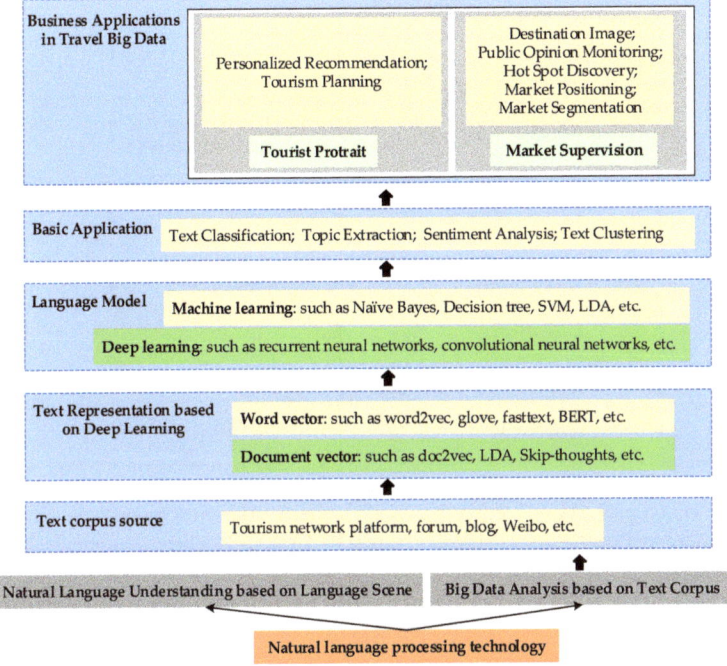

Figure 1. Text corpus-based tourism big data mining.

2. Review Protocol Used in This Review

We have followed a systematic review protocol [38,39] to write this paper, to reduce bias in literature included and to improve the comprehensiveness in our review activities. It is suggested that following an explicit review protocol can help define the source selection and search processes, quality criteria, and information synthesis.

We have used the following digital libraries to search for primary related studies:

- Google Scholar;
- Science Direct;
- ACM Digital Library;
- Citeseer Library;
- Springer Link;
- IEEE explore; and
- Web of Science.

The following queries have been created to conduct the keywords based search:

Text mining; topic extraction, text classification, sentiment classification; text clustering; tourist profile; destination image; market supervision/demand; transfer learning; meta-learning; sentiment aspect; aspect-base sentiment analysis; target-dependent sentiment analysis; NLP; deep learning; machine learning; text representation; word embedding; document vector; supervised learning, semi-supervised learning, unsupervised learning; short text; keyword; attention mechanism; tourism; tourism recommendation; tourism hotspot; crisis events or emergency analysis; tourism dataset; domain adaptability; tourism review. Logical OR, AND, and NOT descriptors have been used also during the literature search.

We have also listed our inclusion criteria in Table 1.

Table 1. Inclusion criteria.

Include	Exclude
Studies focused on text mining techniques based on macro corpus analysis, including topic extraction, text classification, sentiment classification, and text clustering.	NLP based on language scenes which requires knowledge rather than text, such as knowledge of domains and common sense.
Tourism related studies in which text is the main research object, and other data structures can be the auxiliary means. Text corpus-based tourism big data mining related to tourist profiling and market supervision.	Tourism related studies in which other data structures (pictures, videos, etc.) are the main research object, while text can be the auxiliary means. Text corpus-based tourism big data mining related to question answering, or others.
English texts.	All other languages.
Studies published between 2014 and 2019.	Studies published before 2014.
Peer reviewed academic journals or books, conference proceedings.	Dissertations, non-peer reviewed sources.
In person context.	Online context.

Study selection procedure: We first checked the paper titles and then reviewed the abstracts, keywords, results, and conclusions to obtain the first list of studies. Then, we screened the remaining list by the inclusion criteria in Table 1. We then double checked the reference list to identify additional studies that were relevant to our review topic. Finally, we evaluated the quality of remaining list of related studies using the checklist as suggested in [40].

3. Text Corpus-Based Tourism Big Data Mining Techniques

3.1. Text Representations

Recently, text data mining techniques have been mainly based on machine learning and deep learning, which play a decisive role for the improvement of NLP. In order to transform NLP problems into the problem of machine learning, symbols such as text need to be digitized firstly; that is, text representation must be obtained. In 2003, Bengio et al. [41] proposed a word vector model based on N-gram statistical language, which pioneered the neural network as a language model. Since then, a lot of word representations in low-dimensional space have been proposed, which are pre-trained on a large set of unlabeled text corpus. In contrast to high-dimensional space, these word representations or word embeddings can be compared in sematic distance and can be easily applied to other models. Traditionally, word embedding methods such as Word2vec [26,27] and Glove [28] were proposed to create a global word representation which considers the word in all sentences. Currently, more and more works have started to notice the different semantics of a word in different contexts. For example, contextual word vectors (CoVe) [29] capture contextual information by an encoder in an attentional seq-to-seq machine translation model; and embeddings from language model (ELMO) [30] extracts context-sensitive features from a bidirectional language model (biLM). Subsequently, with the proposal of Transformer network, generative pre-training Transformer (OpenAI-GPT) [31] and large-scale pre-training language model based on bidirectional Transformer (BERT) [32] pre-trained language models from Transformers for extracting contextual word embeddings and showed better performance than ever on many tasks [32]. Table 2 provides a directory of existing main pre-trained models which can be used for generating embeddings as an input of the next model training. In addition, the supervised methods for generating word vectors [42–44] can also promote word representations, such as the methods for improving the topics extraction or sentiment classification and so on.

Table 2. Pre-trained models for word embeddings.

Time	Pre-Trained Model	URL	Accessed Data
2013	Word2vec	https://radimrehurek.com/gensim/models/word2vec.html	24 July 2019
2014	Glove	https://nlp.stanford.edu/projects/glove/	24 July 2019
2016	FastText [45]	https://fasttext.cc/	24 July 2019
2016	WordRank [46]	https://radimrehurek.com/gensim/models/wrappers/wordrank.html	24 July 2019
2017	CoVe	https://github.com/salesforce/cove	24 July 2019
2018	ULMFiT [47]	http://nlp.fast.ai/ulmfit	24 July 2019
2018	ELMO	https://github.com/allenai/allennlp/blob/master/tutorials/how_to/elmo.md	24 July 2019
2018	OpenAI-GPT	https://openai.com/blog/language-unsupervised/	24 July 2019
2018	BERT	https://github.com/google-research/bert	24 July 2019

A word is a basic unit of a sentence, paragraph, or document. To better represent a text, converting the word vectors into a short text or long text representation is an efficient operation. Early typical text representations have bag-of-words (BOW) and term frequency-inverse document frequency (TF-IDF) models, but these document vector models are usually too simple and lack context information and word-to-word associations. They often perform poorly on some complex tasks. Latent Dirichlet Allocation (LDA) computes the distribution of topics for documents, which is commonly used for representation of documents. Doc2vec [48] was proposed based on Word2vec, which considered the context information and semantic information, while it is only slightly better than the simple average word vectors of the document in the classification task. Aiming at it, Arora et al. [49] encoded sentences by a linear weighted combination of word vectors for improvement. For a long time, researchers have focused on unsupervised sentence learning, such as Skip-thoughts [50] and its improved Quick-thought [51] afterwards. When the supervised task is suitable for sentence embedding training, such as the natural language inference (NLI) task, the quality of sentence vectors learned by supervised methods can achieve higher performance [52], especially under the framework of multi-task learning [53].

The vector representation for the granularity of words, sentences, documents, etc., is the basis for related machine learning, and the pre-trained models of these vectors provide the premise for the input of other models. In contrast to randomly initialized vectors, the vectors provided by these pre-training models can reduce the data demand and save training time for deep learning, and the captured features of vectors can also significantly improve the performance of the model.

3.2. Text Corpus-Based NLP Techniques in Tourism Data Mining

This section analyzes four basic technical applications of text corpus-based NLP techniques: Topic extraction, text classification, sentiment analysis, and text clustering. These basic technical applications are the basis of related tourism business applications. In order to illustrate them and their applications in tourism, we firstly analyze recent tourism business works based on these techniques and then outline the recent techniques of the basic technical applications.

3.2.1. Topic Extraction

Topic extraction is a technique for extracting topics or aspects from large-scale text data, which can give the decision-maker some insights and help them identify associated sentiments. In tourism, topic extraction can be used to capture tourism public concerns and track hot events, by which tourists can track travel trends and important events and tourism practitioners can find business opportunities or travel crisis in real time, accordingly, to take measures to guide public opinion or promote related fields. Hot topics are often reviewed and reprinted more frequently. Based on this idea, the study [54] filtered out information with high evaluation and reload times, and introduced time distribution calculation methods into LDA to detect hot topics. In the study [55], Structure Topic Model (STM) [56] was adopted to detect negative reviews and how public concerns vary over different hotel grades. In addition, topic extraction can also be used to find tourism characteristics of attractions or build tourism product and user profiles. For example, the study [4] defined the global topic as "scenic spot" to filter noise semantics from tourism corpus, to explore the local topics of "scenic spot" by LDA, and then display the distribution of the attraction types or the local topics in the form of attraction maps. In this study [5], a season topic model based on LDA (STLDA) was proposed to explore the topic characteristics of attractions with seasonal features, which was of great significance for mining related topics with seasons and for personalized recommendations. In this study [57], a topic model was utilized to detect explicit interests by interactions between users for the following users' implicit interest profile building.

Topic extraction has been studied a lot recently and is an important issue for tourism analysis. There are many text mining techniques for topic extraction. Traditionally, keywords are usually used for expressing the topics of documents, and keyword extraction has played an important role in topic extraction for many years. According to existing studies, most of keyword extraction techniques are based on unsupervised learning [58], such as algorithms based on statistical word features (e.g., TF-IDF, Kullback–Leibler divergence, chi-square test, etc.), algorithms based on topic models (e.g., LDA, etc.), and algorithms based on network graphs (e.g., TextRank, Rapid Automatic Keyword Extraction (RAKE) [59], TopicRank [60]). With the appearance of word-distributed representations, some works have also tried to make use of Word2vec to improve keyword extraction, while only considering the similarity calculation of words [61].

Keywords can express topics, but currently, their relevance with document topics mainly depends on the improvement of existing probability topic models [33], such as the LDA model. As a probability generation model, LDA can be easily extended to other probability models. For example, the study [62] considered that different topics in the same corpus are often related, and used this idea as a research perspective to promote topic extraction of the LDA model; some probability topic models for specific tasks such as topic sentiments, time changes, document authors, etc. are also expected to extract the topics related to target task [63]. To extract more relevant topics, some experts have also considered using word-distributed representation to improve the semantics and syntactics of text information. For example, the study [64] introduced the similarity of word embedding into LDA to calculate the relevance of the acquired words; the study [65] improved the way of context acquisition by introducing LDA into Word2vec; the study [66] introduced Word2vec to calculate the distance between the topic vector and the document vector to correct the topics of LDA mining. Moreover, the combination of deep learning and LDA has become another topic extraction method. For example, in this study [67], a novel neural topic model was proposed to acquire the N-gram topic by the deep neural network and then used LDA to obtain the topic representation of the document; the study [68] integrated LDA into language model LSTM for joint training. In addition to the LDA and its extensions, there are also methods for generating subject-related vectors by the neural attention model, such as Attention-based Aspect Extraction (ABAE) [69].

In summary, researches about topic extraction are mostly dependent on the topic probability model such as LDA, and improved aiming at different text structures. Topic extraction in short text often suffers from data sparseness due to the insufficient word co-occurrence and lack of context information. Using long text to assist short text by importing external-related information from Wikipedia and WordNet, etc. [70], or aggregating short text based on the posterior probability of words in original documents [71] can help with the short text task to some extent. Another approach of improving short text task is to enhance the interpretability or the semantical coherence of the topic model, such as informative words rewarding [72]. Besides, as above analysis, LDA ignores the order structure of texts and the meaning of words, so it is one of the research directions that scholars have focused on by exploring the features of words and sentences, etc., to enhance the ability of topic extraction, and will be show great potential in the future. Except for the issue of short text, in business application, users or practitioners may concern different aspects of a topic or aspect related information;

the context information of the topic aspect is often used to explore topic-sensitive content [73]. In order to understand a topic more granularly, the structural relation among topics is also a problem, which is widely concerned such as the exploring the hierarchical structure among topics or the global and local relation [74].

3.2.2. Text Classification

Text classification is a process in which the computer automatically classifies the input texts according to their content, and it includes spam filtering, information retrieval, topic classification, sentiment classification, and so on; sentiment classification of which will be discussed in the Section 3.2.3. In tourism, text classification is generally about topic classification, and the topics of texts in travel mostly involve various aspects of the travel process, such as transportation, accommodation, food, entertainment, and so on. In addition, tourism texts such as tourism comment reviews are often short but contain a lot of information. They usually contain multiple topics but cannot be attributed to one certain aspect or target. Therefore, text classification in the current tourism field is usually carried out by topic extraction, to extract all aspects of the text for targeted analysis [22,75].

Traditionally, text classifications are mainly based on machine learning such as Naive Bayes [76], maximum entropy [77], Support Vector Machine [78], K-nearest neighbor algorithm [78], etc. They usually use keywords or topics to reflect the feature of documents and realize text classification automatically [79], which still plays an important role currently [80]. At present, the mainstream feature extraction techniques characterized by keywords include TF-IDF and information divergence, and more advanced deep learning approaches [81]. Besides, there are some classic feature representation models for words such as Vector Space Model, N-grams [82], etc., but these models have some disadvantages, such as semantic information being missing. With word-distributed representations, text classification no longer relies on the keywords only and begins to pay more attention to the semantics of words themselves. Following this trend, there have emerged a lot of text classification algorithms based on the improvement of word embedding features [45,65,83].

Benefitting from deep learning, various researches on text classification techniques based on deep neural networks have also made significant progress. For example, the representative and innovative algorithms of CNN in text classification include the CNN proposed by Kim [34], character-level convolutional network (ConvNets) proposed by Zhang [84], the CNN-based classification algorithm applied to patent classification [85], the RNN-based text classification algorithms which includes bidirectional RNNs [86], hierarchical attention mechanism (HAN) [35], and the recurrent convolutional network (RCNN) [87]. In addition, the connection between CNNs and RNNs [88], the introduction of multi-task learning frameworks [89], and the increased depth in deep learning models [90] will also improve the performance of text classification to a certain extent.

At present, text classification models are mostly based on supervised learning. Supervised text classification often relies on the integrity of the domain corpus, as well as its annotations, so researchers are more concerned with the improvement of theory but lack of practical applications. In order to solve the issue of few in-domain labeled data, many following studies have been made; Table 3 shows four different strategies: Co-training, training samples extension, meta-learning, and transfer learning. Among them, co-training and training samples extension need auxiliary training with unlabeled data or external knowledge, but as the training samples increase, the noise in the auto-tagging instance will continue to accumulate. Meta-learning or transfer learning attempt to learn general representation or meta knowledge among tasks, but still have to make further improvement, such as in the issue of negative transfer.

Table 3. Strategies of few in-domain labeled data in 2018.

Author-Study	Contribution	Basic Language Model/Classifier
[91]	It proposes a novel co-training algorithm which uses an ensemble of classifiers created in multiple training iterations, with labeled data and unlabeled data trained jointly and with no added computational complexity.	Naïve Bayes; Support Vector Machine
[92]	It uses the knowledge of Wikipedia to extend the training samples, which is realized by network graph construction.	Naïve Bayes; Support Vector Machine; Random Forest
[93]	It introduces an attentive meta-learning method for task-agnostic representation and realizes fast adaption in different tasks, thus having the ability of learning shared representation across tasks.	Temporal Convolutional Networks (TCN)
[47]	It proposes a transfer learning method of universal language model fine-tuning (ULMFiT), which trains on three common text classification tasks; it can prevent overfitting, even with few labeled data in classification tasks by novel fine-tuning techniques.	Averaged stochastic gradient descent Weight-Dropped LSTM (AWD-LSTM) [94]

3.2.3. Sentiment Analysis

In tourism, the application of sentiment classification techniques can help manage obtain tourist sentiment tendency and opinions in real time, thus making appropriate measures. For example, the study [95] proposed a tourist destination recommendation system by analyzing and evaluating the user's sentiment tendency; the study [96] explored the sustainable tourism development path through the sentiment analysis of the user reviews of the shared bicycle system in Spain; and in this study [97], a visual analysis system was designed to analyze regional trends and sentiment changes in visitors.

Text sentiment analysis is the process of automatically classifying the polarity of a given text with subjective sentiments by computer. It includes many tasks, such as sentiment classification, opinion extraction, and so on [98]. We only discuss sentiment classification here. The method of sentiment classification can be divided into two categories: The first one is based on machine learning methods such as neural networks, and the other is based on dictionary-based methods that use pre-defined sentiment dictionaries such as WordNet, HowNet, LIWC, etc., which have sentiment-related terms, and their polarity values. Dictionary-based methods are based on grammatical rules of text analysis, relying on the quality of the sentiment dictionary and its continuous updating, involving more work refinement, such as the extraction and discrimination of evaluation words, and the consideration of the influence of the word contexts, etc. [99]. In addition to the two types of sentiment classification methods, sentiment classification through the integration of machine learning and dictionary-based methods also shows great potential. For example, this research [100] used the sentiment polarity and part of speech in the sentiment dictionary to extract the feature of the text representation combined with convolutional neural networks.

Sentiment classification with machine learning methods is mostly based on supervised learning and relies on the completeness of the labeled training corpus, which is a classification method about features. This research [101] pointed out that feature extraction, feature weight, and sentiment classifier are three essential design elements that affect the accuracy of text sentiment classification. Based on this, sentiment classification with machine learning is mainly carried out around these elements. No matter what kind of design element, the optimal vector representation is sought to achieve better precision and speed for model training. With the development of deep language models and their superiority, sentiment classifiers are more improved and optimized based on recurrent neural networks and convolutional neural networks [102]. Researchers have proposed different feature improvement strategies. For example, for short texts presented on social networks, the study [103] used a two-layer convolutional network to jointly train characters, words, and sentence features. For the long-distance dependence problem of long text, in the study [104], a TopicRNN model was proposed to get the global semantic information, which introduced the topic model to RNN model training to obtain unsupervised feature of document global semantic information. Aiming at the respective characteristics of the classifiers, such as the dependence of the CNN model on window size and step size [105], and the long-distance dependence problem of the mechanism of the RNN model, the study [106] proposed to use LSTM as the pooling layer in CNN to promote sentiment classification. In view of the fact that there are similar contexts in the representation of sentiment words and the opposite of the emotional tendency of words, such as "good" and "bad", the research [107] proposed to introduce sentiment information into the word vector, thus promoting the learning and classification of sentiment words.

In recent years, the attention mechanism has become one of the mainstream techniques of text processing due to its superior performance. In previous text research, the attention mechanism was mainly applied in the recurrent network structure. For example, in this study [35], a hierarchical attention mechanism (HAN) was proposed to achieve sentiment classification, which constructed the sentence representation with the word-level attention mechanism and the document representation with sentence-level attention mechanism. However, the recurrent network is a sequence-dependent structure, which has a disadvantage in training speed and memory consumption. Aiming at these problems, the Transformer model [37] was proposed, which consists entirely of attention mechanisms and applied self-attention mechanism, and has a complete advantage over the structure of recurrent and convolutional sentiment classification [108].

In the last few years, most of the research on sentiment classification focuses on how to improve the classification accuracy of the entire text, but rarely analyzes the sentiment polarity based on the aspects or targets appearing in the text. In tourism analysis, not only is knowing the overall sentiment tendency of the tourists' comments needed, but also knowing the various sentiments of each entity in the tourism or each aspect of the tourist comments is required, so as to better self-evaluate and propose more targeted solutions. Due to the complexity of the process and the lack of related corpora, most of the works are unable to achieve an effective evaluation of aspect extraction and sentiment classification. The research [3] considered the possibility of describing the topic words by considering the distance between the topic words and the sentiment words, and exploring the preferences of tourists for tourism products. This method is simple, but the accuracy of the result is low due to the existence of the virtual target and the implicit evaluation object [109]. The study [22] extracted topics from the destination reviews based on LDA and then analyzed the sentiment state of each topic in more detail or for finer gain. The study [110] used text mining and sentiment analysis techniques to analyze hotel online reviews to explore the characteristics of hotel products that visitors were more concerned about. Most of these methods only make use of the model, while the adaptability of the model to the domain is not well explained.

At present, sentiment analysis based on specific targets or aspects has become a research hotspot for scholars. This method no longer separates the topic model from the sentiment analysis, but unites them into a single model [109,111]. Most works for aspect-based or target-dependent sentiment classification are based on supervised learning and achieve good results, as shown in Tables 4 and 5. While manually labeling data for the supervised model is usually insufficient and costly, unsupervised or semi-supervised models can utilize unlabeled samples for training, which can resolve the problem of insufficient resources. For example, the study [63] incorporated sentiment distribution and sentiment-oriented local topic distribution into the topic probability distribution model, so that the mining of sentiments and local topics was carried out simultaneously. The study [112] proposed to learn specific aspects of word embeddings based on the Topic Word Embeddings model (TWE2), and used the semi-supervised variational autoencoder (SSVAE) to perform aspect-level sentiment analysis.

Table 4. Common aspect-based sentiment analysis (ABSA) and target-dependent sentiment analysis on SemEval 2014 Task 4 in restaurant domain.

Time	Model	Basic Idea	Accuracy (%)
2016	AE-LSTM [113]	The target words given in each sentence of the training corpus are vectorized and added to the LSTM model as input for training together.	76.20
2016	AT-LSTM [113]	An attention mechanism is proposed to capture key parts of a sentence related to a given aspect.	77.90
2018	AF-LSTM [114]	A new association layer that defines two correlation operators, circular convolution and cyclic correlation, is introduced to learn the relationship between sentence words and aspects.	75.44
2015	TD-LSTM [115]	Two LSTM networks are adopted to model separately, based on context before and after target words for target-dependent sentiment analysis tasks.	75.63
2015	TC-LSTM [115]	On the basis of TD-LSTM, target word information is added as an input.	76.01
2016	ATAE-LSTM [113]	On the basis of TD-LSTM, aspect information is introduced in two parts of the model: Input part and hidden part	77.20
2017	IAN [116]	It learns attentions in target and context words interactively, and generates the representations for targets and contexts separately.	78.60
2016	MemNet(k) [117]	It uses deep memory network with multiple computational layers (hops) to classify sentiments at the aspect level, where k is the number of layers.	(k = 2) 78.61 (k = 3) 79.06
2018	Coattention-LSTM Coattention-MemNet(3) [118]	A collaborative attention mechanism is proposed to alternately use target-level and context-level attention mechanisms.	78.8 79.7
2017	BILSTM-ATT-G [119]	Based on the Vanilla Attention Model, this model is extended to differentiate left and right contexts, and uses the gate method to control the output of the data stream.	79.73
2018	TNet-LF TNet-AS [120]	The CNN is used to replace the attention-based recurrent neural network (RNN) to extract the classification features, and the context-preserving transformation (CPT) structure such as lossless forwarding (LF) and adaptive scaling (AS) is used to capture the target entity information and the retention context information.	80.79 80.69
2018	AE-DLSTMs [121]	On the basis of AE-LSTMs, this model captures contextual semantic information in both forward and backward directions in aspect words.	79.57
2018	AELA-DLSTMs [121]	Based on AE-DLSTMs, this model introduces the context position information weight of the aspect word.	80.35
2018	StageI+StageII [122]	It introduces a position attention mechanism based on position context between aspect and context, and also considers the disturbance of other aspects in the same sentence.	80.10
2018	DMN+AttGRU (k = 3) [123]	A dynamic memory network which uses multiple attention blocks of multiple attention mechanisms is proposed to extract sentiment-related features in memory information, where k stands for attention steps.	81.41
2018	MGAN [124]	This model designs an aspect alignment loss to depict aspect-level interactions among aspects with the same context, and to strengthen the attention differences among aspects with the same context and different sentiment polarities.	81.25

In the training process, the pre-trained word vectors in these models were all initialized by 300-dimension Glove embeddings and the sentiment classification was performed in a three-way classification.

Table 5. Common aspect-based sentiment analysis (ABSA) and target-dependent sentiment analysis on subtask 1 (slot 2) SemEval 2016 Task 5 in restaurant domain.

Time	Model	Basic Idea	Accuracy (%)
2019	BERT [125]	Bidirectional Transformer (BERT) is extended with an additional task-specific layer and fine-tuned on each end task	81.54
2019	BERT-PT [125]	On the basis of BERT, two pre-training objectives are used: Masking language model (MLM) and next sentence prediction (NSP), to post-train domain knowledge, and else task (MRC) knowledge.	84.95

The sentiment classification is performed in a three-way classification.

As shown in Tables 4 and 5, the sentiment classification algorithms are all trained on existing data sets from SemEval2014 and SemEval2016 on which they achieved excellent performance, while the limited data sets making them not universally applicable in other new domains. An effective way to enhancing the ability of automatic labeling for target domain is learning shared features from source domain or transferring knowledge from source domain into target domain. Aiming at it, some works have been done attempting to enhance transfer learning, such as importing of domain knowledge into the training process expecting to contribute to the knowledge transfer for realizing cross-domain aspect sentiment classification [126], but which still need human intervention or processing in a semi-supervised manner. As a result, in tourism application, few studies about aspect-based or target-dependent sentiment classification have been made. The study [2] considered using lda2vec to explore the focuses of tourist reviews and also as an input knowledge to enhance the sentiment analysis of these focuses, but still had room for fine-grained sentiment analysis for aspects. The study [127] proposed a novel probability model to judge user sentiment and topic sentiment in an unsupervised manner, which provides a direction for tourism recommendation due to its introduction of user information, but an effective evaluation method is needed.

In summary, the sentiment classification model, improved by the attention mechanism, will be the mainstream trend in the future. In addition, based on the study of sentiment targets or sentiment aspects, the sentiments can be more fine-grained and interpretable, which will be more conducive to the practical application analysis of tourism.

3.2.4. Text Clustering

Text clustering mainly involves unsupervised algorithms that can discover potential knowledge and rules from large-scale text data sets, facilitating the effective organization, abstracting, and navigation of texts. In the field of tourism, text clustering is mainly applied in the research of tourist hotspots or emergencies. For example, the study [128] performed co-occurrence clustering analysis by constructing a high-frequency word co-occurrence matrix in order to acquire hot things, and measured the weights of the connection between the regions within or outside the Tibet by degree centrality in the social network map; the tourist hotspots and their interrelationships were then obtained and tourism planning was further promoted. In this study [129], cohesive hierarchical clustering methods were used to detect the emergencies by using bursty topics to represent texts. Besides, text clustering can also be applied in the subdivision problem of the tourism market in which a clustering method is used to obtain different characteristics of the group for targeted analysis and self-improvement. In this study [130], the collaborative clustering algorithm was used to cluster the five-star hotels and hotel reviews in Rome from two dimensions, which not only solved the feature clustering of each hotel, but also solved the description of the features. As mentioned above, text clustering can be an efficient method for tourism analysis. Next we will review it from the technical perspective.

The object for text clustering can be documents, sentences, paragraphs, and so on. Similarity is the basis of text clustering. At present, the mainstream text similarity calculation method is mainly based on vector space method, including cosine similarity, Manhattan distance, Euclidean distance, and so on. With the development of deep learning, word vectors generated by neural networks such as Word2vec can make words closer in semantic distance, and are more suitable for similarity calculation of various text granularities.

Document clustering techniques include multiple types, such as agglomerative hierarchical clustering algorithm, partitioning clustering algorithm, density-based clustering algorithm, etc. Different clustering algorithms have different requirements for application scenarios, and the prior knowledge of specific tasks [131] must be considered. Currently, there are few researches on text clustering algorithms. The main reason is that the computational overhead of clustering algorithms tends to be large. When the amount of data rises to a certain extent, most clustering algorithms cannot be used, so the time complexity of most clustering algorithms needs to be considered [132]. K-means, which belongs to the partitioning clustering algorithm, is a commonly used text clustering algorithm whose disadvantage is that it cannot effectively determine the number of clusters and select the initial clustering point, and has poor performance on high dimensional data, etc. While compared to other clustering algorithms, K-means is fast and easy to implement on a huge database [36]. Consequently, there are many researches carried out based on K-means, such as through optimization or dynamic definition of the initial clustering point [133,134], improvement of text representation by genetic algorithm, graph structure, deep learning, etc. [135–137], and optimization of algorithm objective function [138].

Text clustering can also be a semi-supervised algorithm, which mainly uses text labels like potential topics as prior knowledge to guide the clustering process, and is a bridge connecting unsupervised clustering and supervised classification problems [139]. The semi-supervised clustering algorithm is usually a combination of unsupervised clustering algorithm and supervised model, which is mainly used to find the similarity between texts and label data samples currently, and can alleviate the demand for data volume and improve the performance of supervised models. With the research and application of large-scale knowledge graph, text clustering algorithms will play more of a role—for example, clustering algorithms can be used to build hierarchical ontological relationships, discover semantic relationships between domain concepts [140], and gradually form large-scale semantic network diagrams, etc.

4. Applications of Text Corpus-Based Tourism Big Data Mining

The tourism process mainly includes five stages: Imagination, planning, scheduling, experience, and sharing [141]. The sharing stage is the most critical stage in the tourism process. Whether tourism behavior occurs or not depends on whether the plan is successfully completed, and the tourism plan depends on other completed visitor shares. If a tourism stakeholder or destination wants to improve their services and attract more visitors, it must know what the tourists are thinking and needs to understand their preferences, needs, and purposes. As tourists, they hope that the journey will involve "zero" conflict, and they can get useful information from the travel network platform. The recommended destination is based on their preferences, and the tour route is greatly optimized.

Tourists share the experience based on their own experience, which can not only reflect their preferences, but also the problems of tourism stakeholders and destinations in time. From the tourism innovative applications based on the techniques of text corpus-based tourism big data mining, this section analyzes the two main tourism application scenarios: Tourist profile and market supervision.

4.1. Tourist Profile

Tourist profile is used to abstract the specific labels from the attribute information of a tourist. The attributes usually include: Demographic characteristics (individual or organization, age, gender, location), mental state and lifestyle (education, profession, purchasing ability, family, property, emotional attitude, interest, fear, etc.), travel preferences, and travel purposes. The tourist attributes are diverse, which leads to that the demand is also diverse, driven by the consumption upgrade [142]. Therefore, tourist market segmentation is of great significance to tourism destinations such as the discovery of market opportunities, the planning of right marketing and competition strategies, and the realization of personalized recommendations.

By dividing their natural attributes, tourists can be divided into female and male groups, youth and old age groups, single and married groups, local and foreign groups, etc. By the analysis of preferences and behaviors, tourists can be divided into more groups such as travel buyers, the decompressions, and so on. Different groups have different characteristics, and individuals with the same attributes may have similarities in tourism behavior [143]. Study [73] has confirmed that differences in tourist attributes can also lead to differences in tourist perceptions. Through the study of the Cape Town tourism market [144], it was found that visitors' age, place of residence, destination stay time, return visits, etc., had an important influence on the perception of tourists, and the sentiments they conveyed [145] also had different characteristics.

Tourist profile are an important means of understanding tourist behavior and meeting the tourist expectation. Since the content of the tourists' comments often reflects their subjective thinking, we can extract information such as preferences, concerns, and purposes of different tourists from the texts. By obtaining their relevant attributes, tourists' profiles can be effectively created. While how to generate user profiles through practical text analysis is still a hot and challenging issue for scholars, through literature research, it has been found that user profiles are mainly obtained by supervised learning, or realized by the feature recognition from data labeled gender, age, occupation, ratings, and so on [14]. In addition, the user attributes for profiles are always treated as isolated in feature recognition; in other words, the relationship between user attributes is ignored, while the attributes are often interrelated. Aiming at this problem, multiple attributes joint learning can be efficient to improve the user attribute prediction [8]. However, although the supervised learning for tourist profiles has achieved good results, it still has limitations because its performance depends entirely on the number of data and its domain. Taking some sample data as the research object, the study [9] extracted the "co-words" from different users in the sample to obtain a universal judgment criterion for each user, but the viewpoints or conclusions derived from the sample were often one-sided due to the limited numbers. By using the text information from a large number of existing users on social media, a unified user vector learning model can be obtained to fill the knowledge gap between the source social media and the target social media, and then the problem of uncertainty of user labels for the target media can be solved [10]. Similar works [15] were also done, which considered matching user accounts on different social networks to build user profiles by user identification based on User Generated Content (UGC) in a supervised manner. These methods are all based on this assumption that the data for the same attribute or the same person has common features, such as commonality of the same gender [13], to resolve the problem of the limited labeled data. In supervised learning, current methods for tourist profiles are usually around gender, age, and other explicit feature predictions. The topic-based model is an unsupervised algorithm which can extract user preferences or hobbies, etc., and is an efficient method for the acquisition of the user's attribute information, except for explicit feature classification [11]. Furthermore, the unsupervised aspect-based or target-dependent sentiment analysis, which is studied a lot currently, can recognize user preference for aspects or the target, and provide a more fine-grained analysis for user profiles [12].

Tourist profile is a feature extraction process and a vital step of the personalized recommendation in tourism big data mining. The personalized recommendation system is a process of intelligent recommending for users according to their preferences, habits, and individual needs. In the field of tourism, the recommendation system is more complicated, because we not only need to consider personal attributes, but also need consider travel characteristics. These two considerations jointly determine tourist decision-making behavior [146]. Travel characteristics include destination type, travel distance, traffic mode, travel expenses, and so on. Different tourist personal attributes have different features in the performance of travel characteristics [147], and tourist characteristics directly influence the choice of travel characteristics, such as the choice of destination.

Mastering the tourist psychological characteristics in travel planning is the critical procedure for a good personalized recommendation system design, and the text reviews become an important supplement to the data sparsity in the tourism recommendation process. By mining user reviews, user preferences, and travel destination, reputation or features can be gained and introduced to the travel recommendation system for final recommendations [148]. Because the topic model can detect tourists' preferences, frequent behaviors, or new travel trends in an unsupervised manner, it has become a hot research direction for scholars. For example, the study [149] mined the feature information of tourists and locations by the topic model, and used knowledge-based filtering techniques to achieve destination recommendations for tourists by semantic similarity. The study [150] proposed a Topic Criterion (TC) model by improving the topic model and the Topic Sentiment Criterion (TSC) model to calculate tourist profiles and item profiles, as well as their matching degrees to achieve project recommendations for potential tourists. In addition, some scholars have also considered the context of travel in the recommendation process, such as seasons, holidays, etc. In the study [95], a text mining technique was used to calculate the user's sentiment tendency toward the destination, and the influence of time elements such as seasons and holidays on the tourists' sentiments were considered comprehensively to promote the tourism recommendation system greatly. Based on the literature research of tourism recommendation system [151,152], we summarize the general framework of the tourism recommendation system based on text mining (shown in Figure 2).

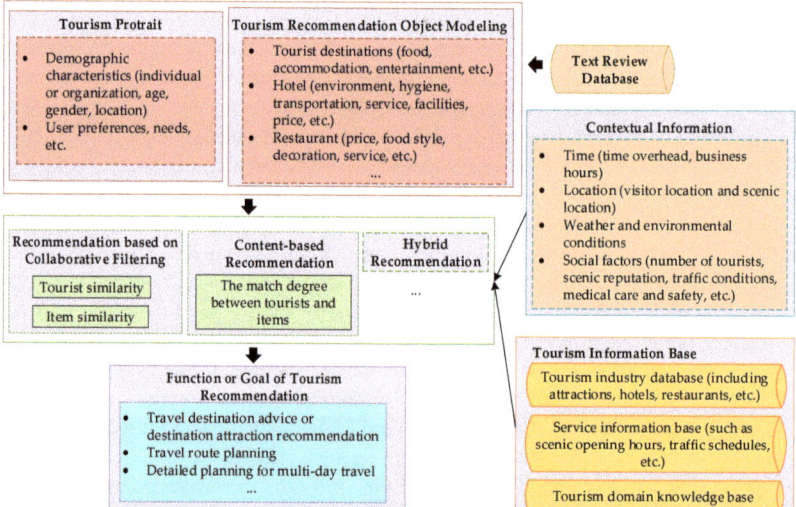

Figure 2. Tourist recommendation system framework based on text mining.

4.2. Market Supervision

The tourism market is the basis for tourism to survive in. Research on the tourism destination market has important theoretical and practical significance for tourism development [50]. The existence of the tourism system depends on the existence of tourist demand, which is always related to aspects of the tourism process such as "food, accommodation, transport, sightseeing, purchase, entertainment", and is diverse due to the difference of tourist natural and social attributes. By the analysis of tourist demand and preferences, researchers or practitioners can assess the market composition of tourism destinations and adjust the tourism market resource allocation or make marketing strategies to maximize the degree of satisfaction of tourists.

In the context of big data, the online tourism market is gradually driven by user data. Texts, as a main component of user-generated content, can accurately reflect the needs of visitors. From the perspective of market or tourism stakeholders, this paper summarizes five aspects of text content analysis: Target topic, dimension and weight of concerns, satisfaction evaluation or preference, the reason for sentiment, and new trend, to assist market strategy planning. The analysis of specific "target topic" of the text can analyze the tourist needs more specifically; "dimension and weight of concerns" is to analyze the tourist demand from their attention to various aspects and compute their weights on the attention; "satisfaction evaluation or preference" is to analyze the sentiment orientation of comments to obtain tourists' satisfaction with the travel experience; "the reason for sentiment" uses sentiment cause detection techniques to detect the cause of sentiment in order to find the reason behind the sentiment; and the "new trend" analyzes the emergence and developing process of new things from the perspective of time series. Next, we will explain with examples in detail. The study [17] explored the key elements of hotel customer comment by the topic model LDA and analyzed the significance of their influence through the perception map of hotel reviews, which are important for the analysis of customer satisfaction. The study [18] combined the three elements of tourist market share, tourist sentiment orientation, and potential tourist awareness to define and calculate the competitiveness of the tourism destination market, the tourists' sentiment orientation of which is obtained through the sentiment analysis model based on text comments. In this study [19], sentiment analysis on a specific topic, "traffic", was conducted to analyze the causes of negative sentiments by using the method of co-occurrence of words and evaluation objects.

The destination image is a reflection of the tourist market, including the national country image, the city image, the scenic spot image, etc. Research on the destination image was first proposed by Gunn [153]. As a basis of market positioning, the destination image has attracted a lot of attention from scientists. Compared with the traditional customer survey method, the method of user-generated text analysis can reflect the various dimensions of the destination image more accurately [154], and the real travel experience of the tourists can effectively improve the accuracy of the destination image evaluation [155]. This research [20] was the early study of using online text content for destination image analysis. With the rapid process of "Internet Tourism", more and more researches have begun to explore text analysis as a means of destination image analysis [16,21].

In the process of evaluating the destination image, it is necessary to recognize the tourists' sentiments and the sentiments for all aspects in their tourism in order to assess the satisfaction of the destination components [21,22]. Specifically, the components which compose the destination image are extracted by text mining techniques, and the sentiment analysis is performed for each component to obtain the satisfaction evaluation. Figure 3 shows the key determinants of tourist satisfaction and their impact from a macro-causal perspective. Customer satisfaction is determined by a combination of customer expectations, perceived quality, and value; it has a direct effect on customer loyalty, which is essential for destinations in gaining competitive advantage [156,157]. Besides, because the determinants of tourist satisfaction may be different for different destinations, it is also a feasible method for studying the constituent variables of the image and their weights [23] to promote the evaluation of destination image.

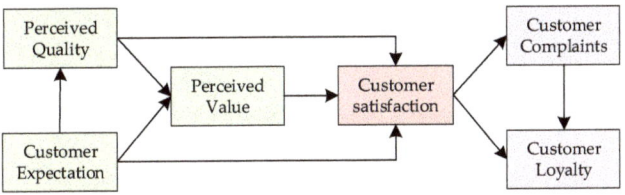

Figure 3. Tourist satisfaction model [18].

From the perspective of tourist behavior, market supervision also includes public sentiment analysis, such as tourism hotspots, crisis events, or emergency analysis, among which tourism hotspots include popular attractions, popular tourist routes, and hot topics. People often show strong concern about current hot spots, hot issues, or public opinion crisis. Especially in the era of highly developed online media, these concerns are often presented in the form of text on the network platform and show high-frequency characteristics. Some scholars take this as a point of view, using statistical word frequency and word frequency co-occurrence to explore tourism hotspots. In the study [24], the location of popular attractions and tourist routes were obtained by mining frequent geographic patterns in travel journals. The study [25] used the maximum confidence and frequent mining patterns to capture neighborhood relationships of the attractions in the tourist log, and further to obtain the most famous sights and frequent tourist routes. Some scholars also use the method of keyword extraction or text clustering to explore the common concerns, get tourist hotspot events, and use sentiment analysis techniques to obtain public opinion orientation with the event [158]. For emergencies or crisis events, due to their real-time characteristics—that is, sudden bursts of growth in a short time—the timing changes of words need to be considered.

For the convenience of readers, we summarize the main contributions, benefits, and main methods of a selected list of informative articles in Table 6.

Table 6. Informative articles about text corpus-based tourism big data mining between 2015 and 2019.

	Contributions	Benefits	Methods
[5]	The topic features of attractions in the context of seasons are firstly explored, which are precisely at the fine-grained season levels.	The proposed a season topic model based on LDA (STLDA) model can distinguish attractions with different seasonal feature distributions, which helps improve personalized recommendations.	Latent Dirichlet Allocation (LDA)
[12]	This paper proposes a sentiment-aspect-region model with the information of Point of Interests (POIs) and geo-tagged reviews to identify the topical-region, topical-aspect, and sentiment for each user; it also proposes an efficient online recommendation algorithm and can provide explanations for recommendations.	POI recommendation, user recommendation, and aspect satisfaction analysis in regions can be achieved by this model.	Probability generative model; expectation-maximization (EM)
[25]	It firstly divides tourism blog contents into semantic word vectors and creatively uses the frequent pattern mining and maximum confidence to capture the neighborhood relationships of the attractions in the tourist log.	Popular attractions and frequent travel routes from massive blog data analysis can be extracted, and thus potential tourists can schedule their travel plans efficiently.	Term Frequency (TF); frequent pattern mining; maximum confidence
[55]	It proposes a negative review detection method by adapting Structure Topic Model (STM); the variation of document-topic proportions with different level of covariates can be easily determined.	It enhances our understanding of the aspects of dissatisfaction in text reviews.	STM
[95]	It employs text mining techniques to access sentiment tendency which is incorporated into an enhanced Singular Value Decomposition (SVD++) model for model amendment also with the temporal influence, such as seasons and holidays on the tourists' sentiments.	It can help alleviate the cold-start problem effectively and thus improve the tourism recommendation system.	SVD++
[127]	It proposes a topic model which can judge users' sentiment distribution and topic sentiment distribution in a topical tree format.	It offers a general model for practitioners to determine why users like or dislike the topics.	Hierarchical probability generative model
[150]	It proposes a Topic Criterion (TC) model and the Topic Sentiment Criterion (TSC) model to calculate tourist profiles and item profiles, as well as their matching degrees to achieve recommendations.	It can be beneficial to tourism recommendation and provide an interpretation of users and item profiles.	LDA; JST (Joint Sentiment-Topic model)

5. Outlook

Tourism big data in the form of text plays an important role in tourism applications. First of all, tourism is a service system, emphasizing the sentiment or value experience of tourism individuals. Text mining techniques have become indispensable to the sentiment judgment and value-oriented analysis in modern tourism applications. Secondly, text mining techniques are experiencing a period of rapid development and are achieving much improvement. Benefit from deep learning techniques such as text classification and sentiment analysis have made many breakthroughs [159].

However, text mining techniques based on deep learning are often less practical in tourism due to the requirements of deep learning for data volume and labeled data, and most of them only use existing data to explore future tourism trends. Aiming at the problem of lack of existing standard tourism corpus and the limitations of deep learning such as interpretability, this paper makes a detailed analysis and puts forward some major trends of future tourism text data mining.

(1) Lack of domain corpus. The languages of the existing tourism corpora are mostly English and the limited multi-language categories make the existing tourism corpora not universally adaptable. In addition, the annotation of the tourism corpus often relies on manual labor, lack of system and formativeness, and the scale of the corpus is usually small. How to automatically and effectively construct a standardized large-scale multi-language tourism corpus has become one of the keys to the successful application of tourism big data. Given the impact of publicly annotated data sets on tourism big data mining and for the convenience of research, we summarize some of the relevant publicly available text data sets currently in the tourism domain, with the data sets described and the dataset sources listed in Table 7.

Table 7. Publicly available tourism data sets.

Name	Description	Source	Accessed Date
Hotel_Reviews 515,000	It contains 515,000 customer reviews with positive and negative aspects and ratings of 1493 luxury hotels across Europe, as well as the location of the hotel.	https://www.kaggle.com/jiashenliu/515k-hotel-reviews-data-in-europe	24 July 2019
TripAdvisor Hotel Review Dataset	It contains 20,490 hotel customer reviews and related review ratings.	https://zenodo.org/record/1219899#.XFSETygzY2w	24 July 2019
Citysearch Restaurant Review Dataset	It contains 35,000 food reviews and lists representative words related to the attributes of each entity. It also includes 3418 sentences with labeled sentiment polarity for the attributes of each entity.	http://dilab.korea.ac.kr/jmts/jmtsdataset.zip	24 July 2019
OpinRank Dataset	It contains 259,000 reviews of 10 different cities (Dubai, Beijing, London, New York, New Delhi, San Francisco, Shanghai, Montreal, Las Vegas, and Chicago), each city of which has approximately 80–700 hotels, with dates, comment title, and full comment included.	https://github.com/kavgan/OpinRank/blob/master/OpinRankDatasetWithJudgments.zip	24 July 2019
SemEval ABSA Restaurant Reviews-English (2014–2016) SemEval ABSA Hotels Domain-English (2015–2016)	It includes multiple English data sets for restaurants and hotels which are composed of comments, with the attributes (E#A pairs) and the target and the corresponding sentiment polarities marked.	http://metashare.ilsp.gr:8080/repository/search/?q=SemEval	24 July 2019
SentiBridge: A Knowledge Base for Entity-Sentiment Representation	The dictionary contains a total of 300,000 entity-sentiment pairs, currently from the three domains of news, travel, and catering.	https://github.com/rainarch/SentiBridge	24 July 2019
ChnSentiCorp-Htl-unba-10000	It contains 7000 positive and 3000 negative hotel reviews in Chinese.	https://download.csdn.net/download/sinat_30045277/9862005	24 July 2019

Table 7. *Cont.*

Name	Description	Source	Accessed Date
TourPedia	It contains two main data sets: Places, and reviews about places. Places contains accommodations, restaurants, attractions, and points of interest, and each place is descripted with address, location, polarity, etc. Reviews about places has some auxiliary information such as rating, time, polarity, place, etc.	http://tour-pedia.org/about/datasets.html	24 July 2019
Museum reviews from TripAdvisor	It contains 1600 museum data including address, category, review, rating, popularity, etc.	https://www.kaggle.com/annecool37/museum-data	24 July 2019

Recently, knowledge transfer has attracted a lot of attention, with attempts to transfer the knowledge learned from the existing large-scale data to the target task to reduce the demand for the target data, and plays a decisive role in putting future research of tourism big data mining into practical applications. At present, transfer learning has made good progress in cross-domain feature extraction and sentiment analysis [160]. For the lack of training data, scholars have proposed some transfer learning models such as few-shot, one-shot and zero-shot, which can learn the relevant features of the data for classification prediction if the training samples in the target area are not provided or only provided a small, and they have achieved good results in the text data mining [161,162]. Recently, the pre-trained BERT model shows great advantages in multi-language and multi-task transfer learning, without substantial task-specific architecture modifications, which makes transfer learning widely applicable to the text mining.

Meta-learning also achieves outstanding results in response to the problem of too little training data in the target domain. The goal of meta-learning is to train a model on multi-task and to obtain common attributes that adapt to a new task, reducing the need for pre-trained data. For example, for the problem of fuzzy learning tasks with the small sample in NLP field, an adaptive metrics meta-learning method has been proposed, which automatically captures the best-weighted combination of metrics from the meta-training task [161].

In addition, the use of semi-supervised and unsupervised learning methods can also reduce the dependence of labeled data. Studies [163] have pointed out that when multilingual transfer learning such as BERT, unsupervised models, and meta-learning are combined, the areas with fewer data resources are very promising.

(2) Limitations of deep learning. The first one is poor interpretability. For a long time, deep learning has been lacking in rigorous mathematical theory, and it is impossible to explain the quality of the results and the variables that lead to the results. In the tourism domain, the interpretable performance of deep learning is more conducive to discover knowledge and understand the nature of the problem, thus the practitioners can make operational service adjustments. The use of attention mechanisms in deep learning also provides an interpretable channel for deep learning. However, for deep learning itself, it still seems to be a black box problem. Some scholars also consider using the knowledge graph to eliminate the semantic gap between NLP and deep learning, which will provide vital support for deep learning interpretability in the future.

The second is the limited expression capability. Text information extraction can be realized by multiple feature learning layers of deep learning model. However, as the complexity of the model increases, the learning ability strengthens, but there exists an over-fitting problem. This problem can be solved by acquiring massive data to a certain extent, while the lack of labeled data and the finiteness of hierarchy in deep learning models restricts the learning ability of deep learning. Currently, transfer learning is an effective way to solve this problem. Besides, some scholars, such as Professor Zhou

Zhihua, have considered the use of non-differentiable models to enhance the expressive ability of deep learning aiming at simulate the diversity of the real world, which is a great challenge for deep learning.

(3) The future trend of text corpus-based tourism application. Tourism has a high degree of social nature. It uses the text information shared in social network media to explore the new vitality of tourism services or develop products by feedbacks from tourists, which is the general way of tourism text data mining currently. Tourism personalized recommendation is a significant and potential direction because it caters to current social needs. However, in tourism recommendation, the cold start problem for tourists or tourism items has always been a difficult task for scholars to explore, and thus fail to solve. Combined with other enriched multimedia content such as videos, photographs, text, links to websites, etc., text-based recommendation will be enhanced [164,165], which is also a supplement for addressing the cold start problem. Besides, how to dynamically explore tourist preferences and how to explore the unknown or unfamiliar tourism area or travel style for tourists will become a hot spot for future research.

This paper mainly reviews the automatic text mining techniques in NLP, which can assist people to acquire information from a large of text data. Text generation techniques will also be necessary for future tourism development and application. From tourism recommendations, NLP is transitioning to the process of assisting people in understanding, which will provide a decisive or interpretable way for tourism. In the future, with the improvement of interactive NLP [166], the machine will be able to understand human language more accurately and communicate more naturally with users, thus providing tourists with real-time intelligent answers and suggestions. In the future, reinforcement learning (RL) [167] will give a powerful impetus to tourism big data because it can adapt to the instant changes in the environment.

For the convenience of readers, we summarize the main key methodologies of the text mining techniques in the surveyed papers in Table 8:

Table 8. Main take-aways for the reader.

Main Take-Aways
Topic probability model is a basic model used in most topic extraction algorithms, which can be improved by enhancing topic coherence of short texts or exploiting the sematic feature of words and text enabled by deep learning.
Language models based on deep learning models such as CNN and RNN, etc., are widely applied in text classification. Focusing on their requirement for abundant labeled data for supervised learning, many strategies have been proposed such as co-training, training samples extension, meta-learning, and transfer learning.
One of the mainstream trends in sentiment classification is to exploit the attention mechanism in deep learning. Based on the study of sentiment targets or sentiment aspects, the sentiments can be more fine-grained and interpretable, which is more conducive to practical application analysis.
K-means is a method often commonly used in text clustering due to its small time complexity. Optimization of initial clustering points, improvement of text representation, and optimization of objective functions are all popular aspects of improvements to K-means-based text clustering.

6. Conclusions

Big data analysis is changing the operating mode of the global tourism economy, providing tourism managers with deeper insights, and infiltrating into all aspects of tourist travels, while driving tourism innovation and development [168]. Tourism text big data mining techniques have made it possible to analyze the behaviors of tourists and realize real-time monitoring of the market. As the key technique of text analysis, NLP is experiencing a period of vigorous development. Both machine learning and current deep learning with high achievements have been greatly applied in NLP. The deep learning language model provides a general learning framework, which can flexibly represent the text, and can be easily extended to different network models—such as standard methods CNN, LSTM, GRU, and various variants of standard methods—which laid the foundation for the deepening of the deep learning theory in the NLP field, and thus provided a solid theoretical basis for the improvement of the text corpus-based tourism big data mining.

This paper systematically summarizes current and potential applications of big data text mining techniques in Internet tourism economy and provides some guides for further research in tourism big data analysis. At present, most of the existing studies on tourism big data mining tend to be driven by data and algorithm innovation. However, tourism data analysis and service evaluations without considering the subjective nature of tourists may be inherently biased. Personalized subjective analysis and evaluation methods, such as Kansei engineering, widely use product evaluation [169], and thus have big potential in tourism big data analysis. Combining data-driven methods with tourism domain knowledge, such as the considering of domain-specific words [170], is also another direction that needs exploration in the future.

Author Contributions: Q.L. and S.L. conceived the conception; Q.L. conducted literature collection and manuscript writing; S.L., J.H. (Jianjun Hu), J.H. (Jie Hu) and S.Z. revised and polished the manuscript. All authors read and approved the final manuscript.

Funding: This research was funded by the National Natural Science Foundation of China under Grant No. 91746116, National Science and Technology Support Program under Grant No. 2014BAH05F02, Science and Technology Program of Guizhou Province Nos. [2015]4011, Nos. [2016]5103, Nos. [2017]5788, and the Science and Technology Project of Guizhou Province under Grant Talents Nos. [2018] 5774-034.

Conflicts of Interest: The authors declare no conflict of interest.

References

1. Ye, Q.; Law, R.; Gu, B.; Chen, W. The influence of user-generated content on traveler behavior: An empirical investigation on the effects of e-word-of-mouth to hotel online bookings. *Comput. Hum. Behav.* **2011**, *27*, 634–639. [CrossRef]
2. Li, Q.; Li, S.; Hu, J.; Zhang, S.; Hu, J. Tourism Review Sentiment Classification Using a Bidirectional Recurrent Neural Network with an Attention Mechanism and Topic-Enriched Word Vectors. *Sustainability* **2018**, *10*, 3313. [CrossRef]
3. Marrese-Taylor, E.; Velásquez, J.D.; Bravo-Marquez, F.; Matsuo, Y. Identifying Customer Preferences about Tourism Products Using an Aspect-based Opinion Mining Approach. *Proc. Comput. Sci.* **2013**, *22*, 182–191. [CrossRef]
4. Xu, J.; Fan, Y.; Bai, B. Knowledge mining and visualizing for scenic spots with probabilistic topic model. *J. Comput. Appl.* **2016**, *36*, 2103–2108.
5. Huang, C.; Wang, Q.; Yang, D.; Xu, F. Topic mining of tourist attractions based on a seasonal context aware LDA model. *Intell. Data Anal.* **2018**, *22*, 383–405. [CrossRef]
6. Al-Horaibi, L.; Khan, M.B. Sentiment analysis of Arabic tweets using text mining techniques. In Proceedings of the First International Workshop on Pattern Recognition, Tokyo, Japan, 11–13 May 2016; p. 100111F.
7. Okazaki, S.; Andreu, L.; Campo, S. Knowledge sharing among tourists via social media: A comparison between Facebook and TripAdvisor. *Int. J. Tour. Res.* **2017**, *19*, 107–119. [CrossRef]
8. Wang, J.; Li, S.; Zhou, G. Joint Learning on Relevant User Attributes in Micro-blog. In Proceedings of the 26th International Joint Conference on Artificial Intelligence, Melbourne, Australia, 19–25 August 2017; pp. 4130–4136.
9. Gu, H.; Wang, J.; Wang, Z.; Zhuang, B.; Su, F. Modeling of User Portrait Through Social Media. In Proceedings of the 2018 IEEE International Conference on Multimedia and Expo (ICME), San Diego, CA, USA, 23–27 July 2018.
10. Wang, J.; Li, S.; Jiang, M.; Wu, H.; Zhou, G. Cross-media User Profiling with Joint Textual and Social User Embedding. In Proceedings of the 27th International Conference on Computational Linguistics, Santa Fe, NM, USA, 21–25 August 2018; pp. 1410–1420.
11. Pennacchiotti, M.; Popescu, A. A Machine Learning Approach to Twitter User Classification. In Proceedings of the International Conference on Weblogs and Social Media, Barcelona, Spain, 17–21 July 2011.

12. Zhao, K.; Cong, G.; Yuan, Q.; Zhu, K.Q. SAR: A Sentiment-aspect-region Model for User Preference Analysis in Geo-tagged Reviews. In Proceedings of the 2015 IEEE 31st International Conference on Data Engineering, Seoul, Korea, 13–17 April 2015; pp. 675–686.
13. Teso, E.; Olmedilla, M.; Martínez-Torres, M.; Toral, S. Application of text mining techniques to the analysis of discourse in eWOM communications from a gender perspective. *Technol. Forecast. Soc. Chang.* **2018**, *129*, 131–142. [CrossRef]
14. Škrlj, B.; Martinc, M.; Kralj, J.; Lavrač, N.; Pollak, S. tax2vec: Constructing Interpretable Features from Taxonomies for Short Text Classification. *arXiv* **2019**, arXiv:1902.00438.
15. Li, Y.; Zhang, Z.; Peng, Y.; Yin, H.; Xu, Q. Matching user accounts based on user generated content across social networks. *Fut. Gen. Comput. Syst.* **2018**, *83*, 104–115. [CrossRef]
16. Költringer, C.; Dickinger, A. Analyzing destination branding and image from online sources: A web content mining approach. *J. Bus. Res.* **2015**, *68*, 1836–1843. [CrossRef]
17. Yue, G.; Barnes, S.J.; Jia, Q. Mining meaning from online ratings and reviews: Tourist satisfaction analysis using latent dirichletallocation. *Tour. Manag.* **2017**, *59*, 467–483. [CrossRef]
18. Wang, Y. *More Important than Ever: Measuring Tourist Satisfaction*; Griffith Institute for Tourism, Griffith University: Queensland, Australia, 2016.
19. Kim, K.; Park, O.; Yun, S.; Yun, H. What makes tourists feel negatively about tourism destinations? Application of hybrid text mining methodology to smart destination management. *Technol. Forecast. Soc. Chang.* **2017**, *123*. [CrossRef]
20. Govers, R.; Go, F.M. Projected destination image online: Website content analysis of pictures and text. *Inf. Technol. Tour.* **2005**, *7*, 73–89. [CrossRef]
21. Chi, T.; Wu, B.; Morrison, A.M.; Zhang, J.; Chen, Y.C. Travel blogs on China as a destination image formation agent: A qualitative analysis using Leximancer. *Tour. Manag.* **2015**, *46*, 347–358. [CrossRef]
22. Ren, G.; Hong, T. Investigating Online Destination Images Using a Topic-Based Sentiment Analysis Approach. *Sustainability* **2017**, *9*, 1765. [CrossRef]
23. Rodrigues, A.I.; Correia, A.; Kozak, M.; Tuohino, A. Lake-destination image attributes: Content analysis of text and pictures. In *Marketing Places and Spaces*; Emerald Group Publishing Limited: Bingley, UK, 2015; pp. 293–314.
24. Yuan, H.; Xu, H.; Qian, Y.; Ye, K. Towards Summarizing Popular Information from Massive Tourism Blogs. In Proceedings of the IEEE International Conference on Data Mining Workshop, Shenzhen, China, 14 December 2014; pp. 409–416.
25. Yuan, H.; Xu, H.; Qian, Y.; Li, Y. Make your travel smarter: Summarizing urban tourism information from massive blog data. *Int. J. Inf. Manag.* **2016**, *36*, 1306–1319. [CrossRef]
26. Mikolov, T.; Chen, K.; Corrado, G.; Dean, J. Efficient Estimation of Word Representations in Vector Space. *arXiv* **2013**, arXiv:1301.3781.
27. Mikolov, T.; Sutskever, I.; Chen, K. Distributed Representations of Words and Phrases and their Compositionality. In Proceedings of the International Conference on Neural Information Processing Systems, Lake Tahoe, CA, USA, 5–10 December 2013; pp. 3111–3119.
28. Pennington, J.; Socher, R.; Manning, C.D. Glove: Global Vectors for Word Representation. In Proceedings of the Empirical Methods in Natural Language Processing, Doha, Qatar, 25–29 October 2014; pp. 1532–1543.
29. McCann, B.; Bradbury, J.; Xiong, C.; Socher, R. Learned in translation: Contextualized word vectors. In Proceedings of the Advances in Neural Information Processing Systems, Long Beach, CA, USA, 4–9 December 2017; pp. 6294–6305.
30. Peters, M.; Neumann, M.; Iyyer, M.; Gardner, M.; Clark, C.; Lee, K.; Zettlemoyer, L. Deep contextualized word representations. *N. Am. Chapter Assoc. Comput. Linguist.* **2018**, *1*, 2227–2237.
31. Radford, A.; Narasimhan, K.; Salimans, T.; Sutskever, I. Improving language understanding by generative pre-training. Available online: https://s3-us-west-2.amazonaws.com/openai-assets/research-covers/languageunsupervised/languageunderstandingpaper.pdf (accessed on 7 June 2018).
32. Devlin, J.; Chang, M.; Lee, K.; Toutanova, K. BERT: Pre-training of Deep Bidirectional Transformers for Language Understanding. *arXiv* **2018**, arXiv:1810.04805.
33. Xu, G.; Wang, H. The Development of Topic Models in Natural Language Processing. *Chin. J. Comput.* **2011**, *34*, 1423–1436. [CrossRef]

34. Kim, Y. Convolutional Neural Networks for Sentence Classification. *Empir. Methods Nat. Lang. Process.* **2014**, 1746–1751. [CrossRef]
35. Yang, Z.; Yang, D.; Dyer, C.; He, X.; Smola, A.; Hovy, E. Hierarchical attention networks for document classification. In Proceedings of the 2016 Conference of the North American Chapter of the Association for Computational Linguistics: Human Language Technologies, San Diego, CA, USA, 13–15 June 2016; pp. 1480–1489.
36. Suyal, H.; Panwar, A.; Negi, A.S. Text Clustering Algorithms: A Review. *Int. J. Comput. Appl.* **2014**, *96*, 36–40. [CrossRef]
37. Vaswani, A.; Shazeer, N.; Parmar, N.; Uszkoreit, J.; Jones, L.; Gomez, A.N.; Kaiser, Ł.; Polosukhin, I. Attention is all you need. In Proceedings of the Advances in neural information processing systems, Long Beach, CA, USA, 4–9 December 2017; pp. 5998–6008.
38. Genc-Nayebi, N.; Abran, A. A systematic literature review: Opinion mining studies from mobile app store user reviews. *J. Syst. Softw.* **2017**, *125*, 207–219. [CrossRef]
39. Moher, D.; Shamseer, L.; Clarke, M.; Ghersi, D.; Liberati, A.; Petticrew, M.; Shekelle, P.; Stewart, L.A. Preferred reporting items for systematic review and meta-analysis protocols (PRISMA-P) 2015 statement. *Syst. Rev.* **2015**, *4*, 1. [CrossRef] [PubMed]
40. Keele, S. *Guidelines for Performing Systematic Literature Reviews in Software Engineering*; Technical Report Ver. 2.3 EBSE Technical Report; EBSE: Durham, UK, 2007.
41. Bengio, Y.; Ducharme, R.; Vincent, P.; Jauvin, C. A neural probabilistic language model. *J. Mach. Learn. Res.* **2003**, *3*, 1137–1155.
42. Qiao, C.; Huang, B.; Niu, G.; Li, D.; Dong, D.; He, W.; Yu, D.; Wu, H. A New Method of Region Embedding for Text Classification. In Proceedings of the International Conference on Learning Representations, Vancouver, BC, Canada, 30 April–3 May 2018.
43. Xiong, S.; Lv, H.; Zhao, W.; Ji, D. Towards Twitter sentiment classification by multi-level sentiment-enriched word embeddings. *Neurocomputing* **2018**, *275*, 2459–2466. [CrossRef]
44. Xiong, S. Improving Twitter Sentiment Classification via Multi-Level Sentiment-Enriched Word Embeddings. *arXiv* **2016**, arXiv:1611.00126. [CrossRef]
45. Joulin, A.; Grave, E.; Bojanowski, P.; Mikolov, T. Bag of Tricks for Efficient Text Classification. *Conf. Eur. Chapter Assoc. Comput. Linguist.* **2017**, *2*, 427–431. [CrossRef]
46. Ji, S.; Yun, H.; Yanardag, P.; Matsushima, S.; Vishwanathan, S.V.N. WordRank: Learning Word Embeddings via Robust Ranking. *Comput. Sci.* **2015**, 658–668. [CrossRef]
47. Howard, J.; Ruder, S. Universal language model fine-tuning for text classification. *arXiv* **2018**, arXiv:1801.06146.
48. Le, Q.V.; Mikolov, T. Distributed Representations of Sentences and Documents. In Proceedings of the International Conference on International Conference on Machine Learning, Beijing, China, 21–26 June 2014; pp. 1188–1196.
49. Arora, S.; Liang, Y.; Ma, T. A Simple but Tough-to-Beat Baseline for Sentence Embeddings. In Proceedings of the International Conference on Learning Representations, Toulon, France, 24–26 April 2017.
50. Kiros, R.; Zhu, Y.; Salakhutdinov, R.R.; Zemel, R.; Urtasun, R.; Torralba, A.; Fidler, S. Skip-thought vectors. In Proceedings of the Advances in Neural Information Processing Systems, Montreal, Canada, 7–12 December 2015; pp. 3294–3302.
51. Logeswaran, L.; Lee, H. An efficient framework for learning sentence representations. *arXiv* **2018**, arXiv:1803.02893.
52. Conneau, A.; Kiela, D.; Schwenk, H.; Barrault, L.; Bordes, A. Supervised Learning of Universal Sentence Representations from Natural Language Inference Data. In Proceedings of the Conference on Empirical Methods in Natural Language Processing, Copenhagen, Denmark, 31 October–4 November 2018; pp. 670–680.
53. Subramanian, S.; Trischler, A.; Bengio, Y.; Pal, C. Learning General Purpose Distributed Sentence Representations via Large Scale Multi-task Learning. In Proceedings of the International Conference on Learning Representations, Vancouver, Canada, 30 April–3 May 2018.
54. Liu, G.; Xu, X.; Zhu, Y.; Li, L. An Improved Latent Dirichlet Allocation Model for Hot Topic Extraction. In Proceedings of the IEEE Fourth International Conference on Big Data and Cloud Computing, Sydney, Australia, 3–5 December 2014; pp. 470–476.
55. Hu, N.; Zhang, T.; Gao, B.; Bose, I. What do hotel customers complain about? Text analysis using structural topic model. *Tour. Manag.* **2019**, *72*, 417–426. [CrossRef]

56. Roberts, M.E.; Stewart, B.M.; Tingley, D.; Lucas, C.; Lederluis, J.; Gadarian, S.K.; Albertson, B.; Rand, D.G. Structural topic models for open ended survey responses. *Am. J. Polit. Sci.* **2014**, *58*, 1064–1082. [CrossRef]
57. Zarrinkalam, F.; Kahani, M.; Bagheri, E. Mining user interests over active topics on social networks. *Inf. Process. Manag.* **2018**, *54*, 339–357. [CrossRef]
58. Rana, T.A.; Cheah, Y.N. Aspect extraction in sentiment analysis: Comparative analysis and survey. *Artif. Intell. Rev.* **2016**, 1–25. [CrossRef]
59. Rose, S.; Engel, D.; Cramer, N.; Cowley, W. Automatic Keyword Extraction from Individual Documents. *Text Min. Appl. Theory* **2010**, 1–20. [CrossRef]
60. Bougouin, A.; Boudin, F.; Daille, B. TopicRank: Graph-Based Topic Ranking for Keyphrase Extraction. In Proceedings of the International Joint Conference on Natural Language Processing, Nagoya, Japan, 14–18 October 2013; pp. 543–551.
61. Ning, J.; Liu, J. Using Word2vec with TextRank to Extract Keywords. *New Technol. Libr. Inf. Serv.* **2016**, *32*, 20–27. [CrossRef]
62. Xun, G.; Li, Y.; Zhao, W.X.; Gao, J.; Zhang, A. A Correlated Topic Model Using Word Embeddings. In Proceedings of the International Joint Conference on Artificial Intelligence, Melbourne, Australian, 19–25 August 2017; pp. 4207–4213.
63. Alam, M.H.; Ryu, W.-J.; Lee, S. Joint multi-grain topic sentiment: Modeling semantic aspects for online reviews. *Inf. Sci.* **2016**, *339*, 206–223. [CrossRef]
64. Yao, L.; Zhang, Y.; Chen, Q.; Qian, H.; Wei, B.; Hu, Z. Mining coherent topics in documents using word embeddings and large-scale text data. *Eng. Appl. Arti. Intell.* **2017**, *64*, 432–439. [CrossRef]
65. Moody, C.E. Mixing dirichlet topic models and word embeddings to make lda2vec. *arXiv* **2016**, arXiv:1605.02019.
66. Wang, Z.; Ma, L.; Zhang, Y. A hybrid document feature extraction method using latent Dirichlet allocation and word2vec. In Proceedings of the 2016 IEEE First International Conference on Data Science in Cyberspace (DSC), Changsha, China, 13–16 June 2016; pp. 98–103.
67. Cao, Z.; Li, S.; Liu, Y.; Li, W.; Ji, H. A novel neural topic model and its supervised extension. In Proceedings of the Twenty-Ninth AAAI Conference on Artificial Intelligence, Austin, TX, USA, 25–30 January 2015; pp. 2210–2216.
68. Lau, J.H.; Baldwin, T.; Cohn, T. Topically driven neural language model. *arXiv* **2017**, arXiv:1704.08012.
69. He, R.; Lee, W.S.; Ng, H.T.; Dahlmeier, D. An Unsupervised Neural Attention Model for Aspect Extraction. In Proceedings of the Meeting of the Association for Computational Linguistics, Vancouver, BC, Canada, 30 July–4 August 2017; pp. 388–397.
70. Qiu, L.; Yu, J. CLDA: An effective topic model for mining user interest preference under big data background. *Complexity* **2018**, *2018*. [CrossRef]
71. Zheng, C.T.; Liu, C.; San Wong, H. Corpus-based topic diffusion for short text clustering. *Neurocomputing* **2018**, *275*, 2444–2458. [CrossRef]
72. Li, X.; Zhang, A.; Li, C.; Ouyang, J.; Cai, Y. Exploring coherent topics by topic modeling with term weighting. *Inf. Process. Manag.* **2018**, *54*, 1345–1358. [CrossRef]
73. Liang, Y.; Liu, Y.; Chen, C.; Jiang, Z. Extracting topic-sensitive content from textual documents—A hybrid topic model approach. *Eng. Appl. Artif. Intell.* **2018**, *70*, 81–91. [CrossRef]
74. Xu, Y.; Yin, J.; Huang, J.; Yin, Y. Hierarchical topic modeling with automatic knowledge mining. *Expert Syst. Appl.* **2018**, *103*, 106–117. [CrossRef]
75. Afzaal, M.; Usman, M.; Fong, A.C.M.; Fong, S.; Zhuang, Y. Fuzzy Aspect Based Opinion Classification System for Mining Tourist Reviews. *Adv. Fuzzy Syst.* **2016**, *2016*, 1–14. [CrossRef]
76. Tang, B.; Kay, S.; He, H. Toward optimal feature selection in naive Bayes for text categorization. *IEEE Trans. Knowl. Data Eng.* **2016**, *28*, 2508–2521. [CrossRef]
77. Hamzah, A.; Widyastuti, N. Opinion classification using maximum entropy and K-means clustering. In Proceedings of the 2016 International Conference on Information & Communication Technology and Systems (ICTS), Surabaya, Indonesia, 12 October 2016; pp. 162–166.
78. Chen, K.; Zhang, Z.; Long, J.; Zhang, H. Turning from TF-IDF to TF-IGM for term weighting in text classification. *Expert Syst. Appl.* **2016**, *66*, 245–260. [CrossRef]
79. An, J.; Chen, Y.P. Keyword extraction for text categorization. In Proceedings of the Active Media Technology, Kagawa, Japan, 19–21 May 2005; pp. 556–561.

80. Hu, J.; Li, S.; Yao, Y.; Yu, L.; Yang, G.; Hu, J. Patent keyword extraction algorithm based on distributed representation for patent classification. *Entropy* **2018**, *20*, 104. [CrossRef]
81. Hu, J.; Li, S.; Hu, J.; Yang, G. A Hierarchical Feature Extraction Model for Multi-Label Mechanical Patent Classification. *Sustainability* **2018**, *10*, 219. [CrossRef]
82. Ogada, K.; Mwangi, W.; Cheruiyot, W. N-gram Based Text Categorization Method for Improved Data Mining. *J. Inf. Eng. Appl.* **2015**, *5*, 35–43.
83. Zhang, H.; Zhong, G. Improving short text classification by learning vector representations of both words and hidden topics. *Knowl. Based Syst.* **2016**, *102*, 76–86. [CrossRef]
84. Zhang, X.; Zhao, J.J.; Lecun, Y. Character-level convolutional networks for text classification. *Neural Inf. Process. Syst.* **2015**, 649–657. [CrossRef]
85. Li, S.; Hu, J.; Cui, Y.; Hu, J. DeepPatent: Patent classification with convolutional neural networks and word embedding. *Scientometrics* **2018**, *117*, 721–744. [CrossRef]
86. Zhou, P.; Qi, Z.; Zheng, S.; Xu, J.; Bao, H.; Xu, B. Text Classification Improved by Integrating Bidirectional LSTM with Two-dimensional Max Pooling. *Int. Conf. Comput. Ling.* **2016**, 3485–3495.
87. Lai, S.; Xu, L.; Liu, K.; Zhao, J. Recurrent convolutional neural networks for text classification. In Proceedings of the 29th AAAI Conference on Artificial Intelligence, Austin, TX, USA, 25–30 January 2015.
88. Sainath, T.N.; Vinyals, O.; Senior, A.; Sak, H. Convolutional, Long Short-Term Memory, fully connected Deep Neural Networks. In Proceedings of the IEEE International Conference on Acoustics, Speech and Signal Processing, Brisbane, QLD, Australia, 19–24 April 2015; pp. 4580–4584.
89. Liu, P.; Qiu, X.; Huang, X. Recurrent neural network for text classification with multi-task learning. *arXiv* **2016**, arXiv:1605.05101.
90. Conneau, A.; Schwenk, H.; Barrault, L.; Lecun, Y.; Conneau, A.; Schwenk, H.; Barrault, L.; Lecun, Y. Very Deep Convolutional Networks for Text Classification. *Comput. Sci.* **2016**, 1107–1116. [CrossRef]
91. Katz, G.; Caragea, C.; Shabtai, A. Vertical Ensemble Co-Training for Text Classification. *ACM Trans. Intell. Syst. Technol. TIST* **2018**, *9*, 21. [CrossRef]
92. Zhu, W.; Liu, Y.; Hu, G.; Ni, J.; Lu, Z. A Sample Extension Method Based on Wikipedia and Its Application in Text Classification. *Wirel. Pers. Commun.* **2018**, *102*, 3851–3867. [CrossRef]
93. Jiang, X.; Havaei, M.; Chartrand, G.; Chouaib, H.; Vincent, T.; Jesson, A.; Chapados, N.; Matwin, S. On the Importance of Attention in Meta-Learning for Few-Shot Text Classification. *arXiv* **2018**, arXiv:1806.00852.
94. Merity, S.; Keskar, N.S.; Socher, R. Regularizing and optimizing LSTM language models. *arXiv* **2017**, arXiv:1708.02182.
95. Zheng, X.; Luo, Y.; Sun, L.; Ji, Z.; Chen, F. A tourism destination recommender system using users' sentiment and temporal dynamics. *J. Intell. Inf. Syst.* **2018**, 1–22. [CrossRef]
96. Serna, A.; Gerrikagoitia, J.K.; Bernabe, U.; Ruiz, T. A Method to Assess Sustainable Mobility for Sustainable Tourism: The Case of the Public Bike Systems. In Proceedings of the Enter Conference | Etourism: Sustaining Culture & Creativity Organized by International Federation for Information Technology & Travel & Tourism, Rome, Italy, 24–26 January 2017.
97. Li, Q.; Wu, Y.; Wang, S.; Lin, M.; Feng, X.; Wang, H. VisTravel: Visualizing tourism network opinion from the user generated content. *J. Vis.* **2016**, *19*, 489–502. [CrossRef]
98. Zong, C. *Statistical Natural Language Processing*; Tsinghua University Press: Beijing, China, 2013.
99. Zhao, Y.; Qin, B.; Liu, T. Sentiment Analysis. *J. Softw.* **2010**, *21*, 1834–1848. [CrossRef]
100. Chen, Z.; Xu, R.; Gui, L.; Lu, Q. Combining Convolutional Neural Networks and Word Sentiment Sequence Features for Chinese Text Sentiment Analysis. *J. Chin. Inf. Process.* **2015**, *29*, 172–178.
101. Fu, Y.; Hao, J.-X.; Li, X.; Hsu, C.H. Predictive Accuracy of Sentiment Analytics for Tourism: A Metalearning Perspective on Chinese Travel News. *J. Travel Res.* **2018**, 0047287518772361. [CrossRef]
102. Zhang, L.; Wang, S.; Liu, B. Deep learning for sentiment analysis: A survey. *Wiley Interdiscip. Rev. Data Min. Knowl. Discov.* **2018**, *8*, e1253. [CrossRef]
103. Santos, C.N.D.; Gatti, M.A.D.C. Deep Convolutional Neural Networks for Sentiment Analysis of Short Texts. In Proceedings of the International Conference on Computational Linguistics, Dublin, Ireland, 23–29 August 2014; pp. 69–78.
104. Dieng, A.B.; Wang, C.; Gao, J.; Paisley, J. Topicrnn: A recurrent neural network with long-range semantic dependency. *arXiv* **2016**, arXiv:1611.01702.

105. Kalchbrenner, N.; Grefenstette, E.; Blunsom, P. A Convolutional Neural Network for Modelling Sentences. *Meet. Assoc. Comput. Ling.* **2014**, 655–665.
106. Hassan, A.; Mahmood, A. Deep Learning approach for sentiment analysis of short texts. In Proceedings of the International Conference on Control and Automation, Ohrid, Macedonia, 3–6 July 2017; pp. 705–710.
107. Tang, D.; Wei, F.; Yang, N.; Zhou, M.; Liu, T.; Qin, B. Learning Sentiment-Specific Word Embedding for Twitter Sentiment Classification. In Proceedings of the Meeting of the Association for Computational Linguistics, Baltimore, MD, USA, 22–27 June 2014; pp. 1555–1565.
108. Ambartsoumian, A.; Popowich, F. Self-Attention: A Better Building Block for Sentiment Analysis Neural Network Classifiers. *Empir. Methods Nat. Lang. Process.* **2018**, 130–139. [CrossRef]
109. Jiang, T.; Wan, C.; Liu, D. Extracting Target-Opinion Pairs Based on Semantic Analysis. *Chin. J. Comput.* **2017**, *40*, 617–633.
110. He, W.; Tian, X.; Tao, R.; Zhang, W.; Yan, G.; Akula, V. Application of social media analytics: A case of analyzing online hotel reviews. *Online Inf. Rev.* **2017**, *41*, 921–935. [CrossRef]
111. Hu, C.; Liang, N. Deeper attention-based LSTM for aspect sentiment analysis. *Appl. Res. Comput.* **2019**, *36*.
112. Fu, X.; Wei, Y.; Xu, F.; Wang, T.; Lu, Y.; Li, J.; Huang, J.Z. Semi-supervised Aspect-level Sentiment Classification Model based on Variational Autoencoder. *Knowl. Based Syst.* **2019**, *171*, 81–92. [CrossRef]
113. Wang, Y.; Huang, M.; Zhao, L. Attention-based LSTM for aspect-level sentiment classification. In Proceedings of the 2016 Conference on Empirical Methods in Natural Language Processing, Austin, TX, USA, 1–5 November 2016; pp. 606–615.
114. Tay, Y.; Tuan, L.A.; Hui, S.C. Learning to attend via word-aspect associative fusion for aspect-based sentiment analysis. In Proceedings of the 32nd AAAI Conference on Artificial Intelligence, New Orleans, LO, USA, 2–7 February 2018.
115. Tang, D.; Qin, B.; Feng, X.; Liu, T. Effective LSTMs for target-dependent sentiment classification. *arXiv* **2015**, arXiv:1512.01100.
116. Ma, D.; Li, S.; Zhang, X.; Wang, H. Interactive attention networks for aspect-level sentiment classification. *arXiv* **2017**, arXiv:1709.00893. [CrossRef]
117. Tang, D.; Qin, B.; Liu, T. Aspect level sentiment classification with deep memory network. *arXiv* **2016**, arXiv:1605.08900. [CrossRef]
118. Yang, C.; Zhang, H.; Jiang, B.; Li, K. Aspect-based sentiment analysis with alternating coattention networks. *Inf. Process. Manag.* **2019**, *56*, 463–478. [CrossRef]
119. Liu, J.; Zhang, Y. Attention modeling for targeted sentiment. In Proceedings of the 15th Conference of the European Chapter of the Association for Computational Linguistics (Volume 2, Short Papers), Valencia, Spain, 3–7 April 2017; pp. 572–577.
120. Li, X.; Bing, L.; Lam, W.; Shi, B. Transformation networks for target-oriented sentiment classification. *arXiv* **2018**, arXiv:1805.01086.
121. Shuang, K.; Ren, X.; Yang, Q.; Li, R.; Loo, J. AELA-DLSTMs: Attention-Enabled and Location-Aware Double LSTMs for aspect-level sentiment classification. *Neurocomputing* **2019**, *334*, 25–34. [CrossRef]
122. Ma, X.; Zeng, J.; Peng, L.; Fortino, G.; Zhang, Y. Modeling multi-aspects within one opinionated sentence simultaneously for aspect-level sentiment analysis. *Fut. Gen. Comput. Syst.* **2019**, *93*, 304–311. [CrossRef]
123. Zhang, Z.; Wang, L.; Zou, Y.; Gan, C. The optimally designed dynamic memory networks for targeted sentiment classification. *Neurocomputing* **2018**, *309*, 36–45. [CrossRef]
124. Fan, F.; Feng, Y.; Zhao, D. Multi-grained attention network for aspect-level sentiment classification. In Proceedings of the 2018 Conference on Empirical Methods in Natural Language Processing, Brussels, Belgium, 31 October–4 November 2018; pp. 3433–3442.
125. Xu, H.; Liu, B.; Shu, L.; Yu, P.S. BERT Post-Training for Review Reading Comprehension and Aspect-based Sentiment Analysis. *arXiv* **2019**, arXiv:1904.02232.
126. Yang, M.; Yin, W.; Qu, Q.; Tu, W.; Shen, Y.; Chen, X. Neural Attentive Network for Cross-Domain Aspect-level Sentiment Classification. *IEEE Trans. Affect. Comput.* **2019**. [CrossRef]
127. Almars, A.; Li, X.; Zhao, X. Modelling user attitudes using hierarchical sentiment-topic model. *Data Knowl. Eng.* **2019**, *119*, 139–149. [CrossRef]
128. Li, J.; Yujie, C.; Zhao, Z. Tibetan Tourism Hotspots: Co-word Cluster Analysis of English Blogs. *Tour. Trib.* **2015**, *30*, 35–43.

129. Ding, S.; Gong, S.; Li, H. A New Method to Detect Bursty Events from Micro-blog Posts Based on Bursty Topic Words and Agglomerative Hierarchical Clustering Algorithm. *New Technol. Libr. Inf. Serv.* **2016**, *32*, 12–20. [CrossRef]
130. Celardo, L.; Iezzi, D.F.; Vichi, M. Multi-mode partitioning for text clustering to reduce dimensionality and noises. In Proceedings of the 13th International Conference on Statistical Analysis of Textual Data, Nice, France, 7–10 June 2016.
131. Allahyari, M.; Pouriyeh, S.; Assefi, M.; Safaei, S.; Trippe, E.D.; Gutierrez, J.B.; Kochut, K. A Brief Survey of Text Mining: Classification, Clustering and Extraction Techniques. *Min. Text Data* **2017**. [CrossRef]
132. Huang, L.-J.; Cheng, M.-Z.; Xiao, Y. Text Clustering Algorithm Based on Random Cluster Core. In Proceedings of the ITM Web of Conferences, Julius, France; 2016; p. 05001.
133. Xiong, C.; Hua, Z.; Lv, K.; Li, X. An Improved K-means Text Clustering Algorithm by Optimizing Initial Cluster Centers. In Proceedings of the International Conference on Cloud Computing & Big Data, Macau, China, 16–18 November 2016.
134. Huan, Z.; Pengzhou, Z.; Zeyang, G. K-means Text Dynamic Clustering Algorithm Based on KL Divergence. In Proceedings of the 2018 IEEE/ACIS 17th International Conference on Computer and Information Science (ICIS), Singapore, 6 June 2018; pp. 659–663.
135. Abualigah, L.M.; Khader, A.T.; Al-Betar, M.A. Unsupervised feature selection technique based on genetic algorithm for improving the Text Clustering. In Proceedings of the 7th International Conference on Computer Science and Information Technology (CSIT), Amman, Jordan, 13–15 July 2016; pp. 1–6.
136. Jin, C.X.; Bai, Q.C. Text Clustering Algorithm Based on the Graph Structures of Semantic Word Co-occurrence. In Proceedings of the International Conference on Information System and Artificial Intelligence, Hangzhou, China, 14–16 July 2017; pp. 497–502.
137. Wang, B.; Liu, W.; Lin, Z.; Hu, X.; Wei, J.; Liu, C. Text clustering algorithm based on deep representation learning. *J. Eng.* **2018**, *2018*, 1407–1414. [CrossRef]
138. Abualigah, L.M.; Khader, A.T.; Al-Betar, M.A. Multi-objectives-based text clustering technique using K-mean algorithm. In Proceedings of the International Conference on Computer Science & Information Technology, Amman, Jordan, 13–15 July 2016.
139. Aggarwal, C.C.; Zhai, C. A survey of text clustering algorithms. In *Mining Text Data*; Springer: Boston, MA, USA, 2012; pp. 77–128.
140. Yu, J.C.X. Ontology Concepts Clustering Based on Encyclopedia Entr. *J. Univ. Electron. Sci. Technol. China* **2017**, *46*, 636–640.
141. Horner, S.; Swarbrooke, J. *Consumer Behaviour in Tourism*; Routledge: London, UK, 2016.
142. Alén, E.; Losada, N.; Domínguez, T. The Impact of Ageing on the Tourism Industry: An Approach to the Senior Tourist Profile. *Soc. Indic. Res.* **2016**, *127*, 1–20. [CrossRef]
143. Liu, Y.; Huang, K.; Bao, J.; Chen, K. Listen to the voices from home: An analysis of Chinese tourists' sentiments regarding Australian destinations. *Tour. Manag.* **2019**, *71*, 337–347. [CrossRef]
144. Ezeuduji, I.O.; November, K.L.; Haupt, C. Tourist Profile and Destination Brand Perception: The Case of Cape Town, South Africa. *Acta Univ. Danub. Oeconomica* **2016**, *12*, 115–132.
145. Padilla, J.J.; Kavak, H.; Lynch, C.J.; Gore, R.J.; Diallo, S.Y. Temporal and Spatiotemporal Investigation of Tourist Attraction Visit Sentiment on Twitter. *PLoS ONE* **2018**, *13*, e0198857. [CrossRef]
146. Pan, M.H.; Yang, X.X.; Pan, Z. Influence Factors of the Old-age Care Tourism Decision Making Behavior based on the Life Course Theory: A Case of Chongqing. *Hum. Geogr.* **2017**, *6*, 154–160. [CrossRef]
147. Qi, S.; Wong, C.U.I.; Chen, N.; Rong, J.; Du, J. Profiling Macau cultural tourists by using user-generated content from online social media. *Inf. Technol. Tour.* **2018**, 1–20. [CrossRef]
148. Zheng, X.; Luo, Y.; Xu, Z.; Yu, Q.; Lu, L. Tourism Destination Recommender System for the Cold Start Problem. *KSII Trans. Internet Inf. Syst.* **2016**, *10*. [CrossRef]
149. Leal, F.; González–Vélez, H.; Malheiro, B.; Burguillo, J.C. Semantic profiling and destination recommendation based on crowd-sourced tourist reviews. In Proceedings of the International Symposium on Distributed Computing and Artificial Intelligence, Porto, Portugal, 21–23 June 2017; pp. 140–147.
150. Rossetti, M.; Stella, F.; Cao, L.; Zanker, M. *Analysing User Reviews in Tourism with Topic Models*; Springer International Publishing: Lugano, Switzerland, 2015; pp. 47–58.
151. Borràs, J.; Moreno, A.; Valls, A. Intelligent tourism recommender systems: A survey. *Expert Syst. Appl.* **2014**, *41*, 7370–7389. [CrossRef]

152. Qiao, X.; Zhang, L. Overseas Applied Studies on Travel Recommender System in the Past Ten Years. *Tour. Trib.* **2014**. [CrossRef]
153. Batat, W.; Phou, S. *Building Understanding of the Domain of Destination Image: A Review*; Springer International Publishing: Atlanta, GA, USA, 2016.
154. Dickinger, A.; Költringer, C.; Körbitz, W. *Comparing Online Destination Image with Conventional Image Measurement—The Case of Tallinn*; Springer: Vienna, Austria, 2011; pp. 165–177.
155. Gunn, C.A. *Vacationscape: Designing Tourist Regions*; Van Nostrand Reinhold: New York, NY, USA, 1988.
156. Castro, J.C.; Quisimalin, M.; de Pablos, C.; Gancino, V.; Jerez, J. Tourism Marketing: Measuring Tourist Satisfaction. *J. Serv. Sci. Manag.* **2017**, *10*, 280. [CrossRef]
157. San Martín, H.; Herrero, A.; García de los Salmones, M.d.M. An integrative model of destination brand equity and tourist satisfaction. *Curr. Iss. Tour.* **2018**, 1–22. [CrossRef]
158. Kim, J.; Bae, J.; Hastak, M. Emergency information diffusion on online social media during storm Cindy in US. *Int. J. Inf. Manag.* **2018**, *40*, 153–165. [CrossRef]
159. Young, T.; Hazarika, D.; Poria, S.; Cambria, E. Recent trends in deep learning based natural language processing. *IEEE Comput. Intell. Mag.* **2018**, *13*, 55–75. [CrossRef]
160. Liao, X.; Wu, X.; Gui, L.; Huang, J.; Chen, G. Cross-Domain Sentiment Classification Based on Representation Learning and Transfer Learning. *Beijing Da Xue Xue Bao* **2019**, *55*, 37–46. [CrossRef]
161. Yu, M.; Guo, X.; Yi, J.; Chang, S.; Potdar, S.; Cheng, Y.; Tesauro, G.; Wang, H.; Zhou, B. Diverse Few-Shot Text Classification with Multiple Metrics. *arXiv* **2018**, arXiv:1805.07513. [CrossRef]
162. Lampinen, A.; Mcclelland, J.L. One-shot and few-shot learning of word embeddings. *arXiv* **2017**, arXiv:1710.10280.
163. Gu, J.; Wang, Y.; Chen, Y.; Li, V.O.K.; Cho, K. Meta-Learning for Low-Resource Neural Machine Translation. *Empir. Methods Nat. Lang. Process.* **2018**, 3622–3631.
164. Stai, E.; Kafetzoglou, S.; Tsiropoulou, E.E.; Papavassiliou, S. A holistic approach for personalization, relevance feedback & recommendation in enriched multimedia content. *Multimed. Tools Appl.* **2018**, *77*, 283–326. [CrossRef]
165. Pouli, V.; Kafetzoglou, S.; Tsiropoulou, E.E.; Dimitriou, A.; Papavassiliou, S. Personalized multimedia content retrieval through relevance feedback techniques for enhanced user experience. In Proceedings of the 13th International Conference on Telecommunications (ConTEL), Graz, Austria, 13–15 July 2015; pp. 1–8.
166. Zhang, H.; Yu, H.; Xu, W. Listen, interact and talk: Learning to speak via interaction. *arXiv* **2017**, arXiv:1705.09906.
167. Sutton, R.S.; Barto, A.G. *Reinforcement Learning: An Introduction*; MIT Press: Cambridge, MA, USA, 2018.
168. Li, J.; Xu, L.; Tang, L.; Wang, S.; Li, L. Big data in tourism research: A literature review. *Tour. Manag.* **2018**, *68*, 301–323. [CrossRef]
169. Quan, H.; Li, S.; Hu, J. Product Innovation Design Based on Deep Learning and Kansei Engineering. *Appl. Sci.* **2018**, *8*, 2397. [CrossRef]
170. Li, W.; Guo, K.; Shi, Y.; Zhu, L.; Zheng, Y. DWWP: Domain-specific new words detection and word propagation system for sentiment analysis in the tourism domain. *Knowl. Based Syst.* **2018**, *146*, 203–214. [CrossRef]

© 2019 by the authors. Licensee MDPI, Basel, Switzerland. This article is an open access article distributed under the terms and conditions of the Creative Commons Attribution (CC BY) license (http://creativecommons.org/licenses/by/4.0/).

Article

A Hybrid Adversarial Attack for Different Application Scenarios †

Xiaohu Du *,‡ , Jie Yu ‡, Zibo Yi, Shasha Li, Jun Ma, Yusong Tan and Qinbo Wu

College of Computer Science and Technology, National University of Defense Technology, Changsha 410073, China; yj@nudt.edu.cn (J.Y.); yizibo14@nudt.edu.cn (Z.Y.); shashali@nudt.edu.cn (S.L.); majun@nudt.edu.cn (J.M.); yusong.tan@nudt.edu.cn (Y.T.); qinbo.wu@nudt.edu.cn (Q.W.)
* Correspondence: duxiaohu18@nudt.edu.cn; Tel.: +86-155-8098-5235
† This paper is an extended version of our paper published in the 6th International Conference on Artificial Intelligence and Security (ICAIS 2020).
‡ These authors contributed equally to this work.

Received: 28 April 2020; Accepted: 15 May 2020; Published: 21 May 2020

Abstract: Adversarial attack against natural language has been a hot topic in the field of artificial intelligence security in recent years. It is mainly to study the methods and implementation of generating adversarial examples. The purpose is to better deal with the vulnerability and security of deep learning systems. According to whether the attacker understands the deep learning model structure, the adversarial attack is divided into black-box attack and white-box attack. In this paper, we propose a hybrid adversarial attack for different application scenarios. Firstly, we propose a novel black-box attack method of generating adversarial examples to trick the word-level sentiment classifier, which is based on differential evolution (DE) algorithm to generate semantically and syntactically similar adversarial examples. Compared with existing genetic algorithm based adversarial attacks, our algorithm can achieve a higher attack success rate while maintaining a lower word replacement rate. At the 10% word substitution threshold, we have increased the attack success rate from 58.5% to 63%. Secondly, when we understand the model architecture and parameters, etc., we propose a white-box attack with gradient-based perturbation against the same sentiment classifier. In this attack, we use a Euclidean distance and cosine distance combined metric to find the most semantically and syntactically similar substitution, and we introduce the coefficient of variation (CV) factor to control the dispersion of the modified words in the adversarial examples. More dispersed modifications can increase human imperceptibility and text readability. Compared with the existing global attack, our attack can increase the attack success rate and make modification positions in generated examples more dispersed. We've increased the global search success rate from 75.8% to 85.8%. Finally, we can deal with different application scenarios by using these two attack methods, that is, whether we understand the internal structure and parameters of the model, we can all generate good adversarial examples.

Keywords: adversarial attack; adversarial example; sentiment classification; deep learning

1. Introduction

In the past few decades, machine learning and deep learning techniques have achieved great success in some applications. However, so far, there are some technologies that have proven to be vulnerable. Some modified inputs can be easily distinguished by humans, but the neural network model will be classified incorrectly [1]. Adversarial attacks on neural networks have attracted a lot of attention. The main target of these attacks is a computer vision model for image classification [2,3]. Since the input features of these models are continuous, we can apply artificially indistinguishable perturbations. Unlike image data, text input consists of individual words represented by word embeddings, but we cannot directly perturb them and find another word because we need to consider whether the context and the grammar are smooth. We call the perturbed words an adversarial example.

The adversarial example is a small modification to the input, which can change the judgment of the classifier but is not easily detected by humans. These adversarial examples expose some of the vulnerabilities of classifiers and can be used to evaluate and improve machine learning models. Liang et al. [4] pointed out that, if we want to produce a very effective adversarial example, we need to solve two problems. The first is to maintain the original meaning of the adversarial example sentences. The second problem is making it difficult for humans to detect that the adversarial examples are modified. Adversarial attacks can be divided into two cases: white-box attacks and black-box attacks. The former can obtain the parameters and structure of the model, while the latter lacks this information. Black-box attacks are more challenging because they often require a large number of queries on the model. White-box attacks have some gradient-based methods for specific models. Alzantot et al. [5] proposed a black-box based genetic algorithm (GA) to generate semantic and grammatically similar adversarial examples. These examples are used to obfuscate the sentiment classification and textual entailment models with good training results; their attack success rates have reached 97% and 70%, respectively. Based on the above work, Wang et al. [6] proposed an improved genetic algorithm (IGA). Compared with GA, IGA can achieve higher attack success rates while maintaining the transferability of the adversarial examples. The use of differential evolution (DE) for generating adversarial images has be proved to be effective [7]. Both GA and DE are population based optimization algorithms. DE has mechanisms in the population selection phase that maintains the diversity. For that, we propose a novel black-box attack for generating adversarial text examples based on differential evolution.

When we understand the model parameters and structure, we can use white-box attack. Most white-box attacks are based on gradient methods. Greedy attack has proven to be a very effective attack method [8]. However, it also has some problems. Tsai et al. [9] pointed out that greedy attack may not guarantee optimal results. Another limitation is that substitute words often appear in the close range of the sentence, especially in front. This greatly reduces the readability of the sentence and even destroys the semantic meaning of the original text. They proposed a "global search" algorithm that computes a perturbation to obtain candidate words, and then replaces the words of the more perturbed locations. The larger the perturbation, the more sensitive the classifier is to changes in the word. Global search results produce better examples than greedy attack and have a higher attack success rate. When generating candidate words, the global search only uses the Euclidean distance to find the nearest word. We consider combining Euclidean distance and cosine distance to find similar words, and find that some of the original attack failed examples can be re-attacked successfully when we use the cosine distance. In the process of generating the adversarial examples, the existing methods modify the word without considering the dispersion of the modified position in the whole sentence. In particular, the word replacement position of a greedy attack is often close in the sentence, which greatly reduces the readability. Our method is essentially to use different metrics to measure embedding distance to find similar words in generating candidate words and introduce the CV in the Generate Adversary Function in [9]. We compare results of different CV weight on the success rate of the attack, and finally get the best CV weight for generating adversarial examples.

In summary, our contributions in this work are as follows:

(1) We propose a novel black-box attack for generating adversarial text examples based on differential evolution.
(2) We use a Euclidean distance and cosine distance combined metric to find the similar words when generating perturbations and candidate words; the results show that the combining metric can increase the attack success rate.
(3) We propose a white-box attack to generate adversarial examples in which the modified words have high semantic relevance and their positions are more dispersed.

(4) Finally, we prove that the global search attack with a coefficient of variation is more similar to the original text and more imperceptible for humans, which is verified by human evaluation.

The rest of this paper is organized as follows: In Section 2, we describe the related works done by the previous scholars, and some of them are our comparison objects. In Section 3, we describe our methods in detail. Section 4 introduces the relevant contents of the experiment, including the target model, data set, experimental parameters, experimental results, and so on. Finally, we analyze and summarize the experiment. Section 5 introduces the final conclusions and future work.

2. Related Work

The first adversarial attack originates in 2014, when Szegedy et al. [1] find that deep neural networks used for image classification could be tricked by a tiny pixel perturbations added to the input image. They found that image classifiers have a high rate of misclassification, but humans have not detected such changes in images. In 2017, Jia et al. [10] are the first to consider generating adversarial examples on text-based deep neural networks. Since then, people have begun to pay attention to generating adversarial examples for text.

2.1. Black-Box Attack on Text

Robin et al. [10] propose a black-box attack in 2017; this is the first job for the reading comprehension system. The attack proposed by the author is to add distracting but meaningless sentences to the end of the paragraph. These distracting sentences do not change the semantics of paragraphs and answers, but they can trip up the neural network model. The distracting sentence can be a carefully generated real sentence or an arbitrary sequence of words using 20 random common words. Finally, the attack is considered successful when the neural network is queried iteratively until the output changes. Later, Yicheng et al. [11] improve the work by changing the position of noise words and expanding the false answer set used to generate the noise words. They provide new adversarial examples that can help train more robust neural models. Yonatan et al. [12] propose in 2018 that interfered with the input data of neural machine translation applications in two ways: synthesis, which changes the order of characters, such as swapping, and randomization in the middle (that is, except for the first and last characters, Randomly change the order of characters); and completely random (that is, randomly change the order of all characters) and keyboard typing error types. They also collect typographical and typographical errors as adversarial examples. These take advantage of typos in the data set. Gao et al. [13] present a novel algorithm, DeepWordBug. They use a new scoring strategy to identify key tokens. If these tokens are modified, it will cause the classifier to misclassify. They use simple character substitution for the highest-ranking tokens to minimize the edit distance of the perturbation, and change the original classification. Their method has achieved good results in tasks such as text classification, sentiment analysis, and spam detection, and reduces the prediction accuracy of the current state-of-the-art deep learning models. In the same year, Alzantot et al. [5] used genetic algorithms (GA) to minimize the number of word replacements in the original text, but, at the same time, they can make the model wrong. They use crossover and mutation operations in genetic algorithms to generate disturbances. Their attack targets are sentiment classification and textually implied DNN models. In 2019, Ren et al. [14] propose a greedy algorithm called probability weighted word saliency (PWWS) for text ad-versarial attack. They think that, compared with images, the main difficulty of generating text adversarial examples is that the text space is discrete, and it is difficult to make small perturbations along the gradient direction. The challenge is that the generated results need to ensure vocabulary correctness, grammatical correctness, and semantic similarity. Therefore, on the basis of the synonym replacement strategy, they introduce a new vocabulary replacement method that is determined by the POS saliency and classification probability. Wang et al. [6] propose an improve genetic algorithm (IGA) based on the above genetic algorithm. Compared with existing genetic-based adversarial attacks, IGA changed from the random initialization of the GA to the first population. Synonyms randomly replace each word to initialize the first population, making the population more diverse. It also allows replacing previously replaced words to avoid local minima. In the cross section, in order to better simulate breeding and biological crossing, the text of the two parents is randomly cut, and the two fragments are merged into a new text, instead of randomly selecting a word from each position of the two parents. In 2020, Jin et al. [15] propose a black-box attack method called TEXTFOOLER. Different from the above method, they define a new method for ranking the importance of words; TEXTFOOLER first obtains the prediction score $F_Y(X)$ for the Y label corresponding to the original text X through the model, and the score $F_Y(X \backslash w_i)$ of X after deleting the word w_i. Then, it calculates the importance score of w_i according to the relationship between $F_Y(X)$, $F_Y(X \backslash w_i)$, Y, and $\hat{Y}$. Finally, it replaces the words according to the importance score. This method achieves good results in text classification and text implication tasks.

To sum up, the above black-box attack method consists of many similarities. Because the black-box does not know the internal structure and specific parameters of the model, scholars attempt to find the optimal replacement in the word space by different methods. Some of them replace the words first and then calculate the prediction score after the replacement, such as multiple iterations of GA to find the optimal replacement. At the same time, they also try to find out the important score of the replacement words and then replace them in order to minimize the word replacement ratio, such as DeepWordBug and TEXTFOOLER. However, they all have the same goal, which is to find an optimal adversarial examples.

2.2. White-Box Attack on Text

In terms of white-box attacks, the related works are not as much as black-box attacks, which are mainly based on gradient methods. Ebrahimi et al. [16] propose a gradient-based white-box attack method to generate adversarial examples. This attack aims at a character level RNN classifier and greatly increases the error rates on text classification and machine translation. Cheng et al. [17] propose a white-box method to generate adversarial examples against NMT and improve the robustness of NMT. Greedy attack proves to be a very effective method of attack [8,9,18], and Yang et al. [8] even show that greedy attack achieves state-of-the-art attack rates across various kinds of models. However, it also has some problems. Tsai et al. [9] propose that it may not guarantee producing the optimal results and sometimes spends too much time because the algorithm needs to search the candidate words for every iteration, at the same time, due to the nature of being greedy, the algorithm can replace sub-optimal words that do not contribute much to the final goal in an earlier position. Another limitation is that replaced words tend to be in a close area of the sentence, especially in the front. This greatly reduces the readability of the sentence and even destroys the semantic meaning of the original text. They propose a "Global Search" algorithm, which obtains candidate words by calculating a perturbation, and then replace the words in the position where the perturbation is larger. The larger the perturbation, the more sensitive the classifier is to the change of the word. Results of global search prove to generate better examples than the greedy attack and higher attack success rate, which is the baseline used in our experiments. In addition, Lei et al. [19] propose a greedy method can be very time consuming when the space of attacks is large and give the optimization scheme.

The related work of white-box attacks have proved to be very effective in text-based attacks, but there are still some problems to be solved, such as a good algorithm in the replacement percentage, attack success rate, word similarity, grammatical correctness, and semantic similarity can still have better results. Based on the strategy of gradient generation perturbation, we propose a new white-box attack method for sentiment classification task and make some progress in the above aspects.

2.3. Different Measures of Textual Similarity

An important problem is that the generated adversarial examples must not only fool the target model, but also keep the perturbation undetected. A good adversarial example should convey the same semantics as the original text, so we need some metrics to quantify the similarity. There are three metrics that used on vectors and documents [20,21].

Euclidean Distance. In text, Euclidean Distance measures the linear distance between two vectors in Euclidean space.

Cosine Similarity. Cosine similarity represents the semantic similarity of two words by calculating the cosine of the angle between two vectors. Cosine distance is more concerned with the direction difference between two vectors. The smaller the angle between two vectors (the larger the cosine value), the greater the similarity.

Word Movers Distance (WMD). WMD [22] mainly reflects the distance between documents, so it is not suitable for finding similar words. Its semantic representation can be based on the embedding vector obtained by word2vec. Of course, it can also be based on other word embedding methods. This algorithm constructs the document distance into a combination of the semantic distances of the words in the two documents. For example, the Euclidean distance is obtained from the word vectors corresponding to any two words in the two documents and then weight and sum. The WMD distance between two documents A and B is:

$$WMD(A,B) = \sum_{i,j=1}^{n} T_{ij} \cdot D(\vec{i}, \vec{j}) \tag{1}$$

where $D(\vec{i}, \vec{j})$ is the Euclidean distance of the word vectors corresponding to the two words i and j. The Bag Of Words model is used to get the word frequency of the word in the document (as the weight of a word in the document), and the problem then becomes how to "carry" all the word units of document A to the corresponding word units of document B with the minimum cost, and finally get the weight matrix T. The WMD algorithm is a special case of the EMD [23] algorithm, and some improved algorithms based on WMD, such as WCD and RWMD.

3. Methods

3.1. Black-Box Attack on Text

In the black-box attack, we adopt the method based on a differential evolution (DE) algorithm to generate an adversarial example, a differential evolution algorithm with a genetic algorithm (GA) has some similarities. It has the choice stage to keep a population diversity mechanism; therefore, in practice, it is expected to be more effective than other types of group evolution algorithms to find a higher quality solution. In a black-box setting, the attacker does not know the model architecture and parameters. They can only use the input provided to query the target model to get prediction results and corresponding confidence scores. The whole algorithm of black-box attack is described in Algorithm 1, which basically follows the idea of differential evolution algorithms. The overall structure of the differential evolution algorithm is similar to the genetic algorithm. It also has mutation, crossover, and selection operations, but it is different from the genetic algorithm. The main difference from the basic genetic algorithm is the mutation operation. For example, in the genetic algorithm, two children are generated by the intersection of two parent individuals, and, in the differential evolution algorithm, the difference vector of two or several individuals is used to perturb. Then, we will get the new individuals. In traditional genetic algorithms, offspring individuals replace their parent individuals with a certain probability, and newly generated individuals in differential evolution only replace individuals in a population when they are better than individuals in the population. In traditional genetic algorithms, offspring individuals replace their parent individuals with a certain probability, and newly generated individuals in differential evolution only replace individuals in a population when they are better than individuals in the population.

Algorithm 1: Black-box Attack on Text

Input: Original text X, target model f, maximum iterations G, initial generation size S
Output: Adversarial text X_{adv}

1:   $y \leftarrow f(X)$
2:   **for** $i = 1 \rightarrow S$ population **do**
3:       $\mathcal{P}_i^0 \leftarrow Mutate(X, w_i)$
4:   **for** $g = 1 \rightarrow G$ generations **do**
5:       **for** $i = 1 \rightarrow S$ population **do**
6:          $F_i^{g-1} = f(\mathcal{P}_i^{g-1})$
7:       $X_{adv} = argmin(F_i^{g-1})$
8:       **if** $f(X_{adv}) \neq y$ **then return** X_{adv}
9:       $\mathcal{P}_1^g \leftarrow X_{adv}$
10:      **for** $i = 2 \rightarrow S$ population **do**
11:         $\mathcal{P}_i^g \leftarrow Differential(\mathcal{P}_i^g, \mathcal{P}_j^g, \mathcal{P}_k^g) \quad 3 \leq i \neq j \neq k \leq S$
12:       $X_{adv} = argmin(f(\mathcal{P}_i^g))$
13:       **if** $f(X_{adv}) \neq y$ **then return** X_{adv}
14:      **else**
15:         Randomly Sample $parent_1$, $parent_2$ from $\mathcal{P}^{g-1}$
16:         $child = Crossover(parent_1, parent_2)$
17:         **if** $f(child) \neq y$ **then return** $child$ as X_{adv}
18:         $\mathcal{P}_i^g \leftarrow Mutate(child, w)$ Randomly word w in child
19:         **if** $f(\mathcal{P}_i^g) \neq y$ **then return** $child$ as X_{adv}

The algorithm consists of the following steps:

Step 1: Mutation Given a text of n words $X = \{w_1, w_2, ..., w_n\}$, we look for the most similar word to replace one of them, then we get the mutated text. We use the counter-fitting method as word embedding from [24]. We use Euclidean distance to calculate the N nearest neighbors of the word to replace, whose cosine similarity with the word to be replaced are smaller than δ, and this word embedding ensures that the neighbors we find are synonyms. Then, we use the Google language model [25] to select the most context-appropriate K words, and replace a word in the original text with these words respectively. Finally, we choose the word with the lowest confidence score of the model to replace, and get the replaced text. We can get an initial population $\mathcal{P}^0$ of S individuals by repeating this process of mutation S times. The prediction score of each individual can be obtained by querying the victim model function f. In each generation of evolution, we select the individual with the lowest prediction score of the target model and make it the first individual $\mathcal{P}_1^{g+1}$ in the next generation. If the prediction tag of one of the members of the population is not the original tag, the attack is completed. However, it is rare that only one word can change the model's prediction, and most of the examples go to the next step.

If there is no sample in the initial population that can change the prediction of the target model, we do a different operation. For all individuals of the g-th generation, $\mathcal{P}^g = \{\mathcal{P}_1^g, \mathcal{P}_2^g, ..., \mathcal{P}_n^g\}$. For each individual, the algorithm continues to generate mutants according to the following formula:

$$\mathcal{P}_i^{g'} = \mathcal{P}_i^g + F \cdot (\mathcal{P}_j^g - \mathcal{P}_k^g) \quad i = 1, 2, ..., n \tag{2}$$

where $\mathcal{P}_j^g$ and $\mathcal{P}_k^g$ are two randomly selected individuals in the population, and $i \neq j \neq k$, and F is the mutation factor, which is generally 0 to 2, so as to obtain the mutant $\mathcal{P}_i^{g'}$. If the prediction tag of one of the individuals after differential operation is not the original tag, the attack is completed. Otherwise, the algorithm proceeds to the next step.

Step 2: Crossover In this step, the new individual is obtained from the mutant individual $\mathcal{P}_i^{g'} = \{\mathcal{P}_{i1}^{g'}, \mathcal{P}_{i2}^{g'}, ..., \mathcal{P}_{in}^{g'}\}$ and the parent individual $\mathcal{P}_i^g = \{\mathcal{P}_{i1}^g, \mathcal{P}_{i2}^g, ..., \mathcal{P}_{in}^g\}$ through a crossover operation.

$$child = \begin{cases} \mathcal{P}_i^{g'} & \text{if rand}[0\ 1] \leq CR \\ \mathcal{P}_i^g & \text{if rand}[0\ 1] > CR \end{cases} \quad (3)$$

where rand [0 1] is a random number between [0 1], and CR is a constant between [0 1], which is called a crossover factor. The greater the value of CR, the greater the probability of crossover. If the prediction tag of one of the individuals after crossover is not the original tag, the attack is completed. Otherwise, the mutation subroutine is applied to the resulting children.

Compared with the genetic algorithm, the black-box attack based on the differential evolution algorithm has a higher attack success rate and a smaller word replacement rate. At the same time, it is also superior to GA in terms of running time because GA uses Perturb every time a new word is generated. Perturb is a multi-step process of finding similar word replacements, which will take a lot of time. The more words a text needs to replace, the more time it takes, such as long sentences. Our method only takes more time to generate the first generation of individuals. In the subsequent evolution process, the difference operation is used to perform subtraction and multiplication based on the existing words, which takes very little time.

3.2. Greedy Search Attack

Greedy search attack is our comparative experiment. We follow the greedy search algorithm in [9,18], which starts from the first word and then selects the word that has the greatest influence on the success of the attack according to different labels in the k nearest of each word. To find the word with the closest Euclidean distance or cosine distance in word space E, if the modification of the word causes the classifier logit output to be larger than the original and the label is pos or the logit output is smaller than the original and the label is neg, the word is replaced. Otherwise, the word is not modified. Finally, the attack is successful until the label of the classifier output is different from the original, and the total number of replacement words is lower than our threshold.

3.3. White-Box Attack on Text

The white-box attack algorithm is described in Algorithm 2. The algorithm is divided into two parts including generating candidate words and modifying the candidate words which have the most influence on the classifier. We use the whole text as the research object. X represents word embedding of the original input text. y and $\hat{y}$ represent the original and adversarial label. For a text of n words, $X = \{w_1, w_2, ..., w_n\}$, and a valid adversarial example X_{adv} should conform to the following requirements:

$$\hat{y} \neq y, \text{ and } Sim(w_i, w_i') \leq threshold \quad (4)$$

where Sim is the distance between w_i and w_i' in the word space. It should be less than a threshold. In the first loop, we obtain a perturbed embedding X' by the gradient-based method, and then traverse every word in X', in order to find the word with the closest Euclidean distance or cosine distance in word space E, and then generate a list of candidate words. In this candidate words list, every word in the original text has been modified. The subsequent second loop will choose to modify these words successively according to priority. We attack the classifier with this list. If the label is not the same as the original input, the loop ends. Otherwise, the algorithm continues to calculate the gradient to get a new X'. After obtaining a list of valid candidate words, we will make a modification order selection.

Algorithm 2: White-box Attack on Text

Input: Original text $X = \{w_1, w_2, ..., w_n\}$, target model f, perturbation δ
Output: Adversarial text X_{adv}
1: $y \leftarrow f(X)$
2: Initialization : $X_{adv} \leftarrow X$, $\delta \leftarrow 0$, success = False, candidates $\leftarrow \varnothing$, finCandidates $\leftarrow \varnothing$
3: Filter out the stop words in X.
4: **while** *not success* **do**
5:    $X' \leftarrow X + \delta$ ◁ *back propagation*
6:    **for** w_i in X' **do**
7:       candidates $\leftarrow$ extracting the top N synonyms using Euclidean and Cosine distance for w_i.
8:       candidates $\leftarrow$ POScheck(candidates)
9:       **for** k_i *in candidates* **do**
10:          $X' \leftarrow$ Replace w_i with k_i in X_{adv}
11:          $P_i \leftarrow f(X')$
12:          $w^* \leftarrow argmax(P_i)$
13:          $finCandidates \leftarrow finCandidates$ append w^*
14:    $\hat{y} \leftarrow f(finCandidates)$
15:    **if** $\hat{y} \neq y$ **then** break
16: $grad \leftarrow ||\delta||_2$
17: $selected \leftarrow 0, list \leftarrow \varnothing, \Omega \leftarrow \varnothing$
18: **while** *not success* **do**
19:    $selectedX = selected.index(0)$
20:    **for** x in $total(grad)$ and $selected[x] \neq 1$ **do**
21:       $CV_1 = CV(list$ append $x), CV_2 = CV(list$ append $selectedX)$
22:       **if** $grad[x] + \lambda \cdot CV_1 > grad[selectedX] + \lambda \cdot CV_2$ **then**
23:          $selectedX \leftarrow x$
24:       $\Omega \leftarrow \Omega$ append x
25:    $selected[selectedX] = 1, list \leftarrow list$ append $selectedX$
26:    **for** w_i in Ω **do**
27:       **if** *distance* < *threshold* and $\frac{i}{len(x)} < r$ **then** $X_{adv} \leftarrow$ Replace w_i
28:       **if** $\hat{y} \neq y$ **then**
29:          success = True
30:          **return** X_{adv}
31:       **else**
32:          **return** None

In the second loop, first, we will take the gradient of the first loop. We set a full 0 tensor with the same dimensions as the original text, with *selected* for recording the position of the selected word, *list* for the sequence of selected words, and *positions* for the last modified order. Then, start the loop selection. First, we select the index number *selectedX* whose value is 0 from the *selected*, the number of words in the text is the traversal range, and the variable is represented by x, when *selected* $[x] \neq 1$, calculating the coefficient of variation CV_1 of x added to the *list* and the CV_2 of the *selectedX* added to the *list*, if the weighted sum of gradient and CV_1 is greater than the sum of gradient and CV_2, we then replace *selectedX* with x, add x to *positions*, update *selected* and *list*, let *selected* [*selectedX*] = 1, and add *selectedX* to *list*. Finally, a modification sequence is generated. Then, we modify them in order until the output of the classifier is different from the original text. In the process, we can set the word distance threshold, word replacement rate, and other parameters, and compare different results under different parameters. The whole attack process of white-box attack is shown in Figure 1.

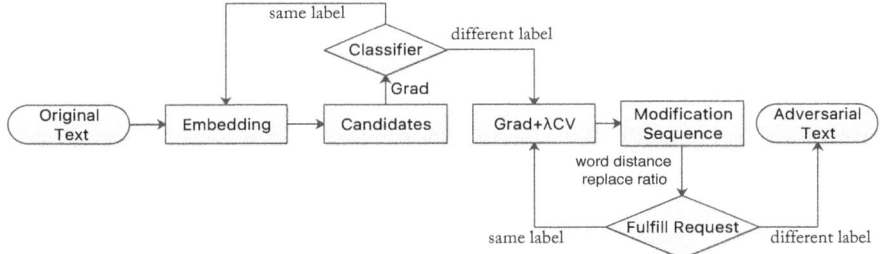

Figure 1. The whole attack process of white-box attack.

Simply put, we combine the gradient of the word we want to modify and coefficient of variation of the text position of all modified words after the word is modified, and use these two data to determine the order of modification.

We can control the degree of dispersion of the word's position by the weight value λ of the CV. When λ is too large, the modified words will be more dispersed. The order of modification is closer to the global search algorithm when λ is smaller; when $\lambda = 0$, the algorithm becomes the global search.

4. Experiments

4.1. Dataset and Target Model

The dataset contains 25,000 IMDB film reviews specifically for sentiment analysis. The mood of the comment is binary. Labels are pos(positive) and neg(negative). We randomly segment 25,000 data into 20,000 examples as training sets and 5000 examples as test sets.

We use the CNN model and some of its hyperparameters [26] as our target model. In this model, there are filter windows of 3, 4, and 5 with 100 feature maps each, a dropout rate of 0.5, and a max pooling layer. The batch size has been modified to 64. We use 20,000 examples to train the model and test the model with 5000 examples. The results of this model are that the accuracy of training sets is 1 and the accuracy of testing sets is 0.89.

4.2. Evaluation

4.2.1. Black-Box Attack Based on Differential Evolution

We randomly sample 200 correctly classified examples from the IMDB test set to evaluate our algorithm. We choose examples of correct classification to avoid the impact of model accuracy. Our purpose is to make the model prediction error, that is, the original prediction is positive. The model will be judged as negative after the adversarial attack, so that our attack is considered successful.

We limit the attacker to maximum G = 20 iterations. We also fix the maximum percentage of each text change to 10% and 20%. We believe that the quality of the text will decrease if the modification ratio exceeds 20%. Although the success rate of black-box attack based on a genetic algorithm has reached 97%, its word replacement rate has reached 25%. If an attack fails within the iteration limit or exceeds a specified threshold, it is considered a failure. Table 1 shows the attack success rate under different F-values and percentage of modified words. From our results, we can see that we can achieve a high success rate by making small changes to the text. In addition, our algorithm is significantly better than the genetic algorithm in word modification percentage and attack success rate.

It is worth noting that, under the 10% replacement rate threshold, GA and DE have only about a 60% attack success rate, which is far lower than the white-box attack algorithm mentioned later. It shows that there is still a lot of room for improvement in a black-box attack. Once the threshold of the word replacement rate is increased to 20%, we see that both GA and DE exceed 90% in the attack success rate, and our method even approaches 100%. This shows that the word replacement rate is an important factor affecting the success rate of attack. Algorithms that do not strictly limit the word replacement rate are not good algorithms.

Table 1. Attack success rate with different word modifiers and F values.

	GA	F = 0.1	F = 0.3	F = 0.5	F = 1.2	F = 1.5
10% modified	58.5%	63%	62.5%	56.5%	55%	53%
20% modified	91%	96%	94.5%	94.5%	96%	97.5%

The mutation factor F can be used to control the degree of scaling of the difference vector between two random individuals. F value has a great influence on the success rate of the final attack. Experiments show that the smaller the F value, the higher the attack success rate at low replacement rates. When the F value is larger, the attack success rate is higher at a relatively higher replacement rate. Moreover, when F is 0.3, the attack success rate of our algorithm is higher than that of the genetic algorithm in terms of 10% and 20% word substitution rate. The example output generated by a black-box attack is shown in Table 2. From the results, the examples we generated can maintain the original sentence form to some extent.

Table 2. Original text and adversarial example of black-box attack.

Original Text Prediction = **Positive**.
absolutely fantastic whatever i say wouldn't do this underrated movie the justice it deserves watch it now fantastic.
Adversarial Text Prediction = **Negative**.
absolutely fantastic whatever i say wouldn't do this underestimated movie the justice it deserve watch it now fantastic.
Original Text Prediction = **Negative**.
poorly directed short film shot on hi def or betacam it appears it screams student film video all the way the premise is limited in scope and the short actually feels a lot longer than it runs some interesting acting moments and some decent production value but not enough to lift this film from the hole it has fallen into.
Adversarial Text Prediction = **Positive**.
poorly directed gunshot film shot on hi def or betacam it appears it shrieks student film video all the way the premises is limited in scope and the short actually feels a lot longest than it runs some interesting acting moments and some decent production value but not enough to lift this film from the hole it has fallen in.

4.2.2. White-Box Attack with the Coefficient of Variation

Our experimental goal is to generate adversarial examples to confuse the classifier. As long as the prediction result of the adversarial example is different from the original comment result, the attack is considered successful. At the same time, we need to exclude the influence of classifier accuracy on the experimental results, so we select 500 correctly classified examples. Our experiments have the same word distance threshold and word replacement rate, the word Euclidean distance is set at 50 and the word replacement rate is set at 0.1, and k is set at 35 in the greedy attack. Finally, we add cosine distance experiments for greedy attack and global attack.

We calculate the attack success rate corresponding to several different cosine distance thresholds. The experimental results are shown in Figure 2. We can see that the smaller the cosine distance is, the higher the success rate the attack will have because the word angle is larger and their similarity is smaller. Greedy attack and global attack without cosine distance had original success rates of 65.8% and 75.8%. In the global attack, there is increased cosine distance, even if the cosine distance is set to 0.9848; the final success rate will increase to 77.4%, while the greedy attack has no new successful examples. There is no significant change in the number of increases between the cosine of 0.9848 and 0.6428. An angle of more than 0.6428 will have a significant increase in the number of successful attacks. In addition, we do an experiment to find candidate words only by cosine distance as a contrast. We find that, in the case of high cosine distance threshold, the attack success rate is very low, but finally when the cosine distance threshold is 0, it can also achieve a high attack success rate, which shows, that in terms of word similarity, the effect of cosine distance is worse than that of European distance. We can use the cosine distance as a supplement of European distance to improve the overall attack success rate. The evaluation of adversarial examples shows that greedy attack still shows that the replacement locations are sometimes close, or even in the front of the text, for which readability is not good, while the replacement position of global attack is relatively random. The following human evaluation also shows this conclusion. The example output generated by black-box attack is shown in Table 3.

Table 3. Original text and three adversarial examples of white-box attack.

Original Text, Prediction = **Negative**.
The Pallbearer is a disappointment and at times extremely boring with a love story that just doesn't work partly with the casting of Gwyneth Paltrow (Julie). Gwyneth Paltrow walks through the entire film with a confused look on her face and its hard to tell what David Schwimmer even sees in her. However The Pallbearer at times is funny particularly the church scene and the group scenes with his friends are a laugh but that's basically it. Watch the Pallbearer for those scenes only and fast forward the rest. Trust me you aren't missing much.
Greedy Attack Text, Prediction = **Positive**.
on despite has given tempered well outside well surprisingly boring with a love story that just doesn't work partly with the casting of Gwyneth Paltrow (Julie). Gwyneth Paltrow walks through the entire film with a confused look on her face and its hard to tell what David Schwimmer even sees in her. However The Pallbearer at times is funny particularly the church scene and the group scenes with his friends are a laugh but that's basically it. Watch the Pallbearer for those scenes only and fast forward the rest. Trust me you aren't missing much.
Global Attack Text, Prediction = **Positive**.
The Pallbearer is a artist and at times extremely boring with affection love story that just doesn't work partly with the american of Paltrow Paltrow (Julie). Paltrow Paltrow walks through the entire film with a confused look on her face and its hard to tell what David Schwimmer even sees in her. However The Pallbearer at times is funny particularly the church scene and the group scenes with his friends are a laugh but that's basically it. Watch the Pallbearer for those scenes only and fast forward the rest. Trust me you aren't missing much.
Global Attack Text with CV, Prediction = **Positive**.
The Pallbearer is affection artist and at times extremely boring with a love story that just doesn't work partly with the casting of Gwyneth Paltrow (Julie). Paltrow Paltrow walks through the entire film with a confused look on her face and its hard to tell what David Schwimmer even sees in her. However The Pallbearer at times is funny particularly the church scene and the group scenes with his friends are affection laugh but that's basically it. Watch the Pallbearer for those scenes only and fast forward the rest. Trust me you aren't missing much.

Because greedy attack may make the word modification position close and result in poor readability, global search improves this situation to some extent, but it does not have the ability to effectively control the dispersion of word modification positions because the modified word is selected from big to small according to the gradient magnitude. We propose a method to control the dispersion of the modified position by adding the coefficient of variation, and control the dispersion degree of the modified position by the weight of CV. We introduced the CV factor into the global search with a combining metric. Finally, we use global attack with the combined metric and set the cosine distance threshold to 0.9848 to maintain the word's high similarity, and compare the attack success rate under different CV weight. We select 500 comments used by greedy attacks and calculate the attack success rate under different CV weight(λ).

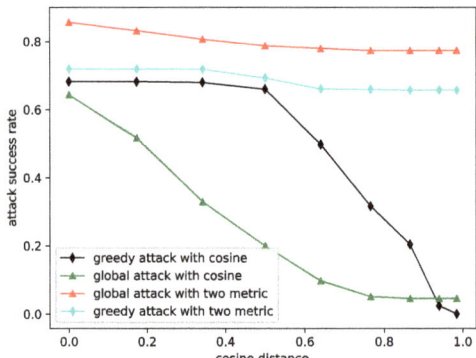

Figure 2. The total success rate of greedy attack and global attack added cosine distance.

In order to prove the validity of adding the CV factor when determining the modification order, we select 50 comments that are correctly classified by the classifier and the algorithm attack is successful, and calculate the CV value of the adversarial examples under different λ. When the CV weight value is 0, our method becomes the global search attack [9].

Experiments shown in Table 4, when λ is larger, the degree of dispersion of the modified positions of the adversarial example is larger (CV value is larger), and the final attack success rate has a slight decrease overall, which indicates that the word with a larger gradient magnitude has more influence on the classifier. We analyze the adversarial examples and find that some examples of the original attack failure will be re-attacked successfully after joining CV, and some examples of the original successful attack will fail the attack after joining CV. Taken as a whole, the attack success rate basically decreases as λ increases, but this change is very small. The experiments also show that even if we set the λ to 30 after we add the cosine distance, the attack success rate still reaches 76.2%, which still exceeds the original global attack success rate of 75.8%. Thus, our methods can improve the attack success rate and make the modification positions in an adversarial example more dispersed.

Table 4. The attack success rate and CV value under different λ.

λ	0	1	5	10	20	30
CV value	0.487	0.589	0.70	0.73	0.827	0.886
attack rate	77.4%	77.6%	76.6%	76.8%	77%	76.2%

4.2.3. Human Evaluation

In order to illustrate that adversarial text with more dispersion words modification could lead to being more similar to the original text and more imperceptible for humans, we select five volunteers to score the similarity between the adversarial examples and the original text from 1 to 5. We randomly chose 10 comments with positive and negative examples and their adversarial examples generated by greedy search, global search, and the global search with CV. This is used to prove the similarity between the original text and adversarial examples. On the other hand, we select 15 comments including the original text, greedy text, global text, and global text with CV, and then ask volunteers to identify which of them are modified adversarial examples. This is used to prove the imperceptibility for humans. After counting all the scoring results, in terms of similarity, we calculate the average score, the global text with CV similarity score is 3.642, the global text score is 3.612, and the greedy text score is 2.91. Because the greedy text often modifies the front words by a large amount, it can obviously find the difference from the original text. In terms of imperceptibility, the global text with CV has a detectable ratio of 0.37, the global text has a detectable ratio of 0.4, and the greedy text has a detectable ratio of

0.46. We find that the scores of global attack and global attack with CV are close, and they are better than greedy attacks.

5. Conclusions and Future Work

In this paper, we propose a hybrid adversarial attack for different scenarios. Specifically, we adopt different attack measures for whether we understand the deep neural network internal structure and specific parameters. If we do not understand the above information, it is suitable for us to use a black-box attack, so we propose a new black-box attack method based on a differential evolution algorithm, and generate adversarial examples with low word substitution ratio and high attack success rate. Since black-box attack does not need to know the model parameters and structure, it also has better universality to attack different natural language processing tasks. At the same time, in the case of a white-box attack, for the problem of greedy search, we propose the factors of increasing CV in the modification position of words to prevent the position of words from being too close. Our algorithm proves that the placement of word modifiers in the adversarial example can be more dispersed with the addition of CV factors. It makes up for the poor readability of the greedy attack example. Our approach maintains a high attack success rate and makes the locations of changes in the adversarial example more diffuse through the CV factor. In pursuit of a high attack success rate, we improve the quality of the adversarial example. We compare the two types of adversarial attacks above against different scenarios with existing attack methods. Our method has a certain degree of improvement in word replacement rate and attack success rate.

In our experiments, although we try to find the most similar words, some of them didn't look the same in real life, according to the example of adversarial actually generated. For example, the substitution of some synonyms does not conform to the context of movie reviews. Therefore, word embedding trained for a specific data set will greatly improve this situation. Word embedding that better reflects word similarity can also enhance our work. At the same time, the adversarial example can reveal the vulnerability of the NLP model, and we can use it to improve the robustness of the model. Although we find what is most similar to a word, in a specific context, the original words should conform the most to the original context. In defense against attack, we can use the idea of adversarial attack to restore the text. Before entering the classifier, we first preprocess the text, which will improve the security and robustness of the model. This will be future work.

Author Contributions: Writing—original draft preparation, X.D.; methodology, X.D. and J.Y.; writing—review and editing, Z.Y., J.Y. and J.M.; supervision, J.Y., Y.T. and Q.W.; funding acquisition, J.Y. and S.L. All authors have read and agreed to the published version of the manuscript.

Funding: This work is supported by the National Key Research and Development Program of China (No. 2018YFB0204301).

Conflicts of Interest: The authors declare no conflict of interest.

References

1. Szegedy, C.; Zaremba, W.; Sutskever, I.; Estrach, J.B.; Erhan, D.; Goodfellow, I.; Fergus, R. Intriguing properties of neural networks. In Proceedings of the 2nd International Conference on Learning Representations (ICLR 2014), Banff, AB, Canada, 14–16 April 2014.
2. Kurakin, A.; Goodfellow, I.J.; Bengio, S. Adversarial Examples in the Physical World. In *Artificial Intelligence Safety and Security*; Chapman and Hall/CRC: London, UK, 2018; pp. 99–112.
3. Dong, Y.; Liao, F.; Pang, T.; Su, H.; Zhu, J.; Hu, X.; Li, J. Boosting adversarial attacks with momentum. In Proceedings of the IEEE Conference on Computer Vision and Pattern Recognition, Salt Lake City, UT, USA, 18–22 June 2018; pp. 9185–9193.
4. Liang, B.; Li, H.; Su, M.; Bian, P.; Li, X.; Shi, W. Deep text classification can be fooled. In Proceedings of the 27th International Joint Conference on Artificial Intelligence, Stockholm, Sweden, 13–19 July 2018; pp. 4208–4215.

5. Alzantot, M.; Sharma, Y.S.; Elgohary, A.; Ho, B.J.; Srivastava, M.; Chang, K.W. Generating Natural Language Adversarial Examples. In Proceedings of the 2018 Conference on Empirical Methods in Natural Language Processing, Brussels, Belgium, 31 October–4 November 2018.
6. Wang, X.; Jin, H.; He, K. Natural language adversarial attacks and defenses in word level. *arXiv* **2019**, arXiv:1909.06723.
7. Su, J.; Vargas, D.V.; Sakurai, K. One pixel attack for fooling deep neural networks. *IEEE Trans. Evol. Comput.* **2019**, *23*, 828–841. [CrossRef]
8. Yang, P.; Chen, J.; Hsieh, C.J.; Wang, J.L.; Jordan, M.I. Greedy attack and gumbel attack: Generating adversarial examples for discrete data. *arXiv* **2018**, arXiv:1805.12316.
9. Tsai, Y.T.; Yang, M.C.; Chen, H.Y. Adversarial Attack on Sentiment Classification. In Proceedings of the 2019 ACL Workshop BlackboxNLP: Analyzing and Interpreting Neural Networks for NLP, Florence, Italy, 28 July–2 Augusy 2019; pp. 233–240.
10. Jia, R.; Liang, P. Adversarial Examples for Evaluating Reading Comprehension Systems. In Proceedings of the 2017 Conference on Empirical Methods in Natural Language Processing, Copenhagen, Denmark, 7–11 September 2017; pp. 2021–2031.
11. Wang, Y.; Bansal, M. Robust Machine Comprehension Models via Adversarial Training. In Proceedings of the 2018 Conference of the North American Chapter of the Association for Computational Linguistics: Human Language Technologies, Volume 2 (Short Papers), New Orleans, LA, USA, 1–6 June 2018; pp. 575–581.
12. Belinkov, Y.; Bisk, Y. Synthetic and natural noise both break neural machine translation. *arXiv* **2017**, arXiv:1711.02173.
13. Gao, J.; Lanchantin, J.; Soffa, M.L.; Qi, Y. *Black-Box Generation of Adversarial Text Sequences to Evade Deep Learning Classifiers*; IEEE: Piscataway, NJ, USA, 2018; pp. 50–56.
14. Ren, S.; Deng, Y.; He, K.; Che, W. Generating Natural Language Adversarial Examples through Probability Weighted Word Saliency. In Proceedings of the 57th Annual Meeting of the Association for Computational Linguistics, Florence, Italy, 28 July–2 Augusy 2019; Association for Computational Linguistics: Stroudsburg, PA, USA, 2019; pp. 1085–1097. [CrossRef]
15. Jin, D.; Jin, Z.; Zhou, J.T.; Szolovits, P. Is BERT Really Robust? A Strong Baseline for Natural Language Attack on Text Classification and Entailment. *arXiv* **2020**, arXiv:2002.06261.
16. Ebrahimi, J.; Rao, A.; Lowd, D.; Dou, D. HotFlip: White-Box Adversarial Examples for Text Classification. In Proceedings of the 56th Annual Meeting of the Association for Computational Linguistics (Volume 2: Short Papers), Melbourne, Australia, 15–20 July 2018; pp. 31–36.
17. Cheng, Y.; Jiang, L.; Macherey, W. Robust Neural Machine Translation with Doubly Adversarial Inputs. In Proceedings of the 57th Annual Meeting of the Association for Computational Linguistics, Florence, Italy, 28 July–2 August 2019; pp. 4324–4333.
18. Kuleshov, V.; Thakoor, S.; Lau, T.; Ermon, S. Adversarial Examples for Natural Language Classification Problems. 2018. Available online: https://openreview.net/forum?id=r1QZ3zbAZ (accessed on 20 May 2020)
19. Lei, Q.; Wu, L.; Chen, P.Y.; Dimakis, A.; Dhillon, I.; Witbrock, M. Discrete Adversarial Attacks and Submodular Optimization with Applications to Text Classification. *arXiv* **2018**, arXiv:1812.00151.
20. Zhang, W.E.; Sheng, Q.Z.; Alhazmi, A.; Li, C. Adversarial attacks on deep learning models in natural language processing: A survey. *arXiv* **2019**, arXiv:1901.06796.
21. Wang, W.; Tang, B.; Wang, R.; Wang, L.; Ye, A. A survey on Adversarial Attacks and Defenses in Text. *arXiv* **2019**, arXiv:1902.07285.
22. Kusner, M.; Sun, Y.; Kolkin, N.; Weinberger, K. From word embeddings to document distances. In Proceedings of the International Conference on Machine Learning, Lille, France, 6–11 July 2015; pp. 957–966.
23. Rubner, Y.; Tomasi, C.; Guibas, L.J. *A Metric for Distributions with Applications to Image Databases*; IEEE: Piscataway, NJ, USA, 1998.
24. Mrkšic, N.; OSéaghdha, D.; Thomson, B.; Gašic, M.; Rojas-Barahona, L.; Su, P.H.; Vandyke, D.; Wen, T.H.; Young, S. Counter-fitting Word Vectors to Linguistic Constraints. In Proceedings of the NAACL-HLT, Atlanta, GA, USA, 12–17 June 2016; pp. 142–148.

25. Chelba, C.; Mikolov, T.; Schuster, M.; Ge, Q.; Brants, T.; Koehn, P.; Robinson, T. One billion word benchmark for measuring progress in statistical language modeling. *arXiv* **2013**, arXiv:1312.3005.
26. Kim, Y. Convolutional Neural Networks for Sentence Classification. In Proceedings of the 2014 Conference on Empirical Methods in Natural Language Processing (EMNLP), Doha, Qatar, 25–29 October 2014; pp. 1746–1751.

© 2020 by the authors. Licensee MDPI, Basel, Switzerland. This article is an open access article distributed under the terms and conditions of the Creative Commons Attribution (CC BY) license (http://creativecommons.org/licenses/by/4.0/).

MDPI
St. Alban-Anlage 66
4052 Basel
Switzerland
Tel. +41 61 683 77 34
Fax +41 61 302 89 18
www.mdpi.com

Applied Sciences Editorial Office
E-mail: applsci@mdpi.com
www.mdpi.com/journal/applsci

www.ingramcontent.com/pod-product-compliance
Lightning Source LLC
LaVergne TN
LVHW070129100526
838202LV00016B/2251